T0184600

Pro Android 5

Dave MacLean

Satya Komatineni

Grant Allen

Apress®

Pro Android 5

ISBN-13 (pbk): 978-1-4302-4680-0

ISBN-13 (electronic): 978-1-4302-4681-7

Managing Director: Welmoed Spahr
Lead Editor: Steve Anglin
Technical Reviewer: Shane Kirk
Editorial Board: Steve Anglin, Louise Corrigan, Jonathan Gennick, Robert Hutchinson, Michelle Lowman, James Markham, Susan McDermott, Matthew Moodie, Jeffrey Pepper, Douglas Pundick, Ben Renow-Clarke, Gwenan Spearing, Steve Weiss
Coordinating Editor: Mark Powers
Copy Editor: Brendan Frost
Compositor: SPi Global
Indexer: SPi Global
Artist: SPi Global
Cover Designer: Anna Ishchenko

Distributed to the book trade worldwide by Springer Science+Business Media New York, 233 Spring Street, 6th Floor, New York, NY 10013. Phone 1-800-SPRINGER, fax (201) 348-4505, e-mail `orders-ny@springer-sbm.com`, or visit `www.springeronline.com`. Apress Media, LLC is a California LLC and the sole member (owner) is Springer Science + Business Media Finance Inc (SSBM Finance Inc). SSBM Finance Inc is a Delaware corporation.

For information on translations, please e-mail `rights@apress.com`, or visit `www.apress.com`.

Apress and friends of ED books may be purchased in bulk for academic, corporate, or promotional use. eBook versions and licenses are also available for most titles. For more information, reference our Special Bulk Sales–eBook Licensing web page at `www.apress.com/bulk-sales`.

Any source code or other supplementary material referenced by the author in this text is available to readers at `www.apress.com/9781430246800`. For detailed information about how to locate your book's source code, go to `www.apress.com/source-code/`.

To my wife Rosie, I never would have made it this far without your love and support. Thank you, you are wonderful, and I love you.

—Dave MacLean

To my late younger brother Sankar Komatineni whose industry, hardship, and zest for life fills me with sadness and joy.

—Satya Komatineni

To all the Android developers out there dreaming of the next great Android app! You are an amazing community, and I can't wait to see what you develop next.

—Grant Allen

Contents at a Glance

Contents

About the Authors

Dave MacLean is a software engineer and architect living and working in Orlando, Florida. Since 1980, he has programmed in many languages, developing solutions ranging from robot automation systems to data warehousing, from web self-service applications to electronic data interchange transaction processors. Dave has worked for Sun Microsystems, IBM, Trimble Navigation, General Motors, Blue Cross Blue Shield of Florida, and several small companies. He has written several books on Android and a few magazine articles. He graduated from the University of Waterloo in Canada with a Systems Design Engineering degree. Visit his blog at `http://davemac327.blogspot.com` or contact him at `davemac327@gmail.com`.

Satya Komatineni has been programming for more than 20 years in the IT and Web space. He has had the opportunity to work with Assembly, C, C++, Rexx, Java, C#, Lisp, HTML, JavaScript, CSS, SVG, relational databases, object databases, and related technologies. He has published more than 30 articles touching many of these areas, both in print and online. He has been a frequent speaker at O'Reilly Open Source Conference, speaking on innovations around Java and Web. Satya has done a considerable amount of original work in creating Aspire, a comprehensive open-source Java-based web framework, and has explored personal web productivity and collaboration tools through his open-source work for `KnowledgeFolders.com`. Satya holds a master's degree in electrical engineering from Indian Institute of Technology and a bachelor's degree in electrical engineering from Andhra University, India. You can find his website at `SatyaKomatineni.com`.

Grant Allen has worked in the IT field for over 20 years, as a CTO, enterprise architect, and database administrator. Grant's roles have covered private enterprise, academia, and the government sector around the world, specializing in global-scale systems design, development, and performance. He is a frequent speaker at industry and academic conferences, on topics ranging from data mining to compliance, and technologies such as databases (DB2, Oracle, SQL Server, MySQL), content management, collaboration, disruptive innovation, and mobile ecosystems like Android. His first Android application was a task list to remind him to finish all his other unfinished Android projects. Grant works for Google, and in his spare time is completing a PhD on building innovative high-technology environments. Grant is the author of *Beginning Android* and lead author of *Oracle SQL Recipes* and *The Definitive Guide to SQLite*.

About the Technical Reviewer

Shane Kirk earned a B.S. in Computer Science from the University of Kentucky in 2000. He's currently a Senior Software Engineer for IDEXX Laboratories in Westbrook, Maine, where he spends his days working on communication solutions for embedded systems. Shane's foray into mobile development began in 2010, shortly after purchasing his first smartphone—a Droid X running Eclair (Android 2.1). He's been hooked on Android ever since.

Acknowledgments

Writing this book took effort not only on the part of the authors, but also from some of the very talented staff at Apress, as well as the technical reviewer. Therefore, we would like to thank Steve Anglin, Matthew Moodie, Douglas Pundick, Mark Powers, Brendan Frost, Ana Panchoo, and Jill Balzano.

We would also like to extend our deepest appreciation to the technical reviewer—Shane Kirk—for his expert appraisals and attention to detail. This book is so much better because of his efforts.

Writing a technical book about a subject that frequently changes is a daunting task. When the documentation didn't say, and the source code didn't reveal, we would search the Internet for answers. And we'd eventually find what we were looking for, buried here and there. To all the other Android developers out there who are working along with us to provide answers, we thank you.

Finally, the authors are deeply grateful to their families for letting us toil away on nights, early mornings, and weekends. It takes great dedication to write a book, and perhaps even more to put up with authors while they write.

Foreword

Way back in 2008, I was given my first Android device. It was the Dream, also known as the G1, and I immediately started tinkering with it. After all, here was a smartphone with the promise of thousands of applications, and who knew how many hundreds of possible handsets. That shows how much I knew at the time! I really should have been thinking in the order of millions of applications, and tens of thousands of devices, because that is where Android is heading today.

Whether it is traditional phones, tablets, cars, in-flight entertainment systems, robots, or any other of the myriad Android devices out there, what makes them great are the applications written by people like you, dear reader! Every day, Android developers push the possibilities of what applications—and Android—can do, and it is that energy that draws me to the community, and to helping in my own small way with books like Pro Android.

One of the best observations about technology and innovation I have heard is that innovation happens when you create something and share it with another person, which they then adapt and use in a totally unexpected way. So let me commend this book to you in that spirit. Enjoy everything Pro Android has to offer you, and take it to create something totally unexpected! We'll be first in line to try it out, whatever it is.

—Grant Allen
New York
May 2015

Introduction

Welcome to the wonderful world of Android. A world where, with a bit of knowledge and effort, you too can write Android applications. To write good applications, however, you will need to dig deeper, to understand the fundamentals of the Android architecture, to understand how applications can work together, to understand how mobile applications are different from all previous forms of programming. The online documentation on Android is fair, but it does not go far enough. You can read the source code, but that's not at all easy.

This book is the culmination of seven years of researching, developing, testing, refining, and writing about Android. We've read all the online documentation, scoured through source code, explored the far reaches of the Internet, and have compiled this book. We've filled in the gaps, anticipated the questions you have, and provided answers. Along the way we've seen APIs come and go and be revised. We've seen major changes in how applications are constructed. At first we all used Activities, but when tablets came along we started using Fragments. We've taken everything we've learned and filled this book with practical guidance to using the latest Android APIs to write interesting applications.

You will still find coverage of the beginning topics, to help the new learner get started developing for Android. You will also find coverage of the more advanced topics, such as Google Maps Android API v2, which is very different from v1. We've updated this edition with the latest information on the available APIs. You will find in-depth coverage of intents, services, broadcast receivers, communication, fragments, widgets, sensors, animation, security, loaders, persistence, Google Cloud Messaging, audio and video, and more. And for every topic there are sample programs that illustrate each API in meaningful ways. All source code is downloadable, so you can copy and paste it into your applications to get a great head start.

Introduction

Chapter 1

Hello Android

Welcome to the book, and welcome to the world of Android development. In a little under ten years, Android has helped change the face of modern mobile computing and telephony and launched a revolution in how applications are developed, and by whom. With this book in your hands, you are now part of the great Android explosion! We're going to assume that you want to get straight at working with Android, so we're not going to bore you with a fireside chat about Android's history, major characters, plaudits, or any other prose. We're going to get straight to it!

In this chapter, you'll start by seeing what you need to begin building applications with the Android software development kit (SDK) and set up your choice of development environment. Next, you step through a "Hello World!" application. Then the chapter explains the Android application life cycle and ends with a discussion about running your applications with Android Virtual Devices (AVDs) and on real devices. So let's get started.

Prerequisites for Android Development

To build applications for Android, you need the Java SE Development Kit (JDK), the Android SDK, and a development environment. Strictly speaking, you can develop your applications using nothing more than a primitive text editor and a handful of command-line tools like Ant. For the purposes of this book, we'll use the commonly available Eclipse IDE, though you are free to adopt Android Studio and its IntelliJ underpinnings—we'll even walk through Android Studio for those who have not seen it. With the exception of a few add-on tools, the examples we share in the book will work equally well between these two IDEs.

The Android SDK requires JDK 6 or 7 (the full JDK, not just the Java Runtime Environment [JRE]) and optionally a supported IDE. Currently, Google directly supports two alternative IDEs, providing some choice. Historically, Eclipse was the first IDE supported by Google for Android development, and developing for Android 4.4 KitKat or 5.0 Lollipop requires Eclipse 3.6.2 or higher (this book uses Eclipse 4.2 or 4.4, also known as Juno and Luna, respectively, and other versions). The alternative environment released and supported by Google for Android is now known as Android Studio. This is a packaged version of IDEA IntelliJ with built-in Android SDK and developer tools.

> **Note** At the time of this writing, Java 8 was available but not yet supported by the Android SDK. In previous versions of the Android SDK, Java 5 was also supported, but this is no longer the case. The latest version of Eclipse (4.4, a.k.a. Juno) was also available, but Android has historically not been reliable on the latest Eclipse right away. Check the system requirements here to find the latest: `http://developer.android.com/sdk/index.html`.

The Android SDK is compatible with Windows (Windows XP, Windows Vista, and Windows 7), Mac OS X (Intel only), and Linux (Intel only). In terms of hardware, you need an Intel machine, the more powerful the better.

To make your life easier, if you choose Eclipse as your IDE, you will want to use Android development tools (ADT). ADT is an Eclipse plug-in that supports building Android applications with the Eclipse IDE.

The Android SDK is made up of two main parts: the tools and the packages. When you first install the SDK, all you get are the base tools. These are executables and supporting files to help you develop applications. The packages are the files specific to a particular version of Android (called a *platform*) or a particular add-on to a platform. The platforms include Android 1.5 through 4.4.2. The add-ons include the Google Maps API, the Market License Validator, and even vendor-supplied ones such as Samsung's Galaxy Tab add-on. After you install the SDK, you then use one of the tools to download and set up the platforms and add-ons.

Remember, you only need to set up and configure one of Eclipse or Android Studio. You can use both if you are so inclined, but it's certainly not required. Let's get started!

Setting Up Your Eclipse Environment

In this section, you walk through downloading JDK 6, the Eclipse IDE, the Android SDK (tools and packages), and ADT. You also configure Eclipse to build Android applications. Google provides a page to describe the installation process (`http://developer.android.com/sdk/installing.html`) but leaves out some crucial steps, as you will see.

Downloading JDK

The first thing you need is the JDK. The Android SDK requires JDK 6 or higher; we've developed our examples using JDK 6 and 7, depending on the version of Eclipse or Android Studio in use. For Windows and Mac OS X, download JDK 7 from the Oracle web site (`www.oracle.com/technetwork/java/javase/ downloads/index.html`) and install it. You only need the JDK, not the bundles. To install the JDK for Linux, open a Terminal window and instruct your package manager to install it. For example, in Debian or Ubuntu try the following:

```
sudo apt-get install sun-java7-jdk
```

This should install the JDK plus any dependencies such as the JRE. If it doesn't, it probably means you need to add a new software source and then try that command again. The web page `https://help.ubuntu.com/community/Repositories/Ubuntu` explains software sources and how to add the connection to third-party software. The process is different depending on which version of Linux you have. After you've done that, retry the command.

With the introduction of Ubuntu 10.04 (Lucid Lynx), Ubuntu recommends using OpenJDK instead of the Oracle/Sun JDK. To install OpenJDK, try the following:

```
sudo apt-get install openjdk-7-jdk
```

If this is not found, set up the third-party software as outlined previously and run the command again. All packages on which the JDK depends are automatically added for you. It is possible to have both OpenJDK and the Oracle/Sun JDK installed at the same time. To switch active Java between the installed versions of Java on Ubuntu, run this command at a shell prompt

```
sudo update-alternatives --config java
```

and then choose which Java you want as the default.

Now that you have a Java JDK installed, it's time to set the `JAVA_HOME` environment variable to point to the JDK install folder. To do this on a Windows XP machine, choose Start ➤ My Computer, right-click, select Properties, choose the Advanced tab, and click Environment Variables. Click New to add the variable or Edit to modify it if it already exists. The value of `JAVA_HOME` is something like `C:\Program Files\Java\jdk1.7.0_79`.

For Windows Vista and Windows 7, the steps to get to the Environment Variables screen are a little different. Choose Start ➤ Computer, right-click, choose Properties, click the link for Advanced System Settings, and click Environment Variables. After that, follow the same instructions as for Windows XP to change the `JAVA_HOME` environment variable.

For Mac OS X, you set `JAVA_HOME` in the `.bashrc` file in your home directory. Edit or create the `.bashrc` file, and add a line that looks like this

```
export JAVA_HOME=path_to_JDK_directory
```

where `path_to_JDK_directory` is probably `/Library/Java/Home`. For Linux, edit your `.bashrc` file and add a line like the one for Mac OS X, except that your path to Java is probably something like `/usr/lib/jvm/java-6-sun` or `/usr/lib/jvm/java-6-openjdk`.

Downloading Eclipse

After the JDK is installed, you can download the Eclipse IDE for Java Developers. (You don't need the edition for Java EE; it works, but it's much larger and includes things you don't need for this book.) The examples in this book use Eclipse 4.2 or 4.4 (on both Linux and Windows environments). You can download all versions of Eclipse from `www.eclipse.org/downloads/`.

> **Note** As an alternative to the individual steps presented here, you can also download the ADT Bundle from the Android developer site. This includes Eclipse with built-in developer tools and the Android SDK in one package. It's a great way to get started quickly, but if you have an existing environment, or just want to know how all the components are stitched together, then following the step-by-step instructions is the way to go.

The Eclipse distribution is a `.zip` file that can be extracted just about anywhere. The simplest place to extract to on Windows is `C:\`, which results in a `C:\eclipse` folder where you find `eclipse.exe`. Depending on your security configuration, Windows may insist on enforcing UAC when running from C:\. For Mac OS X, you can extract to `Applications`. For Linux, you can extract to your home directory or have your administrator put Eclipse into a common place where you can get to it. The Eclipse executable is in the `eclipse` folder for all platforms. You may also find and install Eclipse using Linux's Software Center for adding new applications, although this may not provide you with the latest version.

When you first start up Eclipse, it asks you for a location for the workspace. To make things easy, you can choose a simple location such as `C:\android` or a directory under your home directory. If you share the computer with others, you should put your workspace folder somewhere underneath your home directory.

Downloading the Android SDK

To build applications for Android, you need the Android SDK. As stated before, the SDK comes with the base tools; then you download the package parts that you need and/or want to use. The tools part of the SDK includes an emulator so you don't need a mobile device with the Android OS to develop Android applications. It also has a setup utility to allow you to install the packages that you want to download.

You can download the Android SDK from `http://developer.android.com/sdk`. It ships as a `.zip` file, similar to the way Eclipse is distributed, so you need to unzip it to an appropriate location. For Windows, unzip the file to a convenient location (we used the `C:` drive), after which you should have a folder called something like `C:\android-sdk-windows` that contains the files as shown in Figure 1-1. For Mac OS X and Linux, you can unzip the file to your home directory. Notice that Mac OS X and Linux do not have an SDK Manager executable; the equivalent of the SDK Manager in Mac OS X and Linux is to run the `tools/android` program.

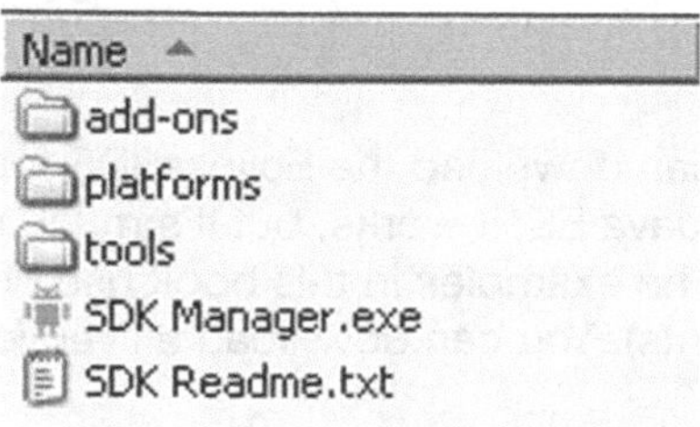

***Figure 1-1.** Base contents of the Android SDK*

An alternative approach (for Windows only) is to download an installer EXE instead of the zip file and then run the installer executable. This executable checks for the Java JDK, unpacks the embedded files for you, and runs the SDK Manager program to help you set up the rest of the downloads.

Whether through using the Windows installer or by executing the SDK Manager, you should install some packages next. When you first install the Android SDK, it does not come with any platform versions (that is, versions of Android). Installing platforms is pretty easy. After you've launched the SDK Manager, you see what is installed and what's available to install, as shown in Figure 1-2. You must add Android SDK tools and platform-tools in order for your environment to work. Because you use it shortly, add at least the Android 1.6 SDK platform, as well as the latest platform shown in your installer.

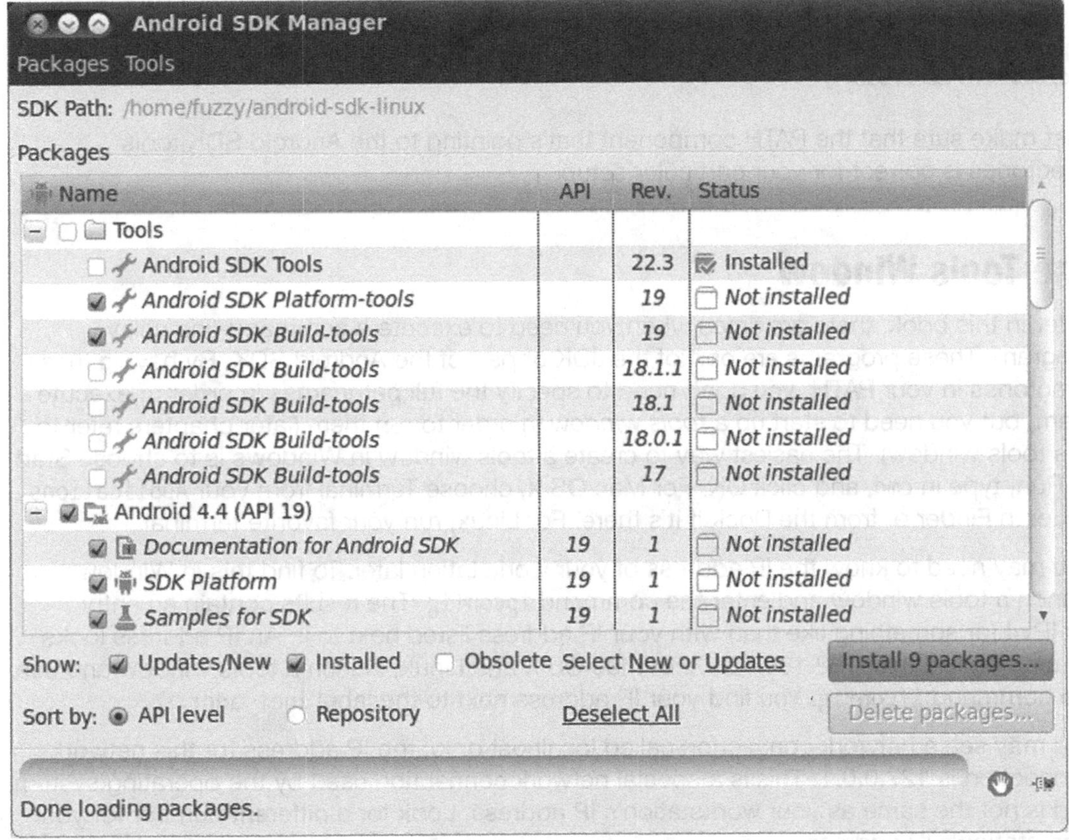

Figure 1-2. Adding packages to the Android SDK

Click the Install button. You need to click Accept for each item you're installing (or Accept All) and then click Install. Android then downloads your packages and platforms to make them available to you. The Google APIs are add-ons for developing applications using Google Maps. You can always come back to add more packages later.

Updating Your PATH Environment Variable

The Android SDK comes with a tools directory that you want to have in your PATH. You also need in your PATH the platform-tools directory you just installed. Let's add them now or, if you're upgrading, make sure they're correct. While you're there, you can also add a JDK bin directory, which will make life easier later.

For Windows, get back to the Environment Variables window. Edit the PATH variable and add a semicolon (;) on the end, followed by the path to the Android SDK tools folder, followed by another semicolon, followed by the path to the Android SDK platform-tools folder, followed by another semicolon, and then `%JAVA_HOME%\bin`. Click OK when you're done. For Mac OS X and Linux, edit your `.bashrc` file and add the Android SDK tools directory path to your PATH variable, as well as the Android SDK `platform-tools` directory and the `$JAVA_HOME/bin` directory. Something like the following works for Linux:

```
export PATH=$PATH:$HOME/android-sdk-linux_x86/tools:$HOME/android-sdk-linux_x86/platform-
tools:$JAVA_HOME/bin
```

Just make sure that the PATH component that's pointing to the Android SDK tools directories is correct for your particular setup.

The Tools Window

Later in this book, there are times when you need to execute a command-line utility program. These programs are part of the JDK or part of the Android SDK. By having these directories in your PATH, you don't need to specify the full pathnames in order to execute them, but you need to start up a *tools window* in order to run them (later chapters refer to this tools window). The easiest way to create a tools window in Windows is to choose Start ➤ Run, type in `cmd`, and click OK. For Mac OS X, choose Terminal from your `Applications` folder in Finder or from the Dock if it's there. For Linux, run your favorite terminal.

You may need to know the IP address of your workstation later. To find this in Windows, launch a tools window and enter the command `ipconfig`. The results contain an entry for IPv4 (or something like that) with your IP address listed next to it. An IP address looks something like this: 192.168.1.25. For Mac OS X and Linux, launch a tools window and use the command `ifconfig`. You find your IP address next to the label `inet addr`.

You may see a network connection called localhost or lo; the IP address for this network connection is 127.0.0.1. This is a special network connection used by the operating system and is not the same as your workstation's IP address. Look for a different number for your workstation's IP address.

Installing ADT

Now you need to install ADT (very recently renamed to GDT, the Google Developer Tools), an Eclipse plug-in that helps you build Android applications. Specifically, ADT integrates with Eclipse to provide facilities for you to create, test, and debug Android applications. You need to use the Install New Software facility in Eclipse to perform the installation. (The instructions for upgrading ADT appear later in this section.) To get started, launch the Eclipse IDE and follow these steps:

1. Select Help ➤ Install New Software.
2. Select the Work With field, type in

   `https://dl-ssl.google.com/android/eclipse/,`

   and press Enter. Eclipse contacts the site and populates the list as shown in Figure 1-3.

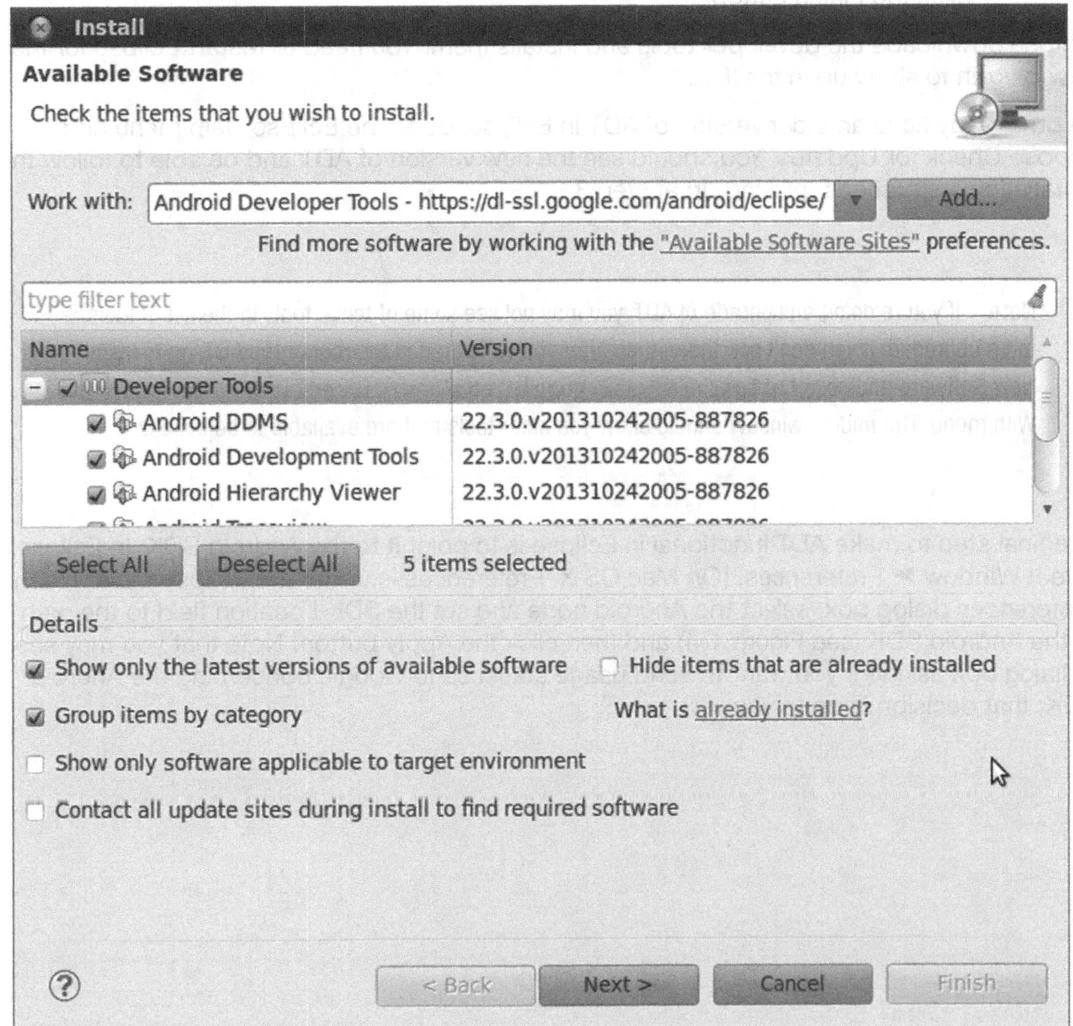

Figure 1-3. Installing ADT using the Install New Software feature in Eclipse

3. You should see an entry named Developer Tools with four child nodes: Android DDMS, Android Development Tools, Android Hierarchy Viewer, and Android Traceview. Just before publishing this book, Google updated the ADT to be part of the more generic Google Developer Tools plugin for Eclipse, or GDT. Look for the same options in the GDT. Select the parent node Developer Tools, make sure the child nodes are also selected, and click the Next button. The versions you see may be newer than these, and that's okay. You may also see additional tools. These tools are explained further in Chapter 11.
4. Eclipse asks you to verify the tools to install. Click Next.
5. You're asked to review the licenses for ADT as well as for the tools required to install ADT. Review the licenses, click "I accept," and then click the Finish button.

Eclipse downloads the developer tools and installs them. You need to restart Eclipse for the new plug-in to show up in the IDE.

If you already have an older version of ADT in Eclipse, go to the Eclipse Help menu and choose Check for Updates. You should see the new version of ADT and be able to follow the installation instructions, picking up at step 3.

> **Note** If you're doing an upgrade of ADT, you may not see some of these tools in the list of tools to be upgraded. If you don't see them, then after you've upgraded the rest of the ADT, go to Install New Software and select `https://dl-ssl.google.com/android/eclipse/` from the Works With menu. The middle window should show you other tools that are available to be installed.

The final step to make ADT functional in Eclipse is to point it to the Android SDK. In Eclipse, select Window ➤ Preferences. (On Mac OS X, Preferences is under the Eclipse menu.) In the Preferences dialog box, select the Android node and set the SDK Location field to the path of the Android SDK (see Figure 1-4) and then click the Apply button. Note that you may see a dialog box asking if you want to send usage statistics to Google concerning the Android SDK; that decision is up to you.

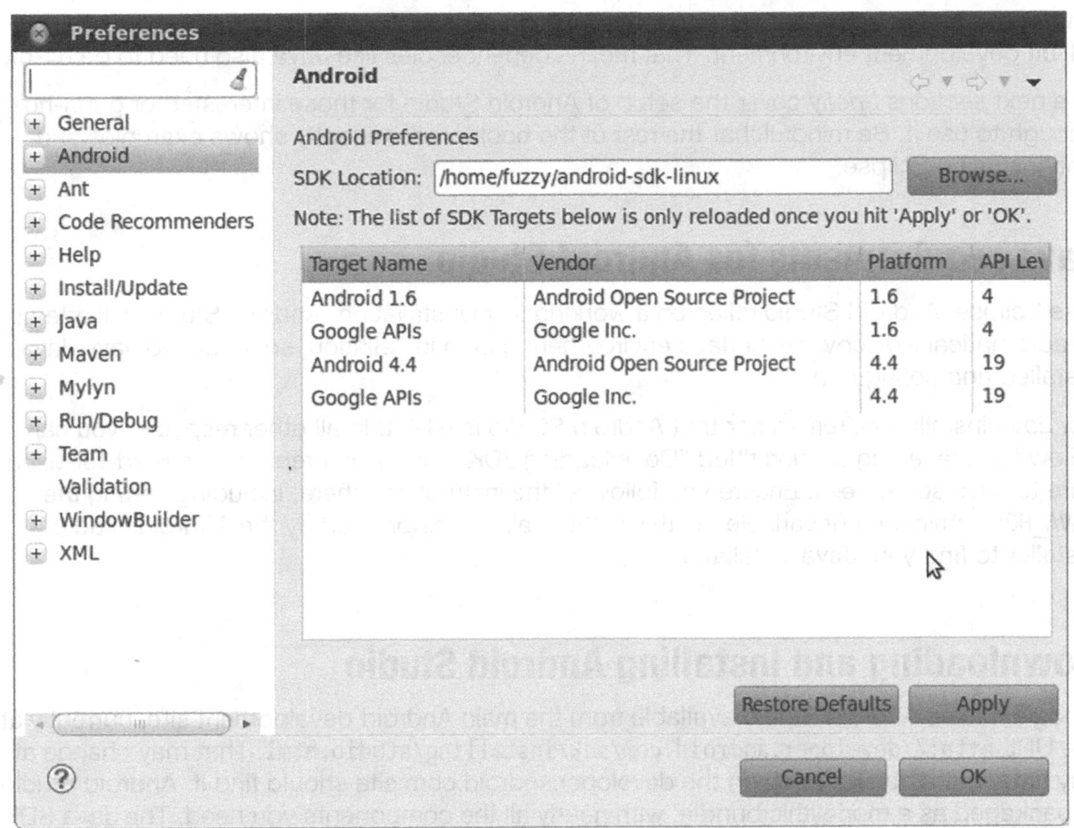

***Figure 1-4.** Pointing ADT to the Android SDK*

You may want to make one more Preferences change on the Android ➤ Build page. The Skip Packaging option should be checked if you'd like to make your file saves faster. By default, the ADT readies your application for launch every time it builds it. By checking this option, packaging and indexing occur only when truly needed.

From Eclipse, you can launch the SDK Manager. To do so, choose Window ➤ Android SDK Manager. You should see the same window as in Figure 1-2.

If you've chosen Eclipse as your IDE, you are almost ready for your first Android application—you can skip the following section on Android Studio and head straight to the "Learning Android's Fundamental Components" section.

Setting Up Your Android Studio Environment

In 2013, Google introduced a second supported development environment, known as Android Studio (or Android Developer Studio at the time of launch). This is based around a popular Java IDE: IDEA IntelliJ. The most important thing to know about Android Studio is that it is still a work in progress. As of this book's writing, the latest version is 1.2. Anyone familiar with the vagaries of version numbers knows that starting with a low number usually means "beware!"

The second most important thing to remember is that Android Studio currently assumes a 64-bit development environment. That means dependencies like Java also need to be 64-bit.

The next sections *briefly* cover the setup of Android Studio for those interested or gung-ho enough to use it. Be mindful that the rest of the book predominantly shows examples and options using Eclipse.

Java requirements for Android Studio

Like Eclipse, Android Studio relies on a working Java installation. Android Studio will attempt to automatically discover your Java environment during installation, so it pays to have Java installed and configured.

For Java installation, remember that Android Studio is 64-bit. In all other respects, you can follow the preceding section titled "Downloading JDK"—we won't repeat that word-for-word here to save some trees. Ensure you follow all the instructions there, including setting the `JAVA_HOME` environment variable, as this is the main indicator used by the Android Studio installer to find your Java installation.

Downloading and Installing Android Studio

Google makes Android Studio available from the main Android development site, currently at the URL `http://developer.android.com/sdk/installing/studio.html`. That may change at any time, but a quick search on the developer.android.com site should find it. Android Studio is packaged as a monolithic bundle, with nearly all the components you need. The Java SDK is the exception—we'll cover that shortly. The package downloaded from the preceding URL will be named something like android-studio-bundle-132.893413-windows.exe for windows, or a similar name with a different extension for OS X and Linux, and includes the following:

- Current latest build of the Android Studio bundle of IntelliJ IDEA
- Built-in Android SDK
- All related Android build tools
- Android Virtual Device images

We'll talk more about these components in later chapters. For a Windows installation run the executable and follow the prompts to choose an installation path, and decide whether Android Studio is made available to all users on the Windows machine, or just the current user. For OS X, open the `.dmg` file and copy the Android Studio entry to your Applications folder. Under Linux, extract the contents of the `.tgz` file to your desired location.

Once installed, you can start Android Studio under Windows from the start menu folder you chose when prompted; under OS X from the Applications folder; and under Linux by running the `./android-studio/bin/studio.sh` file under your installation directory. Whatever the operating system, you should see the Android Studio home screen as depicted in Figure 1-5.

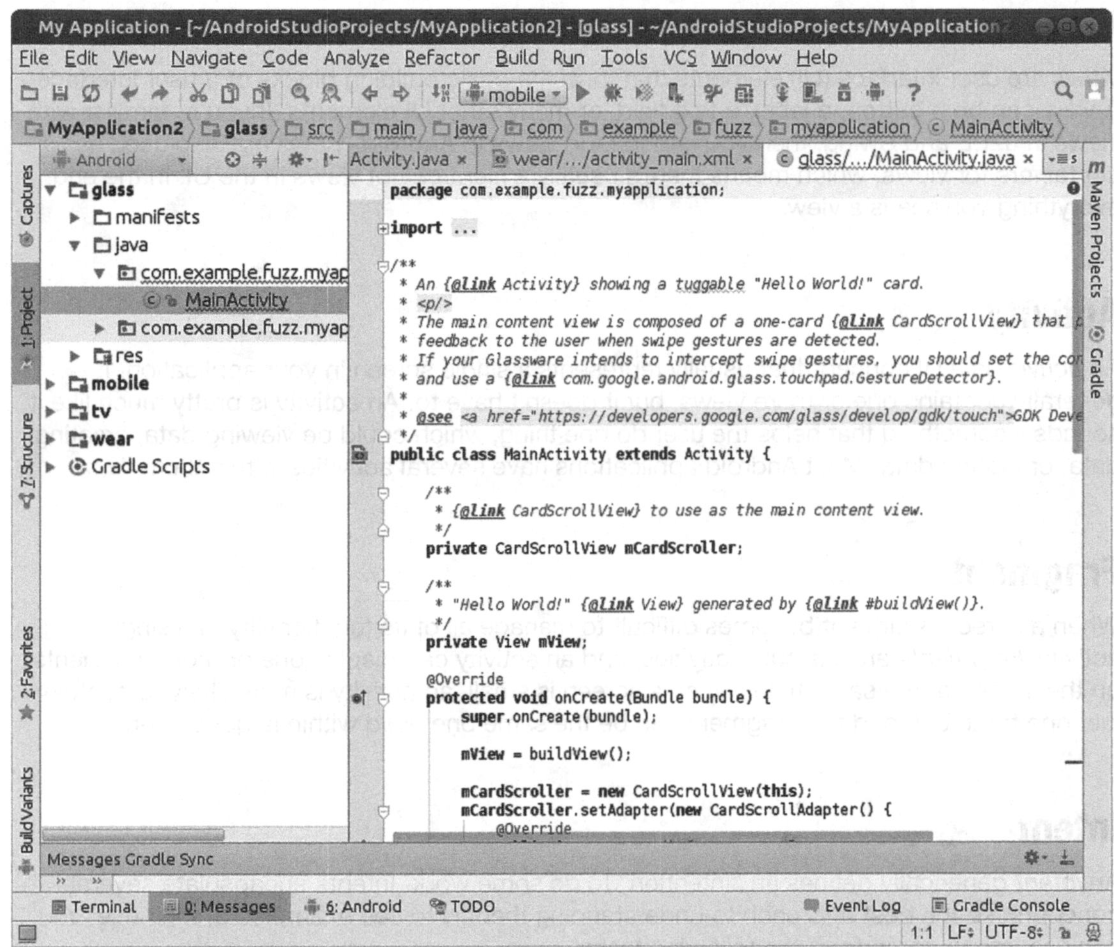

***Figure 1-5.** Android Studio when first launched*

Learning Android's Fundamental Components

Every application framework has some key components that developers need to understand before they can begin to write applications based on the framework. For example, you need to understand JavaServer Pages (JSP) and servlets in order to write Java 2 Platform, Enterprise Edition (J2EE) applications. Similarly, you need to understand views, activities, fragments, intents, content providers, services, and the `AndroidManifest.xml` file when you build applications for Android. You briefly cover these fundamental concepts here and explore them in more detail throughout the book.

View

Views are user interface (UI) elements that form the basic building blocks of a user interface. A view can be a button, a label, a text field, or many other UI elements. If you're familiar with views in J2EE and Swing, then you understand views in Android. Views are also used as containers for views, which means there's usually a hierarchy of views in the UI. In the end, everything you see is a view.

Activity

An *activity* is a UI concept that usually represents a single screen in your application. It generally contains one or more views, but it doesn't have to. An activity is pretty much like it sounds—something that helps the user do one thing, which could be viewing data, creating data, or editing data. Most Android applications have several activities within them.

Fragment

When a screen is large, it becomes difficult to manage all of its functionality in a single activity. *Fragments* are like sub-activities, and an activity can display one or more fragments on the screen at the same time. When a screen is small, an activity is more likely to contain just one fragment, and that fragment can be the same one used within larger screens.

Intent

An *intent* generically defines an "intention" to do some work. Intents encapsulate several concepts, so the best approach to understanding them is to see examples of their use. You can use intents to perform the following tasks:

- Broadcast a message
- Start a service
- Launch an activity
- Display a web page or a list of contacts
- Dial a phone number or answer a phone call

Intents are not always initiated by your application—they're also used by the system to notify your application of specific events (such as the arrival of a text message).

Intents can be explicit or implicit. If you simply say that you want to display a URL, the system decides what component will fulfill the intention. You can also provide specific information about what should handle the intention. Intents loosely couple the action and action handler.

Content Provider

Data sharing among mobile applications on a device is common. Therefore, Android defines a standard mechanism for applications to share data (such as a list of contacts) without exposing the underlying storage, structure, and implementation. Through content providers, you can expose your data and have your applications use data from other applications.

Service

Services in Android resemble services you see in Windows or other platforms—they're background processes that can potentially run for a long time. Android defines two types of services: local services and remote services. Local services are components that are only accessible by the application that is hosting the service. Conversely, remote services are services that are meant to be accessed remotely by other applications running on the device.

An example of a service is a component that is used by an e-mail application to poll for new messages. This kind of service may be a local service if the service is not used by other applications running on the device. If several applications use the service, then it's implemented as a remote service.

AndroidManifest.xml

`AndroidManifest.xml`, which is similar to the `web.xml` file in the J2EE world, defines the contents and behavior of your application. For example, it lists your application's activities and services, along with the permissions and features the application needs to run.

AVDs

An AVD allows developers to test their applications without hooking up an actual Android device (typically a phone or a tablet). AVDs can be created in various configurations to emulate different types of real devices.

Hello World!

Now you're ready to build your first Android application. You start by building a simple "Hello World!" program. Create the skeleton of the application by following these steps:

1. Launch Eclipse, and select File ➤ New ➤ Project. In the New Project dialog box, select Android Application Project and then click Next. You see the New Android Project dialog box, as shown in Figure 1-6. (Eclipse may have added Android Project to the New menu, so you can use it if it's there.) There's also a New Android Project button on the toolbar.

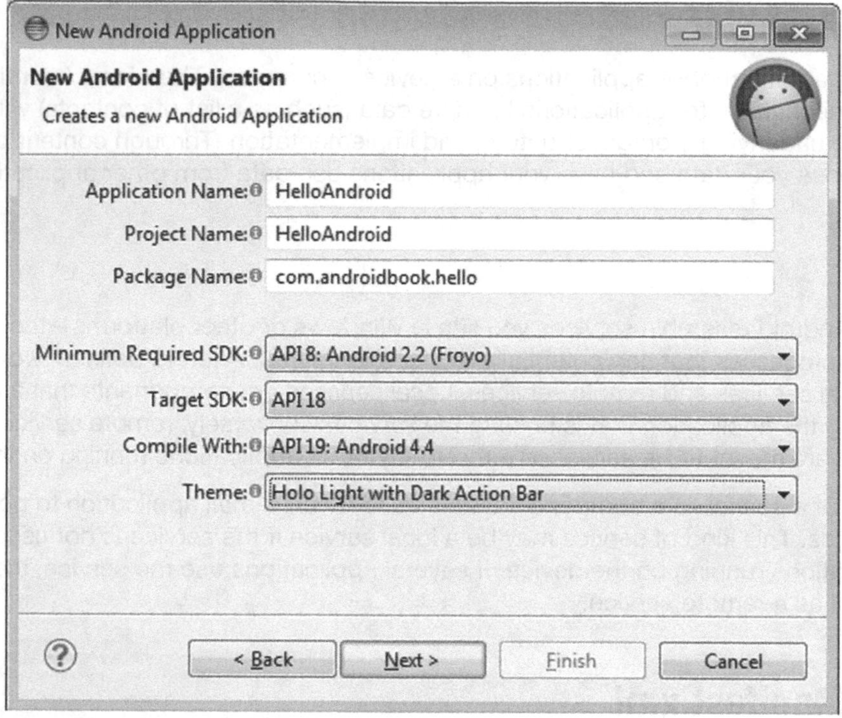

Figure 1-6. Using the New Project Wizard to create an Android application

2. As shown in Figure 1-6, enter **HelloAndroid** as the project name. You need to distinguish this project from other projects you create in Eclipse, so choose a name that will make sense to you when you are looking at all the projects in your Eclipse environment. You will also see the available Build Targets. Select Android 2.2. This is the version of Android you use as your base for the application. You can run your application on later versions of Android, such as 4.3 and 4.4; but Android 2.2 has all the functionality you need for this example, so choose it as your target. In general, it's best to choose the lowest version number you can, because that maximizes the number of devices that can run your application.
3. Leave the Project Name to auto-complete itself based on your Application Name.
4. Use **com.androidbook.hello** as the package name. Like all Java applications, your application must have a base package name, and this is it. This package name will be used as an identifier for your application and must be unique across all applications. For this reason, it's best to start the package name with a domain name that you own. If you don't own one, be creative to ensure that your package name won't likely be used by anyone else. Click Next.

5. The next window provides options for customer launcher icons, the actual directory for the workspace in which you source code and other files are stored, and several other options. Leave all of these at the default, and click Next.

6. The next window shows you the Configure Launcher Icon options and settings, as shown in Figure 1-7. Feel free to play with the options here, though any changes you make are cosmetic and affect the look of the launcher icon when your application is deployed, and not its actual logic. Click Next when ready.

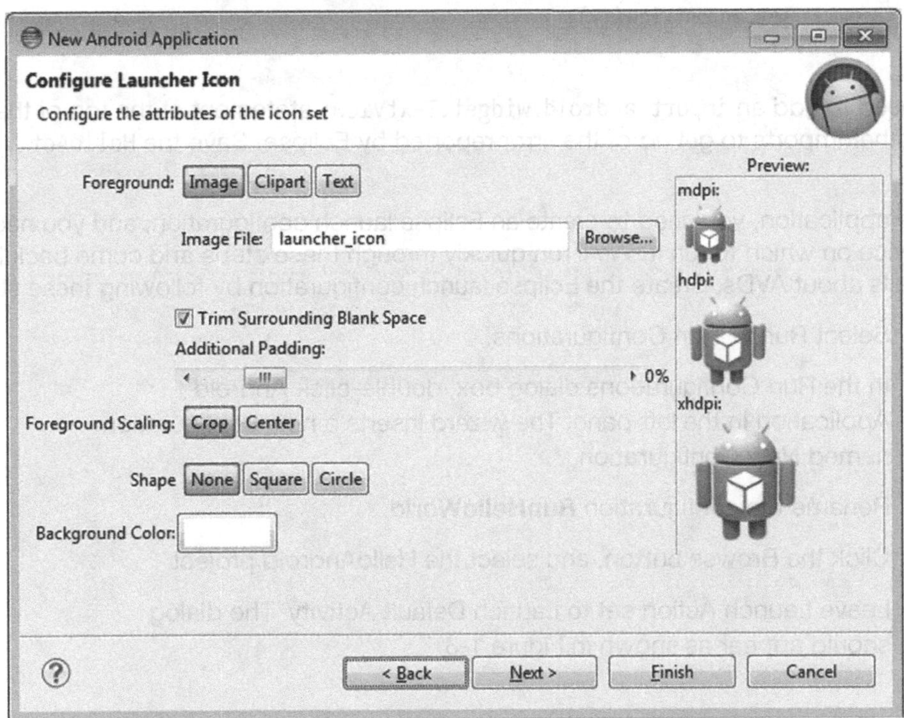

***Figure 1-7.** The Android launcher configuration options for a new Android project*

7. You'll next see the Create Activity screen. Choose Blank Activity as the activity type, and click Next to move to the last screen of the wizard.

8. The final screen of the New Android Application wizard will be the Blank Activity details page. Type **HelloActivity** as the Activity Name. You're telling Android that this activity is the one to launch when your application starts up. You may have other activities in your application, but this is the first one the user sees. Allow the Layout Name to auto-populate with the value `activity_hello`.

9. Click the Finish button, which tells ADT to generate the project skeleton for you. For now, open the HelloActivity.java file under the src folder and modify the onCreate() method as follows:

```
/** Called when the activity is first created. */
    @Override
    public void onCreate(Bundle savedInstanceState) {
        super.onCreate(savedInstanceState);
        /** create a TextView and write Hello World! */
        TextView tv = new TextView(this);
        tv.setText("Hello World!");
        /** set the content view to the TextView */
        setContentView(tv);
    }
```

You will need to add an import android.widget.TextView; statement at the top of the file with the other imports to get rid of the error reported by Eclipse. Save the HelloActivity.java file.

To run the application, you need to create an Eclipse launch configuration, and you need a virtual device on which to run it. We'll run quickly through these steps and come back later to more details about AVDs. Create the Eclipse launch configuration by following these steps:

1. Select Run ➤ Run Configurations.
2. In the Run Configurations dialog box, double-click Android Application in the left pane. The wizard inserts a new configuration named New Configuration.
3. Rename the configuration **RunHelloWorld**.
4. Click the Browse button, and select the HelloAndroid project.
5. Leave Launch Action set to Launch Default Activity. The dialog should appear as shown in Figure 1-8.

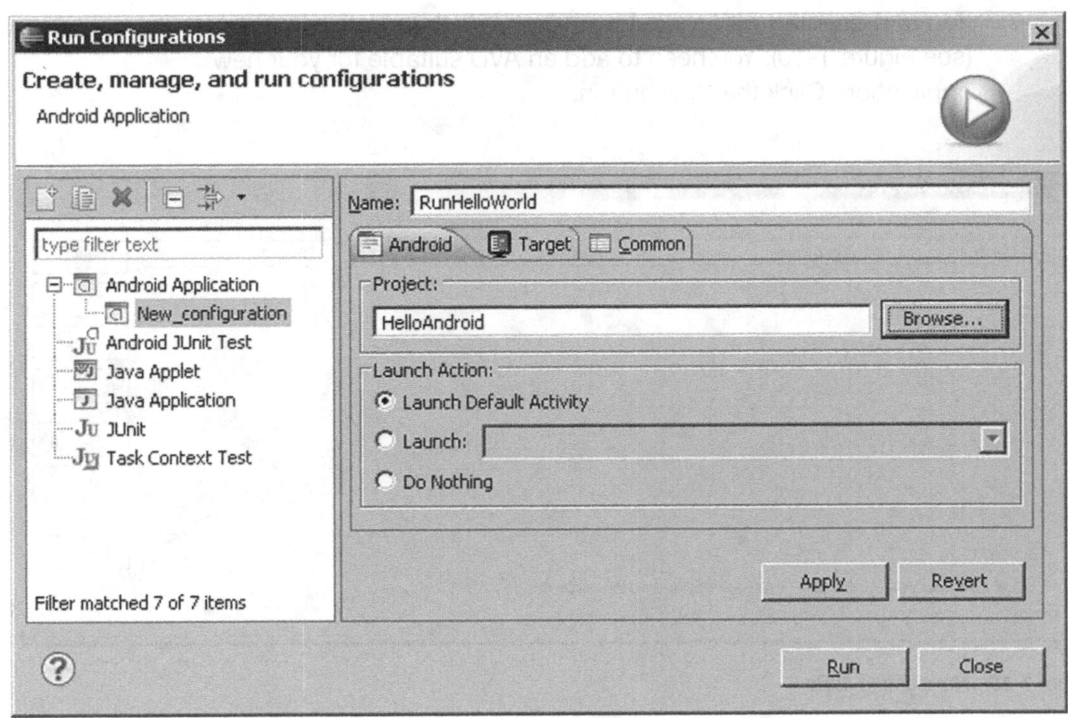

Figure 1-8. Configuring an Eclipse run configuration to run the "Hello World!" application

6. Click Apply and then Run. You're almost there! Eclipse is ready to run your application, but it needs a device on which to run it. As shown in Figure 1-9, you're warned that no compatible targets were found and asked if you'd like to create one. Click Yes.

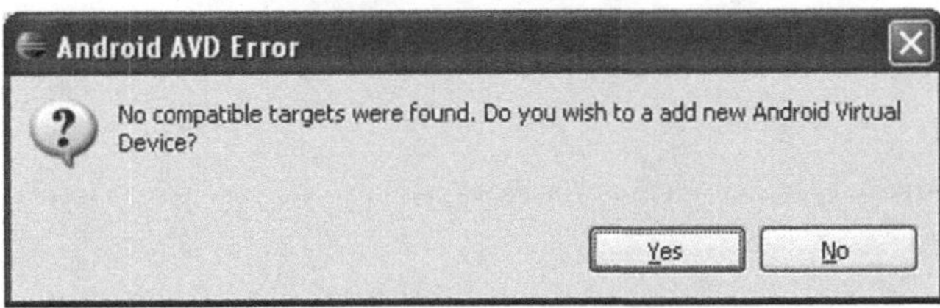

Figure 1-9. Error message warning about targets and asking for a new AVD

7. You're presented with a window that shows the existing AVDs (see Figure 1-10). You need to add an AVD suitable for your new application. Click the New button.

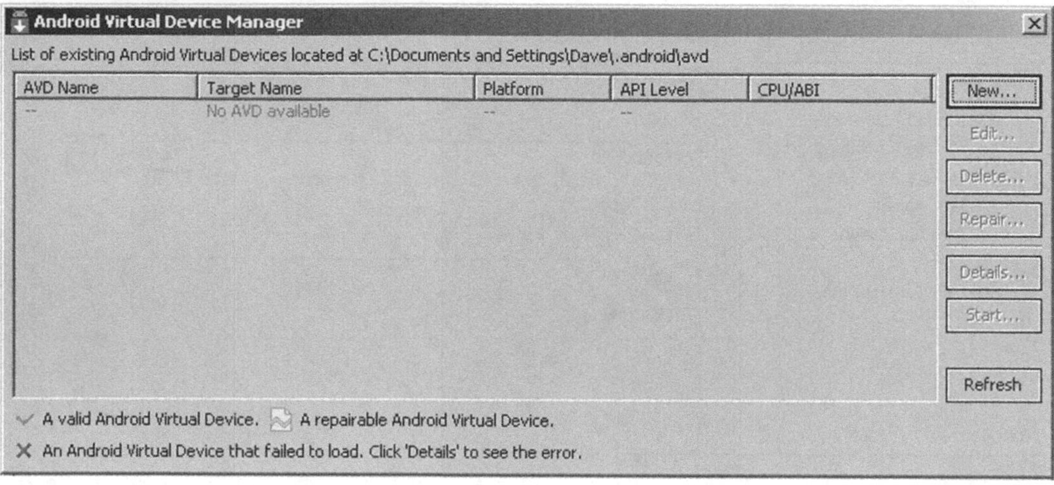

Figure 1-10. The existing AVDs

8. Fill in the Create AVD form as shown in Figure 1-11. Set Name to KitKat, choose Android 4.4 - API Level 19 (or some other version) for the Target, set SD Card Size to 64 (for 64MB), and choose other values as shown. Click Create AVD. The Manager may confirm the successful creation of your AVD. Close the AVD Manager window by clicking X in the upper-right corner.

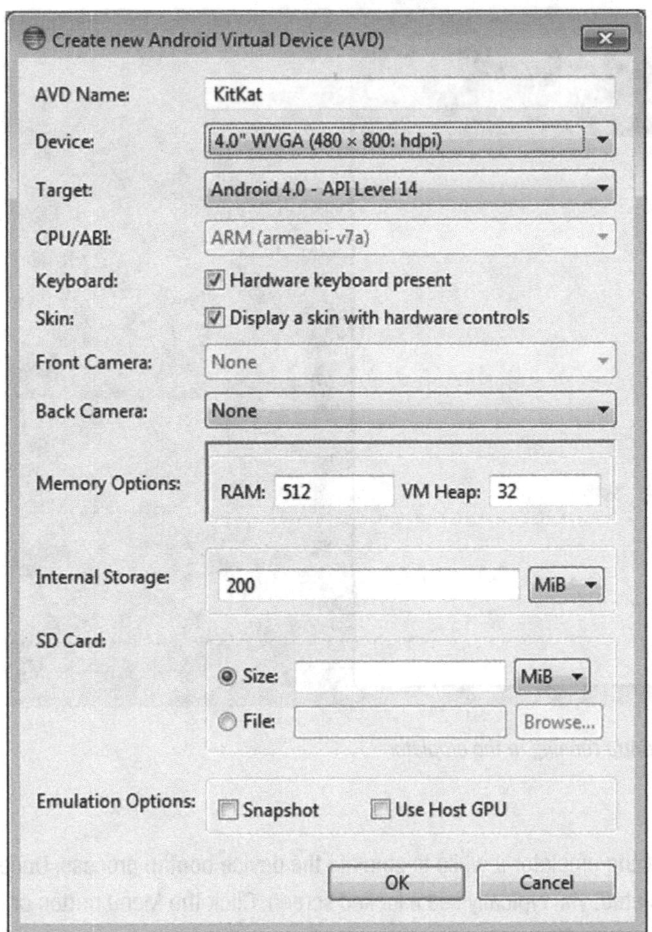

***Figure 1-11.** Configuring an AVD*

> **Note** You're choosing a newer version of the SDK for your AVD, but your application can also run on an older one. This is okay because AVDs with newer SDKs can run applications that require older SDKs. The opposite, of course, is not true: an application that requires features of a newer SDK won't run on an AVD with an older SDK.

9. Select your new AVD from the bottom list. Note that you may need to click the Refresh button to make any new AVDs to show up in the list. Click the OK button.
10. Eclipse launches the emulator with your very first Android app (see Figure 1-12)!

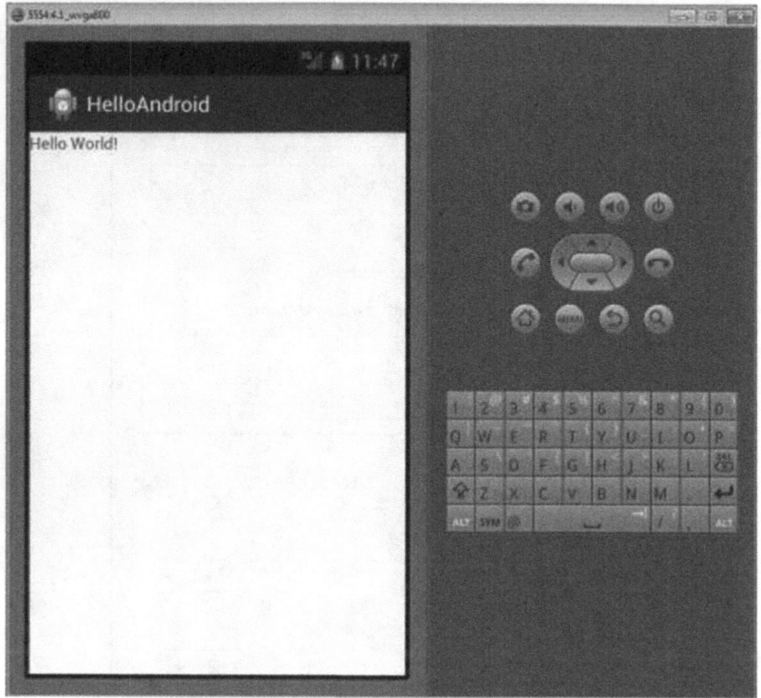

Figure 1-12. HelloAndroidApp running in the emulator

> **Note** It may take the emulator a while to emulate the device bootup process. Once the bootup process has completed, you typically see a locked screen. Click the Menu button or drag the unlock image to unlock the AVD. After unlocking, you should see HelloAndroidApp running in the emulator, as shown in Figure 1-11. Be aware that the emulator starts other applications in the background during the startup process, so you may see a warning or error message from time to time. If you do, you can generally dismiss it to allow the emulator to go to the next step in the startup process. For example, if you run the emulator and see a message like "application abc is not responding," you can either wait for the application to start or simply ask the emulator to forcefully close the application. Generally, you should wait and let the emulator start up cleanly.

Now you know how to create a new Android application and run it in the emulator. Next, we'll look more closely at AVDs, and also how to deploy to a real device.

AVDs

An AVD represents a device and its configuration. For example, you could have an AVD representing a really old Android device running version 1.5 of the SDK with a 32MB SD card. The idea is that you create AVDs you are going to support and then point the emulator to one of those AVDs when developing and testing your application. Specifying (and changing) which AVD to use is very easy and makes testing with various configurations a snap. Earlier, you saw how to create an AVD using Eclipse. You can make more AVDs in Eclipse by choosing Window ➤ Android Virtual Device Manager. You can also create AVDs using the command line with the utility named `android` under the `tools` directory (e.g., `c:\android-sdk-windows\tools\`). `android` allows you to create a new AVD and manage existing AVDs. For example, you can view existing AVDs, move AVDs, and so on by invoking `android` with the "avd" option. You can see the options available for using `android` by running `android -help`. For now, let's just create an AVD.

Running on a Real Device

The best way to test an Android app is to run it on a real device. Any commercial Android device should work when connected to your workstation, but you may need to do a little work to set it up. If you have a Mac, you don't need to do anything except plug it in using the USB cable. Then, on the device itself, choose Settings ➤ Applications ➤ Development (though this may vary by phone and version) and enable USB debugging. On Linux, you probably need to create or modify this file: `/etc/udev/rules.d/51-android.rules`. We put a copy of this file on our web site with the project files; copy it to the proper directory, and modify the username and group values appropriately for your machine. Then, when you plug in an Android device, it will be recognized. Next, enable USB debugging on the device.

For Windows, you have to deal with USB drivers. Google supplies some with the Android packages, which are placed under the `usb_driver` subdirectory of the Android SDK directory. Other device vendors provide drivers for you, so look for them on their web sites. You can also visit the XDA forums, `forum.xda-developers.com`, where advice on sourcing and configuring drivers for a variety of phones and devices is discussed. When you have the drivers set up, enable USB debugging on the device, and you're ready.

Now that your device is connected to your workstation, when you try to launch an app, either it launches directly on the device or (if you have an emulator running or other devices attached) a window opens in which you choose which device or emulator to launch into. If not, try editing your Run Configuration to manually select the target.

Exploring the Structure of an Android Application

Although the size and complexity of Android applications can vary greatly, their structures are similar. Figure 1-13 shows the structure of the "Hello World!" app you just built.

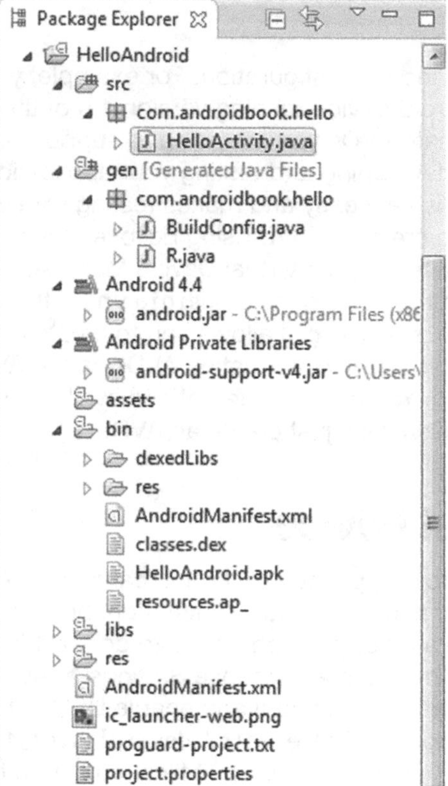

***Figure 1-13.** The structure of the "Hello World!" application*

Android applications have some artifacts that are required and some that are optional. Table 1-1 summarizes the elements of an Android application.

***Table 1-1.** The Artifacts of an Android Application*

Artifact	Description	Required?
`AndroidManifest.xml`	The Android application descriptor file. This file defines the activities, content providers, services, and intent receivers of the application. You can also use this file to declaratively define permissions required by the application, as well as instrumentation and testing options.	Yes
`src`	A folder containing all of the source code of the application.	Yes
`assets`	An arbitrary collection of folders and files.	No
`res`	A folder containing the resources of the application. This is the parent folder of `drawable`, `animator`, `layout`, `menu`, `values`, `xml`, and `raw`.	Yes

(continued)

Table 1-1. (*continued*)

Artifact	Description	Required?
`drawable`	A folder containing the images or image-descriptor files used by the application.	No
`animator`	A folder containing the XML-descriptor files that describe the animations used by the application.	No
`layout`	A folder containing views of the application.	No
`menu`	A folder containing XML-descriptor files for menus in the application.	No
`values`	A folder containing other resources used by the application. Examples of resources found in this folder include strings, arrays, styles, and colors.	No
`xml`	A folder containing additional XML files used by the application.	No
`raw`	A folder containing additional data—possibly non-XML data—that is required by the application.	No

As you can see from Table 1-1, an Android application is primarily made up of three mandatory pieces: the application descriptor, a collection of various resources, and the application's source code. If you put aside the `AndroidManifest.xml` file for a moment, you can view an Android app in this simple way: you have some business logic implemented in code, and everything else is a resource.

Android has also adopted the approach of defining views via markup in XML. You benefit from this approach because you don't have to hard-code your application's views; you can modify the look and feel of the application by editing the markup.

It is also worth noting a few constraints regarding resources. First, Android supports only a single-level list of files within the predefined folders under `res`. For example, there are some similarities between the `assets` folder and the `raw` folder under `res`. Both folders can contain raw files, but the files in `raw` are considered resources, and the files in `assets` are not. So the files in `raw` are localized, accessible through resource IDs, and so on. But the contents of the `assets` folder are considered general-purpose content to be used without resource constraints and support. Note that because the contents of the `assets` folder are not considered resources, you can put an arbitrary hierarchy of folders and files in this folder. (Chapter 3 talks a lot more about resources.)

> **Note** You may have noticed that XML is used quite heavily with Android. You know that XML can be a bloated data format, so does it make sense to rely on XML when you know your target is a device with limited resources? It turns out that the XML you create during development is actually compiled down to binary using the Android Asset Packaging Tool (AAPT). Therefore, when your application is installed on a device, the files on the device are stored as binary. When the file is needed at runtime, the file is read in its binary form and is not transformed back into XML. This gives you the benefits of both worlds—you get to work with XML, and you don't have to worry about taking up valuable resources on the device.

Examining the Application Life Cycle

The life cycle of an Android application is strictly managed by the system, based on the user's needs, available resources, and so on. A user may want to launch a web browser, for example, but the system ultimately decides whether to start the application. Although the system is the ultimate manager, it adheres to some defined and logical guidelines to determine whether an application can be loaded, paused, or stopped. If the user is currently working with an activity, the system gives high priority to that application. Conversely, if an activity is not visible and the system determines that an application must be shut down to free up resources, it shuts down the lower-priority application.

The concept of application life cycle is logical, but a fundamental aspect of Android applications complicates matters. Specifically, the Android application architecture is component- and integration-oriented. This allows a rich user experience, seamless reuse, and easy application integration but creates a complex task for the application life-cycle manager.

Let's consider a typical scenario. A user is talking to someone on the phone and needs to open an e-mail message to answer a question. The user goes to the home screen, opens the mail application, opens the e-mail message, clicks a link in the e-mail, and answers the friend's question by reading a stock quote from a web page. This scenario requires four applications: the home application, a talk application, an e-mail application, and a browser application. As the user navigates from one application to the next, the experience is seamless. In the background, however, the system is saving and restoring application state. For instance, when the user clicks the link in the e-mail message, the system saves metadata on the running e-mail message activity before starting the browser-application activity to launch a URL. In fact, the system saves metadata on any activity before starting another so that it can come back to the activity (when the user backtracks, for example). If memory becomes an issue, the system has to shut down a process running an activity and resume it as necessary.

Android is sensitive to the life cycle of an application and its components. Therefore, you need to understand and handle life-cycle events in order to build a stable application. The processes running your Android application and its components go through various life-cycle events, and Android provides callbacks that you can implement to handle state changes. For starters, you should become familiar with the various life-cycle callbacks for an activity (see Listing 1-1).

Listing 1-1. Life-Cycle Methods of an Activity

```
protected void onCreate(Bundle savedInstanceState);
protected void onStart();
protected void onRestart();
protected void onResume();
protected void onPause();
protected void onStop();
protected void onDestroy();
```

Listing 1-1 shows the list of life-cycle methods that Android calls during the life of an activity. It's important to understand when each of the methods is called by the system in order to ensure that you implement a stable application. Note that you do not need to react to all of these methods. If you do, however, be sure to call the superclass versions as well. Figure 1-14 shows the transitions between states.

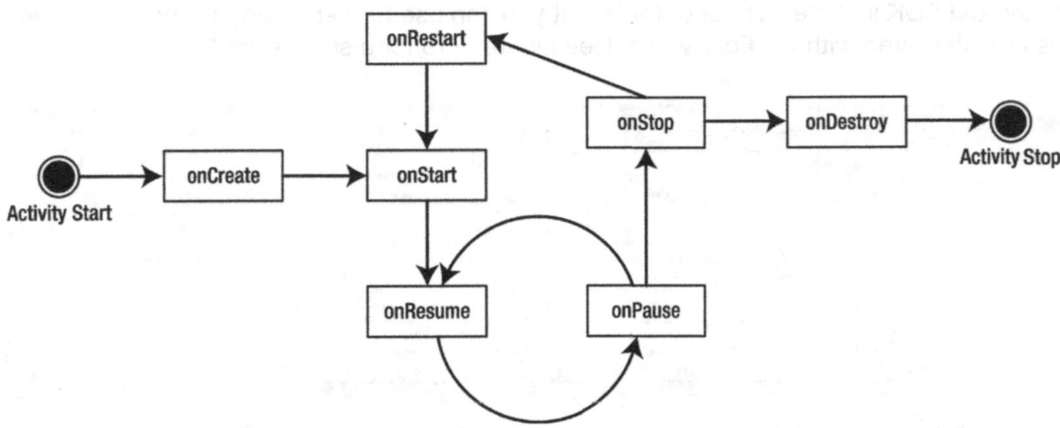

Figure 1-14. State transitions of an activity

The system can start and stop your activities based on what else is happening. Android calls the `onCreate()` method when the activity is freshly created. `onCreate()` is always followed by a call to `onStart()`, but `onStart()` is not always preceded by a call to `onCreate()` because `onStart()` can be called if your application was stopped. When `onStart()` is called, your activity is not visible to the user, but it's about to be. `onResume()` is called after `onStart()`, just when the activity is in the foreground and accessible to the user. At this point, the user can interact with your activity.

When the user decides to move to another activity, the system calls your activity's `onPause()` method. From `onPause()`, you can expect either `onResume()` or `onStop()` to be called. `onResume()` is called, for example, if the user brings your activity back to the foreground. `onStop()` is called if your activity becomes invisible to the user. If your activity is brought back to the foreground after a call to `onStop()`, then `onRestart()` is called. If your activity sits on the activity stack but is not visible to the user, and the system decides to kill your activity, `onDestroy()` is called.

As a developer, you needn't deal with every possible scenario; you mostly handle onCreate(), onResume(), and onPause(). You handle onCreate() to create the user interface for your activity. In this method, you bind data to your widgets and wire up any event handlers for your UI components. In onPause(), you want to persist critical data to your application's data store: it's the last safe method that is called before the system kills your application. onStop() and onDestroy() are not guaranteed to be called, so don't rely on these methods for critical logic.

The takeaway from this discussion? The system manages your application, and it can start, stop, or resume an application component at any time. Although the system controls your components, they don't run in complete isolation with respect to your application. In other words, if the system starts an activity in your application, you can count on an application context in your activity.

Simple Debugging

The Android SDK includes a host of tools that you can use for debugging purposes. These tools are integrated with the Eclipse IDE (see Figure 1-15 for a small sample).

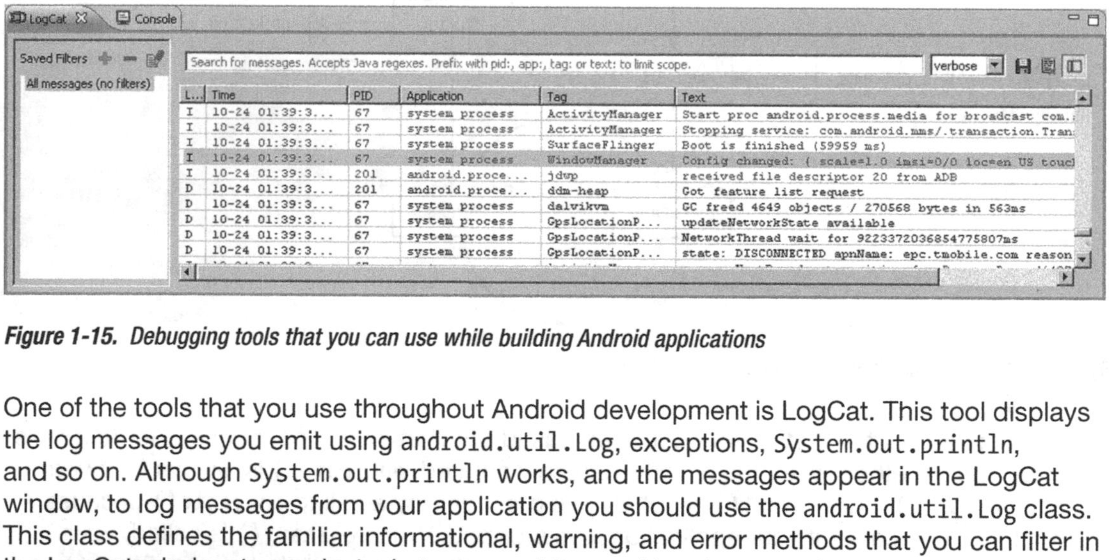

Figure 1-15. Debugging tools that you can use while building Android applications

One of the tools that you use throughout Android development is LogCat. This tool displays the log messages you emit using android.util.Log, exceptions, System.out.println, and so on. Although System.out.println works, and the messages appear in the LogCat window, to log messages from your application you should use the android.util.Log class. This class defines the familiar informational, warning, and error methods that you can filter in the LogCat window to see just what you want to see. Here is a sample Log command:

```
Log.v("string TAG", "This is my verbose message to write to the log");
```

This example shows the static v() method of the Log class, but there are others for different levels of severity. It's best to use the appropriate call level for the message you want to log, and it generally isn't a good idea to leave a verbose call in an app that you want to deploy to production. Keep in mind that logging uses memory and takes CPU resources.

What's particularly nice about LogCat is that you can view log messages when you're running your application in the emulator, but you can also view log messages when you've connected a real device to your workstation and it's in debug mode. In fact, log messages are stored such that you can even retrieve the most recent messages from a device that was disconnected when the log messages were recorded. When you connect a device to your workstation and you have the LogCat view open, you see the last several hundred messages.

Launching the Emulator

Earlier you saw how to launch the emulator from your project in Eclipse. In most cases, you want to launch the emulator first and then deploy and test your applications in a running emulator. To launch an emulator any time, first go to the AVD Manager by running the `Android program` with the `avd` option from the tools directory of the Android SDK or from the Window menu in Eclipse. Once in the Manager, choose the desired AVD from the list, and click Start.

When you click the Start button, the Launch Options dialog opens (see Figure 1-16). This allows you to scale the size of the emulator's window to suit your display and change the startup and shutdown options. The scaling results can sometimes be unexpectedly large or small, so pick the value that works for you based on your screen size and screen density.

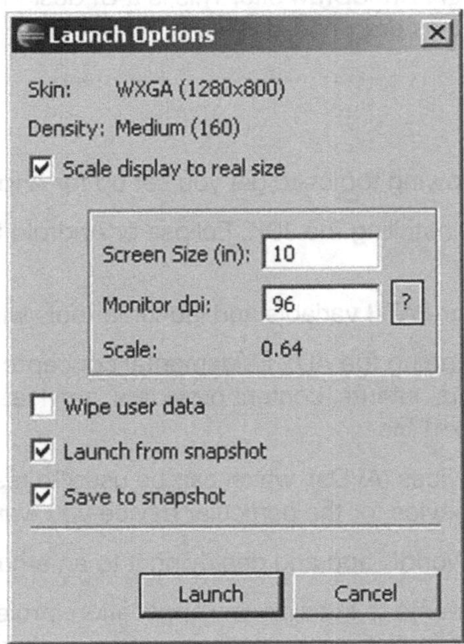

***Figure 1-16.** The Launch Options dialog*

You can also work with snapshots in the Launch Options dialog. Saving to a snapshot causes a somewhat longer delay when you exit the emulator. As the name suggests, you are writing out the current state of the emulator to a snapshot image file, which can then be used the next time you launch to avoid going through an entire Android bootup sequence. Launching goes much faster if a snapshot is present, making the delay at save time well worth it—you basically pick up where you left off.

If you want to start completely fresh, you can choose Wipe User Data. You can also deselect Launch from Snapshot to keep the user data and go through the bootup sequence. Or you can create a snapshot that you like and enable *only* the Launch from Snapshot option; this reuses the snapshot over and over so your startup is fast and the shutdown is fast too, because it doesn't create a new snapshot image file every time it exits. The snapshot image file is stored in the same directory as the rest of the AVD image files. If you didn't enable snapshots when you created the AVD, you can always edit the AVD and enable them there.

References

Here are some helpful references to topics you may wish to explore further:

- `http://developer.samsung.com/`: Samsung's developer site, with many Android-related development tools.
- `http://developer.htc.com/`: HTC site for Android developers.
- `http://developer.android.com/guide/developing/tools/index.html`: Developer documentation for the Android debugging tools.
- `www.droiddraw.org/`: DroidDraw site. This is a UI designer for Android applications that uses drag-and-drop to build layouts.

Summary

This chapter covered the following topics to get you set up for Android development:

- Downloading and installing the JDK, Eclipse or Android Studio, and the Android SDK
- How to modify your PATH variable and launch a tools window
- Installing and upgrading the ADT fundamental concepts of views, activities, fragments, intents, content providers, services, and the `AndroidManifest.xml` file
- Android Virtual Devices (AVDs), which can be used to test apps when you don't have a device (or the particular device you want to test with)
- Building a "Hello World!" app and deploying it to an emulator
- The basic requirements to initialize any application (project name, Android target, application name, package name, main activity, minimum SDK version)
- Where the run configurations are and how to change them
- Connecting a real device to your workstation and running your new apps on it
- The inner structure of an Android app, and the life cycle of an activity
- LogCat, and where to look for the internal messages from apps
- Options available when launching an emulator, such as snapshots and adjusting the screen display size

Chapter 2

Introduction to Android Application Architecture

The first chapter covered the environment and tools necessary to develop Android applications. This chapter will be a broad introductory tour of Android's application architecture. We will do that by doing three things. First, we will present the architecture of an Android app by building one. We will then present the essential components of Android architecture, namely, activities, resources, intents, activity life cycle, and saving state. We will conclude the chapter with a learning roadmap on how to use the rest of the book to create simple to sophisticated mobile apps.

In the **first section** of this chapter, a one-page calculator app will give you a bird's eye view of writing applications using the Android SDK. Creating this app will demonstrate how to create the UI, write Java code to control the UI, and build and deploy the app.

In addition to demonstrating the UI, this calculator app will introduce you to activities, resources, and intents. These concepts go to the heart of Android application architecture. We will cover these topics in detail in the **second section** of the chapter in order to give you a strong footing for understanding the rest of the Android SDK. We will also cover the activity life cycle and a brief overview of the persistence options for your application.

In the **third section** we will give you a roadmap for the rest of the book that addresses basic and advanced aspects of building Android applications. This final section breaks the chapters into a set of learning tracks. This section is a broad introduction to the entire set of Android APIs.

Furthermore, in this chapter you will find answers to the following: How can I create UI with a rich set of controls? How can I store state persistently? How can I read static files that are inputs to the app? How can I reach out and read from or write to the web? What other APIs does Android provide to make my app functional and rich?

Without further ado, let's drop you into the simple calculator application to open up the world of Android.

Exploring a Simple Android Application

The calculator application we want to demonstrate for this chapter is shown in Figure 2-1.

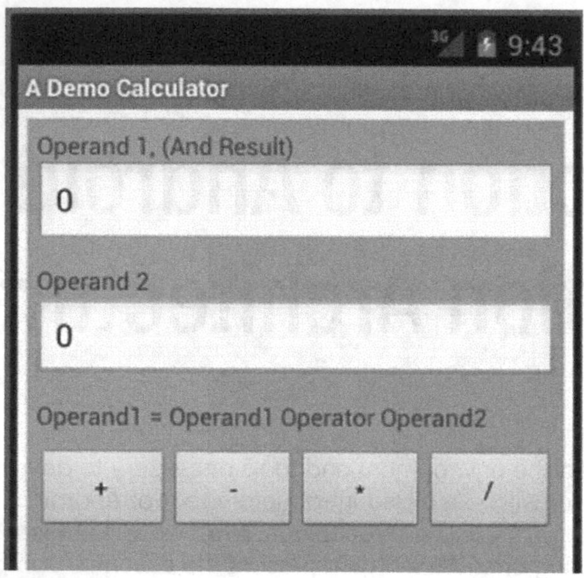

***Figure 2-1.** A Calculator App*

Display in Figure 2-1 is called an activity in Android. This activity has two edit controls at the top representing two numbers. You can enter numbers in these edit boxes and use the operator buttons at the bottom of the figure to perform arithmetical operations. The result of an operation will be shown in the top edit control. These two edit boxes are labeled Operand 1 and Operand 2. To create this type of a calculator application using the Android SDK, you need to perform the following steps:

1. Create a User Interface (UI) definition in a text/xml file (called a layout or a layout file in Android).
2. Write programming logic in a Java file (usually in a class extending the base activity class).
3. Create a configuration file describing your application (this file is always called `AndroidManifest.xml`).
4. Create a project and a directory structure to place the files from steps 1, 2, and 3.
5. Build a deployable package using the project in step 4 (it is called an `.apk` file).

By going through the details of these steps you will get a feel for how Android applications are made. We will go through these steps now.

Defining UI through Layout Files

An Android application resembles a web application in lots of ways. In a web application the UI is your web page. UI of a web page is defined through HTML. An HTML web page is a series of controls like paragraphs, divisions, forms, buttons, etc. UI is constructed similarly in Android. A layout file in Android is like an HTML page, albeit the controls are drawn from the Android SDK instead of HTML. In Android this file is called a layout file. Listing 2-1 shows the layout file that produced the UI of Figure 2-1.

Listing 2-1. An Android Layout File that Defines UI for an Activity

```
<?xml version="1.0" encoding="utf-8"?>
<!--
*********************************************
* calculator_layout.xml
* corresponding activity: CalculatorMainActivity.java
* prefix: cl_ (Used for prefixing unique identifiers)
*
* Use:
*    Demonstrate a simple calculator
*    Demonstrate text views, edit text, buttons, business logic
*********************************************
-->
<LinearLayout xmlns:android="http://schemas.android.com/apk/res/android"
    android:orientation="vertical"
    android:layout_width="match_parent" android:layout_height="match_parent"
    android:layout_margin="5dp" android:padding="5dp"
    android:background="@android:color/darker_gray"
    >
    <!-- Operand 1 -->
    <TextView android:layout_width="match_parent"
        android:layout_height="wrap_content"
        android:text="Operand 1, (And Result)"
        />
    <EditText android:layout_width="match_parent" android:layout_height="wrap_content"
        android:id="@+id/editText1"  android:text="0"
        android:inputType="numberDecimal"/>
    <!-- Operand 2 -->
    <TextView android:layout_width="match_parent"
        android:layout_height="wrap_content"
        android:text="Operand 2"
        android:layout_marginTop="10dp"
        />
    <EditText android:layout_width="match_parent"
       android:layout_height="wrap_content"
       android:text="0"
       android:id="@+id/editText2"
       android:inputType="numberDecimal">
    </EditText>
```

```
    <!--  Buttons for Various Operators -->
    <TextView android:layout_width="match_parent"
        android:layout_height="wrap_content"
        android:text="Operand1 = Operand1 Operator Operand2"
        android:layout_marginTop="10dp"
        />
<LinearLayout
    android:orientation="horizontal"
    android:layout_marginTop="10dp"
    android:layout_width="match_parent"
    android:layout_height="wrap_content">
    <Button android:text="+" android:id="@+id/plusButton"
       android:layout_weight="1"
       android:layout_width="wrap_content"
       android:layout_height="wrap_content">
    </Button>
    <Button android:text="-" android:id="@+id/minusButton"
       android:layout_weight="1"
       android:layout_width="wrap_content"
       android:layout_height="wrap_content">
    </Button>
    <Button android:text="*" android:id="@+id/multiplyButton"
       android:layout_weight="1"
       android:layout_width="wrap_content"
       android:layout_height="wrap_content">
    </Button>
    <Button android:text="/" android:id="@+id/divideButton"
       android:layout_weight="1"
       android:layout_width="wrap_content"
       android:layout_height="wrap_content">
    </Button>
</LinearLayout>
</LinearLayout>
```

Let's go through this calculator XML layout file of Listing 2-1 line by line. This file looks complicated compared to Figure 2-1. Yes, it is verbose, but you will see shortly it is simple in its architecture.

Specifying Comments in Layout Files

As a good practice the comments at the top of the layout XML file in Listing 2-1 indicate what this file name is, what UI activity will be used to display this file, what the purpose of this file is, and briefly what controls are in this layout file.

Adding Views and View Groups in Layout Files

Each XML node in a layout file represents a UI control. These controls can be either views or containers of other views. A container of other views is called a `ViewGroup`. For example, a button is a view. A `LinearLayout` in Listing 2-1 is a `ViewGroup` that places all its child views either vertically down or horizontally across. So, a `LinearLayout` is like an HTML `div` that lays out its children either across or down.

Specifying Control Properties in Layout Files

The UI controls in the calculator layout file are `LinearLayout`, `TextView`, `EditText`, and a `button`. Each of these controls represents a Java object when painted on the screen. Being an object, each of these controls has properties. If the controls belong to the core Android SDK, their properties are prefixed with `"android:"` as in `"android:orientation"` for the `LinearLayout` control. The majority, if not all, of the controls that you normally use in your apps are from the core Android SDK. When you write your own controls they are called custom controls. These custom controls allow you to define custom properties. See the "Roadmap" section of this chapter for more on custom controls.

Indicating ViewGroup Properties

Some of the control properties are labeled as `"android:layout_,"` such as `android:layout_width`. These properties, although mentioned in a given XML node, like a `button`, are read and used by parent node, like `LinearLayout`, to place the children. Parent nodes are view groups like the `LinearLayout`. You can see this difference in how `padding` and `margins` are defined for the first `LinearLayout` node in the layout file of listing 2-1. The property `padding` belongs to the topmost `LinearLayout` object in this example, whereas the property for margins of that same topmost `LinearLayout`, the `layout_margin` property, belongs to the parent of the `LinearLayout`, which is an implicit view group provided by the Android framework. So for padding you say `android:padding`, and for margins you say `android:layout_margin`. Notice the presence or lack of `"layout_"` prefix. If you want to know what properties an object (or control) supports, you can use `Ctrl-Space in eclipse` to see a set of suggestions for the properties for that object. Depending on your development environment you can easily find an equivalent set of key combinations to do the same.

Controlling Width and Height of a Control

Two often-used properties for a control are its layout width and layout height. The layout parent of a control manages these values. Values for these properties are typically `match_parent` and `wrap_content`. If you say your `TextView` is set to `match_parent` for its width, the width of the control matches up with the parent width. When a `TextView` is set for its height `wrap_content`, then its height will be just sufficient to contain all its text in the vertical direction. Of course, these two properties are available to all child controls of a layout, not just the text control. These two layout control properties, `match_parent` and `wrap_content`, also apply to the height of a control as well.

Introducing Resources and Backgrounds

Although we are in the middle of explaining the controls in the layout file, this is a good place to introduce resources. Layout files are, and are made up of, resources. In the calculator layout file, we have set the background of the entire view by setting the background on the root `LinearLayout` control. This instruction looked like the following:

```
android:background="@android:color/darker_gray"
```

Every view or control in Android supports the background property. Backgrounds are usually identified as resources. In this example, the background is pointing to a resource, coming from the Android package, which is of type color whose referenced value is darker gray.

A number of inputs to your application are represented as resources in Android. Some example resources are image files, entire layout files, colors, strings, XML files, menus, and many other things as listed in the Android SDK. For instance, the entire calculator layout file we are talking about is itself a resource.

As you can see from the calculator layout file, resources are of different types. In Android they are further broadly classified as "value based" or "file based." Examples of resources that are values are strings and colors. Examples of resources that are files are images or layout files. Listing 2-2 shows an example of creating value-based resources that are strings and colors.

Listing 2-2. Example of Value-Based Resources

```
<?xml version="1.0" encoding="utf-8"?>
<!-- this file will be in /res/values subdirectory  -->
<resources>
    <string name="hello">Hello World, CalculatorMainActivity!</string>
    <string name="app_name">A Demo Calculator</string>
    <color name="red">#FF0000</color>
    <color name="blue">#0000FF</color>
</resources>
```

You can have any number of value-based files as long as they are all under the /res/values subdirectory. Each file will start with the resources root node. You can use Ctrl-Space to discover what other possible value-based resources are available.

Turning to file-based resources, Listing 2-3 shows an example of placing a number of file-based resources under their respective resource subdirectories.

Listing 2-3. Example of File-Based Resources

```
/res/layout/page1_layout.xml (A layout file for say page 1)
/res/drawable/page1_background.jpg (An example image file)
/res/drawable-hdpi/page1_background.jpg (Same image file for a different density)
/res/xml/some_preferences.xml (example of an input file for your app)
```

Any of these resources, be it file based or value based, can be referenced in the layout files using the "@" resource reference syntax. For example, in the calculator layout file in Listing 2-1 the background can be set literally and explicitly as a color value between the quotes, such as "#FFFFFF," or point to a resource reference (indicated by a starting @color/red) that is already defined as a color resource (as in Listing 2-2). In this syntax led by "@," the type of referenced resource is "color." Some of the key words for other types of resources are string (for strings), drawable (for images), etc.

In Listing 2-1, the way to read the value of the background property of the LinearLayout, namely, @android:color/darker_gray, is as follows: Use the value of the resource identified as darker_gray in the Android core framework and whose resource type is color. With this knowledge of resource reference syntax, take a look at the calculator layout file listing one more time and you will be able to read it where each control has properties and each property has a value that is either directly specified or references a resource that is elsewhere defined in a resource file.

The indirection of a control property value defined as a resource reference has an advantage. A resource can be customized for languages, device density variation, and a variety of factors without altering the compiled Java source code. For example when you supply background images you can place a number of these images in different directories and name them using the convention specified by Android. Then Android knows how to locate the right image, given its name, depending on the device your app is running on.

Working with Text Controls in the Layout File

In the calculator layout example we have used two text-based controls. One is a `TextView` control, which is used as a label; the other is an `EditText` control, which is used for taking input text. We have already shown you how to set the width and height of any view by using the attributes that start with "`layout_`". Every text-based control also has an attribute called `text`. In our examples we have directly specified the literal text as a value for this property. The recommendation is to use instead a resource reference. For example:

```
android:text="Literal text"  //what we did for clarity
or
android:text="@string/LiteralTextId" //doing it properly
```

The latter resource ID, `LiteralTextId`, then can be defined in a file in the `/res/values` subdirectory much like in Listing 2-2.

`EditText` control in the calculator layout has an attribute `inputType` to provide the necessary constraints and validations that need to take place when data is typed into the editable field. Refer to the documentation to see a large number of constraints that are available for editable fields. Alternatively, you can use eclipse ADT to discover the available input types on the fly during coding.

Working with Autogenerated IDs for Controls

To manipulate the controls that are in the calculator layout of Listing 2-1, we need a way to turn them into Java objects. This is done by locating these controls using a unique ID in the currently loaded layout file of an activity. Let's look at one example in the layout file where an `EditText` control is given an ID of `editText2` as follows:

```
android:id="@+id/editText2"
```

This format tells Android that `ID` of this `EditText` control is a resource of type `ID` and its integer value should be known in Java as `editText2`. The + is a convenience to allocate a new unique integer for `editText2`. If you don't have the + sign, then Android looks for an integer-valued resource defined with an ID that is called `editText2`. With the convenience of + we can avoid separately defining a resource first and then use it. In some cases, you may have a need for a well-known ID that is shared by multiple pieces of code, in which case you will remove the + and take the multiple steps of defining the ID first and then using its name in multiple places. You will see in the programming logic section (soon to follow) how these control IDs are used to locate the controls and manipulate them.

Implementing Programming Logic

To see the calculator layout on the screen of your device, you need a Java class derived from the Android SDKs class `activity`. Such an `activity` represents a window in your mobile application. So you need to craft a calculator activity by extending the Android base `activity` class as shown in Listing 2-4.

Listing 2-4. Programming Logic: Implementing an Activity Class

```
/**
 * Activity name: CalculatorMainActivity
 * Layout file: calculator_layout.xml
 * Layout shortcut prefix for ids: cl_
 * Menu file: none
 * Purpose and Logic
 * ******************
 * 1. Demonstrate business logic for a simple calculator
 * 2. Load the calculator_layout.xml as layout
 * 3. Setup button callbacks
 * 4. Respond to button clicks
 * 5. Read values from edit text controls
 * 6. Perform operation and update result edit control
 */
public class CalculatorMainActivity extends Activity
implements OnClickListener
{
    private EditText number1EditText;
    private EditText number2EditText;

    /** Called when the activity is first created. */
    @Override
    public void onCreate(Bundle savedInstanceState) {
        super.onCreate(savedInstanceState);
        setContentView(R.layout.calculator_layout);
        gatherControls();
        setupButtons();
    }
    private void gatherControls()   {
        number1EditText = (EditText)this.findViewById(R.id.editText1);
        number2EditText = (EditText)this.findViewById(R.id.editText2);
        number2EditText.requestFocus();
    }
    private void setupButtons()    {
        Button b = (Button)this.findViewById(R.id.plusButton);
        b.setOnClickListener(this);

        b = (Button)this.findViewById(R.id.minusButton);
        b.setOnClickListener(this);
```

```
        b = (Button)this.findViewById(R.id.multiplyButton);
        b.setOnClickListener(this);

        b = (Button)this.findViewById(R.id.divideButton);
        b.setOnClickListener(this);
    }
    @Override
    public void onClick(View v)     {
        String sNum1 = number1EditText.getText().toString();
        String sNum2 = number2EditText.getText().toString();
        double num1 = getDouble(sNum1);
        double num2 = getDouble(sNum2);
        Button b = (Button)v;

        double value = 0;
        if (b.getId() == R.id.plusButton)   {
            value = plus(num1, num2);
        }
        else if (b.getId() == R.id.minusButton)    {
            value = minus(num1, num2);
        }
        else if (b.getId() == R.id.multiplyButton)    {
            value = multiply(num1, num2);
        }
        else if (b.getId() == R.id.divideButton)   {
            value = divide(num1, num2);
        }
        number1EditText.setText(Double.toString(value));
    }

    private double plus(double n1, double n2)    {
        return n1 + n2;
    }
    private double minus(double n1, double n2)    {
        return n1 - n2;
    }
    private double multiply(double n1, double n2)   {
        return n1 * n2;
    }
    private double divide(double n1, double n2)    {
        if (n2 == 0)     {
            return 0;
        }
        return n1 / n2;
    }
    private double getDouble(String s)     {
        if (validString(s))          {
            return Double.parseDouble(s);
        }
        return 0;
    }
```

```
    private boolean invalidString(String s)    {
        return !validString(s);
    }
    private boolean validString(String s)    {
        if (s == null)    {
            return false;
        }
        if (s.trim().equalsIgnoreCase(""))    {
            return false;
        }
        return true;
    }
}
```

In this listing, the calculator activity is called `CalculatorMainActivity`. Once you have this activity, you can load the calculator layout into it in order to see the calculator screen of Figure 2-1.

Let's learn a bit about an activity in Android. A programmer does not need to instantiate an activity directly. An activity can be instantiated by the Android framework based on user's actions. In that sense, an activity is a "*managed component*" managed by Android.

An activity can get partially hidden or completely hidden when another UI with higher priority sits on top of it (for example, due to a phone call). Or, an activity that is in the background can be temporarily removed due to memory constraint. In these circumstances, the activity can be automatically brought back when a user revisits the application.

Loading the Layout File into an Activity

As the activity is event driven, an activity relies on callbacks. The first callback of importance is the `onCreate()` callback. In the calculator activity given in Listing 2-4, you can easily locate this method. This is where we will load the calculator layout into the calculator activity. This is done through the method `setContentView()`. The input to this method is an identifier for the calculator layout file.

A nice feature of Android is what it does with the various resources including the layout files. It autogenerates a java class called `R.java` where it defines integer IDs for all the resources be they value based or file based. In the activity given in Listing 2-4, the variable `R.layout.calculator_layout` points to the calculator layout file (which itself is in Listing 2-1).

When you are dipping your toes into the Android framework, the other mysterious thing in `onCreate()` is the `savedInstanceBundle`. As the Android framework may stop and restart (even re-create) activities, it needs a way to pass the last state of the activity to the `onCreate()` method. That is what the `savedInstanceBundle` is. It is a collection of key value pairs holding the previous state of the activity. You will learn about this aspect of state management in more detail later in the chapter, and also in Chapter 9, where we cover what happens when a device is rotated. For the implementation of the calculator example we simply call the super class's method to pass on that state bundle.

Gathering Controls

The next two methods, gatherControls() and setupButtons(), set up the interaction model for the calculator. In the gatherControls() method you obtain java references for the edit controls that you need to manipulate (read or write to) and save them locally in the calculator activity class. You do this by using the findViewById() method on the base activity class. The findViewById() method takes as input the ID of the control that is in the layout file. Here also Android autogenerates these IDs and places them into the R.java class. In your eclipse project you can see this file in the /gen subdirectory. Listing 2-5 shows the generated R.java file for this calculator project. (If you were to try this project yourself, these IDs may differ. So use this listing primarily to understand concepts.)

Listing 2-5. Autogenerated Resource IDs: R.java

```
public final class R {
    public static final class attr {
    }
    public static final class drawable {
        public static final int background=0x7f020000;
        public static final int icon=0x7f020001;
    }
    public static final class id {
        public static final int divideButton=0x7f050005;
        public static final int editText1=0x7f050000;
        public static final int editText2=0x7f050001;
        public static final int minusButton=0x7f050003;
        public static final int multiplyButton=0x7f050004;
        public static final int plusButton=0x7f050002;
    }
    public static final class layout {
        public static final int calculator_layout=0x7f030000;
    }
    public static final class string {
        public static final int app_name=0x7f040001;
        public static final int hello=0x7f040000;
    }
}
```

Notice how R.java uses a different class prefix for each resource type. This allows the programmer in eclipse to quickly separate the IDs by what their type is. So, for example, all IDs for layout files are prefixed with R.layout, and all image IDs are prefixed with R.drawable, and all strings with R.string, etc. However, there is a caution while working these IDs. Even if you have ten layout files the IDs for all the controls are generated into a single namespace such as R.id.* (where "id" is an example of a resource type). So you may want to get into the habit of naming controls in the layout files with some prefix indicating which layout files they belong to.

Setting Up Buttons

Some of the controls in the calculator layout of Listing 2-1 are the calculator buttons. They are the buttons representing operators: +, -, x, and /. We need code to be invoked when these buttons are pressed. The way to do that is by registering a callback object on the button controls. These callback objects must implement the `View.OnClickListener` interface. The calculator activity in addition to extending the `activity` class also implements the `View.OnClickListener` interface, allowing us to register our activity as the one that needs to be called back when each button is pressed. As you can see in the code of the activity (Listing 2-4), this is done by calling the `setOnClickListener` on each button.

Responding to Button Clicks: Tying It All Together

When any of the operator buttons is clicked, the `onClick()` method in the calculator activity given in Listing 2-4 gets called. In this method we will investigate the ID of the `view` that called back. This calling view should be one of the buttons. In this method we will read the values from both the `EditText` controls (the operand values) and then invoke a method that is specific to each operator. The operator method will calculate the result and update the `EditText`, which is labeled Result.

Updating the AndroidManifest.XML

So far we have the UI (in terms of the layout file) and we have the business logic in terms of the calculator activity. Every Android app must have its configuration file. This file is called the `AndroidManifest.xml`. This is available in the root directory of the project. Listing 2-6 shows the `AndroidManifest.xml` for this project.

Listing 2-6. Application Configuration File: AndroidManifest.xml

```
<?xml version="1.0" encoding="utf-8"?>
<manifest xmlns:android="http://schemas.android.com/apk/res/android"
      package="com.androidbook.calculator"
      android:versionCode="1"
      android:versionName="1.0">
    <uses-sdk android:minSdkVersion="14" />
    <application android:icon="@drawable/icon" android:label="@string/app_name">
        <activity android:name=".CalculatorMainActivity"
            android:theme="@android:style/Theme.Light"
                  android:label="@string/app_name">
            <intent-filter>
                <action android:name="android.intent.action.MAIN" />
                <category android:name="android.intent.category.LAUNCHER" />
            </intent-filter>
        </activity>

    </application>
</manifest>
```

The package attribute of this manifest file follows a naming structure similar to the java namespaces. In the calculator app, the package is set to `com.androidbook.calculator`. This is like giving a name and a unique identifier to your app. Once you sign this app and install it on an app publisher like the Google Play Store, only you will be able to update it or release subsequent versions of it. The `uses-sdk` directive indicates the API for which this app is backward compatible. The application node has a number of properties including its label and an icon that will show up in the Android device apps menu. Inside an application node we need to define all of the activities that make up this application. Each activity is identified by its respective java classname. If the activity classname is not fully qualified, then the java package is assumed to be the same as the application package identified. Theme for the activity indicates a set of properties that the views belonging to that activity will inherit. It is like setting a CSS style on the HTML UI. Android comes with a few default styles. Choosing a light theme is good for contrast while taking screen shots (as shown in Figure 2-1). Chapter 7 is dedicated to using styles and themes in your apps.

In the Android application manifest file an activity can specify a series of intent filters. `Intent` is a programming concept that is unique to Android. Android relies heavily on these intents. Android uses intent objects to invoke application components including activities. An intent object can contain an explicit activity classname so that when you invoke that intent you end up invoking the activity. Or instead of having an explicit classname, an intent can indicate a generic action like VIEW to view a web page. When you invoke such an intent with a generic action Android will present all possible activities that can satisfy that action. Activities register with Android through the manifest file that they can respond to some actions through an intent filter. Listing 2-7 shows how you can invoke an activity through an intent object.

***Listing 2-7.** Using an Intent Object to Invoke an Activity*

```
//currentActivity refers to the activity in which this code runs
Intent i = new Intent(currentActivity,SomeTargetActivity.class);
currentActivity.startActivity(i); //start the target activity
```

Although we used `currentActivity` as the value of the first argument to create an intent, all it needs is a base class reference called Context. A `context` reference represents the application context in which a component like an activity runs. Coming back to the intent object, it has a number of flags and extra data elements that you can use to control the behavior of the target activity that the intent is invoking. Listing 2-8 shows an example.

***Listing 2-8.** Using Extras on an Intent Object*

```
//currentActivity refers to the activity in which this code runs
Intent intent = new Intent(currentActivity,SomeTargetActivity.class);
intent.setFlags(Intent.FLAG_ACTIVITY_CLEAR_TOP
                | Intent.FLAG_ACTIVITY_SINGLE_TOP);
intent.putExtra("some-key", "some-value");
currentActivity.startActivity(intent);
```

In this example, we want the target activity to be brought to the top of the window or activity stack and close any other activities that were on top of it before. As one invokes activities from other activities they sit on top of each other. This stack allows the back button to navigate back to the previous activity in the stack. When you go back, the current top activity is finished and the previous activity is shown in the foreground. The code in Listing 2-8 is like going back to the last position of the target activity, making that the top instance, and removing/finishing all recent activities above that. `Extras` on intent are a set of key value pairs that you can pass to the target activity from the source activity. Activities are pretty isolated from each other. They don't share their local variables between each other. Instead, they should pass their data through objects that can be serialized and deserialized. Android uses an interface similar to `Serializable` called `Parcelable` that allows greater flexibility and efficiency.

Ultimately, every activity is almost always started by an intent object. You can get the intent object anywhere in your target activity by calling `getIntent()`. Once you get the intent object, you can get its extras and see if there is any pertinent data that you need.

Complete study of intents and their variations is a large topic. We will return to talk more about intents later in this chapter after concluding our discussion on the calculator app. We have also included a URL for the free dedicated chapter on intents from our previous editions at the end of this chapter.

Placing the Files in the Android Project

Let's return to our main line of thought, the calculator app. By now you have the three files you need to create the calculator application. Use what you have learned in the first chapter to create an empty Android project and adjust that project to place these three files. These files are given in Listing 2-9 along with their parent directories.

***Listing 2-9.** Placement of Files for the Calculator App*

```
/res/layout/calculator_layout.xml
/src/com/androidbook/calculator/CalculatorActivity.java
/AndroidManifest.xml
```

Figure 2-2 shows the structure of your Android project in eclipse. You can see the relative locations of the files of Listing 2-9.

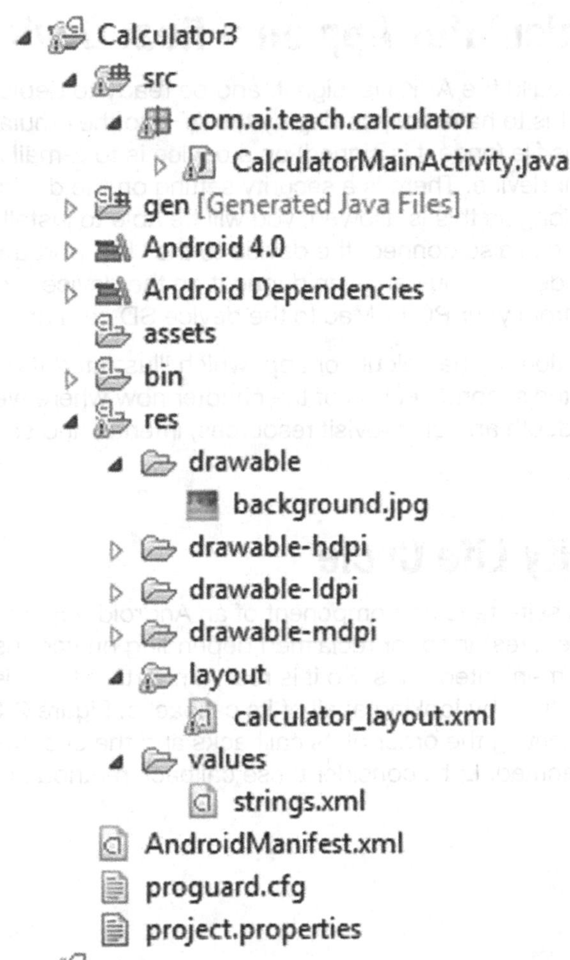

***Figure 2-2.** A calculator app directory structure*

The directory structure in Figure 2-1 also shows you where other resources like images and strings are placed. You can also see the directory structure for the device-dependent image files in Figure 2-2. This is how Android solves the localization multilingual support as well by using different resource subdirectory suffixes. You will learn about the other subdirectories of an Android project as you go through this book.

Testing the Calculator App on a Real Device

All that is left now is to build the APK file, sign it, and be ready to deploy. The simplest way to test your project is to have eclipse deploy the APK to the emulator and test it. The simplest way to test this file (once it is signed) on a device is to e-mail it to yourself and open the e-mail on your device. There is a security setting on the device to allow APKs from unverified sources. As long as this is allowed, you will be able to install the APK file and run it on your device. Or you can also connect the device to the USB port and have eclipse deploy the APK directly to the device. You can even debug it on the device through eclipse. You can also copy the APK file from your PC or Mac to the device SD card and install it from there.

This concludes our section on the calculator app, which illustrated the nature of Android apps. We will move to the second section of the chapter now where we will talk about activities in a lot more depth and also revisit resources, intents, and saving state. Let's start with activities.

Android Activity Life Cycle

An Android activity is a self-standing component of an Android application that can be started, stopped, paused, restarted, or reclaimed depending on various events including user-initiated and system-initiated ones. So it is really important to review the architecture of the life cycle of an activity by looking at all of its callbacks. Figure 2-3 shows the life cycle of an activity by documenting the order of its callbacks and the circumstances under which those callbacks are executed. Let's consider these callback methods one by one.

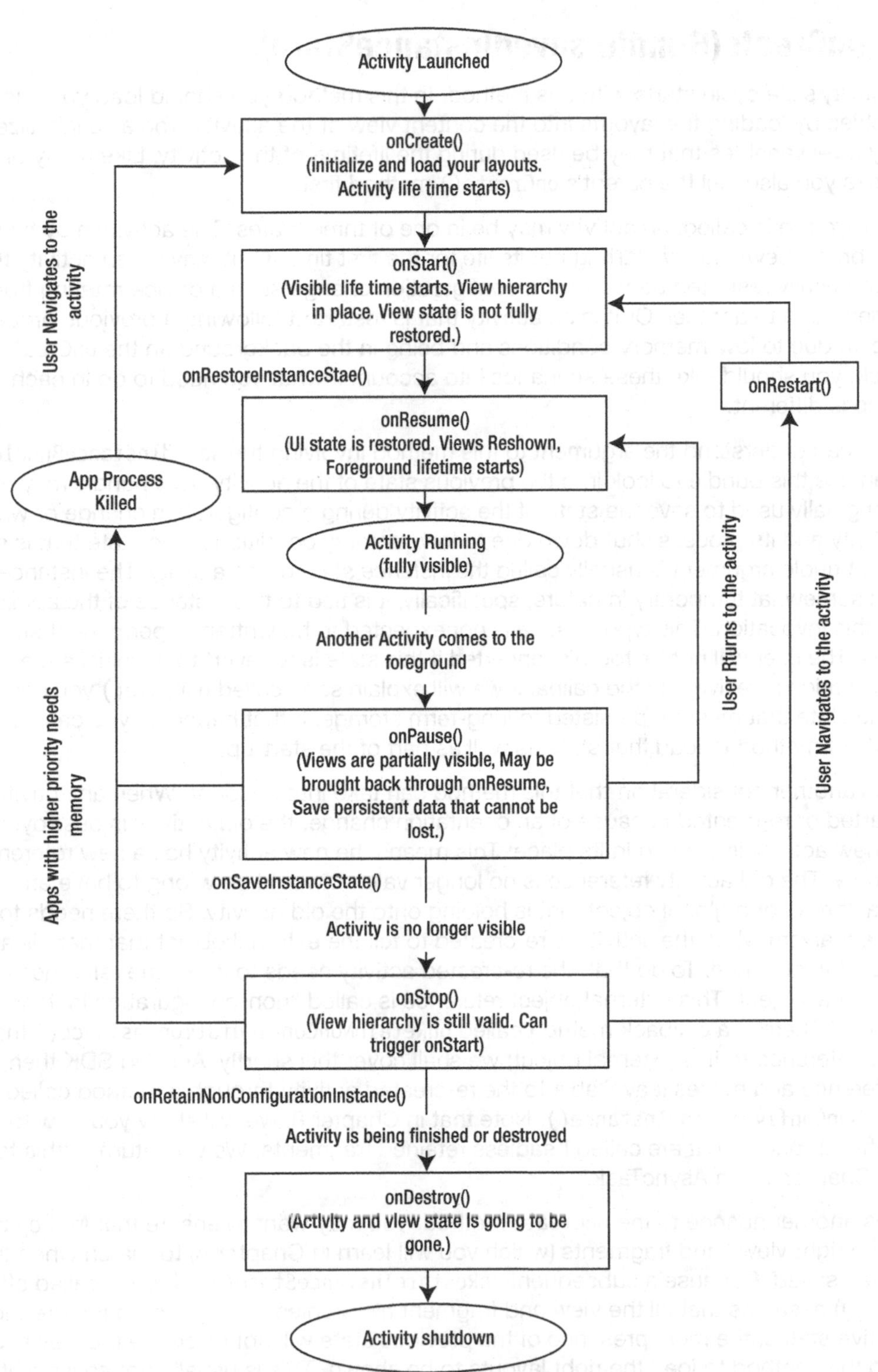

***Figure 2-3.** Annotated Android activity life cycle*

void onCreate(Bundle savedInstanceState)

The activity's life cycle starts with this method. In this method you should load your view hierarchies by loading the layouts into the content view of the activity. You also initialize any activity level variables that may be used during the lifetime of the activity. Like many of the callbacks you also call the parent's `onCreate()` method first.

When `onCreate` is called, an activity may be in one of three states. The activity may have been a brand-new activity starting out its life for the first time. Or it may be an activity that is automatically restarted because of a configuration change such a device rotating from one orientation to another. Or it is an activity that is restarted following a previous process shutdown due to low-memory conditions and being in the background. In the `onCreate` callback, you should take these scenarios into account if what you need to do in each scenario is different.

Now we can understand the argument to this method involving the `savedInstanceBundle`. You can use this bundle to look into the previous state of the activity. This bundle may have been originally used to save the state of the activity during a configuration change or when the activity and its process shut down due to low-memory conditions. The state that is saved into this bundle argument is usually called the *instance state* of the activity. The instance state is somewhat temporary in nature; specifically, it is tied to this instance of the application during this invocation. This type of state is not expected to be written to permanent storage like files. The user will not be too disconcerted if this state is to revert to an initial state when the application is revived. In the callback we will explain soon called `onPause()` you can save the state that must be persisted to long-term storage. If that happens, you can use the `onCreate()` method to load that state as well as part of the start-up.

There is another consideration that this method can take into account. When an activity is restarted or re-created because of an orientation change, the old activity is destroyed and a new activity is created in its place. This means the new activity has a new reference in memory. The old activity reference is no longer valid. It would be wrong to have an external thread or a global object that is holding onto the old activity. So there needs to be a mechanism when the activity is re-created to tell the external object that there is a new activity reference. To do that, the re-created activity needs to know the reference of that external object. This external object reference is called "non-configuration instance reference." There is a callback method called `onRetainNonConfigurationInstance()` that can return a reference to this external object; we shall cover this shortly. Android SDK then keeps this reference and makes it available to the re-created activity through a method called `getLastNonConfigurationInstance()`. Note that in Chapter 8, we will show you how to do this better through what are called headless retained fragments. We will return to this topic also in Chapter 15 on AsyncTask.

There is another nuance to the `onCreate` method. You may want to ensure that in the layouts you have right views and fragments (which you will learn in Chapter 8) to match when the state was saved. Because a subsequent `onRestoreInstanceState()` (which is called after `onStart()`) assumes that all the view and fragment hierarchies are present to restore their respective states, the mere presence of the previous state will not re-create the views. So it is up to this method to load the right layouts to be shown. This is usually not an issue if you don't delete or add views during the interaction with the activity.

void onStart()

After being created, this method pushes the activity into a visible state. In other words this method starts the "visible life cycle" of the activity. This method is called right after `onCreate()`. This method assumes that the view hierarchies are loaded and available from the `onCreate()`. You normally don't need to do override this method and if you do, make sure you call the parent's `onStart()` first. In Figure 2-2 note that this method can also be called from another callback called `onRestart`.

You must be aware that the `onRestoreInstanceState` method is called after this method. So you shouldn't make assumptions about the state of the views in this method. So try not to manipulate the state of the views in this method. Do that refinement in the subsequent `onRestoreInstanceState` or the `onResume` method. Because this is a counterpart of the `onStop()`, do the reverse should you have stopped something in `onStop()` or in `onPause()`. If you see something is being done in this method, look at it with caution and make sure it is what you want. Also know that the start-and-stop cycle can happen multiple times during the overall current cycle of the activity.

This method can also be called when the activity is shown after being hidden first, because another activity has come to the top of the visibility stack. In those cases this method is called after the `onRestart()`, which itself is triggered after the `onStop()`. So there are two paths into this method: either `onCreate()` or `onRestart()`. In both cases the view hierarchies are expected to be established and available prior to this callback.

void onRestoreInstanceState(Bundle savedInstanceState)

If an activity is to be legitimately closed by a user, then the state that user is willing to discard is the instance state. For example, when the user chooses a back button, then he/she is informing Android that he/she no longer is interested in this activity and that the activity can be closed, discarding all its state that is not yet saved. So this state, which is transitory and only valid for the life of the activity while it is in memory, is the instance state.

If the system choses to close the activity, because there is a change in orientation, then the user will expect that transitory (instance) state right back when the activity is restarted. To facilitate this, Android calls this `onRestoreInstanceState` method with a bundle that contains the saved instance state. (See the `onSavedInstanceState` method explanation.)

In contrast to instance state, the persistent state of an activity is something the user expects to see even after the activity finishes and is no longer in play. This persistence state may have been created during the activity or may even exist before the activity is created. This type of state, especially when it is created with the help of the activity, must be explicitly saved to an external persistent store like a file. If the activity doesn't use an explicit "save" button for such needs, then the "`onPause`" method needs to be used to save such implicit persistent states. This is because no method after `onPause` is guaranteed to be called in case of low-memory conditions. You shouldn't rely on the instance state if the information is too important to lose.

void onResume()

The callback method onResume is the precursor to having the activity fully visible. This is also the start of the foreground cycle for the activity. In this foreground cycle the activity can move between onResume() and onPause() multiple times as other activities, notifications, or dialogs with more urgency come on top and go.

By the time this method is called, we can expect the views and their state fully restored. You can take this opportunity to tweak final state changes. As this method doesn't have a bundle, you need to rely on the information from onCreate or onRestoreInstanceState methods to fine-tune state if further needed.

If you had stopped any counters or animations during onPause you can restart them here. You can also keep track of the case if the views are really destroyed or not by following the previous callback methods (whether onResume is a result of onCreate, onRestart, or onPause) and do the minimum possible to adjust the view state. Typically you will not do state management here but only those tasks that need to be turned on or off based on visibility.

void onPause()

This callback indicates that the activity is about to go into background. You should stop any counters or animations that were running when the activity was fully visible. The activity may go to onResume or proceed to onStop. Going to onResume will bring the activity to the foreground. Going to onStop will take the activity into a background state.

As per the SDK, it is also the last method that is guaranteed to be called before the activity and the process is completely reclaimed. So it is the last opportunity that a developer has to save any non-instance and persistent data to a file.

Android SDK also waits for this method to return before making the foreground activity fully active. So you want to be brief in this method. Also notice that this method has no bundle that is passed. This is an indication that this method is for storing persistent data and also in an external storage medium such as a file or a network.

You can also use this method to stop any counters, animations, or status displays of a background task. You can resume them in onResume.

void onStop()

The callback method onStop() moves the activity from partially visible to the background state while keeping all of the view hierarchies intact. This is the counterpart of onStart. The activity can be taken back to the visible cycle by calling onStart. This state transition of going from onStop to onStart during the same activity life cycle goes through the onRestart() method.

After this call, the activity is no longer visible. But keep in mind that this may not be called after onPause under low-memory conditions. Because of this uncertainty do not use this method to start or stop services that are outside of this process. Do that in onPause instead and resume them in onResume. However, you can use this method to control services or work that is inside your process. This is because, as long as the process is active, this method is going to get called. If the whole process is taken down then those dependent tasks or global variables will go away anyway.

void onSaveInstanceState(Bundle saveStateBundle)

The control goes to `onDestroy()` coming out of `onStop` if the process is still in memory. However, if Android realizes that activity is being closed without the user's expectation then it would call the `onSaveInstanceState()` before calling `onDestroy()`. Orientation change is a very concrete example of this. The SDK warns that the timing of `onSaveInstanceState()` is not predictable whether before or after `onStop()`.

The default implementation of this method already saves the state of views. However if there is some explicit state that is not known to the views you need to save it in the bundle object and retrieve it back in the `onRestoreInstanceState` method. You do need to call the parent's `onSaveInstanceState()` method first so that views have an opportunity to save their state themselves. There are some restrictions and rules for the views to be able to save their state. The chapters on UI controls (Chapters 3, 4, and 5) and configuration change (Chapter 9) go into more detail on this subject.

void onRestart()

This method is called when the activity transitions from background state to partially visible state, i.e., going from `onStop` to `onStart`. You can use this knowledge in `onStart` if you want to optimize code there based on whether it is a fresh start or a restart. When it is a restart the view and their state are fairly intact.

You can do things in this method that would have been done in `onStart`, but optimized when the activity is not visible, but too expensive to be done multiple times in `onResume`.

Object onRetainNonConfigurationInstance()

This callback method is in place to deal with activity re-creation due to configuration changes. This method returns an object reference in your process memory that needs to be retied to the activity once it is re-created. We explained this in more detail previously when we described the `onCreate` method.

When the activity is re-created, the object that is returned from this method is made available through the method `getLastNonConfigurationInstance()`. Now in `onCreate()` the new activity can use the previously established resources and object references. Importantly, if those previous resources are holding to the old activity reference, then the resources can be told to use the new one.

This dilemma exists because during an orientation change Android doesn't kill the process, but just discards the old activity, re-creates the activity in the new orientation, and expects the programmer to supply new layouts, etc., to suit the new configuration. So the working objects are still there holding onto an old activity. This is the method in association with its "get" counterpart to overcome this obstacle.

When you read Chapter 8, you will learn that this method is deprecated and you will use in its place what are called headless retained fragments. These headless retained fragments have the additional benefit of being able to track the activity life cycle and not just the reference to the activity.

void onDestroy()

`onDestroy()` is the counterpart of `onCreate()`. The activity is going to finish after onDestroy. An activity can finish for two primary reasons.

One is an explicit close. This can happen when the user has explicitly caused the activity to finish either by clicking a button that is provided to indicate that the user is done or by using a back button leaving the activity to go to the previous activity. Under such circumstances the activity will not be brought back by the system unless the user chooses the activity again. In this scenario the activity life cycle ends with the onDestroy method.

The second reason an activity can close is involuntary. When the orientation of a device changes, the Android SDK will forcefully close the activity and call the `onDestroy` method followed by re-creating the activity and calling the `onCreate` again.

When an activity is in the background and if the system needs memory, Android may shut down the process and may not have an opportunity to call the `onDestroy` method. Due to this uncertainty, much like onStop, don't use this method to control tasks or services that are outside the process in which the activity had been running. However, if the process is still in memory the onDestroy will be called as part of the life cycle and you can place cleanup code in onDestroy as long as that code belongs to this process.

General Notes on Activity Callbacks

Use Figure 2-3 to guide you to see the order of these callbacks and how best to use them. If you were to override a callback you need to call back the parent method. The SDK documentation explicitly indicates which derived methods are required to call back their parent equivalents. Also refer to the SDK documentation to learn during which callbacks the system will not kill the process due to low-memory conditions. Also notice that only a handful of callbacks carry instance state bundle.

More on Resources

We want to tell you little more about how resources are used in Android applications. In the calculator layout file, you have seen some of the resources used like strings, images, IDs, etc.

Other resources that are not so obvious include dimensions, drawables, string arrays, language terms for plurals, xml files, and all types of input files. In Android, something is treated as a resource a) if it is an input to your program and is part of the apk file and b) if the value or content of the input can have different values based on language, locale, or orientation of the device, generally called a configuration change.

Directory Structure of Resources

All resources in Android are placed under the /res subdirectory of the root of your application package. Listing 2-10 shows an example of what a /res may look like:

Listing 2-10. Android Resource and Assets Directory Structure

```
/res/values/strings.xml
           /colors.xml
           /dimens.xml
           /attrs.xml
           /styles.xml
    /drawable/*.png
             /*.jpg
             /*.gif
             /*.9.png
             /*.xml
    /anim/*.xml`
    /layout/*.xml
    /raw/*.*
    /xml/*.xml
/assets/*.*/*.*
```

We will cover attrs.xml and styles.xml in Chapter 7. The xml files in the anim subdirectory define animations that can be applied to various views. We will cover these animation-related resources in the animations chapter (Chapter 18). The xml files in the xml subdirectory get compiled away to binary and their resource IDs can be used to read them. We will show an example of this shortly. The /raw subdirectory holds files that get placed, as they are, without getting converted to any binary format.

The /assets directory, which is a sibling of /res, is not part of the resource hierarchy. This means that the files in this subdirectory do not change based on language or a locale. Android does not generate any IDs for these files. This directory is more like a static local storage for any files that are used as inputs, such as configuration files for your application.

Except for the assets directory, every other artifact in the /res subdirectory will end up generating an ID in R.* namespace, as you have seen before. Each distinct resource type will have its own namespace under R.*, as in R.id, R.string, or R.drawable, etc.

Reading Resources from Java Code

In layout files, as you have seen the in calculator layout, one resource can refer to other resources. For example, the calculator layout resource file referenced the string and color references. This approach is common. Alternatively, you can also use Java API to retrieve the resource values using the method Activity.getResources(). This method returns a reference to the Android SDK java class resources. You can use methods on this class to get to the values of each resource identified in your local R.* namespace. Listing 2-11 shows an illustration of this approach:

Listing 2-11. Reading Resource Values in Java Code

```
Resources res = activity.getResources();
//Retrieving a color resource
int somecolor  = res.getColor(R.color.main_back_ground_color);
// Using a drawable resource
ColorDrawable redDrawable=(ColorDrawable)res.getDrawable(R.drawable.red_rectangle);
```

Runtime Behavior of Drawable Resources

The drawable directory is an interesting case worth covering to demonstrate the fluency of Android's architecture. As shown earlier, this directory can contain images that can be set as backgrounds. This directory also allows XML files that know how to get converted to `drawable` java objects which can then be used as backgrounds that are rendered at runtime. Listing 2-12 shows an example of this:

Listing 2-12. Example of a Shape Drawable XML Resource File

```
<?xml version="1.0" encoding="utf-8"?>
<shape xmlns:android="http://schemas.android.com/apk/res/android"
    android:shape="rectangle">
    <solid android:color="#f0600000"/>
    <stroke android:width="3dp" android:color="#ffff8080"/>
    <corners android:radius="13dp" />
    <padding android:left="10dp" android:top="10dp"
        android:right="10dp" android:bottom="10dp" />
</shape>
```

If you place a file like this in the drawable subdirectory and call it `background1.xml`, it will result in an ID called `R.drawable.background1`. You can then use that ID as if it were a background image for any view that is drawn with a rectangular border. Other possible shapes are ovals, lines, and rings.

Similar to the shape xml file, each allowed XML file in the drawable directory defines a drawable that defines a particular way to draw. Examples of these drawables include bitmaps that can be decorated with certain behavior, or images that can transition from one image to another, layered drawables that are collections of other drawables, drawables that can be selected based on input parameters, drawables that can respond to progress by showing multiple images, drawables that can clip other drawables, etc... See the following URL for a number of sophisticated things you can do using these runtime drawable objects:

`http://androidbook.com/item/4236`

Using Arbitrary XML Files as Resources

Android also allows arbitrary XML files to be used as resources which can then be localized or tuned for each device. Listing 2-13 is an example of reading and processing an XML-based resource file from the /res/xml subdirectory.

Listing 2-13. Reading an XML Resource File

```
private String readAnXMLFile(Activity activity) throws XmlPullParserException, IOException {
   StringBuffer sb = new StringBuffer();
   Resources res = activity.getResources();
   XmlResourceParser xpp = res.getXml(R.xml.test);

   xpp.next();
   int eventType = xpp.getEventType();
    while (eventType != XmlPullParser.END_DOCUMENT) {
        if(eventType == XmlPullParser.START_DOCUMENT) {
           sb.append("******Start document");
        }
        else if(eventType == XmlPullParser.START_TAG)  {
           sb.append("\nStart tag "+xpp.getName());
        }
        else if(eventType == XmlPullParser.END_TAG) {
           sb.append("\nEnd tag "+xpp.getName());
        }
        else if(eventType == XmlPullParser.TEXT) {
           sb.append("\nText "+xpp.getText());
        }
        eventType = xpp.next();
    }//eof-while
    sb.append("\n******End document");
    return sb.toString();
}//eof-function
```

Working with Raw Resource Files

Android also allows any type of non-compiled files as resources. Listing 2-14 is an example of reading a file that is placed in the /res/raw subdirectory. Being a resource even the raw files that are in this directory can be customized for language or a device configuration. Android generates IDs automatically for these files as well, as they are resources like any other resource.

Listing 2-14. Reading a Raw Resource File

```
String getStringFromRawFile(Activity activity) throws IOException {
      Resources r = activity.getResources();
      InputStream is = r.openRawResource(R.raw.test);
      //assuming you have a function to convert a stream to a string
      String myText = convertStreamToString(is);
      is.close(); //take care of exceptions etc.
      return myText;
}
```

Reading Files from the Assets Directory

Although usually clubbed with resources, the /assets directory is a bit different. This directory does not sit under the /res path, so the files in this directory do not behave like resource files. Android does not generate resource IDs for these files in the R.* namespace. These files are not customizable based on locale or device configuration. Listing 2-15 shows an example of reading a file that is placed in the /assets subdirectory.

Listing 2-15. Reading a File from Assets Directory

```
String getStringFromAssetFile(Activity activity) {
    AssetManager am = activity.getAssets();
    InputStream is = am.open("test.txt");
    String s = convertStreamToString(is);
    is.close();
    return s;
}
```

Thus far, we have used an activity reference to get hold of the resources or an AssetManager object as in Listing 2-15. In reality, all we need is the base class of the activity, the context object.

Reading Resources and Assets Without an Activity Reference

Sometimes you may need to read an XML resource file or an asset file from the bowels of source code, where it is intrusive to pass the activity reference. For these cases, you can use the following approach to obtain the application context and then use that reference instead to get to the assets and resources.

When Android loads your application (in order to invoke any of its components), it instantiates and calls an application object to inform that the application could initialize itself. This application classname is specified in the Android manifest file. If MyApplication.java is your application java class, then it can be specified in the Android manifest file as shown in Listing 2-16.

Listing 2-16. Specifying an Application Class in the Manifest File

```
<application android:name=".MyApplication"
        android:icon="@drawable/icon" .../>
```

Listing 2-17 shows how we can code the MyApplication and also shows how we can capture the application context in a global variable.

Listing 2-17. Sample Code for an Application that Captures Application Context

```
public class MyApplication extends Application {
   //Make sure to check for null for this variable
   public static volatile Context s_appContext = null;

   @Override
   public void onConfigurationChanged(Configuration newConfig) {
      super.onConfigurationChanged(newConfig);
   }
   @Override
   public void onCreate() {
      super.onCreate();
      MyApplication.s_appContext = this.getApplicationContext();
   }
   @Override
   public void onLowMemory() {
      super.onLowMemory();
   }
   @Override
   public void onTerminate() {
      super.onTerminate();
   }
}
```

With the application context captured in a global variable, we now can get to the asset manager to read our assets as in Listing 2-18.

Listing 2-18. Using Application Object to Get to Application Asset Files

```
AssetManager am = MyApplication.s_appContext.getAssets();
InputStream is = am.open(filename);
```

Understanding Resource Directories, Language, and Locale

Let's wrap up the idea of Android resources by pointing out how resource directories are used to load resources based on language, locale, or a configuration change of the device like say orientation. See how in Listing 2-19 a layout file with the same name is located in multiple layout directories starting with same prefix of layout but with different qualifiers such as "`port`" for portrait and "`land`" for landscape. There are a large number of these qualifiers available in the SDK documentation. We also cover some of these aspects in Chapter 9 (Configuration Changes). Listing 2-19 shows an example of how layout files are arranged by portrait or landscape configuration:

Listing 2-19. Demonstrating Resource Qualifiers

```
\res\layout\main_layout.xml
\res\layout-port\main_layout.xml
\res\layout-land\main_layout.xml
```

More on Intents

We have talked about how intents are used to invoke activities. We want cover few more essential aspects of intents now. Listing 2-20 shows how intents are used to invoke a number of prebuilt Google applications.

Listing 2-20. Sample Code Using Intents

```
public class IntentsUtils {
    public static void invokeWebBrowser(Activity activity)    {
       Intent intent = new Intent(Intent.ACTION_VIEW);
       intent.setData(Uri.parse("http://www.google.com"));
       activity.startActivity(intent);
    }
    public static void invokeWebSearch(Activity activity)    {
       Intent intent = new Intent(Intent.ACTION_WEB_SEARCH);
       intent.setData(Uri.parse("http://www.google.com"));
       activity.startActivity(intent);
    }
    public static void dial(Activity activity)    {
       Intent intent = new Intent(Intent.ACTION_DIAL);
       activity.startActivity(intent);
    }
    public static void call(Activity activity)    {
       Intent intent = new Intent(Intent.ACTION_CALL);
       intent.setData(Uri.parse("tel:555-555-5555"));
       activity.startActivity(intent);
    }
    public static void showMapAtLatLong(Activity activity)    {
       Intent intent = new Intent(Intent.ACTION_VIEW);
       //geo:lat,long?z=zoomlevel&q=question-string
       intent.setData(Uri.parse("geo:0,0?z=4&q=business+near+city"));
       activity.startActivity(intent);
    }
}
```

Notice how these intents do not invoke a specific activity by its classname but rather use the target qualities of suitable activities. For example to invoke a browser to view a web page, the intent simply says the action is `ACTION_VIEW` and the data portion of the intent is set to the web address. Android then looks around to see all the activities that know how to show the type of data requested in the data attribute. It will then give the user an option which of the activities that the user wants to choose to open the URL. These types of intents that don't specify the classname of the component to invoke are called implicit intents. We will cover this in a little bit more detail shortly.

Starting Activities for Results

Listing 2-21 shows an example of an activity where one of its methods is invoking a target activity in order to obtain a result when that target activity is completed. This is done through the method `invokePick()` in as shown in Listing 2-21.

Listing 2-21. Using Intents to Get Results from Activities

```
public class SomeActivity extends Activity {
.....
//Call this method to start a target activity that knows how to pick a note
//Use a data URI that tells the target activity which list of notes to show
public static void invokePick(Activity activity) {
  Intent pickIntent = new Intent(Intent.ACTION_PICK);
  int requestCode = 1;
  pickIntent.setData(Uri.parse(
     "content://com.google.provider.NotePad/notes"));
  activity.startActivityForResult(pickIntent, requestCode);
}

//the following method will be called when the target activity finishes
//Notice the outputIntent object that is passed back which could
//contain additional information

@Override
protected void
onActivityResult(int requestCode,int resultCode, Intent outputIntent) {
   super.onActivityResult(requestCode, resultCode, outputIntent);
   parseResult(this, requestCode, resultCode, outputIntent);
}
public static void parseResult(Activity activity
    , int requestCode, int resultCode , Intent outputIntent)
{
    if (requestCode != 1)  {
     Log.d("Test", "Someone else called this. not us");
     return;
    }
    if (resultCode != Activity.RESULT_OK)  {
      Log.d("Test", "Result code is not ok:" + resultCode);
              return;
    }
    Log.d("Test", "Result code is ok:" + resultCode);
    Uri selectedUri = outputIntent.getData();
    Log.d("Test", "The output uri:" + selectedUri.toString());

    //Proceed to display the note
    outputIntent.setAction(Intent.ACTION_VIEW);
    startActivity(outputIntent);
}
```

The constants RESULT_OK, RESULT_CANCELED, and RESULT_FIRST_USER are all defined in the activity class. The constant RESULT_FIRST_USER is used as a starting number for user-defined activity results. The numerical values of these constants are shown in Listing 2-22:

Listing 2-22. Result Values from Returned Activities

```
RESULT_OK = -1;
RESULT_CANCELED = 0;
RESULT_FIRST_USER = 1;
```

To make the PICK functionality work, the implementing or the target activity that is responding should have code that explicitly addresses the needs of an ACTION_PICK. Let's look at an example of how this is done in the Google sample NotePad application. (See the references section, where you can find this application.) When the item is selected in the list of items, the intent that invoked the target activity is checked to see whether it's an ACTION_PICK intent. If it is, the data URI of the selected note item is set in a new intent and returned through setResult() as shown in Listing 2-23. The calling activity then can investigate the returned intent to see what data it has in it. See the method parseResult() in Listing 2-21.

Listing 2-23. Target Activity Returning a Result through a Data URI

```
@Override
protected void onListItemClick(ListView l, View v, int position, long id) {
    Uri uri = ContentUris.withAppendedId(getIntent().getData(), id);

    String action = getIntent().getAction();
    if (Intent.ACTION_PICK.equals(action) ||
            Intent.ACTION_GET_CONTENT.equals(action))    {
        // The caller is waiting for us to return a note selected by
        // the user.  They have clicked on one, so return it now.
        setResult(RESULT_OK, new Intent().setData(uri));
        finish();
    }
    ...other ways of how this activity may have been invoked
}
```

Exercising the GET_CONTENT Action

ACTION_GET_CONTENT is similar to ACTION_PICK. In the case of ACTION_PICK, you are specifying a data URI that points to a collection of items, like a list of notes from a NotePad-like application. You will expect the intent action to pick one of the notes and return it to the caller. In the case of ACTION_GET_CONTENT, you indicate to Android that you need an item of a particular MIME type. Android searches for activities that can either create one of those items or choose from an existing set of items that satisfy that MIME type.

Using ACTION_GET_CONTENT, you can pick a note from a collection of notes supported by the NotePad application using the code shown in Listing 2-24:

Listing 2-24. Invoking Activities for Creating Content

```
public static void invokeGetContent(Activity activity) {
      Intent pickIntent = new Intent(Intent.ACTION_GET_CONTENT);
      int requestCode = 2;
      pickIntent.setType("vnd.android.cursor.item/vnd.google.note");
      activity.startActivityForResult(pickIntent, requestCode);
}
```

Notice how the intent type is set to the MIME type of a single note. Contrast this with the ACTION_PICK code, where it explicitly indicated a URL that points to a collection of notes (like a web URL that can retrieve a page worth of data).

For an activity to respond to ACTION_GET_CONTENT, the activity has to register an intent filter indicating that the activity can provide an item of that MIME type. Listing 2-25 shows how the SDK's NotePad application accomplishes this:

Listing 2-25. Activity Filter for Get Content

```
<activity android:name="NotesList" android:label="@string/title_notes_list">
......
<intent-filter>
    <action android:name="android.intent.action.GET_CONTENT" />
    <category android:name="android.intent.category.DEFAULT" />
    <data android:mimeType="vnd.android.cursor.item/vnd.google.note" />
      </intent-filter>
......
</activity>
```

The rest of the code for responding to onActivityResult() is identical to the previous ACTION_PICK example. If there are multiple activities that can return the same MIME type, Android will show you the chooser dialog to let you pick an activity.

Relating Intents and Activities

An intent is used to start not only activities but also other components like a service or a broadcast receiver. These components are covered in later chapters. You can see these components as having certain attributes. One attribute of a component may be the category to which this component belongs. Another attribute may be what type of data this component can view, edit, update, or delete. Another attribute may be what type of actions a component can respond to. If you were to look upon these components as entities in a database, their attributes can be seen as columns. Then an intent can be seen as a where clause that specifies all or some of those characteristics to choose a component like an activity to start. Listing 2-26 is an example of demonstrating how to query for all activities that are categorized as CATEGORY_LAUNCHER.

Listing 2-26. Querying Activities that Match an Intent

```
Intent mainIntent = new Intent(Intent.ACTION_MAIN, null);
mainIntent.addCategory(Intent.CATEGORY_LAUNCHER);
PackageManager pm = getPackageManager();
List<ResolveInfo> list = pm.queryIntentActivities(mainIntent, 0);
```

PackageManager is a key class that allows you to discover activities that match certain intents without invoking them. You can cycle through the received activities and invoke them as you see fit, based on the ResolveInfo API. Listing 2-27 is an extension to the preceding code that walks through the list of activities and invokes one of the activities if it matches a name. In the code, we have used an arbitrary name to test it:

Listing 2-27. Walking Through a Matched Activity List for an Intent

```
for(ResolveInfo ri: list) {
    //ri.activityInfo.
    Log.d("test",ri.toString());
    String packagename = ri.activityInfo.packageName;
    String classname = ri.activityInfo.name;
    Log.d("test", packagename + ":" + classname);
    if (classname.equals("com.ai.androidbook.resources.TestActivity")) {
        Intent ni = new Intent();
        ni.setClassName(packagename,classname);
        activity.startActivity(ni);
    }
}
```

Understanding Explicit and Implicit Intents

When you specify an explicit activity name (or a component name like a service or a broadcast receiver) in an intent, such an intent is called an explicit intent. When this intent is used to start an activity, that activity is invoked irrespective of what else is there in that intent such as its category or data.

As you have seen, an intent does not have to have an activity specified explicitly to invoke it. An intent can rely on an activity's action attribute, category attribute, or data attribute. These intents that omit the explicit activity or component class are called implicit intents. When you use an implicit intent to invoke an activity it is paramount that the activity must have as one of its categories CATEGORY_DEFAULT. If you expect your activity to be explicitly started by an intent, then you don't need to specify any category at all to that activity. Listing 2-28 shows an example of minimally registering an activity in an Android manifest file so that it can be invoked by an explicit intent.

Listing 2-28. Minimal Activity Definition

```
<activity android:name="com.androidbook.asynctask.TestProgressBarDriverActivity"
      android:label="Test Progress bars"/>
```

If you want to invoke this activity through an implicit intent without specifying its classname, like through an action say, then you need to add the following intent filters, one for the action and one for the needed mandatory category of default, as shown in Listing 2-29.

***Listing 2-29.** An Activity Definition with Filters*

```
<activity android:name="com.androidbook.asynctask.TestProgressBarDriverActivity"
        android:label="Test Progress bars">
      <intent-filter>
           <action android:name="com.androidbook.intent.action.ME" />
           <category android:name="android.intent.category.DEFAULT" />
      </intent-filter>
</activity>
```

Saving State in Android

As you reviewed the calculator app, your next likely need is how to store the data of an Android app. Let's briefly cover the available options. There are five ways to store data in Android: 1) shared preferences, 2) internal files, 3) external files, 4) SQLlite, and 5) network storage in the cloud.

Shared preferences API is a sophisticated API in the Android SDK to save, display, and manipulate preferences for your applications. Although this feature is intended and tailored for preferences it can be used for saving arbitrary state of your application. Shared preferences are internal to the application and device. Android does not make this data available to other applications. A user is not expected to directly manipulate this data by mounting onto a USB port. This data is removed automatically when the application is removed. These shared preferences are covered in detail in Chapter 11.

While shared preferences data is structured key/value pair data and follows a few other semantics imposed, internal files are stand-alone files that you can write to without a predefined structure. We haven't found a compelling advantage of using internal files over shared preferences, or the other way, especially for small- to medium-sized state. So for most apps you can choose one or the other.

Unlike internal files, which are stored on the internal storage of the device, external files are stored on the SD card. These become public files that other apps including the user could see outside the context of your application. The external files can be used to store data that makes sense even outside of your app such as image files or video files. For strictly the internal state of the app, internal files are a better option.

The external files may also be an option if the state is very large running into tens of megabytes. Usually when that happens you don't want to save the state as a monolithic file anyway and opt for more granular storage as a relational database like the SQLlite.

We will give a quick overview and brief code samples in Chapter 25 on how to use preferences, internal files, and external files to store your app state. One of the tricks is to persist java object tree directly using JSON and GSOn while giving consideration to see if this level of granularity is appropriate. If you are not familiar with JSON, it is an object transport and storage format for JavaScript-based objects. It is also generally applicable any object structure as well including java objects and often used that way lately. The GSON is a Google library that converts Java objects to and from JSON strings.

SQLlite is a really good option that is recommended to store the state of an app. The short drawback is your logic to save and read data become verbose and cumbersome. You can probably use O/R mapping libraries to overcome this mismatch between java objects and its relational representation. SQLlite is also often used to store data that needs to be shared by multiple applications through a concept called content providers. This is the central topic of Chapter 25.

Finally, cloud-based network storage is coming into its own. For example a number of MBAAS (Mobile Backend as a Service) platforms such as parse.com support storing the mobile data directly in the cloud for both online and offline usage. This model is going to be increasingly relevant as you start making your app available on multiple devices for the same user or being able to collaborate with other users. This topic is covered in great detail in our companion book *Expert Android* from Apress.

Many time for your apps the GSON option to store app state in an internal file is really the quickest and most practical way to go. Of course you do want to analyze the granularity of the solution and see if this simpler approach won't become a burden on computing power or battery life. If your app gains lot of popularity you may want to use a second release with SQLlite by optimizing storage speed or use cloud storage if that is more appropriate for that release.

Roadmap for Learning Android and the Rest of the Book

Let's quickly review what we have covered so far. In the one-pager application you have seen how the UI is put together, how the business logic is coded in Java, and then how the application is defined to the Android sdk using the Android manifest file. We explained what resources are, how they reference each other, how they are referenced in layout files, and even how to read your input files as resources. We have shown you what intents are, their intricacies, and how to use them to invoke or discover activities. We have covered the activity's life cycle, which is really important to understand Android architecture. We have also given a quick rundown of how you can save the state of your application. This is a pretty good foundation to plan and write simple applications.

We now want to follow up this bird's eye view of Android applications with a roadmap of becoming an expert app developer on the Android platform. This roadmap divides the chapters of this book into the following six key learning tracks:

- Track 1: UI essentials for your Android applications
- Track 2: Saving state
- Track 3: Preparing/taking your application to Google Play
- Track 4: Making your application robust
- Track 5: Bringing finesse to your apps
- Track 6: Integrating with other devices and the cloud

Among these six tracks, the first three are the basic tracks that you must know well to write Android apps that are useful to you and the larger community. Tracks 4, 5, and 6 are there to make your apps better and feature rich in subsequent releases. We will talk about what chapters make up each track and what you are expected to gain from that track.

Track 1: UI Essentials for Your Android Applications

Android has a number of UI controls and layouts out of the box to write very feature rich-applications. Some examples are buttons, various TextViews, EditText controls, checkboxes, RadioButtons, date and time controls, list controls, controls to show analog and digital clocks, controls to show images and videos, controls to pick numbers, etc. We will cover a number of these in **Chapter 3**. In that chapter, we will also cover the essential layouts that are needed to compose the UI from those controls.

Once you are able to use the basic controls to construct your UI, the one control that you absolutely need in your apps is the list control. We did not cover list control as a basic control because it is a bit involved. Also Android has a number of features and approaches to do list-based applications. So we have dedicated a separate chapter for list controls and the data adapters that are necessary to populate those list controls. These aspects are covered in **Chapter 4**.

Once you master the basic controls, basic layouts, and list controls, you will start looking around for more sophisticated layouts like the grid and table layouts. These are covered in **Chapter 5** under "Using Advanced Layouts."

Menus are covered in **Chapter 6**. Android's menu infrastructure includes context menus, pop-up menus, option icons in an action bar, etc.

Your mobile app is not really complete without refining it through styling, much like CSS. **Chapter 7** covers how styles and themes work in Android.

Dialogs are essential in any UI. Dialogs are a bit involved in Android. To understand dialogs in Android you have to first understand the concept of fragments. Architecture of dialogs is only one aspect of fragments. Fragments are now core to the Android UI. **Chapter 8** explains what fragments are and in **Chapter 10** we cover dialogs, building upon Chapter 8.

In mobile apps, you cannot write an app without understanding what happens to your application when the device orientation changes. Programming correctly for orientation change is not trivial in Android. How to program for orientation and other device configuration changes is covered in **Chapter 9**.

For any reasonably useful application you will likely need to know all these UI essentials. So Track 1 is an essential track.

Track 2: Saving State

Once you know how to construct the UI of your application, the next need you will run into is to save the state of your application. Refer to the earlier section on saving state to see what options are available and in which chapters those options are covered. Track 2 is also an essential track as you should know how to save state.

Track 3: Preparing/Taking Your Application to the Market

By completing Tracks 1 and 2 you can build a pretty reasonable application that you can deploy to the marketplace. **Chapter 30** shows you how you can take your app to the Google Play store.

Track 4: Making Your Application Robust

Track 4 is an advanced track getting into the internals of Android. You will need to go through the chapters in this track to solidify your understanding of how Android works. We start this track with **Chapter 12** on compatibility library. This chapter teaches how to make your app run well on older releases while using features that are available only on the newer platforms.

Android allows you to run code in your application even though you are not actively using the application in the foreground. It could be the music you are playing in the background, or it could be backing up your images to a cloud, etc. This type of code is called a Service in Android. Working with services is covered in **Chapter 13**. These services can be triggered by a direct user action or through alarms or broadcast events. Alarm manager is covered in **Chapter 17**.

When you use intents to invoke components such as activities or services you are targeting a single component. Android also supports a publish-and-subscribe protocol where an intent can be used to invoke multiple components that register for it at the same time. These components are called receivers or broadcast receivers. A broadcast receiver is a piece of code in your application that is executed in response to a broadcasted event even if your application had not been started or was just dormant at the time of the event. How to work with broadcast receivers is covered in **Chapter 16**.

As you start using more and more features of Android such as services, broadcast receivers, and content providers you will need to understand how Android uses a single main thread to run the code in these components. This threading model is covered in detail in **Chapter 14**. Knowing this will help you write code that is robust. In this track, you will also learn about the very useful `AsyncTask`, which is used to simplify offloading work from the main thread. This API is often used from UI to read messages from the web or check for e-mails, etc. `AsyncTask` is covered in **Chapter 15**.

Track 5: Bringing Finesse to Your Apps

To make your apps look appealing, one of the first things you can do is to add a little or a lot of animation. This is covered in **Chapter 18**. Touch-based interfaces are now the norm. Manipulating your environment with drag and drop is more natural. You want to employ sensors to write apps that integrate with the external world better. These touch screens, drag and drop, and sensors are respectively covered in **Chapters 22, 23, and 24**.

Home screen widgets are a wonderful way to extract pieces of your app and make it available on any home screen of your choosing. This personalization feature, when used innovatively with value in mind, makes the interaction with the device simple and joyful. Widgets are covered in **Chapter 21**.

Map- and location-based apps are made for mobile devices. This topic is covered in **Chapter 19**.

You can very easily integrate audio and video into your apps on Android. This API is covered in **Chapter 20**.

Track 6: Integrating with Other Devices and the Cloud

You can use Google cloud messaging to reach out to the users of your mobile applications. Google cloud messaging is covered in **Chapter 29**. With NFC and Bluetooth capabilities in Android you can start interacting with your physical environment in your apps. We hope to post some material on these topics to the online companion for the book.

Final Track: Getting a Helping Hand from Expert Android

Now, we are going to talk about a few topics that are not covered in this book. You may want to consider these topics, should you find them relevant to your needs. Most of these are based on our research for the *Expert Android* book that we published in early 2014 through Apress.

Android has a public API to write custom components that can work and behave differently than what come out of the box. You can write custom views where you can control what to draw and how to draw, which can then coexist with other controls that are out of the box like a button or a text control. You can also combine multiple existing controls into a compound control that can then behave like an independent control. You can also design new layouts that suit your display needs. There are a lot of tricky things to create these custom components well. You have to understand the core Android view architecture. This material is covered over three chapters and 100 pages in the *Expert Android* book from Apress.

If your apps are form based, you will need to write a lot of code to validate the form input. You really need a framework to handle this. *Expert Android* has a chapter on creating a small form processing framework that is really useful and will reduce errors and the amount of code you need to write.

MBAAS, Mobile Backend as a Service, is a needed technology for mobile apps and is now pretty widely available. The facilities an MBAAS offers are user logins, social logins, user management, savind data on behalf of users in the cloud, communication with the users, collaboration between the users themselves, etc. In *Expert Android* we have multiple chapters dedicated to an MBAAS platform called Parse.

OpenGL has come a long way on Android with now-substantial support for the new generation of programmable GPUs. Android has been supporting ES 2.0 for some time now. In *Expert Android* we have over 100 pages of coverage on OpenGL. We start at the beginning and explain all the concepts without needing to refer to external books, although we do give an extensive bibliography on OpenGL. We cover ES 2.0 really well and provide guidance to combine OpenGL and regular views to pave the way for 3D components.

Federated search protocol of Android is powerful as you can use it in quite a few imaginative ways. *Expert Android* fully explores its fundamentals and also some alternate ways of using it optimally.

Android provides an increasingly large set of features for debugging. These topics are covered in *Expert Android*. A cell phone is ultimately a talking device, although it is used less and less often for that. We have a chapter on utilizing the telephony API in *Expert Android* as well.

As We Leave You Now with the Rest of the Book

Finally, you may be wondering why you should even become a mobile developer. We can cite two strong arguments, one of which never existed before. The familiar one is to be part of an IT organization for their mobile programming efforts. The IT opportunities are on the rise but not fully realized yet unlike what happened with the Web programming paradigm when it came into being. We expect this need, however, to be a gradually increasing demand.

On the other hand, the immediate and exciting opportunity is for you to become an independent app publisher. The availability of a sales channel for the apps that you write is a unique one in the software industry. Not every one of us is going to be a rising star in an IT organization. The independent developer path gives an avenue for you to grow at your own pace and in a direction that satisfies you. Luck and patience might even make you rich. At least you can add value to the society while meeting your needs.

Should you decide to venture into the Android mobile programming space, you want to be prepared with the right hardware that makes this experience bearable. If you are buying a Windows laptop see if you can get one with at least 8G of memory, solid-state hard drive, and a reasonably fast processor. Expect to spend about $1,000 to $1,500. If you are buying a Mac laptop, a similar configuration may cost you about $2,500. A good fast configuration is important for Android development. If you are a seasoned Java programmer, given this investment, and this book in hand, if you follow the tracks laid out here you can become a competent mobile Android app developer in about six months.

References

Here are additional resources for the topics discussed in this chapter.

- `http://androidbook.com/free-android-chapters`: You can use this URL to download detailed chapters on resources and intents (made available free from previous editions due to space limitations).
- `http://androidbook.com/working-with-avds`: You will find at this URL notes on installing Android, working with AVDs, signing APK files, and more to get you started with Android.
- `http://androidbook.com/item/3574`: This URL shows how to run an Android application on a device from the eclipse ADT. This link also shows you how to hook up your device through a USB port to your development computer.
- `http://androidbook.com/item/4629`: This URL talks about key callback functions on an activity. Monitoring the activity callbacks is a good way to get a handle on the activity life cycle. You can copy the code from here to create a base activity that can monitor and log these callbacks for you.

- `http://androidbook.com/item/4440`: This URL talks about how you can use GSON and JSON for persistence needs of your application. This article suggests an easy way to persist data on the device for your apps.
- *Expert Android* from Apress talks about passing objects through Android bundles as parcelables in depth.
- `http://developer.android.com/guide/topics/resources/index.html`: Android SDK roadmap to the documentation on resources.
- `http://developer.android.com/guide/topics/resources/available-resources.html`: Android documentation of various types of resources available.
- `http://developer.android.com/guide/topics/resources/providing-resources.html#AlternativeResources`: A list of various configuration qualifiers provided by the latest Android SDK.
- `http://developer.android.com/guide/practices/screens_support.html`: Guidelines on how to design Android applications for multiple screen sizes.
- `http://developer.android.com/reference/android/content/res/Resources.html`: Various Java methods available to read resources.
- `http://developer.android.com/reference/android/R.html`: Resources as defined to the core Android platform.
- `http://androidbook.com/item/3542`: Our research on plurals, string arrays, resource qualifiers, and alternate resources, as well as links to other references.
- `http://androidbook.com/item/4236`: Using drawable resources to control backgrounds.
- `http://developer.android.com/training/notepad/index.html`: A beginner's guide, yet a comprehensive introduction to Android applications through a NotePad example.
- `http://developer.android.com/reference/android/content/Intent.html`: Overview of intents, including well-known actions, extras, and so on.
- `http://developer.android.com/guide/appendix/g-app-intents.html`: Lists the intents for a set of Google applications. Here, you will see here how to invoke Browser, Map, Dialer, and Google Street View.
- `http://developer.android.com/reference/android/content/IntentFilter.html`: Talks about intent filters and is useful when you are registering intent filters for activities and other components in the manifest file.
- `http://developer.android.com/guide/topics/intents/intents-filters.html`: Goes into the resolution rules of intent filters.

- `http://developer.android.com/training/notepad/index.html`: URL where you can download the sample code for a NotePad application. This is a good sample application that features a number of Android APIs. A good place to go after the calculator application.
- `http://developer.android.com/samples/index.html`: This is the primary link to browse through the various samples presented for the Android SDK by Google.
- `http://developer.android.com/training/index.html`: This is the primary learning site from Google that presents a series of lessons to learn Android.
- `https://code.google.com/p/openintents/`: A web effort to make various Android applications work together.
- `http://androidbook.com/item/4623`: A roadmap for learning Android. Although some of these points are covered here, see this URL for the latest guidance on learning and maximizing Android.
- `http://androidbook.com/item/4764`: This is a knowledge folder containing a series of articles and tidbits on programming with Android basic UI.
- `http://www.androidbook.com/proandroid5/projects`. Look here for a list of downloadable projects related to this book. For this chapter, look for a ZIP file called ProAndroid5_Ch02_Calculator.zip.

Summary

This chapter laid out everything you need to understand to create mobile applications with the Android SDK. You have seen how UI is constructed. You know what activities are. You know the intricacies of the activity life cycle. You understood resources and intents. You know how to save state. Finally, you got to see the breadth of the Android SDK by reading the learning tracks that summarized the rest of the book. We hope these first two chapters gave you a head start for your development efforts with the Android SDK.

Chapter 3

Building Basic User Interfaces and Using Controls

The previous chapter gave you a crash course in some of the UI elements available in Android, and how to put them together quickly to create the calculator application. While that was fun, we hope you started thinking about what other UI widgets are available in Android, over and above the TextView, EditText, and Button controls introduced in Chapter 2.

In this chapter, we are going to discuss user interfaces and controls in detail. We will begin by discussing the general philosophy of UI development in Android, and then we'll describe many of the UI controls that ship with the Android SDK. These are the building blocks of the interfaces you'll create. In the subsequent chapters, we will also discuss view adapters and layout managers, and you'll see how they build on the basic controls we introduce in this chapter.

By the end of this chapter, you'll have a solid understanding of the many UI controls available in the stock Android toolset, and how to lay out UI controls into screens and populate them with data.

UI Development in Android

UI development in Android is fun. It's fun because it's relatively easy. With Android, we have a simple-to-understand framework with a limited set of out-of-the-box controls. The available screen area is generally limited—on phones if not on tablets—and this guides the underlying philosophy of "simple power" for Android controls. Android also takes care of a lot of the heavy lifting normally associated to designing and building quality UIs. This, combined with the fact that the user usually wants to do one specific action, allows us to easily build a good UI to deliver a good user experience.

The Android SDK ships with a host of controls that you can use to build UIs for your application. Similar to other SDKs, the Android SDK provides text fields, buttons, lists, grids, and so on. In addition, Android provides a collection of controls that are appropriate for mobile devices.

At the heart of the common controls are two classes: `android.view.View` and `android.view.ViewGroup`. As the name of the first class suggests, the `View` class represents a general-purpose `View` object. The common controls in Android ultimately extend the `View` class. `ViewGroup` is also a view, but it contains other views too. `ViewGroup` is the base class for a list of layout classes. Android, like Swing, uses the concept of *layouts* to manage how controls are laid out within a container view. Using layouts, as we'll see, makes it easy for us to control the position and orientation of the controls in our UIs.

You can choose from several approaches to build UIs in Android. You can construct UIs entirely in code. You can also define UIs in XML. You can even combine the two—define the UI in XML and then refer to it, and modify it, in code. To demonstrate this, in this chapter we are going to build a simple UI using each of these three approaches.

Before we get started, let's define some nomenclature. In this book and other Android literature, you will find the terms *view*, *control*, *widget*, *container*, and *layout* in discussions regarding UI development. If you are new to Android programming or UI development in general, you might not be familiar with these terms. We'll briefly describe them before we get started (see Table 3-1).

***Table 3-1.** UI Nomenclature*

Term	Description
View, widget, control	Each of these represents a UI element. Examples include a button, a grid, a list, a window, a dialog box, and so on. The terms *view*, *widget*, and *control* are used interchangeably in this chapter.
Container	This is a view used to contain other views. For example, a grid can be considered a container because it contains cells, each of which is a view.
Layout	This is a visual arrangement of containers and views and can include other layouts. We will work with layouts in this chapter and return for a full exploration of Android's Layout features in Chapter 5.

Figure 3-1 shows a screenshot of the application that we are going to build. Next to the screenshot is the layout hierarchy of the controls and containers in the application.

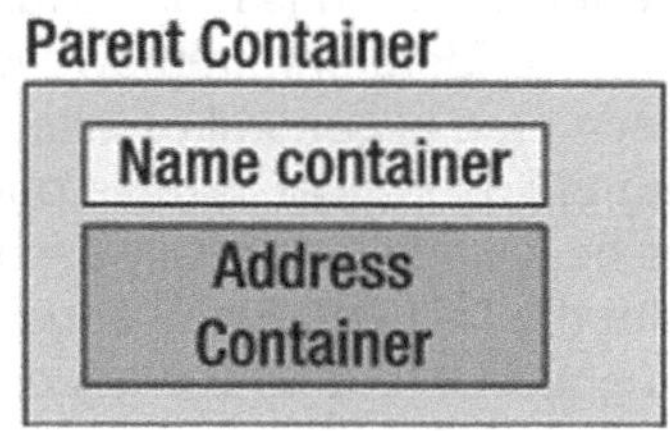

***Figure 3-1.** The UI and layout of an activity*

We will refer to this layout hierarchy as we discuss the sample programs. For now, know that the application has one activity. The UI for the activity is composed of three containers: a container that contains a person's name, a container that contains the address, and an outer parent container for the child containers.

Building a UI Completely in Code

The first example, Listing 3-1, demonstrates how to build the UI entirely in code. To try this, create a new Android Application project using a project name of `controls`, a package name of `com.androidbook.controls`, and with an activity named `MainActivity` and then copy the code from Listing 3-1 into your `MainActivity` class.

> **Note** We will give you a URL at the end of the chapter that you can use to download projects from this chapter. This will allow you to import these projects into Eclipse directly instead of copying and pasting code.

Listing 3-1. Creating a Simple User Interface Entirely in Code

```
package com.androidbook.controls;
import android.app.Activity;
import android.os.Bundle;
import android.view.ViewGroup.LayoutParams;
import android.widget.LinearLayout;
import android.widget.TextView;
public class MainActivity extends Activity
{
    private LinearLayout nameContainer;

    private LinearLayout addressContainer;

    private LinearLayout parentContainer;

    /** Called when the activity is first created. */
    @Override
    public void onCreate(Bundle savedInstanceState)
    {
        super.onCreate(savedInstanceState);

        createNameContainer();

        createAddressContainer();

        createParentContainer();

        setContentView(parentContainer);
    }
```

```
    private void createNameContainer()
    {
        nameContainer = new LinearLayout(this);

        nameContainer.setLayoutParams(new LayoutParams(LayoutParams.FILL_PARENT,
                LayoutParams.WRAP_CONTENT));
        nameContainer.setOrientation(LinearLayout.HORIZONTAL);

        TextView nameLbl = new TextView(this);
        nameLbl.setText("Name: ");

        TextView nameValue = new TextView(this);
        nameValue.setText("John Doe");

        nameContainer.addView(nameLbl);
        nameContainer.addView(nameValue);
    }
    private void createAddressContainer()
    {
        addressContainer = new LinearLayout(this);

        addressContainer.setLayoutParams(new LayoutParams(LayoutParams.FILL_PARENT,
                LayoutParams.WRAP_CONTENT));
        addressContainer.setOrientation(LinearLayout.VERTICAL);

        TextView addrLbl = new TextView(this);
        addrLbl.setText("Address:");

        TextView addrValue = new TextView(this);
        addrValue.setText("911 Hollywood Blvd");

        addressContainer.addView(addrLbl);
        addressContainer.addView(addrValue);
    }

    private void createParentContainer()
    {
        parentContainer = new LinearLayout(this);

        parentContainer.setLayoutParams(new LayoutParams(LayoutParams.FILL_PARENT,
                LayoutParams.FILL_PARENT));
        parentContainer.setOrientation(LinearLayout.VERTICAL);

        parentContainer.addView(nameContainer);
        parentContainer.addView(addressContainer);
    }
}
```

As shown in Listing 3-1, the activity contains three `LinearLayout` objects. We will be discussing layouts in much more depth in Chapter 5, but there's a little chicken-and-egg issue of needing to know just a little about layouts so one can learn about the many basic controls. For now, it's enough to know that layout objects contain logic to position objects within a portion of the screen. A LinearLayout, for example, knows how to lay out controls either vertically or horizontally. Layout objects can contain any type of view—even other layouts.

The nameContainer object contains two TextView controls: one for the label Name: and the other to hold the actual text for the name (such as John Doe). The addressContainer also contains two TextView controls. The difference between the two containers is that the nameContainer is laid out horizontally and the addressContainer is laid out vertically. Both of these containers live within the parentContainer, which is the root view of the activity. After the containers have been built, the activity sets the content of the view to the root view by calling setContentView(parentContainer). When it comes time to render the UI of the activity, the root view is called to render itself. The root view then calls its children to render themselves, and the child controls call their children, and so on, until the entire UI is rendered.

As shown in Listing 3-1, we have several LinearLayout controls. Two of them are laid out vertically, and one is laid out horizontally. The nameContainer is laid out horizontally. This means the two TextView controls appear side by side horizontally. The addressContainer is laid out vertically, which means the two TextView controls are stacked one on top of the other. The parentContainer is also laid out vertically, which is why the nameContainer appears above the addressContainer. Note a subtle difference between the two vertically laid-out containers, addressContainer and parentContainer. parentContainer is set to take up the entire width and height of the screen:

```
parentContainer.setLayoutParams(new LayoutParams(LayoutParams.FILL_PARENT,
        LayoutParams.FILL_PARENT));
```

and addressContainer wraps its content vertically:

```
addressContainer.setLayoutParams(new LayoutParams(LayoutParams.FILL_PARENT,
        LayoutParams.WRAP_CONTENT));
```

Said another way, WRAP_CONTENT means the view should take just the space it needs in that dimension and no more, up to what the containing view will allow. For the addressContainer, this means the container will take two lines vertically, because that's all it needs for the dummy address we have provided.

Building a UI Completely in XML

Now let's build the same UI in XML (see Listing 3-2). XML layout files are stored under the resources (/res/) directory in a folder called layout. To try this example, create a new Android project in Eclipse. By default, you will get an XML layout file named activity_main.xml, located under the res/layout folder. Double-click activity_main.xml to see the contents. Eclipse will display a visual editor for your layout file. You probably have a string at the top of the view that says "Hello World, MainActivity!" or something like that. Click the activity_main.xml tab at the bottom of the view to see the XML of the activity_main.xml file. This reveals a LinearLayout and a TextView control. Using either the Layout or activity_main.xml tab, or both, re-create Listing 3-2 in the activity_main.xml file. Save it.

Listing 3-2. Creating a User Interface Entirely in XML

```
<?xml version="1.0" encoding="utf-8"?>
<LinearLayout xmlns:android="http://schemas.android.com/apk/res/android"
    android:orientation="vertical" android:layout_width="fill_parent"
    android:layout_height="fill_parent">
    <!-- NAME CONTAINER -->
    <LinearLayout        android:orientation="horizontal" android:layout_width="fill_parent"
        android:layout_height="wrap_content">

            <TextView  android:layout_width="wrap_content"
        android:layout_height="wrap_content" android:text="Name:" />

            <TextView android:layout_width="wrap_content"
        android:layout_height="wrap_content" android:text="John Doe" />

    </LinearLayout>

    <!-- ADDRESS CONTAINER -->
    <LinearLayout        android:orientation="vertical" android:layout_width="fill_parent"
        android:layout_height="wrap_content">

            <TextView android:layout_width="fill_parent"
        android:layout_height="wrap_content" android:text="Address:" />

            <TextView android:layout_width="fill_parent"
        android:layout_height="wrap_content" android:text="911 Hollywood Blvd" />
    </LinearLayout>

</LinearLayout>
```

Under your new project's `src` directory, there is a `.java` file containing an `Activity` class definition. Double-click that file to see its contents. Notice the statement `setContentView(R.layout.activity_main)`. The XML snippet shown in Listing 3-2, combined with a call to `setContentView(R.layout.activity_main)`, will render the same UI as before when we generated it completely in code. The XML file is self-explanatory, but note that we have three container views defined. The first `LinearLayout` is the equivalent of our parent container. This container sets its orientation to vertical by setting the corresponding property like this: `android:orientation="vertical"`. The parent container contains two `LinearLayout` containers, which represent `nameContainer` and `addressContainer`.

Running this application will produce the same UI as our previous example application. The labels and values will be displayed as shown in Figure 3-1.

Building a UI in XML with Code

Listing 3-2 is a contrived example. It doesn't make any sense to hard-code the values of the `TextView` controls in the XML layout. Ideally, we should design our UIs in XML and then reference the controls from code. This approach enables us to bind dynamic data to the controls defined at design time. In fact, this is the recommended approach. It is fairly easy to build layouts in XML and then use code to populate the dynamic data.

Listing 3-3 shows the same UI with slightly different XML. This XML assigns IDs to the TextView controls so that we can refer to them in code.

Listing 3-3. Creating a User Interface in XML with IDs

```
<?xml version="1.0" encoding="utf-8"?>
<LinearLayout xmlns:android="http://schemas.android.com/apk/res/android"
    android:orientation="vertical" android:layout_width="fill_parent"
    android:layout_height="fill_parent">
    <!-- NAME CONTAINER -->
    <LinearLayout        android:orientation="horizontal" android:layout_width="fill_parent"
        android:layout_height="wrap_content">

            <TextView android:layout_width="wrap_content"
        android:layout_height="wrap_content" android:text="@string/name_text" />

            <TextView android:id="@+id/nameValue"
        android:layout_width="wrap_content" android:layout_height="wrap_content" />

    </LinearLayout>

    <!-- ADDRESS CONTAINER -->
    <LinearLayout xmlns:android="http://schemas.android.com/apk/res/android"
        android:orientation="vertical" android:layout_width="fill_parent"
        android:layout_height="wrap_content">

            <TextView android:layout_width="fill_parent"
        android:layout_height="wrap_content" android:text="@string/addr_text" />

            <TextView android:id="@+id/addrValue"
        android:layout_width="fill_parent" android:layout_height="wrap_content" />
    </LinearLayout>

</LinearLayout>
```

In addition to adding the IDs to the TextView controls that we want to populate from code, we also have label TextView controls that we're populating with text from our strings resource file. These are the TextViews without IDs that have an android:text attribute. The actual strings for these TextViews will come from our strings.xml file in the /res/values folder. Listing 3-4 shows what our strings.xml file might look like.

Listing 3-4. strings.xml File for Listing 3-3

```
<?xml version="1.0" encoding="utf-8"?>
<resources>
    <string name="app_name">Common Controls</string>
    <string name="name_text">Name:</string>
    <string name="addr_text">Address:</string>
</resources>
```

The code in Listing 3-5 demonstrates how you can obtain references to the controls defined in the XML to set their properties. You might put this into your onCreate() method for your activity.

Listing 3-5. Referring to Controls in Resources at Runtime

```
setContentView(R.layout.activity_main);
TextView nameValue = (TextView)findViewById(R.id.nameValue);
nameValue.setText("John Doe");
TextView addrValue = (TextView)findViewById(R.id.addrValue);
addrValue.setText("911 Hollywood Blvd.");
```

The code in Listing 3-5 is straightforward, but note that we load the resource by calling `setContentView(R.layout.activity_main)` before calling `findViewById()`—we cannot get references to views if they have not been loaded yet.

The developers of Android have done a nice job of making just about every aspect of a control settable via XML or code. It's usually a good idea to set the control's attributes in the XML layout file rather than using code. However, there will be a variety of times when you need to use code, such as setting a value to be displayed to the user.

FILL_PARENT vs. MATCH_PARENT

The constant `FILL_PARENT` was deprecated in Android 2.2 and replaced with `MATCH_PARENT`. This was strictly a name change, though. The value of this constant is still –1. Similarly, for XML layouts, `fill_parent` was replaced with `match_parent`. So what value do you use? Instead of `FILL_PARENT` or `MATCH_PARENT`, you could simply use the value –1, and you'd be fine. However, this isn't very easy to read, and you don't have an equivalent unnamed value to use with your XML layouts. There's a better way.

Depending on which Android APIs you need to use in your application, you can either build your application against a version of Android before 2.2 and rely on forward compatibility or build your application against version 2.2 or later of Android and set `minSdkVersion` to the lowest version of Android your application will run on. For example, if you only need APIs that existed in Android 1.6, build against Android 1.6 and use `FILL_PARENT` and `fill_parent`. Your application should run with no problems in all later versions of Android including 2.2 and beyond. If you need APIs from Android 2.2 or later, go ahead and build against that version of Android, use `MATCH_PARENT` and `match_parent`, and set `minSdkVersion` to something older: for example, `4` (for Android 1.6). You can still deploy an Android application built in Android 2.2 to an older version of Android, but you'll have to be careful about the classes and/or methods that aren't in the earlier releases of the Android SDK. There are ways around this, such as using reflection or creating wrapper classes to handle differences in Android versions. We will cover those advanced topics in later chapters.

Understanding Android's Common Controls

We will now start our discussion of the common controls in the Android SDK. We'll start with text controls and then cover buttons, check boxes, radio buttons, lists, grids, date and time controls, and a map-view control. These will go hand in hand with the layout controls we'll introduce in Chapter 4.

Text Controls

Text controls are likely to be the first type of control that you'll work with in Android. Android has a complete but not overwhelming set of text controls. In this section, we are going to discuss the `TextView`, `EditText`, `AutoCompleteTextView`, and `MultiAutoCompleteTextView` controls. Figure 3-2 shows the controls in action.

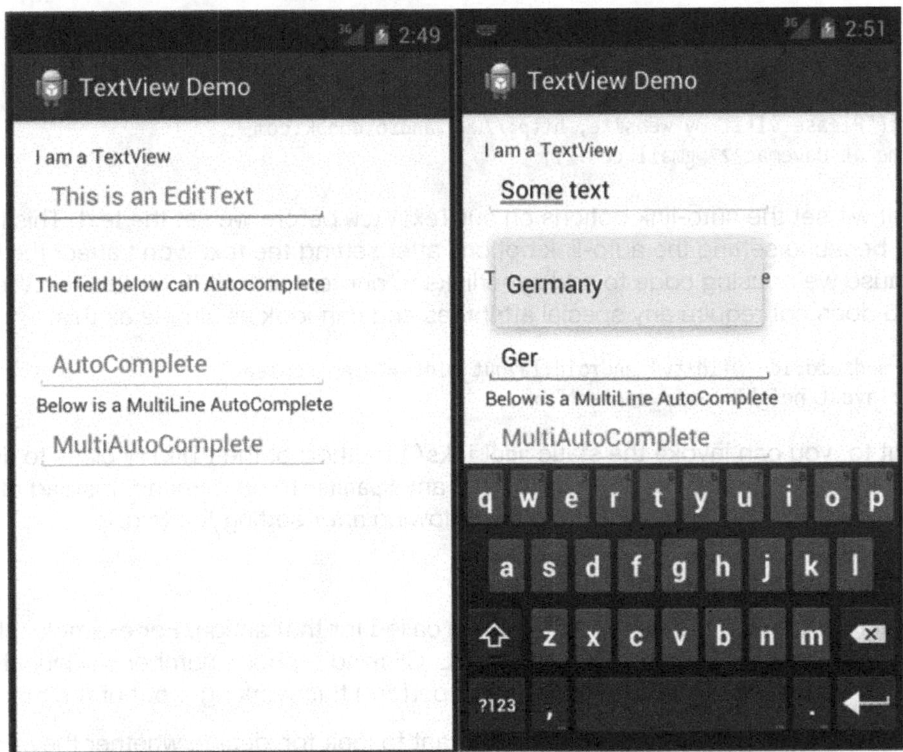

Figure 3-2. Text controls in Android

TextView

You've already seen a simple XML specification for a `TextView` control, in Listing 3-3, and how to handle `TextViews` in code in Listing 3-4. Notice how we specified the ID, width, height, and value of the text in XML and how we set the value using the `setText()` method. The `TextView` control knows how to display text but does not allow editing. This might lead you to conclude that the control is essentially a dummy label. Not true. The `TextView` control has a few interesting properties that make it very handy. If you know that the content of the `TextView` is going to contain a web URL or an e-mail address, for example, you can set the `autoLink` property to `email|web`, and the control will find and highlight any e-mail addresses and URLs. Moreover, when the user clicks one of these highlighted items, the system will take care of launching the e-mail application with the e-mail address or a browser with the URL. In XML, this attribute would be inside the `TextView` tag and would look something like this:

```
<TextView ...    android:autoLink="email|web"  ...    />
```

You specify a pipe-delimited set of values including web, email, phone, or map, or use none (the default) or all. If you want to set autoLink behavior in code instead of using XML, the corresponding method call is setAutoLinkMask(). You would pass it an int representing the combination of values sort of like before, such as Linkify.EMAIL_ADDRESSES|Linkify.WEB_URLS. To achieve this functionality, TextView is utilizing the android.text.util.Linkify class. Listing 3-6 shows an example of auto-linking with code.

Listing 3-6. Using Linkify on Text in a TextView

```
TextView tv =(TextView)this.findViewById(R.id.tv);
tv.setAutoLinkMask(Linkify.ALL);
tv.setText("Please visit my website, http://www.androidbook.com
or email me at davemac327@gmail.com.");
```

Notice that we set the auto-link options on our TextView before we set the text. This is important because setting the auto-link options after setting the text won't affect the existing text. Because we're using code to add hyperlinks to our text, our XML for the TextView in Listing 3-6 does not require any special attributes and can look as simple as this:

```
<TextView android:id="@+id/tv" android:layout_width="wrap_content"
  android:layout_height="wrap_content"/>
```

If you want to, you can invoke the static addLinks() method of the Linkify class to find and add links to the content of any TextView or any Spannable on demand. Instead of using setAutoLinkMask(), we could have done the following *after* setting the text:

```
Linkify.addLinks(tv, Linkify.ALL);
```

Clicking a link will cause the default intent to be called for that action. For example, clicking a web URL will launch the browser with the URL. Clicking a phone number will launch the phone dialer, and so on. The Linkify class can perform this work right out of the box.

Linkify can also detect custom patterns you want to look for, decide whether they are a match for something you decide needs to be clickable, and set up how to fire an intent to make a click turn into some sort of action. We won't go into those details here, but know that these things can be done.

There are many more features of TextView to explore, from font attributes to minLines and maxLines and many more. These are fairly self-explanatory, and you are encouraged to experiment to see how you might be able to use them. Although you should keep in mind that some functionality in the TextView class is not applicable to a read-only field, the functionality is there for the subclasses of TextView, one of which we will cover next.

EditText

The EditText control is a subclass of TextView. As suggested by the name, the EditText control allows for text editing. EditText is not as powerful as the text-editing controls that you find on the Internet, but users of Android-based devices probably won't type documents directly into an EditText control—they'll type a couple of paragraphs at most or use a more fully functional HTML-based page instead. Therefore, the class has limited but appropriate functionality and may even surprise you. For example, one of the most significant properties of an EditText is the inputType. You can set the inputType property to textAutoCorrect to have the control correct common misspellings. You can set it to textCapWords to have the control capitalize words. Other options expect only phone numbers or passwords.

There are older, now deprecated, ways of specifying capitalization, multiline text, and other features. If these are specified without an inputType property, they can be read; but if inputType is specified, these older properties are ignored.

The old default behavior of the EditText control is to display text on one line and expand as needed. In other words, if the user types past the first line, another line will appear, and so on. You could, however, force the user to a single line by setting the singleLine property to true. In this case, the user will have to continue typing on the same line. With inputType, if you don't specify textMultiLine, the EditText will default to single-line only. So if you want the old default behavior of multiline typing, you need to specify inputType with textMultiLine.

One of the nice features of EditText is that you can specify hint text. This text will be displayed slightly faded and disappears as soon as the user starts to type text. The purpose of the hint is to let the user know what is expected in this field, without the user having to select and erase default text. In XML, this attribute is android:hint="your hint text here" or android:hint="@string/your_hint_name", where your_hint_name is a resource name of a string to be found in /res/values/strings.xml. In code, you would call the setHint() method with either a CharSequence or a resource ID.

AutoCompleteTextView

The AutoCompleteTextView control is a TextView with auto-complete functionality. In other words, as the user types in the TextView, the control can display suggestions for selection. Listing 3-7 demonstrates the AutoCompleteTextView control with XML and with the corresponding code.

Listing 3-7. Using an AutoCompleteTextView Control

```
<AutoCompleteTextView android:id="@+id/actv"
    android:layout_width="fill_parent"  android:layout_height="wrap_content" />
AutoCompleteTextView actv = (AutoCompleteTextView) this.findViewById(R.id.actv);

ArrayAdapter<String> aa = new ArrayAdapter<String>(this,
                android.R.layout.simple_dropdown_item_1line,
                new String[] {"English", "Hebrew", "Hindi", "Spanish",
                "German", "Greek" });

actv.setAdapter(aa);
```

The AutoCompleteTextView control shown in Listing 3-7 suggests a language to the user. For example, if the user types **en**, the control suggests English. If the user types **gr**, the control recommends Greek, and so on.

If you have used a suggestion control or a similar auto-complete control, you know that controls like this have two parts: a text-view control and a control that displays the suggestion(s). That's the general concept. To use a control like this, you have to create the control, create the list of suggestions, tell the control the list of suggestions, and possibly tell the control how to display the suggestions. Alternatively, you could create a second control for the suggestions and then associate the two controls.

Android has made this simple, as is evident from Listing 3-7. To use an `AutoCompleteTextView`, you can define the control in your layout file and reference it in your activity. You then create an adapter class that holds the suggestions and define the ID of the control that will show the suggestion (in this case, a simple list item). In Listing 3-7, the second parameter to the `ArrayAdapter` tells the adapter to use a simple list item to show the suggestion. The final step is to associate the adapter with the `AutoCompleteTextView`, which you do using the `setAdapter()` method. Don't worry about the adapter for the moment; we'll cover those later in this chapter.

MultiAutoCompleteTextView

If you have played with the `AutoCompleteTextView` control, you know that the control offers suggestions only for the *entire* text in the text view. In other words, if you type a sentence, you don't get suggestions for each word. That's where `MultiAutoCompleteTextView` comes in. You can use the `MultiAutoCompleteTextView` to provide suggestions as the user types. For example, Figure 3-2 shows that the user typed the word **English** followed by a comma, and then **Ge**, at which point the control suggested **German**. If the user were to continue, the control would offer additional suggestions.

Using the `MultiAutoCompleteTextView` is like using the `AutoCompleteTextView`. The difference is that you have to tell the control where to start suggesting again. For example, in Figure 3-2, you can see that the control can offer suggestions at the beginning of the sentence and after it sees a comma. The `MultiAutoCompleteTextView` control requires that you give it a tokenizer that can parse the sentence and tell it whether to start suggesting again. Listing 3-8 demonstrates using the `MultiAutoCompleteTextView` control with the XML and then the Java code.

***Listing 3-8.** Using the MultiAutoCompleteTextView Control*

```
<MultiAutoCompleteTextView android:id="@+id/mactv"
    android:layout_width="fill_parent"  android:layout_height="wrap_content" />

MultiAutoCompleteTextView mactv = (MultiAutoCompleteTextView) this
                .findViewById(R.id.mactv);
ArrayAdapter<String> aa2 = new ArrayAdapter<String>(this,
                android.R.layout.simple_dropdown_item_1line,
new String[] {"English", "Hebrew", "Hindi", "Spanish", "German", "Greek" });

mactv.setAdapter(aa2);

mactv.setTokenizer(new MultiAutoCompleteTextView.CommaTokenizer());
```

The only significant differences between Listings 3-7 and 3-8 are the use of `MultiAutoCompleteTextView` and the call to the `setTokenizer()` method. Because of the `CommaTokenizer` in this case, after a comma is typed into the `EditText` field, the field will again make suggestions using the array of strings. Any other characters typed in will not trigger the field to make suggestions. So even if you were to type **French Spani**, the partial word *Spani* would not trigger the suggestion because it did not follow a comma. Android provides another tokenizer for e-mail addresses called `Rfc822Tokenizer`. You can always create your own tokenizer if you want to.

Button Controls

Buttons are common in any widget toolkit, and Android is no exception. Android offers the typical set of buttons as well as a few extras. In this section, we will discuss three types of button controls: the basic button, the image button, and the toggle button. Figure 3-3 shows a UI with these controls. The button at the top is the basic button, the middle button is an image button, and the last one is a toggle button.

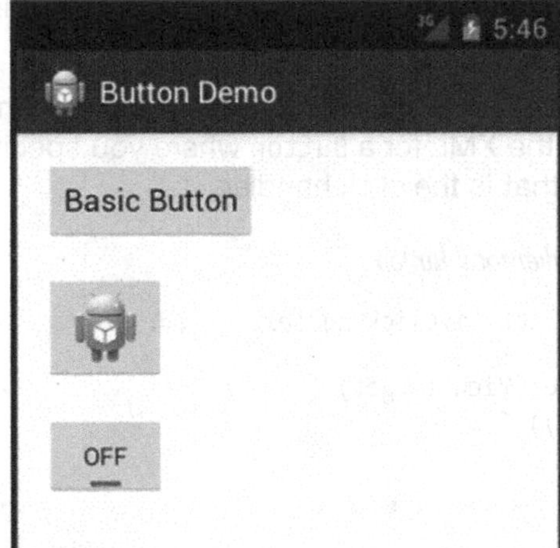

***Figure 3-3.** Android button controls*

Let's get started with the basic button.

The Button Control

The basic button class in Android is `android.widget.Button`. There's not much to this type of button, beyond how you use it to handle click events. Listing 3-9 shows a fragment of an XML layout for the `Button` control, plus some Java that we might set up in the `onCreate()` method of our activity. Our basic button would look like the top button in Figure 3-3.

***Listing 3-9.** Handling Click Events on a Button*

```
<Button android:id="@+id/button1"
    android:text="@string/basicBtnLabel"
    android:layout_width="fill_parent"
    android:layout_height="wrap_content" />
```

```
Button button1 = (Button)this.findViewById(R.id.button1);
button1.setOnClickListener(new OnClickListener()
{
     public void onClick(View v)
     {
        Intent intent = new Intent(Intent.ACTION_VIEW,
                            Uri.parse("http://www.androidbook.com"));
        startActivity(intent);
     }
});
```

Listing 3-9 shows how to register for a button-click event. You register for the on-click event by calling the `setOnClickListener()` method with an `OnClickListener`. In Listing 3-9, an anonymous listener is created on the fly to handle click events for `button1`. When the button is clicked, the `onClick()` method of the listener is called and, in this case, launches the browser to our web site.

Since Android SDK 1.6, there is an easier way to set up a click handler for your button or buttons. Listing 3-10 shows the XML for a `Button` where you specify an attribute for the handler, plus the Java code that is the click handler.

Listing 3-10. Setting Up a Click Handler for a Button

```
<Button   ...    android:onClick="myClickHandler"    ...  />

    public void myClickHandler(View target) {
        switch(target.getId()) {
        case R.id.button1:
        ...
```

The handler method will be called with target set to the `View` object representing the button that was clicked. Notice how the `switch` statement in the click handler method uses the resource IDs of the buttons to select the logic to run. Using this method means you won't have to explicitly create each `Button` object in your code, and you can reuse the same method across multiple buttons. This makes things easier to understand and maintain. This works with the other button types as well.

The ImageButton Control

Android provides an image button via `android.widget.ImageButton`. Using an image button is similar to using the basic button (see Listing 3-11). Our image button would look like the middle button in Figure 3-3.

Listing 3-11. Using an `ImageButton`

```
<ImageButton android:id="@+id/imageButton2"
    android:layout_width="wrap_content" android:layout_height="wrap_content"
    android:onClick="myClickHandler"
    android:src="@drawable/icon"  />

ImageButton imageButton2 = (ImageButton)this.findViewById(R.id.imageButton2);
imageButton2.setImageResource(R.drawable.icon);
```

Here we've created the image button in XML and set the button's image from a drawable resource. The image file for the button must exist under /res/drawable. In our case, we're simply reusing the Android icon for the button. We also show in Listing 3-11 how you can set the button's image dynamically by calling setImageResource() method on the button and passing it a resource ID. Note that you only need to do one or the other. You don't need to specify the button image both in the XML file and in code.

One of the nice features of an image button is that you can specify a transparent background for the button. The result will be a clickable image that acts like a button but can look like whatever you want it to look like. Just set android:background="@null" for the image button.

Because your image may be something very different than a standard button, you can customize how the button looks in the two other states it can be in when used in your UI. Besides appearing as normal, buttons can have focus, and they can be pressed. Having *focus* simply means the button is currently where events will go. You can direct focus to a button using the arrow keys on the keypad or D-pad, for example. *Pressed* means that the button's appearance changes when it has been pressed but before the user has let go. To tell Android what the three images are for our button, and which one is which, we set up a selector. This is a simple XML file, imagebuttonselector, that resides in the /res/drawable folder of our project. This is somewhat counterintuitive, because this is an XML file and not an image file, yet that is where the selector file must go. The content of a selector file will look like Listing 3-12.

***Listing 3-12.** Using a Selector with an ImageButton*

```
<?xml version="1.0" encoding="utf-8"?>
    <selector xmlns:android="http://schemas.android.com/apk/res/android">
     <item android:state_pressed="true"
          android:drawable="@drawable/button_pressed" /> <!-- pressed -->
     <item android:state_focused="true"
          android:drawable="@drawable/button_focused" /> <!-- focused -->
     <item android:drawable="@drawable/icon" /> <!-- default -->
    </selector>
```

There are several things to note about the selector file. First, you do not specify a <resources> tag as in values XML files. Second, the order of the button images is important. Android will test each item in the selector, in order, to see if it matches. Therefore, you want the normal image to be last so it is used only if the button is not pressed and if the button does not have focus. If the normal image was listed first, it would always match and be selected even if the button is pressed or has focus. Of course, the drawables you refer to must exist in the /res/drawables folder. In the definition of your button in the layout XML file, you want to set the android:src property to the selector XML file as if it were a regular drawable, like so:

```
<Button   ...   android:src="@drawable/imagebuttonselector"   ...  />
```

The ToggleButton Control

The ToggleButton control, like a check box or a radio button, is a two-state button. This button can be in either the On or Off state. As shown in Figure 3-3, the ToggleButton's default behavior is to show a colored bar when in the On state and a grayed-out bar when in the Off state. Moreover, the default behavior also sets the button's text to On when it's in the On state and Off when it's in the Off state. You can modify the text for the ToggleButton if On/Off is not appropriate for your application. For example, if you have a background process that you want to start and stop via a ToggleButton, you could set the button's text to Stop and Run by using android:textOn and android:textOff properties.

Listing 3-13 shows an example. Our toggle button is the bottom button in Figure 3-3, and it is in the On position, so the label on the button says Stop.

Listing 3-13. The Android ToggleButton

```
<ToggleButton android:id="@+id/cctglBtn"
        android:layout_width="wrap_content"
        android:layout_height="wrap_content"
        android:text="Toggle Button"
        android:textOn="Stop"
        android:textOff="Run"/>
```

Because ToggleButtons have on and off text as separate attributes, the android:text attribute of a ToggleButton is not really used. It's available because it has been inherited (from TextView), but in this case, you don't need to use it.

The CheckBox Control

The CheckBox control is another two-state button that allows the user to toggle its state. The difference is that, for many situations, the users don't view it as a button that invokes immediate action. From Android's point of view, however, it is a button, and you can do anything with a check box that you can do with a button.

In Android, you can create a check box by creating an instance of android.widget.CheckBox. See Listing 3-14 and Figure 3-4.

Listing 3-14. Creating Check Boxes

```
<LinearLayout xmlns:android="http://schemas.android.com/apk/res/android"
    android:orientation="vertical"
    android:layout_width="fill_parent"
    android:layout_height="fill_parent">

<CheckBox android:id="@+id/chickenCB"
    android:text="Chicken"
    android:checked="true"
    android:layout_width=""wrap_content"
    android:layout_height="wrap_content" />
```

```
<CheckBox android:id="@+id/fishCB"
    android:text="Fish"
    android:layout_width="wrap_content"
    android:layout_height="wrap_content" />

<CheckBox android:id="@+id/steakCB"
    android:text="Steak"
    android:checked="true"
    android:layout_width="wrap_content"
    android:layout_height="wrap_content" />

</LinearLayout>
```

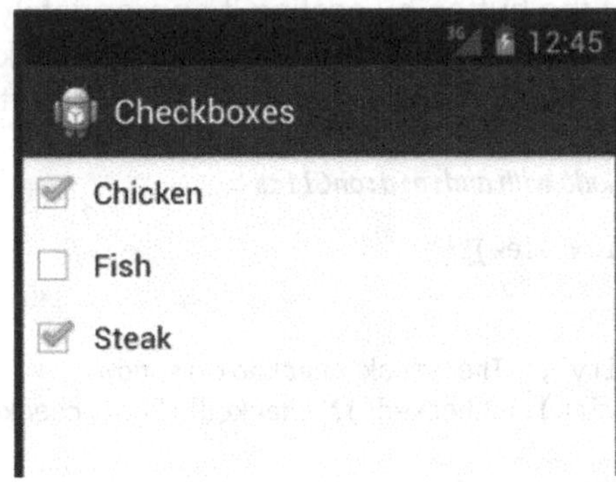

Figure 3-4. Using the CheckBox control

You manage the state of a check box by calling `setChecked()` or `toggle()`. You can obtain the state by calling `isChecked()`.

If you need to implement specific logic when a check box is checked or unchecked, you can register for the on-checked event by calling `setOnCheckedChangeListener()` with an implementation of the `CompoundButton.OnCheckedChangeListener` interface. You'll then have to implement the onCheckedChanged() method, which will be called when the check box is checked or unchecked. Listing 3-15 show some code that deals with a `CheckBox`.

Listing 3-15. Using Check Boxes in Code

```
public class CheckBoxActivity extends Activity {
    /** Called when the activity is first created. */
    @Override
    public void onCreate(Bundle savedInstanceState) {
        super.onCreate(savedInstanceState);
        setContentView(R.layout.checkbox);

        CheckBox fishCB = (CheckBox)findViewById(R.id.fishCB);

        if(fishCB.isChecked())
            fishCB.toggle();        // flips the checkbox to unchecked if it was checked
```

```
        fishCB.setOnCheckedChangeListener(
                new CompoundButton.OnCheckedChangeListener() {

            @Override
            public void onCheckedChanged(CompoundButton arg0, boolean isChecked) {
                Log.v("CheckBoxActivity", "The fish checkbox is now "
                        + (isChecked?"checked":"not checked"));
            }});
    }
}
```

The nice part of setting up the OnCheckedChangeListener is that you are passed the new state of the CheckBox button. You could instead use the OnClickListener technique as we used with basic buttons. When the onClick() method is called, you would need to determine the new state of the button by casting it appropriately and then calling isChecked() on it. Listing 3-16 shows what this code might look like if we added android:onClick="myClickHandler" to the XML definition of our CheckBox buttons.

Listing 3-16. ***Using Check Boxes in Code with android:onClick***

```
public void myClickHandler(View view) {
    switch(view.getId()) {
    case R.id.steakCB:
        Log.v("CheckBoxActivity", "The steak checkbox is now " +
                (((CheckBox)view).isChecked()?"checked":"not checked"));
    }
}
```

The Switch Control

The Switch widget was introduced in Android 4.0 and provides very similar behavior to the CheckBox. In fact, the two widgets are so similar, you'll almost certainly get a sense of deja vu when reviewing the code for a Switch object. Many people (including some of this book's authors) believe that the Switch was introduced for aesthetic reasons more than anything. The trend in UI design in the last few years has been toward the skewmorphic ideal of widgets looking like real-world things, and a Switch is a concrete selector in the real world—not many kitchen appliances have a CheckBox after all.

The Switch similarities to the CheckBox control extend to common methods for examining and changing state. This mimicking of methods includes setChecked() to turn the Switch on, isChecked() to test current state, and so on. One aesthetic difference offered by the Switch widget is the ability to change the associated text between states. Additional methods are available to control this text:

- getTextOn(): returns the text displayed if the Switch is on.
- getTextOff(): returns the text displayed if the Switch is off.
- setTextOn(): sets the text to be displayed if the Switch is on. While good design would usually mean one wouldn't change the text, there are a few cases where a live update of some metric in the switch text can be helpful.
- setTextOff(): sets the text to be displayed if the Switch is off.

An example layout including a Switch is shown in Listing 3-17.

Listing 3-17. Creating a Layout Using a Switch

```
<LinearLayout xmlns:android="http://schemas.android.com/apk/res/android"
    android:orientation="vertical"
    android:layout_width="fill_parent"
    android:layout_height="fill_parent">

    <Switch
        android:id="@+id/switchdemo"
        android:layout_width="wrap_content"
        android:layout_height="wrap_content"
        android:text="This switch is: off" />

</LinearLayout>
```

> **Caution** Remember that "switch" is a reserved word in Java. So we use an ID that doesn't clash.

The code for our example Switch in Listing 3-18 should provoke those feelings of deja vu we mentioned with respect to the CheckBox control.

Listing 3-18. Controlling Switch Behavior in Code

```
public class SwitchDemo extends Activity
  implements CompoundButton.OnCheckedChangeListener {
  Switch sw;

  @Override
  public void onCreate(Bundle icicle) {
    super.onCreate(icicle);
    setContentView(R.layout.main);

    sw=(Switch)findViewById(R.id.switchdemo);
    sw.setOnCheckedChangeListener(this);
  }

  public void onCheckedChanged(CompoundButton buttonView,
                               boolean isChecked) {
    if (isChecked) {
      sw.setTextOn("This switch is: on");
    }
    else {
      sw.setTextOff("This switch is: off");
    }
  }
}
```

The results of our Switch work are showing in Figure 3-5.

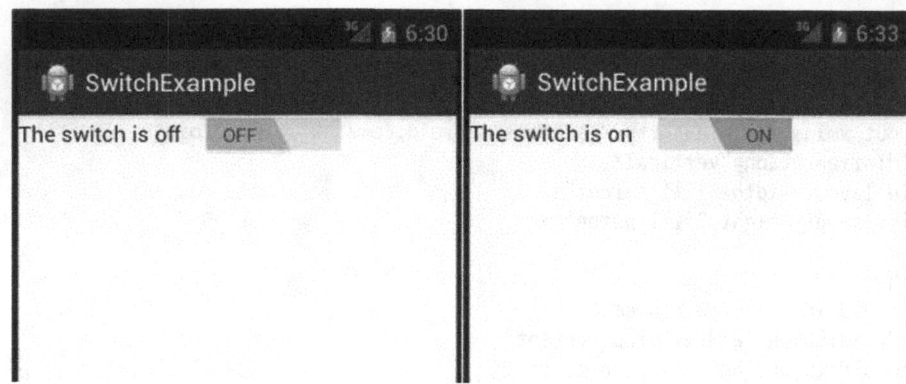

Figure 3-5. Using the Switch control

The RadioButton Control

RadioButton controls are an integral part of any UI toolkit. A radio button gives the users several choices and forces them to select a single item. To enforce this single-selection model, radio buttons generally belong to a group, and each group is forced to have only one item selected at a time.

To create a group of radio buttons in Android, first create a RadioGroup, and then populate the group with radio buttons. Listing 3-19 and Figure 3-6 show an example.

Listing 3-19. Using Android RadioButton Widgets

```
<LinearLayout xmlns:android="http://schemas.android.com/apk/res/android"
    android:orientation="vertical"
   android:layout_width="fill_parent"
    android:layout_height="fill_parent">

    <RadioGroup
        android:id="@+id/rBtnGrp"
        android:layout_width="wrap_content"
        android:layout_height="wrap_content"
        android:orientation="vertical" >

        <RadioButton
            android:id="@+id/chRBtn"
            android:text="Chicken"
            android:layout_width="wrap_content"
            android:layout_height="wrap_content"/>

        <RadioButton
            android:id="@+id/fishRBtn"
            android:text="Fish"
            android:checked="true"
            android:layout_width="wrap_content"
            android:layout_height="wrap_content"/>
```

```
        <RadioButton
            android:id="@+id/stkRBtn"
            android:text="Steak"
            android:layout_width="wrap_content"
            android:layout_height="wrap_content"/>

    </RadioGroup>

</LinearLayout>
```

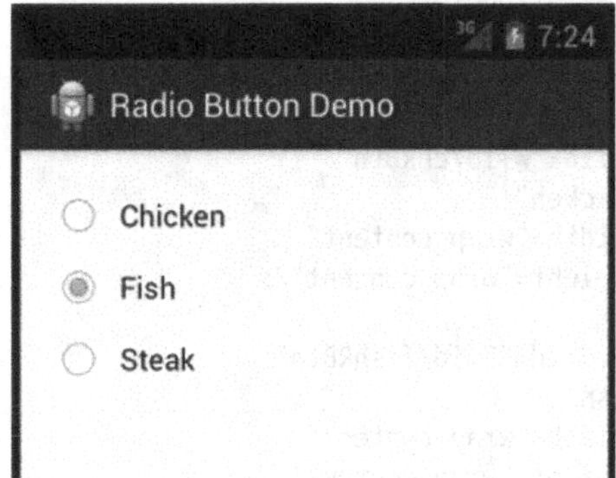

***Figure 3-6.** Using radio buttons*

In Android, you implement a radio group using `android.widget.RadioGroup` and a radio button using `android.widget.RadioButton`.

Note that the radio buttons within the radio group are, by default, unchecked to begin with, although you can set one to checked in the XML definition, as we did with Fish in Listing 3-19. To set one of the radio buttons to the checked state programmatically, you can obtain a reference to the radio button and call `setChecked()`:

```
RadioButton steakBtn = (RadioButton)this.findViewById(R.id.stkRBtn);
steakBtn.setChecked(true);
```

You can also use the `toggle()` method to toggle the state of the radio button. As with the `CheckBox` control, you will be notified of `on-checked` or `on-unchecked` events if you call the `setOnCheckedChangeListener()` with an implementation of the `OnCheckedChangeListener` interface. There is a slight difference here, though. This is a different class than before. This time, it's technically the `RadioGroup.OnCheckedChangeListener` class acting for the RadioGroup, whereas before it was the `CompoundButton.OnCheckedChangeListener` class.

The `RadioGroup` can also contain views other than the radio button. For example, Listing 3-20 adds a `TextView` after the last radio button. Also note that the first radio button (`anotherRadBtn`) lies outside the radio group.

Listing 3-20. A RadioGroup with More Than Just RadioButtons

```
<LinearLayout xmlns:android="http://schemas.android.com/apk/res/android"
        android:orientation="vertical"  android:layout_width="fill_parent"
        android:layout_height="fill_parent">

    <RadioButton android:id="@+id/anotherRadBtn"
        android:text="Outside"
        android:layout_width="wrap_content"
        android:layout_height="wrap_content"/>

    <RadioGroup android:id="@+id/radGrp"
        android:layout_width="wrap_content"
        android:layout_height="wrap_content">

        <RadioButton android:id="@+id/chRBtn"
            android:text="Chicken"
            android:layout_width="wrap_content"
            android:layout_height="wrap_content"/>

          <RadioButton android:id="@+id/fishRBtn"
            android:text="Fish"
            android:layout_width="wrap_content"
            android:layout_height="wrap_content"/>

        <RadioButton android:id="@+id/stkRBtn"
            android:text="Steak"
            android:layout_width="wrap_content"
            android:layout_height="wrap_content"/>

        <TextView android:text="My Favorite"
            android:layout_width="wrap_content"
            android:layout_height="wrap_content"/>

    </RadioGroup>
</LinearLayout>
```

Listing 3-20 shows that you can have non-RadioButton controls inside a radio group. You should also know that the radio group can only enforce single-selection on the radio buttons in its own container. That is, the radio button with ID anotherRadBtn will not be affected by the radio group shown in Listing 3-20 because it is not one of the group's children.

You can manipulate the RadioGroup programmatically. For example, you can obtain a reference to a radio group and add a radio button (or other type of control). Listing 3-21 demonstrates this concept.

Listing 3-21. Adding a RadioButton to a RadioGroup in Code

```
RadioGroup radGrp = (RadioGroup)findViewById(R.id.radGrp);
RadioButton newRadioBtn = new RadioButton(this);
newRadioBtn.setText("Pork");
radGrp.addView(newRadioBtn);
```

Once a user has checked a radio button within a radio group, the user cannot uncheck it by clicking it again. The only way to clear all radio buttons in a radio group is to call the `clearCheck()` method on the `RadioGroup` programmatically.

Of course, you want to do something interesting with the `RadioGroup`. You probably don't want to poll each `RadioButton` to determine whether it's checked. Fortunately, the `RadioGroup` has several methods to help you out. We demonstrate those with Listing 3-22. The XML for this code is in Listing 3-20.

***Listing 3-22.** Using a RadioGroup Programmatically*

```
public class RadioGroupActivity extends Activity {
        protected static final String TAG = "RadioGroupActivity";

        /** Called when the activity is first created. */
        @Override
        public void onCreate(Bundle savedInstanceState) {
            super.onCreate(savedInstanceState);
            setContentView(R.layout.radiogroup);

            RadioGroup radGrp = (RadioGroup)findViewById(R.id.radGrp);

            int checkedRadioButtonId = radGrp.getCheckedRadioButtonId();

            radGrp.setOnCheckedChangeListener(new RadioGroup.OnCheckedChangeListener() {
                @Override
                public void onCheckedChanged(RadioGroup arg0, int id) {
                    switch(id) {
                    case -1:
                        Log.v(TAG, "Choices cleared!");
                        break;
                    case R.id.chRBtn:
                        Log.v(TAG, "Chose Chicken");
                        break;
                    case R.id.fishRBtn:
                        Log.v(TAG, "Chose Fish");
                        break;
                    case R.id.stkRBtn:
                        Log.v(TAG, "Chose Steak");
                        break;
                    default:
                        Log.v(TAG, "Huh?");
                        break;
                    }
                }});
        }
}
```

We can always get the currently checked `RadioButton` using `getCheckedRadioButtonId()`, which returns the resource ID of the checked item or –1 if nothing is checked (possible if there's no default and the user hasn't chosen an option yet). We showed this in our `onCreate()` method previously, but in reality, you'd want to use it at the appropriate time to read the user's current choice. We can also set up a listener to be notified immediately when the user chooses one of the RadioButtons. Notice that the onCheckedChanged() method takes a RadioGroup parameter, allowing you to use the same OnCheckedChangeListener for multiple RadioGroups. You may have noticed the switch option of −1. This can also occur if the RadioGroup is cleared through code using clearCheck().

The ImageView Control

One of the basic controls we haven't covered yet is the ImageView control. This is used to display an image, where the image can come from a file, a content provider, or a resource such as a drawable. You can even specify just a color, and the ImageView will display that color. Listing 3-23 shows some XML examples of ImageViews, followed by some code that shows how to create an ImageView.

Listing 3-23. ImageViews in XML and in Code

```
<ImageView android:id="@+id/image1"
  android:layout_width="wrap_content"  android:layout_height="wrap_content"
  android:src="@drawable/icon" />

<ImageView android:id="@+id/image2"
  android:layout_width="125dip"  android:layout_height="25dip"
  android:src="#555555" />

<ImageView android:id="@+id/image3"
  android:layout_width="wrap_content"  android:layout_height="wrap_content" />

<ImageView android:id="@+id/image4"
  android:layout_width="wrap_content"  android:layout_height="wrap_content"
  android:src="@drawable/manatee02"
  android:scaleType="centerInside"
  android:maxWidth="35dip"  android:maxHeight="50dip"
  />

  ImageView imgView = (ImageView)findViewById(R.id.image3);

  imgView.setImageResource( R.drawable.icon );

  imgView.setImageBitmap(BitmapFactory.decodeResource(
            this.getResources(), R.drawable.manatee14) );

  imgView.setImageDrawable(
            Drawable.createFromPath("/mnt/sdcard/dave2.jpg") );

  imgView.setImageURI(Uri.parse("file://mnt/sdcard/dave2.jpg"));
```

In this example, we have four images defined in XML. The first is simply the icon for our application. The second is a gray bar that is wider than it is tall. The third definition does not specify an image source in the XML, but we associate an ID with this one (image3) that we can use from our code to set the image. The fourth image is another of our drawable image files where we not only specify the source of the image file but also set the maximum dimensions of the image on the screen and define what to do if the image is larger than our maximum size. In this case, we tell the ImageView to center and scale the image so it fits inside the size we specified.

In the Java code of Listing 3-23 we show several ways to set the image of image3. We first of course must get a reference to the ImageView by finding it using its resource ID. The first setter method, setImageResource(), simply uses the image's resource ID to locate the image file to supply the image for our ImageView. The second setter uses the BitmapFactory to read in an image resource into a Bitmap object and then sets the ImageView to that Bitmap. Note that we could have done some modifications to the Bitmap before applying it to our ImageView, but in our case, we used it as is. In addition, the BitmapFactory has several methods of creating a Bitmap, including from a byte array and an InputStream. You could use the InputStream method to read an image from a web server, create the Bitmap image, and then set the ImageView from there.

The third setting uses a Drawable for our image source. In this case, we're showing the source of the image coming from the SD card. You'll need to put some sort of image file out on the SD card with the proper name for this to work for you. Similar to BitmapFactory, the Drawable class has a few different ways to construct Drawables, including from an XML stream.

The final setter method takes the URI of an image file and uses that as the image source. For this last call, don't think that you can use any image URI as the source. This method is really only intended to be used for local images on the device, not for images that you might find through HTTP. To use Internet-based images as the source for your ImageView, you'd most likely use BitmapFactory and an InputStream.

Date and Time Controls

Date and time controls are common in many widget toolkits. Android offers several date- and time-based controls, some of which we'll discuss in this section. Specifically, we are going to introduce the DatePicker, TimePicker, DigitalClock, and AnalogClock controls.

The DatePicker and TimePicker Controls

As the names suggest, you use the DatePicker control to select a date and the TimePicker control to pick a time. Listing 3-24 and Figure 3-7 show examples of these controls.

Listing 3-24. The DatePicker and TimePicker Controls in XML

```
<LinearLayout xmlns:android="http://schemas.android.com/apk/res/android"
        android:orientation="vertical"
        android:layout_width="fill_parent"
        android:layout_height="fill_parent">

  <TextView android:id="@+id/dateDefault"
    android:layout_width="fill_parent" android:layout_height="wrap_content" />
```

```
  <DatePicker android:id="@+id/datePicker"
    android:layout_width="wrap_content" android:layout_height="wrap_content" />

  <TextView android:id="@+id/timeDefault"
    android:layout_width="fill_parent" android:layout_height="wrap_content" />

  <TimePicker android:id="@+id/timePicker"
    android:layout_width="wrap_content" android:layout_height="wrap_content" />

</LinearLayout>
```

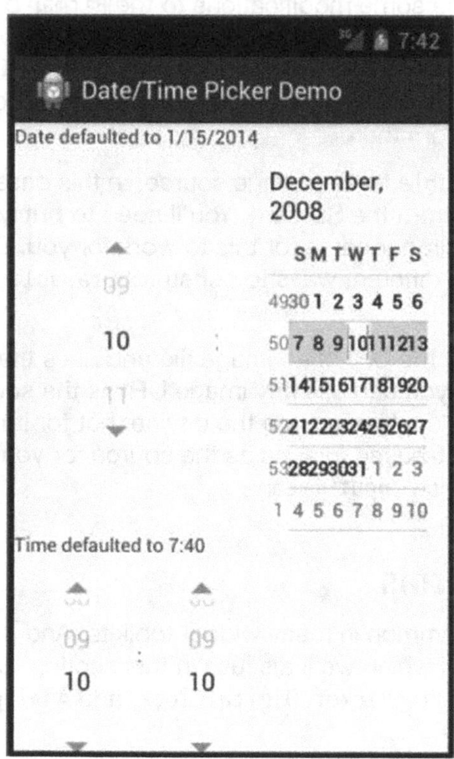

Figure 3-7. *The `DatePicker` and `TimePicker` UIs*

If you look at the XML layout, you can see that defining these controls is easy. As with any other control in the Android toolkit, you can access the controls programmatically to initialize them or to retrieve data from them. For example, you can initialize these controls as shown in Listing 3-23.

Listing 3-25. *Initializing the `DatePicker` and `TimePicker` with Date and Time, Respectively*

```
public void onCreate(Bundle savedInstanceState) {
    super.onCreate(savedInstanceState);
    setContentView(R.layout.datetimepicker);

    TextView dateDefault = (TextView)findViewById(R.id.dateDefault);
    TextView timeDefault = (TextView)findViewById(R.id.timeDefault);
```

```
    DatePicker dp = (DatePicker)this.findViewById(R.id.datePicker);
    // The month, and just the month, is zero-based. Add 1 for display.
    dateDefault.setText("Date defaulted to " + (dp.getMonth() + 1) + "/" +
            dp.getDayOfMonth() + "/" + dp.getYear());
    // And here, subtract 1 from December (12) to set it to December
    dp.init(2008, 11, 10, null);

    TimePicker tp = (TimePicker)this.findViewById(R.id.timePicker);

    java.util.Formatter timeF = new java.util.Formatter();
    timeF.format("Time defaulted to %d:%02d", tp.getCurrentHour(),
                    tp.getCurrentMinute());
    timeDefault.setText(timeF.toString());

    tp.setIs24HourView(true);
    tp.setCurrentHour(new Integer(10));
    tp.setCurrentMinute(new Integer(10));
}
```

Listing 3-25 sets the date on the DatePicker to December 10, 2008. Note that for the month, the internal value is zero-based, which means that January is 0 and December is 11. For the TimePicker, the number of hours and minutes is set to 10. Note also that this control supports 24-hour view. If you do not set values for these controls, the default values will be the current date and time as known to the device.

Finally, note that Android offers versions of these controls as modal windows, such as DatePickerDialog and TimePickerDialog. These controls are useful if you want to display the control to the user and force the user to make a selection. We'll cover dialogs in more detail in Chapter 8.

The TextClock and AnalogClock Controls

Android also offers TextClock and AnalogClock controls (see Figure 3-8).

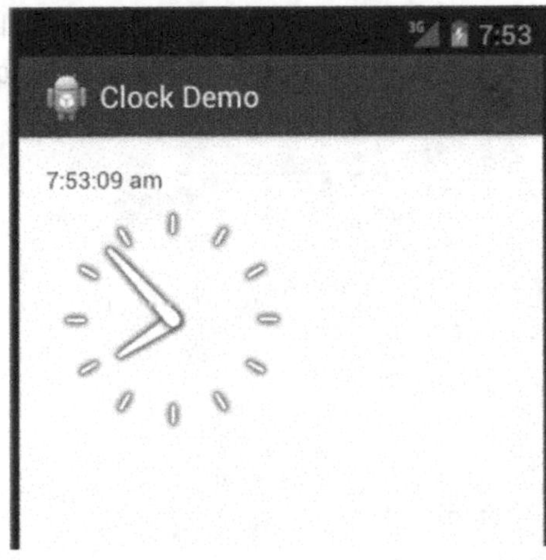

Figure 3-8. Using the AnalogClock and DigitalClock

As shown, the text clock supports seconds in addition to hours and minutes. The analog clock in Android is a two-handed clock, with one hand for the hour indicator and the other hand for the minute indicator. To add these to your layout, use the XML as shown in Listing 3-26.

Listing 3-26. Adding a DigitalClock or an AnalogClock in XML

```
<TextClock
  android:layout_width="wrap_content" android:layout_height="wrap_content"
  android:format12Hour="hh:mm:ss aa" android:format24Hour="kk:mm:ss" />

<AnalogClock
  android:layout_width="wrap_content" android:layout_height="wrap_content" />
```

These two controls are really just for displaying the current time, as they don't let you modify the date or time. In other words, they are controls whose only capability is to display the current time. Thus, if you want to change the date or time, you'll need to stick to the DatePicker/TimePicker or DatePickerDialog/TimePickerDialog. The nice part about these two clocks, though, is that they will update themselves without you having to do anything. That is, the seconds tick away in the TextClock, and the hands move on the AnalogClock without anything extra from us.

The MapView Control

With the introduction of Google Play Services, Android's approach to displaying map-based data underwent some changes. However, the vast majority of developers still favor the original MapView Control for a range of reasons—backward compatibility, simplicity, and so on. As the name suggests, the com.google.android.maps.MapView control can display a map. You can instantiate this control either via XML layout or code, but the activity that uses it must extend MapActivity. MapActivity takes care of multithreading requests to load a map, perform caching, and so on.

> **Note** Strictly, the MapView is part of the Google API, not the stock Android API. In order to test code etc. for MapView, ensure your emulator is created against a version of the SDK with the Google APIs included.

Listing 3-27 shows an example instantiation of a MapView.

Listing 3-27. Creating a MapView Control via XML Layout

```
<LinearLayout xmlns:android="http://schemas.android.com/apk/res/android"
        android:orientation="vertical" android:layout_width="fill_parent"
        android:layout_height="fill_parent">

    <com.google.android.maps.MapView
        android:layout_width="fill_parent"
        android:layout_height="fill_parent"
        android:enabled="true"
        android:clickable="true"
        android:apiKey="myAPIKey"
        />

</LinearLayout>
```

We'll discuss the location-based services in detail in Chapter 19. This is also where you'll learn how to obtain your own mapping API key.

References

Here are some helpful references to topics you may wish to explore further:

- http://www.androidbook.com/proandroid5/projects: A list of downloadable projects related to this book. For this chapter, look for a ZIP file called ProAndroid5_Ch03_Controls.zip. This ZIP file contains all projects from this chapter, listed in separate root directories. There is also a README.TXT file that describes exactly how to import projects into Eclipse from one of these ZIP files.
- http://developer.android.com/resources/articles/index.html: Several "Layout Tricks"–type technical articles that are well worth reading. They get into performance aspects of designing and building UIs in Android. Look for other articles in this list related to building UIs.

Summary

Let's conclude this chapter by quickly enumerating what you have learned about building user interfaces:

- How XML resources define UI appearances, and how code fills in the data
- The full range of basic User Interface controls available in Android
- A hint of what's to come with List views in Chapter 4 and Layouts in Chapter 5.

Chapter 4

Adapters and List Controls

In Chapter 3, we introduced a range of basic User Interface controls with which you can construct Android applications. If you recall the examples on TextView, one of the types of controls we explored was the AutoCompleteTextView, which when coupled with a source of data—an adapter—was able to prompt the user with a range of predetermined values. In this chapter, we'll explore adapters further, and the wider topic of list controls that enable construction of more elaborate and sophisticated screen designs.

Understanding Adapters

Before we get into the details of list controls of Android, we need to talk about adapters. List controls are used to display collections of data. But instead of using a single type of control to manage both the display and the data, Android separates these two responsibilities into list controls and adapters. List controls are classes that extend `android.widget.AdapterView` and include `ListView`, `GridView`, `Spinner`, and `Gallery` (see Figure 4-1).

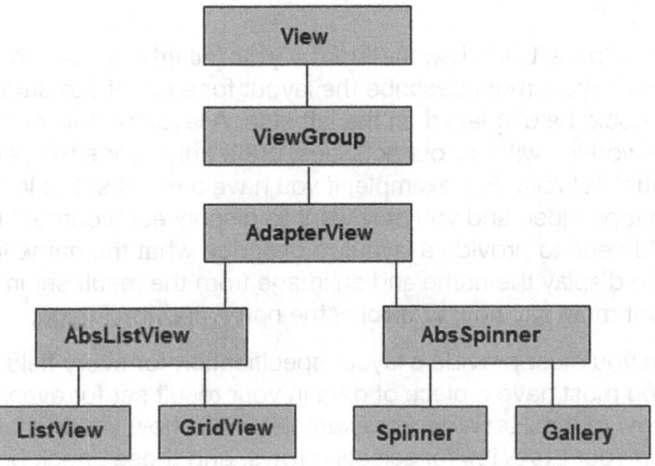

***Figure 4-1.** `AdapterView` class hierarchy*

AdapterView itself extends android.widget.ViewGroup, which means that ListView, GridView, and so on are container controls. In other words, list controls contain collections of child views. The purpose of an adapter is to manage the data for an AdapterView and to provide the child views for it. Let's see how this works by examining the SimpleCursorAdapter.

Getting to Know SimpleCursorAdapter

The SimpleCursorAdapter is depicted in Figure 4-2.

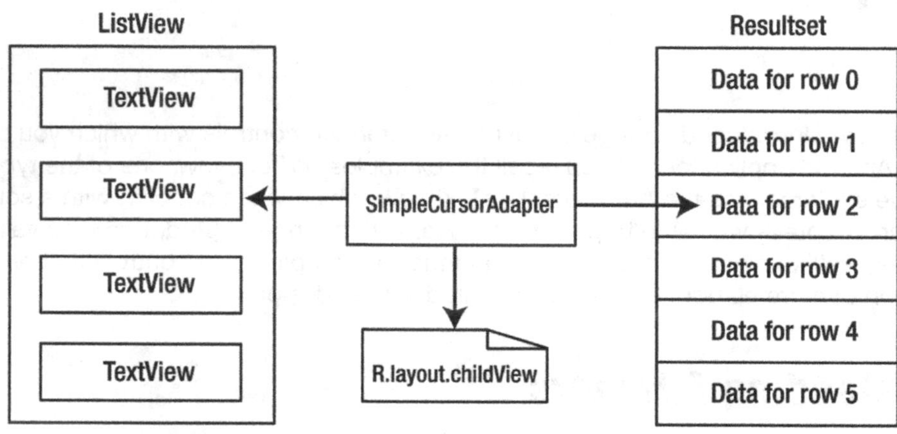

Figure 4-2. *The SimpleCursorAdapter*

This is a very important picture to understand. On the left side is the AdapterView; in this example, it is a ListView made up of TextView children. On the right side is the data; in this example, it's represented as a result set of data rows that came from a query against a content provider.

To map the data rows to the ListView, the SimpleCursorAdapter needs to have a child layout resource ID. The child layout must describe the layout for each of the data elements from the right side that should be displayed on the left side. A layout in this case is just like the layouts we've been working with for our activities, but it only needs to specify the layout of a single row of our ListView. For example, if you have a result set of information from the Contacts content provider, and you only want to display each contact name in your ListView, you would need to provide a layout to describe what the name field should look like. If you wanted to display the name and an image from the result set in each row of the ListView, your layout must say how to display the name and the image.

This does not mean you must provide a layout specification for every field in your result set, nor does it mean you must have a piece of data in your result set for everything you want to include in each row of the ListView. For example, we'll show you in a bit how you can have check boxes in your ListView for selecting rows, and those check boxes don't need to be set from data in a result set. We'll also show you how to get to data in the result set that is not part of the ListView. And although we've just talked about ListViews, TextViews, cursors, and result sets, please keep in mind that the adapter concept is more general than this. The left side can be a gallery, and the right side can be a simple array of images. But let's keep things fairly simple for now and look at SimpleCursorAdapter in more detail.

The simplest constructor of SimpleCursorAdapter looks like this:

```
SimpleCursorAdapter(Context context, int childLayout, Cursor c, String[] from, int[] to)
```

This adapter converts a row from the cursor to a child view for the container control. The definition of the child view is defined in an XML resource (childLayout parameter). Note that because a row in the cursor might have many columns, you tell the SimpleCursorAdapter which columns you want to select from the row by specifying an array of column names (using the from parameter).

Similarly, because each column you select must be mapped to a View in the layout, you must specify the IDs in the to parameter. There's a one-to-one mapping between the column you select and a View that displays the data in the column, so the from and to parameter arrays must have the same number of elements. As we mentioned before, the child view could contain other types of views; they don't have to be TextViews. You could use an ImageView, for example.

There is a careful collaboration going on between the ListView and our adapter. When the ListView wants to display a row of data, it calls the getView() method of the adapter, passing in the position to specify the row of data to be displayed. The adapter responds by building the appropriate child view using the layout that was set in the adapter's constructor and by pulling the data from the appropriate record in the result set. The ListView, therefore, doesn't have to deal with how the data exists on the adapter side; it only needs to call for child views as needed. This is a critical point, because it means our ListView doesn't necessarily need to create every child view for every data row. It really only needs to have as many child views as are necessary for what's visible in the display window. If only ten rows are being displayed, technically the ListView needs to have only ten child layouts instantiated, even if there are hundreds of records in our result set. In reality, more than ten child layouts get instantiated, because Android usually keeps extras on hand to make it faster to bring a new row to visibility. The conclusion you should reach is that the child views managed by the ListView can be recycled. We'll talk more about that a little later.

Figure 4-2 reveals some flexibility in using adapters. Because the list control uses an adapter, you can substitute various types of adapters based on your data and child view. For example, if you are not going to populate an AdapterView from a content provider or database, you don't have to use the SimpleCursorAdapter. You can opt for an even "simpler" adapter—the ArrayAdapter.

Getting to Know ArrayAdapter

The ArrayAdapter is the simplest of the adapters in Android. It specifically targets list controls and assumes that TextView controls represent the list items (the child views). Creating a new ArrayAdapter can look as simple as this:

```
ArrayAdapter<String> adapter = new ArrayAdapter<String>(this,
                android.R.layout.simple_list_item_1,
                new String[]{"Dave","Satya","Dylan"});
```

We still pass the context (`this`) and a childLayout resource ID. But instead of passing a `from` array of data field specifications, we pass in an array of strings as the actual data. We don't pass a cursor or a `to` array of `View` resource IDs. The assumption here is that our child layout consists of a single `TextView`, and that's what the `ArrayAdapter` will use as the destination for the strings that are in our data array.

Now we're going to introduce a nice shortcut for the `childLayout` resource ID. Instead of creating our own layout file for the list items, we can take advantage of predefined layouts in Android. Notice that the prefix on the resource for the child layout resource ID is `android.` Instead of looking in our local `/res` directory, Android looks in its own. You can browse to this folder by navigating to the Android SDK folder and looking under `platforms/<android-version>/data/res/layout`. There you'll find `simple_list_item_1.xml` and can see inside that it defines a simple `TextView`. That `TextView` is what our `ArrayAdapter` will use to create a view (in its `getView()` method) to give to the `ListView`. Feel free to browse through these folders to find predefined layouts for all sorts of uses. We'll be using more of these later.

`ArrayAdapter` has other constructors. If the childLayout is not a simple `TextView`, you can pass in the row layout resource ID plus the resource ID of the `TextView` to receive the data. When you don't have a ready-made array of strings to pass in, you can use the `createFromResource()` method. Listings 4-1, 4-2, and 4-3 show an example in which we create an `ArrayAdapter` for a spinner.

Listing 4-1. Manifest Fragment for Creating an `ArrayAdapter` from a String-Resource File

```
<Spinner android:id="@+id/spinner"
    android:layout_width="wrap_content"  android:layout_height="wrap_content" />
```

Listing 4-2. Code Fragment for Creating an `ArrayAdapter` from a String-Resource File

```
Spinner spinner = (Spinner) findViewById(R.id.spinner);

ArrayAdapter<CharSequence> adapter = ArrayAdapter.createFromResource(this,
        R.array.planets, android.R.layout.simple_spinner_item);

adapter.setDropDownViewResource(android.R.layout.simple_spinner_dropdown_item);

spinner.setAdapter(adapter);
```

Listing 4-3. The Actual String-Resource File

```
<?xml version="1.0" encoding="utf-8"?>
<!-- This file is /res/values/planets.xml -->
<resources>
  <string-array name="planets">
    <item>Mercury</item>
    <item>Venus</item>
    <item>Earth</item>
    <item>Mars</item>
    <item>Jupiter</item>
```

```
    <item>Saturn</item>
    <item>Uranus</item>
    <item>Neptune</item>
  </string-array>
</resources>
```

The first listing is the XML layout for a spinner. The second Java listing in shows how you can create an ArrayAdapter whose data source is defined in a string resource file. Using this method allows you to not only externalize the contents of the list to an XML file but also use localized versions. We'll talk about spinners a little later, but for now, know that a spinner has a view to show the currently selected value, plus a list view to show the values that can be selected from. It's basically a drop-down menu. Listing 4-3 is the XML resource file called /res/values/planets.xml, which is read in to initialize the ArrayAdapter.

Worth mentioning is that the ArrayAdapter allows for dynamic modifications to the underlying data. For example, the add() method will append a new value on the end of the array. The insert() method will add a new value at a specified position within the array. And remove() takes an object out of the array. You can also call sort() to reorder the array. Of course, once you've done this, the data array is out of sync with the ListView, so that's when you call the notifyDataSetChanged() method of the adapter. This method will resync the ListView with the adapter.

The following list summarizes the adapters that Android provides:

- ArrayAdapter<T>: This is an adapter on top of a generic array of arbitrary objects. It's meant to be used with a ListView.
- CursorAdapter: This adapter, also meant to be used in a ListView, provides data to the list via a cursor.
- SimpleAdapter: As the name suggests, this adapter is a simple adapter. It is generally used to populate a list with static data (possibly from resources).
- ResourceCursorAdapter: This adapter extends CursorAdapter and knows how to create views from resources.
- SimpleCursorAdapter: This adapter extends ResourceCursorAdapter and creates TextView/ImageView views from the columns in the cursor. The views are defined in resources.

We've covered enough of adapters to start showing you some real examples of working with adapters and list controls (also known as AdapterViews). Let's get to it.

Using Adapters with AdapterViews

Now that you've been introduced to adapters, it is time to put them to work for us, providing data for list controls. In this section, we're going to first cover the basic list control, the ListView. Then, we'll describe how to create your own custom adapter, and finally, we'll describe the other types of list controls: GridViews, spinners, and the gallery.

The Basic List Control: ListView

The `ListView` control displays a list of items vertically. That is, if we've got a list of items to view and the number of items extends beyond what we can currently see in the display, we can scroll to see the rest of the items. You generally use a `ListView` by writing a new activity that extends `android.app.ListActivity`. `ListActivity` contains a `ListView`, and you set the data for the `ListView` by calling the `setListAdapter()` method.

As we described previously, adapters link list controls to the data and help prepare the child views for the list control. Items in a `ListView` can be clicked to take immediate action or selected to act on the set of selected items later. We're going to start really simple and then add functionality as we go.

Displaying Values in a ListView

Figure 4-3 shows a `ListView` control in its simplest form.

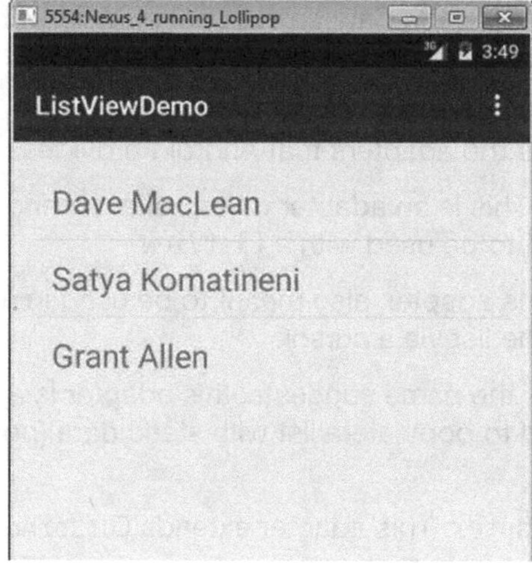

***Figure 4-3.** Using the `ListView` control*

For this exercise, we will place a `ListView` into a default Android layout, with no special tweaks or changes, so you can see how they fit within a typical main layout XML file. Listing 4-4 shows the Java code for our activity.

***Listing 4-4.** Adding Items to a `ListView`*

```
public class MainActivity extends Activity {

    private ListView listView1;
    private ArrayAdapter<String> listAdapter1;

    @Override
    protected void onCreate(Bundle savedInstanceState) {
        super.onCreate(savedInstanceState);
        setContentView(R.layout.activity_main);
```

```
        listView1 = (ListView) findViewById(R.id.listView1);

        String[] someColors = new String[] { "Red", "Orange", "Yellow",
                "Green", "Blue", "Indigo", "Violet", "Black", "White"};
        ArrayList<String> colorArrayList = new ArrayList<String>();
        colorArrayList.addAll( Arrays.asList(someColors) );

        listAdapter1 = new ArrayAdapter<String>(this, android.R.id.text1,
                colorArrayList);

        listView1.setAdapter( listAdapter1 );
    }
...
}
```

Listing 4-2 creates a `ListView` control populated with the list of colors we specify in an array, `someColors`. In our example, we take the contents of the array and map the `String` color names to a `TextView` control (`android.R.id.text1`). After that, we create an array adapter and set the list's adapter. The adapter class has the smarts to take the rows in whatever data source you provide to populate the UI.

We could have taken advantage of the very basic `ListActivity` supplying the main layout, as there are no other UI elements or complexity to take care of. However we've chosen to deploy the ListView within a typical new project and utilize the basic activity. We're also using an Android-provided layout for our child view (resource ID `android.R.layout.simple_list_item_1`), which contains an Android-provided `TextView` (resource ID `android.R.id.text1`). All in all, pretty simple to set up.

We can extend this example, and your understanding, by showing how to replace the Android-provided layout for the child view with one of our own design. Create a new empty file in the `res/layout` folder of your project and name it `simple_list_row.xml`. Listing 4-5 shows the XML for our own layout for a simple `TextView` to represent each line to be rendered in our `ListView` (or any other layout that refers to this `simple_list_row` layout).

Listing 4-5. Creating a Custom TextView Child View for List Rendering

```
<TextView xmlns:android="http://schemas.android.com/apk/res/android"
  android:id="@+id/rowTextView"
  android:layout_width="fill_parent"
  android:layout_height="wrap_content"
  android:padding="12dp"
  android:textSize="24sp" >
</TextView>
```

We need only change the reference that binds the chosen layout for use in the ListView in our code, to use the new simple_list_row layout, like so:

```
listAdapter1 = new ArrayAdapter<String>(this, R.layout.simple_list_row,
        colorArrayList);
```

Note that when we refer to our own custom layout in this way, we drop the leading "android" reference. We can now run this example to see the complete effect, as shown in Figure 4-4.

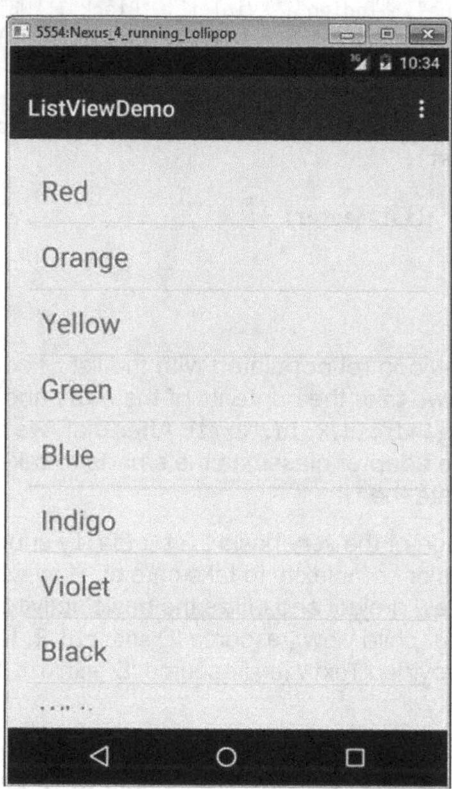

Figure 4-4. The ListView example in action

Clickable Items in a ListView

Of course, when you run this example, you'll see that you're able to scroll up and down the list to see all your color names, but that's about it. What if we want to do something a little more interesting with this example, like have the application respond when a user clicks one of the items in our `ListView`? Listing 4-6 shows a modification to our example to accept user input.

Listing 4-6. Accepting User Input on a `ListView`

```
public class MainActivity extends Activity {

    private ListView listView1;
    private ArrayAdapter<String> listAdapter1;

    @Override
    protected void onCreate(Bundle savedInstanceState) {
        super.onCreate(savedInstanceState);
        setContentView(R.layout.activity_main);
```

```
        listView1 = (ListView) findViewById(R.id.listView1);

        String[] someColors = new String[] { "Red", "Orange", "Yellow",
                "Green", "Blue", "Indigo", "Violet", "Black", "White"};
        ArrayList<String> colorArrayList = new ArrayList<String>();
        colorArrayList.addAll( Arrays.asList(someColors) );

        listAdapter1 = new ArrayAdapter<String>(this, android.R.layout.simple_list_item_1,
                colorArrayList);

        listView1.setAdapter( listAdapter1 );

        listView1.setOnItemClickListener(new OnItemClickListener() {

          @Override
          public void onItemClick(AdapterView<?> parent, View view, int position
              , long id) {
            String itemValue = (String) listView1.getItemAtPosition(position);
            Toast.makeText(getApplicationContext(), itemValue,
                Toast.LENGTH_LONG).show();
          }
        });
    }
...
}
```

Our activity is now implementing the OnItemClickListener interface, which means we'll receive a callback when the user clicks something in our ListView. As you can see by our onItemClick() method, we get a lot of information about what was clicked, including the view receiving the click, the position of the clicked item in the ListView, and the ID of the item according to our adapter. We cast accordingly before calling the makeText() method to work with the color's name. The position value represents where this item is in relation to the overall list of items in the ListView, and it's zero-based. Therefore, the first item in the list is at position 0.

The ID value depends entirely on the adapter and the source of the data. In our example, we happen to be querying strings with the names of colors in an array, so the ID according to this adapter is the position of the entry in the array from the content provider. But your data source in other situations may not be as straightforward as this, so you should not think that you can always know things like ordering in advance as we've done in this example. If we were using an SimpleCursorAdapter that had read its values from the system's Contacts database, the ID given to us will be the underlying _ID of the record, and that could be any value depending on the age of the contact in the system.

When we discussed ArrayAdapters before, we mentioned the notifyDataSetChanged() method to have the adapter update the ListView if the data has changed. Some adapters, such as the SimpleCursorAdapter, are aware of updates that happen to underlying datasources such as the Contacts content provider and will dynamically update ListView contents for you based on changes. With ArrayAdapters, however, you will need to invoke the notifyDataSetChanged() method yourself.

That was pretty easy to do. We generated our own ListView of color names, and by clicking a color we showed a message to the user. But what if we want to select a bunch of names first and then do something with the subset of people? For the next example application, we're going to modify the layout of a list item to include a check box, and we're going to add a button to the UI to then act on the subset of selected items.

Adding Other Controls with a ListView

If you want additional controls in your main layout, you can provide your own layout XML file, put in a ListView, and add other desired controls. For example, you could add a button below the ListView in the UI to submit an action on the selected items, as shown in Figure 4-5.

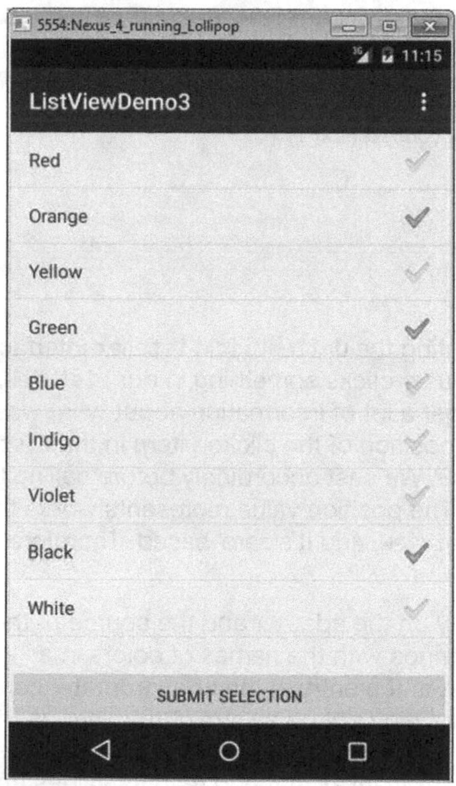

***Figure 4-5.** An additional button that lets the user submit the selected item(s)*

The main layout for this example is in Listing 4-7, and it contains the UI definition of the activity—the ListView and the Button.

Listing 4-7. ***Overriding the `ListView` Referenced by `Our Activity`***

```
<LinearLayout xmlns:android="http://schemas.android.com/apk/res/android"
    xmlns:tools="http://schemas.android.com/tools"
    android:orientation="vertical"
    android:layout_width="match_parent"
    android:layout_height="match_parent"
    tools:context="com.artifexdigital.android.listviewdemo3.MainActivity" >

    <ListView
        android:id="@+id/listView1"
        android:layout_width="match_parent"
        android:layout_height="wrap_content"
        android:layout_weight="1" />

    <Button
        android:id="@+id/button1"
        android:layout_width="match_parent"
        android:layout_height="wrap_content"
        android:onClick="doClick"
        android:text="Submit selection" />

</LinearLayout>
```

Notice the way we have to specify the height and weight of the `ListView` in `LinearLayout`. We want our button to appear on the screen at all times no matter how many items are in our `ListView`, and we don't want to be scrolling all the way to the bottom of the page just to find the button. To accomplish this, we set the `layout_height` to `wrap_content` and then use `layout_weight` to say that this control should take up all available room from the parent container. This trick allows room for the button and retains our ability to scroll the `ListView`. We'll talk more about layouts and weights later in this chapter.

The activity implementation would then look like Listing 4-8.

Listing 4-8. ***Reading User Input from the `ListActivity`***

```
public class MainActivity extends Activity {

    private ListView listView1;
    private ArrayAdapter<String> listAdapter1;

    @Override
    protected void onCreate(Bundle savedInstanceState) {
        super.onCreate(savedInstanceState);
        setContentView(R.layout.activity_main);

        listView1 = (ListView) findViewById(R.id.listView1);

        String[] someColors = new String[] { "Red", "Orange", "Yellow",
                "Green", "Blue", "Indigo", "Violet", "Black", "White"};
        ArrayList<String> colorArrayList = new ArrayList<String>();
        colorArrayList.addAll( Arrays.asList(someColors) );
```

```
        listAdapter1 = new ArrayAdapter<String>(this, android.R.layout.simple_list_item_checked,
                colorArrayList);

        listView1.setAdapter( listAdapter1 );


        listView1.setChoiceMode(listView1.CHOICE_MODE_MULTIPLE);

        listView1.setOnItemClickListener(new OnItemClickListener() {

          @Override
          public void onItemClick(AdapterView<?> parent, View view, int position
              , long id) {
            String itemValue = (String) listView1.getItemAtPosition(position);
            Toast.makeText(getApplicationContext(), itemValue,
                Toast.LENGTH_LONG).show();
          }
        });
    }


    public void doClick(View view) {
      int count=listView1.getCount();
      SparseBooleanArray viewItems = listView1.getCheckedItemPositions();
      for(int i=0; i<count; i++) {
        if(viewItems.get(i)) {
          String selectedColor = (String) listView1.getItemAtPosition(i);
          Log.v("ListViewDemo", selectedColor + " is checked at position " + i);
        }
      }
    }
}
```

Within the setup of the adapter, we're passing another of the Android-provided views for a ListView line item (android.R.layout.simple_list_item_checked), which results in each row having a TextView and a CheckBox. If you look inside this layout file, you will see another subclass of TextView, this one called CheckedTextView. This special type of TextView is intended for use with ListViews. See, we told you there were some interesting things in that Android layout folder! You will see that the ID of the CheckedTextView is text1, which is what we needed to pass in our views array to the constructor of the SimpleCursorAdapter.

Because we want the user to be able to select our rows, we set the choice mode to CHOICE_MODE_MULTIPLE. By default, the choice mode is CHOICE_MODE_NONE. The other possible value is CHOICE_MODE_SINGLE. If you want to use that choice mode for this example, you would want to use a different layout, most likely android.R.layout.simple_list_item_single_choice.

In this example, we've implemented a basic button that calls the doClick() method of our activity. To keep things simple, we just want to write out to LogCat the names of the items that were checked by the user. The good news is that the solution is pretty easy; the bad news is that Android has evolved so the best solution depends on which version of Android you're targeting. The ListView solution we've shown here has worked since Android 1 (although we took the Android 1.6 shortcut on the button callback). That is, the getCheckedItemPositions()

method is old, but it still works. The return value is an array that can tell you whether an item has been checked. So, we iterate through the array. `viewItems.get(i)` will return true if the corresponding row in our `ListView` has been checked. Our data is accessible directly from the `ListView`, using the `getItemAtPosition()` method of the `ListView`. In our case, the object returned from `getItemAtPosition()` would turn out to be a `String` object. As we said before, in other situations, we might get some other type of object, such as a `CursorWrapper`, when working with some specific content providers like the `Contacts` provider discussed later in this book. You have to understand your data source and your adapter to know what to expect.

If we go ahead and hit the Submit Selection button shown in Figure 4-5, we can watch the log cat window in Eclipse or Android Studio as it emits the data from our selection as implemented in the `doClick()` method. This is shown in Figure 4-6.

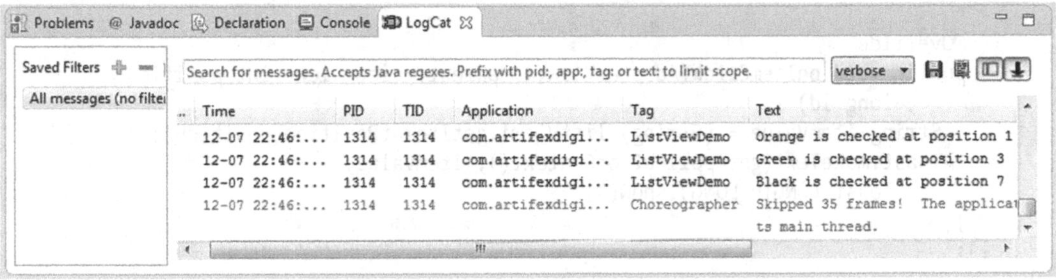
Problems
Javadoc
Declaration
Console
LogCat
Saved Filters
All messages (no filte
Search for messages. Accepts Java regexes. Prefix with pid:, app:, tag: or text: to limit scope.
verbose
Time
PID
TID
Application
Tag
Text
12-07 22:46:... 1314 1314 com.artifexdigi... ListViewDemo Orange is checked at position 1
12-07 22:46:... 1314 1314 com.artifexdigi... ListViewDemo Green is checked at position 3
12-07 22:46:... 1314 1314 com.artifexdigi... ListViewDemo Black is checked at position 7
12-07 22:46:... 1314 1314 com.artifexdigi... Choreographer Skipped 35 frames! The applica
ts main thread.

***Figure 4-6.** Using user input from a ListView for further processing*

Another Way to Read Selections from a ListView

Android 1.6 introduced another method for retrieving a list of the checked rows from a `ListView`: `getCheckItemIds()`. Then, in Android 2.2, this method was deprecated and replaced with `getCheckedItemIds()`. It was a subtle name change, but the way you use the method is basically the same. Listing 4-9 shows the Java code changes we'd make to reflect this evolution of dealing with checked items in a list. For the XML layout of `list.xml`, we can continue to use the file in Listing 4-7.

***Listing 4-9.** Another Way of Reading User Input from the `ListActivity`*

```
public class MainActivity extends Activity {

    private ListView listView1;
    private ArrayAdapter<String> listAdapter1;

    @Override
    protected void onCreate(Bundle savedInstanceState) {
        super.onCreate(savedInstanceState);
        setContentView(R.layout.activity_main);

        listView1 = (ListView) findViewById(R.id.listView1);
```

```
        String[] someColors = new String[] { "Red", "Orange", "Yellow",
                "Green", "Blue", "Indigo", "Violet", "Black", "White"};
        ArrayList<String> colorArrayList = new ArrayList<String>();
        colorArrayList.addAll( Arrays.asList(someColors) );

        listAdapter1 = new ArrayAdapter<String>(this, android.R.layout.simple_list_item_checked,
                colorArrayList);

        listView1.setAdapter( listAdapter1 );


        listView1.setChoiceMode(listView1.CHOICE_MODE_MULTIPLE);

        listView1.setOnItemClickListener(new OnItemClickListener() {

          @Override
          public void onItemClick(AdapterView<?> parent, View view, int position
              , long id) {
            String itemValue = (String) listView1.getItemAtPosition(position);
            Toast.makeText(getApplicationContext(), itemValue,
                Toast.LENGTH_LONG).show();
          }
        });
    }

...

    public void doClick(View view) {
        if(!listAdapter1.hasStableIds()) {
            Log.v(TAG, "Data is not stable");
            return;
        }
        long[] viewItems = listView1.getCheckedItemIds();
        for(int i=0; i<viewItems.length; i++) {
          String selectedColor = (String) listView1.getItemAtPosition(i);
          Log.v("ListViewDemo", selectedColor + " is checked at position " + i);
        }
      }
    }
}
```

In this example application, when we click the button, our callback calls the method getCheckedItemIds(). Whereas in our last example, we got an array of positions of the checked items in the ListView, this time we get an array of IDs of the records from the adapter that have been checked in the ListView. We can bypass the ListView and the cursor now, because the IDs can be used to drive whatever action we desire.

We've shown you how to work with ListViews from a variety of scenarios. We've shown that adapters do a lot of the work to support a ListView. Next, we'll cover the other types of list controls, starting with the GridView.

The GridView Control

Most widget toolkits offer one or more grid-based controls. Android has a GridView control that can display data in the form of a grid. Note that although we use the term *data* here, the contents of the grid can be text, images, and so on.

The GridView control displays information in a grid. The usage pattern for the GridView is to define the grid in the XML layout (see Listings 4-10 and 4-11) and then bind the data to the grid using an android.widget.ListAdapter.

Listing 4-10. Definition of a GridView in an XML Layout

```
<RelativeLayout xmlns:android="http://schemas.android.com/apk/res/android"
    xmlns:tools="http://schemas.android.com/tools"
    android:layout_width="match_parent"
    android:layout_height="match_parent"
    tools:context="com.artifexdigital.android.gridviewdemo.MainActivity" >

    <GridView
        android:id="@+id/gridView1"
        android:layout_width="fill_parent"
        android:layout_height="fill_parent"
        android:padding="10dp"
        android:verticalSpacing="10dp"
        android:horizontalSpacing="10dp"
        android:numColumns="auto_fit"
        android:columnWidth="100dp"
        android:stretchMode="columnWidth"
        android:gravity="center" />

</RelativeLayout>
```

Listing 4-11. Java Implementation for the GridView

```
public class MainActivity extends Activity {

    private GridView gridView1;
    private ArrayAdapter<String> listAdapter1;

    @Override
    protected void onCreate(Bundle savedInstanceState) {
        super.onCreate(savedInstanceState);
        setContentView(R.layout.activity_main);

        gridView1 = (GridView) findViewById(R.id.gridView1);

        String[] someColors = new String[] { "Red", "Orange", "Yellow",
                 "Green", "Blue", "Indigo", "Violet", "Black", "White"};

        ArrayList<String> colorArrayList = new ArrayList<String>();
        colorArrayList.addAll( Arrays.asList(someColors) );
```

```
        listAdapter1 = new ArrayAdapter<String>(this,
                android.R.layout.simple_list_item_1, colorArrayList);

        gridView1.setAdapter( listAdapter1 );

    }
}
```

Listing 4-10 defines a simple GridView in an XML layout. The grid is then loaded into the activity's content view. The generated UI is shown in Figure 4-7.

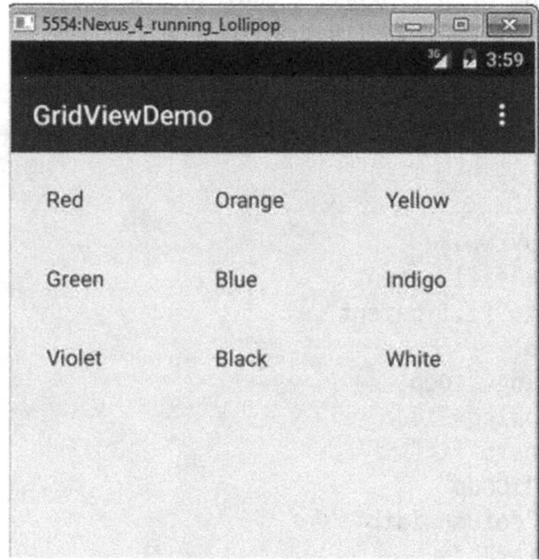

***Figure 4-7.** A GridView populated with colors*

The grid shown in Figure 4-7 displays the names of the colors from our array. We have decided to show a TextView with the color names, but you could easily generate a grid filled with images or other controls. We've again taken advantage of predefined layouts in Android. In fact, this example looks very much like Listing 4-7 except for a few important differences. We must call setContentView() to set the layout for our GridView; there are no default views to fall back on. And to set the adapter, we call setAdapter() on the GridView object instead of calling setListAdapter() on Activity.

You've no doubt noticed that the adapter used by the grid is a ListAdapter. Lists are generally one-dimensional, whereas grids are two-dimensional. We can conclude, then, that the grid actually displays list-oriented data. And it turns out that the list is displayed by rows. That is, the list goes across the first row, then across the second row, and so on.

As before, we have a list control that works with an adapter to handle the data management and the generation of the child views. The same techniques we used before should work just fine with GridViews. One exception relates to making selections: there is no way to specify multiple choices in a GridView, as we did in Listing 4-7.

The Spinner Control

The Spinner control is like a drop-down menu. It is typically used to select from a relatively short list of choices. If the choice list is too long for the display, a scrollbar is automatically added for you. You can instantiate a Spinner via XML layout as simply as this:

```
<Spinner
    android:id="@+id/spinner"  android:prompt="@string/spinnerprompt"
    android:layout_width="wrap_content"  android:layout_height="wrap_content" />
```

Although a spinner is technically a list control, it will appear to you more like a simple TextView control. In other words, only one value will be displayed when the spinner is at rest. The purpose of the spinner is to allow the user to choose from a set of predetermined values: when the user clicks the small arrow, a list is displayed, and the user is expected to pick a new value. Populating this list is done in the same way as the other list controls: with an adapter.

Because a spinner is often used like a drop-down menu, it is common to see the adapter get the list choices from a resource file. An example that sets up a spinner using a resource file is shown in Listing 4-12. Notice the new attribute called android:prompt for setting a prompt at the top of the list to choose from. The actual text for our spinner prompt is in our /res/values/strings.xml file. As you should expect, the Spinner class has a method for setting the prompt in code as well.

Listing 4-12. Code to Create a Spinner from a Resource File

```
public class SpinnerActivity extends Activity {
    /** Called when the activity is first created. */
    @Override
    public void onCreate(Bundle savedInstanceState) {
        super.onCreate(savedInstanceState);
        setContentView(R.layout.spinner);

        Spinner spinner = (Spinner)findViewById(R.id.spinner);

        ArrayAdapter<CharSequence> adapter = ArrayAdapter.createFromResource(this,
                R.array.planets, android.R.layout.simple_spinner_item);

        adapter.setDropDownViewResource(android.R.layout.simple_spinner_dropdown_item);

        spinner.setAdapter(adapter);
    }
}
```

You may recall seeing the planets.xml file in Listing 4-1. We show in this example how a Spinner control is created; the adapter is set up and then associated to the spinner. See Figure 4-8 for what this looks like in action.

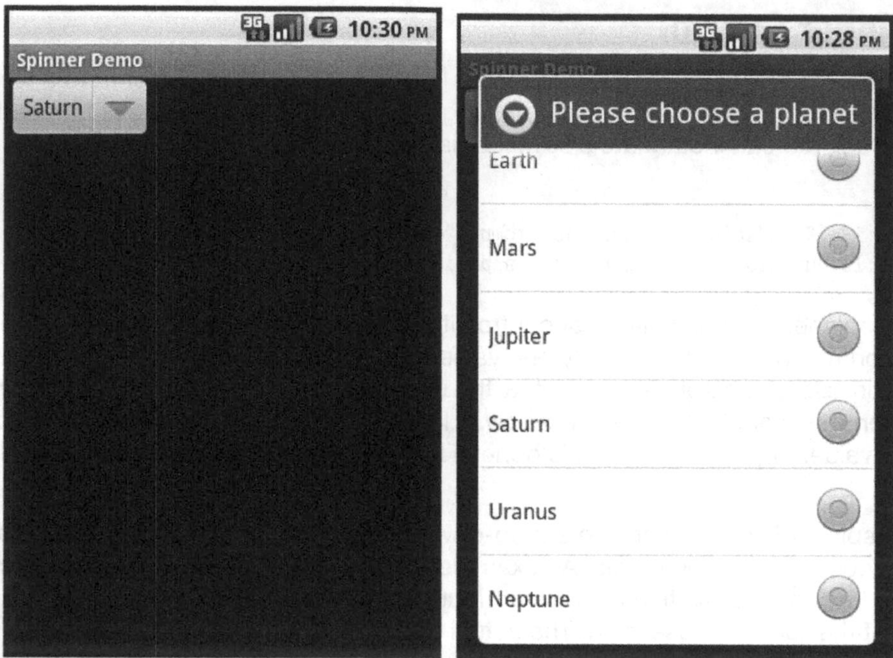

Figure 4-8. A spinner for choosing a planet

One of the differences from our earlier list controls is that we've got an extra layout to contend with when working with a spinner. The left side of Figure 4-8 shows the normal mode of a spinner, where the current selection is shown. In this case, the current selection is Saturn. Next to the word is a downward-pointing arrow indicating that this control is a spinner and can be used to pop up a list to select a different value. The first layout, supplied as a parameter to the `ArrayAdapter.createFromResource()` method, defines how the spinner looks in normal mode. On the right side of Figure 4-8, we show the spinner in the pop-up list mode, waiting for the user to choose a new value. The layout for this list is set using the `setDropDownViewResource()` method. Again in this example, we're using Android-provided layouts for these two needs, so if you want to inspect the definition of either of these layouts, you can visit the Android `res/layout` folder. And of course, you can specify your own layout definition for either of these to get the effect you want.

The Gallery Control

The `Gallery` control is a horizontally scrollable list control that always focuses at the center of the list. This control generally functions as a photo gallery in touch mode. You can instantiate a `Gallery` via either XML layout or code:

```
<Gallery
    android:id="@+id/gallery"
    android:layout_width="fill_parent"
    android:layout_height="wrap_content"
/>
```

The Gallery control is typically used to display images, so your adapter is likely going to be specialized for images. We'll show you a custom image adapter in next section on custom adapters. Visually, a gallery looks like Figure 4-9.

Figure 4-9. A gallery with images of manatees

Summary

In this chapter, we've expanded your understanding and proficiency with UI components in the following ways:

- The main list controls available in Android
- How to use adapters to populate the data in a list control

Chapter 5

Building More Advanced UI Layouts

In the previous chapters we reviewed many of the standard layouts provided with Android, which cover a broad array of possible UI approaches. When the stock layouts offered by Android don't quite do what you want, where do you turn? In this chapter, we will quickly explore how Android provides you with the ability to build your own custom layouts and manage the related adapters for populating them with useful data.

Creating Custom Adapters

Standard adapters in Android are easy to use, but they have some limitations. To address this, Android provides an abstract class called `BaseAdapter` that you can extend if you need a custom adapter. You would use a custom adapter if you had special data-management needs or if you wanted more control over how to display child views. You might also use a custom adapter to improve performance by using caching techniques. We're going to show you how to build a custom adapter next.

Listing 5-1 shows what the XML layout and the Java code could look like for a custom adapter. For this next example, our adapter is going to deal with images of manatees, so we'll call it `ManateeAdapter`. We're going to create it inside of an activity as well.

***Listing 5-1.** Our Custom Adapter: `ManateeAdapter`*

```
<?xml version="1.0" encoding="utf-8"?>
<!-- This file is at /res/layout/gridviewcustom.xml -->
<GridView xmlns:android="http://schemas.android.com/apk/res/android"
    android:id="@+id/gridview"
    android:layout_width="fill_parent"
    android:layout_height="fill_parent"
```

```
    android:padding="10dip"
    android:verticalSpacing="10dip"
    android:horizontalSpacing="10dip"
    android:numColumns="auto_fit"
    android:gravity="center"
    />
```

Java Implementation

```
public class GridViewCustomAdapter extends Activity
{
    @Override
    protected void onCreate(Bundle savedInstanceState)
    {
        super.onCreate(savedInstanceState);
        setContentView(R.layout.gridviewcustom);
        GridView gv = (GridView)findViewById(R.id.gridview);
        ManateeAdapter adapter = new ManateeAdapter(this);
        gv.setAdapter(adapter);
    }

    public static class ManateeAdapter extends BaseAdapter {
        private static final String TAG = "ManateeAdapter";
        private static int convertViewCounter = 0;
        private Context mContext;
        private LayoutInflater mInflater;
        static class ViewHolder {
            ImageView image;
        }

        private int[] manatees = {
                R.drawable.manatee00, R.drawable.manatee01, R.drawable.manatee02,
// ... many more manatees here - see the sample code folder
                R.drawable.manatee32, R.drawable.manatee33 };

        private Bitmap[] manateeImages = new Bitmap[manatees.length];
        private Bitmap[] manateeThumbs = new Bitmap[manatees.length];

        public ManateeAdapter(Context context) {
            Log.v(TAG, "Constructing ManateeAdapter");
            this.mContext = context;
            mInflater = LayoutInflater.from(context);
```

```
        for(int i=0; i<manatees.length; i++) {
            manateeImages[i] = BitmapFactory.decodeResource(
                    context.getResources(), manatees[i]);
            manateeThumbs[i] = Bitmap.createScaledBitmap(manateeImages[i],
                    100, 100, false);
        }
    }

    @Override
    public int getCount() {
        Log.v(TAG, "in getCount()");
        return manatees.length;
    }

    public int getViewTypeCount() {
        Log.v(TAG, "in getViewTypeCount()");
        return 1;
    }

    public int getItemViewType(int position) {
        Log.v(TAG, "in getItemViewType() for position " + position);
        return 0;
    }

    @Override
    public View getView(int position, View convertView, ViewGroup parent) {
        ViewHolder holder;

        Log.v(TAG, "in getView for position " + position +
                ", convertView is " +
                ((convertView == null)?"null":"being recycled"));

        if (convertView == null) {
            convertView = mInflater.inflate(R.layout.gridimage, null);
            convertViewCounter++;
            Log.v(TAG, convertViewCounter + " convertViews have been created");
            holder = new ViewHolder();
            holder.image = (ImageView) convertView.findViewById(R.id.gridImageView);
            convertView.setTag(holder);
        } else {
            holder = (ViewHolder) convertView.getTag();
        }
```

```
            holder.image.setImageBitmap( manateeThumbs[position] );

            return convertView;
        }

        @Override
        public Object getItem(int position) {
            Log.v(TAG, "in getItem() for position " + position);
            return manateeImages[position];
        }

        @Override
        public long getItemId(int position) {
            Log.v(TAG, "in getItemId() for position " + position);
            return position;
        }
    }
}
```

When you run this application, you should see a display that looks like Figure 5-1.

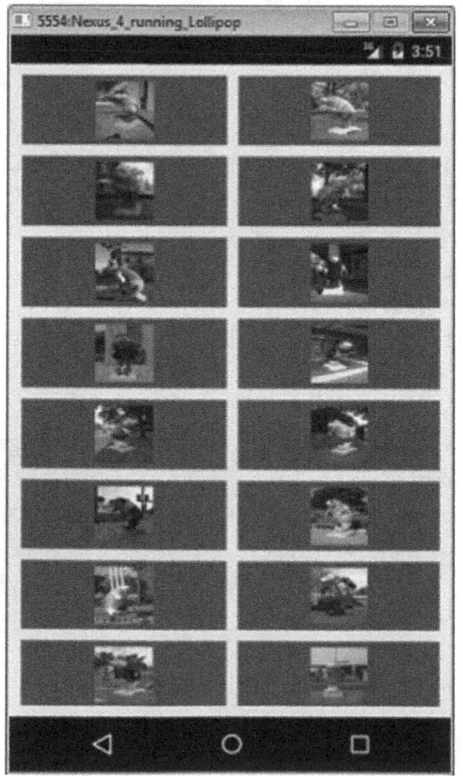

***Figure 5-1.** A `GridView` with images of manatees*

There is a lot to explain in this example, even though it looks relatively simple. We'll start with our Activity class, which looks a lot like the ones we've been working with throughout this section of the chapter. There's a main layout from gridviewcustom.xml, which contains just a GridView definition. We need to get a reference to the GridView from inside the layout, so we define and set gv. We instantiate our ManateeAdapter, passing it our context, and we set the adapter on our GridView. This is pretty standard stuff so far, although you've no doubt noticed that our custom adapter doesn't use nearly as many parameters as predefined adapters when being created. This is mainly because we're in complete control over this particular adapter, and we're using it with only this application. If we were making this adapter more general, we would most likely be setting more parameters. But let's keep going.

Our job inside an adapter is to manage the passing of data into Android View objects. The View objects will be used by the list control (a GridView in this case). The data comes from some data source. In the earlier examples, the data came via a cursor object that was passed into the adapter. In our custom case here, our adapter knows all about the data and where it comes from. The list control will ask for things so it knows how to build the UI. It is also kind enough to pass in views for recycling when it has a view it no longer needs. It may seem a bit strange to think that our adapter must know how to construct views, but in the end, it all makes sense.

When we instantiate our custom adapter ManateeAdapter, it is customary to pass in the context and for the adapter to hold onto it. It is often very useful to have it available when needed. The second thing we want to do in our adapter is to hang onto the inflater. This will help performance when we need to create a new view to return to the list control. The third thing that is typical in an adapter is to create a ViewHolder object, to contain the View objects for the data we are managing. Taking this approach also acts as a performance optimization, saving us from repeatedly looking up the Views. For this example, we are simply storing an ImageView, but if we had additional fields to deal with, we would add them into the definition of ViewHolder. For example, if we had a ListView where each row contained an ImageView and two TextViews, our ViewHolder would have an ImageView and two TextViews.

Because we're dealing with images of manatees in this adapter, we set up an array of their resource IDs to be used during construction to create bitmaps. We also define an array of bitmaps to use as our data list.

As you can see from our ManateeAdapter constructor, we save the context, create and hang onto an inflater, and then we iterate through the image resource IDs and build an array of bitmaps. This bitmap array will be our data.

As you learned previously, setting the adapter will cause our GridView to call methods on the adapter to set itself up with data to display. For example, our GridView gv will call the adaptor's getCount() method to determine how many objects there are for displaying. It will also call the getViewTypeCount() method to determine how many different types of views could be displayed within the GridView. For our purposes in this example, we set this to 1. However, if we had a ListView and wanted to put separators in between regular rows of data, we would have two types of views and would need to return 2 from getViewTypeCount(). You could have as many different view types as you like, as long as you appropriately return the correct count from this method. Related to this method is getItemViewType(). We just said that we could have more than one type of view to return from the adapter, but to keep things simpler, `getItemViewType()` needs to return only an integer value to indicate which of our view types is at a particular position in the data. Therefore, if we had two types of views to return, `getItemViewType()` would need to return either 0 or 1 to indicate which type. If we have three types of views, this method needs to return 0, 1, or 2.

If our adapter is dealing with separators in a `ListView`, it must treat the separators as data. That means there is a position in the data that is taken up by a separator. When `getView()` is called by a list control to retrieve the appropriate view for that position, `getView()` will need to return a separator as a view instead of regular data as a view. And when asked in `getItemViewType()` for the view type for that position, we need to return the appropriate integer value that we've decided matches that view type. The other thing you should do if using separators is to implement the `isEnabled()` method. This should return true for list items and false for separators because separators should not be selectable or clickable.

The most interesting method in `ManateeAdapter` is the `getView()` method call. Once the `GridView` has determined how many items are available, it starts to ask for the data. Now, we can talk about recycling views. A list control can only show as many child views on the display as will fit. That means there's no point in calling `getView()` for every piece of data in the adapter; it only makes sense to call `getView()` for as many items as can be displayed. As gv gets child views back from the adapter, it is determining how many will fit on the display. When the display is full of child views, gv can stop calling `getView()`.

If you look at LogCat after starting this example application, you will see the various calls, but you will also see that `getView()` stops being called before all images have been requested. If you start scrolling up and down the `GridView`, you will see more calls to `getView()` in LogCat, and you will notice that, once we've created a certain number of child views, `getView()` is being called with `convertView` set to something, not null. This means we're now recycling child views—and that's very good for performance.

If we get a nonnull `convertView` value from gv in `getView()`, it means gv is recycling that view. By reusing the view passed in, we avoid having to inflate an XML layout, and we avoid having to find the `ImageView`. By linking a `ViewHolder` object to the `View` that we return, we can be much faster at recycling the view the next time it comes back to us. All we have to do in `getView()` is reacquire the `ViewHolder` and assign the right data into the view.

For this example, we wanted to show that the data placed into the view is not necessarily exactly what exists in the data. The `createScaledBitmap()` method is creating a smaller version of the data for display purposes. The point is that our list control does not call the `getItem()` method. This method would be called by our other code that wants to do something with the data if the user acts on the list control. Once again, for any adapter, it is very important that you understand what it is doing. You don't necessarily want to rely on data in the view from the list control, as created by `getView()` in the adapter. Sometimes, you will need to call the adapter's `getItem()` method to get the actual data to be operated on. And sometimes, as we did in the earlier `ListView` examples, you'll want to go to a cursor for the data. It all depends on the adapter and where the data is ultimately coming from. Although we used the `createScaledBitmap()` method in our example, Android 2.2 introduced another class that might have been helpful here: `ThumbnailUtils`. This class has some static methods for generating thumbnail images from bitmaps and videos.

The last thing to point out from this example is the getItemId() method call. In our earlier examples with ListViews and contacts, the item ID was the _ID value from the content provider. For this example, we don't really need to use anything other than position for the item ID. The point of item IDs is to provide a mechanism to refer to the data separately from its position. This is especially true when the data has a life away from this adapter, as is the case with our contacts. When we have this kind of direct control over the data, as we do with our images of manatees, and we understand how to get to the actual data in our application, it is a common shortcut to simply use position as the item ID. This is particularly true in our case, because we don't even allow adding or removal of data.

Other Controls in Android

There are many, many controls in Android that you can use. We've covered quite a few so far, and more will be covered in later chapters (such as MapView in Chapter 19 and VideoView and MediaController in Chapter 20). You will find that the other controls, because they're all descended from View, have a lot in common what the ones we've covered here. For now, we'll just mention a few of the controls you might want to explore further on your own.

ScrollView is a control for setting up a View container with a vertical scrollbar. This is useful when you have too much to fit onto a single screen.

The ProgressBar and RatingBar controls are like sliders. The first shows the progress of some operation visually (perhaps a file download or music playing), and the second shows a rating scale of stars.

The Chronometer control is a timer that counts up. There's a CountDownTimer class if you want something to help you display a countdown timer, but it's not a View class.

The Switch control, which functions like a ToggleButton but visually has a side-to-side presentation, was introduced in Android 4.0, along with the Space view, a lightweight view that can be used in layouts to more easily create spaces between other views.

WebView is a very special view for displaying HTML. It can do a lot more than that, including handling cookies and JavaScript and linking to Java code in your application. But before you go implementing a web browser inside your application, you should carefully consider invoking the on-device web browser to let it do all that heavy lifting.

That completes our introduction of controls in this chapter. We'll now move on to styles and themes for modifying the look and feel of our controls and then to layouts for arranging our controls on screens.

Styles and Themes

Android provides several ways to alter the style of views in your application. We'll first cover using markup tags in strings and then how to use Spannables to change specific visual attributes of text. But what if you want to control how things look using a common specification for several views or across an entire activity or application? We'll discuss Android styles and themes to show you how.

Using Styles

Sometimes, you want to highlight or style a portion of the View's content. You can do this statically or dynamically. Statically, you can apply markup directly to the strings in your string resources, as shown here:

```
<string name="styledText"><i>Static</i> style in a <b>TextView</b>.</string>
```

You can then reference it in your XML or from code. Note that you can use the following HTML tags with string resources: <i>, <b>, and <u> for italics, bold, and underlined, respectively, as well as <sup> (superscript), <sub> (subscript), <strike> (strikethrough), <big>, <small>, and <monospace>. You can even nest these to get, for example, small superscripts. This works not just in TextViews but also in other views, like buttons. Figure 5-2 shows what styled and themed text looks like, using many of the examples in this section.

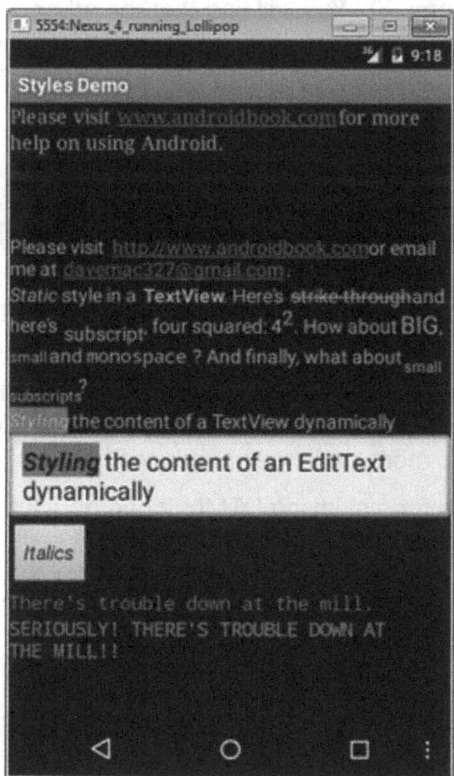

***Figure 5-2.** Examples of styles and themes*

Styling a TextView control's content programmatically requires a little additional work but allows for much more flexibility (see Listing 5-2), because you can style it at runtime. This flexibility can only be applied to a Spannable, though, which is how EditText normally manages the internal text, whereas TextView does not normally use Spannable. Spannable is basically a String to which you can apply styles. To get a TextView to store text as a Spannable, you can call setText() this way:

```
tv.setText("This text is stored in a Spannable", TextView.BufferType.SPANNABLE);
```

Then, when you call tv.getText(), you'll get a Spannable.

As shown in Listing 5-2, you can get the content of the EditText (as a Spannable object) and then set styles for portions of the text. The code in the listing sets the text styling to bold and italics and sets the background to red. You can use all the styling options as we have with the HTML tags as described previously, and then some.

Listing 5-2. Applying Styles Dynamically to the Content of an EditText

```
EditText et =(EditText)this.findViewById(R.id.et);
et.setText("Styling the content of an EditText dynamically");
Spannable spn = (Spannable) et.getText();
spn.setSpan(new BackgroundColorSpan(Color.RED), 0, 7,
            Spannable.SPAN_EXCLUSIVE_EXCLUSIVE);
spn.setSpan(new StyleSpan(android.graphics.Typeface.BOLD_ITALIC),
            0, 7, Spannable.SPAN_EXCLUSIVE_EXCLUSIVE);
```

These two techniques for styling work only on the one view they're applied to. Android provides a style mechanism to define a common style to be reused across views, as well as a theme mechanism, which basically applies a style to an entire activity or the entire application. To begin with, we need to talk about styles.

A *style* is a collection of View attributes that is given a name so you can refer to that collection by its name and assign that style by name to views. For example, Listing 5-3 shows a resource XML file, saved in /res/values, that we could use for all error messages.

Listing 5-3. Defining a Style to Be Used Across Many Views

```
<?xml version="1.0" encoding="utf-8"?>
<resources>
    <style name="ErrorText">
        <item name="android:layout_width">fill_parent</item>
        <item name="android:layout_height">wrap_content</item>
        <item name="android:textColor">#FF0000</item>
        <item name="android:typeface">monospace</item>
    </style>
</resources>
```

The size of the view is defined as well as the font color (red) and typeface. Notice how the name attribute of the item tag is the XML attribute name we used in our layout XML files, and the value of the item tag no longer requires double quotes. We can now use this style for an error TextView, as shown in Listing 5-4.

Listing 5-4. Using a Style in a View

```
<TextView  android:id="@+id/errorText"
    style="@style/ErrorText"
    android:text="No errors at this time"
    />
```

It is important to note that the attribute name for a style in this `View` definition does not start with `android:`. Watch out for this, because everything seems to use `android:` except the style. When you've got many views in your application that share a style, changing that style in one place is much simpler; you need to modify the style's attributes only in the one resource file. You can, of course, create many different styles for various controls. Buttons could share a common style, for example, that's different from the common style for text in menus.

One really nice aspect of styles is that you can set up a hierarchy of them. We could define a new style for really bad error messages and base it on the style of `ErrorText`. Listing 5-5 shows how this might look.

Listing 5-5. Defining a Style from a `Parent` Style

```
<?xml version="1.0" encoding="utf-8"?>
<resources>
    <style name="ErrorText.Danger" >
        <item name="android:textStyle">bold</item>
    </style>
</resources>
```

This example shows that we can simply name our child style using the parent style as a prefix to the new style name. Therefore, `ErrorText.Danger` is a child of `ErrorText` and inherits the style attributes of the parent. It then adds a new attribute for `textStyle`. This can be repeated again and again to create a whole tree of styles.

As was the case for adapter layouts, Android provides a large set of styles that we can use. To specify an Android-provided style, use syntax like this:

```
style="@android:style/TextAppearance"
```

This style sets the default style for text in Android. To locate the master Android `styles.xml` file, visit the `Android SDK/platforms/<android-version>/data/res/values/` folder. Inside this file, you will find quite a few styles that are ready-made for you to use or extend. Here's a word of caution about extending the Android-provided styles: the previous method of using a prefix won't work with Android-provided styles. Instead, you must use the parent attribute of the style tag, like this:

```
<style name="CustomTextAppearance" parent="@android:style/TextAppearance">
    <item  ... your extensions go here ...    />
</style>
```

You don't always have to pull in an entire style on your view. You could choose to borrow just a part of the style instead. For example, if you want to set the color of the text in your TextView to a system style color, you could do the following:

```
<EditText android:id="@+id/et2"
    android:layout_width="fill_parent"  android:layout_height="wrap_content"
    android:textColor="?android:textColorSecondary"
    android:text="@string/hello_world" />
```

Notice that in this example, the name of the textColor attribute value starts with the ? character instead of the @ character. The ? character is used so Android knows to look for a style value in the current theme. Because we see ?android, we look in the Android system theme for this style value.

Using Themes

One problem with styles is that you need to add an attribute specification of style= "@style/..." to every view definition that you want it to apply to. If you have some style elements you want applied across an entire activity, or across the whole application, you should use a theme instead. A *theme* is really just a style applied broadly; but in terms of defining a theme, it's exactly like a style. In fact, themes and styles are fairly interchangeable: you can extend a theme into a style or refer to a style as a theme. Typically, only the names give a hint as to whether a style is intended to be used as a style or a theme.

To specify a theme for an activity or an application, add an attribute to the <activity> or <application> tag in the AndroidManifest.xml file for your project. The code might look like this:

```
<activity android:theme="@style/MyActivityTheme">
<application android:theme="@style/MyApplicationTheme">
<application android:theme="@android:style/Theme.NoTitleBar">
```

You can find the Android-provided themes in the same folder as the Android-provided styles, with the themes in a file called themes.xml. When you look inside the themes file, you will see a large set of styles defined, with names that start with Theme. You will also notice that within the Android-provided themes and styles, there is a lot of extending going on, which is why you end up with styles called Theme.Dialog.AppError, for example.

This concludes our discussion of the Android control set. As we mentioned in the beginning of the chapter, building UIs in Android requires you to master two things: the control set and the layout managers. In the next section, we are going to discuss the Android layout managers.

Understanding Layout Managers

Android offers a collection of view classes that act as containers for views. These container classes are called *layouts* (or *layout managers*), and each implements a specific strategy to manage the size and position of its children. For example, the `LinearLayout` class lays out its children either horizontally or vertically, one after the other. All layout managers derive from the `View` class, therefore you can nest layout managers inside of one another.

The layout managers that ship with the Android SDK include the commonly used ones defined in Table 5-1.

Table 5-1. Android Layout Managers

Layout Manager	Description
`LinearLayout`	Organizes its children either horizontally or vertically
`TableLayout`	Organizes its children in tabular form
`RelativeLayout`	Organizes its children relative to one another or to the parent
`FrameLayout`	Allows you to dynamically change the control(s) in the layout
`GridLayout`	Organizes its children in a grid arrangement

We will discuss these layout managers in the sections that follow. The layout manager called `AbsoluteLayout` has been deprecated and will not be covered in this book.

The LinearLayout Layout Manager

The `LinearLayout` layout manager is the most basic. This layout manager organizes its children either horizontally or vertically based on the value of the `orientation` property. We've used `LinearLayout` in several of our examples so far. Listing 5-6 shows `LinearLayout` with a horizontal configuration.

Listing 5-6. LinearLayout with a Horizontal Configuration

```
<LinearLayout xmlns:android="http://schemas.android.com/apk/res/android"
    android:orientation="horizontal"
    android:layout_width="fill_parent"  android:layout_height="wrap_content">

    <!-- add children here-->

</LinearLayout>
```

You can create a vertically oriented `LinearLayout` by setting the value of `orientation` to `vertical`. Because layout managers can be nested, you could, for example, construct a vertical layout manager that contained horizontal layout managers to create a fill-in form, where each row had a label next to an `EditText` control. Each row would be its own horizontal layout, but the rows as a collection would be organized vertically.

Understanding Weight and Gravity

The `orientation` attribute is the first important attribute recognized by the `LinearLayout` layout manager. Other important properties that can affect size and position of child controls are weight and gravity.

You use *weight* to assign size importance to a control relative to the other controls in the container. Suppose a container has three controls: one has a weight of 1, whereas the others have a weight of 0. In this case, the control whose weight equals 1 will consume the empty space in the container. *Gravity* is essentially alignment. For example, if you want to align a label's text to the right, you would set its gravity to `right`. There are quite a few possible values for `gravity`, including `left`, `center`, `right`, `top`, `bottom`, `center_vertical`, `clip_horizontal`, and others. See `developer.android.com` for details on these and the other values of gravity.

> **Note** Layout managers extend `android.widget.ViewGroup`, as do many control-based container classes such as `ListView`. Although the layout managers and control-based containers extend the same class, the layout manager classes, by convention if not strict requirement, deal with the sizing and position of controls and not user interaction with child controls.

Now let's look at an example involving the weight and gravity properties (see Figure 5-3).

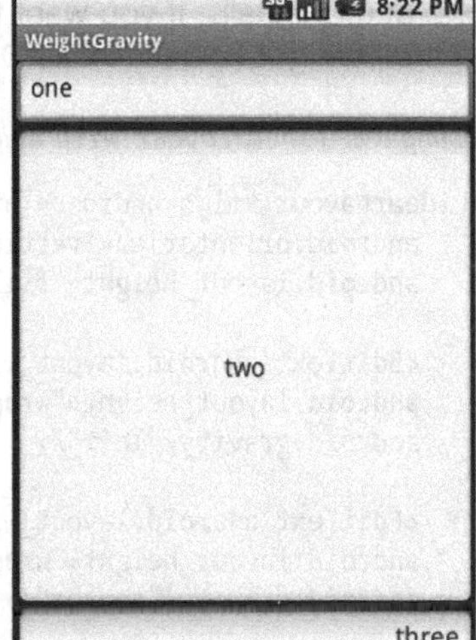

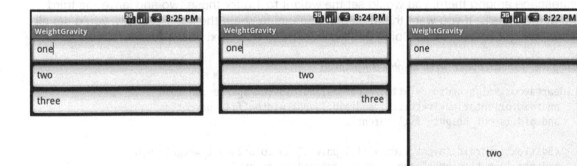

***Figure 5-3.* Using the `LinearLayout` layout manager**

Figure 5-3 shows three UIs that utilize `LinearLayout`, with different weight and gravity settings. The UI on the left uses the default settings for weight and gravity. The XML layout for this first UI is shown in Listing 5-7.

Listing 5-7. Three Text Fields Arranged Vertically in a LinearLayout, Using Default Values for Weight and Gravity

```
<LinearLayout xmlns:android="http://schemas.android.com/apk/res/android"
    android:orientation="vertical" android:layout_width="fill_parent"
    android:layout_height="fill_parent">

    <EditText android:layout_width="fill_parent"
        android:layout_height="wrap_content"
        android:text="one"/>
    <EditText android:layout_width="fill_parent"
        android:layout_height="wrap_content"
        android:text="two"/>
    <EditText android:layout_width="fill_parent"
        android:layout_height="wrap_content"
        android:text="three"/>
</LinearLayout>
```

The UI in the center of Figure 5-3 uses the default value for weight but sets `android:gravity` for the controls in the container to `left`, `center`, and `right`, respectively. The last example sets the `android:layout_weight` attribute of the center component to 1.0 and leaves the others to the default value of 0.0 (see Listing 5-8). By setting the weight attribute to 1.0 for the middle component and leaving the weight attributes for the other two components at 0.0, we are specifying that the center component should take up all the remaining whitespace in the container and that the other two components should remain at their ideal size.

Similarly, if you want two of the three controls in the container to share the remaining whitespace among them, you would set the weight to 1.0 for those two and leave the third one at 0.0. Finally, if you want the three components to share the space equally, you'd set all of their weight values to 1.0. Doing this would expand each text field equally.

Listing 5-8. `LinearLayout` with Weight Configurations

```
<LinearLayout xmlns:android="http://schemas.android.com/apk/res/android"
    android:orientation="vertical" android:layout_width="fill_parent"
    android:layout_height="fill_parent">

    <EditText android:layout_width="fill_parent" android:layout_weight="0.0"
    android:layout_height="wrap_content" android:text="one"
    android:gravity="left"/>

    <EditText android:layout_width="fill_parent" android:layout_weight="1.0"
    android:layout_height="wrap_content" android:text="two"
    android:gravity="center"/>

    <EditText android:layout_width="fill_parent" android:layout_weight="0.0"
    android:layout_height="wrap_content" android:text="three"
    android:gravity="right"
    />
</LinearLayout>
```

android:gravity vs. android:layout_gravity

Note that Android defines two similar gravity attributes: android:gravity and android:layout_gravity. Here's the difference: android:gravity is a setting used by the view, whereas android:layout_gravity is used by the container (android.view.ViewGroup). For example, you can set android:gravity to center to have the text in the EditText centered within the control. Similarly, you can align an EditText to the far right of a LinearLayout (the container) by setting android:layout_gravity="right". See Figure 5-4 and Listing 5-9.

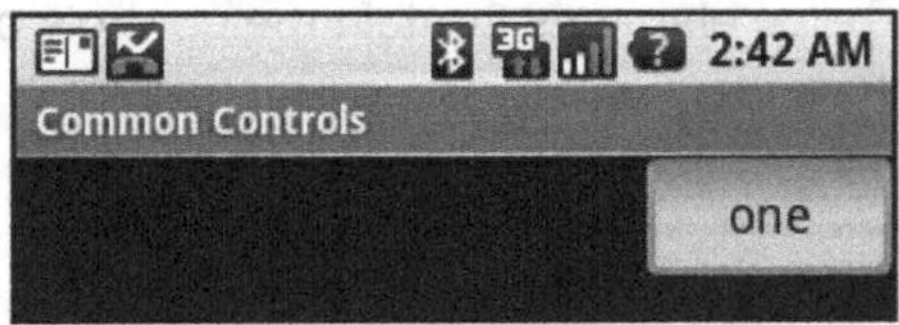

***Figure 5-4.** Applying gravity settings*

***Listing 5-9.** Understanding the Difference Between android:gravity and android:layout_gravity*

```
<LinearLayout xmlns:android="http://schemas.android.com/apk/res/android"
    android:orientation="vertical" android:layout_width="fill_parent"
    android:layout_height="fill_parent">

    <EditText android:layout_width="wrap_content" android:gravity="center"
    android:layout_height="wrap_content" android:text="one"
 android:layout_gravity="right"/>
</LinearLayout>
```

As shown in Figure 5-4, the text is centered in the EditText, which is aligned to the right of the LinearLayout.

The TableLayout Layout Manager

The TableLayout layout manager is an extension of LinearLayout. This layout manager structures its child controls into rows and columns. Listing 5-10 shows an example.

***Listing 5-10.** A Simple TableLayout*

```
<?xml version="1.0" encoding="utf-8"?>
<TableLayout xmlns:android="http://schemas.android.com/apk/res/android"
    android:layout_width="fill_parent"  android:layout_height="fill_parent">

  <TableRow>
    <TextView android:text="First Name:"
        android:layout_width="wrap_content"  android:layout_height="wrap_content" />

    <EditText android:text="Edgar"
        android:layout_width="wrap_content"  android:layout_height="wrap_content" />
  </TableRow>
```

```
  <TableRow>
    <TextView android:text="Last Name:"
        android:layout_width="wrap_content"  android:layout_height="wrap_content" />
    <EditText android:text="Poe"
        android:layout_width="wrap_content"  android:layout_height="wrap_content" />
  </TableRow>
</TableLayout>
```

To use this layout manager, you create an instance of TableLayout and place TableRow elements within it. These TableRow elements contain the controls of the table. The UI for Listing 5-10 is shown in Figure 5-5.

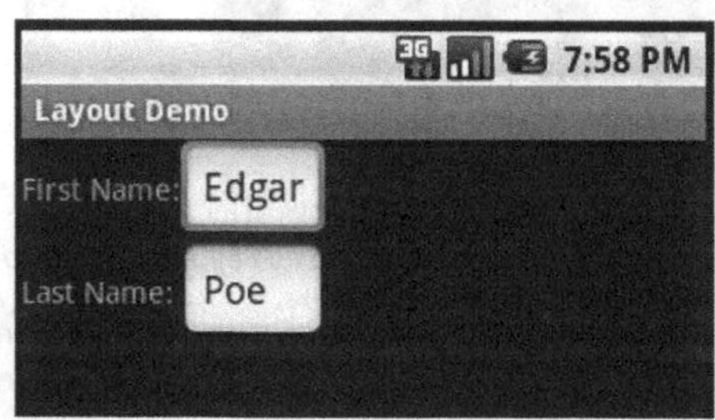

***Figure 5-5.** The TableLayout layout manager*

There are a number of more complex layouts possible with TableLayout, including nesting, asymmetrical rows and columns, and more. We have a bonus section on more options for TableLayout on the book website, www.androidbook.com.

The RelativeLayout Layout Manager

Another interesting layout manager is RelativeLayout. As the name suggests, this layout manager implements a policy where the controls in the container are laid out relative to either the container or another control in the container. Listing 5-11 and Figure 5-6 show an example.

***Listing 5-11.** Using a RelativeLayout Layout Manager*

```
<RelativeLayout xmlns:android="http://schemas.android.com/apk/res/android"
        android:layout_width="fill_parent"
        android:layout_height="wrap_content">

<TextView android:id="@+id/userNameLbl"
        android:layout_width="fill_parent"  android:layout_height="wrap_content"
        android:text="Username: "
        android:layout_alignParentTop="true" />
```

```
<EditText android:id="@+id/userNameText"
        android:layout_width="fill_parent"  android:layout_height="wrap_content"
        android:layout_toRightOf="@id/userNameLbl" />

<TextView android:id="@+id/pwdLbl"
        android:layout_width="wrap_content"  android:layout_height="wrap_content"
        android:layout_below="@id/userNameText"
        android:text="Password: " />

<EditText android:id="@+id/pwdText"
        android:layout_width="fill_parent"  android:layout_height="wrap_content"
        android:layout_toRightOf="@id/pwdLbl"
        android:layout_below="@id/userNameText" />

<TextView android:id="@+id/pwdCriteria"
        android:layout_width="fill_parent"  android:layout_height="wrap_content"
        android:layout_below="@id/pwdText"
        android:text="Password Criteria... " />

<TextView android:id="@+id/disclaimerLbl"
        android:layout_width="fill_parent"  android:layout_height="wrap_content"
        android:layout_alignParentBottom="true"
        android:text="Use at your own risk... " />

</RelativeLayout>
```

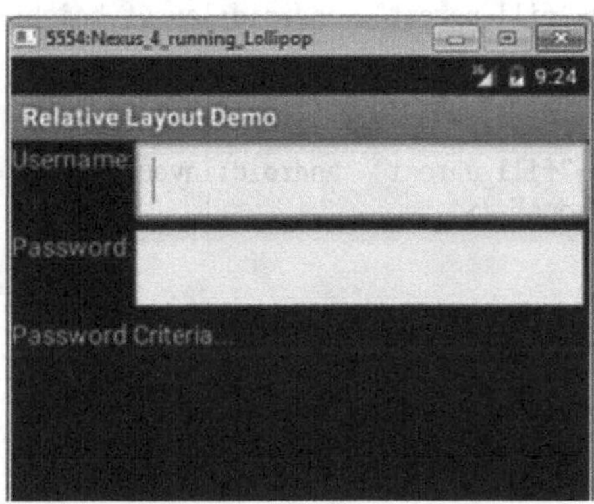

***Figure 5-6.** A UI laid out using the `RelativeLayout` layout manager*

As shown, the UI looks like a simple login form. The username label is pinned to the top of the container, because we set `android:layout_alignParentTop` to `true`. Similarly, the Username input field is positioned below the Username label because we set `android:layout_below`. The Password label appears below the Username label, and the Password input field appears below the Password label. The disclaimer label is pinned to the bottom of the container because we set `android:layout_alignParentBottom` to `true`.

Besides these three layout attributes, you can also specify layout_above, layout_toRightOf, layout_toLeftOf, layout_centerInParent, and several more. Working with RelativeLayout is fun due to its simplicity. In fact, once you start using it, it'll become your favorite layout manager—you'll find yourself going back to it over and over again.

The FrameLayout Layout Manager

The layout managers that we've discussed so far implement various layout strategies. In other words, each one has a specific way that it positions and orients its children on the screen. With these layout managers, you can have many controls on the screen at one time, each taking up a portion of the screen. Android also offers a layout manager that is mainly used to display a single item: FrameLayout. You mainly use this utility layout class to dynamically display a single view, but you can populate it with many items, setting one to visible while the others are invisible. Listing 5-12 demonstrates using FrameLayout.

Listing 5-12. Populating FrameLayout

```
<?xml version="1.0" encoding="utf-8"?>
<FrameLayout xmlns:android="http://schemas.android.com/apk/res/android"
    android:id="@+id/frmLayout"
    android:layout_width="fill_parent"  android:layout_height="fill_parent">

     <ImageView
        android:id="@+id/oneImgView" android:src="@drawable/one"
        android:scaleType="fitCenter"
        android:layout_width="fill_parent"  android:layout_height="fill_parent"/>
    <ImageView
        android:id="@+id/twoImgView" android:src="@drawable/two"
        android:scaleType="fitCenter"
        android:layout_width="fill_parent"  android:layout_height="fill_parent"
        android:visibility="gone" />

</FrameLayout>

public class FrameLayoutActivity extends Activity{
    private ImageView one = null;
    private ImageView two = null;
    @Override
    protected void onCreate(Bundle savedInstanceState) {
        super.onCreate(savedInstanceState);
        setContentView(R.layout.listing6_48);

        one = (ImageView)findViewById(R.id.oneImgView);
        two = (ImageView)findViewById(R.id.twoImgView);
```

```
        one.setOnClickListener(new OnClickListener(){

            public void onClick(View view) {
                two.setVisibility(View.VISIBLE);

                view.setVisibility(View.GONE);
            }});

        two.setOnClickListener(new OnClickListener(){

            public void onClick(View view) {
                one.setVisibility(View.VISIBLE);

                view.setVisibility(View.GONE);
            }});
    }
}
```

Listing 5-12 shows the layout file as well as the `onCreate()` method of the activity. The idea of the demonstration is to load two `ImageView` objects in the `FrameLayout`, with only one of the `ImageView` objects visible at a time. In the UI, when the user clicks the visible image, we hide one image and show the other one.

Look at Listing 5-12 more closely now, starting with the layout. You can see that we define a `FrameLayout` with two `ImageView` objects (an `ImageView` is a control that knows how to display images). Notice that the second `ImageView`'s visibility is set to `gone`, making the control invisible. Now, look at the `onCreate()` method. In the `onCreate()` method, we register listeners to click events on the `ImageView` objects. In the click handler, we hide one `ImageView` and show the other.

As we said earlier, you generally use `FrameLayout` when you need to dynamically set the content of a view to a single control. Although this is the general practice, the control will accept many children, as we demonstrated. Listing 5-12 adds two controls to the layout but has one of the controls visible at a time. `FrameLayout`, however, does not force you to have only one control visible at a time. If you add many controls to the layout, `FrameLayout` will simply stack the controls, one on top of the other, with the last one on top. This can create an interesting UI. For example, Figure 5-7 shows a `FrameLayout` control with two `ImageView` objects that are visible. You can see that the controls are stacked, and that the top one is partially covering the image behind it.

Figure 5-7. *`FrameLayout` with two `ImageView` objects*

Another interesting aspect of the `FrameLayout` is that if you add more than one control to the layout, the size of the layout is computed as the size of the largest item in the container. In Figure 5-7, the top image is actually much smaller than the image behind it, but because the size of the layout is computed based on the largest control, the image on top is stretched.

Also note that if you put many controls inside a `FrameLayout` with one or more of them invisible to start, you might want to consider using `setMeasureAllChildren(true)` on your `FrameLayout`. Because the largest child dictates the layout size, you'll have a problem if the largest child is invisible to begin with: when it becomes visible, it is only partially visible. To ensure that all items are rendered properly, call `setMeasureAllChildren()` and pass it a value of `true`. The equivalent XML attribute for `FrameLayout` is `android:measureAllChildren="true"`.

The GridLayout Layout Manager

Android 4.0 brought with it a new layout manager called `GridLayout`. As you might expect, it lays out views in a grid pattern of rows and columns, somewhat like `TableLayout`. However, it's easier to use than `TableLayout`. With a `GridLayout`, you can specify a row and column value for a view, and that's where it goes in the grid. This means you don't need to specify a view for every cell, just those that you want to hold a view. Views can span multiple grid cells. You can even put more than one view into the same grid cell.

When laying out views, you must not use the weight attribute, because it does not work in child views of a GridLayout. You can use the layout_gravity attribute instead. Other interesting attributes you can use with GridLayout child views include layout_column and layout_columnSpan to specify the left-most column and the number of columns the view takes up, respectively. Similarly, there are layout_row and layout_rowSpan attributes. Interestingly, you do not need to specify layout_height and layout_width for GridLayout child views; they default to WRAP_CONTENT.

Customizing the Layout for Various Device Configurations

By now, you know very well that Android offers a host of layout managers that help you build UIs. If you've played around with the layout managers we've discussed, you know that you can combine the layout managers in various ways to obtain the look and feel you want. But even with all the layout managers, building UIs—and getting them right—can be a challenge. This is especially true for mobile devices. Users and manufacturers of mobile devices are getting more and more sophisticated, and that makes the developer's job even more challenging.

One of the challenges is building a UI for an application that displays in various screen configurations. For example, what would your UI look like if your application were displayed in portrait versus landscape mode? If you haven't run into this yet, your mind is probably racing right now, wondering how to deal with this common scenario. Interestingly, and fortunately, Android provides some support for this use case.

Here's how it works: when building a layout, Android will find and load layouts from specific folders based on the configuration of the device. A device can be in one of three configurations: portrait, landscape, or square (square is rare). To provide different layouts for the various configurations, you have to create specific folders for each configuration from which Android will load the appropriate layout. As you know, the default layout folder is located at res/layout. To support portrait display, create a folder called res/layout-port. For landscape, create a folder called res/layout-land. And for a square, create one called res/layout-square.

A good question at this point is, "With these three folders, do I need the default layout folder (res/layout)?" Generally, yes. Android's resource-resolution logic looks in the configuration-specific directory first. If Android doesn't find a resource there, it goes to the default layout directory. Therefore, you should place default layout definitions in res/layout and the customized versions in the configuration-specific folders.

Another trick is to use the <include /> tag in a layout file. This allows you to create common chunks of layout code (for example, in the default layout directory) and include them in layouts defined in layout-port and layout-land. An include tag might look like this:

```
<include layout="@layout/common_chunk1" />
```

If the concept of include interests you, you should also check out the <merge /> tag and the ViewStub class in the Android API. These give you even more flexibility when organizing layouts, without duplicating views.

Note that the Android SDK does not offer any APIs for you to programmatically specify which configuration to load—the system simply selects the folder based on the configuration of the device. You can, however, set the orientation of the device in code, for example, using the following:

```
import android.content.pm.ActivityInfo;
...
setRequestedOrientation(ActivityInfo.SCREEN_ORIENTATION_LANDSCAPE);
```

This forces your application to appear on the device in landscape mode. Go ahead and try it in one of your earlier projects. Add the code to your onCreate() method of an activity, run it in the emulator, and see your application sideways.

Summary

Let's conclude this chapter by quickly enumerating what you have learned about building user interfaces:

- The main types of layouts and when to use each
- Views supported in Android and how to define them both in XML and via code
- Styles and themes you can use to manage the look and feel of your application from a common set of resources

Chapter 6

Working with Menus and Action Bars

Android SDK supports regular menus, submenus, context menus, icon menus, and secondary menus. Android 3.0 introduced the action bar, which integrates well with menus. We will cover both menus and action bars in this chapter.

Like many other chapters in the book, we will present the essential code snippets that you can use to work with menus and action bars. The completer code context for these snippets is available in the downloadable application that is specifically developed for this chapter. The link for these downloadable projects is given in the "Resources" section at the end of this chapter.

Working with Menus Through XML Files

In Android the easiest way to work with menus is through XML menu resource files. This XML approach to menu creation offers several advantages, such as the ability to name menus, order them automatically, and allocate IDs. As XML menus are resources, you also get the localization support for the menu text and icons.

Creating XML Menu Resource Files

A sample menu XML file is given Listing 6-1. You see in this listing a series of menu items grouped together under a group XML node. You can specify an ID for the group using the `@+id` resource reference approach. You can use this ID in Java code to get access to the menu group and manage it when needed. Grouping is optional and you can omit the group XML node.

Each menu XML file has a series of menu items with their menu item IDs tied to symbolic names. The title indicates the menu title, and the orderInCategory indicates the order in which the menu item appears in the menu. You can refer to the Android SDK documentation for all the possible attributes for these XML tags. The reference URL is provided in the "Resources" section of this chapter.

Listing 6-1. Menu XML Resource File with Menu Definitions

```
<menu xmlns:android="http://schemas.android.com/apk/res/android">
    <group android:id="@+id/menuGroup_Main">
        <item android:id="@+id/menu_item1"
            android:orderInCategory="1"
            android:title="item1 text" />
        <item android:id="@+id/menu_item2"
            android:orderInCategory="2"
            android:enabled="true"
            android:icon="@drawable/some-file"
            android:title="item2 text" />
        <item android:id="@+id/menu_item3"
            android:orderInCategory="3"
            android:title="item3 text" />
    </group>
</menu>
```

All the child menu items in Listing 6-1 are allocated menu item IDs based on their names (example: menu_item1) in this XML file. Let's see now how we take this menu XML file and associate it with an activity.

Populating Activity Menu from Menu XML Files

Assume that the name of the menu XML file is my_menu.xml. You need to place this file in the /res/menu subdirectory. Placing the file in /res/menu automatically generates a resource ID called R.menu.my_menu.

The key class in Android menu support is android.view.Menu. Every activity in Android is associated with one menu object of this type. In the life cycle of an activity Android calls a method called onCreateOptionsMenu() to populate this Menu object. In this method we load the XML menu file into the Menu object. This is shown in Listing 6-2.

Listing 6-2. Using Menu Inflater

```
//This callback method is available on every activity class
@Override
public boolean onCreateOptionsMenu(Menu menu) {
   super.onCreateOptionsMenu(menu);
   MenuInflater inflater = getMenuInflater(); //from activity
   inflater.inflate(R.menu.my_menu, menu);

   //It is important to return true to see the menu
   return true;

}
```

Once the menu items are populated, the code should return `true` to make the menu visible. If this method returns `false`, the menu is invisible.

Responding to XML-Based Menu Items

You respond to menu items in the `onOptionsItemSelected()` callback method. Android not only generates a resource ID for the XML menu file (as used in Listing 6-2) but also generates the necessary menu item IDs to help you distinguish between the menu items. The code in Listing 6-3 illustrates how to respond to menu items.

Listing 6-3. Responding to Menu Items from an XML Menu Resource File

```
@Override
public void onOptionsItemSelected (MenuItem item){
   if (item.getItemId() == R.id.menu_item1){
        //do something
        //for items handled
        return true;
   }
   else if (item.getItemId() == R.id.menu_item2){
        //do something
        return true;
   }
   //for the rest
   ...return super.onOptionsItemSelected(item);
}
```

Notice how the menu item names from the XML menu resource file have automatically generated menu item IDs in the `R.id` space.

Starting in SDK 3.0, you can also use the android:onClick attribute of a menu item to directly indicate the name of a method in an activity that is attached to this menu. This activity method is then called with the menu item object as the sole input. This feature is only available in 3.0 and above. Listing 6-4 shows an example.

Listing 6-4. Specifying a Menu Callback Method in an XML Menu Resource File

```
<item android:id="... "
        android:onClick="a-method-name-in-your-activity"
       ...
</item>
```

It is this simple to work with menu items in Android. Let's explore the Java API for the menus a bit now.

Working with Menus in Java Code

As indicated the key class in Android menu support is android.view.Menu. Every activity in Android is associated with one menu object of this type. The menu object then contains a number of menu items and submenus. Menu items are represented by android.view.MenuItem. Submenus are represented by android.view.SubMenu.

Prior to SDK 3.0, onCreateOptionsMenu() is called the first time an activity's options menu is accessed. Starting with 3.0, this method is called as part of activity creation. Also note that this method is called only once for the life cycle of the activity. If you want to add menus dynamically you will need to use the method onPrepareOptionsMenu(), which is covered a little later. The code in Listing 6-5 shows how to add three menu items using a single group ID along with incremental menu item IDs and order IDs.

Listing 6-5. Adding Menu Items

```
@Override
public boolean onCreateOptionsMenu(Menu menu){
   super.onCreateOptionsMenu(menu);
   menu.add(0            // Group
        ,1              // item id
        ,0              //order
        ,"item1");      // title

   menu.add(0,2,1,"item2");
   menu.add(0,3,2,"item3");
   //It is important to return true to see the menu
   return true;
}
```

You should also call the base-class implementation of this method to give the system an opportunity to populate the menu with system menu items (no system menu items are defined so far).

The arguments to create the menu item are explained in Listing 6-5. The last argument is the name or title of the menu item. Instead of free text, you can use a string resource through the R.java constants file. The group, menu item, and order IDs are all optional; you can use

Menu.NONE if you don't want to specify any of them. If Menu.NONE is specified for a group, then the items are outside of any group. If Menu.NONE is specified for an item, then this might be a submenu or a separator. If Menu.NONE is specified for the order, Android will choose some mechanism to order them.

Working with Menu Groups

Now, let's look at how to work with menu groups. Listing 6-6 shows how you add two groups of menus: Group 1 and Group 2.

Listing 6-6. Using Group IDs to Create Menu Groups

```
@Override
public boolean onCreateOptionsMenu(Menu menu) {
   //Group 1
   int group1 = 1;
   menu.add(group1,1,1,"g1.item1");
   menu.add(group1,2,2,"g1.item2");

   //Group 2
   int group2 = 2;
   menu.add(group2,3,3,"g2.item1");
   menu.add(group2,4,4,"g2.item2");

   return true; // it is important to return true
}
```

Android provides a set of methods on the android.view.Menu class that are based on group IDs. You can manipulate a group's menu items using the methods shown in Listing 6-7:

Listing 6-7. Menu Group–Related Methods

```
removeGroup(id)
setGroupCheckable(id, checkable, exclusive)
setGroupEnabled(id,enabled)
setGroupVisible(id,visible)
```

removeGroup() removes all menu items from that group, given the group ID. You can enable or disable menu items in a given group using the setGroupEnabled method(). Similarly, you can control the visibility of a group of menu items using setGroupVisible().

setGroupCheckable() is interesting. You can use this method to show a check mark on a menu item when that menu item is selected. When applied to a group, it enables this functionality for all menu items within that group. If this method's exclusive flag is set, only one menu item within that group is allowed to go into a checked state. The other menu items remain unchecked.

You now know how to populate an activity's main menu with a set of menu items and group them according to their nature. The way you respond to these menu items is identical to how you would have responded to for their XML counterparts except that the menu items IDs are explicitly controlled by the programmer.

Responding to Menu Items Through Listeners

You usually respond to menus by overriding onOptionsItemSelected(); a menu item also allows you to register a listener that could be used as a callback. This approach is a two-step process. In the first step, you implement the MenuItem.OnMenuItemClickListener interface. Then, you take an instance of this implementation and pass it to the menu item. When the menu item is clicked, the menu item calls the onMenuItemClick() method of the MenuItem.OnMenuItemClickListener interface (see Listing 6-8).

Listing 6-8. Using a Listener as a Callback for a Menu Item Click

```
//Step 1
public class MyResponse implements MenuItem.OnMenuItemClickListener{
   public MyResponse(...someargs...){} //a constructor
   @override
   public boolean OnMenuItemClick(MenuItem item) {
      //do your thing
      return true;
   }
}

//Step 2
MyResponse myResponse = new MyResponse(..your args..);//supply your args
menuItem.setOnMenuItemClickListener(myResponse);
...
```

The onMenuItemClick() method is called when the menu item has been invoked. This code executes as soon as the menu item is clicked, even before the onOptionsItemSelected() method is called. If onMenuItemClick() returns true, no other callbacks are executed—including the onOptionsItemSelected() callback method. This means that the listener code takes precedence over the onOptionsItemSelected() method.

Using an Intent to Respond to Menu Items

You can also associate a menu item with an intent by using the MenuItem's method setIntent(intent). When an intent is associated with a menu item, and nothing else handles the menu item, then the default behavior is to invoke the intent using startActivity(intent). For this to work, all the handlers—especially the onOptionsItemSelected() method—should call the parent class's onOptionsItemSelected() method for those menu items that are not handled.

Understanding Expanded Menus

If an application has more menu items than it can display on the main screen, Android shows a More menu item to allow the user to see the rest. This menu, called an expanded menu, appears automatically when there are too many menu items to display in the limited amount of space.

Working with Icon Menus

Android supports not only text but also images or icons as part of its menu repertoire. Creating an icon menu item is straightforward. You create a regular text-based menu item as before, and then you use the `setIcon()` method on the `MenuItem` class to set the image. You need to use the image's resource ID, so you must generate it first by placing the image or icon in the `/res/drawable` directory. For example, if the icon's file name is `balloons`, then the resource ID is `R.drawable.balloons`. Listing 6-9 demonstrates how to add an icon to a menu item.

Listing 6-9. Attaching an Icon to a Menu Item

```
//add a menu item and remember it so that you can use it
//subsequently to set the icon on it.
MenuItem item = menu.add(...);//supply the menu item details
item.setIcon(R.drawable.balloons);
```

The icon shows as long as the menu item is displayed on the main application screen. If it's displayed as part of the expanded menu, the icon doesn't show, just the text. There is an icon tag available as well to indicate the icon in an XML menu resource file. There are conditions under which Android may choose not to show the icons and recommends that text is always provided.

Working with Submenus

A `Menu` object can have multiple `SubMenu` objects. Each `SubMenu` object is added to the `Menu` object through a call to the `Menu.addSubMenu()` method (see Listing 6-10). You add menu items to a submenu the same way that you add menu items to a menu. This is because `SubMenu` is also derived from a `Menu` object. However, you cannot add additional submenus to a submenu.

Listing 6-10. Adding Submenus

```
private void addSubMenu(Menu menu){
   //Secondary items are shown just like everything else
   int base=Menu.FIRST + 100;
   SubMenu sm = menu.addSubMenu(base,base+1,Menu.NONE,"submenu");
   sm.add(base,base+2,base+2,"sub item1");
   sm.add(base,base+3,base+3,"sub item2");
   sm.add(base,base+4,base+4,"sub item3");

   //the following is ok
   sm.setIcon(R.drawable.icon48x48_1);

   //This will result in runtime exception
   //sm.addSubMenu("try this");
}
```

> **Note** SubMenu, as a subclass of the Menu object, continues to carry the addSubMenu() method. The compiler won't complain if you add a submenu to another submenu, but you'll get a runtime exception if you try to do it.

The Android SDK documentation also suggests that submenus do not support icon menu items. When you add an icon to a menu item and then add that menu item to a submenu, the menu item ignores that icon, even if you don't see a compile-time or runtime error. However, the submenu itself can have an icon.

Working with Context Menus

Android supports the idea of context menus through an action called a long click. A long click is a long press held down slightly longer than usual on any Android view. An activity owns a regular options menu, whereas a view owns a context menu. This is to be expected, because the long clicks that activate context menus apply to the view being clicked. So an activity can have only one options menu but many context menus.

Registering a View for a Context Menu

The first step in implementing a context menu is to register a view for the context menu in an activity's onCreate() method. You can register a TextView for a context menu by using the code in Listing 6-11. You first find the TextView and then call registerForContextMenu() on the activity using the TextView as an argument. This sets up the TextView for context menus.

Listing 6-11. Registering a TextView for a Context Menu

```
@Override
public void onCreate(Bundle savedInstanceState) {
    super.onCreate(savedInstanceState);
    setContentView(R.layout.main);

    TextView tv = (TextView)this.findViewById(R.id.textViewId);
    registerForContextMenu(tv);
}
```

Populating a Context Menu

Once a view like the TextView in this example is registered for context menus, Android calls the onCreateContextMenu() method with this view as the argument. This is where you can populate the context menu items for that context menu. The onCreateContextMenu() callback method provides three arguments to work with. Listing 6-12 demonstrates the onCreateContextMenu() method.

Listing 6-12. The onCreateContextMenu() Method

```
@Override
public void onCreateContextMenu(ContextMenu menu, View v, ContextMenuInfo menuInfo){
        menu.setHeaderTitle("Sample Context Menu");
        menu.add(200, 200, 200, "item1");
}
```

The first argument is a preconstructed ContextMenu object, the second is the view (such as the TextView) that generated the callback, and the third is the ContextMenuInfo class. For a lot of simple cases, you can just ignore the ContextMenuInfo object. However, some views may pass extra information through this object. In those cases, you need to cast the ContextMenuInfo class to a subclass and then use the additional methods to retrieve the additional information.

Some examples of classes derived from ContextMenuInfo include AdapterContextMenuInfo and ExpandableListContextMenuInfo. Views that are AdapterViews such as the ListView in Android use the AdapterContextMenuInfo class to pass the row ID within that view for which the context menu is being displayed. In a sense, you can use this class to further clarify the object underneath the touch or the click, even within a given composite view.

Responding to Context Menu Items

Android provides a callback method similar to onOptionsItemSelected() called onContextItemSelected(). Listing 6-13 demonstrates onContextItemSelected().

Listing 6-13. Responding to Context Menus

```
//This method is available for all activities @Override
 public boolean onContextItemSelected(MenuItem item) {
     if (item.getItemId() == some-menu-item-id)     {
        //handle this menu item
        return true;
     }
... other exception processing
}
```

Incorporating Dynamic Menus

So far, we've talked about static menus—you set them up once, and they don't change dynamically according to what's onscreen. If you want to create dynamic menus, use the onPrepareOptionsMenu() method that Android provides on an activity class. This method resembles onCreateOptionsMenu() except that it is called every time a menu is displayed prior to displaying. You should use onPrepareOptionsMenu() along with the onCreateOptionsMenu() to effectively manage your menu if it has dynamic menu options. onPrepareOptionMenu() is where you want to enable or disable some menu items or menu groups based on what you are displaying. For 3.0 and above when you want to change a menu, because a menu-related component like the action bar is always displayed, you have to explicitly call a new provisioned method called `Activity.invalidateOptionsMenu()`, which in turn invokes the `onCreateOptionsMenu()` and redraws the menu and thereby also results in calling `onPrepareOptionsMenu()` prior to the display. You can call this method any time something changes in your application state that would require a change to the menu.

Working with Pop-up Menus

Android 3.0 introduced another type of menu called a pop-up menu. SDK 4.0 enhanced this slightly by adding a couple of utility methods (for example, `PopupMenu.inflate`) to the `PopupMenu` class. (See the `PopupMenu` API documentation to learn about these methods. Listing 6-14 also draws attention to this difference.)

A pop-up menu can be invoked against any view in response to any UI event. An example of a UI event is a button click or a click on an image view. Figure 6-1 shows a pop-up menu invoked against a view.

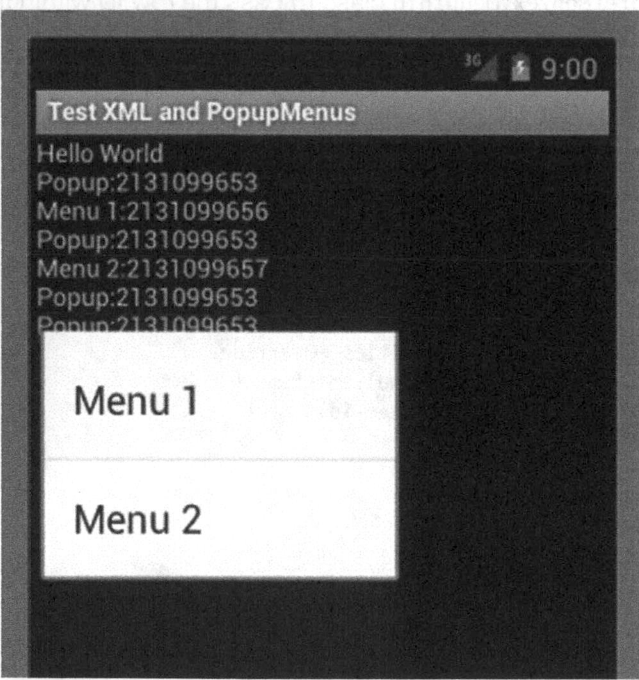

***Figure 6-1.** Pop-up menu attached to a text view*

To create a pop-up menu like the one in Figure 6-1, start with a regular XML menu file and use the Java code in Listing 6-14 to load this menu XML as a pop-up menu. See the downloadable project for this chapter if you want to see the full implementation.

Listing 6-14. Working with a Pop-up Menu

```
//Other activity code goes here...
//Invoke the following method to show a popup menu
private void showPopupMenu() {
    //Get hold of a view to anchor the popup
    TextView tv = findViewById(R.id.SOME_TEXT_VIEW_ID);

    //instantiate a popup menu. var "this" stands for activity
    PopupMenu popup = new PopupMenu(this, tv);

    //the following code for 3.0 sdk
    //popup.getMenuInflater().inflate(R.menu.popup_menu, popup.getMenu());
    //Or in sdk 4.0 and above
    popup.inflate(R.menu.popup_menu);
    popup.setOnMenuItemClickListener(new PopupMenu.OnMenuItemClickListener() {
        public boolean onMenuItemClick(MenuItem item) {
            //do something here
            return true; } } );
    popup.show();
}
```

As you can see, a pop-up menu behaves much like an options menu. The key differences are as follows:

- A pop-up menu is used on demand, whereas an options menu is always available.
- A pop-up menu is anchored to a view, whereas an options menu belongs to the entire activity.
- A pop-up menu uses its own menu item callback, whereas the options menu uses the `onOptionsItemSelected()` callback on the activity.

Exploring Action Bars

Introduced in Android 3.0 and expanded in Android 4.0, an `ActionBar` extends the reach of menus into the title bar of an activity. This allows frequently used actions easily available to the user without searching through option menus or context menus. In addition to icons and menu items, an action bar can accommodate other views such as tabs, or a list, or a search box to help with navigation. Figure 6-2 shows an action bar in tabbed navigation mode.

Figure 6-2. An activity with a tabbed action bar

You can see the various parts of an action bar here. The icon at upper left on the action bar is called a Home icon. Clicking this Home icon sends a callback to the option menu with menu ID `android.R.id.home`. Followed by the home icon is the title area for this activity. Then you see a set of tabs (or a drop-down list if this were to be a list-based action bar). In the middle, you see search view. Towards the end, you see a set of action icons. The last part of this action bar is a dotted vertical line representing the menu for this activity. When you click on that icon, a standard drop-down menu will appear (See Figure 6-3).

The action bar you see in Figure 6-1 is a tabbed action bar. The two other modes of an action bar are a standard and a list. In a list action bar, the tabs are replaced by a drop-down list. In a standard action bar, there is no area set aside for a list or tabs. Now, let's show you how to implement a simple standard action bar.

Implementing a Standard Action Bar

Listing 6-15 presents sample source code for implementing a standard navigation action bar for an activity.

Listing 6-15. ***Standard Navigation Action Bar Activity***

```
public class StandardNavigationActionBarActivity extends Activity {
     //    ..... other code
    @Override
    public void onCreate(Bundle savedInstanceState)     {
        super.onCreate(savedInstanceState);

        ActionBar bar = this.getActionBar();
        bar.setTitle("Some title of your choosing");
        bar.setNavigationMode(ActionBar.NAVIGATION_MODE_STANDARD);
    }
    public boolean onCreateOptionsMenu(Menu mainMenu) {
       //load the menu xml file into the mainMenu object as usual here
       return true;
    }
}
```

As you can see from Listing 6-15, it is easy to work with an action bar. Notice in that listing how we have used the `getActionBar()` to get access to the action bar object and then set its title and navigation mode. Any menu you set in the `onCreateOptionsMenu()` can be invoked directly from the action bar as shown in Figure 6-3. (However, when a menu is presented in this fashion from an action bar, due to space limitations, the system may not show the icons along with menu text.)

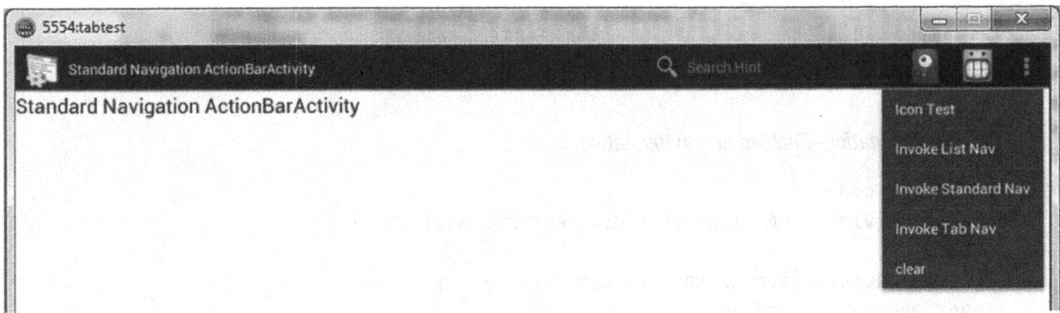

***Figure 6-3.** An activity with an action bar and expanded menu*

With the introduction of action bar, the menu XML file is enhanced with new attributes to indicate some menu items to be shown in the action bar directly as icons. (You can see these icons in action bar above the expanded menu in Figure 6-3). The XML menu file example in Listing 6-16 demonstrates how a menu item can be specified to become an icon directly on the action bar.

***Listing 6-16.** Menu XML File for This Project*

```
<!-- /res/menu/menu.xml -->
<menu
xmlns:android="http://schemas.android.com/apk/res/android">
    <!-- This group uses the default category. -->
    <group android:id="@+id/menuGroup_Main">
        <!-- a regular menu item -->
        <item android:id="@+id/menu_da_clear"
            android:title="clear" />
        <!--item to be shown directly on the action bar-->
        <item android:id="@+id/menu_action_icon1"
            android:title="Action Icon1"
            android:icon="@drawable/creep001"
            android:showAsAction="ifRoom"/>
        <!-- ..other menu items-->
    </group>
</menu>
```

The menu items that are to be shown on the action bar are indicated with the tag `showAsAction`. In the preceding code, this attribute is set to `"ifRoom"`. The other possible values for this XML tag are as follows: `always`, `never`, `withText`, `collapseActionView`. You can also accomplish the same effect with a Java API available on the `MenuItem` class. The option `always` means "show this item as a button in the action bar." The option `never` means "never show this item." The option `withText` means "show this item with its text label and the icon." The option `collapseActionView` means "collapse the space taken by the action view of this action menu item when not selected." Because these actions are merely menu items, they behave as such and call the `onOptionsItemSelected()` callback method of the activity class.

Implementing a Tabbed Action Bar

Listing 6-17 shows how to setup a tabbed action bar.

Listing 6-17. Tab-Navigation–Enabled Action Bar Activity

```
//Activity Source code
public class TabNavigationActionBarActivity extends Activity {
    @Override
    public void onCreate(Bundle savedInstanceState)   {
        super.onCreate(savedInstanceState);
        workwithTabbedActionBar();
    }
    public void workwithTabbedActionBar()    {
        ActionBar bar = this.getActionBar();
        bar.setTitle(tag);
        bar.setNavigationMode(ActionBar.NAVIGATION_MODE_TABS);
        TestTabListener tl = new TestTabListener();
        Tab tab1 = bar.newTab();
        tab1.setText("Tab1");  tab1.setTabListener(tl);   bar.addTab(tab1);
        Tab tab2 = bar.newTab();
        tab2.setText("Tab2");   tab2.setTabListener(tl);   bar.addTab(tab2);
    }
}//eof-class
```

A tabbed action bar, as the name suggests, has multiple tabs. In Listing 6-17 you see that there are a few additional methods and classes that are used to work with tabbed action bars. Unlike a standard action bar, a tabbed action bar requires a tab listener for each tab. This listener needs to implement the `TabListener` interface. In Listing 6-18 the class `TestTabListener` implements the `TabListener` interface. If you forget to call the `setTabListener()` method on a tab that is added to the action bar, you get a runtime error indicating that a listener is needed. Listing 6-18 shows the code for the `TestTabListener` class.

Listing 6-18. Tab Listener to Respond to Tab Actions

```
public class TestTabListener implements ActionBar.TabListener {
   // constructor code
    public TestTabListener(){}
   // callbacks
    public void onTabReselected(Tab tab, FragmentTransaction ft)  {
       //apply necessary logic here
    }
    public void onTabSelected(Tab tab, FragmentTransaction ft)   {
       //apply necessary logic here
    }
    public void onTabUnselected(Tab tab, FragmentTransaction ft)   {
       //apply necessary logic here
    }
}
```

As tabs are selected and unselected, the callback methods in Listing 6-18 will be called. Action bar is a property of the activity and does not cross activity boundaries. In other words, one cannot use an action bar to control or influence multiple activities. Each activity must provision its own action bars. Any commonality of actions between action bars is left to the programmer to orchestrate.

In Listing 6-17, once we obtained the action bar for an activity, we set its navigation mode to `ActionBar.NAVIGATION_MODE_TABS`. The other two possible action bar navigation modes are `NAVIGATION_MODE_LIST` and `NAVIGATION_MODE_STANDARD`. Let's see now how to implement a list-based action bar.

Implementing a List-Based Action Bar

To be able to initialize an action bar with list navigation mode, you need the following two things:

- A spinner adapter that can be used populate the drop-down list of navigation choices.
- A list navigation listener so that when one of the list items is picked you can get a callback.

Listing 6-19 presents the `SimpleSpinnerArrayAdapter` that implements the `SpinnerAdapter` interface. As stated earlier, the goal of this class is to give a list of items to show.

***Listing 6-19.** Creating a Spinner Adapter for List Navigation*

```
public class SimpleSpinnerArrayAdapter extends ArrayAdapter<String>
implements SpinnerAdapter {
    public SimpleSpinnerArrayAdapter(Context ctx)    {
        super(ctx,
          android.R.layout.simple_spinner_item,
          new String[]{"one","two"});

        this.setDropDownViewResource(
          android.R.layout.simple_spinner_dropdown_item);
    }
    public View getDropDownView(int position, View convertView, ViewGroup parent) {
        return super.getDropDownView(
          position, convertView, parent);
    }
}
```

There is no SDK class that directly implements the `SpinnerAdapter` interface required by list navigation. So, you derive this class from an `ArrayAdapter` and provide a simple implementation for the `SpinnerAdapter`. At the end of the chapter is a reference URL on spinner adapters for further reading. Let's move on now to the list navigation listener. This is a simple class implementing the `ActionBar.OnNavigationListener`. Listing 6-20 shows the code for this class.

Listing 6-20. Creating a List Listener for List Navigation

```
public class ListListener implements ActionBar.OnNavigationListener {
    //simple constructor...
    public ListListener(){}
    //needed callback to respond to actions
    public boolean onNavigationItemSelected(int itemPosition, long itemId)  {
        //respond and return true
        return true;
    }
}
```

You now have what you require to set up a list navigation action bar. The source code necessary for working with a list-based action bar is shown in Listing 6-21.

Listing 6-21. List Navigation Action Bar Activity

```
//Activity Source code
public class TabNavigationActionBarActivity extends Activity {
    @Override
    public void onCreate(Bundle savedInstanceState)   {
        super.onCreate(savedInstanceState);
        workwithTabbedActionBar();
    }
   public void workwithListActionBar()  {
       ActionBar bar = this.getActionBar();
       bar.setTitle("title");
       bar.setNavigationMode(ActionBar.NAVIGATION_MODE_LIST);
       bar.setListNavigationCallbacks(
          new SimpleSpinnerArrayAdapter(this),
          new ListListener());
   }
}//eof-class
```

Figure 6-4 shows how a list bar action bar looks when expanded.

***Figure 6-4.** An activity with an opened navigation list*

That concludes how we can use an action bar for regular menus, tabbed navigation, and list-based navigation. Let's see now how we can embed a search view like the one shown in Figure 6-2.

Exploring Action Bar and Search View

This section shows how to use a search widget in the action bar. You need the following to use search in your action bar:

1. Define a menu item in a menu XML file pointing to a search view class provided by the SDK. You also need an activity into which you can load this menu. This is often called the *search invoker activity*.
2. Create another activity that can take the query from the search view in step 1 and provide results. This is often called the *search results activity*.
3. Create an XML file that allows you to customize the search view in the action bar. This file is often called `searchable.xml` and resides in the `res/xml` subdirectory.
4. Declare the search results activity in the manifest file. This definition needs to point to the XML file defined in step 3.
5. In your menu setup for the search invoker activity, indicate that the search view needs to target the search results activity from step 2.

Let's start with the Search view widget.

Defining a Search View Widget as a Menu Item

To define a search view to appear in the action bar of your activity, you need to define a menu item in one of your menu XML files, as shown in Listing 6-22.

***Listing 6-22.** Search View Menu Item Definition*

```
<item android:id="@+id/menu_search"
    android:title="Search"
    android:showAsAction="ifRoom"
    android:actionViewClass="android.widget.SearchView"
    />
```

The key element in Listing 6-22 is the `actionViewClass` attribute pointing to `android.widget.SearchView`. You saw the other attributes earlier in the chapter when you declared your normal menu items to appear as action icons in the action bar.

Creating a Search Results Activity

To enable search in your application, you need an activity that can respond to a search query. This can be like any other activity. An example is shown in Listing 6-23.

Listing 6-23. Search Results Activity

```
public class SearchResultsActivity extends Activity {
    public static String tag = "SearchResultsActivity ";
    @Override
    public void onCreate(Bundle savedInstanceState) {
        super.onCreate(savedInstanceState);
        final Intent queryIntent = getIntent();
        doSearchQuery(queryIntent);
    }
    @Override
    public void onNewIntent(final Intent newIntent) {
        super.onNewIntent(newIntent);
        final Intent queryIntent = getIntent();
        doSearchQuery(queryIntent);
    }
    private void doSearchQuery(final Intent queryIntent) {
        final String queryAction = queryIntent.getAction();
        if (!(Intent.ACTION_SEARCH.equals(queryAction)))    {
            Log.d(tag,"intent NOT for search");
            return;
        }
        final String queryString = queryIntent.getStringExtra(SearchManager.QUERY);
        Log.d(tag, queryString);
    }
}//eof-class
```

In Listing 6-23, the activity checks to see whether the action that invoked it is initiated by search. Or, this activity could have been newly created or just brought to the top, in which case it needs to do something identical to the `onCreate()` method in its `onNewIntent()` method as well. On the other hand, if this activity is invoked by search, it retrieves the query string using an extra parameter called `SearchManager.QUERY`. Then the activity logs what that string is. In a real scenario, you would use that string to paint matching results.

Specifying a Searchable XML File

As indicated in the earlier steps, let's look at the XML file that is required and customizes the search widget; see Listing 6-24.

Listing 6-24. Searchable XML File

```
<!-- /res/xml/searchable.xml -->
<searchable xmlns:android="http://schemas.android.com/apk/res/android"
    android:label="@string/search_label"
    android:hint="@string/search_hint"
/>
```

The hint attribute will appear on the search view widget as a hint that disappears when you start typing. The label doesn't play a significant role in the action bar. However, when you use the same search results activity in a search dialog, the dialog has the label defined here. You can learn more about searchable XML attributes at the following URL:

http://developer.android.com/guide/topics/search/searchable-config.html

Defining the Search Results Activity in the Manifest File

Now let's see how to tie this XML file to the search results activity. This is done in the manifest file as part of defining the search results activity: see Listing 6-25. Notice the metadata definition pointing to the searchable XML file resource.

***Listing 6-25.** Tying an Activity to Its Searchable.xml*

```
<activity android:name=".SearchResultsActivity"
   android:label="Search Results">
     <intent-filter>
        <action android:name="android.intent.action.SEARCH"/>
     </intent-filter>
     <meta-data android:name="android.app.searchable"
                android:resource="@xml/searchable"/>
</activity>
```

Identifying the Search Target for the Search View Widget

So far, you have the search view in your action bar, and you have the activity that can respond to search. You need to tie together these two pieces using Java code. You do this in the onCreateOptions() callback of the search-invoking activity as part of setting up your menu. The function in Listing 6-26 can be called from onCreateOptions() to link the search view widget and the search results activity.

***Listing 6-26.** Tying the Search View Widget to the Search Results Activity*

```
private void setupSearchView(Menu menu) {
  //Step1: Locate the search view widget
  SearchView searchView = (SearchView) menu.findItem(R.id.menu_search).getActionView();
  //report error and return if searchView is null

  //Step2: get SearchManager and searchableInfo
  SearchManager
  searchManager = (SearchManager)getSystemService(Context.SEARCH_SERVICE);
  ComponentName cn = new ComponentName(this,SearchResultsActivity.class);
  SearchableInfo info = searchManager.getSearchableInfo(cn);
  //report error and return if searchable info is null

  //Step3: set searchableInfo on the searchview widget
  searchView.setSearchableInfo(info);
  // Do not iconify the widget; expand it by default
   searchView.setIconifiedByDefault(false);
}
```

Let's walk through what is happening in Listing 6-26. The goal of this code is to tell the search view where it can find the `searchable.xml` that defines the search behavior. To do this, the first step is to get a reference to the `SearchView`. This is done through the `Menu` object. The second step is to ask the system-wide search manager what searchable XML file is tied to the activity `SearchResultsActivity`. This is done by calling the method `getSearchableInfo` on the `SearchManager` system service. Once we have the `SearchableInfo` object representing the XML file, we pass that information to the `SearchView` object. With all this in place, now if you type something in the search box, that information will be passed to the search results activity, which will show the results.

Android Search API is a large API with a lot of nuances that, due to space, we have not included in this book. There are three suggestions. We have provided a URL in the "Resources" section that points to a series of articles and notes on the Google search API. We also have a large chapter on Search from the previous edition made available online. The link to this is also in the "Resources" section. We have also updated that Search material from the previous edition and added that content to the *Expert Android* edition from Apress.

Resources

As you learn about and work with Android menus and action bars, you may want to keep the following URLs handy:

- `http://developer.android.com/guide/topics/ui/menus.html`: Primary document from Google describing how to work with menus.
- `http://developer.android.com/guide/topics/resources/menu-resource.html`: Information about various XML tags you can use in a menu resource.
- `http://developer.android.com/reference/android/app/ActionBar.html`: API URL for the `ActionBar` class.
- `http://www.androidbook.com/item/3624`: Our research on action bar, including a list of further references, sample code, links to examples, and UI figures representing various action bar modes.
- `http://www.androidbook.com/item/3627`: To set up list navigation mode, you need to understand how drop-down lists and spinners work. This brief article shows a few samples and reference links on how to use spinners in Android.
- `http://www.androidbook.com/item/3885`: Explains how search works, to help you utilize the action bar to its full extent.
- `http://www.androidicons.com`: Web site from which a couple of the icons used in this chapter are borrowed. These icons are under Creative Commons License 3.0.
- `http://www.androidbook.com/item/3302`: "Pleasing Android Layouts." A few notes and sample code for simple layouts.

- http://www.androidbook.com/item/4060: You will find here a free copy of the Search chapter from the previous edition. This provides extensive coverage on Android search.
- http://androidbook.com/proandroid5/projects: Project download URL for this book. The downloadable project ZIP files for this chapter are ProAndroid5_ch06_TestMenus.zip and ProAndroid5_ch06_TestActionBar.zip.

Summary

Menus and action bars are an integral part of writing mobile apps. This chapter covers regular menus, context menus, pop-up menus, standard action bars, tabbed action bars, and list-based action bars. This chapter also covers the basics of how to embed a search view widget in an action bar.

Chapter 7

Styles and Themes

Thus far, we have covered some fundamentals of the Android user interface (UI). In this chapter, we are going to discuss styles and themes, which help to encapsulate control-appearance attributes for easier setup and maintenance. Android provides several ways to alter the style of views in your application, in XML and in code. We'll first cover using markup tags in strings and then how to use spannables to change specific visual attributes of text. But what if you want to control how things look using a common specification for several views or across an entire activity or application? We'll discuss Android styles and themes to show you how.

Using Styles

Sometimes, you want to highlight or style a portion of the View's content. You can do this statically or dynamically. Statically, you can apply markup directly to the strings in your string resources, as shown here:

```
<string name="styledText"><i>Static</i> style in a <b>TextView</b>.</string>
```

You can then reference it in your XML or from code. Note that you can use the following HTML tags with string resources: <i>, <b>, and <u>, for italics, bold, and underlined, respectively, as well as <sup> (superscript), <sub> (subscript), <strike> (strikethrough), <big>, <small>, and <monospace>. You can even nest these to get, for example, small superscripts. This works not just in TextViews but also in other views, like buttons. Figure 7-1 shows what styled and themed text looks like, using many of the examples in this section.

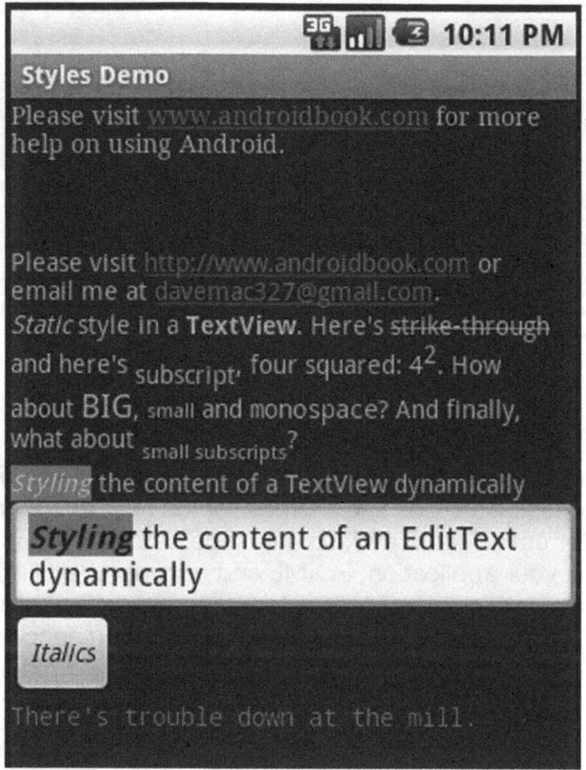

***Figure 7-1.** Examples of styles and themes*

Styling a `TextView` control's content programmatically requires a little additional work but allows for much more flexibility (see Listing 7-1), because you can style it at runtime. This flexibility can only be applied to a spannable, though, which is how `EditText` normally manages the internal text, whereas `TextView` does not normally use `Spannable`. `Spannable` is basically a `String` that you can apply styles to. To get a `TextView` to store text as a spannable, you can call `setText` this way:

```
tv.setText("This text is stored in a Spannable", TextView.BufferType.SPANNABLE);
```

Then, when you call `tv.getText`, you'll get a spannable.

As shown in Listing 7-1, you can get the content of the `EditText` (as a `Spannable` object) and then set styles for portions of the text. The code in the listing sets the text styling to bold and italics and sets the background to red. You can use all the styling options as we have with the HTML tags as described previously, and then some.

***Listing 7-1.** Applying Styles Dynamically to the Content of an `EditText`*

```
EditText et =(EditText)this.findViewById(R.id.et);
et.setText("Styling the content of an EditText dynamically");
Spannable spn = (Spannable) et.getText();
```

```
spn.setSpan(new BackgroundColorSpan(Color.RED), 0, 7,
        Spannable.SPAN_EXCLUSIVE_EXCLUSIVE);
spn.setSpan(new StyleSpan(android.graphics.Typeface.BOLD_ITALIC),
        0, 7, Spannable.SPAN_EXCLUSIVE_EXCLUSIVE);
```

These two techniques for styling only work on the one view they're applied to. Android provides a style mechanism to define a common style to be reused across views, as well as a theme mechanism, which basically applies a style to an entire activity or the entire application. To begin with, we need to talk about styles.

A *style* is a collection of View attributes that is given a name so you can refer to that collection by its name and assign that style by name to views. For example, Listing 7-2 shows a resource XML file, saved in /res/values, that we could use for all error messages.

Listing 7-2. ***Defining a Style to Be Used Across Many Views***

```
<?xml version="1.0" encoding="utf-8"?>
<resources>
    <style name="ErrorText">
        <item name="android:layout_width">fill_parent</item>
        <item name="android:layout_height">wrap_content</item>
        <item name="android:textColor">#FF0000</item>
        <item name="android:typeface">monospace</item>
    </style>
</resources>
```

The size of the view is defined as well as the font color (red) and typeface. Notice how the name attribute of the item tag (e.g., android:layout_width) is the XML attribute name we used in our layout XML files in earlier chapters, and the value of the item tag no longer requires double quotes. We can now use this style for an error TextView, as shown in Listing 7-3.

Listing 7-3. ***Using a Style in a View***

```
<TextView  android:id="@+id/errorText"
    style="@style/ErrorText"
    android:text="No errors at this time"
    />
```

It is important to note that the attribute name for a style in this View definition does not start with android:. Watch out for this, because everything seems to use android: except the style. When you've got many views in your application that share a style, changing that style in one place is much simpler; you only need to modify the style's attributes in the one resource file.

You can, of course, create many different styles for various controls. For example, buttons could share a common style that is different from the common style for text in menus. It is common to see text attributes managed with styles, including android:textColor, android:textStyle, and android:textSize. Other common attributes used with styles include the padding values, android:background, and colors.

One really nice aspect of styles is that you can set up a hierarchy of them. We could define a new style for really bad error messages and base it on the style of ErrorText. Listing 7-4 shows how this might look.

Listing 7-4. Defining a Style from a Parent Style

```
<?xml version="1.0" encoding="utf-8"?>
<resources>
    <style name="ErrorText.Danger" >
        <item name="android:textStyle">bold</item>
    </style>
</resources>
```

This example shows that we can simply name our child style using the parent style as a prefix to the new style name. Therefore, ErrorText.Danger is a child of ErrorText and inherits the style attributes of the parent. It then adds a new attribute for textStyle. This can be repeated again and again to create a whole tree of styles.

As was the case for adapter layouts, Android provides a large set of styles that we can use. To specify an Android-provided style, use syntax like this:

```
style="@android:style/TextAppearance"
```

This style sets the default style for text in Android. To locate the master Android styles.xml file, visit the Android SDK/platforms/<android-version>/data/res/values/ folder, where you installed the Android SDK; <android-version> is the particular version of Android you want to see styles for. Inside this file, you will find quite a few styles that are ready-made for you to use or extend. A quick note about @android:style/TextAppearance: this style does not set android:layout_height or android:layout_width, so a View specification would need more than this style to compile properly.

Here's a word of caution about extending the Android-provided styles: the previous method of using a prefix won't work with Android-provided styles. Instead, you must use the parent attribute of the style tag, like this:

```
<style name="CustomTextAppearance" parent="@android:style/TextAppearance">
    <item  ... your extensions go here ...    />
</style>
```

You don't always have to pull in an entire style on your view. You could choose to borrow just a part of the style instead. For example, if you want to set the color of the text in your TextView to a system style color, you could do the following:

```
<TextView android:id="@+id/tv2"
    android:layout_width="fill_parent"  android:layout_height="wrap_content"
    android:textColor="?android:textColorSecondary"
    android:text="@string/hello_world" />
```

Notice that in this example, the name of the textColor attribute value starts with the ? character instead of the @ character. The ? character is used so Android knows to look for a style value in the current theme. Because we see ?android, we look in the Android system theme for this style value.

Using Themes

One problem with styles is that you need to add an attribute specification of `style="@style/..."` to every view definition that you want it to apply to. If you have some style elements you want applied across an entire activity, or across the whole application, you should use a theme instead. A *theme* is really just a style applied broadly; but in terms of defining a theme, it's exactly like a style. In fact, themes and styles are fairly interchangeable: you can extend a theme into a style or refer to a style as a theme. Typically, only the names give a hint as to whether a style is intended to be used as a style or a theme.

To specify a theme for an activity or an application, you would add an attribute to the `<activity>` or `<application>` tag in the `AndroidManifest.xml` file for your project. The code might look like one of these:

```
<activity android:theme="@style/MyActivityTheme">
<application android:theme="@style/MyApplicationTheme">
<application android:theme="@android:style/Theme.NoTitleBar">
```

You can find the Android-provided themes in the same folder as the Android-provided styles, with the themes in a file called `themes.xml`. When you look inside the themes file, you will see a large set of styles defined, with names that start with `Theme`. It might be good to read that last line a few times. Put another way, all styles and themes are of type style, even if the style *name* has "Theme" in it. You will also notice that within the Android-provided themes and styles, there is a lot of extending going on, which is why you end up with styles called `Theme.Dialog.AppError`, for example.

References

Here are some helpful references to topics you may wish to explore further:

- `www.androidbook.com/proandroid5/projects`: A list of downloadable projects related to this book. For this chapter, look for a ZIP file called `ProAndroid5_Ch07_Styles.zip`. This ZIP file contains all projects from this chapter, listed in separate root directories. There is also a `README.TXT` file that describes exactly how to import projects into your IDE from one of these ZIP files.
- `http://developer.android.com/guide/topics/ui/themes.html`: The Android guide to styles and themes.

Summary

Let's conclude this chapter by quickly enumerating what you have learned about styles and themes:

- Styles are just collections of view attributes for easy reuse across views, activities, and applications.
- You can make your own styles, use a predefined style, or extend an existing style.
- Themes are what you call a style when it is applied to an activity or application.

Chapter 8

Fragments

So far, we've explored several bits and pieces of an Android application, and you've run some simple applications tailored to a smartphone-sized screen. All you had to think about was how to lay out the UI controls on the screen for an activity, and how one activity flowed to the next, and so on. For the first two major releases of Android, small screens were it. Then came the Android tablets: devices with screen sizes of 10". And that complicated things. Why? Because now there was so much screen real estate that a simple activity had a hard time filling a screen while at the same time keeping to a single function. It no longer made sense to have an e-mail application that showed only headers in one activity (filling a large screen), and a separate activity to show an individual e-mail (also filling a large screen). With that much room to work with, an application could show a list of e-mail headers down the left side of the screen and the selected e-mail contents on the right side of the screen. Could it be done in a single activity with a single layout? Well, yes, but you couldn't reuse that activity or layout for any of the smaller-screen devices.

One of the core classes introduced in Android 3.0 was the `Fragment` class, especially designed to help developers manage application functionality so it would provide great usability as well as lots of reuse. This chapter will introduce you to the fragment, what it is, how it fits into an application's architecture, and how to use it. Fragments make a lot of interesting things possible that were difficult before. At about the same time, Google released a fragment SDK that works on old Androids. So even if you weren't interested in writing applications for tablets, you may have found that fragments made your life easier on non-tablet devices. Now it's easier than ever to write great applications for smartphones and tablets and even TVs and other devices.

Let's get started with Android fragments.

What Is a Fragment?

This first section will explain what a fragment is and what it does. But first, let's set the stage to see why we need fragments. As you learned earlier, an Android application on small-screen devices uses activities to show data and functionality to a user, and each activity has a fairly simple, well-defined purpose. For example, an activity might show the user a list of contacts from their address book. Another activity might allow the user to type an e-mail. The Android application is the series of these activities grouped together to achieve a larger purpose, such as managing an e-mail account via the reading and sending of messages. This is fine for a small-screen device, but when the user's screen is very large (10" or larger), there's room on the screen to do more than just one simple thing. An application might want to let the user view the list of e-mails in their inbox and at the same time show the currently selected e-mail text next to the list. Or an application might want to show a list of contacts and at the same time show the currently selected contact in a detail view.

As an Android developer, you know that this functionality could be accomplished by defining yet another layout for the xlarge screen with `ListViews` and layouts and all sorts of other views. And by "yet another layout" we mean layouts in addition to those you've probably already defined for the smaller screens. Of course, you'll want to have separate layouts for the portrait case as well as the landscape case. And with the size of an xlarge screen, this could mean quite a few views for all the labels and fields and images and so on that you'll need to lay out and then provide code for. If only there were a way to group these view objects together and consolidate the logic for them, so that chunks of an application could be reused across screen sizes and devices, minimizing how much work a developer has to do to maintain their application. And that is why we have fragments.

One way to think of a fragment is as a sub-activity. And in fact, the semantics of a fragment are a lot like an activity. A fragment can have a view hierarchy associated with it, and it has a life cycle much like an activity's life cycle. Fragments can even respond to the Back button like activities do. If you were thinking, "If only I could put multiple activities together on a tablet's screen at the same time," then you're on the right track. But because it would be too messy to have more than one activity of an application active at the same time on a tablet screen, fragments were created to implement basically that thought. This means fragments are contained within an activity. Fragments can only exist within the context of an activity; you can't use a fragment without an activity. Fragments can coexist with other elements of an activity, which means you do *not* need to convert the entire user interface of your activity to use fragments. You can create an activity's layout as before and only use a fragment for one piece of the user interface.

Fragments are not like activities, however, when it comes to saving state and restoring it later. The fragments framework provides several features to make saving and restoring fragments much simpler than the work you need to do on activities.

How you decide when to use a fragment depends on a few considerations, which are discussed next.

When to Use Fragments

One of the primary reasons to use a fragment is so you can reuse a chunk of user interface and functionality across devices and screen sizes. This is especially true with tablets. Think of how much can happen when the screen is as large as a tablet's. It's more like a desktop than a phone, and many of your desktop applications have a multipane user interface. As described earlier, you can have a list and a detail view of the selected item on screen at the same time. This is easy to picture in a landscape orientation with the list on the left and the details on the right. But what if the user rotates the device to portrait mode so that now the screen is taller than it is wide? Perhaps you now want the list to be in the top portion of the screen and the details in the bottom portion. But what if this application is running on a small screen and there's just no room for the two portions to be on the screen at the same time? Wouldn't you want the separate activities for the list and for the details to be able to share the logic you've built into these portions for a large screen? We hope you answered yes. Fragments can help with that. Figure 8-1 makes this a little clearer.

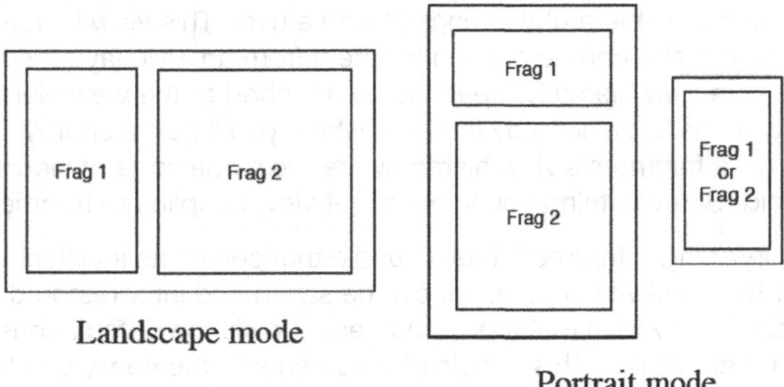

***Figure 8-1.** Fragments used for a tablet UI and for a smartphone UI*

In landscape mode, two fragments may sit nicely side by side. In portrait mode, we might be able to put one fragment above the other. But if we're trying to run the same application on a device with a smaller screen, we might need to show either fragment 1 or fragment 2 but not both at the same time. If we tried to manage all these scenarios with layouts, we'd be creating quite a few, which means difficulty trying to keep everything correct across many separate layouts. When using fragments, our layouts stay simple; each activity layout deals with the fragments as containers, and the activity layouts don't need to specify the internal structure of each fragment. Each fragment will have its own layout for its internal structure and can be reused across many configurations.

Let's go back to the rotating orientation example. If you've had to code for orientation changes of an activity, you know that it can be a real pain to save the current state of the activity and to restore the state once the activity has been re-created. Wouldn't it be nice if your activity had chunks that could be easily retained across orientation changes, so you could avoid all the tearing down and re-creating every time the orientation changed? Of course it would. Fragments can help with that.

Now imagine that a user is in your activity, and they've been doing some work. And imagine that the user interface has changed within the same activity, and the user wants to go back a step, or two, or three. In an old-style activity, pressing the Back button will take the user out of the activity entirely. With fragments, the Back button can step backward through a stack of fragments while staying inside the current activity.

Next, think about an activity's user interface when a big chunk of content changes; you'd like to make the transition look smooth, like a polished application. Fragments can do that, too.

Now that you have some idea of what a fragment is and why you'd want to use one, let's dig a little deeper into the structure of a fragment.

The Structure of a Fragment

As mentioned, a fragment is like a sub-activity: it has a fairly specific purpose and almost always displays a user interface. But where an activity is subclassed from `Context`, a fragment is extended from `Object` in package `android.app`. A fragment is *not* an extension of `Activity`. Like activities, however, you will always extend `Fragment` (or one of its subclasses) so you can override its behavior.

A fragment can have a view hierarchy to engage with a user. This view hierarchy is like any other view hierarchy in that it can be created (inflated) from an XML layout specification or created in code. The view hierarchy needs to be attached to the view hierarchy of the surrounding activity if it is to be seen by the user, which you'll get to shortly. The view objects that make up a fragment's view hierarchy are the same sorts of views that are used elsewhere in Android. So everything you know about views applies to fragments as well.

Besides the view hierarchy, a fragment has a bundle that serves as its initialization arguments. Similar to an activity, a fragment can be saved and later restored automatically by the system. When the system restores a fragment, it calls the default constructor (with no arguments) and then restores this bundle of arguments to the newly created fragment. Subsequent callbacks on the fragment have access to these arguments and can use them to get the fragment back to its previous state. For this reason, it is imperative that you

- Ensure that there's a default constructor for your fragment class.
- Add a bundle of arguments as soon as you create a new fragment so these subsequent methods can properly set up your fragment, and so the system can restore your fragment properly when necessary.

An activity can have multiple fragments in play at one time; and if a fragment has been switched out with another fragment, the fragment-switching transaction can be saved on a back stack. The back stack is managed by the fragment manager tied to the activity. The back stack is how the Back button behavior is managed. The fragment manager is discussed later in this chapter. What you need to know here is that a fragment knows which activity it is tied to, and from there it can get to its fragment manager. A fragment can also get to the activity's resources through its activity.

Also similar to an activity, a fragment can save state into a bundle object when the fragment is being re-created, and this bundle object gets given back to the fragment's `onCreate()` callback. This saved bundle is also passed to `onInflate()`, `onCreateView()`, and `onActivityCreated()`. Note that this is not the same bundle as the one attached as initialization arguments. This bundle is one in which you are likely to store the current state of the fragment, not the values that should be used to initialize it.

A Fragment's Life Cycle

Before you start using fragments in sample applications, you need understand the life cycle of a fragment. Why? A fragment's life cycle is more complicated than an activity's life cycle, and it's very important to understand *when* you can do things with fragments. Figure 8-2 shows the life cycle of a fragment.

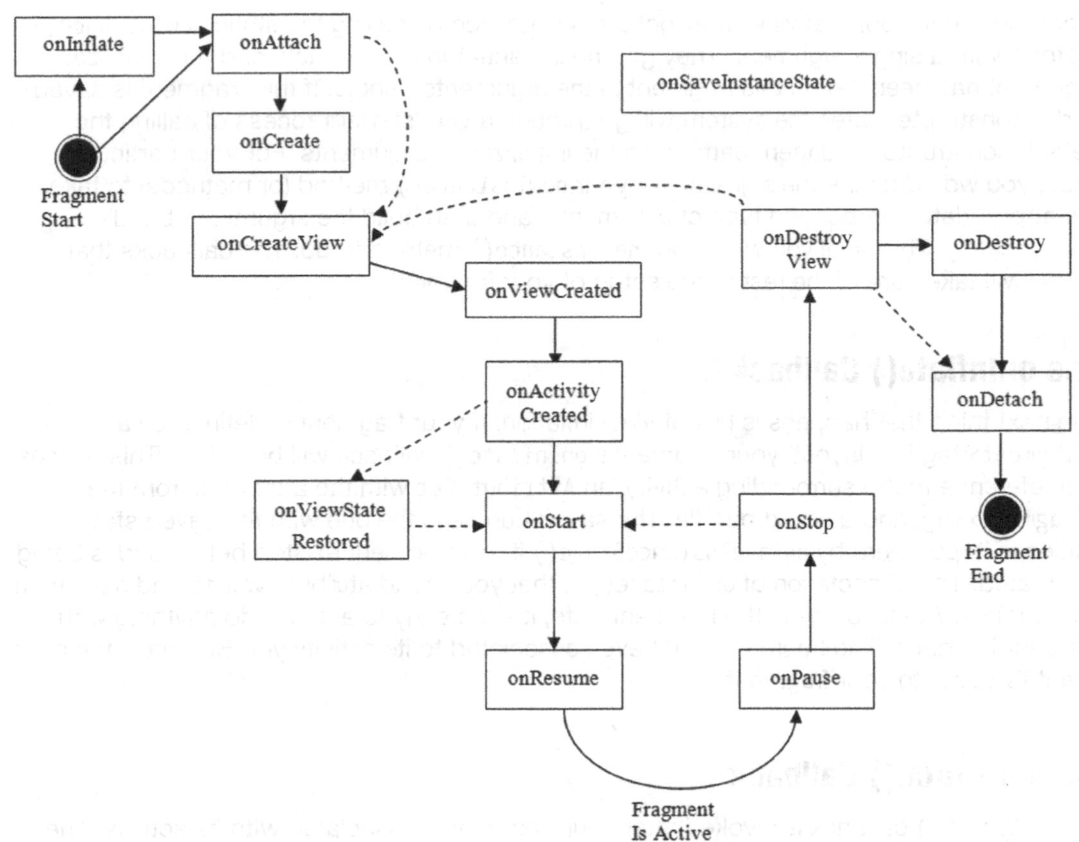

Figure 8-2. Life cycle of a fragment

If you compare this to Figure 2-3 (the life cycle for an activity), you'll notice several differences, due mostly to the interaction required between an activity and a fragment. A fragment is very dependent on the activity in which it lives and can go through multiple steps while its activity goes through one.

At the very beginning, a fragment is instantiated. It now exists as an object in memory. The first thing that is likely to happen is that initialization arguments will be added to your fragment object. This is definitely true in the situation where the system is re-creating your fragment from a saved state. When the system is restoring a fragment from a saved state, the default constructor is invoked, followed by the attachment of the initialization arguments bundle. If you are doing the creation of the fragment in code, a nice pattern to use is that in Listing 8-1, which shows a factory type of instantiator within the `MyFragment` class definition.

Listing 8-1. Instantiating a Fragment Using a Static Factory Method

```
public static MyFragment newInstance(int index) {
    MyFragment f = new MyFragment();
    Bundle args = new Bundle();
    args.putInt("index", index);
    f.setArguments(args);
    return f;
}
```

From the client's point of view, they get a new instance by calling the static `newInstance()` method with a single argument. They get the instantiated object back, and the initialization argument has been set on this fragment in the arguments bundle. If this fragment is saved and reconstructed later, the system will go through a very similar process of calling the default constructor and then reattaching the initialization arguments. For your particular case, you would define the signature of your `newInstance()` method (or methods) to take the appropriate number and type of arguments, and then build the arguments bundle appropriately. This is all you want your `newInstance()` method to do. The callbacks that follow will take care of the rest of the setup of your fragment.

The onInflate() Callback

The next thing that happens is layout view inflation. If your fragment is defined by a `<fragment>` tag in a layout, your fragment's `onInflate()` callback will be called. This passes in a reference to the surrounding activity, an `AttributeSet` with the attributes from the `<fragment>` tag, and a saved bundle. The saved bundle is the one with the saved state values in it, put there by `onSaveInstanceState()` if this fragment existed before and is being re-created. The expectation of `onInflate()` is that you'll read attribute values and save them for later use. At this stage in the fragment's life, it's too early to actually do anything with the user interface. The fragment is not even associated to its activity yet. But that's the next event to occur to your fragment.

The onAttach() Callback

The `onAttach()` callback is invoked after your fragment is associated with its activity. The activity reference is passed to you if you want to use it. You can at least use the activity to determine information about your enclosing activity. You can also use the activity as a context to do other operations. One thing to note is that the `Fragment` class has a `getActivity()` method that will always return the attached activity for your fragment should you need it. Keep in mind that all during this life cycle, the initialization arguments bundle is available to you from the fragment's `getArguments()` method. However, once the fragment is attached to its activity, you can't call `setArguments()` again. Therefore, you can't add to the initialization arguments except in the very beginning.

The onCreate() Callback

Next up is the `onCreate()` callback. Although this is similar to the activity's `onCreate()`, the difference is that you should not put code in here that relies on the existence of the activity's view hierarchy. Your fragment may be associated to its activity by now, but you haven't yet been notified that the activity's `onCreate()` has finished. That's coming up. This callback gets the saved state bundle passed in, if there is one. This callback is about as early as possible to create a background thread to get data that this fragment will need. Your fragment code is running on the UI thread, and you don't want to do disk input/output (I/O) or network accesses on the UI thread. In fact, it makes a lot of sense to fire off a background thread to get things ready. Your background thread is where blocking calls should be. You'll need to hook up with the data later, perhaps using a handler or some other technique.

> **Note** One of the ways to load data in a background thread is to use the Loader class. This will be covered in Chapter 28.

The onCreateView() Callback

The next callback is onCreateView(). The expectation here is that you will return a view hierarchy for this fragment. The arguments passed into this callback include a LayoutInflater (which you can use to inflate a layout for this fragment), a ViewGroup parent (called *container* in Listing 8-2), and the saved bundle if one exists. It is very important to note that you should not attach the view hierarchy to the ViewGroup parent passed in. That association will happen automatically later. You will very likely get exceptions if you attach the fragment's view hierarchy to the parent in this callback—or at least odd and unexpected application behavior.

***Listing 8-2.** Creating a Fragment View Hierarchy in onCreateView()*

```
@Override
public View onCreateView(LayoutInflater inflater,
            ViewGroup container, Bundle savedInstanceState) {
        if(container == null)
            return null;

        View v = inflater.inflate(R.layout.details, container, false);
        TextView text1 = (TextView) v.findViewById(R.id.text1);
        text1.setText(myDataSet[ getPosition() ] );
        return v;
}
```

The parent is provided so you can use it with the inflate() method of the LayoutInflater. If the parent container value is null, that means this particular fragment won't be viewed because there's no view hierarchy for it to attach to. In this case, you can simply return null from here. Remember that there may be fragments floating around in your application that aren't being displayed. Listing 8-2 shows a sample of what you might want to do in this method.

Here you see how you can access a layout XML file that is just for this fragment and inflate it to a view that you return to the caller. There are several advantages to this approach. You could always construct the view hierarchy in code, but by inflating a layout XML file, you're taking advantage of the system's resource-finding logic. Depending on which configuration the device is in, or for that matter which device you're on, the appropriate layout XML file will be chosen. You can then access a particular view within the layout—in this case, the text1 TextView field—to do what you want with. To repeat a very important point: do not attach the fragment's view to the container parent in this callback. You can see in Listing 8-2 that you use a container in the call to inflate(), but you also pass false for the attachToRoot parameter.

The onViewCreated() Callback

This one is called right after onCreateView() but before any saved state has been put into the UI. The view object passed in is the same view object that got returned from onCreateView().

The onActivityCreated() Callback

You're now getting close to the point where the user can interact with your fragment. The next callback is `onActivityCreated()`. This is called after the activity has completed its `onCreate()` callback. You can now trust that the activity's view hierarchy, including your own view hierarchy if you returned one earlier, is ready and available. This is where you can do final tweaks to the user interface before the user sees it. It's also where you can be sure that any other fragment for this activity has been attached to your activity.

The onViewStateRestored() Callback

This one is relatively new, introduced with JellyBean 4.2. Your fragment will have this callback called when the view hierarchy of this fragment has all state restored (if applicable). Previously you had to make decisions in `onActivityCreated()` about tweaking the UI for a restored fragment. Now you can put that logic in this callback knowing definitely that this fragment is being restored from a saved state.

The onStart() Callback

The next callback in your fragment life cycle is `onStart()`. Now your fragment is visible to the user. But you haven't started interacting with the user just yet. This callback is tied to the activity's `onStart()`. As such, whereas previously you may have put your logic into the activity's `onStart()`, now you're more likely to put your logic into the fragment's `onStart()`, because that is also where the user interface components are.

The onResume() Callback

The last callback before the user can interact with your fragment is `onResume()`. This callback is tied to the activity's `onResume()`. When this callback returns, the user is free to interact with this fragment. For example, if you have a camera preview in your fragment, you would probably enable it in the fragment's `onResume()`.

So now you've reached the point where the app is busily making the user happy. And then the user decides to get out of your app, either by Back'ing out, or by pressing the Home button, or by launching some other application. The next sequence, similar to what happens with an activity, goes in the opposite direction of setting up the fragment for interaction.

The onPause() Callback

The first undo callback on a fragment is `onPause()`. This callback is tied to the activity's `onPause()`; just as with an activity, if you have a media player in your fragment or some other shared object, you could pause it, stop it, or give it back via your `onPause()` method. The same good-citizen rules apply here: you don't want to be playing audio if the user is taking a phone call.

The onSaveInstanceState() Callback

Similar to activities, fragments have an opportunity to save state for later reconstruction. This callback passes in a Bundle object for this fragment to be used as the container for whatever state information you want to hang onto. This is the saved-state bundle passed to the callbacks covered earlier. To prevent memory problems, be careful about what you save into this bundle. Only save what you need. If you need to keep a reference to another fragment, don't try to save or put the other fragment, rather just save the identifier for the other fragment such as its tag or ID. When this fragment runs onViewStateRestored(), then you could re-establish connections to the other fragments that this fragment depends on.

Although you may see this method usually called right after onPause(), the activity to which this fragment belongs calls it when it feels that the fragment's state should be saved. This can occur any time before onDestroy().

The onStop() Callback

The next undo callback is onStop(). This one is tied to the activity's onStop() and serves a purpose similar to an activity's onStop(). A fragment that has been stopped could go straight back to the onStart() callback, which then leads to onResume().

The onDestroyView() Callback

If your fragment is on its way to being killed off or saved, the next callback in the undo direction is onDestroyView(). This will be called after the view hierarchy you created on your onCreateView() callback earlier has been detached from your fragment.

The onDestroy() Callback

Next up is onDestroy(). This is called when the fragment is no longer in use. Note that it is still attached to the activity and is still findable, but it can't do much.

The onDetach() Callback

The final callback in a fragment's life cycle is onDetach(). Once this is invoked, the fragment is not tied to its activity, it does not have a view hierarchy anymore, and all its resources should have been released.

Using setRetainInstance()

You may have noticed the dotted lines in the diagram in Figure 8-2. One of the cool features of a fragment is that you can specify that you don't want the fragment completely destroyed if the activity is being re-created and therefore your fragments will be coming back also. Therefore, Fragment comes with a method called setRetainInstance(), which takes a boolean parameter to tell it "Yes; I want you to hang around when my activity restarts" or "No; go away, and I'll create a new fragment from scratch." A good place to call setRetainInstance() is in the onCreate() callback of a fragment, but in onCreateView() works, as does onActivityCreated().

If the parameter is `true`, that means you want to keep your fragment object in memory and not start over from scratch. However, if your activity is going away and being re-created, you'll have to detach your fragment from this activity and attach it to the new one. The bottom line is that if the retain instance value is `true`, you won't actually destroy your fragment instance, and therefore you won't need to create a new one on the other side. The dotted lines on the diagram mean you would skip the `onDestroy()` callback on the way out, you'd skip the `onCreate()` callback when your fragment is being re-attached to your new activity, and all other callbacks would fire. Because an activity is re-created most likely for configuration changes, your fragment callbacks should probably assume that the configuration has changed, and therefore should take appropriate action. This would include inflating the layout to create a new view hierarchy in `onCreateView()`, for example. The code provided in Listing 8-2 would take care of that as it is written. If you choose to use the retain-instance feature, you may decide not to put some of your initialization logic in `onCreate()` because it won't always get called the way the other callbacks will.

Sample Fragment App Showing the Life Cycle

There's nothing like seeing a real example to get an appreciation for a concept. You'll use a sample application that has been instrumented so you can see all these callbacks in action. You're going to work with a sample application that uses a list of Shakespearean titles in one fragment; when the user clicks one of the titles, some text from that play will appear in a separate fragment. This sample application will work in both landscape and portrait modes on a tablet. Then you'll configure it to run as if on a smaller screen so you can see how to separate the text fragment into an activity. You'll start with the XML layout of your activity in landscape mode in Listing 8-3, which will look like Figure 8-3 when it runs.

***Listing 8-3.** Your Activity's Layout XML for Landscape Mode*

```
<?xml version="1.0" encoding="utf-8"?>
<!-- This file is res/layout-land/main.xml -->
<LinearLayout xmlns:android="http://schemas.android.com/apk/res/android"
        android:orientation="horizontal"
        android:layout_width="match_parent"
        android:layout_height="match_parent">

    <fragment class="com.androidbook.fragments.bard.TitlesFragment"
            android:id="@+id/titles" android:layout_weight="1"
            android:layout_width="0px"
            android:layout_height="match_parent" />
    <FrameLayout
            android:id="@+id/details" android:layout_weight="2"
            android:layout_width="0px"
            android:layout_height="match_parent" />

</LinearLayout>
```

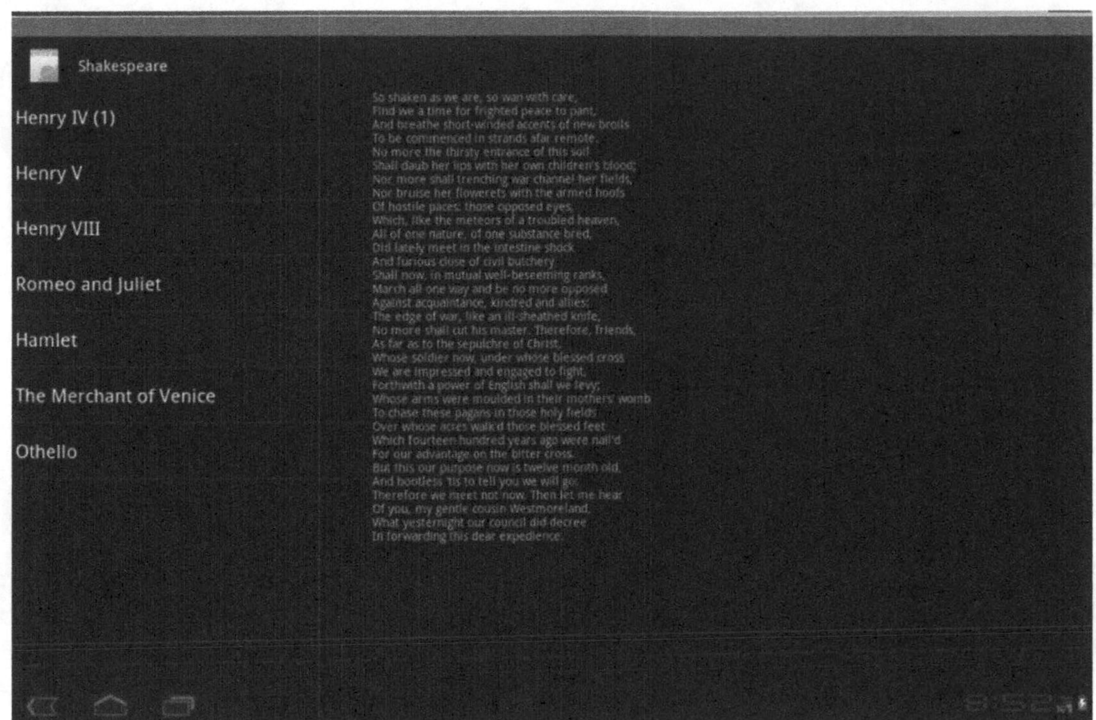

Figure 8-3. ***The user interface of your sample fragment application***

> **Note** At the end of the chapter is the URL you can use to download the projects in this chapter. This will allow you to import these projects into your IDE (such as Eclipse or Android Studio) directly.

This layout looks like a lot of other layouts you've seen throughout the book, horizontally left to right with two main objects. There's a special new tag, though, called `<fragment>`, and this tag has a new attribute called `class`. Keep in mind that a fragment is not a view, so the layout XML is a little different for a fragment than it is for everything else. The other thing to keep in mind is that the `<fragment>` tag is just a placeholder in this layout. You should not put child tags under `<fragment>` in a layout XML file.

The other attributes for a fragment look familiar and serve a purpose similar to that for a view. The fragment tag's `class` attribute specifies your extended class for the titles of your application. That is, you must extend one of the Android `Fragment` classes to implement your logic, and the `<fragment>` tag must know the name of your extended class. A fragment has its own view hierarchy that will be created later by the fragment itself. The next tag is a `FrameLayout`—not another `<fragment>` tag. Why is that? We'll explain in more detail later, but for now, you should be aware that you're going to be doing some transitions on the text, swapping out one fragment with another. You use the `FrameLayout` as the view container to hold the current text fragment. With your titles fragment, you have one—and only one—

fragment to worry about: no swapping and no transitions. For the area that displays the Shakespearean text, you'll have several fragments.

The MainActivity Java code is in Listing 8-4. Actually, the listing only shows the interesting code. The code is instrumented with logging messages so you can see what's going on through LogCat. Please review the source code files for ShakespeareInstrumented from the web site to see all of it.

Listing 8-4. ***Interesting Source Code from*** `MainActivity`

```
public boolean isMultiPane() {
    return getResources().getConfiguration().orientation
            == Configuration.ORIENTATION_LANDSCAPE;
}

/**
 * Helper function to show the details of a selected item, either by
 * displaying a fragment in-place in the current UI, or starting a
 * whole new activity in which it is displayed.
 */
public void showDetails(int index) {
    Log.v(TAG, "in MainActivity showDetails(" + index + ")");

    if (isMultiPane()) {
        // Check what fragment is shown, replace if needed.
        DetailsFragment details = (DetailsFragment)
                getFragmentManager().findFragmentById(R.id.details);
        if ( (details == null) ||
             (details.getShownIndex() != index) ) {
            // Make new fragment to show this selection.
            details = DetailsFragment.newInstance(index);

            // Execute a transaction, replacing any existing
            // fragment with this one inside the frame.
            Log.v(TAG, "about to run FragmentTransaction...");
            FragmentTransaction ft
                    = getFragmentManager().beginTransaction();
            ft.setTransition(
                    FragmentTransaction.TRANSIT_FRAGMENT_FADE);
            //ft.addToBackStack("details");
            ft.replace(R.id.details, details);
            ft.commit();
        }

    } else {
        // Otherwise you need to launch a new activity to display
        // the dialog fragment with selected text.
        Intent intent = new Intent();
        intent.setClass(this, DetailsActivity.class);
        intent.putExtra("index", index);
        startActivity(intent);
    }
}
```

This is a very simple activity to write. To determine multipane mode (that is, whether you need to use fragments side by side), you just use the orientation of the device. If you're in landscape mode, you're multipane; if you're in portrait mode, you're not. The helper method `showDetails()` is there to figure out how to show the text when a title is selected. The index is the position of the title in the title list. If you're in multipane mode, you're going to use a fragment to show the text. You're calling this fragment a `DetailsFragment`, and you use a factory-type method to create one with the index. The interesting code for the `DetailsFragment` class is shown in Listing 8-5 (minus all of the logging code). As we did before in `TitlesFragment`, the various callbacks of `DetailsFragment` have logging added so we can watch what happens via LogCat. You'll come back to your `showDetails()` method later.

Listing 8-5. Source Code for DetailsFragment

```
public class DetailsFragment extends Fragment {

    private int mIndex = 0;

    public static DetailsFragment newInstance(int index) {
        Log.v(MainActivity.TAG, "in DetailsFragment newInstance(" +
                                index + ")");

        DetailsFragment df = new DetailsFragment();

        // Supply index input as an argument.
        Bundle args = new Bundle();
        args.putInt("index", index);
        df.setArguments(args);
        return df;
    }

    public static DetailsFragment newInstance(Bundle bundle) {
        int index = bundle.getInt("index", 0);
        return newInstance(index);
    }

    @Override
    public void onCreate(Bundle myBundle) {
        Log.v(MainActivity.TAG,
              "in DetailsFragment onCreate. Bundle contains:");
        if(myBundle != null) {
            for(String key : myBundle.keySet()) {
                Log.v(MainActivity.TAG, "    " + key);
            }
        }
        else {
            Log.v(MainActivity.TAG, "    myBundle is null");
        }
        super.onCreate(myBundle);

        mIndex = getArguments().getInt("index", 0);
    }
```

```
    public int getShownIndex() {
        return mIndex;
    }

    @Override
    public View onCreateView(LayoutInflater inflater,
            ViewGroup container, Bundle savedInstanceState) {
        Log.v(MainActivity.TAG,
                "in DetailsFragment onCreateView. container = " +
                container);

        // Don't tie this fragment to anything through the inflater.
        // Android takes care of attaching fragments for us. The
        // container is only passed in so you can know about the
        // container where this View hierarchy is going to go.
        View v = inflater.inflate(R.layout.details, container, false);
        TextView text1 = (TextView) v.findViewById(R.id.text1);
        text1.setText(Shakespeare.DIALOGUE[ mIndex ] );
        return v;
    }
}
```

The DetailsFragment class is actually fairly simple as well. Now you can see how to instantiate this fragment. It's important to point out that you're instantiating this fragment in code because your layout defines the ViewGroup container (a FrameLayout) that your details fragment is going to go into. Because the fragment is not itself defined in the layout XML for the activity, as your titles fragment was, you need to instantiate your details fragments in code.

To create a new details fragment, you use your newInstance() method. As discussed earlier, this factory method invokes the default constructor and then sets the arguments bundle with the value of index. Once newInstance() has run, your details fragment can retrieve the value of index in any of its callbacks by referring to the arguments bundle via getArguments(). For your convenience, in onCreate() you can save the index value from the arguments bundle to a member field in your DetailsFragment class.

You might wonder why you didn't simply set the mIndex value in newInstance(). The reason is that Android will, behind the scenes, re-create your fragment using the default constructor. Then it sets the arguments bundle to what it was before. Android won't use your newInstance() method, so the only reliable way to ensure that mIndex is set is to read the value from the arguments bundle and set it in onCreate(). The convenience method getShownIndex() retrieves the value of that index. Now the only method left to describe in the details fragment is onCreateView(). And this is very simple, too.

The purpose of onCreateView() is to return the view hierarchy for your fragment. Remember that based on your configuration, you could want all kinds of different layouts for this fragment. Therefore, the most common thing to do is utilize a layout XML file for your fragment. In your sample application, you specify the layout for the fragment to be details.xml using the resource R.layout.details. The XML for details.xml is in Listing 8-6.

Listing 8-6. The `details.xml` Layout File for the Details Fragment

```
<?xml version="1.0" encoding="utf-8"?>
<!-- This file is res/layout/details.xml -->
<LinearLayout
  xmlns:android="http://schemas.android.com/apk/res/android"
  android:layout_width="match_parent"
  android:layout_height="match_parent">
  <ScrollView android:id="@+id/scroller"
      android:layout_width="match_parent"
      android:layout_height="match_parent">
    <TextView android:id="@+id/text1"
        android:layout_width="match_parent"
        android:layout_height="match_parent" />
  </ScrollView>
</LinearLayout>
```

For your sample application, you can use the exact same layout file for details whether you're in landscape mode or in portrait mode. This layout is not for the activity, it's just for your fragment to display the text. Because it could be considered the default layout, you can store it in the `/res/layout` directory and it will be found and used even if you're in landscape mode. When Android goes looking for the details XML file, it tries the specific directories that closely match the device's configuration, but it will end up in the `/res/layout` directory if it can't find the `details.xml` file in any of the other places. Of course, if you want to have a different layout for your fragment in landscape mode, you could define a separate `details.xml` layout file and store it under `/res/layout-land`. Feel free to experiment with different `details.xml` files.

When your details fragment's `onCreateView()` is called, you will simply grab the appropriate `details.xml` layout file, inflate it, and set the text to the text from the `Shakespeare` class. The entire Java code for `Shakespeare` is not shown here, but a portion is in Listing 8-7 so you understand how it was done. For the complete source, access the project download files, as described in the "References" section at the end of this chapter.

Listing 8-7. Source Code for `Shakespeare.java`

```
public class Shakespeare {
    public static String TITLES[] = {
            "Henry IV (1)",
            "Henry V",
            "Henry VIII",
            "Romeo and Juliet",
            "Hamlet",
            "The Merchant of Venice",
            "Othello"
    };
    public static String DIALOGUE[] = {
        "So shaken as we are, so wan with care,\n...
... and so on ...
```

Now your details fragment view hierarchy contains the text from the selected title. Your details fragment is ready to go. And you can return to `MainActivity`'s `showDetails()` method to talk about `FragmentTransactions`.

FragmentTransactions and the Fragment Back Stack

The code in showDetails() that pulls in your new details fragment (partially shown again in Listing 8-8) looks rather simple, but there's a lot going on here. It's worth spending some time to explain what is happening and why. If your activity is in multipane mode, you want to show the details in a fragment next to the title list. You may already be showing details, which means you may have a details fragment visible to the user. Either way, the resource ID R.id.details is for the FrameLayout for your activity, as shown in Listing 8-3. If you have a details fragment sitting in the layout because you didn't assign any other ID to it, it will have this ID. Therefore, to find out if there's a details fragment in the layout, you can ask the fragment manager using findFragmentById(). This will return null if the frame layout is empty or will give you the current details fragment. You can then decide if you need to place a new details fragment in the layout, either because the layout is empty or because there's a details fragment for some other title. Once you make the determination to create and use a new details fragment, you invoke the factory method to create a new instance of a details fragment. Now you can put this new fragment into place for the user to see.

***Listing 8-8.** Fragment Transaction Example*

```
public void showDetails(int index) {
    Log.v(TAG, "in MainActivity showDetails(" + index + ")");

    if (isMultiPane()) {
        // Check what fragment is shown, replace if needed.
        DetailsFragment details = (DetailsFragment)
                getFragmentManager().findFragmentById(R.id.details);
        if (details == null || details.getShownIndex() != index) {
            // Make new fragment to show this selection.
            details = DetailsFragment.newInstance(index);

            // Execute a transaction, replacing any existing
            // fragment with this one inside the frame.
            Log.v(TAG, "about to run FragmentTransaction...");
            FragmentTransaction ft
                    = getFragmentManager().beginTransaction();
            ft.setTransition(
                    FragmentTransaction.TRANSIT_FRAGMENT_FADE);
            //ft.addToBackStack("details");
            ft.replace(R.id.details, details);
            ft.commit();
        }
            // The rest was left out to save space.
}
```

A key concept to understand is that a fragment must live inside a view container, also known as a *view group*. The ViewGroup class includes such things as layouts and their derived classes. FrameLayout is a good choice as the container for the details fragment in the main.xml layout file of your activity. A FrameLayout is simple, and all you need is a simple container for your fragment, without the extra baggage that comes with other types of layouts. The FrameLayout is where your details fragment is going to go. If you had instead specified another <fragment> tag in the activity's layout file instead of a FrameLayout, you would not be able to replace the current fragment with a new fragment (i.e., swap fragments).

The FragmentTransaction is what you use to do your swapping. You tell the fragment transaction that you want to replace whatever is in your frame layout with your new details fragment. You could have avoided all this by locating the resource ID of the details TextView and just setting the text of it to the new text for the new Shakespeare title. But there's another side to fragments that explains why you use FragmentTransactions.

As you know, activities are arranged in a stack, and as you get deeper and deeper into an application, it's not uncommon to have a stack of several activities going at once. When you press the Back button, the topmost activity goes away, and you are returned to the activity below, which resumes for you. This can continue until you're at the home screen again.

This was fine when an activity was just single-purpose, but now that an activity can have several fragments going at once, and because you can go deeper into your application without leaving the topmost activity, Android really needed to extend the Back button stack concept to include fragments as well. In fact, fragments demand this even more. When there are several fragments interacting with each other at the same time in an activity, and there's a transition to new content across several fragments at once, pressing the Back button should cause each of the fragments to roll back one step *together*. To ensure that each fragment properly participates in the rollback, a FragmentTransaction is created and managed to perform that coordination.

Be aware that a back stack for fragments is not required within an activity. You can code your application to let the Back button work at the activity level and not at the fragment level at all. If there's no back stack for your fragments, pressing the Back button will pop the current activity off the stack and return the user to whatever was underneath. If you choose to take advantage of the back stack for fragments, you will want to uncomment in Listing 8-8 the line that says `ft.addToBackStack("details")`. For this particular case, you've hardcoded the tag parameter to be the string `"details"`. This tag should be an appropriate string name that represents the state of the fragments at the time of the transaction. The tag is not necessarily a name for a specific fragment but rather for the fragment transaction and all the fragments in the transaction. You will be able to interrogate the back stack in code using the tag value to delete entries, as well as pop entries off. You will want meaningful tags on these transactions to be able to find the appropriate ones later.

Fragment Transaction Transitions and Animations

One of the very nice things about fragment transactions is that you can perform transitions from an old fragment to a new fragment using transitions and animations. These are not like the animations coming later, in Chapter 18. These are much simpler and do not require in-depth graphics knowledge. Let's use a fragment transaction transition to add special effects when you swap out the old details fragment with a new details fragment. This can add polish to your application, making the switch from the old to the new fragment look smooth.

One method to accomplish this is `setTransition()`, as shown in Listing 8-8. However, there are a few different transitions available. You used a fade in your example, but you can also use the `setCustomAnimations()` method to describe other special effects, such as sliding one fragment out to the right as another slides in from the left. The custom animations use the new object animation definitions, not the old ones. The old anim XML files use tags such as `<translate>`, whereas the new XML files use `<objectAnimator>`. The old standard

XML files are located in the /data/res/anim directory under the appropriate Android SDK platforms directory (such as platforms/android-11 for Honeycomb). There are some new XML files located in the /data/res/animator directory here, too. Your code could be something like

```
ft.setCustomAnimations(android.R.animator.fade_in, android.R.animator.fade_out);
```

which will cause the new fragment to fade in as the old fragment fades out. The first parameter applies to the fragment entering, and the second parameter applies to the fragment exiting. Feel free to explore the Android animator directory for more stock animations. If you'd like to create your own, there's section on the object animator in Chapter 18 to help you. The other very important bit of knowledge you need is that the transition calls need to come before the replace() call; otherwise, they will have no effect.

Using the object animator for special effects on fragments can be a fun way to do transitions. There are two other methods on FragmentTransaction you should know about: hide() and show(). Both of these methods take a fragment as a parameter, and they do exactly what you'd expect. For a fragment in the fragment manager associated to a view container, the methods simply hide or show the fragment in the user interface. The fragment does not get removed from the fragment manager in the process, but it certainly must be tied into a view container in order to affect its visibility. If a fragment does not have a view hierarchy, or if its view hierarchy is not tied into the displayed view hierarchy, then these methods won't do anything.

Once you've specified the special effects for your fragment transaction, you have to tell it the main work that you want done. In your case, you're replacing whatever is in the frame layout with your new details fragment. That's where the replace() method comes in. This is equivalent to calling remove() for any fragments that are already in the frame layout and then add() for your new details fragment, which means you could just call remove() or add() as needed instead.

The final action you must take when working with a fragment transaction is to commit it. The commit() method does not cause things to happen immediately but rather schedules the work for when the UI thread is ready to do it.

Now you should understand why you need to go to so much trouble to change the content in a simple fragment. It's not just that you want to change the text; you might want a special graphics effect during the transition. You may also want to save the transition details in a fragment transaction that you can reverse later. That last point may be confusing, so we'll clarify.

This is not a transaction in the truest sense of the word. When you pop fragment transactions off the back stack, you are not undoing all the data changes that may have taken place. If data changed within your activity, for example, as you created fragment transactions on the back stack, pressing the Back button does not cause the activity data changes to revert back to their previous values. You are merely stepping back through the user interface views the way you came in, just as you do with activities, but in this case it's for fragments. Because of the way fragments are saved and restored, the inner state of a fragment that has been restored from a saved state will depend on what values you saved with the fragment and how you manage to restore them. So your fragments may look the same as they did previously but your activity will not, unless you take steps to restore activity state when you restore fragments.

In your example, you're only working with one view container and bringing in one details fragment. If your user interface were more complicated, you could manipulate other fragments within the fragment transaction. What you are actually doing is beginning the transaction, replacing any existing fragment in your details frame layout with your new details fragment, specifying a fade-in animation, and committing the transaction. You commented out the part where this transaction is added to the back stack, but you could certainly uncomment it to take part in the back stack.

The FragmentManager

The `FragmentManager` is a component that takes care of the fragments belonging to an activity. This includes fragments on the back stack and fragments that may just be hanging around. We'll explain.

Fragments should only be created within the context of an activity. This occurs either through the inflation of an activity's layout XML or through direct instantiation using code like that in Listing 8-1. When instantiated through code, a fragment usually gets attached to the activity using a fragment transaction. In either case, the `FragmentManager` class is used to access and manage these fragments for an activity.

You use the `getFragmentManager()` method on either an activity or an attached fragment to retrieve a fragment manager. You saw in Listing 8-8 that a fragment manager is where you get a fragment transaction. Besides getting a fragment transaction, you can also get a fragment using the fragment's ID, its tag, or a combination of bundle and key. The fragment's ID will either be the fragment's resource ID if the fragment was inflated from XML, or it will be the container's resource ID if the fragment was placed into a view using a fragment transaction. A fragment's tag is a String that you can assign in the fragment's XML definition, or when the fragment is placed in a view via a fragment transaction. The bundle and key method of retrieving a fragment only works for fragments that were persisted using the `putFragment()` method.

For getting a fragment, the getter methods include `findFragmentById()`, `findFragmentByTag()`, and `getFragment()`. The `getFragment()` method would be used in conjunction with `putFragment()`, which also takes a bundle, a key, and the fragment to be put. The bundle is most likely going to be the `savedState` bundle, and `putFragment()` will be used in the `onSaveInstanceState()` callback to save the state of the current activity (or another fragment). The `getFragment()` method would probably be called in `onCreate()` to correspond to `putFragment()`, although for a fragment, the bundle is available to the other callback methods, as described earlier.

Obviously, you can't use the `getFragmentManager()` method on a fragment that has not been attached to an activity yet. But it's also true that you can attach a fragment to an activity without making it visible to the user yet. If you do this, you should associate a `String` tag to the fragment so you can get to it in the future. You'd most likely use this method of `FragmentTransaction` to do this:

```
public FragmentTransaction add (Fragment fragment, String tag)
```

In fact, you can have a fragment that does not exhibit a view hierarchy. This might be done to encapsulate certain logic together such that it could be attached to an activity, yet still retain some autonomy from the activity's life cycle and from other fragments. When an activity goes through a re-create cycle due to a device-configuration change, this non-UI fragment could remain largely intact while the activity goes away and comes back again. This would be a good candidate for the `setRetainInstance()` option.

The fragment back stack is also the domain of the fragment manager. Whereas a fragment transaction is used to put fragments onto the back stack, the fragment manager can take fragments off the back stack. This is usually done using the fragment's ID or tag, but it can be done based on position in the back stack or just to pop the topmost fragment.

Finally, the fragment manager has methods for some debugging features, such as turning on debugging messages to LogCat using `enableDebugLogging()` or dumping the current state of the fragment manager to a stream using `dump()`. Note that you turned on fragment manager debugging in the `onCreate()` method of your activity in Listing 8-4.

Caution When Referencing Fragments

It's time to revisit the earlier discussion of the fragment's life cycle and the arguments and saved-state bundles. Android could save one of your fragments at many different times. This means that at the moment your application wants to retrieve that fragment, it's possible that it is not in memory. For this reason, we caution you *not* to think that a variable reference to a fragment is going to remain valid for a long time. If fragments are being replaced in a container view using fragment transactions, any reference to the old fragment is now pointing to a fragment that is possibly on the back stack. Or a fragment may get detached from the activity's view hierarchy during an application configuration change such as a screen rotation. Be careful.

If you're going to hold onto a reference to a fragment, be aware of when it could get saved away; when you need to find it again, use one of the getter methods of the fragment manager. If you want to hang onto a fragment reference, such as when an activity is going through a configuration change, you can use the `putFragment()` method with the appropriate bundle. In the case of both activities and fragments, the appropriate bundle is the `savedState` bundle that is used in `onSaveInstanceState()` and that reappears in `onCreate()` (or, in the case of fragments, the other early callbacks of the fragment's life cycle). You will probably never store a direct fragment reference into the arguments bundle of a fragment; if you're tempted to do so, please think very carefully about it first.

The other way you can get to a specific fragment is by querying for it using a known tag or known ID. The getter methods described previously will allow retrieval of fragments from the fragment manager this way, which means you have the option of just remembering the tag or ID of a fragment so that you can retrieve it from the fragment manager using one of those values, as opposed to using `putFragment()` and `getFragment()`.

Saving Fragment State

Another interesting class was introduced in Android 3.2: `Fragment.SavedState`. Using the `saveFragmentInstanceState()` method of `FragmentManager`, you can pass this method a fragment, and it returns an object representing the state of that fragment. You can then use that object when initializing a fragment, using `Fragment`'s `setInitialSavedState()` method. Chapter 9 discusses this in more detail.

ListFragments and <fragment>

There are still a few more things to cover to make your sample application complete. The first is the TitlesFragment class. This is the one that is created via the main.xml file of your main activity. The <fragment> tag serves as your placeholder for where this fragment will go and does not define what the view hierarchy will look like for this fragment. The interesting code for your TitlesFragment is in Listing 8-9. For all of the code please refer to the source code files. TitlesFragment displays the list of titles for your application.

Listing 8-9. TitlesFragment Java Code

```
public class TitlesFragment extends ListFragment {
    private MainActivity myActivity = null;
    int mCurCheckPosition = 0;

    @Override
    public void onAttach(Activity myActivity) {
        Log.v(MainActivity.TAG,
            "in TitlesFragment onAttach; activity is: " + myActivity);
        super.onAttach(myActivity);
        this.myActivity = (MainActivity)myActivity;
    }


    @Override
    public void onActivityCreated(Bundle savedState) {
        Log.v(MainActivity.TAG,
            "in TitlesFragment onActivityCreated. savedState contains:");
        if(savedState != null) {
            for(String key : savedState.keySet()) {
                Log.v(MainActivity.TAG, "    " + key);
            }
        }
        else {
            Log.v(MainActivity.TAG, "    savedState is null");
        }
        super.onActivityCreated(savedState);

        // Populate list with your static array of titles.
        setListAdapter(new ArrayAdapter<String>(getActivity(),
                android.R.layout.simple_list_item_1,
                Shakespeare.TITLES));

        if (savedState != null) {
            // Restore last state for checked position.
            mCurCheckPosition = savedState.getInt("curChoice", 0);
        }

        // Get your ListFragment's ListView and update it
        ListView lv = getListView();
        lv.setChoiceMode(ListView.CHOICE_MODE_SINGLE);
        lv.setSelection(mCurCheckPosition);
```

```
        // Activity is created, fragments are available
        // Go ahead and populate the details fragment
        myActivity.showDetails(mCurCheckPosition);
    }
    @Override
    public void onSaveInstanceState(Bundle outState) {
        Log.v(MainActivity.TAG, "in TitlesFragment onSaveInstanceState");
        super.onSaveInstanceState(outState);
        outState.putInt("curChoice", mCurCheckPosition);
    }

    @Override
    public void onListItemClick(ListView l, View v, int pos, long id) {
        Log.v(MainActivity.TAG,
            "in TitlesFragment onListItemClick. pos = "
            + pos);
        myActivity.showDetails(pos);
        mCurCheckPosition = pos;
    }

    @Override
    public void onDetach() {
        Log.v(MainActivity.TAG, "in TitlesFragment onDetach");
        super.onDetach();
        myActivity = null;
    }
}
```

Unlike DetailsFragment, for this fragment you don't do anything in the onCreateView() callback. This is because you're extending the ListFragment class, which contains a ListView already. The default onCreateView() for a ListFragment creates this ListView for you and returns it. It's not until onActivityCreated() that you do any real application logic. By this time in your application, you can be sure that the activity's view hierarchy, plus this fragment's, has been created. The resource ID for that ListView is android.R.id.list1, but you can always call getListView() if you need to get a reference to it, which you do in onActivityCreated(). Because ListFragment manages the ListView, do not attach the adapter to the ListView directly. You must use the ListFragment's setListAdapter() method instead. The activity's view hierarchy is now set up, so you're safe going back into the activity to do the showDetails() call.

At this point in your sample activity's life, you've added a list adapter to your list view, you've restored the current position (if you came back from a restore, due perhaps to a configuration change), and you've asked the activity (in showDetails()) to set the text to correspond to the selected Shakespearean title.

Your TitlesFragment class also has a listener on the list so when the user clicks another title, the onListItemClick() callback is called, and you switch the text to correspond to that title, again using the showDetails() method.

Another difference between this fragment and the earlier details fragment is that when this fragment is being destroyed and re-created, you save state in a bundle (the value of the current position in the list), and you read it back in onCreate(). Unlike the details fragments that get swapped in and out of the FrameLayout on your activity's layout, there is just one titles fragment to think about. So when there is a configuration change and your titles fragment is going through a save-and-restore operation, you want to remember where you were. With the details fragments, you can re-create them without having to remember the previous state.

Invoking a Separate Activity When Needed

There's a piece of code we haven't talked about yet, and that is in showDetails() when you're in portrait mode and the details fragment won't fit properly on the same page as the titles fragment. If the screen real estate won't permit feasible viewing of a fragment that would otherwise be shown alongside the other fragments, you will need to launch a separate activity to show the user interface of that fragment. For your sample application, you implement a details activity; the code is in Listing 8-10.

***Listing 8-10.** Showing a New Activity When a Fragment Doesn't Fit*

```
public class DetailsActivity extends Activity {

    @Override
    public void onCreate(Bundle savedInstanceState) {
        Log.v(MainActivity.TAG, "in DetailsActivity onCreate");
        super.onCreate(savedInstanceState);

        if (getResources().getConfiguration().orientation
                == Configuration.ORIENTATION_LANDSCAPE) {
            // If the screen is now in landscape mode, it means
            // that your MainActivity is being shown with both
            // the titles and the text, so this activity is
            // no longer needed. Bail out and let the MainActivity
            // do all the work.
            finish();
            return;
        }

        if(getIntent() != null) {
            // This is another way to instantiate a details
            // fragment.
            DetailsFragment details =
                DetailsFragment.newInstance(getIntent().getExtras());

            getFragmentManager().beginTransaction()
                .add(android.R.id.content, details)
                .commit();
        }
    }
}
```

There are several interesting aspects to this code. For one thing, it is really easy to implement. You make a simple determination of the device's orientation, and as long as you're in portrait mode, you set up a new details fragment within this details activity. If you're in landscape mode, your MainActivity is able to display both the titles fragment and the details fragment, so there is no reason to be displaying this activity at all. You may wonder why you would ever launch this activity if you're in landscape mode, and the answer is, you wouldn't. However, once this activity has been started in portrait mode, if the user rotates the device to landscape mode, this details activity will get restarted due to the configuration change. So now the activity is starting up, and it's in landscape mode. At that moment, it makes sense to finish this activity and let the `MainActivity` take over and do all the work.

Another interesting aspect about this details activity is that you never set the root content view using `setContentView()`. So how does the user interface get created? If you look carefully at the `add()` method call on the fragment transaction, you will see that the view container to which you add the fragment is specified as the resource `android.R.id.content`. This is the top-level view container for an activity, and therefore when you attach your fragment view hierarchy to this container, your fragment view hierarchy becomes the only view hierarchy for the activity. You used the very same `DetailsFragment` class as before with the other `newInstance()` method to create the fragment (the one that takes a bundle as a parameter), then you simply attached it to the top of the activity's view hierarchy. This causes the fragment to be displayed within this new activity.

From the user's point of view, they are now looking at just the details fragment view, which is the text from the Shakespearean play. If the user wants to select a different title, they press the Back button, which pops this activity to reveal your main activity (with the titles fragment only). The other choice for the user is to rotate the device to get back to landscape mode. Then your details activity will call `finish()` and go away, revealing the also-rotated main activity underneath.

When the device is in portrait mode, if you're not showing the details fragment in your main activity, you should have a separate `main.xml` layout file for portrait mode like the one in Listing 8-11.

***Listing 8-11.** The Layout for a Portrait Main Activity*

```
<?xml version="1.0" encoding="utf-8"?>
<!-- This file is res/layout/main.xml -->
<LinearLayout xmlns:android="http://schemas.android.com/apk/res/android"
        android:orientation="vertical"
        android:layout_width="match_parent"
        android:layout_height="match_parent">

    <fragment class="com.androidbook.fragments.bard.TitlesFragment"
            android:id="@+id/titles"
            android:layout_width="match_parent"
            android:layout_height="match_parent" />

</LinearLayout>
```

Of course, you could make this layout whatever you want it to be. For your purposes here, you simply make it show the titles fragment by itself. It's very nice that your titles fragment class doesn't need to include much code to deal with the device reconfiguration.

Take a moment to view this application's manifest file. In it you find the main activity with a category of `LAUNCHER` so that it will appear in the device's list of apps. Then you have the separate `DetailsActivity` with a category of `DEFAULT`. This allows you to start the details activity from code but will not show the details activity as an app in the App list.

Persistence of Fragments

When you play with this sample application, make sure you rotate the device (pressing Ctrl+F11 rotates the device in the emulator). You will see that the device rotates, and the fragments rotate right along with it. If you watch the LogCat messages, you will see a lot of them for this application. In particular, during a device rotation, pay careful attention to the messages about fragments; not only does the activity get destroyed and re-created, but the fragments do also.

So far, you only wrote a tiny bit of code on the titles fragment to remember the current position in the titles list across restarts. You didn't do anything in the details fragment code to handle reconfigurations, and that's because you didn't need to. Android will take care of hanging onto the fragments that are in the fragment manager, saving them away, then restoring them when the activity is being re-created. You should realize that the fragments you get back after the reconfiguration is complete are very likely not the same fragments in memory that you had before. These fragments have been reconstructed for you. Android saved the arguments bundle and the knowledge of which type of fragment it was, and it stored the saved-state bundles for each fragment that contain saved-state information about the fragment to use to restore it on the other side.

The LogCat messages show you the fragments going through their life cycles in sync with the activity. You will see that your details fragment gets re-created, but your `newInstance()` method does not get called again. Instead, Android uses the default constructor, attaches the arguments bundle to it, and then starts calling the callbacks on the fragment. This is why it is so important not to do anything fancy in the `newInstance()` method: when the fragment gets re-created, it won't do it through `newInstance()`.

You should also appreciate by now that you've been able to reuse your fragments in a few different places. The titles fragment was used in two different layouts, but if you look at the titles fragment code, it doesn't worry about the attributes of each layout. You could make the layouts rather different from each other, and the titles fragment code would look the same. The same can be said of the details fragment. It was used in your main landscape layout and within the details activity all by itself. Again, the layout for the details fragment could have been very different between the two, and the code of the details fragment would be the same. The code of the details activity was very simple, also.

So far, you've explored two of the fragment types: the base `Fragment` class and the `ListFragment` subclass. `Fragment` has other subclasses: the `DialogFragment`, `PreferenceFragment`, and `WebViewFragment`. We'll cover `DialogFragment` and `PreferenceFragment` in Chapters 10 and 11, respectively.

Communications with Fragments

Because the fragment manager knows about all fragments attached to the current activity, the activity or any fragment in that activity can ask for any other fragment using the getter methods described earlier. Once the fragment reference has been obtained, the activity or fragment could cast the reference appropriately and then call methods directly on that activity or fragment. This would cause your fragments to have more knowledge about the other fragments than might normally be desired, but don't forget that you're running this application on a mobile device, so cutting corners can sometimes be justified.

A code snippet is provided in Listing 8-12 to show how one fragment might communicate directly with another fragment. The snippet would be part of one of your extended `Fragment` classes, and `FragmentOther` is a different extended `Fragment` class.

Listing 8-12. Direct Fragment-to-Fragment Communication

```
FragmentOther fragOther =
        (FragmentOther)getFragmentManager().findFragmentByTag("other");
fragOther.callCustomMethod( arg1, arg2 );
```

In Listing 8-12, the current fragment has direct knowledge of the class of the other fragment and also which methods exist on that class. This may be okay because these fragments are part of one application, and it can be easier to simply accept the fact that some fragments will know about other fragments. We'll show you a cleaner way to communicate between fragments in the `DialogFragment` sample application in Chapter 10.

Using startActivity() and setTargetFragment()

A feature of fragments that is very much like activities is the ability of a fragment to start an activity. `Fragment` has a `startActivity()` method and `startActivityForResult()` method. These work just like the ones for activities; when a result is passed back, it will cause the `onActivityResult()` callback to fire on the fragment that started the activity.

There's another communication mechanism you should know about. When one fragment wants to start another fragment, there is a feature that lets the calling fragment set its identity with the called fragment. Listing 8-13 shows an example of what it might look like.

Listing 8-13. Fragment-to-Target-Fragment Setup

```
mCalledFragment = new CalledFragment();
mCalledFragment.setTargetFragment(this, 0);
fm.beginTransaction().add(mCalledFragment, "work").commit();
```

With these few lines, you've created a new `CalledFragment` object, set the target fragment on the called fragment to the current fragment, and added the called fragment to the fragment manager and activity using a fragment transaction. When the called fragment starts to run, it will be able to call `getTargetFragment()`, which will return a reference to the calling fragment. With this reference, the called fragment could invoke methods on the calling fragment or even access view components directly. For example, in Listing 8-14, the called fragment could set text in the UI of the calling fragment directly.

Listing 8-14. Target Fragment-to-Fragment Communication

```
TextView tv = (TextView)
    getTargetFragment().getView().findViewById(R.id.text1);
tv.setText("Set from the called fragment");
```

References

Here are some helpful references to topics you may wish to explore further:

- `www.androidbook.com/proandroid5/projects`: A list of downloadable projects related to this book. The file called `ProAndroid5_Ch08_Fragments.zip` contains all projects from this chapter, listed in separate root directories. There is also a `README.TXT` file that describes exactly how to import projects into an IDE from one of these zip files. It includes some projects that use the Fragment Compatibility SDK for older Androids as well.
- `http://developer.android.com/guide/components/fragments.html`: The Android Developer's Guide page to fragments.
- `http://developer.android.com/design/patterns/multi-pane-layouts.html`: Android design guidelines for multipane layouts.
- `http://developer.android.com/training/basics/fragments/index.html`: Android training page for fragments.

Summary

This chapter introduced the `Fragment` class and its related classes for the manager, transactions, and subclasses. This is a summary of what's been covered in this chapter:

- The `Fragment` class, what it does, and how to use it.
- Why fragments cannot be used without being attached to one and only one activity.
- That although fragments can be instantiated with a static factory method such as `newInstance()`, you must always have a default constructor and a way to save initialization values into an initialization arguments bundle.
- The life cycle of a fragment and how it is intertwined with the life cycle of the activity that owns the fragment.
- `FragmentManager` and its features.
- Managing device configurations using fragments.
- Combining fragments into a single activity, or splitting them between multiple activities.
- Using fragment transactions to change what's displayed to a user, and animating those transitions using cool effects.

- New behaviors that are possible with the Back button when using fragments.
- Using the `<fragment>` tag in a layout.
- Using a `FrameLayout` as a placeholder for a fragment when you want to use transitions.
- `ListFragment` and how to use an adapter to populate the data (very much like a `ListView`).
- Launching a new activity when a fragment can't fit onto the current screen, and how to adjust when a configuration change makes it possible to see multiple fragments again.
- Communicating between fragments, and between a fragment and its activity.

Chapter 9

Responding to Configuration Changes

We've covered a fair bit of material so far, and now seems like a good time to cover configuration changes. When an application is running on a device, and the device's configuration changes (for example, is rotated 90 degrees), your application needs to respond accordingly. The new configuration will most likely look different from the previous configuration. For example, switching from portrait to landscape mode means the screen went from being tall and narrow to being short and wide. The UI elements (buttons, text, lists, and so on) will need to be rearranged, resized, or even removed to accommodate the new configuration.

In Android, a configuration change by default causes the current activity to go away and be re-created. The application itself keeps on running, but it has the opportunity to change how the activity is displayed in response to the configuration change. In the rare case that you need to handle a configuration change without destroying and re-creating your activity, Android provides a way to handle that as well.

Be aware that configuration changes can take on many forms, not just device rotation. If a device gets connected to a dock, that's also a configuration change. So is changing the language of the device. Whatever the new configuration is, as long as you've designed your activity for that configuration, Android takes care of most everything to transition to it, giving the user a seamless experience.

This chapter will take you through the process of a configuration change, from the perspectives of both activities and fragments. We'll show you how to design your application for those transitions and how to avoid traps that could cause your application to crash or misbehave.

The Default Configuration Change Process

The Android operating system keeps track of the current configuration of the device it's running on. Configuration includes lots of factors, and new ones get added all the time. For example, if a device is plugged into a docking station, that represents a change in the device configuration. When a configuration change is detected by Android, callbacks are invoked in running applications to tell them a change is occurring, so an application can properly respond to the change. We'll discuss those callbacks a little later, but for now let's refresh your memory with regard to resources.

One of the great features of Android is that resources get selected for your activity based on the current configuration of the device. You don't need to write code to figure out which configuration is active; you just access resources by name, and Android gets the appropriate resources for you. If the device is in portrait mode and your application requests a layout, you get the portrait layout. If the device is in landscape mode, you get the landscape layout. The code just requests a layout without specifying which one it should get. This is powerful because as new configuration factors get introduced, or new values for configuration factors, the code stays the same. All a developer needs to do is decide if new resources need to be created, and create them as necessary for the new configuration. Then, when the application goes through a configuration change, Android provides the new resources to the application, and everything continues to function as desired.

Because of a great desire to keep things simple, Android destroys the current activity when the configuration changes and creates a new one in its place. This might seem rather harsh, but it's not. It is a bigger challenge to take a running activity and figure out which parts would stay the same and which would not, and then only work with the pieces that need to change.

An activity that's about to be destroyed is properly notified first, giving you a chance to save anything that needs to be saved. When the new activity gets created, it has the opportunity to restore state using data from the previous activity. For a good user experience, obviously you do not want this save and restore to take very long.

It's fairly easy to save any data that you need saved and then let Android throw away the rest and start over, as long as the design of the application and its activities is such that activities don't contain a lot of non-UI stuff that would take a long time to re-create. Therein lies the secret to successful configuration change design: do not put "stuff" inside an activity that cannot be easily re-created during a configuration change.

Keep in mind that our application is not being destroyed, so anything that is in the application context, and not a part of our current activity, will still be there for the new activity. Singletons will still be available, as well as any background threads we might have spun off to do work for our application. Any databases or content providers that we were working with will also still be around. Taking advantage of these makes configuration changes quick and painless. Keep data and business logic outside of activities if you can.

The configuration change process is somewhat similar between activities and fragments. When an activity is being destroyed and re-created, the fragments within that activity get destroyed and re-created. What we need to worry about then is state information about our fragments and activity, such as data currently being displayed to the user, or internal values that we want to preserve. We will save what we want to keep, and pick it up again on the other side when the fragments and activities are being re-created. You'll want to protect data that can't easily be re-created by not letting it get destroyed in the default configuration change process.

The Destroy/Create Cycle of Activities

There are three callbacks to be aware of when dealing with default configuration changes in activities:

- onSaveInstanceState()
- onCreate()
- onRestoreInstanceState()

The first is the callback that Android will invoke when it detects that a configuration change is happening. The activity has a chance to save state that it wants to restore when the new activity gets created at the end of the configuration change. The onSaveInstanceState() callback will be called prior to the call to onStop(). Whatever state exists can be accessed and saved into a Bundle object. This object will get passed in to both of the other callbacks (onCreate() and onRestoreInstanceState()) when the activity is re-created. You only need to put logic in one or the other to restore your activity's state.

The default onSaveInstanceState() callback does some nice things for you. For example, it goes through the currently active view hierarchy and saves the values for each view that has an android:id. This means if you have an EditText view that has received some user input, that input will be available on the other side of the activity destroy/create cycle to populate the EditText before the user gets control back. You do not need to go through and save this state yourself. If you do override onSaveInstanceState(), be sure to call super.onSaveInstanceState() with the bundle object so it can take care of this for you. It's not the views that are saved, only the attributes of their state that should persist across the destroy/create boundary.

To save data in the bundle object, use methods such as putInt() for integers and putString() for strings. There are quite a few methods in the android.os.Bundle class; you are not limited to integers and strings. For example, putParcelable() can be used to save complex objects. Each put is used with a string key, and you will retrieve the value later using the same key used to put the value in. A sample onSaveInstanceState() might look like Listing 9-1.

Listing 9-1. ***Sample onSaveInstanceState()***

```
@Override
public void onSaveInstanceState(Bundle icicle) {
    super.onSaveInstanceState(icicle);
    icicle.putInt("counter", 1);
}
```

Sometimes the bundle is called icicle because it represents a small frozen piece of an activity. In this sample, you only save one value, and it has a key of counter. You could save more values by simply adding more put statements to this callback. The counter value in this example is somewhat temporary because if the application is completely destroyed, the current value will be lost. This could happen if the user turned off their device, for example. In Chapter 11, you'll learn about ways to save values more permanently. This instance state is only meant to hang onto values while the application is running this time. Do not use this mechanism for state that is important to keep for a longer term.

To restore activity state, you access the bundle object to retrieve values that you believe are there. Again, you use methods of the Bundle class such as getInt() and getString() with the appropriate key passed to tell which value you want back. If the key does not exist in the Bundle, a value of 0 or null is passed back (depending on the type of the object being requested). Or you can provide a default value in the appropriate getter method. Listing 9-2 shows a sample onRestoreInstanceState() callback.

Listing 9-2. Sample onRestoreInstanceState()

```
@Override
public void onRestoreInstanceState(Bundle icicle) {
    super.onRestoreInstanceState(icicle);
    int someInt = icicle.getInt("counter", -1);
    // Now go do something with someInt to restore the
    // state of the activity. -1 is the default if no
    // value was found.
}
```

It's up to you whether you restore state in onCreate() or in onRestoreInstanceState(). Many applications will restore state in onCreate() because that is where a lot of initialization is done. One reason to separate the two would be if you're creating an activity class that could be extended. The developers doing the extending might find it easier to just override onRestoreInstanceState() with the code to restore state, as compared to having to override all of onCreate().

What's very important to note here is that you need to be very concerned with references to activities and views and other objects that need to be garbage-collected when the current activity is fully destroyed. If you put something into the saved bundle that refers back to the activity being destroyed, that activity can't be garbage collected. This is very likely a memory leak that could grow and grow until your application crashes. Objects to avoid in bundles include Drawables, Adapters, Views, and anything else that is tied to the activity context. Instead of putting a Drawable into the bundle, serialize the bitmap and save that. Or better yet, manage the bitmaps outside of the activity and fragment instead of inside. Add some sort of reference to the bitmap to the bundle. When it comes time to re-create any Drawables for the new fragment, use the reference to access the outside bitmaps to regenerate your Drawables.

The Destroy/Create Cycle of Fragments

The destroy/create cycle for fragments is very similar to that of activities. A fragment in the process of being destroyed and re-created will have its onSaveInstanceState() callback called, allowing the fragment to save values in a Bundle object for later. One difference is that six fragment callbacks receive this Bundle object when a fragment is being re-created: onInflate(), onCreate(), onCreateView(), onActivityCreated(), onViewCreated(), and onViewStateRestored(). The last two callbacks are more recent, from Honeycomb 3.2 and JellyBean 4.2 respectively. This gives us lots of opportunities to rebuild the internal state of our reconstructed fragment from its previous state.

Android guarantees only that onSaveInstanceState() will be called for a fragment sometime before onDestroy(). That means the view hierarchy may or may not be attached when onSaveInstanceState() is called. Therefore, don't count on traversing the view hierarchy inside of onSaveInstanceState(). For example, if the fragment is on the fragment back stack, no UI will be showing, so no view hierarchy will exist. This is OK of course because if no UI is showing, there is no need to attempt to capture the current values of views to save them. You need to check if a view exists before trying to save its current value, and not consider it an error if the view does not exist.

Just like with activities, be careful not to include items in the bundle object that refer to an activity or to a fragment that might not exist later when this fragment is being re-created. Keep the size of the bundle as small as possible, and as much as possible store long-lasting data outside of activities and fragments and simply refer to it from your activities and fragments. Then your destroy/create cycles will go that much faster, you'll be much less likely to create a memory leak, and your activity and fragment code should be easier to maintain.

Using FragmentManager to Save Fragment State

Fragments have another way to save state, in addition to, or instead of, Android notifying the fragments that their state should be saved. With Honeycomb 3.2, the FragmentManager class got a saveFragmentInstanceState() method that can be called to generate an object of the class Fragment.SavedState. The methods mentioned in the previous sections for saving state do so within the internals of Android. While we know that the state is being saved, we do not have any direct access to it. This method of saving state gives you an object that represents the saved state of a fragment and allows you to control if and when a fragment is created from that state.

The way to use a Fragment.SavedState object to restore a fragment is through the setInitialSavedState() method of the Fragment class. In Chapter 8, you learned that it is best to create new fragments using a static factory method (for example, newInstance()). Within this method, you saw how a default constructor is called and then an arguments bundle is attached. You could instead call the setInitialSavedState() method to set it up for restoration to a previous state.

There are a few caveats you should know about this method of saving fragment state:

- The fragment to be saved must currently be attached to the fragment manager.
- A new fragment created using this saved state must be the same class type as the fragment it was created from.
- The saved state cannot contain dependencies on other fragments. Other fragments may not exist when the saved fragment is re-created.

Using setRetainInstance on a Fragment

A fragment can avoid being destroyed and re-created on a configuration change. If the setRetainInstance() method is called with an argument of true, the fragment will be retained in the application when its activity is being destroyed and re-created. The fragment's onDestroy() callback will not be called, nor will onCreate(). The onDetach() callback will be called because the fragment must be detached from the activity that's going away, and onAttach() and onActivityCreated() will be called because the fragment is attached to a new activity. This only works for fragments that are not on the back stack. It is especially useful for fragments that do not have a UI.

This feature is very powerful in that you can use a non-UI fragment to handle references to your data objects and background threads, and call `setRetainInstance(true)` on this fragment so it won't get destroyed and re-created on a configuration change. The added bonus is that during the normal configuration change process, the non-UI fragment callbacks `onDetach()` and `onAttach()` will switch the activity reference from the old to the new.

Deprecated Configuration Change Methods

A couple of methods on `Activity` have been deprecated, so you should no longer use them:

- `getLastNonConfigurationInstance()`
- `onRetainNonConfigurationInstance()`

These methods previously allowed you to save an arbitrary object from an activity that was being destroyed, to be passed to the next instance of the activity that was being created. Although they were useful, you should now use the methods described earlier instead to manage data between instances of activities in the destroy/create cycle.

Handling Configuration Changes Yourself

So far, you've seen how Android handles configuration changes for you. It takes care of destroying and re-creating activities and fragments, pulling in the best resources for the new configuration, retaining any user-entered data, and giving you the opportunity to execute some extra logic in some callbacks. This is usually going to be your best option. But when it isn't, when you have to handle a configuration change yourself, Android provides a way out. This isn't recommended because it is then completely up to you to determine what needs to change due to the change, and then for you to take care of making all the changes. As mentioned before, there are many configuration changes besides just an orientation change. Luckily, you don't necessarily have to handle all configuration changes yourself.

The first step to handling configuration changes yourself is to declare in the `<activity>` tag in `AndroidManifest.xml` file which changes you're going to handle using the `android:configChanges` attribute. Android will handle the other configuration changes using the previously described methods. You can specify as many configuration change types as needed by or'ing them together with the '|' symbol, like this:

```
<activity ...   android:configChanges="orientation|keyboardHidden" ... >
```

The complete list of configuration change types can be found on the reference page for R.attr. Be aware that if you target API 13 or higher and you need to handle `orientation`, you also need to handle `screenSize`.

The default process for a configuration change is the invoking of callbacks to destroy and re-create the activity or fragment. When you've declared that you will handle the specific configuration change, the process changes so only the `onConfigurationChanged()` callback is invoked instead, on the activity and its fragments. Android passes in a Configuration object so the callback knows what the new configuration is. It is up to the callback to determine what might have changed; however, since you likely handle only a small number of configuration changes yourself, it shouldn't be too hard to figure this out.

You'd really only want to handle a configuration change yourself when there is very little to be done, when you could skip destroying and re-creating. For example, if the activity layout for portrait and landscape is the same layout and all image resources are the same, destroying and re-creating the activity doesn't really accomplish anything. In this case it would be fairly safe to declare that you will handle the orientation configuration change. During an orientation change of your activity, the activity would remain intact and simply re-render itself in the new orientation using the existing resources such as the layout, images, strings, etc. But it's really not that big a deal to just let Android take care of things if you can.

References

Here are some helpful references to topics you may wish to explore further:

- `www.androidbook.com/proandroid5/projects`: A list of downloadable projects related to this book. For this chapter, look for a ZIP file called `ProAndroid5_Ch09_ConfigChanges.zip`. This ZIP file contains all the projects from this chapter, listed in separate root directories. There is also a `README.TXT` file that describes exactly how to import projects into your IDE from one of these ZIP files.
- `http://developer.android.com/guide/topics/fundamentals/activities.html#SavingActivityState`: The Android Developer's Guide, which discusses saving and restoring state.
- `http://developer.android.com/guide/topics/resources/runtime-changes.html`: The Android API Guide for Handling Runtime Changes.

Summary

Let's conclude this chapter by quickly enumerating what you have learned about handling configuration changes:

- Activities by default get destroyed and re-created during configuration changes. So do fragments.
- Avoid putting lots of data and logic into activities so configuration changes occur quickly.
- Let Android provide the appropriate resources.
- Use singletons to hold data outside of activities to make it easier to destroy and re-create activities during configuration changes.
- Take advantage of the default `onSaveInstanceState()` callback to save UI state on views with `android:ids`.
- If a fragment can survive with no issues across an activity destroy-and-create cycle, use `setRetainInstance()` to tell Android it doesn't need to destroy and create the fragment.

Chapter 10

Working with Dialogs

The Android SDK offers extensive support for dialogs. A dialog is a smaller window that pops up in front of the current window to show an urgent message, to prompt the user for a piece of input, or to show some sort of status like the progress of a download. The user is generally expected to interact with the dialog and then return to the window underneath to continue with the application. Technically, Android allows a dialog fragment to also be embedded within an activity's layout, and we'll cover that as well.

Dialogs that are explicitly supported in Android include the alert, prompt, pick-list, single-choice, multiple-choice, progress, time-picker, and date-picker dialogs. (This list could vary depending on the Android release.) Android also supports custom dialogs for other needs. The primary purpose of this chapter is not to cover every single one of these dialogs but to cover the underlying architecture of Android dialogs with a sample application. From there you should be able to use any of the Android dialogs.

It's important to note that Android 3.0 added dialogs based on fragments. The expectation from Google is that developers will only use fragment dialogs, even in the versions of Android before 3.0. This can be done with the fragment-compatibility library. For this reason, this chapter focuses on `DialogFragment`.

Using Dialogs in Android

Dialogs in Android are asynchronous, which provides flexibility. However, if you are accustomed to a programming framework where dialogs are primarily synchronous (such as Microsoft Windows, or JavaScript dialogs in web pages), you might find asynchronous dialogs a bit unintuitive. With a synchronous dialog, the line of code after the dialog is shown does not run until the dialog has been dismissed. This means the next line of code could interrogate which button was pressed, or what text was typed into the dialog. In Android however, dialogs are asynchronous. As soon as the dialog has been shown, the next line of code runs, even though the user hasn't touched the dialog yet. Your application has to deal with this fact by implementing callbacks from the dialog, to allow the application to be notified of user interaction with the dialog.

This also means your application has the ability to dismiss the dialog from code, which is powerful. If the dialog is displaying a busy message because your application is doing something, as soon as your application has completed that task, it can dismiss the dialog from code.

Understanding Dialog Fragments

In this section, you learn how to use dialog fragments to present a simple alert dialog and a custom dialog that is used to collect prompt text.

DialogFragment Basics

Before we show you working examples of a prompt dialog and an alert dialog, we would like to cover the high-level idea of dialog fragments. Dialog-related functionality uses a class called `DialogFragment`. A `DialogFragment` is derived from the class `Fragment` and behaves much like a fragment. You will then use the `DialogFragment` as the base class for your dialogs. Once you have a derived dialog from this class such as

```
public class MyDialogFragment extends DialogFragment { ... }
```

you can then show this dialog fragment `MyDialogFragment` as a dialog using a fragment transaction. Listing 10-1 shows a code snippet to do this.

***Listing 10-1.** Showing a Dialog Fragment*

```
public class SomeActivity extends Activity
{
    //....other activity functions
    public void showDialog()
    {
        //construct MyDialogFragment
        MyDialogFragment mdf = MyDialogFragment.newInstance(arg1,arg2);
        FragmentManager fm = getFragmentManager();
        FragmentTransaction ft = fm.beginTransaction();
        mdf.show(ft,"my-dialog-tag");
    }
    //....other activity functions
}
```

> **Note** We provide a link to a downloadable project at the end of this chapter in the "References" section. You can use this download to experiment with the code and the concepts presented in this chapter.

From Listing 10-1, the steps to show a dialog fragment are as follows:

1. Create a dialog fragment.
2. Get a fragment transaction.
3. Show the dialog using the fragment transaction from step 2.

Let's talk about each of these steps.

Constructing a Dialog Fragment

When constructing a dialog fragment, the rules are the same as when building any other kind of fragment. The recommended pattern is to use a factory method such as `newInstance()` as you did before. Inside that `newInstance()` method, you use the default constructor for your dialog fragment, and then you add an arguments bundle that contains your passed-in parameters. You don't want to do other work inside this method because you must make sure that what you do here is the same as what Android does when it restores your dialog fragment from a saved state. And all that Android does is to call the default constructor and re-create the arguments bundle on it.

Overriding onCreateView

When you inherit from a dialog fragment, you need to override one of two methods to provide the view hierarchy for your dialog. The first option is to override `onCreateView()` and return a view. The second option is to override `onCreateDialog()` and return a dialog (like the one constructed by an `AlertDialog.Builder`, which we'll get to shortly).

Listing 10-2 shows an example of overriding the `onCreateView()`.

***Listing 10-2.** Overriding `onCreateView()` of a DialogFragment*

```
public class MyDialogFragment extends DialogFragment
    implements View.OnClickListener
{
    .....other functions
    public View onCreateView(LayoutInflater inflater,
            ViewGroup container, Bundle savedInstanceState)
    {
        //Create a view by inflating desired layout
        View v = inflater.inflate(R.layout.prompt_dialog, container, false);

        //you can locate a view and set values
        TextView tv = (TextView)v.findViewById(R.id.promptmessage);
        tv.setText(this.getPrompt());

        //You can set callbacks on buttons
        Button dismissBtn = (Button)v.findViewById(R.id.btn_dismiss);
        dismissBtn.setOnClickListener(this);
```

```
        Button saveBtn = (Button)v.findViewById(R.id.btn_save);
        saveBtn.setOnClickListener(this);
        return v;
    }
    .....other functions
}
```

In Listing 10-2, you are loading a view identified by a layout. Then you look for two buttons and set up callbacks on them. This is very similar to how you created the details fragment in Chapter 8. However, unlike the earlier fragments, a dialog fragment has another way to create the view hierarchy.

Overriding onCreateDialog

As an alternate to supplying a view in onCreateView(), you can override onCreateDialog() and supply a dialog instance. Listing 10-3 supplies sample code for this approach.

Listing 10-3. Overriding onCreateDialog() of a DialogFragment

```
public class MyDialogFragment extends DialogFragment
    implements DialogInterface.OnClickListener
{
    .....other functions
    @Override
    public Dialog onCreateDialog(Bundle icicle)
    {
        AlertDialog.Builder b = new AlertDialog.Builder(getActivity())
          .setTitle("My Dialog Title")
          .setPositiveButton("Ok", this)
          .setNegativeButton("Cancel", this)
          .setMessage(this.getMessage());
        return b.create();
    }
    .....other functions
}
```

In this example, you use the alert dialog builder to create a dialog object to return. This works well for simple dialogs. The first option of overriding onCreateView() is equally easy and provides much more flexibility.

AlertDialog.Builder is actually a carryover from pre-3.0 Android. This is one of the old ways to create a dialog, and it's still available to you to create dialogs within DialogFragments. As you can see, it's fairly easy to build a dialog by calling the various methods available, as we've done here.

Displaying a Dialog Fragment

Once you have a dialog fragment constructed, you need a fragment transaction to show it. Like all other fragments, operations on dialog fragments are conducted through fragment transactions.

The show() method on a dialog fragment takes a fragment transaction as an input. You can see this in Listing 10-1. The show() method uses the fragment transaction to add this dialog to the activity and then commits the fragment transaction. However, the show() method does not add the transaction to the back stack. If you want to do this, you need to add this transaction to the back stack first and then pass it to the show() method. The show() method of a dialog fragment has the following signatures:

```
public int show(FragmentTransaction transaction, String tag)
public int show(FragmentManager manager, String tag)
```

The first show() method displays the dialog by adding this fragment to the passed-in transaction with the specified tag. This method then returns the identifier of the committed transaction.

The second show() method automates getting a transaction from the transaction manager. This is a shortcut method. However, when you use this second method, you don't have an option to add the transaction to the back stack. If you want that control, you need to use the first method. The second method could be used if you wanted to simply display the dialog, and you had no other reason to work with a fragment transaction at that time.

A nice thing about a dialog being a fragment is that the underlying fragment manager does the basic state management. For example, even if the device rotates when a dialog is being displayed, the dialog is reproduced without you performing any state management.

The dialog fragment also offers methods to control the frame in which the dialog's view is displayed, such as the title and the appearance of the frame. Refer to the DialogFragment class documentation to see more of these options; this URL is provided at the end of this chapter.

Dismissing a Dialog Fragment

There are two ways you can dismiss a dialog fragment. The first is to explicitly call the dismiss() method on the dialog fragment in response to a button or some action on the dialog view, as shown in Listing 10-4.

Listing 10-4. Calling dismiss()

```
if (someview.getId() == R.id.btn_dismiss)
{
    //use some callbacks to advise clients
    //of this dialog that it is being dismissed
    //and call dismiss
    dismiss();
    return;
}
```

The dialog fragment's dismiss() method removes the fragment from the fragment manager and then commits that transaction. If there is a back stack for this dialog fragment, then the dismiss() pops the current dialog out of the transaction stack and presents the previous fragment transaction state. Whether there is a back stack or not, calling dismiss() results in calling the standard dialog fragment destroy callbacks, including onDismiss().

One thing to note is that you can't rely on onDismiss() to conclude that a dismiss() has been called by your code. This is because onDismiss() is also called when a device configuration changes and hence is not a good indicator of what the user did to the dialog itself. If the dialog is being displayed when the user rotates the device, the dialog fragment sees onDismiss() called even though the user did not press a button in the dialog. Instead, you should always rely on explicit button clicks on the dialog view.

If the user presses the Back button while the dialog fragment is displayed, this causes the onCancel() callback to fire on the dialog fragment. By default, Android makes the dialog fragment go away, so you don't need to call dismiss() on the fragment yourself. But if you want the calling activity to be notified that the dialog has been cancelled, you need to invoke logic from within onCancel() to make that happen. This is a difference between onCancel() and onDismiss() with dialog fragments. With onDismiss(), you can't be sure exactly what happened that caused the onDismiss() callback to fire. You might also have noticed that a dialog fragment does not have a cancel() method, just dismiss(); but as we said, when a dialog fragment is being cancelled by pressing the Back button, Android takes care of cancelling/dismissing it for you.

The other way to dismiss a dialog fragment is to present another dialog fragment. The way you dismiss the current dialog and present the new one is slightly different than just dismissing the current dialog. Listing 10-5 shows an example.

Listing 10-5. Setting Up a Dialog for a Back Stack

```
if (someview.getId() == R.id.btn_invoke_another_dialog)
{
    Activity act = getActivity();
    FragmentManager fm = act.getFragmentManager();
    FragmentTransaction ft = fm.beginTransaction();
    ft.remove(this);

    ft.addToBackStack(null);
    //null represents no name for the back stack transaction

    HelpDialogFragment hdf =
        HelpDialogFragment.newInstance(R.string.helptext);
    hdf.show(ft, "HELP");
    return;
}
```

Within a single transaction, you're removing the current dialog fragment and adding the new dialog fragment. This has the effect of making the current dialog disappear visually and making the new dialog appear. If the user presses the Back button, because you've saved this transaction on the back stack, the new dialog is dismissed and the previous dialog is displayed. This is a handy way of displaying a help dialog, for example.

Implications of a Dialog Dismiss

When you add any fragment to a fragment manager, the fragment manager does the state management for that fragment. This means when a device configuration changes (for example, the device rotates), the activity is restarted and the fragments are also restarted. You saw this earlier when you rotated the device while running the Shakespeare sample application in chapter 8.

A device-configuration change doesn't affect dialogs because they are also managed by the fragment manager. But the implicit behavior of `show()` and `dismiss()` means you can easily lose track of a dialog fragment if you're not careful. The `show()` method automatically adds the fragment to the fragment manager; the `dismiss()` method automatically removes the fragment from the fragment manager. You may have a direct pointer to a dialog fragment before you start showing the fragment. But you can't add this fragment to the fragment manager and later call `show()`, because a fragment can only be added once to the fragment manager. You may plan to retrieve this pointer through restore of the activity. However, if you show and dismiss this dialog, this fragment is implicitly removed from the fragment manager, thereby denying that fragment's ability to be restored and repointed (because the fragment manager doesn't know this fragment exists after it is removed).

If you want to keep the state of a dialog after it is dismissed, you need to maintain the state outside of the dialog either in the parent activity or in a non-dialog fragment that hangs around for a longer time.

DialogFragment Sample Application

In this section, you review a sample application that demonstrates these concepts of a dialog fragment. You also examine communication between a fragment and the activity that contains it. To make it all happen, you need five Java files:

- `MainActivity.java`: The main activity of your application. It displays a simple view with help text in it and a menu from which dialogs can be started.
- `PromptDialogFragment.java`: An example of a dialog fragment that defines its own layout in XML and allows input from the user. It has three buttons: Save, Dismiss (cancel), and Help.
- `AlertDialogFragment.java`: An example of a dialog fragment that uses the `AlertBuilder` class to create a dialog within this fragment. This is the old-school way of creating a dialog.
- `HelpDialogFragment.java`: A very simple fragment that displays a help message from the application's resources. The specific help message is identified when a help dialog object is created. This help fragment can be shown from both the main activity and the prompt dialog fragment.
- `OnDialogDoneListener.java`: An interface that you require your activity to implement in order to get messages back from the fragments. Using an interface means your fragments don't need to know much about the calling activity, except that it must have implemented this interface. This helps encapsulate functionality where it belongs. From the activity's point of view, it has a common way to receive information back from fragments without needing to know too much about them.

There are three layouts for this application: for the main activity, for the prompt dialog fragment, and for the help dialog fragment. Note that you don't need a layout for the alert dialog fragment because the AlertBuilder takes care of that layout for you internally. When you're done, the application looks like Figure 10-1.

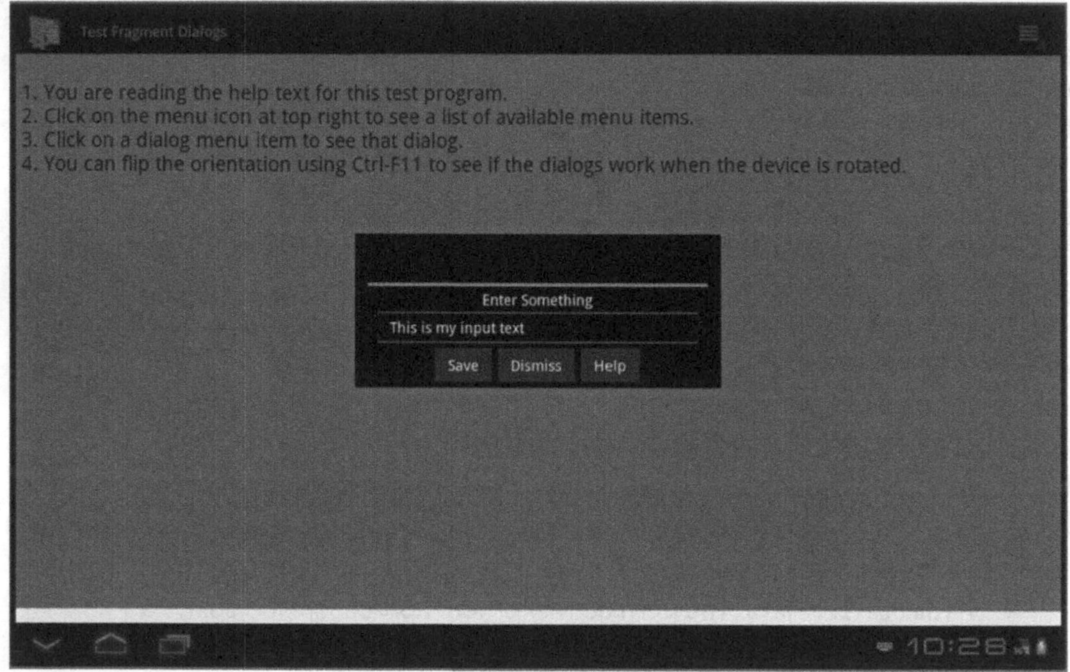

***Figure 10-1.** The user interface for the dialog fragment sample application*

Dialog Sample: MainActivity

Let's get to the source code, which you can download from the book's web site (see the "References" section). We'll use the DialogFragmentDemo project. Open up the source code for MainActivity.java before we continue.

The code for the main activity is very straightforward. You display a simple page of text and set up a menu. Each menu item invokes an activity method, and each method does basically the same thing: gets a fragment transaction, creates a new fragment, and shows the fragment. Note that each fragment has a unique tag that's used with the fragment transaction. This tag becomes associated with the fragment in the fragment manager, so you can locate these fragments later by tag name. The fragment can also determine its own tag value with the getTag() method on Fragment.

The last method definition in the main activity is onDialogDone(), which is a callback that is part of the OnDialogDoneListener interface that your activity is implementing. As you can see, the callback supplies a tag of the fragment that is calling you, a boolean value indicating whether the dialog fragment was cancelled, and a message. For your purposes, you merely want to log the information to LogCat; you also show it to the user using Toast. Toast will be covered later in this chapter.

Dialog Sample: OnDialogDoneListener

So that you can know when a dialog has gone away, create a listener interface that your dialog callers implement. The code of the interface is in OnDialogDoneListener.java.

This is a very simple interface, as you can see. You choose only one callback for this interface, which the activity must implement. Your fragments don't need to know the specifics of the calling activity, only that the calling activity must implement the `OnDialogDoneListener` interface; therefore the fragments can call this callback to communicate with the calling activity. Depending on what the fragment is doing, there could be multiple callbacks in the interface. For this sample application, you're showing the interface separately from the fragment class definitions. For easier management of code, you could embed the fragment listener interface inside of the fragment class definition itself, thus making it easier to keep the listener and the fragment in sync with each other.

Dialog Sample: PromptDialogFragment

Now let's look at your first fragment, `PromptDialogFragment`, whose layout is in /res/layout/prompt_dialog.xml and Java code is under /src in PromptDialogFragment.java.

This prompt dialog layout looks like many you've seen previously. There is a `TextView` to serve as the prompt; an `EditText` to take the user's input; and three buttons for saving the input, dismissing (cancelling) the dialog fragment, and popping a help dialog.

The `PromptDialogFragment` Java code starts out looking just like your earlier fragments. You have a `newInstance()` static method to create new objects, and within this method you call the default constructor, build an arguments bundle, and attach it to your new object. Next, you have something new in the `onAttach()` callback. You want to make sure the activity you just got attached to has implemented the `OnDialogDoneListener` interface. In order to test that, you cast the activity passed in to the `OnDialogDoneListener` interface. Here's that code:

```
try {
    OnDialogDoneListener test = (OnDialogDoneListener)act;
}
catch(ClassCastException cce) {
    // Here is where we fail gracefully.
    Log.e(MainActivity.LOGTAG, "Activity is not listening");
}
```

If the activity does not implement this interface, a `ClassCastException` is thrown. You could handle this exception and deal with it more gracefully, but this example keeps the code as simple as possible.

Next up is the `onCreate()` callback. As is common with fragments, you don't build your user interface here, but you can set the dialog style. This is unique to dialog fragments. You can set both the style and the theme yourself, or you can set just style and use a theme value of zero (0) to let the system choose an appropriate theme for you. Here's that code:

```
int style = DialogFragment.STYLE_NORMAL, theme = 0;
setStyle(style,theme);
```

In onCreateView() you create the view hierarchy for your dialog fragment. Just like other fragments, you do not attach your view hierarchy to the view container passed in (that is, by setting the attachToRoot parameter to false). You then proceed to set up the button callbacks, and you set the dialog prompt text to the prompt that was passed originally to newInstance().

The onCancel() and onDismiss() callbacks are not shown because all they do is logging; you'll be able to see when these callbacks fire during the fragment's lifecycle.

The final callback in the prompt dialog fragment is for the buttons. Once again, you grab a reference to your enclosing activity and cast it to the interface you expect the activity to have implemented. If the user pressed the Save button, you grab the text as entered and call the interface's callback onDialogDone(). This callback takes the tag name of this fragment, a boolean indicating whether this dialog fragment was cancelled, and a message, which in this case is the text typed by the user. Here it is from the MainActivity:

```
public void onDialogDone(String tag, boolean cancelled,
                              CharSequence message) {
    String s = tag + " responds with: " + message;
    if(cancelled)
        s = tag + " was cancelled by the user";
    Toast.makeText(this, s, Toast.LENGTH_LONG).show();
    Log.v(LOGTAG, s);
}
```

To finish handling a click on the Save button, you then call dismiss() to get rid of the dialog fragment. Remember that dismiss() not only makes the fragment go away visually, but also pops the fragment out of the fragment manager so it is no longer available to you.

If the button pressed is Dismiss, you again call the interface callback, this time with no message, and then you call dismiss(). And finally, if the user pressed the Help button, you don't want to lose the prompt dialog fragment, so you do something a little different. We described this earlier. In order to remember the prompt dialog fragment so you can come back to it later, you need to create a fragment transaction to remove the prompt dialog fragment and add the help dialog fragment with the show() method; this needs to go onto the back stack. Notice, too, how the help dialog fragment is created with a reference to a resource ID. This means your help dialog fragment can be used with any help text available to your application.

Dialog Sample: HelpDialogFragment

You created a fragment transaction to go from the prompt dialog fragment to the help dialog fragment, and you placed that fragment transaction on the back stack. This has the effect of making the prompt dialog fragment disappear from view, but it's still accessible through the fragment manager and the back stack. The new help dialog fragment appears in its place and allows the user to read the help text. When the user dismisses the help dialog fragment, the fragment back stack entry is popped, with the effect of the help dialog fragment being dismissed (both visually and from the fragment manager) and the prompt dialog fragment restored to view. This is a pretty easy way to make all this happen. It is very simple yet very powerful; it even works if the user rotates the device while these dialogs are being displayed.

Look at the source code of the HelpDialogFragment.java file and its layout (help_dialog.xml). The point of this dialog fragment is to display help text. The layout is a TextView and a Close button. The Java code should be starting to look familiar to you. There's a newInstance() method to create a new help dialog fragment, an onCreate() method to set the style and theme, and an onCreateView() method to build the view hierarchy. In this particular case, you want to locate a string resource to populate the TextView, so you access the resources through the activity and choose the resource ID that was passed in to newInstance(). Finally, onCreateView() sets up a button-click handler to capture the clicks of the Close button. In this case, you don't need to do anything interesting at the time of dismissal.

This fragment is called two ways: from the activity and from the prompt dialog fragment. When this help dialog fragment is shown from the main activity, dismissing it simply pops the fragment off the top and reveals the main activity underneath. When this help dialog fragment is shown from the prompt dialog fragment, because the help dialog fragment was part of a fragment transaction on the back stack, dismissing it causes the fragment transaction to be rolled back, which pops the help dialog fragment but restores the prompt dialog fragment. The user sees the prompt dialog fragment reappear.

Dialog Sample: AlertDialogFragment

We have one last dialog fragment to show you in this sample application: the alert dialog fragment. Although you could create an alert dialog fragment in a way similar to the help dialog fragment, you can also create a dialog fragment using the old AlertBuilder framework that has worked for many releases of Android. Look at the source code in AlertDialogFragment.java.

You don't need a layout for this one because the AlertBuilder takes care of that for you. Note that this dialog fragment starts out like any other, but instead of an onCreateView() callback, you have a onCreateDialog() callback. You implement either onCreateView() or onCreateDialog() but not both. The return from onCreateDialog() is not a view; it's a dialog. Of interest here is that to get parameters for the dialog, you should be accessing your arguments bundle. In this example application, you only do this for the alert message, but you could access other parameters through the arguments bundle as well.

Notice also that with this type of dialog fragment, you need your fragment class to implement the DialogInterface.OnClickListener, which means your dialog fragment must implement the onClick() callback. This callback is fired when the user acts on the embedded dialog. Once again, you get a reference to the dialog that fired and an indication of which button was pressed. As before, you should be careful not to depend on an onDismiss() because this could fire when there is a device configuration change.

Dialog Sample: Embedded Dialogs

There's one more feature of a DialogFragment that you may have noticed. In the main layout for the application, under the text, is a FrameLayout that can be used to hold a dialog. In the application's menu, the last item causes a fragment transaction to add a new instance of a PromptDialogFragment to the main screen. Without any modifications, the dialog fragment can be displayed embedded in the main layout, and it functions as you would expect.

One thing that is different about this technique is that the code to show the embedded dialog is not the same as the code to do a pop-up dialog. The embedded dialog code looks like this:

```
ft.add(R.id.embeddedDialog, pdf, EMBED_DIALOG_TAG);
ft.commit();
```

This looks just the same as in Chapter 8, when we displayed a fragment in a `FrameLayout`. This time, however, you make sure to pass in a tag name, which is used when the dialog fragment notifies your activity of the user's input.

Dialog Sample: Observations

When you run this sample application, make sure you try all the menu options in different orientations of the device. Rotate the device while the dialog fragments are displayed. You should be pleased to see that the dialogs go with the rotations; you do not need to worry about a lot of code to manage the saving and restoring of fragments due to configuration changes.

The other thing we hope you appreciate is the ease with which you can communicate between the fragments and the activity. Of course, the activity has references, or can get references, to all the available fragments, so it can access methods exposed by the fragments themselves. This isn't the only way to communicate between fragments and the activity. You can always use the getter methods on the fragment manager to retrieve an instance of a managed fragment, and then cast that reference appropriately and call a method on that fragment directly. You can even do this from within another fragment. The degree to which you isolate your fragments from each other with interfaces and through activities, or build in dependencies with fragment-to-fragment communication, is based on how complex your application is and how much reuse you want to achieve.

Working with Toast

A `Toast` is like a mini alert dialog that has a message and displays for a certain amount of time and then goes away automatically. It does not have any buttons. So it can be said that it is a transient alert message. It's called `Toast` because it pops up like toast out of a toaster.

Listing 10-10 shows an example of how you can show a message using `Toast`.

***Listing 10-10.** Using `Toast` for Debugging*

```
//Create a function to wrap a message as a toast
//show the toast
public void reportToast(String message)
{
    String s = MainActivity.LOGTAG + ":" + message;
    Toast.makeText(activity, s, Toast.LENGTH_SHORT).show();
}
```

The makeText() method in Listing 10-10 can take not only an activity but any context object, such as the one passed to a broadcast receiver or a service, for example. This extends the use of Toast outside of activities.

References

- www.androidbook.com/proandroid5/projects: This chapter's test project. The name of the ZIP file is ProAndroid5_ch10_Dialogs.zip. The download includes an example of the date- and time-picker dialogs in PickerDialogFragmentDemo.
- http://developer.android.com/guide/topics/ui/dialogs.html: Android SDK document that provides an excellent introduction to working with Android dialogs. You will find here an explanation of how to use managed dialogs and various examples of available dialogs.
- http://developer.android.com/reference/android/content/DialogInterface.html: The many constants defined for dialogs.
- http://developer.android.com/reference/android/app/AlertDialog.Builder.html: API documentation for the AlertDialog builder class.
- http://developer.android.com/reference/android/app/ProgressDialog.html: API documentation for ProgressDialog.
- http://developer.android.com/guide/topics/ui/controls/pickers.html: An Android tutorial for using the date-picker and time-picker dialogs.

Summary

This chapter discussed asynchronous dialogs and how to use dialog fragments, including the following topics:

- What a dialog is and why you use one
- The asynchronous nature of a dialog in Android
- The three steps of getting a dialog to display on the screen
- Creating a fragment
- Two methods for how a dialog fragment can create a view hierarchy
- How a fragment transaction is involved in displaying a dialog fragment, and how to get one
- What happens when the user presses the Back button while viewing a dialog fragment

- The back stack, and managing dialog fragments
- What happens when a button on a dialog fragment is clicked, and how you deal with it
- A clean way to communicate back to the calling activity from a dialog fragment
- How one dialog fragment can call another dialog fragment and still get back to the previous dialog fragment
- The `Toast` class and how it can be used as a simple alert pop-up

Chapter 11

Working with Preferences and Saving State

Android offers a robust and flexible framework for dealing with settings, also known as preferences. And by settings, we mean those feature choices that a user makes and saves to customize an application to their liking. (In this chapter, the terms settings and preferences will be used interchangeably.) For example, if the user wants a notification via a ringtone or vibration or not at all, that is a preference the user saves; the application remembers the choice until the user changes it. Android provides simple APIs that hide the management and persisting of preferences. It also provides prebuilt user interfaces that you can use to let the user make preference selections. Because of the power built into the Android preferences framework, we can also use preferences for more general-purpose storing of application state, to allow our application to pick up where it left off, should our application go away and come back later. As another example, a game's high scores could be stored as preferences, although you'll want to use your own UI to display them.

This chapter covers how to implement your own settings screens for your application, how to interact with Android system settings, and how to use settings to secretly save application state, and it also provides best-practice guidance. You'll discover how to make your settings look good on small screens as well as larger screens such as those found on tablets.

Exploring the Preferences Framework

Android's preferences framework builds from the individual settings choices, to a hierarchy of screens that contain settings choices. Settings could be binary settings such as on/off, or text input, or a numeric value, or could be a selection from a list of choices. Android uses a `PreferenceManager` to provide settings values to applications. The framework takes care of making and persisting changes, and notifying the application when a setting changes or is about to change. While settings are persisted in files, applications don't deal directly with the files. The files are hidden away, and you'll see shortly where they are.

As with views covered in Chapter 3, preferences can be specified with XML, or by writing code. For this chapter, you'll work with a sample application that demonstrates the different types of choices. XML is the preferred way to specify a preference, so that is how the application was written. XML specifies the lowest-level settings, plus how to group settings together into categories and screens. For reference, the sample application for this chapter presents the following settings as shown in Figure 11-1.

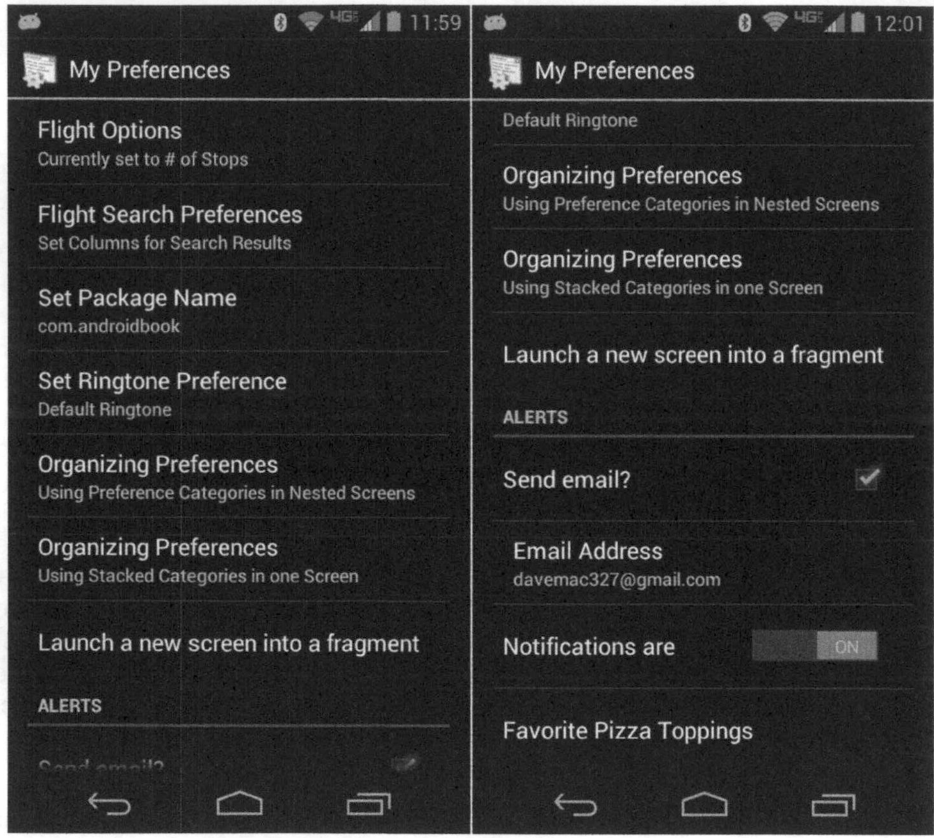

***Figure 11-1.** The main settings from the sample app preference UI. Due to the screen's height, it has been shown with the top on the left and the bottom on the right. Notice the overlap between the two images*

Android provides an end-to-end preferences framework. This means the framework lets you define your preferences, display the setting(s) to the user, and persist the user's selection to the data store. You define your preferences in XML under `/res/xml/`. To show preferences to the user, you write an activity class that extends a predefined Android class called `android.preference.PreferenceActivity` and use fragments to handle the screens of preferences. The framework takes care of the rest (displaying and persisting). Within your application, your code will get references to specific preferences. With a preference reference, you can get the current value of the preference.

In order for preferences to be saved across user sessions, the current values must be saved somewhere. The Android framework takes care of persisting preferences in an XML file within the application's `/data/data` directory on the device (see Figure 11-2).

Threads | Heap | Allocation Tracker | File Explorer

Name	Size	Date	Time	Permissions
⊞ acct		2013-11-24	12:11	drwxr-xr-x
⊞ cache		2013-11-24	13:15	drwxrwx---
⊞ config		2013-11-24	12:11	dr-x------
d		2013-11-24	12:11	lrwxrwxrwx
⊟ data		2012-10-13	14:40	drwxrwx--x
⊟ data		2013-11-24	12:16	drwxrwx--x
⊟ com.androidbook.preferences.main		2013-11-24	12:16	drwxr-x--x
⊞ cache		2013-11-24	12:16	drwxrwx--x
⊞ lib		2013-11-24	12:16	drwxr-xr-x
⊟ shared_prefs		2013-11-24	12:28	drwxrwx--x
com.androidbook.preferences.main_preferences.xml	380	2013-11-24	12:28	-rw-rw----

***Figure 11-2.** Path to an application's saved preferences*

> **Note** You will be able to inspect shared preferences files in the emulator only. On a real device, the shared preferences files are not readable due to Android security (unless you have root privileges, of course).

The default preferences file path for an application is `/data/data/[PACKAGE_NAME]/shared_prefs/[PACKAGE_NAME]_preferences.xml`, where `[PACKAGE_NAME]` is the package of the application. Listing 11-1 shows the `com.androidbook.preferences.main_preferences.xml` data file for this example.

***Listing 11-1.** Saved Preferences for Our Example*

```
<?xml version='1.0' encoding='utf-8' standalone='yes' ?>
<map>
<boolean name="notification_switch" value="true" />
<string name="package_name_preference">com.androidbook.win</string>
<boolean name="potato_selection_pref" value="true" />
<boolean name="show_airline_column_pref" value="true" />
<string name="flight_sort_option">2</string>
<boolean name="alert_email" value="false" />
<set name="pizza_toppings">
<string>pepperoni</string>
<string>cheese</string>
<string>olive</string>
</set>
<string name="alert_email_address">davemac327@gmail.com</string>
</map>
```

As you can see, values are stored in a map, with preference keys as names to the data values. Some of the values look cryptic and do not match what is displayed to the user. For example, the value for flight_sort_option is 2. Android does not store the displayed text as the value of the preference; rather, it stores a value that the user won't see, that you can use independently of what the user sees. You want the freedom to change the displayed text based on the user's language, and you also want the ability to tweak the displayed text while keeping the same stored value in the preferences file. You might even be able to do simpler processing of the preference if the value is an integer instead of some display string. What you don't have to worry about is parsing this data file. The Android preferences framework provides a nice API for dealing with preferences, which will be described in more detail later in this chapter.

If you compare the preferences map in Listing 11-1 with the screenshots in Figure 11-1, you will notice that not all preferences are listed with values in the preferences XML data file. This is because the preference data file does not automatically store a default value for you. You'll see shortly how to deal with default values.

Now that you've seen where the values are saved, you need to see how to define the screens to display to the user so they can make selections. Before you see how to collect preferences together into screens, you'll learn about the different types of preferences you can use, and then you'll see how to put them together into screens. Each persisted value in the /data/data XML file is from a specific preference. So let's understand what each of these means.

Understanding CheckBoxPreference and SwitchPreference

The simplest of the preferences are the `CheckBoxPreference` and `SwitchPreference`. These share a common parent class (`TwoStatePreference`) and are either on (value is true) or off (value is false). For the sample application, a screen was created with five `CheckBoxPreferences`, as shown in Figure 11-3. Listing 11-2 shows what the XML looks like for a `CheckBoxPreference`.

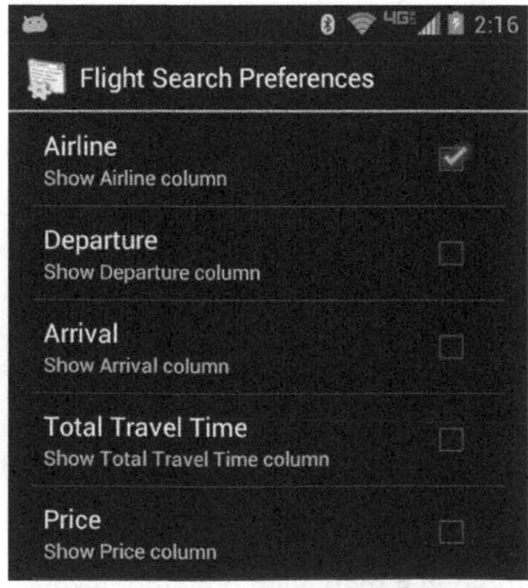

***Figure 11-3.** The user interface for the check box preference*

Listing 11-2. Using CheckBoxPreference

```
<CheckBoxPreference
        android:key="show_airline_column_pref"
        android:title="Airline"
        android:summary="Show Airline column" />
```

> **Note** We will give you a URL at the end of the chapter that you can use to download projects from this chapter. This will allow you to import these projects into your IDE directly. The main sample application is called PrefDemo. You should refer to that project until you come to the Saving State section.

This example shows the minimum that's required to specify a preference. The key is the reference to, or name of, the preference, the title is the title displayed for the preference, and summary is a description of what the preference is for or a status of the current setting. Looking back on the saved values in Listing 11-1, you will see a `<boolean>` tag for "show_airline_column_pref" (the key), and it has an attribute value of true, which indicates that the preference is checked on.

With `CheckBoxPreference`, the state of the preference is saved when the user sets the state. In other words, when the user checks or unchecks the preference control, its state is saved immediately.

The `SwitchPreference` is very similar except that the visual display is different. Instead of a check box in the user interface, the user sees an on-off switch, as shown in Figure 11-1 next to "Notifications are".

One other useful feature of `CheckBoxPreference` and `SwitchPreference` is that you can set different summary text depending on whether it's checked. The XML attributes are `summaryOn` and `summaryOff`. If you look in the main.xml file for the `CheckBoxPreference` called "potato_selection_pref" you will see an example of this.

Before you learn the other preference types, now would be a good time to understand how to access this preference to read its value and perform other operations.

Accessing a Preference Value in Code

Now that you have a preference defined you need to know how to access the preference in code so you can read the value. Listing 11-3 shows code to access the `SharedPreferences` object in Android where the preferences exist. This code is from the `MainActivity.java` file in the `setOptionText()` method.

Listing 11-3. Accessing the CheckBoxPreference

```
    SharedPreferences prefs =
            PreferenceManager.getDefaultSharedPreferences(this);
//  This is the other way to get to the shared preferences:
//  SharedPreferences prefs = getSharedPreferences(
//          "com.androidbook.preferences.main_preferences", 0);
    boolean showAirline = prefs.getBoolean("show_airline_column_pref", false);
```

Using the reference to preferences, it is straightforward to read the current value of the show_airline_column_pref preference. As shown in Listing 11-3, there are two ways to get to the preferences. The first way shown is to get the default preferences for the current context. In this case, the context is that of the MainActivity of our application. The second case, which is shown commented out, retrieves the preferences using a package name. You could use whatever package name you want in case you need to store different sets of preferences in different files.

Once you have a reference to the preferences, you call the appropriate getter method with the key of the preference and a default value. Since show_airline_column_pref is a TwoStatePreference, the value returned is a boolean. The default value for show_airline_column_pref is hard-coded here as false. If this preference has not yet been set at all, the hard-coded value (false) will be assigned to showAirline. However, that by itself does not persist the preference to false for future use, nor does it honor any default value that might have been set in the XML specification for this preference. If the XML specification uses a resource value to specify the default value, then the same resource could be referred to in code to set the default value, as shown in the following for a different preference:

```
String flight_option = prefs.getString(
        resources.getString(R.string.flight_sort_option),
        resources.getString(R.string.flight_sort_option_default_value));
```

Notice here that the key for the preference is also using a string resource value (R.string.flight_sort_option). This can be a wise choice since it makes typos less likely. If the resource name is typed wrong you'll very likely get a build error. If you use just simple strings, it is possible for a typo to go unnoticed, except that your preferences won't work.

We showed one way to read a default value for a preference in code. Android provides another way that is a bit more elegant. In onCreate(), you can do the following instead:

```
PreferenceManager.setDefaultValues(this, R.xml.main, false);
```

Then, in setOptionText(), you would have done this to read the option value:

```
String option = prefs.getString(
    resources.getString(R.string.flight_sort_option), null);
```

The first call will use main.xml to find the default values and generate the preferences XML data file for us using the default values. If we already have an instance of the SharedPreferences object in memory, it will update that too. The second call will then find a value for flight_sort_option, because we took care of loading defaults first.

After running this code the first time, if you look in the shared_prefs folder, you will see the preferences XML file even if the preferences screen has not yet been invoked. You will also see another file called _has_set_default_values.xml. This file tells your application that the preferences XML file has already been created with the default values. The third argument to setDefaultValues()—that is, false—indicates that you want the defaults set in the preferences XML file only if it hasn't been done before. Android remembers this information through the existence of this new XML file. However, Android remembers even if you upgrade your application and add new settings with new default values, which means this trick won't set those new defaults. Your best option is to always use a resource for the default value, and always provide that resource as the default value when getting the current value of a preference.

Understanding ListPreference

A list preference contains radio buttons for each option, and the default (or current) selection is preselected. The user is expected to select one and only one of the choices. When the user chooses an option, the dialog is immediately dismissed and the choice is saved in the preferences XML file. Figure 11-4 shows what this looks like.

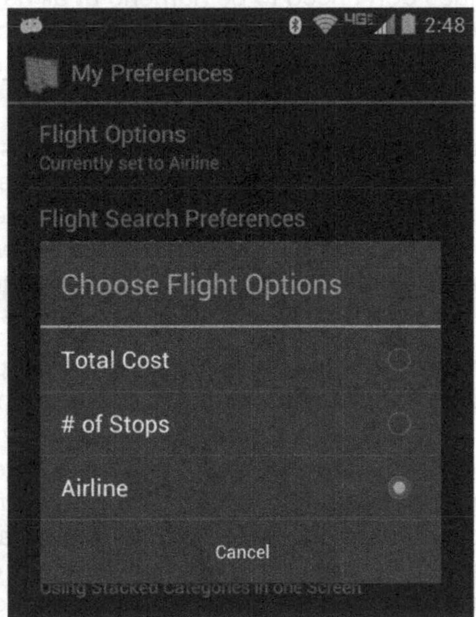

***Figure 11-4.** The user interface for the ListPreference*

Listing 11-4 contains an XML fragment that represents the flight-option preference setting. This time the file contains references to strings and to arrays, which would be the more common way to specify these rather than hard-coding the strings. As mentioned before, the value of a list preference as stored in the XML data file under the /data/data/{package} directory is not the same as what the user sees in the user interface. The name of the key is stored in the data file, along with a hidden value that the user does not see. Therefore, to get a ListPreference to work, there needs to be two arrays: the values displayed to the user and the strings used as key values. This is where you can easily get tripped up. The entries array holds the strings displayed to the user, and the entryValues array holds the strings that will be stored in the preferences data XML file.

Listing 11-4. Specifying a ListPreference in XML

```
<ListPreference
  android:key="@string/flight_sort_option"
  android:title="@string/listTitle"
  android:summary="@string/listSummary"
  android:entries="@array/flight_sort_options"
  android:entryValues="@array/flight_sort_options_values"
  android:dialogTitle="@string/dialogTitle"
  android:defaultValue="@string/flight_sort_option_default_value" />
```

The elements between the two arrays correspond to each other positionally. That is, the third element in the entryValues array corresponds to the third element in the entries array. It is tempting to use 0, 1, 2, etc., as entryValues but it is not required, and it could cause problems later when the arrays must be modified. If our option were numeric in nature (for example, a countdown timer starting value), then we could have used values such as 60, 120, 300, and so on. The values don't need to be numeric at all as long as they make sense to the developer; the user doesn't see these values unless you choose to expose them. The user only sees the text from the first string array flight_sort_options. The example application for this chapter shows it both ways.

A word of caution here: because the preferences XML data file is storing only the value and not the text, should you ever upgrade your application and change the text of the options or add items to the string arrays, any value stored in the preferences XML data file should still line up with the appropriate text after the upgrade. The preferences XML data file is kept during the application upgrade. If the preferences XML data file had a "1" in it, and that meant "# of Stops" before the upgrade, it should still mean "# of Stops" after the upgrade.

Since the entryValues array is not seen by the end user, it is best practice to store it once and only once within your application. Therefore, make one and only one /res/values/prefvaluearrays.xml file to contain these arrays. The entries array is very likely to be created multiple times per application, for different languages or perhaps different device configurations. Therefore, make separate prefdisplayarrays.xml files for each variation that you need. For example, if your application will be used in English and in French, there will be separate prefdisplayarrays.xml files for English and French. You do not want to include the entryValues array in each of these other files. It is imperative though that there are the same numbers of array elements between entryValues and entries arrays. The elements must line up. When you make changes, be careful to keep everything in alignment. Listing 11-5 contains the source of ListPreference files for the example.

Listing 11-5. Other ListPreference Files from Our Example

```
<?xml version="1.0" encoding="utf-8"?>
<!-- This file is /res/values/prefvaluearrays.xml -->
<resources>
<string-array name="flight_sort_options_values">
    <item>0</item>
    <item>1</item>
    <item>2</item>
</string-array>
<string-array name="pizza_toppings_values">
    <item>cheese</item>
    <item>pepperoni</item>
    <item>onion</item>
    <item>mushroom</item>
    <item>olive</item>
    <item>ham</item>
    <item>pineapple</item>
</string-array>
<string-array name="default_pizza_toppings">
    <item>cheese</item>
    <item>pepperoni</item>
</string-array>
</resources>

<?xml version="1.0" encoding="utf-8"?>
<!-- This file is /res/values/prefdisplayarrays.xml -->
<resources>
<string-array name="flight_sort_options">
    <item>Total Cost</item>
    <item># of Stops</item>
    <item>Airline</item>
</string-array>
<string-array name="pizza_toppings">
    <item>Cheese</item>
    <item>Pepperoni</item>
    <item>Onions</item>
    <item>Portobello Mushrooms</item>
    <item>Black Olives</item>
    <item>Smoked Ham</item>
    <item>Pineapple</item>
</string-array>
</resources>
```

Also, don't forget that your default value as specified in the XML source file must match an `entryValue` in the array from prefvaluearrays.xml.

For a ListPreference, the value of the preference is a `String`. If you are using number strings (e.g., 0, 1, 1138) as `entryValues`, you could convert those to integers or whatever you need in your code, as is used in the flight_sort_options_values array.

Your code is likely going to want to display the user-friendly text from the preference's entries array. This example took a shortcut, because array indices were used for the elements in `flight_sort_options_values`. By simply converting the value to an `int`, you know which string to read from `flight_sort_options`. Had you used some other set of values for `flight_sort_options_values`, you would need to determine the index of the element that is your preference and then turn around and use that index to grab the text of your preference from `flight_sort_options`. `ListPreference`'s helper method `findIndexOfValue()` can help with this, by providing the index into the values array so you can then easily get the corresponding display text from the entries array.

Returning now to Listing 11-4, there are several strings for titles, summaries, and more. The string called `flight_sort_option_default_value` sets the default value to `1` to represent "# of Stops" in the example. It is usually a good idea to choose a default value for each option. If you don't choose a default value and no value has yet been chosen, the methods that return the value of the option will return `null`. Your code would have to deal with `null` values in this case.

Understanding EditTextPreference

The preferences framework also provides a free-form text preference called `EditTextPreference`. This preference allows you to capture raw text rather than ask the user to make a selection. To demonstrate this, let's assume you have an application that generates Java code for the user. One of the preference settings of this application might be the default package name to use for the generated classes. Here, you want to display a text field to the user for setting the package name for the generated classes. Figure 11-5 shows the UI, and Listing 11-6 shows the XML.

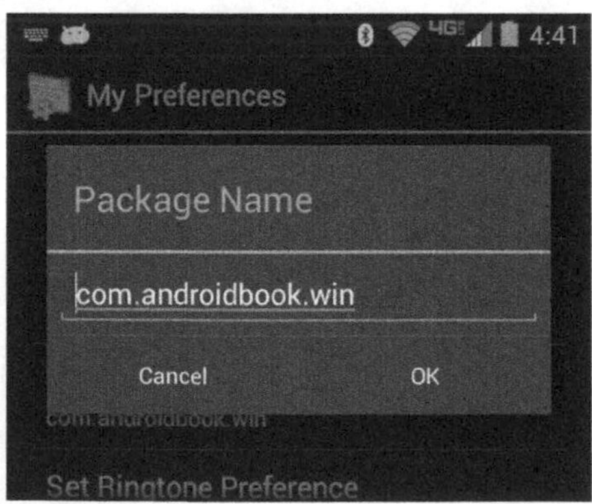

***Figure 11-5.** Using the `EditTextPreference`*

Listing 11-6. An Example of an EditTextPreference

```
<EditTextPreference
        android:key="package_name_preference"
        android:title="Set Package Name"
        android:summary="Set the package name for generated code"
        android:dialogTitle="Package Name" />
```

When Set Package Name is selected, the user is presented with a dialog to input the package name. When the OK button is clicked, the preference is saved to the preference store.

As with the other preferences, you can obtain the value of the preference by calling the appropriate getter method, in this case getString().

Understanding MultiSelectListPreference

And finally, a preference called MultiSelectListPreference was introduced in Android 3.0. The concept is somewhat similar to a ListPreference, but instead of only being able to select one item in the list, the user can select several or none. In Listing 11-1, the MultiSelectListPreference stores a <set name="pizza_toppings"> tag in the preferences XML data file, instead of a single value. The other significant difference with a MultiSelectListPreference is that the default value is an array just like the entryValues array. That is, the array for the default values must contain zero or more of the elements from the entryValues array for this preference. This can also be seen in the sample application for this chapter; just view the end of the main.xml file in the /res/xml directory.

To get the current value of a MultiSelectListPreference, use the getStringSet() method of SharedPreferences. To retrieve the display strings from the entries array, you would need to iterate through the set of strings that is the value of this preference, determine the index of the string, and use the index to access the proper display string from the entries array.

Updating AndroidManifest.xml

Because there are two activities in the sample application, we need two activity tags in AndroidManifest.xml. The first one is a standard activity of category LAUNCHER. The second one is for a PreferenceActivity, so set the action name according to convention for intents, and set the category to PREFERENCE as shown in Listing 11-7. You probably don't want the PreferenceActivity showing up on the Android page with all our other applications, which is why you don't use LAUNCHER for it. You would need to make similar changes to AndroidManifest.xml if you were to add other preference activities.

Listing 11-7. `PreferenceActivity` Entry in `AndroidManifest.xml`

```
<activity android:name=".MainPreferenceActivity"
          android:label="@string/prefTitle">
    <intent-filter>
        <action android:name=
"com.androidbook.preferences.main.intent.action.MainPreferences" />
        <category
            android:name="android.intent.category.PREFERENCE" />
    </intent-filter>
</activity>
```

Using PreferenceCategory

The preferences framework provides support for you to organize your preferences into categories. If you have a lot of preferences, for example, you can use `PreferenceCategory`, which groups preferences under a separator label. Figure 11-6 shows what this could look like. Notice the separators called "`MEATS`" and "`VEGETABLES`." You can find the specifications for these in `/res/xml/main.xml`.

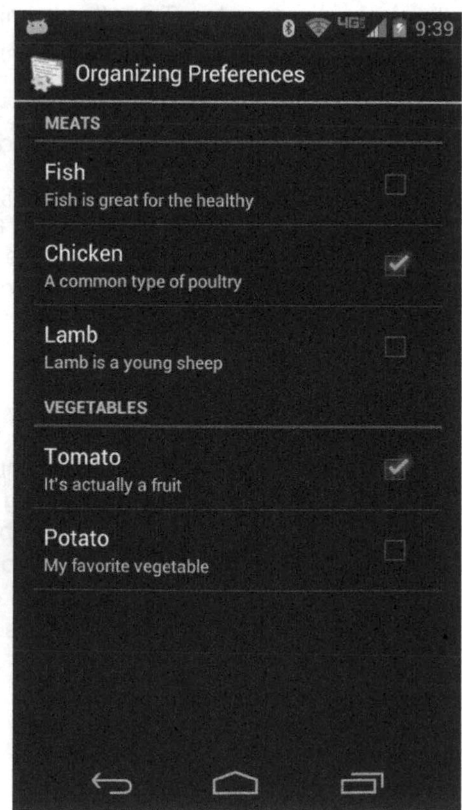

Figure 11-6. Using `PreferenceCategory` to organize preferences

Creating Child Preferences with Dependency

Another way to organize preferences is to use a preference dependency. This creates a parent-child relationship between preferences. For example, you might have a preference that turns on alerts; and if alerts are on, there might be several other alert-related preferences to choose from. If the main alerts preference is off, the other preferences are not relevant and should be disabled. Listing 11-8 shows the XML, and Figure 11-7 shows what it looks like.

Listing 11-8. Preference Dependency in XML

```
<PreferenceScreen>
    <PreferenceCategory
            android:title="Alerts">

        <CheckBoxPreference
                android:key="alert_email"
                android:title="Send email?" />

        <EditTextPreference
                android:key="alert_email_address"
                android:layout="?android:attr/preferenceLayoutChild"
                android:title="Email Address"
                android:dependency="alert_email" />

    </PreferenceCategory>
</PreferenceScreen>
```

Figure 11-7. Preference dependency

Preferences with Headers

Android 3.0 introduced a new way to organize preferences. You see this on tablets under the main Settings app. Because tablet screen real estate offers much more room than a smartphone does, it makes sense to display more preference information at the same time. To accomplish this, you use preference headers. Take a look at Figure 11-8.

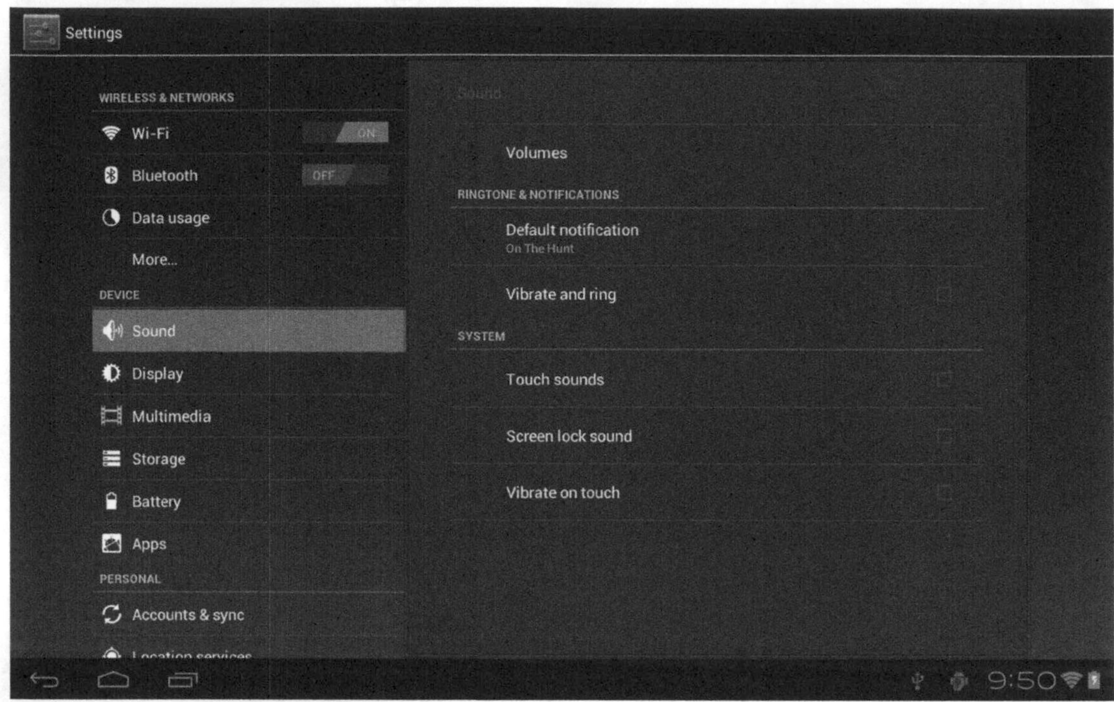

***Figure 11-8.** Main Settings page with preference headers*

Notice that headers appear down the left side, like a vertical tab bar. As you click each item on the left, the screen to the right displays the preferences for that item. In Figure 11-8, Sound is chosen, and the sound preferences are displayed at right. The right side is a `PreferenceScreen` object, and this setup uses fragments. Obviously, we need to do something different than what has been discussed so far in this chapter.

The big change from Android 3.0 was the addition of headers to `PreferenceActivity`. This also means using a new callback within `PreferenceActivity` to do the headers setup. Now, when you extend `PreferenceActivity`, you'll want to implement this method:

```
public void onBuildHeaders(List<Header> target) {
    loadHeadersFromResource(R.xml.preferences, target);
}
```

Please refer to the PrefDemo sample application for the complete source code. The `preferences.xml` file contains some new tags that look like this:

```
<preference-headers
        xmlns:android="http://schemas.android.com/apk/res/android">
    <header android:fragment="com.example.PrefActivity$Prefs1Fragment"
            android:icon="@drawable/ic_settings_sound"
            android:title="Sound"
            android:summary="Your sound preferences" />
    ...
```

Each header tag points to a class that extends PreferenceFragment. In the example just given, the XML specifies an icon, the title, and summary text (which acts like a subtitle). Prefs1Fragment is an inner class of PreferenceActivity that could look something like this:

```
public static class Prefs1Fragment extends PreferenceFragment {
    @Override
    public void onCreate(Bundle savedInstanceState) {
        super.onCreate(savedInstanceState);
        addPreferencesFromResource(R.xml.sound_preferences);
    }
}
```

All this inner class needs to do is pull in the appropriate preferences XML file, as shown. That preferences XML file contains the types of preference specifications we covered earlier, such as ListPreference, CheckBoxPreference, PreferenceCategory, and so on. What's very nice is that Android takes care of doing the right thing when the screen configuration changes and when the preferences are displayed on a small screen. Headers behave like old preferences when the screen is too small to display both headers and the preference screen to the right. That is, you only see the headers; and when you click a header, you then see only the appropriate preference screen.

PreferenceScreens

The top-level container for preferences is a PreferenceScreen. Before tablets and PreferenceFragments, you could nest PreferenceScreens, and when the user clicked on a nested PreferenceScreen item, the new PreferenceScreen would replace the currently displayed PreferenceScreen. This worked fine on a small screen, but doesn't look as good on a tablet, especially if you started with headers and fragments. What you probably want is for the new PreferenceScreen to appear where the current fragment is.

To make a PreferenceScreen work inside of a fragment, all you need to do is specify a fragment class name for that PreferenceScreen. Listing 11-9 shows the XML from the sample application.

Listing 11-9. PreferenceScreen invoked via a PreferenceFragment

```
<PreferenceScreen
    android:title="Launch a new screen into a fragment"
    android:fragment="com.androidbook.preferences.main.BasicFrag" />
```

When the user clicks on this item, the current fragment is replaced with BasicFrag, which then loads a new XML layout for a PreferenceScreen as specified in nested_screen_basicfrag.xml. In this case, we chose not to make the BasicFrag class an inner class of the MainPreferenceActivity class, mainly because there is no sharing needed from the outer class, and to show you that you can do it this way if you prefer.

Dynamic Preference Summary Text

You've probably seen preferences where the preference summary contains the current value. This is actually a little harder to implement than you might think. To accomplish this feat, you create a listener callback that detects when a preference value is about to change, and you then update the preference summary accordingly. The first step is for your PreferenceFragment to implement the OnPreferenceChangeListener interface. You then need to implement the onPreferenceChange() callback. Listing 11-10 shows an example. The pkgPref object in the callback was set earlier to the preference in the onCreate() method.

Listing 11-10. Setting Up a Preference Listener

```
public boolean onPreferenceChange(Preference preference,
                                  Object newValue) {
    final String key = preference.getKey();
    if ("package_name_preference".equals(key)) {
        pkgPref.setSummary(newValue.toString());
    }
    ...
    return true;
}
```

You have to register the fragment as a listener in onResume() using setOnPreferenceChange Listener(this) on each preference you want to listen on, and unregister in onPause() by calling it again with null. Now every time there is a pending change to a preference you've registered for, this callback will be invoked passing in the preference and the potential new value. The callback returns a boolean indicating whether to proceed with setting the preference to the new value (true) or not (false). Assuming you would return true to allow the new setting, this is where you can update the summary value as well. You could also validate the new value and reject the change. Perhaps you want a MultiSelectListPreference to have a maximum number of checked items. You could count the selected items in the callback and reject the change if there are too many.

Saving State with Preferences

Preferences are great for allowing users to customize applications to their liking, but we can use the Android preference framework for more than that. When your application needs to keep track of some data between invocations of the application, preferences are one way to accomplish the task even if the user can't see the data in preference screens. Please find the sample application called SavingStateDemo to follow along with the complete source code.

The Activity class has a getPreferences(int mode) method. This, in reality, simply calls getSharedPreferences() with the class name of the activity as the tag plus the mode as passed in. The result is an activity-specific shared preferences file that you can use to store data about this activity across invocations. A simple example of how you could use this is shown in Listing 11-11.

Listing 11-11. Using Preferences to Save State for an Activity

```
    final String INITIALIZED = "initialized";
    private String someString;

[ ... ]

    SharedPreferences myPrefs = getPreferences(MODE_PRIVATE);

    boolean hasPreferences = myPrefs.getBoolean(INITIALIZED, false);
    if(hasPreferences) {
        Log.v("Preferences", "We've been called before");
        // Read other values as desired from preferences file...
        someString = myPrefs.getString("someString", "");
    }
    else {
        Log.v("Preferences", "First time ever being called");
        // Set up initial values for what will end up
        // in the preferences file
        someString = "some default value";
    }

[ ... ]

    // Later when ready to write out values
    Editor editor = myPrefs.edit();
    editor.putBoolean(INITIALIZED, true);
    editor.putString("someString", someString);
    // Write other values as desired
    editor.commit();
```

What this code does is acquire a reference to preferences for our activity class and check for the existence of a boolean "preference" called `initialized`. We write "preference" in double quotation marks because this value is not something the user is going to see or set; it's merely a value that we want to store in a shared preferences file for use next time. If we get a value, the shared preferences file exists, so the application must have been called before. You could then read other values out of the shared preferences file. For example, someString could be an activity variable that should be set from the last time this activity ran or set to the default value if this is the first time.

To write values to the shared preferences file, you must first get a preferences `Editor`. You can then put values into preferences and commit those changes when you're finished. Note that, behind the scenes, Android is managing a `SharedPreferences` object that is truly shared. Ideally, there is never more than one `Editor` active at a time. But it is very important to call the `commit()` method so that the `SharedPreferences` object and the shared preferences XML file get updated. In the example, the value of `someString` is written out to be used the next time this activity runs.

You can access, write, and commit values any time to your preferences file. Possible uses for this include writing out high scores for a game or recording when the application was last run. You can also use the `getSharedPreferences()` call with different names to manage separate sets of preferences, all within the same application or even the same activity.

MODE_PRIVATE was used for mode in our examples thus far. Because the shared preferences files are always stored within your application's /data/data/{package} directory and therefore are not accessible to other applications, you only need to use MODE_PRIVATE.

Using DialogPreference

So far, you've seen how to use the out-of-the-box capabilities of the preferences framework, but what if you want to create a custom preference? What if you want something like the slider of the Brightness preference under Screen Settings? This is where DialogPreference comes in. DialogPreference is the parent class of EditTextPreference and ListPreference. The behavior is a dialog that pops up, displays choices to the user, and is closed with a button or via the Back button. But you can extend DialogPreference to set up your own custom preference. Within your extended class, you provide your own layout, your own click handlers, and custom code in onDialogClosed() to write the data for your preference to the shared preferences file.

Reference

Here are helpful references to topics you may wish to explore further:

- http://developer.android.com/design/patterns/settings.html: Android's Design Guide to Settings. Some good advice about laying out Settings screens and options.
- http://developer.android.com/guide/topics/ui/settings.html: Android's API Guide to Settings. This page describes the Settings framework.
- http://developer.android.com/reference/android/provider/Settings.html: Reference page that lists the settings constants for calling a system settings activity.
- www.androidbook.com/proandroid5/projects: A list of downloadable projects related to this book. For this chapter, look for the file ProAndroid5_Ch11_Preferences.zip. This ZIP file contains all the projects from this chapter, listed in separate root directories. There is also a README.TXT file that describes how to import projects into your IDE from one of these ZIP files.

Summary

This chapter talked about managing preferences in Android:

- Types of preferences available
- Reading the current values of preferences into your application
- Setting default values from embedded code and by writing the default values from the XML file to the saved preferences file
- Organizing preferences into groups, and defining dependencies between preferences
- Callbacks on preferences to validate changes and to set dynamic summary text
- Using the preferences framework to save and restore information from an activity across invocations
- Creating a custom preference

Chapter 12

Using the Compatibility Library for Older Devices

The Android platform has gone through an impressive evolution since it was first introduced several years ago. While the intention has always been for Android to power lots of different types of devices, it wasn't architected from the beginning to meet that goal. Instead, the Google engineers have added, removed, and changed APIs in order to provide new features. One of the biggest changes was the creation of fragments in order to handle larger screen sizes such as on tablets and TVs. But there have been other changes such as with ActionBar and Menus.

The new APIs created a difficult problem for developers who wanted their applications to run on the new devices with the new APIs, as well as older devices that did not have those APIs. Many older devices do not get Android upgrades. Even if Google added the new APIs to a revision of the old Android OS, the old devices aren't going to get that new revision, because of the testing and support required from both the device manufacturer and the cellular carrier. The solution that Google came up with was to create compatibility libraries that could be linked into an application so it could take advantage of the new API functionality yet still run on an older version of Android. The library figures out how to use the older APIs to implement the new features. If the same application runs on a newer version of Android that already has those new features, the compatibility library calls through to the underlying APIs present in that newer version of Android.

This chapter will dive into the compatibility libraries and explain how to use them and what to watch out for. If you aren't developing applications for older versions of Android, you could safely skip this chapter as you won't need the libraries. The libraries are only useful if you want to include the functionality of a new API in an application that will run on an old version of Android that doesn't have that new API.

It All Started with Tablets

The Android operating system was doing fine until it came time to support tablets. The basic building block of an application was the activity, meant to perform a single task for the user and to fill the screen of the device. But tablets offered more real estate so the user could see and do a few things at a time on one screen. So with Honeycomb (Android 3.0), Google introduced fragments. This was a whole new concept, which changed how developers created UIs and the logic that ran behind them. And this would have been fine, except that there were still plenty of Android devices (e.g., smartphones) in the wild which did not support fragments. What Google figured out is that a compatibility library could be written to provide comparable implementations of `Fragment`, etc., that used the existing APIs in the older versions of Android. If an application linked in the compatibility library, it could work with fragments even though the older version of Android didn't support fragments in the OS.

The Google engineers then looked at other features and APIs in new Android and provided compatibility library features and APIs to match, so that these features could also be used in older versions of Android without having to release updates to those older versions of Android. In addition to support for Fragments, compatibility libraries provide support for Loaders, RenderScript, ActionBar, and others.

The compatibility library doesn't always make things perfectly the same between old and new. For example, the new Activity class is aware of fragments. To use the compatibility library, you must extend the `FragmentActivity` class instead of `Activity`; it is the `FragmentActivity` class that works with fragments in old Android versions.

When you use the compatibility library, you will use those classes for your application regardless of which version of Android it will run on. In other words, you would only use `FragmentActivity` in your application and it will do the right thing in all versions of Android, including Android 3.0 and later. You would not try to include in the same application both `Activity` for Android 3.0+ and `FragmentActivity` for Android below 3.0. When `FragmentActivity` is executing on Android 3.0 and above, it can pretty much call straight through to the underlying `Activity` class. There is no real penalty to using a compatibility library on a recent Android version.

Adding the Library to Your Project

As of this writing, there are four compatibility libraries; together the collection is called the Android Support Library, revision 22.1.1:

- v4—contains `FragmentActivity`, `Fragment`, `Loader`, and quite a few other classes introduced after Android 3.0. The number 4 represents Android API version 4 (i.e., Donut 1.6). It means this library can be used for applications that run on Android API version 4 and above.
- v7—makes available the `ActionBar`, `CardView`, `GridLayout`, `MediaRouter`, `Palette` and `RecyclerView` classes. This library can be used with Android API version 7 (i.e., Eclair 2.1) and above. There are actually six libraries here: appcompat, cardview, gridlayout, mediarouter, palette and recyclerview

- v8—adds RenderScipt capability to Android API version 8 (i.e., Froyo 2.2) and above. RenderScript allows for parallelization of work across device processors (CPU cores, GPUs, DSPs) and was introduced in Android API version 11 (i.e., Honeycomb 3.0).
- v13—adds some special `Fragment` functionality for things like tabbed and pager interfaces. This library also contains many of the classes from v4 so it can be included in your application without requiring other libraries.
- v17—adds Leanback features related to Android TV applications

For a complete list of all compatibility functionality by version number, please see the references at the end of this chapter.

To download the Android Support Library to your computer, use the Android SDK Manager and look for it at the bottom of the list under Extras. If you're using Android Studio, download the Android Support Repository. Otherwise, download Android Support Library instead. The files will be placed under your Android SDK directory. The Android Support Library can be found in `extras/android/support/`, and the Android Support Repository can be found in `extras/android/m2repository`.

As you can see from the preceding bullet list, not all features of the Android Support Library are available on all older versions of Android. Therefore you must properly set `android:minSdkVersion` in your AndroidManifest.xml file. If you are using a compatibility library feature from v7, `android:minSdkVersion` should not be lower than 7.

Including the v7 Support Library

There's very little chance that you'd ever want to include the v4 library and not the v7 library. Since the v7 library requires that the v4 library also be included to provide the necessary classes for v7 to function properly, you'll want to include both. If you are using Eclipse, the ADT plug-in makes all of this pretty easy. When you create a new Android project in Eclipse, you specify the minimum version of Android that it will run on. If ADT thinks that you might want the compatibility library included, it will automatically include it.

For example, if you specify a target SDK of 16 (JellyBean 4.1) but a minimum SDK of 8 (Froyo 2.2), ADT will automatically set up an appcompat v7 library project, include that library project in your new application, and also include the v4 library as well in your application. The resources from the v7 library are therefore available to your application without you having to do extra work. However, if you want to use either of the other two v7 libraries (gridlayout and/or mediarouter), those will require a little extra work, as will now be explained. By creating a library project and including that in your application, it will include the compatibility library resources that your application will need.

You will manually do something similar to what ADT did to automatically include the v7 appcompat library into your project. To start, you will choose File ➤ Import, then Existing Android Code Into Workspace, then navigate to the extras folder where the Android SDK is on your workstation. Locate the v7 gridlayout or mediarouter folder and choose that. See Figure 12-1.

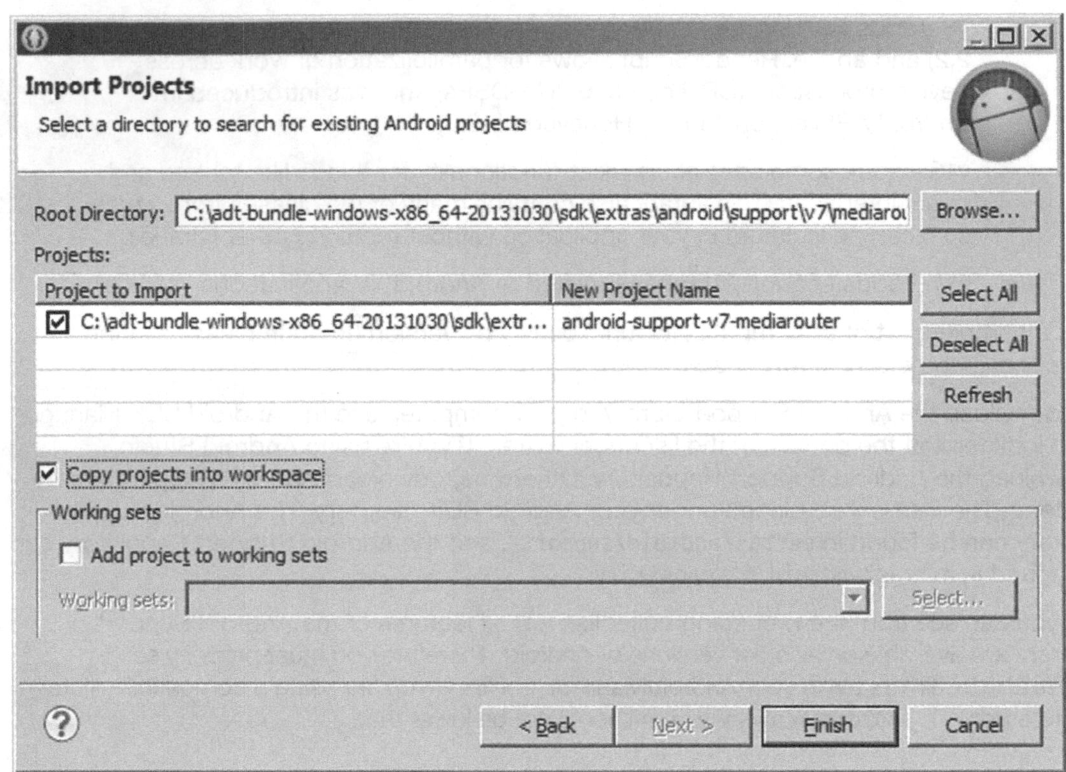

Figure 12-1. Importing the v7 mediarouter compatibility library

Click Finish and you will get a new library project. If you chose to create a library project for v7 mediarouter, you will see that it is missing some functionality so it has errors. You need to add in the v7 appcompat library to clear that up. Right-click the mediarouter library project in Eclipse and choose Properties. In the list on the left choose Android. Now click the Add... button in the Library section. See Figure 12-2.

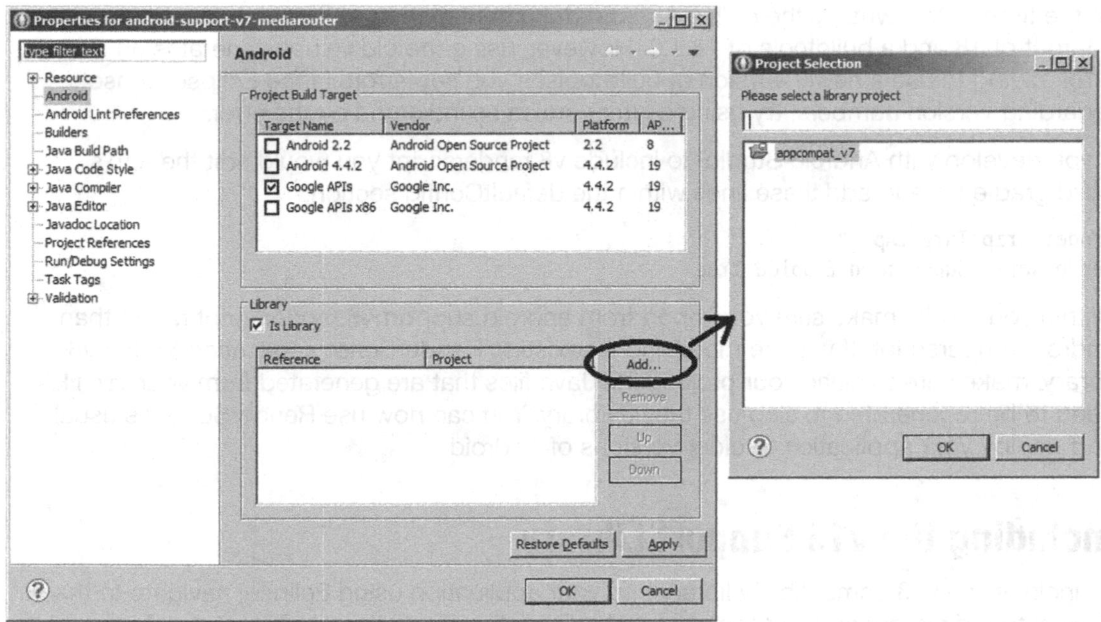

Figure 12-2. Adding appcompat_v7 to the v7 mediarouter compatibility library

Select the appcompat_v7 library and click OK. That should clear up the errors in mediarouter. Now when you want to include mediarouter in your application project, simply follow the same procedure but right-click your application project, and when you click the Add… button for Library, chose the mediarouter library.

With Android Studio, adding a v7 compatibility library is just as easy. By default, if you create a new project with a minimum SDK value less than your target SDK, you will very likely get the v7 appcompat library added in automatically. You can check this by looking for the following line in the app's build.gradle configuration file in the dependencies section:

```
compile 'com.android.support:appcompat-v7:22.0.0'
```

Therefore, to add one of the other v7 libraries, you would insert another similar compile line to the dependencies section, but use the appropriate name such as cardview or mediarouter.

Including the v8 Support Library

If you want to use the v8 renderscript compatibility library, and you develop with Eclipse, you simply add the following three lines to the application project's `project.properties` file regardless of the target version of your application:

```
renderscript.target=22
renderscript.support.mode=true
sdk.buildtools=22.1.1
```

At the time of this writing, the online Android documentation says that you should use a target of 18 and a buildtools of 18.1.0. However, using the old values generates an error saying to use a newer version of buildtools. If you see errors in the Eclipse Console regarding version numbers, try using a later version as indicated by the error.

If you develop with Android Studio, to include v8 renderscript you would edit the app's build.gradle file and add these lines within the defaultConfig section:

```
renderscriptTargetApi 22
renderscriptSupportModeEnabled true
```

Within your code, make sure you import from android.support.v8.renderscript rather than android.renderscript. If you are modifying an existing RenderScript application for the v8 library, make sure to clean your project; the Java files that are generated from your `.rs` files need to be regenerated to also use the v8 library. You can now use RenderScript as usual and deploy your application to older versions of Android.

Including the v13 Support Library

To include the v13 compatibility library into your application using Eclipse, navigate to the SDK extras directory and find the v13 jar file. Copy this file to the /libs directory of your application project. Once the v13 jar file is in place, right-click it to pull up the menu, and then choose Build Path ➤ Add to Build Path. There's a good chance you already have the v4 and v7 appcompat libraries in your application courtesy of ADT. You may choose to get rid of those if you don't need the functionality from either one. For example, if the minimum SDK for your application is v11, you can use the native `ActionBar` class without the need for the v7 appcompat support library.

The v13 jar file contains many of the same classes as v4, so you don't want to cause any problems by having the same classes in twice. If you're going to have all three libraries in your application (i.e., v4, v7, and v13), then at least ensure that v13 is ordered before v4. This can be done in the Configure Build Path dialog box.

If you're using Android Studio, just make sure the SDK Manager has downloaded the Support Repository, then add the following compile line to the app's build.gradle file just like you do for v7 libraries:

```
compile 'com.android.support:support-v13:22.0.0'
```

Including the v17 Support Library

Finally, including the v17 compatibility library is done the same way as for the v13 support library.

Including Just the v4 Support Library

If you really must have the v4 support library and none of the others, you would follow the same procedure as for the v13 library.

Retrofitting an App with the Android Support Library

To get a better feel for how this all works, you're going to bring back a fragment app you worked on in Chapter 8 and will make it work for older versions of Android that don't natively support fragments.

Use File ➤ Import, choose General, then Existing Projects into Workspace. Navigate to the ShakespeareInstrumented project from Chapter 8 and choose that. Check "Copy projects into workspace" before hitting Finish.

Now you're going to retrofit this application to work on versions of Android lower than API version 11. The following works when you don't need resources from the compatibility library, since it worries only about copying in the JAR file.

1. Right-click your project and choose Android Tools ➤ Add Support Library.... Accept the license and click OK.
2. Now go into `MainActivity.java` and change the base class from `Activity` to `FragmentActivity`. You need to fix the `import` line from `android.app.Activity` to `android.support.v4.app.FragmentActivity`. Also fix the imports for `Fragment`, `FragmentManager`, and `FragmentTransaction` to use the ones from the support library.
3. Find the method calls for `getFragmentManager()` and change these to `getSupportFragmentManager()`. Do this also for `DetailsActivity.java`.
4. For `DetailsFragment.java`, change the import for `Fragment` to the one for the support library `Fragment` (i.e., `android.support.v4.app.Fragment`).
5. In `TitlesFragment.java`, change the import for `ListFragment` to the one for the support library `ListFragment` (i.e., `android.support.v4.app.ListFragment`).

The newer versions of Android use different animators from old Android. You may need to fix animations in `MainActivity.java` in the `showDetails()` method. Pick one of the commented out calls to `setCustomAnimations()`, then play with the in and out animations. Anything that relies on an `ObjectAnimator` class will not work on older devices since this class was introduced with API version 11 (i.e., Honeycomb 3.0). It will compile but since that class has not been implemented in older Android and has not been included in the compatibility libraries, you will get a runtime exception. In other words, avoid R.animator. Try using R.anim instead. You can copy into your project anim resource files that you'd like to use, or you can try referring to `android.R.anim` files.

Now you can go into `AndroidManifest.xml` and change the `minSdkVersion` from 11 to 8. That should be all you need to do. Try running this application on a Froyo device or emulator. If all went well you should now be seeing a fragment-based application running on a pre–Android 3.0 OS.

References

Here are some helpful references to topics you may wish to explore further:

- `http://developer.android.com/tools/support-library/index.html`: The Android Developer's Guide on the Support Library package.
- `http://developer.android.com/tools/support-library/features.html`: Android documentation on the main features of each compatibility library.
- `http://developer.android.com/tools/support-library/setup.html`: Android documentation on setting up a compatibility library for your project, for both Eclipse and Android Studio. At the time of this writing, these pages were not as current as this chapter. However, things change. If you experience trouble, check the online documentation or contact the book's authors.

Summary

Let's conclude this chapter by quickly enumerating what you have learned about the Android compatibility libraries:

- To get your application working on the broadest array of devices, use the compatibility libraries and code to their APIs rather than the latest and greatest APIs.
- The v7 support libraries come with resources that must be included in your application for the APIs to work properly.

Chapter 13

Exploring Packages, Processes, Threads, and Handlers

In the book thus far, we have focused on the essentials of how to program for the Android platform. In this chapter we want to go under the hood a bit to address the process and threading model for Android programs. This discussion will lead us to signing packages, sharing data between packages, using compile-time libraries, the nature of Android components and how they use threads, and finally the need for handlers and how one can code handlers.

As you go through this chapter, keep in mind that the word "package" is overloaded. Sometimes it refers to the Java language package, and sometimes it refers to the APK files that Android applications are deployed as.

Understanding Packages and Processes

We will start with Android packages and the process model. When you develop an application in Android, you end up with an `.apk` file. You sign this `.apk` file and deploy it to the device. Each`.apk` file is uniquely identified by a unique java-language-style package name, as shown in the manifest file shown in Listing 13-1.

Listing 13-1. Providing a Package Name in the Manifest File

```
<manifest xmlns:android="http://schemas.android.com/apk/res/android"
      package="com.androidbook.testapp"
      ...>
      ...rest of the xml nodes
</manifest>
```

If you were the developer of this package, no one other than you could update this application once it is deployed. The Android application package name is reserved for you. This tie-up happens when you sign and register your app with various app publishers. So choose this Android application package name very similar to the way that Java packages are named. This needs to be unique in the world. Once you publish the app, you cannot change this package name, as this defines your application's identity.

Android uses the package name as the name of the process that runs the components of this package. Android also allocates a unique user ID for this process to run under. This user ID is essentially the user ID for the underlying Linux OS. As this user ID is determined at the time of the install on a particular device, it will be different on each device where your app is installed. You can discover this information by looking at the details of the installed package through the developer tools in the Android Emulator. For example, a package detail screen for the installed browser application looks like Figure 13-1. (Please note that this image or tool where you look this up may vary from release to release. The image in Figure 13-1 is taken from the developer tools application on the Android Emulator.)

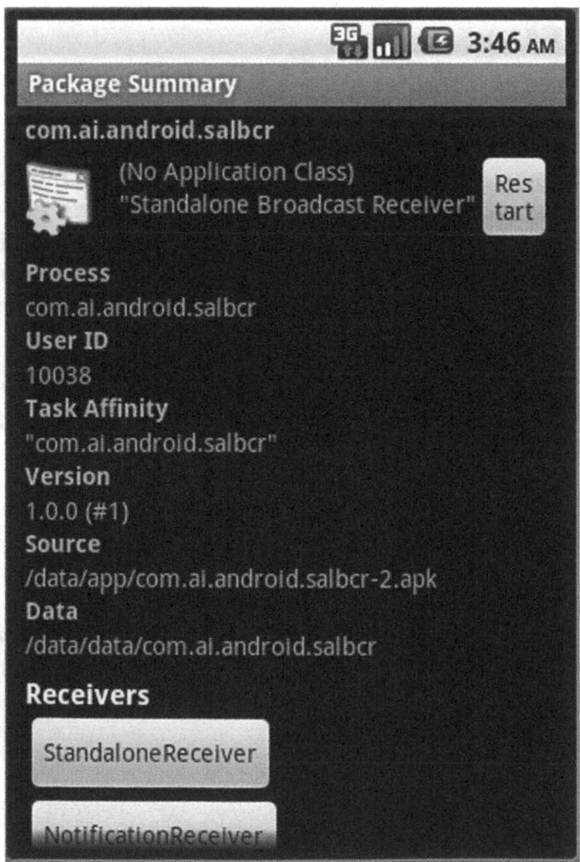

Figure 13-1. Android package details

Figure 13-1 shows the name of the process as indicated by the Java package name in the manifest file and the unique user ID allocated to this package. Any resources created by this process or package will be secured under that Linux user ID. This screen also lists the components inside this package. Examples of components are activities, services, and broadcast receivers. Do note that this image may vary depending on the Android release. Through the settings of the device or the emulator, you can also uninstall the package so that it can be removed.

Because a process is tied to a package name, and a package name is tied to its signature, signatures play a role in securing the data belonging to a package. A package is typically signed with a self-signed PKI (Public Key Infrastructure) certificate. A certificate identifies who the author of the package is. These certificates need not be issued by a certificate authority. This means the information in the certificate is not approved or validated by any authority. This means one can create a certificate that says that their name is Google. The only assurance is that this package name is reserved to that user if no one had claimed it in the marketplace before, and any subsequent updates to that package are given only to that user (identified by that certificate).

All assets that are installed or created through this package belong to the user whose ID is assigned to the package. If your intention is to allow a set of cooperating applications that depend on a common set of data, you have an option to explicitly specify a user ID that is unique to you and common for your needs. This shared user ID is also defined in the manifest file, similar to the definition of a package name. Listing 13-2 shows an example.

Listing 13-2. Shared User ID Declaration

```
<manifest xmlns:android="http://schemas.android.com/apk/res/android"
      package="com.androidbook.somepackage"
      sharedUserId="com.androidbook.mysharedusrid"
      ...
>
...the rest of the xml nodes
</manifest>
```

Multiple applications can specify the same shared user ID if they share the same signature (signed with the same PKI certificate). Having a shared user ID allows multiple applications to share data and even run in the same process. To avoid the duplication of a shared user ID, use a convention similar to naming a Java class. Here are some examples of shared user IDs found in the Android system:

```
"android.uid.system"
"android.uid.phone"
```

> **Note** A shared ID must be specified as a raw string and not a string resource.

As a note of caution, if you are planning to use shared user IDs, the recommendation is to use them from the start. Otherwise, they don't work well when you upgrade your application from a nonshared user ID to one with a shared ID. One of the cited reasons is that Android will not run chown on the old resources because of the user ID change.

A Code Pattern for Sharing Data

This section explores the opportunities when two applications want to share resources and data through the use of a shared user ID. The resources and data of each package are owned and protected by that package's context during runtime. You need access to the context of the package from which you want to share the resources or data.

You can use the createPackageContext() API on any existing context object (such as your activity) to get a reference to the target context that you want to interact with. Listing 13-3 provides an example.

Listing 13-3. Using the createPackageContext() API

```
//Use the appropriate try/catch to detect errors
//Identify package you want to use
String targetPackageName="com.androidbook.samplepackage1";

//Decide on an appropriate context flag
int flag=Context.CONTEXT_RESTRICTED;

//Get the target context through one of your activities
//Need to catch NameNotFoundException
Activity myContext = ......;
Context targetContext =
        myContext.createPackageContext(targetPackageName, flag);

//Use context to resolve file paths
Resources res = targetContext.getResources();
File path = targetContext.getFilesDir();
```

Notice how we are able to get a reference to the context of a given package name such as com.androidbook.samplepackage1. This targetContext in Listing 13-3 is identical to the context that is passed to the target application when that application is launched. As the name of the method indicates (in its "create" prefix), each call returns a new context object. However, the documentation assures us that this returned context object is designed to be lightweight, meaning it doesn't consume a lot of memory and is optimized to refer the target package's resources, assets, and code.

This API is applicable regardless of whether both contexts share a user ID. If you share the user ID, it is well and good. If you don't share a user ID, the target application would need to declare its resources accessible to outside users.

The CONTEXT_RESTRICTED flag indicates that you are interested in just loading the resources and the assets and not the code. So using this flag allows the system to detect if the layouts contain references to callback code. Example of a callback would be a button in a layout referring to a method that would be called. This callback code exists in the source context.

So, you would want the system to throw an exception so that you can detect that condition or ignore that particular XML tag. In essence, you are telling the system that you are using the context in a restricted sense and the target context is free to make suitable assumptions based on that flag. The bottom line appears to be that if you are interested in not using the code from the target context, use this flag.

`CONTEXT_INCLUDE_CODE` allows you to load Java classes at runtime from the target context into your process and call that code. Documentation indicates that you may receive a security exception if it is not safe to load the code. However, it is not clear under what circumstances the code is considered unsafe. One educated guess is that the target context does not have a shared user ID as that of the source context. You can overcome this restriction by also specifying the `CONTEXT_IGNOR_SECURITY` along with the `CONTEXT_INCLUDE_CODE`. These two flags together load the target context code into the source context code all the time, ignoring even if the target context belongs to a different user. Although code is borrowed and runs in the client process, it will not have permissions to the target context data. So, be sure what that code does when let loose on your data. This approach is often used for utility code that can be shared.

Understanding Library Projects

As we talk through sharing code and resources, one question worth asking is, will the idea of a "library" project help? Starting with ADT 0.9.7 Eclipse plug-in, Android supports the idea of library projects. The approach to building libraries has been changing a bit since then, while the central idea remains in all recent releases.

A library project is a collection of Java code and resources that looks like a regular Android project but never ends up in an `.apk` file by itself. Instead, the code and resources of a library project become part of another project and get compiled into that main project's `.apk` file. As libraries are purely a compile-time concept, each development tool may craft this facility differently.

Here are some additional facts about these library projects:

- A library project can have its own package name distinct from the main application.
- A library project can use other JAR files.
- Eclipse ADT will compile the library Java source files into a JAR file that is then compiled with the application project.
- Except for the Java files (which become a jar file), the rest of the files belonging to a library project (such as resources) are kept with the library project. The presence of the library project is required in order to compile the application project that includes that library as a dependency.
- Starting with SDK Tools 15.0, the resource IDs generated for library projects in their respective R.java files are not final. (This is explained later in the chapter.)

- Both the library project and the main project can access the resources from the library project through their respective `R.java` files. This means the ID names are duplicated and available in both R.java files.
- If you would like to distinguish resource IDs between the two projects (library and main), you can use different resource prefixes, such as `lib_` for the library project resources.
- A main project can reference any number of library projects.
- Components, such as an activity, of a library need to be defined in the target main project manifest file. When this is done, the component name from the library package must be fully qualified with the library package name.
- It is not necessary to define the components in a library manifest file, although it may be a good practice to know quickly what components it supports.
- Creating a library project starts with creating a regular Android project and then choosing the `Is Library` flag in its properties window.
- You can set the dependent library projects for a main project through the project properties screen as well.
- Clearly, being a library project, any number of main projects can include a library project.
- One library project cannot reference another library project as of the releases (Android 4.4, API 19, SDK Tools 19, ADT 22.3), although there seems to be a desire to be able to do so in future releases.

To create a library project, you start by creating a regular Android project. Once the project is set up, right-click the project name and click the properties context menu to show the properties dialog for the library project. This dialog is shown in Figure 13-2. (The available build targets in this figure may vary with your version of the Android SDK.) Simply select Is Library from this dialog to set up this project as a library project.

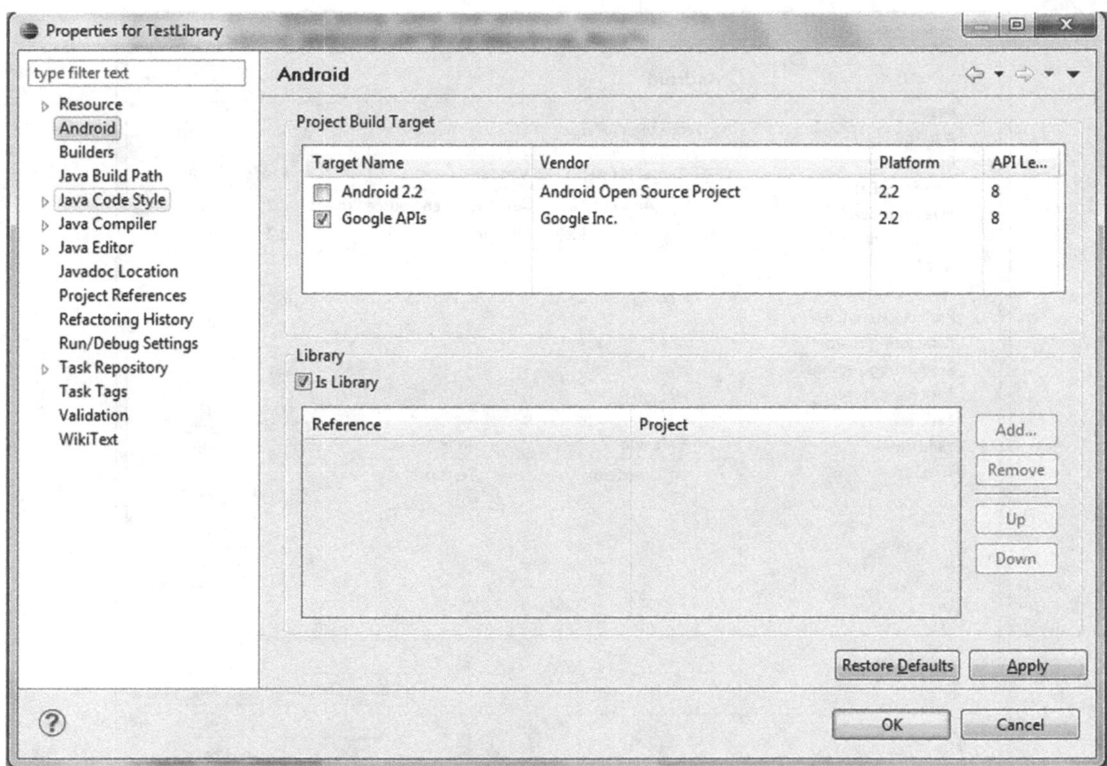

***Figure 13-2.** Designating a project as a library project*

You can use the following project properties dialog (see Figure 13-3) to indicate that a main project depends on the library project that was created earlier.

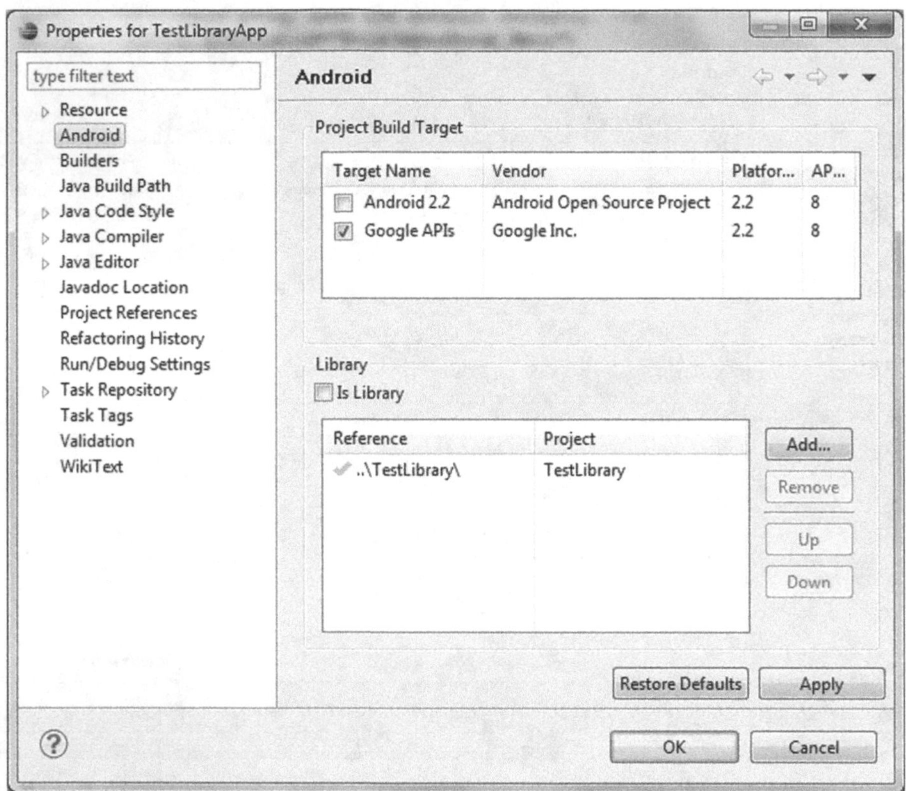

***Figure 13-3.** Declaring a library project dependency*

Notice the Add button in the dialog. You can use this to add the library in Figure 13-3 as a reference. You don't need to do anything else.

Once the library project is set up as a dependency for the main application project, the library project appears as a compiled JAR file in the application project under the node `Android Dependencies`.

Android doesn't package `R.class` files from the libraries in their respective jar files. Instead, it relies on the source `R.java` file that is re-created and made available in the main application project for each of the libraries. That means you have an R.java file for each of the libraries in the gen subdirectory of the main project.

To avoid hard-coded constants being in the compiled source code of the libraries, Android creates the library R.java files such that all the constants in that file are non-final. During the final compilation of the main project, new constant values are allocated so that these constant values are unique across all the libraries and the main project. Had we given final constant values during library compilation, then those numbers could collide between libraries. Allocation of IDs uniquely for a given set of names must be done one time. Once these numbers are allocated to the IDs during the compile of the main project, they can become final in that main project.

There is an implication tied to the fact that IDs in the library's R.java file are not final. It is common to use a switch statement to respond to menu items based on a menu item ID. This language construct will fail at compile time when done in the library code if the IDs are not final. This is because the case statement in a switch clause has to be a numerical constant number.

So, the switch statement in Listing 13-4 will not compile unless the IDs (such as R.id.menu_item_1) are actual literal numbers or static finals.

Listing 13-4. ***Sample switch Statement to Demonstrate Non-Final Variables***

```
switch(menuItem.getItemId()) {
   case R.id.menu_item_1:
        Statement1;
        break;
   case 0x7778888: // as an example for R.id.menu_item_2:
        statement;
        statement;
        break;
   default:
        statement;
        statement;
}
```

Because the IDs are defined as non-final for library projects, we are forced to use if/else statements instead of switch/case clauses. Because the same constants re-created from the library's R.java files are final, you can use freely the switch clause in your final project.

As you can see, library projects are compile-time constructs. Clearly, any resources that belong to the library get absorbed and merged into the main project. There is not a question of sharing at runtime, because there is just one package file with the name of the main package. In short, libraries offer a way to share resources between related projects at compile time.

Understanding Components and Threads

We started off this chapter establishing that each package runs in its own process. We will now explain the organization of threads within this process. This will lead us to why we need handlers to offload the work from the main thread and also to communicate with the main thread.

Most code in an Android application runs in the context of a component such as an activity or a service. Most of the time, there is only one thread running in an Android process, called the main thread. We will talk about the implications of sharing this main thread among various components. Primarily, this can lead to Application Not Responding (ANR) messages (the "A" stands for "application" and not "annoying"). We will show you how you can use handlers, messages, and threads to break the dependency on the main thread when long-running operations are needed.

An Android process has four primary component types: Activity, Service, ContentProvider, and a BroadcastReceiver. Most code you write in an Android application is part of one of these components or called by one of these components. Each of these components gets its own XML node under an application node specification in the Android project manifest file. To recall, here are these nodes in Listing 13-5:

Listing 13-5. How Components Are Declared in the Manifest File

```
<manifest...>
  <application>
     <activity/>
     <service/>
     <receiver/>
     <provider/>
  </application>
</manifest>
```

With some exceptions (such as external process calls to content providers), Android uses the same thread to process (or run through) code in these components. This thread is called the main thread of the application. When these components are called, the call can be either a synchronous call, such as when you call a content provider for data, or a deferred one through a message queue, such as when you invoke functionality by calling a start service or show a dialog.

Figure 13-4 describes the relationship between threads and these four components. This diagram shows how threads weave through the Android framework and its components. The diagram does not indicate the order in which a thread might weave through the various components. The diagram is merely showing that the processing continues from one component to another in a sequential fashion.

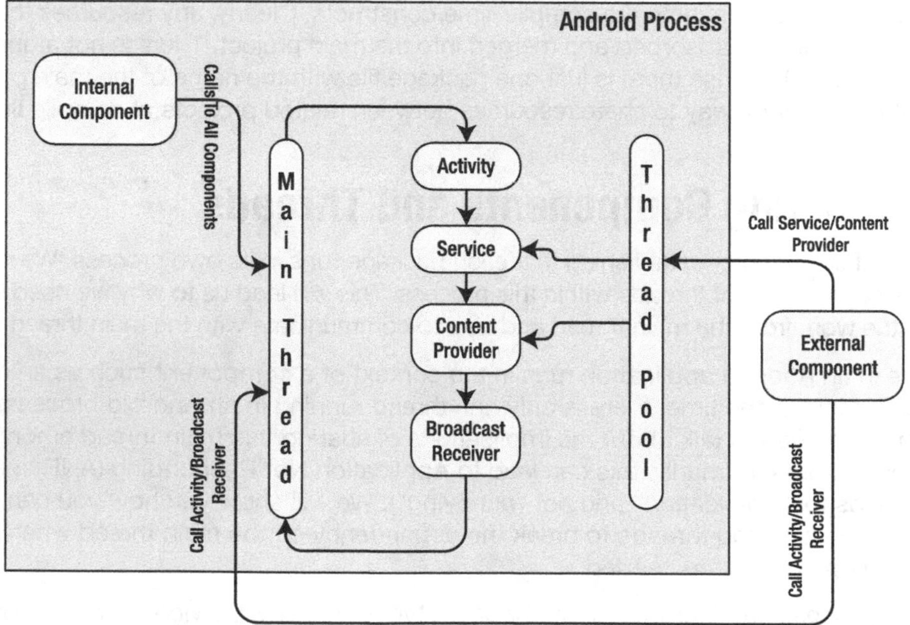

Figure 13-4. *Android components and threading framework*

As indicated in Figure 13-4, the main thread does the heavy lifting. It runs through all the components by using a message queue. As you select menus or buttons on the device screen, the device will translate these actions as messages and drop them onto the main queue of the process that is in focus. The main thread sits in a loop and processes each message. If any message takes more than five seconds or so, Android throws an ANR message.

Similarly, in response to a menu item, if you were to invoke a broadcast message, Android again drops a message on the main queue of the package process from which the registered receiver is to be invoked. The main thread will come around to that message at a later time to invoke the receiver. The main thread does the work for a broadcast receiver as well. If the main thread is busy responding to a menu action, the broadcast receiver will have to wait until the main thread gets freed up.

The same is true with a service. When you start a local service with `Activity.startService` from a menu item, a message is dropped onto the main queue, and the main thread will come around to process it via the service code.

Calls to a local content provider are slightly different. A content provider still runs on the main thread for a local call, but a call to it is synchronous and does not use message queues.

You may ask, "Why is it important whether most code in an Android application runs on the main thread or otherwise?" This is important because the main thread has the responsibility to get back to its queue so that UI events are responded to. As a consequence, you should not hold up the main thread. If there is something that is going to take longer than five seconds, you should get that done in a separate thread or defer it by asking the main thread to come back to it when it is freed up from other processing.

When external clients or components outside of the process make a call to the content provider for data, then that call is allocated a thread from a thread pool. The same is true with external clients connecting to services.

Let's look at what handlers are and how they function in the next section.

Understanding Handlers

We have briefly referred to the idea of deferring work on a main thread if needed. This is done through handlers. Handlers are extensively used throughout Android so that the main UI thread is not held up. They also play a role in communicating with the main thread from other spawned worker threads.

A handler is a mechanism to drop a message on the main queue (more precisely, the queue attached to the thread on which the handler is instantiated) so that the message can be processed at a later point in time by that circulating thread. The message that is dropped has an internal reference pointing to the handler that dropped it.

When the main thread gets around to processing that message, it invokes the handler that dropped the message through a callback method on the handler object. This callback method is called `handleMessage`. Figure 13-5 presents this relationship between handlers, messages, and the main thread.

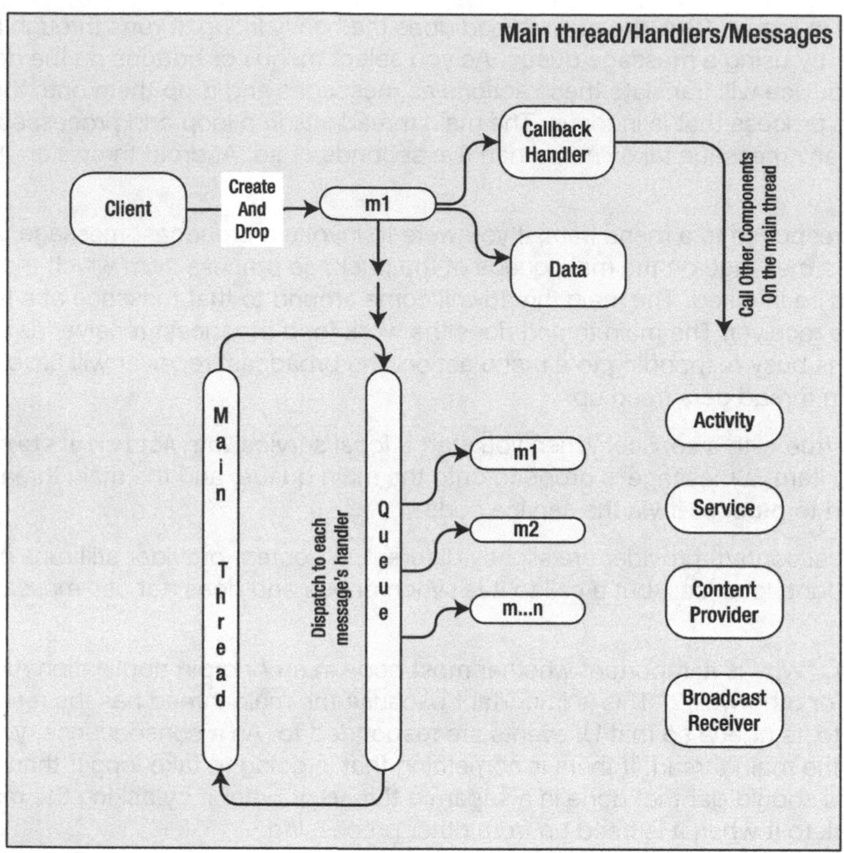

***Figure 13-5.** Handler, message, message queue relationship*

Figure 13-5 illustrates the key players that work together when we talk about handlers: main thread, main thread queue, handler, and a message. Out of these four, we are not exposed to the main thread or the queue directly. We primarily deal with the handler object and the message object. Even between these two, the handler object coordinates most of the work.

Although a handler allows us to drop a message onto the queue, it is the message object that actually holds a reference back to the handler. The message object also holds a data structure that can be passed back to the handler.

Working with a handler and messages is best understood through an example. For the example, we will have a menu item that invokes a function, and that function, in turn, performs an action five times at one-second intervals and reports back to the invoking activity each time.

If we didn't mind holding up the main thread, we could have coded this scenario like the pseudo code in Listing 13-6.

Listing 13-6. Holding Up the Main Thread with a Sleep Method

```
public class SomeActivity  {
    ....other methods
    void respondToMenuItem()     {
        //Prove that we are on the main thread
        Utils.logThreadSignature();
        //simulate an operation that takes longer than 5 seconds
        for (int i=0;i<6;i++)        {
            sleepFor(1000);// put main thread to sleep for 1 sec
            dosomething();
            SomeTextView.setText("did something. Counter:" + Integer.toString(i));
         }
    }
}
```

This will satisfy the requirement of the use case. However, if we do this, we are holding up the main thread, and we are guaranteed to have an ANR. We can use a handler to avoid the ANR in the previous example. Pseudo code to do this via a handler will look like Listing 13-7.

Listing 13-7. Instantiating a Handler from the Main Thread

```
void respondToMenuItem(){
    SomeHandlerDerivedFromHandler myHandler =
                new SomeHandlerDerivedFromHandler();
    myHandler.doDeferredWork(); //invoke a function in 1 sec intervals
    //note that doDeferredWork() is not part of the SDK
    //we will show you the code for this shortly
}
```

Now, the call `respondToMenuItem()` will allow the main thread to go back to its loop. The instantiated handler knows that it is invoked on the main thread and hooks itself up to the queue. The method `doDeferredWork()` will schedule work so that the main thread can get back to this work once it is free.

To investigate this protocol, let's see the actual source code for a proper handler. The code in Listing 13-8 in the next section demonstrates this handler, which is called `DeferWorkHandler`. In the previous pseudo code of Listing 13-7, the indicated handler `SomeHandlerDerivedFromHandler` is equivalent to this `DeferWorkHandler`. Similarly, the indicated method `doDeferredWork()` (of Listing 13-7) is implemented on the `DeferWorkHandler` in Listing 13-8.

Listing 13-8. DeferWorkHandler Source Code

```
public class DeferWorkHandler extends Handler  {
    //Keep track of how many times we sent the message
    private int count = 0;

    //A parent driver activity we can use to inform of status.
    private TestHandlersDriverActivity parentActivity = null;
```

```
    //During construction we take in the parent driver activity.
    public DeferWorkHandler(TestHandlersDriverActivity inParentActivity){
        parentActivity = inParentActivity;
    }
    //Callback method that gets called by the main thread
    @Override
    public void handleMessage(Message msg)     {
        //Use the message object to get to its data
        String pm = new String("message called:" + count + ":" +
                msg.getData().getString("message"));
        //you can access the parent activity and invoke UI calls on it here
        parentActivity.someControl.somemethod(); //example only

        //logic to invoke itself multiple times if needed
        if (count > 5)      {
            return;
        }
        count++; //increment count
        sendTestMessage(1); //reinvoke again by sending a message
    }
    //method called by the client
    public void doDeferredWork()    {
        count = 0;
        sendTestMessage(1);
    }
    //Preparing and sending the message
    public void sendTestMessage(long interval)    {
        Message m = this.obtainMessage();
        prepareMessage(m);
        this.sendMessageDelayed(m, interval * 1000);
    }
    public void prepareMessage(Message m)    {
        Bundle b = new Bundle();
        b.putString("message", "Hello World");
        m.setData(b);
        return ;
    }
}
```

Let's look at the key aspects of this source code. The first is that the handler is derived from the base class handler. In the constructor of the handler, we use a pointer to the parent activity so that we can use the UI controls of the activity to report what needs to be reported or to act upon. Then we code a method (doDeferredWork) to encapsulate what this handler is expected to do for us. Notice that the doDeferredWork() is not an overridden method and you can call this method whatever name that you would like. It is in this method that you work with messages to eventually call the overridden handleMessage(). Also, it is in this handleMessage() that you actually put the real code that is originally deferred from the main thread.

The base handler offers a series of methods to send messages to the queue to be responded to later. These methods are used in the doDeferredWork(). sendMessage() and sendMessageDelayed() are two examples of these send methods. sendMessageDelayed(), which we used in the example, allows us to drop a message on the main queue with a given amount of time delay. sendMessage(), in contrast, drops the message immediately to be processed when the main thread gets around to it.

When you call sendMessage() or sendMessageDelayed(), you will need an instance of the message object. It is best that you ask the handler to give it to you, because when the handler returns the message object, it hides itself in the belly of the message. That way, when the main thread comes along, it knows which handler to call based solely on the message. In Listing 13-8, the message is obtained using the following code:

```
Message m = this.obtainMessage();
```

The variable this refers to is the handler object instance. As the name indicates, the method does not create a new message but instead gets one from a global message pool. At a later point, once this message is processed, it will be recycled. The method obtainMessage() has the variations shown in Listing 13-9.

Listing 13-9. Constructing a Message Through a Handler

```
obtainMessage();
obtainMessage(int what);
obtainMessage(int what, Object object);
obtainMessage(int what, int arg1, int arg2)
obtainMessage(int what, int arg1, int arg2, Object object);
```

Each method variation sets the corresponding fields on the message object. There are some restrictions on the object argument when the message crosses process boundaries. In such cases, it needs to be Parcelable. It is much safer and compatible in such cases to use the setData() method explicitly on the message object, which takes a Bundle. In Listing 13-8, we have used setData(). You are encouraged to use arg1 or arg2 instead if what you are intending to pass are simple indicators that can be accommodated with integer values.

The argument what (in Listing 13-9) allows you to dequeue message or enquire if there are messages of this type in the queue. See the operations on the handler class for more details.

Once we obtain a message from the handler, we can optionally modify the data contents of that message. In our example, we have used the setData() function by passing it a Bundle object. After we have categorized or identified the data of the message, we can send the message to the queue through sendMessage() or sendMessageDelayed(). When these methods are called, the main thread will return to attending the queue.

Once the messages are delivered to the queue, the handler sits and waits (figuratively speaking) until the main thread retrieves those messages and calls the handler's handleMessage().

If you want to see this handler and main thread interaction more clearly, you can write a logcat message when you are sending the message and in the handleMessage() callback. You will notice the time stamps differ as the main thread would have taken a few more milliseconds to come back to the handleMessage() method.

In our example, each `handleMessage()`, after processing one message, sends another message to the queue so that it can be called again. It does this five times, and when the counter reaches five, it quits sending messages to the queue. This is one way to break up the work into multiple chunks, although there are better ways to do this either through a worker thread or through a class `AsyncTask`. The essential `AsyncTask` is covered in the next chapter. Let's cover the explicit worker threads option briefly now.

Using Worker Threads

When we use a handler like the one in the previous section, the code is still executed on the main thread. Each call to `handleMessage()` still should return within the time stipulations of the main thread (in other words, each message invocation should complete in less than five seconds to avoid Application Not Responding). If your goal is to extend that time of execution further, you will need to start a separate thread, keep the thread running until it finishes the work, and allow for that subthread to report back to the main activity, which is running on the main thread. This type of a subthread is often called a worker thread.

It is a no-brainer to start a separate thread while responding to a menu item. However, the clever trick is to allow the worker thread to post a message to the queue of the main thread that something is happening and that the main thread should look at it when it gets to that message. It is also an error to call UI methods on a non-UI thread. So, you will need this handler that is tied to the main thread to call UI methods from a worker thread.

A reasonable solution that involves a worker thread is as follows:

1. Create a handler in the main thread while responding to the menu item. Keep it aside.
2. Create a separate thread (a worker thread) that does the actual work. Pass the handler from step 1 to the worker thread. This handler allows the worker thread to communicate with the main thread.
3. The worker thread code can now do the actual work for longer than five seconds and, while doing it, can call the handler to send status messages to communicate with the main thread.
4. These status messages now get processed by the main thread, because the handler belonged to the main thread. The main thread can process these messages while the worker thread is doing its work.

You can see the sample code for this interaction in the downloadable project for this chapter. An alternate and probably more straightforward way to communicate with the UI thread from a worker thread is to get hold of the activity pointer and call the method `Activity.runOnUiThread(Runnable action)`. Of course you need to create a Runnable object for coordination.

References

Here are some useful links to further strengthen your understanding of this chapter:

- `http://developer.android.com/guide/publishing/app-signing.html`: A must-read for signing `.apk` files.
- `http://developer.android.com/guide/developing/projects/projects-eclipse.html`: Primary SDK reference for Android libraries.
- `http://developer.android.com/guide/topics/fundamentals.html`: SDK reference on Android component life cycles.
- `http://www.androidbook.com/item/3493`: A layman's introduction to what it means to sign digitally.
- `http://www.androidbook.com/item/3279`: Our research on understanding Android packages. You will see how to sign `.apk` files, further links to how to share data between packages, more on shared user IDs, and instructions to install and uninstall packages.
- `http://www.androidbook.com/item/3908`: Our research notes on all aspects of Android library support, including older screen shots, newer screen shots, useful URLs, sample code, and more.
- `http://android-developers.blogspot.com/2011/10/changes-to-library-projects-in-android.html`: What has changed in libraries at the time of Android 4.0 and the reasons for the change? This blog also talks about future directions for working with libraries.
- `http://tools.android.com/tips/non-constant-fields`: Insightful discussion of the role of non-final variables and how they affect `switch` statements.
- `http://tools.android.com/knownissues`: Android documentation of known issues in the SDK Tools and the ADT releases. Also note the domain name of this URL; this site is dedicated to all aspects of Android tooling.
- `http://docs.oracle.com/javase/7/docs/technotes/tools/windows/keytool.html`: Excellent documentation on `keytool`, `jarsigner`, and the signing process itself.
- `http://www.androidbook.com/proandroid5/projects`: A list of downloadable projects related to this book. For this chapter, look for a file called `ProAndroid5_Ch13_TestAndroidLibraries.zip`. This ZIP file contains two projects: one a library and the other that uses this library. Also take a look at a project called `ProAndroid5_Ch13_TestHandlers.zip`, which contains the code to work with handlers including worker threads.

Summary

This chapter gave you a quick run-down on how packages, processes, components, and threads interact in an Android application. This chapter has also documented the library support for sharing assets between multiple applications. This chapter also has introduced handlers, a key concept in the Android SDK. In the next chapter, we will give detailed coverage of `AsyncTask`, which combines the worker threads and handlers into a simpler programming abstraction to use.

Chapter 14

Building and Consuming Services

The Android platform provides a complete software stack. This means you get an operating system and middleware, as well as working applications (such as a phone dialer). Alongside all of this, you have an SDK that you can use to write applications for the platform. Thus far, we've seen that we can build applications that directly interact with the user through a user interface. We have not, however, discussed background services or the possibilities of building components that run in the background.

In this chapter, we are going to focus on building and consuming services in Android. First we'll discuss consuming HTTP services, and then we'll cover a nice way to do simple background tasks, and finally we'll discuss interprocess communication—that is, communication between applications on the same device.

Consuming HTTP Services

Android applications and mobile applications in general are small apps with a lot of functionality. One of the ways that mobile apps deliver such rich functionality on such a small device is that they pull information from various sources. For example, most Android smartphones come with the Maps application, which provides sophisticated mapping functionality. We, however, know that the application is integrated with the Google Maps API and other services, which provide most of the sophistication.

That said, it is likely that the applications you write will also leverage information from other applications and APIs. A common integration strategy is to use HTTP. For example, you might have a Java servlet available on the Internet that provides services you want to leverage from one of your Android applications. How do you do that with Android? Interestingly, the Android SDK ships with a variation of Apache's `HttpClient` (`http://hc.apache.org/httpcomponents-client-ga/`), which is universally used. The Android version has been modified for Android, but the APIs are very similar to the APIs in the Apache version.

The Apache HttpClient is a comprehensive HTTP client. It offers full support for the HTTP protocol. In this section, we will discuss using the HttpClient to make HTTP GET and HTTP POST calls. If you are working with RESTful services, you would probably use the other HTTP operations as well (PUT, DELETE, etc.).

Using the HttpClient for HTTP GET Requests

Here's one of the general patterns for using the HttpClient:

1. Create an HttpClient (or get an existing reference).
2. Instantiate a new HTTP method, such as PostMethod or GetMethod.
3. Set HTTP parameter names/values.
4. Execute the HTTP call using the HttpClient.
5. Process the HTTP response.

Listing 14-1 shows how to execute an HTTP GET using the HttpClient.

> **Note** We give you a URL at the end of the chapter that you can use to download projects from this chapter. This will allow you to import these projects into your IDE directly. Also, because the code attempts to use the Internet, you will need to add android.permission.INTERNET to your manifest file when making HTTP calls using HttpClient.
>
> Also note that in the following examples, all web services calls should be put into background threads so as not to block the main UI thread. See later in this chapter, as well as Chapter 15, for an excellent deep-dive on how to do that. For the purposes of this chapter, those details are excluded to help with understanding services.

Listing 14-1. Using HttpClient and HttpGet: HttpGetDemo.java

```
public class HttpGetDemo extends Activity {
    /** Called when the activity is first created. */
    @Override
    public void onCreate(Bundle savedInstanceState) {
        super.onCreate(savedInstanceState);
        setContentView(R.layout.main);

        BufferedReader in = null;
        try {

            HttpClient client = new DefaultHttpClient();
            HttpGet request = new HttpGet("http://code.google.com/android/");
            HttpResponse response = client.execute(request);
```

```
            in = new BufferedReader(
                    new InputStreamReader(
                        response.getEntity().getContent()));

            StringBuffer sb = new StringBuffer("");
            String line = "";
            String NL = System.getProperty("line.separator");
            while ((line = in.readLine()) != null) {
                sb.append(line + NL);
            }
            in.close();

            String page = sb.toString();
            System.out.println(page);
        } catch (Exception e) {
            e.printStackTrace();
        } finally {
            if (in != null) {
                try {
                    in.close();
                } catch (IOException e) {
                    e.printStackTrace();
                }
            }
        }
    }
}
```

The HttpClient is able to consume the various HTTP request types, such as HttpGet, HttpPost, and so on. Listing 14-1 uses the HttpClient to get the contents of the http://code.google.com/android/ URL. The actual HTTP request is executed with the call to client.execute(). After executing the request, the code reads the entire response into a string object. Note that the BufferedReader is closed in the finally block, which also closes the underlying HTTP connection.

For our example we embedded the HTTP logic inside of an activity, but we don't need to be within the context of an activity to use HttpClient. You can use it from within the context of any Android component or use it as part of a stand-alone class. In fact, you shouldn't use HttpClient directly within an activity, because a web call could take a while to complete and cause an Application Not Responding (ANR) pop-up. We'll cover that topic later in this chapter. For now we're going to cheat a little so we can focus on how to make HttpClient calls.

The code in Listing 14-1 executes an HTTP request without passing any HTTP parameters to the server. You can pass name/value parameters as part of the request by appending name/value pairs to the URL, as shown in Listing 14-2.

***Listing 14-2.** Adding Parameters to an HTTP GET Request*

```
HttpGet request =
    new HttpGet("http://somehost/Upload.aspx?one=value1&two=value2");
client.execute(request);
```

When you execute an HTTP GET, the parameters (names and values) of the request are passed as part of the URL. Passing parameters this way has some limitations. Namely, the length of a URL should be kept below 2,048 characters. If you have more than this amount of data to submit, you should use HTTP POST instead. The POST method is more flexible and passes parameters as part of the request body.

Using the HttpClient for HTTP POST Requests (a Multipart Example)

Making an HTTP POST call is very similar to making an HTTP GET call (see Listing 14-3). This example is called SimpleHTTPPost.

Listing 14-3. Making an HTTP POST Request with the `HttpClient`

```
HttpClient client = new DefaultHttpClient();
HttpPost request = new HttpPost(
        "http://www.androidbook.com/akc/display");
List<NameValuePair> postParameters = new ArrayList<NameValuePair>();
postParameters.add(new BasicNameValuePair("url", "DisplayNoteIMPURL"));
postParameters.add(new BasicNameValuePair("reportId", "4788"));
postParameters.add(new BasicNameValuePair("ownerUserId", "android"));
postParameters.add(new BasicNameValuePair("aspire_output_format", "embedded-xml"));
UrlEncodedFormEntity formEntity = new UrlEncodedFormEntity(
        postParameters);
request.setEntity(formEntity);
HttpResponse response = client.execute(request);
```

The code in Listing 14-3 would replace the three lines in Listing 14-1 where the `HttpGet` is used. Everything else could stay the same. To make an HTTP POST call with the `HttpClient`, you have to call the `execute()` method of the `HttpClient` with an instance of `HttpPost`. When making HTTP POST calls, you generally pass URL-encoded name/value form parameters as part of the HTTP request. To do this with the `HttpClient`, you have to create a list that contains instances of `NameValuePair` objects and then wrap that list with a `UrlEncodedFormEntity` object. The `NameValuePair` wraps a name/value combination, and the `UrlEncodedFormEntity` class knows how to encode a list of `NameValuePair` objects suitable for HTTP calls (generally POST calls). After you create a `UrlEncodedFormEntity`, you can set the entity type of the `HttpPost` to the `UrlEncodedFormEntity` and then execute the request.

In Listing 14-3, we created an `HttpClient` and then instantiated the `HttpPost` with the URL of the HTTP endpoint. Next, we created a list of `NameValuePair` objects and populated it with several name/value parameters. We then created a `UrlEncodedFormEntity` instance, passing the list of `NameValuePair` objects to its constructor. Finally, we called the `setEntity()` method of the POST request and then executed the request using the `HttpClient` instance.

HTTP POST is actually much more powerful than this. With an HTTP POST, we can pass simple name/value parameters, as shown in Listing 14-3, as well as complex parameters such as files. HTTP POST supports another request-body format known as a multipart POST. With this type of POST, you can send name/value parameters as before, along with arbitrary files. Unfortunately, the version of `HttpClient` shipped with Android does not directly support multipart POST. To achieve this goal in the past, we've recommended that you grab three other libraries: Apache Commons IO, Mime4j, and HttpMime.

Now we recommend that you download the Ion library, which has two dependencies. All three jar files can be found at these two sites:

- `https://github.com/koush/ion#jars` (ion and androidasync)
- `https://code.google.com/p/google-gson/downloads/list` (gson)

Listing 14-4 demonstrates a multipart POST using Android. This example is called MultipartHTTPPost.

***Listing 14-4.** Making a Multipart POST Call*

```
public class TestMultipartPost extends Activity {
    /** Called when the activity is first created. */
    @Override
    public void onCreate(Bundle savedInstanceState) {
        super.onCreate(savedInstanceState);
        setContentView(R.layout.main);

        try {
            Ion.with(this, "http://www.androidbook.com/akc/update/PublicUploadTest")
            .setMultipartParameter("field1", "This is field number 1")
            .setMultipartParameter("field2", "Field 2 is shorter")
            .setMultipartFile("datafile",
                    new File(Environment.getExternalStorageDirectory()+"/testfile.txt"))
            .asString()
            .setCallback(new FutureCallback<String>() {
                   @Override
                    public void onCompleted(Exception e, String result) {
                       System.out.println(result);
                    }});

        } catch(Exception e) {
            // Do something about exceptions
            System.out.println("Got exception: " + e);
        }
    }
}
```

Note The multipart example uses several `.jar` files that are not included as part of the Android runtime. To ensure that the `.jar` files will be packaged as part of your `.apk` file, you need to add them as external `.jar` files in Eclipse. To do this, right-click your project in Eclipse, select Properties, choose Java Build Path, select the Libraries tab, and then select Add External JARs.

Following these steps will make the `.jar` files available during compile time as well as runtime.

To execute a multipart POST using the Ion library, you simply put together the appropriate calls to build a URL, add parameters, define the return type, and set up a callback method. This will run asynchronously and the callback will be invoked on the UI thread once a response is received from the web server. In the example, the result string is written to LogCat. Your application is probably going to receive back a JsonObject which the callback would then process. But realize that the response from the web server has already been converted into a JsonObject for you, making the processing in the callback that much easier. Listing 14-4 adds three parts to the request: two string parts and a text file. To run this example yourself you will need to put a testfile.txt file onto the external storage area of your device or emulator.

Finally, if you are building an application that requires you to pass a multipart POST to a web resource, you'll likely have to debug the solution using a dummy implementation of the service on your local workstation. When you're running applications on your local workstation, normally you can access the local machine by using `localhost` or IP address `127.0.0.1`. With Android applications, however, you will not be able to use `localhost` (or `127.0.0.1`) because the device or emulator will be its own `localhost`. You don't want to point this client to a service on the Android device; you want to point to your workstation. To refer to your development workstation from the application running in the device or emulator, you'll have to use your workstation's IP address in the URL.

SOAP, JSON, and XML Parsers

What about SOAP? There are lots of SOAP-based web services on the Internet, but to date, Google has not provided direct support in Android for calling SOAP web services. Google instead prefers REST-like web services, seemingly to reduce the amount of computing required on the client device. However, the tradeoff is that the developer must do more work to send data and to parse the returned data. Ideally, you will have some options for how you can interact with your web services. Some developers have used the kSOAP2 developer kit to build SOAP clients for Android. We won't be covering that approach, but it's out there if you're interested.

> **Note** The original kSOAP2 source is located here: `http://ksoap2.sourceforge.net/`. The open source community has (thankfully!) contributed a version of kSOAP2 for Android, and you can find out more about it here: `http://code.google.com/p/ksoap2-android/`.

One approach that's been used successfully is to implement your own services on the Internet, which can talk SOAP (or whatever) to the destination service. Then your Android application only needs to talk to your services, and you now have complete control. If the destination services change, you might be able to handle that without having to update and release a new version of your application. You'd only have to update the services on your server. A side benefit of this approach is that you could more easily implement a paid subscription model for your application. If a user lets their subscription lapse, you can turn them off at your server.

Android *does* have support for JavaScript Object Notation (JSON). This is a fairly common method of packaging data between a web server and a client. The JSON parsing classes make it very easy to unpack data from a response so your application can act on it. Or dig deeper into the Gson package referenced earlier in this chapter. Gson is a JSON Java library from Google, and its main benefit is how easy it is to parse JSON input into Java objects, and vice versa. It's also very fast.

Android also has a couple of XML parsers that you can use to interpret the responses from the HTTP calls; the recommended one is XMLPullParser.

Dealing with Exceptions

Dealing with exceptions is part of any program, but software that makes use of external services (such as HTTP services) must pay additional attention to exceptions because the potential for errors is magnified. There are several types of exceptions that you can expect while making use of HTTP services. These are transport exceptions, protocol exceptions, and timeouts. You should understand when these exceptions could occur.

Transport exceptions can occur due to a number of reasons, but the most likely scenario with a mobile device is poor network connectivity. Protocol exceptions (e.g., ClientProtocolException) are exceptions at the HTTP protocol layer. These include authentication errors, invalid cookies, and so on. You can expect to see protocol exceptions if, for example, you have to supply login credentials as part of your HTTP request but fail to do so. Timeouts, with respect to HTTP calls, come in two flavors: connection timeouts and socket timeouts. A connection timeout (e.g., ConnectTimeoutException) can occur if the `HttpClient` is not able to connect to the HTTP server—if, for example, the server is not available. A socket timeout (e.g., SocketTimeoutException) can occur if the `HttpClient` fails to receive a response within a defined time period. In other words, the `HttpClient` was able to connect to the server, but the server failed to return a response within the allocated time limit.

Now that you understand the types of exceptions that might occur, how do you deal with them? Fortunately, the `HttpClient` is a robust framework that takes most of the burden off your shoulders. In fact, the only exception types that you'll have to worry about are the ones that you'll be able to manage easily. The `HttpClient` takes care of transport exceptions by detecting transport issues and retrying requests (which works very well with this type of exception). Protocol exceptions are exceptions that can generally be flushed out during development. Timeouts are the most likely exceptions that you'll have to deal with. A simple and effective approach to dealing with both types of timeouts—connection timeouts and socket timeouts—is to wrap the `execute()` method of your HTTP request with a `try/catch` and then retry if a failure occurs.

When using the `HttpClient` as part of a real-world application, you need to pay some attention to multithreading issues that might come up. Let's delve into these now.

Addressing Multithreading Issues

The examples we've shown so far created a new `HttpClient` for each request. In practice, however, you could create one `HttpClient` for the entire application and use that for all of your HTTP communication. It's possible to associate a connection pool with this HttpClient, which you'll now see. With one `HttpClient` servicing all of your HTTP requests, you should pay attention to multithreading issues that could surface if you make simultaneous requests through the same `HttpClient`. Fortunately, the `HttpClient` provides facilities that make this easy—all you have to do is create the `DefaultHttpClient` using a `ThreadSafeClientConnManager`, as shown in Listing 14-5. This example project is HttpSingleton.

Listing 14-5. Creating an `HttpClient` for Multithreading: `CustomHttpClient.java`

```
public class CustomHttpClient {
    private static HttpClient customHttpClient;

    /** A private Constructor prevents instantiation */
    private CustomHttpClient() {
    }

    public static synchronized HttpClient getHttpClient() {
        if (customHttpClient == null) {
            HttpParams params = new BasicHttpParams();
            HttpProtocolParams.setVersion(params, HttpVersion.HTTP_1_1);
            HttpProtocolParams.setContentCharset(params,
                    HTTP.DEFAULT_CONTENT_CHARSET);
            HttpProtocolParams.setUseExpectContinue(params, true);
            HttpProtocolParams.setUserAgent(params,
                    System.getProperty("http.agent")
                    // Could also have used the following which is browser-oriented as opposed to
                    // device-oriented:
                    // new WebView(getApplicationContext()).getSettings().getUserAgentString()
            );

            ConnManagerParams.setTimeout(params, 1000);

            HttpConnectionParams.setConnectionTimeout(params, 5000);
            HttpConnectionParams.setSoTimeout(params, 10000);

            SchemeRegistry schReg = new SchemeRegistry();
            schReg.register(new Scheme("http",
                            PlainSocketFactory.getSocketFactory(), 80));
            schReg.register(new Scheme("https",
                            SSLSocketFactory.getSocketFactory(), 443));
            ClientConnectionManager conMgr = new
                            ThreadSafeClientConnManager(params,schReg);

            customHttpClient = new DefaultHttpClient(conMgr, params);
        }
        return customHttpClient;
    }

    public Object clone() throws CloneNotSupportedException {
        throw new CloneNotSupportedException();
    }
}
```

If your application needs to make more than a few HTTP calls, you should create an HttpClient that services all your HTTP requests. The simplest way to do this is to create a singleton class that can be accessed from anywhere in the application, as we've shown here. This is a fairly standard Java pattern in which we synchronize access to a getter method, and that getter method returns the one and only HttpClient object for the singleton, creating it the first time as necessary.

Now, take a look at the getHttpClient() method of CustomHttpClient. This method is responsible for creating our singleton HttpClient. We set some basic parameters, some timeout values, and the schemes that our HttpClient will support (that is, HTTP and HTTPS). Notice that when we instantiate the DefaultHttpClient(), we pass in a ClientConnectionManager. The ClientConnectionManager is responsible for managing HTTP connections for the HttpClient. Because we want to use a single HttpClient for all the HTTP requests (requests that could overlap if we're using threads), we create a ThreadSafeClientConnManager.

We also show you a simpler way of collecting the response from the HTTP request, using a BasicResponseHandler. The code for our activity that uses our CustomHttpClient is in Listing 14-6.

Listing 14-6.* Using Our *CustomHttpClient:HttpActivity.java

```
public class HttpActivity extends Activity
{
    private HttpClient httpClient;
    @Override
    public void onCreate(Bundle savedInstanceState)
    {
        super.onCreate(savedInstanceState);
        setContentView(R.layout.main);

        httpClient = CustomHttpClient.getHttpClient();
        getHttpContent();
    }

    public void getHttpContent()
    {
        try {
            HttpGet request = new HttpGet("http://www.google.com/");
            String page = httpClient.execute(request,
                    new BasicResponseHandler());
            System.out.println(page);
        } catch (IOException e) {
            // covers:
            //      ClientProtocolException
            //      ConnectTimeoutException
            //      ConnectionPoolTimeoutException
            //      SocketTimeoutException
            e.printStackTrace();
        }
    }
}
```

For this sample application, we do a simple HTTP get of the Google home page. We also use a BasicResponseHandler object to take care of rendering the page as a big String, which we then write out to LogCat. As you can see, adding a BasicResponseHandler to the execute() method is very easy to do.

You may be tempted to take advantage of the fact that each Android application has an associated Application object. By default, if you don't define a custom application object, Android uses android.app.Application. Here's the interesting thing about the application object: there will always be exactly one application object for your application, and all of your components can access it (using the global context object). It is possible to extend the Application class and add functionality such as our CustomHttpClient. However, in our case there is really no reason to do this within the Application class itself, and you will be much better off not messing with the Application class when you can simply create a separate singleton class to handle this type of need.

Fun with Timeouts

There are other terrific advantages to setting up a single HttpClient for our application to use. We can modify the properties of it in one place, and everyone can take advantage of it. For example, if we want to set up common timeout values for our HTTP calls, we can do that when creating our HttpClient by calling the appropriate setter functions against our HttpParams object. Please refer to Listing 14-5 and the getHttpClient() method. Notice that there are three timeouts we can play with. The first is a timeout for the connection manager, and it defines how long we should wait to get a connection out of the connection pool managed by the connection manager. In our example, we set this to 1 second. About the only time we might ever have to wait is if all connections from the pool are in use. The second timeout value defines how long we should wait to make a connection over the network to the server on the other end. Here, we used a value of 2 seconds. And lastly, we set a socket timeout value to 4 seconds to define how long we should wait to get data back for our request.

Corresponding to the three timeouts described previously, we could get these three exceptions: ConnectionPoolTimeoutException, ConnectTimeoutException, or SocketTimeoutException. All three of these exceptions are subclasses of IOException, which we've used in our HttpActivity instead of catching each subclass exception separately.

If you investigate each of the parameter-setting classes that we used in getHttpClient(), you might discover even more parameters that you would find useful.

We've described for you how to set up an HttpClient with a pool of connections for use across your application. And the implication is that every time you need to use a connection, the various settings will apply to your particular needs. But what if you want different settings for a particular message? Thankfully, there's an easy way to do that as well. We showed you how to use an HttpGet or an HttpPost object to describe the request to be made across the network. In a similar way to how we set HttpParams on our HttpClient, you can set HttpParams on both HttpGet and HttpPost objects. The settings you apply at the message level will override the settings at the HttpClient level without changing the HttpClient settings. Listing 14-7 shows what this might look like if we wanted to have a socket timeout of 1 minute instead of 4 seconds for one particular request. You would use these lines in place of the lines in the try block of getHttpContent() in Listing 14-6.

Listing 14-7. Overriding the Socket Timeout at the Request Level

```
HttpGet request = new HttpGet("http://www.google.com/");
HttpParams params = request.getParams();
HttpConnectionParams.setSoTimeout(params, 60000);   // 1 minute
request.setParams(params);
String page = httpClient.execute(request,
        new BasicResponseHandler());
System.out.println(page);
```

Using the HttpURLConnection

Android provides another way to deal with HTTP services, and that is using the `java.net.HttpURLConnection` class. This is not unlike the `HttpClient` classes we've just covered, but `HttpURLConnection` tends to require more statements to get things done. HttpURLConnection is also not threadsafe. On the other hand, this class is much smaller and lightweight than `HttpClient`, so you can simply create the ones you need. Starting with the Gingerbread release, it is also fairly stable, so you should consider it for apps on more recent devices when you just need basic HTTP features and you want a compact application.

Using the AndroidHttpClient

Android 2.2 introduced a new subclass of `HttpClient` called `AndroidHttpClient`. The idea behind this class is to make things easier for the developer of Android apps by providing default values and logic appropriate for Android apps. For example, the timeout values for the connection and the socket (that is, operation) default to 20 seconds each. The connection manager defaults to the `ThreadSafeClientConnManager`. For the most part, it is interchangeable with the `HttpClient` we used in the previous examples. There are a few differences, though, that you should be aware of:

- To create an `AndroidHttpClient`, you invoke the static `newInstance()` method of the `AndroidHttpClient` class, like this:

  ```
  AndroidHttpClient httpClient = AndroidHttpClient.newInstance
  ("my-http-agent-string");
  ```

- Notice that the parameter to the `newInstance()` method is an HTTP agent string. You most likely don't want to hardcode this, so you have two options as follows, which unfortunately can return different strings. The second one is probably the one you want to use as it looks more like what a browser would send (at least in our experiments).

  ```
  // The first option is a device-level agent string
  String httpAgent = System.getProperty("http.agent");
  // This second option looks like a browser's agent string
  httpAgent = new WebView(context).getSettings().getUserAgentString();
  ```

  Of course, you are also free to build your own agent string using anything available to your app; it's the server that's going to parse it to better understand the device, and if you control the server, you can use whatever values you sent from the app.

- When execute() is called on this client, you must be in a thread separate from the main UI thread. This means that you'll get an exception if you simply attempt to replace our previous HttpClient with an AndroidHttpClient. It is bad practice to make HTTP calls from the main UI thread, so AndroidHttpClient won't let you. We'll be covering threading issues in the next section.
- You must call close() on the AndroidHttpClient instance when you are done with it. This is so memory can be freed up properly.
- There are some handy static methods for dealing with compressed responses from a server, including
  - modifyRequestToAcceptGzipResponse(HttpRequest request)
  - getCompressedEntity(byte[] data, ContentResolver resolver)
  - getUngzippedContent(HttpEntity entity)

Once you've acquired an instance of the AndroidHttpClient, you cannot modify any parameter settings in it, nor can you add any parameter settings to it (such as the HTTP protocol version, for example). Your options are to override settings within the HttpGet object as shown previously or to not use the AndroidHttpClient.

This concludes our discussion of using HTTP services with the HttpClient. For a great tutorial on using HttpClient and these other concepts, please check out the Apache site at http://hc.apache.org/httpcomponents-client-ga/tutorial/html/.

We've shown you how to operate with HTTP-based services. But what if we wanted to run some background processing that lasted longer than a short while, or what if we wanted to invoke some non-UI functionality that exists in another Android application? For these needs, Android provides services. We will discuss them next.

Using Android Services

Android supports the concept of services. *Services* are components that run in the background, without a user interface. You can think of these components as similar to Windows services or Unix daemons. Similar to these types of services, Android services can be always available but don't have to be actively doing something. More important, Android services can have life cycles separate from activities. When an activity pauses, stops, or gets destroyed, there may be some processing that you want to continue. Services are good for that too.

Android supports two types of services: local services and remote services. A *local service* is a service that is only accessible to the application that is hosting it, and it is not accessible from other applications running on the device. Generally, these types of services simply support the application that is hosting the service. A *remote service* is accessible from other applications on the device in addition to the application hosting the service. Remote services define themselves to clients using Android Interface Definition Language (AIDL). We're going to talk about both of these types of services, although in the next few chapters, we're going deep into local services. Therefore, we will introduce them here but not spend that much time on them. We'll cover remote services in more detail in this chapter.

Understanding Services in Android

The Android Service class is a wrapper of sorts for code that has service-like behavior. However, a Service object does not create its own threads automatically. For a Service object to use threads, the developer must make it happen. This means that without adding threading to a service, the code of the service will run on the main thread. If our service is performing operations that will complete quickly, this won't be a problem. If our service might run for a while, we definitely want to involve threading. Keep in mind there is nothing wrong with using AsyncTasks to do threading within services.

Android supports the concept of a service for two reasons:

- First, to allow you to implement background tasks easily.
- Second, to allow you to do interprocess communication between applications running on the same device.

These two reasons correspond to the two types of services that Android supports: local services and remote services. An example of the first case might be a local service implemented as part of an e-mail application. The service could handle the sending of a new e-mail to the e-mail server, complete with attachments and retries. As this could take a while to complete, a service is a nice way of wrapping up that functionality so the main thread can kick it off and get back to the user. Plus, if the e-mail activity goes away, you still want the sent e-mails to be delivered. An example of the second case, as we'll see later, is a language translation application. Suppose you have several applications running on a device, and you need a service to accept text that needs to be translated from one language to another. Rather than repeat the logic in every application, you could write a remote translation service and have the applications talk to the service.

A local service gets initialized either by a client binding to it using bindService(), or by a client starting it using startService(). Remote services are typically always initialized with bindService(). A bound service gets instantiated when the first client binds to it, and destroyed when the last client unbinds from it. As clients come in and out of the foreground, they can bind and unbind as needed, to ensure that the service isn't running unnecessarily. This helps to preserve battery life. However, it is unwise to bind in onResume() and unbind in onPause() because that could cause a lot of unnecessary starting and stopping of the service. It's better to bind and unbind in onCreate() and onDestroy(), or in onStart() and onStop(). Binding is only allowed from an Application Context, an Activity, another Service, or a Content Provider. That means not from Fragments and not from Broadcast Receivers.

When a service is instead started with startService(), it will remain running until it is stopped, either by a client or by telling itself to stop. For a local service that wants to perform work in the background, consider instantiating it with startService() so it can remain running even if the activity that started it goes away. Technically a Broadcast Receiver can start a service using startService(), since the service can then continue to exist once the short-lived Broadcast Receiver terminates. If you do create a service that will run in the background even when the activities have gone away, you may want to implement onBind() for when the user wants to regain control of the service. A new activity could bind to the existing service and then call service methods on it.

There are examples of local services that do not create background threads, but this may not be very useful in practice. A service does not inherently create any threads, so code of a service will by default run on the main UI thread. There may not be any real advantage to wrapping this code in a service then, since you could just call methods of a class to execute that logic. It is more common for a local service to have its own threads of execution, which can be started either when the first client binds to it, or because of a startService() command.

Now, we can begin a detailed examination of the two types of services. We will start by talking about local services and then discuss remote services. As mentioned before, local services are services that are called only by the application that hosts them. Remote services are services that support a remote procedure call (RPC) mechanism. These services allow external clients, on the same device, to connect to the service and use its facilities. There are two main ways of calling remote services: using an AIDL interface and using a Messenger. Both will be covered.

> **Note** The second type of service in Android is known by several names: remote service, AIDL-supporting service, AIDL service, external service, and RPC service. These terms all refer to the same type of service—one that's meant to be accessed remotely by other applications running on the device.

Understanding Local Services

Local services are services that are generally started via `Context.startService()`. Once started, these types of services will continue to run until a client calls `Context.stopService()` on the service or the service itself calls `stopSelf()`. Note that when `Context.startService()` is called and the service has not already been created, the system will instantiate the service and call the service's `onStartCommand()` method. Keep in mind that calling `Context.startService()` after the service has been started (that is, while it exists) will not result in another instance of the service, but will reinvoke the running service's `onStartCommand()` method. Here are a couple of examples of local services:

- A service to monitor sensor data from the device and do analysis, issuing alerts if a certain condition is realized. This service might run constantly.
- A task-executor service that lets your application's activities submit jobs and queue them for processing. This service might only run for the duration of the operation to submit the job.

Listing 14-8 demonstrates a local service by implementing a service that executes background tasks. We'll end up with four artifacts required to create and consume the service: `BackgroundService.java` (the service itself), `main.xml` (a layout file for the activity), `MainActivity.java` (an activity class to call the service), and `AndroidManifest.xml`. Listing 14-8 only contains `BackgroundService.java`. We'll dissect this code first and then move on to the other three.

Listing 14-8. Implementing a Local Service: `BackgroundService.java`

```
public class BackgroundService extends Service
{
    private static final String TAG = "BackgroundService";
    private NotificationManager notificationMgr;
    private ThreadGroup myThreads = new ThreadGroup("ServiceWorker");

    @Override
    public void onCreate() {
        super.onCreate();

        Log.v(TAG, "in onCreate()");
        notificationMgr =(NotificationManager)getSystemService(
               NOTIFICATION_SERVICE);
        displayNotificationMessage("Background Service is running");
    }

    @Override
    public int onStartCommand(Intent intent, int flags, int startId) {
        super.onStartCommand(intent, flags, startId);

        int counter = intent.getExtras().getInt("counter");
        Log.v(TAG, "in onStartCommand(), counter = " + counter +
               ", startId = " + startId);

        new Thread(myThreads, new ServiceWorker(counter),
            "BackgroundService")
                .start();

        return START_STICKY;
    }

    class ServiceWorker implements Runnable
    {
        private int counter = -1;
        public ServiceWorker(int counter) {
            this.counter = counter;
        }

        public void run() {
            final String TAG2 = "ServiceWorker:" +
                Thread.currentThread().getId();
            // do background processing here... we'll just sleep...
            try {
                Log.v(TAG2, "sleeping for 10 seconds. counter = " +
                    counter);
                Thread.sleep(10000);
                Log.v(TAG2, "... waking up");
            } catch (InterruptedException e) {
                Log.v(TAG2, "... sleep interrupted");
            }
        }
    }
```

```
    @Override
    public void onDestroy()
    {
        Log.v(TAG, "in onDestroy(). Interrupting threads and cancelling notifications");
        myThreads.interrupt();
        notificationMgr.cancelAll();
        super.onDestroy();
    }

    @Override
    public IBinder onBind(Intent intent) {
        Log.v(TAG, "in onBind()");
        return null;
    }

    private void displayNotificationMessage(String message)
    {

        PendingIntent contentIntent =
            PendingIntent.getActivity(this, 0,
                new Intent(this, MainActivity.class), 0);

        Notification notification = new NotificationCompat.Builder(this)
            .setContentTitle(message)
            .setContentText("Touch to turn off service")
            .setSmallIcon(R.drawable.emo_im_winking)
            .setTicker("Starting up!!!")
            // .setLargeIcon(aBitmap)
            .setContentIntent(contentIntent)
            .setOngoing(true)
            .build();

        notificationMgr.notify(0, notification);
    }
}
```

The structure of a Service object is somewhat similar to an activity. There is an onCreate() method where you can do initialization, and an onDestroy() where you do cleanup. Services don't pause or resume the way activities do, so we don't use onPause() or onResume() methods. In this example, we won't be binding to the local service, but because Service requires an implementation of the onBind() method, we provide one that simply returns null. It's worth mentioning that you could have a local service that implements onBind() and does not use onStartCommand().

Going back to our onCreate() method, we don't need to do much except to notify the user that this service has been created. We do this using the NotificationManager. You've probably noticed the notification bar at the top left of an Android screen. By pulling down on this, the user can view messages of importance, and by touching notifications can act on the notifications, which usually means returning to some activity related to the notification. With services, because they can be running, or at least existing, in the background without a visible activity, there has to be some way for the user to get back in touch with the service, perhaps to turn it off. Therefore, we create a Notification object, populate it with a PendingIntent, which will get us back to our control activity, and post it. This all happens in the displayNotificationMessage() method. Note that our Notification object needs to exist as long as our service exists, so we use setOngoing(true) to keep it in the notifications list until we clear it ourselves from our service's onDestroy() method. The method we used in onDestroy() to clear our notification is cancelAll() on the NotificationManager.

There's another thing you need to have for this example to work. You'll need to create a drawable named emo_im_winking and place it within your project's drawable folder. A good source of drawables for this demonstration purpose is to look under the Android platform folder at Android SDK/platforms/<version>/data/res/drawable, where <version> is the version you're interested in. Unfortunately, you can't reliably refer to Android system drawables from your code, so you'll need to copy what you want over to your project's drawables folder. If you choose a different drawable file for your example, just go ahead and rename the resource ID in the constructor for the Notification.

When an intent is sent into our service using startService(), onCreate() is called if necessary, and our onStartCommand() method is called to receive the caller's intent. In our case, we're not going to do anything special with it, except to unpack the counter and use it to start a background thread. In a real-world service, we would expect any data to be passed to us via the intent, and this could include URIs, for example. Notice the use of a ThreadGroup when creating the Thread. This will prove to be useful later when we want to get rid of our background threads. Also notice the startId parameter. This is set for us by Android and is a unique identifier of the service calls since this service was started.

Our ServiceWorker class is a typical runnable and is where the work happens for our service. In our particular case, we're simply logging some messages and sleeping. We're also catching any interruptions and logging them. One thing we're not doing is manipulating the user interface. We're not updating any views for example. Because we're not on the main thread anymore, we cannot touch the UI directly. There are ways for our ServiceWorker to effect changes in the user interface, and we'll get into those details in the next few chapters.

The last item to pay attention to in our BackgroundService is the onDestroy() method. This is where we perform the cleanup. For our example, we want to get rid of the threads we created earlier, if any are still around. If we don't do this, they could simply hang around and take up memory. Second, we want to get rid of our notification message. Because our service is going away, there's no longer any need for the user to get to the activity to get rid of it. In a real-world application, however, we might want to keep our workers working. If our service is sending e-mails, we certainly don't want to simply kill off the threads. Our example is overly simple, because we imply through the use of the interrupt() method that you can easily kill off background threads. In reality, however, the most you can do is interrupt. This won't necessarily kill off a thread, though. There are deprecated methods for killing threads, but you should not use these. They can cause memory and stability problems for you and your users. Interrupting works in our example, because we're doing sleeps, which can be interrupted.

It's worthwhile taking a look at the ThreadGroup class because it provides ways for you to get access to your threads. We created a single ThreadGroup object within our service and then used that when creating our individual threads. Within our onDestroy() method of the service, we simply interrupt() on the ThreadGroup, and it issues an interrupt to each thread in the ThreadGroup.

So there you have the makings of a simple local service. Before we show you the code for our activity, Listing 14-9 shows the XML layout file for our user interface.

***Listing 14-9.** Implementing a Local Service: `main.xml`*

```
<?xml version="1.0" encoding="utf-8"?>
<!-- This file is /res/layout/main.xml -->
<LinearLayout xmlns:android="http://schemas.android.com/apk/res/android"
    android:orientation="vertical"
    android:layout_width="fill_parent"
    android:layout_height="fill_parent"
    >
<Button  android:id="@+id/startBtn"
    android:layout_width="wrap_content"
    android:layout_height="wrap_content"
    android:text="Start Service"  android:onClick="doClick" />
<Button  android:id="@+id/stopBtn"
    android:layout_width="wrap_content"
    android:layout_height="wrap_content"
    android:text="Stop Service"  android:onClick="doClick" />
</LinearLayout>
```

We're going to show two buttons on the user interface, one to do `startService()` and the other to do `stopService()`. We could have chosen to use a ToggleButton, but then you would not be able to call `startService()` multiple times in a row. This is an important point. There is not a one-to-one relationship between `startService()` and `stopService()`. When `stopService()` is called, the service object will be destroyed, and all threads created from all `startService()` calls should also go away. Now, let's look at the code for our activity in Listing 14-10.

***Listing 14-10.** Implementing a Local Service: `MainActivity.java`*

```
public class MainActivity extends Activity
{
    private static final String TAG = "MainActivity";
    private int counter = 1;

    @Override
    public void onCreate(Bundle savedInstanceState)
    {
        super.onCreate(savedInstanceState);
        setContentView(R.layout.main);
    }

    public void doClick(View view) {
        switch(view.getId()) {
        case R.id.startBtn:
            Log.v(TAG, "Starting service... counter = " + counter);
            Intent intent = new Intent(MainActivity.this,
                    BackgroundService.class);
```

```
            intent.putExtra("counter", counter++);
            startService(intent);
            break;
        case R.id.stopBtn:
            stopService();
        }
    }

    private void stopService() {
        Log.v(TAG, "Stopping service...");
        if(stopService(new Intent(MainActivity.this,
                    BackgroundService.class)))
            Log.v(TAG, "stopService was successful");
        else
            Log.v(TAG, "stopService was unsuccessful");
    }

    @Override
    public void onDestroy()
    {
        stopService();
        super.onDestroy();
    }
}
```

Our MainActivity looks a lot like other activities you've seen. There's a simple onCreate() to set up our user interface from the main.xml layout file. There's a doClick() method to handle the button callbacks. In our example, we're calling startService() when the Start Service button is pressed, and we're calling stopService() when the Stop Service button is pressed. When we start the service, we want to pass in some data, which we do via the intent. We chose to pass the data in the Extras bundle, but we could have added it using setData() if we had a URI. When we stop the service, we check to see the return result. It should normally be true, but if the service was not running, we could get a return of false. Last, when our activity dies, we want to stop the service, so we also stop the service in our onDestroy() method. There's one more item to discuss, and that's the AndroidManifest.xml file, which we show in Listing 14-11.

Listing 14-11. Implementing a Local Service: AndroidManifest.xml

```
<?xml version="1.0" encoding="utf-8"?>
<manifest xmlns:android="http://schemas.android.com/apk/res/android"
      package="com.androidbook.services.simplelocal"
      android:versionCode="1"
      android:versionName="1.0">
    <uses-sdk android:minSdkVersion="8" />
    <application android:icon="@drawable/icon"
            android:label="@string/app_name">
        <activity android:name=".MainActivity"
                android:label="@string/app_name"
                android:launchMode="singleTop" >
```

```
        <intent-filter>
          <action android:name="android.intent.action.MAIN" />
          <category android:name="android.intent.category.LAUNCHER" />
        </intent-filter>
      </activity>
      <service android:name="BackgroundService"/>
  </application>

</manifest>
```

In addition to our regular <activity> tags in the manifest file, we now have a <service> tag. Because this is a local service that we're calling explicitly using the class name, we don't need to put much into the <service> tag. All that is required is the name of our service. But there is one other thing to point out about this manifest file. Our service creates a notification so that the user can get back to our MainActivity if, for example, the user pressed the Home key on MainActivity without stopping the service.

The MainActivity is still there; it's just not visible. One way to get back to the MainActivity is to click the notification that our service created. The notification manager delivers our intent back to our application and would normally cause a new instance of MainActivity to handle the new intent. To prevent this from happening, we set an attribute in our manifest file for MainActivity called android:launchMode, and we set it to singleTop. This will help ensure that the existing invisible MainActivity will be brought forward and displayed, rather than creating another MainActivity.

When you run this application, you will see our two buttons. By clicking the Start Service button, you will be instantiating the service and calling onStartCommand(). Our code logs several messages to LogCat, so you can follow along. Go ahead and click Start Service several times in a row, even quickly. You will see threads created to handle each request. You'll also notice that the value of counter is passed along through to each ServiceWorker thread. When you press the Stop Service button, our service will go away, and you'll see the log messages from our MainActivity's stopService() method, from our BackgroundService's onDestroy() method, and possibly from ServiceWorker threads if they got interrupted.

You should also notice the notification message when the service has been started. With the service running, go ahead and press the Back button from our MainActivity and notice that the notification message disappears. This means our service has gone away also. To restart our MainActivity, click Start Service to get the service going again. Now, press the Home button. Our MainActivity disappears from view, but the notification remains, meaning our service is still in existence. Go ahead and click the notification, and you'll again see our MainActivity.

Note that our example uses an activity to interface with the service, but any component in your application can use the service. This includes other services, activities, generic classes, and so on. Also note that our service does not stop itself; it relies on the activity to do that for it. There are some methods available to a service to allow the service to stop itself, namely stopSelf() and stopSelfResult(). Obviously, if we have multiple clients for this service, we wouldn't want the service to be stopped by one if the others are still using it. For a started service with multiple clients, it is more likely you'd put logic in the service itself to decide when the service can or should be stopped, and the service would use one of the stop*() methods to do that.

Our BackgroundService is a typical example of a service that is used by the components of the application that is hosting the service. In other words, the application that is running the service is also the only consumer. Because the service does not support clients from outside its process, the service is a local service. The critical methods of a local service are onCreate(), onStartCommand(), onBind(), stop*(), and onDestroy().

There's another option with a local service, and that is for the case where you'll only have one instance of the service with one background thread. In this case, in the onCreate() method of the BackgroundService, we could create a thread that does the service's heavy lifting. We could create and start the thread in onCreate() rather than onStartCommand(). We could do this because onCreate() is called only once, and we want the thread to be created only once during the life of the service. One thing we wouldn't have in onCreate(), though, is the content of the intent passed by startService(). If we need that, we might as well use the pattern as described previously, and we'd just know that onStartCommand() should be called only once.

Android has yet another way to implement a local service that includes a background thread automatically: the IntentService. A subclass of Service, IntentService receives the incoming Intent from a startService() call, creates a background (worker) thread for you, and invokes the callback onHandleIntent(Intent intent). If another intent is delivered to this service before the worker thread has completed the earlier intent, the new intent will sit and wait until the previous intent has been processed, at which time the next intent in the queue will get passed to the onHandleIntent() method. When all intents from the inbound queue have completed processing, the service will stop itself (no need for you to do that).

This concludes our introduction to local services. Remember that we'll get into more details of local services in subsequent chapters. Let's move on to AIDL services—the more complicated type of service.

Understanding AIDL Services

In the previous section, we showed you how to write an Android service that is consumed by the application that hosts the service. Now, we are going to show you how to build a service that can be consumed by other processes via remote procedure call (RPC). As with many other RPC-based solutions, in Android you need an interface definition language (IDL) to define the interface that will be exposed to clients. In the Android world, this IDL is called Android Interface Definition Language (AIDL). To build a remote service, you do the following:

1. Write an AIDL file that defines your interface to clients. The AIDL file uses Java syntax and has an .aidl extension. Use the same package name inside your AIDL file as the package for your Android project.
2. Add the AIDL file to your Eclipse project under the src directory. The Android Eclipse plug-in will call the AIDL compiler to generate a Java interface from the AIDL file (the AIDL compiler is called as part of the build process).
3. Implement a service, and return the interface from the onBind() method.
4. Add the service configuration to your AndroidManifest.xml file. The sections that follow show you how to execute each step.

Defining a Service Interface in AIDL

To demonstrate an example of a remote service, we are going to write a stock-quoter service. This service will provide a method that takes a ticker symbol and returns the stock value. To write a remote service in Android, the first step is to define the service interface definition in an AIDL file. Listing 14-12 shows the AIDL definition of `IStockQuoteService`. This file goes into the same place as a regular Java file would for your `StockQuoteService` project.

Listing 14-12. The AIDL Definition of the Stock-Quoter Service

```
// This file is IStockQuoteService.aidl
package com.androidbook.services.stockquoteservice;
interface IStockQuoteService
{
        double getQuote(String ticker);
}
```

The `IStockQuoteService` accepts the stock-ticker symbol as a string and returns the current stock value as a double. When you create the AIDL file, the Android Eclipse plug-in runs the AIDL compiler to process your AIDL file (as part of the build process). If your AIDL file compiles successfully, the compiler generates a Java interface suitable for RPC communication. Note that the generated file will be in the package named in your AIDL file—`com.androidbook.services.stockquoteservice` in this case.

Listing 14-13 shows the generated Java file for our `IStockQuoteService` interface. The generated file will be put into the gen folder of our Eclipse project.

Listing 14-13. The Compiler-Generated Java File

```
 /*
 * This file is auto-generated.  DO NOT MODIFY.
 * Original file: C:\\android\\StockQuoteService\\src\\com\\androidbook\\↵
services\\stockquoteservice\\IStockQuoteService.aidl
 */
package com.androidbook.services.stockquoteservice;
import java.lang.String;
import android.os.RemoteException;
import android.os.IBinder;
import android.os.IInterface;
import android.os.Binder;
import android.os.Parcel;
public interface IStockQuoteService extends android.os.IInterface
{
/** Local-side IPC implementation stub class. */
public static abstract class Stub extends android.os.Binder implements↵
com.androidbook.services.stockquoteservice.IStockQuoteService
{
private static final java.lang.String DESCRIPTOR =↵
"com.androidbook.services.stockquoteservice.IStockQuoteService";
```

```
/** Construct the stub at attach it to the interface. */
public Stub()
{
this.attachInterface(this, DESCRIPTOR);
}
/**
 * Cast an IBinder object into an IStockQuoteService interface,
 * generating a proxy if needed.
 */
public static com.androidbook.services.stockquoteservice.IStockQuoteService➥
asInterface(android.os.IBinder obj)
{
if ((obj==null)) {
return null;
}
android.os.IInterface iin = (android.os.IInterface)obj.queryLocalInterface(DESCRIPTOR);
if (((iin!=null)&&(iin instanceof com.androidbook.services.stockquoteservice.
IStockQuoteService))) {
return ((com.androidbook.services.stockquoteservice.IStockQuoteService)iin);
}
return new com.androidbook.services.stockquoteservice.IStockQuoteService.Stub.Proxy(obj);
}
public android.os.IBinder asBinder()
{
return this;
}
@Override public boolean onTransact(int code, android.os.Parcel data,➥
     android.os.Parcel reply, int flags) throws android.os.RemoteException
{
switch (code)
{
case INTERFACE_TRANSACTION:
{
reply.writeString(DESCRIPTOR);
return true;
}
case TRANSACTION_getQuote:
{
data.enforceInterface(DESCRIPTOR);
java.lang.String _arg0;
_arg0 = data.readString();
double _result = this.getQuote(_arg0);
reply.writeNoException();
reply.writeDouble(_result);
return true;
}
}
return super.onTransact(code, data, reply, flags);
}
```

```
private static class Proxy implements
        com.androidbook.services.stockquoteservice.IStockQuoteService
{
private android.os.IBinder mRemote;
Proxy(android.os.IBinder remote)
{
mRemote = remote;
}
public android.os.IBinder asBinder()
{
return mRemote;
}
public java.lang.String getInterfaceDescriptor()
{
return DESCRIPTOR;
}
public double getQuote(java.lang.String ticker) throws android.os.RemoteException
{
android.os.Parcel _data = android.os.Parcel.obtain();
android.os.Parcel _reply = android.os.Parcel.obtain();
double _result;
try {
_data.writeInterfaceToken(DESCRIPTOR);
_data.writeString(ticker);
mRemote.transact(Stub.TRANSACTION_getQuote, _data, _reply, 0);
_reply.readException();
_result = _reply.readDouble();
}
finally {
_reply.recycle();
_data.recycle();
}
return _result;
}
}
static final int TRANSACTION_getQuote = (IBinder.FIRST_CALL_TRANSACTION + 0);
}
public double getQuote(java.lang.String ticker) throws android.os.RemoteException;
}
```

Note the following important points regarding the generated classes:

- The interface we defined in the AIDL file is implemented as an interface in the generated code (that is, there is an interface named `IStockQuoteService`).
- A static abstract class named `Stub` extends `android.os.Binder` and implements `IStockQuoteService`. Note that the class is an abstract class.

- An inner class named Proxy implements the IStockQuoteService that proxies the Stub class.
- The AIDL file must reside in the package where the generated files are supposed to be (as specified in the AIDL file's package declaration).

Now, let's move on and implement the AIDL interface in a service class.

Implementing an AIDL Interface

In the previous section, we defined an AIDL file for a stock-quoter service and generated the binding file. Now, we are going to provide an implementation of that service. To implement the service's interface, we need to write a class that extends android.app.Service and implements the IStockQuoteService interface. The class we are going to write we'll call StockQuoteService. To expose the service to clients, our StockQuoteService will need to provide an implementation of the onBind() method, and we'll need to add some configuration information to the AndroidManifest.xml file. Listing 14-14 shows an implementation of the IStockQuoteService interface. This file also goes into the src folder of the StockQuoteService project.

Listing 14-14. The IStockQuoteService Service Implementation

```
public class StockQuoteService extends Service
{
    private static final String TAG = "StockQuoteService";
    public class StockQuoteServiceImpl extends IStockQuoteService.Stub
    {
        @Override
        public double getQuote(String ticker) throws RemoteException
        {
            Log.v(TAG, "getQuote() called for " + ticker);
            return 20.0;
        }
    }

    @Override
    public void onCreate() {
        super.onCreate();
        Log.v(TAG, "onCreate() called");
    }

    @Override
    public void onDestroy()
    {
        super.onDestroy();
        Log.v(TAG, "onDestroy() called");
    }
```

```
    @Override
    public IBinder onBind(Intent intent)
    {
        Log.v(TAG, "onBind() called");
        return new StockQuoteServiceImpl();
    }
}
```

The StockQuoteService.java class in Listing 14-14 resembles the local BackgroundService we created earlier, but without the NotificationManager. The important difference is that we now implement the onBind() method. Recall that the Stub class generated from the AIDL file was an abstract class and that it implemented the IStockQuoteService interface. In our implementation of the service, we have an inner class that extends the Stub class called StockQuoteServiceImpl. This class serves as the remote-service implementation, and an instance of this class is returned from the onBind() method. With that, we have a functional AIDL service, although external clients cannot connect to it yet.

To expose the service to clients, we need to add a service declaration in the AndroidManifest.xml file, and this time, we need an intent filter to expose the service. Listing 14-15 shows the service declaration for the StockQuoteService. The <service> tag is a child of the <application> tag.

Listing 14-15. Manifest Declaration for the IStockQuoteService

```
<?xml version="1.0" encoding="utf-8"?>
<manifest xmlns:android="http://schemas.android.com/apk/res/android"
      package="com.androidbook.services.stockquoteservice"
      android:versionCode="1"
      android:versionName="1.0">
    <application android:icon="@drawable/icon"
        android:label="@string/app_name">
      <service android:name="StockQuoteService">
        <intent-filter>
                <action android:name=
                        "com.androidbook.services.stockquoteservice.IStockQuoteService" />
        </intent-filter>
      </service>
    </application>
    <uses-sdk android:minSdkVersion="4" />
</manifest>
```

As with all services, we define the service we want to expose with a <service> tag. For an AIDL service, we also need to add an <intent-filter> with an <action> entry for the service interface we want to expose.

With this in place, we have everything we need to deploy the service. When you are ready to deploy the service application from Eclipse, just go ahead and choose Run As the way you would for any other application. Eclipse will comment in the Console that this application has no Launcher, but it will deploy the app anyway, which is what we want. Let's now look at how we would call the service from another application (on the same device, of course).

Calling the Service from a Client Application

When a client talks to a service, there must be a protocol or contract between the two. With Android, the contract is in our AIDL file. So the first step in consuming a service is to take the service's AIDL file and copy it to your client project. When you copy the AIDL file to the client project, the AIDL compiler creates the same interface-definition file that was created when the service was implemented (in the service-implementation project). This exposes to the client all of the methods, parameters, and return types on the service. Let's create a new project and copy the AIDL file:

1. Create a new Android project named `StockQuoteClient`. Use a different package name, such as `com.androidbook.stockquoteclient`. Use `MainActivity` for the Create Activity field.

2. Create a new Java package in this project named `com.androidbook.services.stockquoteservice` in the `src` directory.

3. Copy the `IStockQuoteService.aidl` file from the `StockQuoteService` project to this new package. Note that after you copy the file to the project, the AIDL compiler will generate the associated Java file.

The service interface that you regenerate serves as the contract between the client and the service. The next step is to get a reference to the service so we can call the `getQuote()` method. With remote services, we have to call the `bindService()` method rather than the `startService()` method. Listing 14-16 shows an activity class that acts as a client of the `IStockQuoteService` service. Listing 14-17 contains the layout file for the activity.

Listing 14-16 shows our `MainActivity.java` file. Realize that the package name of the client activity is not that important—you can put the activity in any package you'd like. However, the AIDL artifacts that you create are package-sensitive because the AIDL compiler generates code from the contents of the AIDL file.

Listing 14-16. A Client of the `IStockQuoteService` Service

```
public class MainActivity extends Activity {
    private static final String TAG = "StockQuoteClient";
    private IStockQuoteService stockService = null;
    private ToggleButton bindBtn;
    private Button callBtn;

    /** Called when the activity is first created. */
    @Override
    public void onCreate(Bundle savedInstanceState) {
        super.onCreate(savedInstanceState);
        setContentView(R.layout.main);

        bindBtn = (ToggleButton)findViewById(R.id.bindBtn);
        callBtn = (Button)findViewById(R.id.callBtn);
    }
```

```
public void doClick(View view) {
    switch(view.getId()) {
    case R.id.bindBtn:
        if(((ToggleButton) view).isChecked()) {
            bindService(new Intent(
                IStockQuoteService.class.getName()),
                serConn, Context.BIND_AUTO_CREATE);
        }
        else {
            unbindService(serConn);
            callBtn.setEnabled(false);
        }
        break;
    case R.id.callBtn:
        callService();
        break;
    }
}

private void callService() {
    try {
        double val = stockService.getQuote("ANDROID");
        Toast.makeText(MainActivity.this,
                "Value from service is " + val,
                Toast.LENGTH_SHORT).show();
    } catch (RemoteException ee) {
        Log.e("MainActivity", ee.getMessage(), ee);
    }
}

private ServiceConnection serConn = new ServiceConnection() {

    @Override
    public void onServiceConnected(ComponentName name,
        IBinder service)
    {
        Log.v(TAG, "onServiceConnected() called");
        stockService = IStockQuoteService.Stub.asInterface(service);
        bindBtn.setChecked(true);
        callBtn.setEnabled(true);
    }

    @Override
    public void onServiceDisconnected(ComponentName name) {
        Log.v(TAG, "onServiceDisconnected() called");
        bindBtn.setChecked(false);
        callBtn.setEnabled(false);
        stockService = null;
    }
};
```

```
    protected void onDestroy() {
        Log.v(TAG, "onDestroy() called");
        if(callBtn.isEnabled())
            unbindService(serConn);
        super.onDestroy();
    }
}
```

The activity displays our layout and grabs a reference to the Call Service button so we can properly enable it when the service is running and disable it when the service is stopped. When the user clicks the Bind button, the activity calls the `bindService()` method. Similarly, when the user clicks UnBind, the activity calls the `unbindService()` method. Notice that three parameters are passed to the `bindService()` method: an `Intent` with the name of the AIDL service, a `ServiceConnection` instance, and a flag to autocreate the service.

***Listing 14-17.** The IStockQuoteService Service Client Layout*

```
<?xml version="1.0" encoding="utf-8"?>
<!-- This file is /res/layout/main.xml -->
<LinearLayout xmlns:android="http://schemas.android.com/apk/res/android"
    android:orientation="vertical"
    android:layout_width="fill_parent"
    android:layout_height="fill_parent" >

<ToggleButton android:id="@+id/bindBtn"
    android:layout_width="wrap_content"
    android:layout_height="wrap_content"
    android:textOff="Bind"  android:textOn="Unbind"
    android:onClick="doClick" />

<Button android:id="@+id/callBtn"
    android:layout_width="wrap_content"
    android:layout_height="wrap_content"
    android:text="Call Service"  android:enabled="false"
    android:onClick="doClick" />
</LinearLayout>
```

With a bound service, such as an AIDL service, you need to provide an implementation of the `ServiceConnection` interface. This interface defines two methods: one called by the system when a connection to the service has been established and one called when the connection to the service has been destroyed. In our activity implementation, we define the `ServiceConnection` for the `IStockQuoteService`. When we call the `bindService()` method, we pass in the reference to this (i.e., `serConn`). When the connection to the service is established, the `onServiceConnected()` callback is invoked, and we then obtain a reference to the `IStockQuoteService` using the `Stub` and enable the Call Service button.

Note that the `bindService()` call is an asynchronous call. It is asynchronous because the process or service might not be running and thus might have to be created or started. And we cannot wait on the main thread for the service to start. Because `bindService()` is asynchronous, the platform provides the `ServiceConnection` callback, so we know when the service has been started and when the service is no longer available. These `ServiceConnection` callbacks will run on the main thread though, so they'll have access to the UI components if necessary.

Please notice the `onServiceDisconnected()` callback. This does *not* get invoked when we unbind from the service. It is invoked if the service crashes or if Android decides to kill the service, for example if memory is getting low. If this callback fires, we should not think that we're still connected, and we might need to reinvoke the `bindService()` call. That is why we change the status of our buttons in the UI when this callback is invoked. But notice we said "we might need to reinvoke the `bindService()` call." Android could restart our service for us and invoke our `onServiceConnected()` callback. You can try this yourself by running the client, binding to the service, and using DDMS to do a Stop on the Stock Quote Service application.

When you run this example, watch the log messages in LogCat to get a feel for what is going on behind the scenes.

In our service examples thus far, we have strictly dealt with passing simple Java primitive types. Android services actually support passing complex types, too. This is very useful, especially for AIDL services, because you might have an open-ended number of parameters that you want to pass to a service, and it's unreasonable to pass them all as simple primitives. It makes more sense to package them as complex types and then pass them to the service.

Let's see how we can pass complex types to services.

Passing Complex Types to Services

Passing complex types to and from services requires more work than passing Java primitive types. Before embarking on this work, you should get an idea of AIDL's support for nonprimitive types:

- AIDL supports `String` and `CharSequence`.
- AIDL allows you to pass other AIDL interfaces, but you need to have an `import` statement for each AIDL interface you reference (even if the referenced AIDL interface is in the same package).
- AIDL allows you to pass complex types that implement the `android.os.Parcelable` interface. You need to have an `import` statement in your AIDL file for these types.
- AIDL supports `java.util.List` and `java.util.Map`, with a few restrictions. The allowable data types for the items in the collection include Java primitive, `String`, `CharSequence`, and `android.os.Parcelable`. You do not need `import` statements for `List` or `Map`, but you do need them for the `Parcelables`.
- Nonprimitive types, other than `String`, require a directional indicator. Directional indicators include `in`, `out`, and `inout`. `in` means the value is set by the client, `out` means the value is set by the service, and `inout` means both the client and service set the value. Android avoids serializing the values if they're not flowing in the indicated direction, which helps overall performance.

The Parcelable interface tells the Android runtime how to serialize and deserialize objects during the marshalling and unmarshalling process. Listing 14-18 shows a Person class that implements the Parcelable interface.

Listing 14-18.** **Implementing the Parcelable Interface

```
// This file is Person.java
package com.androidbook.services.stock2;
import android.os.Parcel;
import android.os.Parcelable;

public class Person implements Parcelable {
    private int age;
    private String name;
    public static final Parcelable.Creator<Person> CREATOR =
        new Parcelable.Creator<Person>()
    {
        public Person createFromParcel(Parcel in) {
            return new Person(in);
        }

        public Person[] newArray(int size) {
            return new Person[size];
        }
    };

    public Person() {
    }

    private Person(Parcel in) {
        readFromParcel(in);
    }

    @Override
    public int describeContents() {
        return 0;
    }

    @Override
    public void writeToParcel(Parcel out, int flags) {
        out.writeInt(age);
        out.writeString(name);
    }

    public void readFromParcel(Parcel in) {
        age = in.readInt();
        name = in.readString();
    }

    public int getAge() {
        return age;
    }
```

```
    public void setAge(int age) {
        this.age = age;
    }

    public String getName() {
        return name;
    }

    public void setName(String name) {
        this.name = name;
    }
}
```

To get started on implementing this, create a new Android Project in Eclipse called StockQuoteService2. For Create Activity, use a name of MainActivity, and use a package of com.androidbook.services.stock2. Then add the Person.java file from Listing 14-18 to the com.androidbook.services.stock2 package of our new project.

The Parcelable interface defines the contract for the marshalling and unmarshalling of objects. Underlying the Parcelable interface is the Parcel container object. The Parcel class is a fast serialization/deserialization mechanism specially designed for interprocess communication within Android. The class provides methods that you use to flatten your members to the container and to expand the members back from the container. To properly implement an object for interprocess communication, we have to do the following:

1. Implement the Parcelable interface. This means that you implement writeToParcel() and readFromParcel(). The write method will write the object to the parcel, and the read method will read the object from the parcel. Note that the order in which you write properties must be the same as the order in which you read them.

2. Add a static final property to the class with the name CREATOR. The property needs to implement the android.os.Parcelable.Creator<T> interface.

3. Provide a constructor for the Parcelable that knows how to create the object from the Parcel.

4. Define a Parcelable class in an .aidl file that matches the .java file containing the complex type. The AIDL compiler will look for this file when compiling your AIDL files. An example of a Person.aidl file is shown in Listing 14-19. This file should be in the same place as Person.java.

> **Note** Seeing Parcelable might have triggered the question, why is Android not using the built-in Java serialization mechanism? It turns out that the Android team came to the conclusion that the serialization in Java is far too slow to satisfy Android's interprocess-communication requirements. So the team built the Parcelable solution. The Parcelable approach requires that you explicitly serialize the members of your class, but in the end, you get a much faster serialization of your objects.
>
> Also realize that Android provides two mechanisms that allow you to pass data to another process. The first is to pass a bundle to an activity using an intent, and the second is to pass a Parcelable to a service. These two mechanisms are not interchangeable and should not be confused. That is, the Parcelable is not meant to be passed to an activity. If you want to start an activity and pass it some data, use a Bundle. Parcelable is meant to be used only as part of an AIDL definition.

Listing 14-19. An Example of a Person.aidl File

```
// This file is Person.aidl
package com.androidbook.services.stock2;
parcelable Person;
```

You will need an .aidl file for each Parcelable in your project. In this case, we have just one Parcelable, which is Person. You may notice that you don't get a Person.java file created in the gen folder. This is to be expected. We already have this file from when we created it previously.

Now, let's use the Person class in a remote service. To keep things simple, we will modify our IStockQuoteService to take an input parameter of type Person. The idea is that clients will pass a Person to the service to tell the service who is requesting the quote. The new IStockQuoteService.aidl looks like Listing 14-20.

Listing 14-20. Passing Parcelables to Services

```
// This file is IStockQuoteService.aidl
package com.androidbook.services.stock2;
import com.androidbook.services.stock2.Person;

interface IStockQuoteService
{
    String getQuote(in String ticker,in Person requester);
}
```

The getQuote() method now accepts two parameters: the stock's ticker symbol and a Person object to specify who is making the request. Note that we have directional indicators on the parameters because the parameters include nonprimitive types and that we have an import statement for the Person class. The Person class is also in the same package as the service definition (com.androidbook.services.stock2).

The service implementation now looks like Listing 14-21, with the MainActivity layout in Listing 14-22.

Listing 14-21. The StockQuoteService2 Implementation

```
package com.androidbook.services.stock2;
// This file is StockQuoteService2.java

import android.app.Notification;
import android.app.NotificationManager;
import android.app.PendingIntent;
import android.app.Service;
import android.content.Intent;
import android.os.IBinder;
import android.os.RemoteException;

public class StockQuoteService2 extends Service
{
    private NotificationManager notificationMgr;

    public class StockQuoteServiceImpl extends IStockQuoteService.Stub
    {
        public String getQuote(String ticker, Person requester)
                throws RemoteException {
            return "Hello " + requester.getName() +
                "! Quote for " + ticker + " is 20.0";
        }
    }

    @Override
    public void onCreate() {
        super.onCreate();

        notificationMgr =
          (NotificationManager)getSystemService(NOTIFICATION_SERVICE);

        displayNotificationMessage(
              "onCreate() called in StockQuoteService2");
    }

    @Override
    public void onDestroy()
    {
        displayNotificationMessage(
              "onDestroy() called in StockQuoteService2");
        // Clear all notifications from this service
        notificationMgr.cancelAll();
        super.onDestroy();
    }
```

```
    @Override
    public IBinder onBind(Intent intent)
    {
        displayNotificationMessage(
                "onBind() called in StockQuoteService2");
        return new StockQuoteServiceImpl();
    }

    private void displayNotificationMessage(String message)
    {
        PendingIntent contentIntent =
                PendingIntent.getActivity(this, 0, new Intent(this, MainActivity.class), 0);

        Notification notification = new NotificationCompat.Builder(this)
            .setContentTitle("StockQuoteService2")
            .setContentText(message)
            .setSmallIcon(R.drawable.emo_im_happy)
            .setTicker(message)
            // .setLargeIcon(aBitmap)
            .setContentIntent(contentIntent)
            .setOngoing(true)
            .build();

        notificationMgr.notify(R.id.app_notification_id, notification);
    }
}
```

Listing 14-22. The StockQuoteService2 Layout

```
<?xml version="1.0" encoding="utf-8"?>
<!-- This file is /res/layout/main.xml -->
<LinearLayout xmlns:android="http://schemas.android.com/apk/res/android"
    android:orientation="vertical"
    android:layout_width="fill_parent"
    android:layout_height="fill_parent" >
<TextView
    android:layout_width="fill_parent"
    android:layout_height="wrap_content"
    android:text="This is where the service could ask for help." />
</LinearLayout>
```

The differences between this implementation and the previous one are that we brought back the notifications, and we now return the stock value as a string and not a double. The string returned to the user contains the name of the requester from the Person object, which demonstrates that we read the value sent from the client and that the Person object was passed correctly to the service.

There are a few other things that need to be done to make this work:

1. Find the emo_im_happy.png image file from under Android SDK/platforms/android-19/data/res/drawable-mdpi, and copy it to the /res/drawable directory of our project. Or change the name of the resource in the code, and put whatever image you want in the drawables folder.
2. Add a new <item type="id" name="app_notification_id"/> tag to the /res/values/strings.xml file.
3. We need to modify the application in the AndroidManifest.xml file as shown in Listing 14-23.

Listing 14-23. Modified <application> in AndroidManifest.xml File for StockQuoteService2

```
<?xml version="1.0" encoding="utf-8"?>
<manifest xmlns:android="http://schemas.android.com/apk/res/android"
      package="com.androidbook.services.stock2"
      android:versionCode="1"
      android:versionName="1.0">
    <uses-sdk android:minSdkVersion="8" />
    <application android:icon="@drawable/icon"
            android:label="@string/app_name">
        <activity android:name=".MainActivity"
                android:label="@string/app_name"
                android:launchMode="singleTop" >
            <intent-filter>
                <action android:name="android.intent.action.MAIN" />
            </intent-filter>
        </activity>
      <service android:name="StockQuoteService2">
        <intent-filter>
            <action android:name="com.androidbook.services.stock2.IStockQuoteService" />
        </intent-filter>
      </service>
    </application>

</manifest>
```

While it is OK to use the dot notation for our android:name=".MainActivity" attribute, it is not OK to use dot notation inside of our <action> tag inside the service's <intent-filter> tag. We need to spell it out; otherwise, our client will not find the service specification.

Last, we'll use the default MainActivity.java file that simply displays a basic layout with a simple message. We showed you earlier how to launch to the activity from a notification. This activity would serve that purpose also in real life, but for this example, we'll keep that part simple. Now that we have our service implementation, let's create a new Android project called StockQuoteClient2. Use com.dave for the package and MainActivity for the activity name. To implement a client that passes the Person object to the service, we need to copy everything that the client needs from the service project to the client project. There needs to be a new src package called com.androidbook.services.stock2 to receive these copied files. In our previous example, all we needed was the IStockQuoteService.aidl file. We also need to copy the Person.java and Person.aidl files, because the Person object is now part of the interface. After you copy these three files to the com.androidbook.services.stock2 src package of the client project, modify main.xml according to Listing 14-24, and modify MainActivity.java according to Listing 14-25. Or simply import this project from the source code on our web site.

Listing 14-24. Updated main.xml for StockQuoteClient2

```
<?xml version="1.0" encoding="utf-8"?>
<!-- This file is /res/layout/main.xml -->
<LinearLayout xmlns:android="http://schemas.android.com/apk/res/android"
    android:orientation="vertical"
    android:layout_width="fill_parent"
    android:layout_height="fill_parent" >

<ToggleButton android:id="@+id/bindBtn"
    android:layout_width="wrap_content"
    android:layout_height="wrap_content"
    android:textOff="Bind"  android:textOn="Unbind"
    android:onClick="doClick" />

<Button android:id="@+id/callBtn"
    android:layout_width="wrap_content"
    android:layout_height="wrap_content"
    android:text="Call Service" android:enabled="false"
    android:onClick="doClick" />
</LinearLayout>
```

Listing 14-25. Calling the Service with a Parcelable

```
package com.dave;
// This file is MainActivity.java
import com.androidbook.services.stock2.IStockQuoteService;
import com.androidbook.services.stock2.Person;

public class MainActivity extends Activity {

    protected static final String TAG = "StockQuoteClient2";
    private IStockQuoteService stockService = null;
    private ToggleButton bindBtn;
    private Button callBtn;

    /** Called when the activity is first created. */
    @Override
    public void onCreate(Bundle savedInstanceState) {
        super.onCreate(savedInstanceState);
        setContentView(R.layout.main);

        bindBtn = (ToggleButton)findViewById(R.id.bindBtn);
        callBtn = (Button)findViewById(R.id.callBtn);
    }
```

```
public void doClick(View view) {
    switch(view.getId()) {
    case R.id.bindBtn:
        if(((ToggleButton) view).isChecked()) {
            bindService(new Intent(
                IStockQuoteService.class.getName()),
                serConn, Context.BIND_AUTO_CREATE);
        }
        else {
            unbindService(serConn);
            callBtn.setEnabled(false);
        }
        break;
    case R.id.callBtn:
        callService();
        break;
    }
}

private void callService() {
    try {
        Person person = new Person();
        person.setAge(47);
        person.setName("Dave");
        String response = stockService.getQuote("ANDROID", person);
        Toast.makeText(MainActivity.this,
                    "Value from service is "+response,
                    Toast.LENGTH_SHORT).show();
    } catch (RemoteException ee) {
        Log.e("MainActivity", ee.getMessage(), ee);
    }
}

private ServiceConnection serConn = new ServiceConnection() {

    @Override
    public void onServiceConnected(ComponentName name,
        IBinder service)
    {
        Log.v(TAG, "onServiceConnected() called");
        stockService = IStockQuoteService.Stub.asInterface(service);
        bindBtn.setChecked(true);
        callBtn.setEnabled(true);
    }

    @Override
    public void onServiceDisconnected(ComponentName name) {
        Log.v(TAG, "onServiceDisconnected() called");
        bindBtn.setChecked(false);
        callBtn.setEnabled(false);
        stockService = null;
    }
};
```

```
    protected void onDestroy() {
        if(callBtn.isEnabled())
            unbindService(serConn);
        super.onDestroy();
    }
}
```

This is now ready to run. Remember to send over the service to the device or emulator before you send over the client to run. The user interface should look like Figure 14-1.

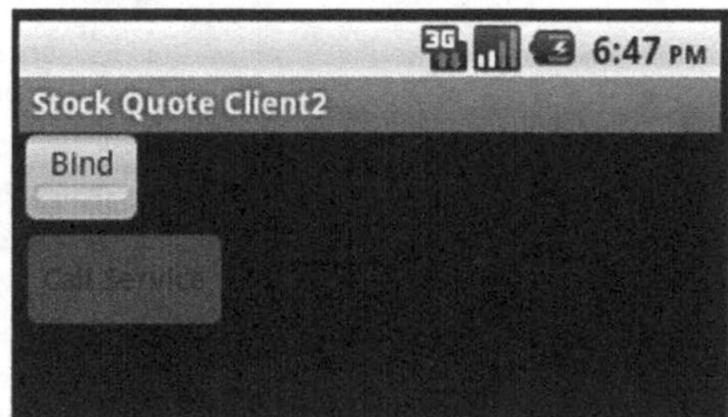

Figure 14-1. *User interface of* `StockQuoteClient2`

Let's take a look at what we've got. As before, we bind to our service, and then we can invoke a service method. The `onServiceConnected()` method is where we get told that our service is running, so we can then enable the Call Service button so the button can invoke the `callService()` method. As shown, we create a new `Person` object and set its `Age` and `Name` properties. We then execute the service and display the result from the service call. The result looks like Figure 14-2.

Value from service is Hello Dave! Quote for ANDROID is 20.0

Figure 14-2. ***Result from calling the service with a*** `Parcelable`

Notice that when the service is called, you get a notification in the status bar. This is coming from the service itself. We briefly touched on Notifications earlier as a way for a service to communicate to the user. Normally, services are in the background and do not display any sort of UI. But what if a service needs to interact with the user? While it's tempting to think that a service can invoke an activity, a service should *never* invoke an activity directly. A service should instead create a notification, and the notification should be how the user gets to the desired activity. This was shown in our last exercise. We defined a simple layout and activity implementation for our service. When we created the notification within the service, we set the activity in the notification. The user can touch the notification, and it will take the user to our activity that is part of this service. This will allow the user to interact with the service.

Notifications are saved so that you can get to them by pulling down from the status bar to see them. Note the fact that we reuse the same ID for every message. This means that we are updating the one and only notification every time, rather than creating new notification entries. Therefore, if you go to the Notifications screen in Android after clicking Bind,

Call Again, and Unbind a few times, you will only see one message in Notifications, and it will be the last one sent by `StockQuoteService2`. If we used different IDs, we could have multiple notification messages, and we could update each one separately. Notifications can also be set with additional user "prompts" such as sound, lights, and/or vibration.

It is also useful to see the artifacts of the service project and the client that calls it (see Figure 14-3).

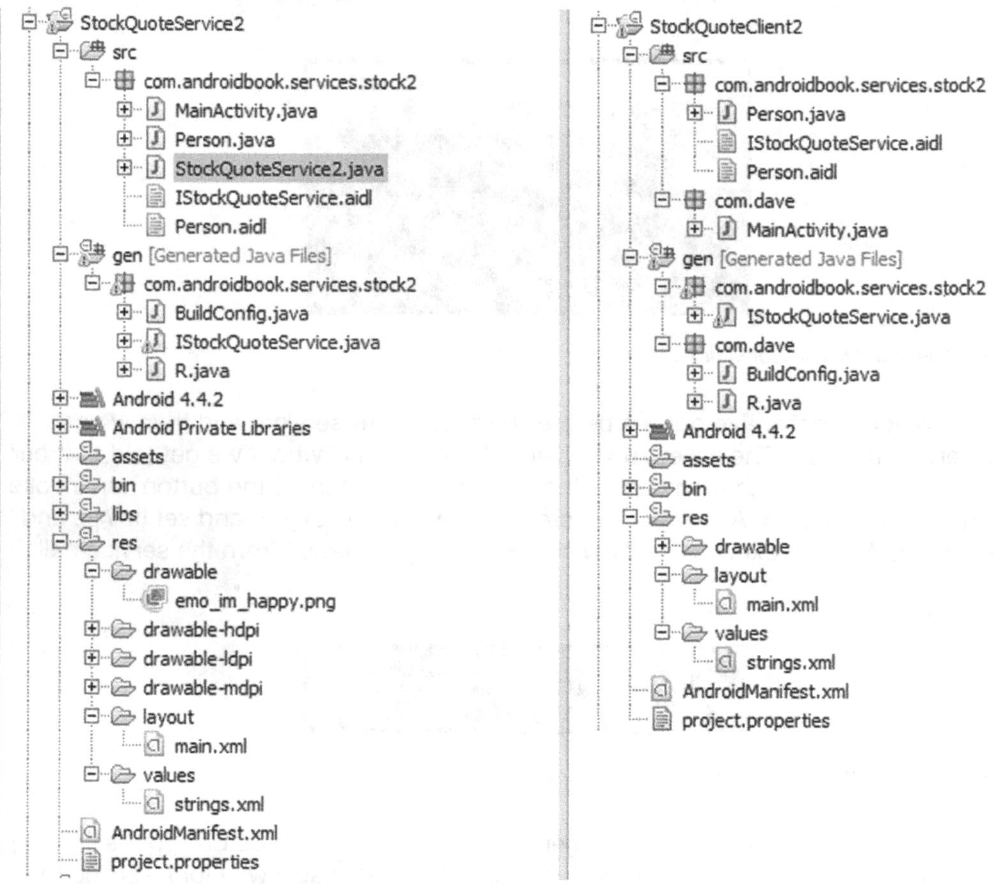

***Figure 14-3.** The artifacts of the service and the client*

Figure 14-3 shows the Eclipse project artifacts for the service (left) and the client (right). Note that the contract between the client and the service consists of the AIDL artifacts and the `Parcelable` objects exchanged between the two parties. This is the reason that we see `Person.java`, `IStockQuoteService.aidl`, and `Person.aidl` on both sides. Because the AIDL compiler generates the Java interface, stub, proxy, and so on from the AIDL artifacts, the build process creates the `IStockQuoteService.java` file on the client side when we copy the contract artifacts to the client project.

Now you know how to exchange complex types between services and clients. Let's briefly touch on another important aspect of calling services: synchronous versus asynchronous service invocation.

All of the calls that you make on services are synchronous. This brings up the obvious question: Do you need to implement all of your service calls in a worker thread? Not necessarily. On most other platforms, it's common for a client to use a service that is a complete black box, so the client would have to take appropriate precautions when making service calls. With Android, you will likely know what is in the service (generally because you wrote the service yourself), so you can make an informed decision. If you know that the method you are calling is doing a lot of heavy lifting, you should consider using a secondary thread to make the call. If you are sure that the method does not have any bottlenecks, you can safely make the call on the UI thread. If you conclude that it's best to make the service call within a worker thread, you can create the thread and then call the service. You can then communicate the result to the UI thread.

Messengers and Handlers

There is one more way to communicate with a service in Android, and that is with Messengers and Handlers. This mechanism is built on top of AIDL services, but without you having to see or deal with AIDL. Like AIDL services, you use it when the service is in a separate process from the client. Both the client and the service will implement a Messenger and a Handler, and proceed to send messages back and forth. You don't need to specify any .aidl files; everything is coded in your Java classes. This is a fairly common way to do inter-process service calls on Android, and is significantly easier than messing with AIDL yourself.

Here's a quick overview of how it works. The client binds to the service, and sets up a Messenger and Handler to receive responses from the service. A callback within the Handler takes care of messages sent back by the service. The client also creates a Messenger to send messages to the service. On the service side, there's a similar Messenger and Handler to receive the incoming messages from clients. A message coming in from a client includes a Messenger to use for any replies to that client. Therefore, the service creates only one Messenger while a client creates two. The client side is asynchronous, with the service response coming later. A problem with the service call generates a RemoteException that the client can capture and act upon.

Let's see an example of how this works. This sample application has two parts: a MessengerClient and a MessengerService. They will run as separate processes on a device. The client will use a non-UI fragment to contain the service client connection. This means the client activity can go away and be recreated due to a configuration change, and the underlying service connection remains in place. This is a preferred way to connect to a service from an activity since you don't want to have to reconstruct the service client connection just because the device has been rotated for example. Listing 14-26 shows the significant code from MessengerService.java to set up the Handler and Messenger. For a full listing, refer to the MessengerService source project for this chapter.

Listing 14-26. Messenger/Handler-Based Service Code

```
public class MessengerService extends Service {
    NotificationManager mNM;
    ArrayList<Messenger> mClients = new ArrayList<Messenger>();
    int mValue = 0;
    public static final int MSG_REGISTER_CLIENT = 1;
    public static final int MSG_UNREGISTER_CLIENT = 2;
    public static final int MSG_SET_SIMPLE_VALUE = 3;
    public static final int MSG_SET_COMPLEX_VALUE = 4;
    public static final String TAG = "MessengerService";
    /**
     * Handler of incoming messages from clients.
     */
    class IncomingHandler extends Handler {
        @Override
        public void handleMessage(Message msg) {
            switch (msg.what) {
                case MSG_REGISTER_CLIENT:
                    mClients.add(msg.replyTo);
                    Log.v(TAG, "Registering client");
                    break;
                case MSG_UNREGISTER_CLIENT:
                    mClients.remove(msg.replyTo);
                    Log.v(TAG, "Unregistering client");
                    break;
                case MSG_SET_SIMPLE_VALUE:
                    mValue = msg.arg1;
                    Log.v(TAG, "Receiving arg1: " + mValue);
                    showNotification("Received arg1: " + mValue);
                    for (int i=mClients.size()-1; i>=0; i--) {
                        try {
                            mClients.get(i).send(Message.obtain(null,
                                    MSG_SET_SIMPLE_VALUE, mValue, 0));
                        } catch (RemoteException e) {
                            // The client is dead.  Remove it from the list;
                            // we are going through the list from back to front
                            // so this is safe to do inside the loop.
                            mClients.remove(i);
                        }
                    }
                    break;
                case MSG_SET_COMPLEX_VALUE:
                    Bundle mBundle = msg.getData();
                    Log.v(TAG, "Receiving bundle: ");
                    if(mBundle != null) {
                        showNotification("Got complex msg: myDouble = "
                                + mBundle.getDouble("myDouble"));
                        for(String key : mBundle.keySet()) {
                            Log.v(TAG, "    " + key);
                        }
                    }
                    break;
```

```
                default:
                    Log.v(TAG, "Got some other message: " + msg.what);
                    super.handleMessage(msg);
            }
        }
    }

    // Target for clients to send messages to IncomingHandler.
    final Messenger mMessenger = new Messenger(new IncomingHandler());

    @Override
    public void onCreate() {
        mNM = (NotificationManager)getSystemService(NOTIFICATION_SERVICE);
        // Display a notification about us starting.
        Log.v(TAG, "Service is starting");
        showNotification(getText(R.string.remote_service_started));
    }

    @Override
    public void onDestroy() {
        // Cancel the persistent notification.
        mNM.cancel(R.string.remote_service_started);

        // Tell the user we stopped.
        Toast.makeText(this, R.string.remote_service_stopped, Toast.LENGTH_SHORT).show();
    }

    /**
     * When binding to the service, we return an interface to our messenger
     * for sending messages to the service.
     */
    @Override
    public IBinder onBind(Intent intent) {
        return mMessenger.getBinder();
    }

    /**
     * Show a notification while this service is running. Note that
     * we don't include an intent since we're just a service here. The
     * service stops when the client tells it to.
     */
    private void showNotification(CharSequence text) {
        Notification notification = new NotificationCompat.Builder(this)
            .setContentTitle("MessengerService")
            .setContentText(text)
            .setSmallIcon(android.R.drawable.ic_dialog_info)
            .setTicker(text)
            .setOngoing(true)
            .build();

        mNM.notify(R.string.remote_service_started, notification);
    }

}
```

In this sample, clients register with the service, unregister with the service, send a simple message, or send a complex message. When a client registers, the service remembers it by saving the passed-in client `Messenger` (i.e., `msg.replyTo`) in `mClients`. If a simple message is received, the service sends a copy of the received argument value to all known clients. Notice how replies are sent to each client using the `Messengers` in `mClients` that came from each client. The Message's what field is just an int to indicate what service operation is being called. Based upon the what operation, the service will extract the appropriate arguments. Since a Message object has two int arguments available, the simple case uses just one of those Message fields. When more complex data must be sent, a Bundle object is created, populated, and attached to the Message for transmission to the service.

Be aware that a service has a 1MB buffer for passed data (in and out) for all in-process service calls, so you'll want to keep Message data to a minimum. If there are a lot of simultaneous service calls, you could exceed the buffer and get a TransactionTooLargeException.

On the client side, there's a MainActivity and a ClientFrag (the non-UI fragment). For simplicity's sake the activity provides the UI to the user without using a UI fragment. Listing 14-27 shows the MainActivity. For a full listing of the project, please see the MessengerClient project for this chapter.

Listing 14-27. Messenger/Handler-Based Client Activity Code

```
public class MainActivity extends FragmentActivity implements ISampleServiceClient {

    protected static final String TAG = "MessengerClient";
    private TextView mCallbackText;
    private ClientFrag clientFrag;

    @Override
    protected void onCreate(Bundle savedInstanceState) {
        super.onCreate(savedInstanceState);
        setContentView(R.layout.activity_main);

        mCallbackText = (TextView)findViewById(R.id.callback);

        // Get a non-UI fragment to handle the service interface.
        // If our activity gets destroyed and recreated, the fragment
        // will still be around and we just need to re-fetch it.
        if((clientFrag = (ClientFrag) getSupportFragmentManager()
                .findFragmentByTag("clientFrag")) == null) {
            updateStatus("Creating a clientFrag. No service yet.");
            clientFrag = ClientFrag.getInstance();
            getSupportFragmentManager().beginTransaction()
                .add(clientFrag, "clientFrag")
                .commit();
        }
        else {
            updateStatus("Found existing clientFrag, will use it");
        }
    }
```

```
    public void doClick(View view) {
        switch(view.getId()) {
        case R.id.startBtn:
            clientFrag.doBindService();
            break;
        case R.id.stopBtn:
            clientFrag.doUnbindService();
            break;
        case R.id.simpleBtn:
            clientFrag.doSendSimple();
            break;
        case R.id.complexBtn:
            clientFrag.doSendComplex();
            break;
        }
    }

    @Override
    public void updateStatus(String status) {
        mCallbackText.setText(status);
    }
}
```

Notice how there's no mention of a service in this activity, just a TextView, buttons, and a client fragment. The updateStatus() method is as a result of the ISampleServiceClient interface that this activity implements, and all it needs to do is set the text in the UI as passed in. The buttons simply invoke a method of the client fragment. In a real application, there would be more business and UI logic in this activity or in other fragments that are separate from the service call.

The client fragment is where the fun is. Listing 14-28 shows the code from the client fragment.

***Listing 14-28.** Messenger/Handler-Based Client Fragment Code*

```
public class ClientFrag extends Fragment {
    private static final String TAG = "MessengerClientFrag";
    static private ClientFrag mClientFrag = null;
    // application context will be used to bind to the service because
    // fragments can't bind and activities can go away.
    private Context appContext = null;

    // Messenger for sending to service.
    Messenger mService = null;
    // Flag indicating whether we have called bind on the service.
    boolean mIsBound;

    // Instantiation method for the client fragment. We just want one
    // and we use setRetainInstance(true) so it hangs around during
    // configuration changes.
```

```
public static ClientFrag getInstance() {
    if(mClientFrag == null) {
        mClientFrag = new ClientFrag();
        mClientFrag.setRetainInstance(true);
    }
    return mClientFrag;
}

// Handler for response messages from the service
class IncomingHandler extends Handler {
    @Override
    public void handleMessage(Message msg) {
        switch (msg.what) {
            case MessengerService.MSG_SET_SIMPLE_VALUE:
                updateStatus("Received from service: " + msg.arg1);
                break;
            default:
                break;
        }
        super.handleMessage(msg);
    }
}

// Need a Messenger to receive responses. Send this with the
// Messages to the service.
final Messenger mMessenger = new Messenger(new IncomingHandler());

private ServiceConnection mConnection = new ServiceConnection() {
    public void onServiceConnected(ComponentName className,
            IBinder service) {
        // This is called when the connection with the service has been
        // established, giving us the service object we can use to
        // interact with the service.  We are communicating with our
        // service through a Messenger, so get a client-side
        // representation of that from the raw service object.
        mService = new Messenger(service);
        updateStatus("Attached.");

        // We want to monitor the service for as long as we are
        // connected to it. This is not strictly necessary. You
        // do not need to register with the service before using
        // it. But if this failed you'd have an early warning.
        try {
            Message msg = Message.obtain(null,
                    MessengerService.MSG_REGISTER_CLIENT);
            msg.replyTo = mMessenger;
            mService.send(msg);
        } catch (RemoteException e) {
            // In this case the service has crashed before we could even
            // do anything with it; we can count on soon being
```

```
            // disconnected (and then reconnected if it can be restarted)
            // so there is no need to do anything here.
            Log.e(TAG, "Could not establish a connection to the service: " + e);
        }
    }

    public void onServiceDisconnected(ComponentName className) {
        // This is called when the connection with the service has been
        // unexpectedly disconnected -- that is, its process crashed.
        mService = null;
        updateStatus("Disconnected.");
    }
};

public void doBindService() {
    // Establish a connection with the service. We use the String name
    // of the service since it exists in a separate process and we do
    // not want to require the service jar in the client. We also grab
    // the application context and bind the service to that since the
    // activity context could go away on a configuration change but the
    // application context will always be there.
    appContext = getActivity().getApplicationContext();
    if(mIsBound = appContext.bindService(
        new Intent("com.androidbook.messengerservice.MessengerService"),
                mConnection, Context.BIND_AUTO_CREATE)
        ) {
        updateStatus("Bound to service.");
    }
    else {
        updateStatus("Bind attempt failed.");
    }
}

public void doUnbindService() {
    if (mIsBound) {
        // If we have received the service, and hence registered with
        // it, then now is the time to unregister. Note that the
        // replyTo value is only used by the service to unregister
        // this client. No response message will come back to the client.
        if (mService != null) {
            try {
                Message msg = Message.obtain(null,
                        MessengerService.MSG_UNREGISTER_CLIENT);
                msg.replyTo = mMessenger;
                mService.send(msg);
            } catch (RemoteException e) {
                // There is nothing special we need to do if the service
                // has crashed.
            }
        }
```

```
            // Detach our existing connection.
            appContext.unbindService(mConnection);
            mIsBound = false;
            updateStatus("Unbound.");
        }
    }

    // If you can simplify and send only one or two integers, this
    // is the easy way to do it.
    public void doSendSimple() {
        try {
            Message msg = Message.obtain(null,
                MessengerService.MSG_SET_SIMPLE_VALUE, this.hashCode(), 0);
            mService.send(msg);
            updateStatus("Sending simple message.");
        } catch (RemoteException e) {
            Log.e(TAG, "Could not send a simple message to the service: " + e);
        }
    }

    // If you have more complex data, throw it into a Bundle and
    // add it to the Message. Can also pass Parcelables if you like.
    public void doSendComplex() {
        try {
            Message msg = Message.obtain(null,
                MessengerService.MSG_SET_COMPLEX_VALUE);
            Bundle mBundle = new Bundle();
            mBundle.putString("stringArg", "This is a string to pass");
            mBundle.putDouble("myDouble", 1138L);
            mBundle.putInt("myInt", 42);
            msg.setData(mBundle);
            mService.send(msg);
            updateStatus("Sending complex message.");
        } catch (RemoteException e) {
            Log.e(TAG, "Could not send a complex message to the service: " + e);
        }
    }

    private void updateStatus(String status) {
        // Make sure the latest status is updated in the GUI, which
        // is handled by the parent activity.
        ISampleServiceClient uiContext = (ISampleServiceClient) getActivity();
        if(uiContext != null) {
            uiContext.updateStatus(status);
        }
    }
}
```

The client fragment code is fairly straightforward. When the user clicks the Bind Service button, the client fragment binds to the remote service and sets up the ServiceConnection. Binding is done from the application context. This is preferred because fragments can't bind services, but activities and applications can. However, because the activity could go away during a configuration change, it's better to bind to the application which will always be there. When the ServiceConnection gets connected, an outgoing Messenger is set up to send the MSG_REGISTER_CLIENT register client message to the service. The client does not wait for a reply from the service but does go back to waiting for the user's next interaction. This prevents the dreaded ANR pop-up. Pressing Send Simple creates a simple message and sends it.

For a simple message, the service does a reply message which is received by the client's handler and processed. All the client handler does is update the TextView with the value received from the service. Notice that the client fragment uses the parent activity's ISampleServiceClient interface to call an appropriate method to update the UI. This is because the client fragment is non-UI and we would prefer not to embed UI logic within it. An interface keeps the client fragment separate from the activity and makes it easy to let the activity go away and come back during a configuration change. Pressing Send Complex creates a message with a bundle containing several different values, which is sent to the service. The service will use the double value in a notification to prove that the value was properly transmitted from client to service. The service does not send a reply message for the complex message.

One thing to be aware of with this mechanism for inter-process service calls: the service's handler is working from a queue of incoming messages and is therefore single-threaded by default. There will not be multiple threads processing the incoming service messages unless you create some yourself. Since the client is not blocking on a reply from the service, a client application would not crash if the service took a while to respond to a message. However, it would be something to keep in mind if you'll have multiple clients of the service. AIDL services can more easily handle requests simultaneously, so it might be a better choice if you need more predictable response times.

If your client is sending messages to multiple services, you could use a single Messenger/Handler pair to process reply messages from those services. You just have to put that same Messenger into each outbound Message and each service should reply back.

The other thing to be aware of is that the client has no guarantee that the service will *ever* respond. There are no timeouts inherent in a Messenger/Handler interaction. You will be notified through `onServiceDisconnected()` if the service dies, but not if it hangs or takes too long. Therefore, to be sure that the service responds in a timely fashion, the client could choose to set a timer, or an alarm to wake it up again. If the reply comes back before the timer/alarm goes off, the client handler could clear it. If the timer/alarm wakes up the client, it means the service took too long and the client could then take appropriate action.

References

Here are some helpful references to topics you may wish to explore further:

- www.androidbook.com/proandroid5/projects: A list of downloadable projects related to this book. For this chapter, look for a ZIP file called ProAndroid5_Ch14_Services.zip. This ZIP file contains all projects from this chapter, listed in separate root directories. There is also a README.TXT file that describes exactly how to import projects into your IDE from one of these ZIP files.
- http://hc.apache.org/httpcomponents-client-ga/tutorial/html/: Great tutorials on using the HttpClient classes, including authentication and the use of cookies.
- http://developer.android.com/guide/components/bound-services.html: Android Developer Guide on Bound Services.

Summary

This chapter was all about services, specifically:

- We talked about consuming external HTTP services using the Apache HttpClient.
- With regard to using the HttpClient, we showed you how to do HTTP GET calls and HTTP POST calls.
- We also showed you how to do multipart POSTs.
- You learned that SOAP can be done from Android, but it's not the preferred way to call web services.
- We talked about how you could set up an Internet proxy to manage a SOAP service on your application's behalf from a server somewhere, so your application can use RESTful services to your proxy and keep the application simpler.
- We then covered exception handling and the likely types of exceptions that your application is likely to experience (timeouts mostly).
- You saw how to use the ThreadSafeClientConnManager to share a common HttpClient inside your application.
- You learned how to check and set timeout values for connections to the network.
- We covered a couple of options for making connections to web services, including HttpURLConnection and AndroidHttpClient.

- We explained the difference between local services and remote services. Local services are services that are consumed by the components (such as activities) in the same process as the service. Remote services are services whose clients are outside the process hosting the services.
- You learned that even though a service is meant to be on a separate thread, it is still up to the developer to create and manage the background threads associated with services.
- You discovered how to start and stop local services, and how to create and bind to a remote service.
- You saw how the `NotificationManager` is used to track running services.
- We covered how to pass data to a service, using Parcelables for the complex types.
- You learned how to use Messengers and Handlers to call remote services.

Chapter 15

Advanced AsyncTask and Progress Dialogs

In Chapter 13, we covered handlers and worker threads to run long-running tasks while the main thread kept the UI house in order. Android SDK has recognized this as a pattern and abstracted the handler and thread details into a utility class called AsyncTask. You can use AsyncTask to run tasks that take longer than five seconds in the context of UI. (We will cover how to run really long-running tasks, ranging from minutes to even hours, through "Long-Running Receivers and Services" in Chapter 16.)

This chapter will start with the basics of an AsyncTask and move to the code needed to present progress dialogs and progress bars that show the status of an AsyncTask correctly even if the device changes its configuration. Let's start by introducing the AsyncTask through pseudocode in Listing 15-1.

Listing 15-1. Usage Pattern for an AsyncTask by an Activity

```
public class MyActivity {
    void respondToMenuItem()    { //menu handler
       performALongTask();
    }
    void performALongTask()    { //using an AsyncTask
        //Derive from an AsyncTask, and Instantiate this AsyncTask
        MyLongTask myLongTask = new MyLongTask(...CallBackObjects...);
        myLongTask.execute(...someargs...); //start the work on a worker thread
        //have the main thread get back to its UI business
    }

    //Hear back from the AsyncTask
    void someCallBackFromAsyncTask(SomeParameterizedType x)    {
        //Although invoked by the AsyncTask this code runs on the main thread.
        //report back to the user of the progress
    }
}
```

Use of an AsyncTask starts with extending from AsyncTask first like the MyLongTask in Listing 15-1. Once you have the AsyncTask object instantiated, you can call execute() method on that object. The execute() method internally starts a separate thread to do the actual work. The AsyncTask implementation will in turn invoke a number of callbacks to report the beginning of the task, the progress of the task, and the end of the task. Listing 15-2 shows pseudocode to extend an AsyncTask and the methods that need to be overridden. (Please note that this is pseudocode and not intended to be compiled. The @override annotation is added to explicitly state that they are overridden from the base class.)

Listing 15-2. Extending an AsyncTask: An Example

```
public class MyLongTask extends AsyncTask<String,Integer,Integer> {
    //... constructors stuff
    //Calling execute() will result in calling all of these methods
    @Override
    void onPreExecute(){} //Runs on the main thread

    //This is where you do all the work and runs on the worker thread
    @Override
    Integer doInBackground(String... params){}

    //Runs on the main thread again once it finishes
    @Override
    void onPostExecute(Integer result){}

    //Runs on the main thread
    @Override
    void onProgressUpdate(Integer... progressValuesArray){}
    //....other methods
}
```

execute() method in Listing 15-1 is called on the main thread. This call will trigger a series of methods in Listing 15-2, starting with onPreExecute(). The onPreExecute() is called on the main thread as well. You can use this method to set up your environment to execute the task. You can also use this method to set up a dialog box or initiate a progress bar to indicate to the user that the work has started. After the completion of the onPreExecute(), execute() method will return and the main thread of the activity continues with its UI responsibilities. By that time the execute() would have spawned a new worker thread so that doInBackground() method is scheduled to be executed on that worker thread. You will do all your heavy lifting in this doInBackground() method. As this method runs on a worker thread, the main thread is not affected and you will not get the "application not responding" message. From the doInBackground() method you have a facility (you will see this shortly) to call the onProgressUpdate() to report the progress. This onProgressUpdate() method runs on the main thread so that you can affect the UI on the main thread.

Essentials of a Simple AsyncTask

Let's get into the details of extending the AsyncTask. The AsyncTask class uses generics to provide type safety to its methods, including the overridden methods. You can see these generics when you look at the partial definition (Listing 15-3) of the AsyncTask class. (Please note that Listing 15-3 is an extremely pruned-down version of the AsyncTask class. It's really just the elements of its interface most commonly used by client code.)

Listing 15-3. A Quick Look at the AsyncTask Class Definition

```
public class AsyncTask<Params, Progress, Result> {
    //A client will call this method
    AsyncTask<Params, Progress, Result>    execute(Params... params);

    //Do your work here. Frequently triggers onProgressUpdate()
    Result doInBackGround(Params... params);

    //Callback: After the work is complete
    void onPostExecute(Result result);

    //Callback: As the work is progressing
    void onProgressUpdate(Progress... progressValuesArray);
}
```

Studying Listing 15-3, you can see that the AsyncTask (through generics) needs the following three parameterized types (Params, Progress, and Result) when you extend it. Let's explain these types briefly:

- Params (The type of parameters to the execute() method): When extending AsyncTask, you will need to indicate the type of parameters that you will pass to the execute() method. If you say your Params type is String, then the execute() method will expect any number of strings separated by commas in its invocation such as execute(s1,s2,s3) or execute(s1,s2,s3,s4,s5).
- Progress (Parameter types to the progress callback method): This type indicates the array of values passed back to the caller while reporting progress through the callback onProgressUpdate(Progress... progressValuesArray). The ability to pass an array of progress values allows situations where multiple aspects of a task can be monitored and reported on. For example, this feature could be used if an AsyncTask is working on multiple subtasks.
- Result (Type used to report the result through onPostExecute() method): This type indicates the type of the return value that is sent back as the final result from the execution through the callback onPostExecute(Result finalResult).

Knowing now the needed generic types for an AsyncTask, suppose we decide on the following parameters for our specific AsyncTask: Params: A String, Result: An int, Progress: An Integer. Then, we can declare an extended AsyncTask class as shown in Listing 15-4.

Listing 15-4. Extending the Generic AsyncTask Through Concrete Types

```
public class MyLongTask
extends AsyncTask<String,Integer,Integer>
{
   //...other constructors stuff
   //...other methods
   //Concrete methods based on the parameterized types
   protected Integer doInBackground(String... params);
   protected void onPostExecute(Integer result);
   protected void onProgressUpdate(Integer... progressValuesArray);

   //....other methods
}
```

Notice how this concrete class in Listing 15-4, `MyLongTask`, has disambiguated the type names and arrived at function signatures that are type safe.

Implementing Your First AsyncTask

Let's now look at a simple, but complete, implementation of `MyLongTask`. We have amply commented the code in Listing 15-5 inline to indicate which methods run on which thread. Also pay attention to the constructor of `MyLongTask` where it receives object references of the calling context (usually an activity) and also a specific simple interface such as `IReportBack` to log progress messages.

The `IReportBack` interface is not critical to your understanding because it is merely a wrapper to a log. Same is true with the `Utils` class as well. You can see these additional classes in both of the downloadable projects for this chapter. The URL for the downloadable projects is in the references section at the end of this chapter. Listing 15-5 shows the complete code for `MyLongTask`.

Listing 15-5. Complete Source Code for Implementing an AsyncTask

```
//The following code is in MyLongTask.java (ProAndroid5_Ch15_TestAsyncTask.zip)
//Use menu item: Test Async1 to invoke this code
public class MyLongTask extends AsyncTask<String,Integer,Integer>
{
    IReportBack r; // an interface to report back log messages
    Context ctx;   //The activity to start a dialog
    public String tag = null;  //Debug tag
    ProgressDialog pd = null;  //To start, report, and stop a progress dialog

    //Constructor now
    MyLongTask(IReportBack inr, Context inCtx, String inTag)   {
        r = inr;  ctx = inCtx;  tag = inTag;
    }
    //Runs on the main ui thread
    protected void onPreExecute()    {
        Utils.logThreadSignature(this.tag);
        pd = ProgressDialog.show(ctx, "title", "In Progress...",true);
    }
```

```
    //Runs on the main ui thread. Triggered by publishProgress called multiple times
    protected void onProgressUpdate(Integer... progress) {
        Utils.logThreadSignature(this.tag);
        Integer i = progress[0];
        r.reportBack(tag, "Progress:" + i.toString());
    }
    protected void onPostExecute(Integer result)       {
        //Runs on the main ui thread
        Utils.logThreadSignature(this.tag);
        r.reportBack(tag, "onPostExecute result:" + result);
        pd.cancel();
    }
    //Runs on a worker thread. May even be a pool if there are more tasks.
    protected Integer doInBackground(String...strings)     {
        Utils.logThreadSignature(this.tag);
        for(String s :strings)          {
            Log.d(tag, "Processing:" + s);
        }
        for (int i=0;i<3;i++)          {
            Utils.sleepForInSecs(2);
            publishProgress(i); //this calls onProgressUpdate
        }
        return 1; //this value is then passed to the onPostExecute as input
    }
}
```

We will go into the details of each of the methods highlighted in Listing 15-5 after covering briefly how a client would make use of (or call) MyLongTask.

Calling an AsyncTask

Once we have the class MyLongTask implemented, a client will utilize this class as shown in Listing 15-6.

Listing 15-6. Calling an AsyncTask

```
//You will find this class AsyncTester.java(ProAndroid5_Ch15_TestAsyncTask.zip)
//Use menu item: Test Async1 to invoke this code
void respondToMenuItem() {
   //An interface to log some messages back to the activity
   //See downloadable project if you need the details.
   IReportBack reportBackObject = this;
   Context ctx = this;    //activity
   String tag = "Task1"; //debug tag

   //Instantiate and execute the long task
   MyLongTask mlt = new MyLongTask(reportBackObject,ctx,tag);
   mlt.execute("String1","String2","String3");
}
```

Notice how the execute() method is called in Listing 15-6. Because we have indicated one of the generic types as a String and that the execute() methods takes a variable number of arguments for this type, we can pass any number of strings to the execute() method. In the example in Listing 15-6, we have passed three string arguments. You can pass more or less as you need.

Once we call the execute() method on the AsyncTask, this will result in a call to the onPreExecute() method followed by a call to the doInBackground() method. The system will also call the onPostExecute() callback once the doInBackground() method finishes. Refer to Listing 15-5 for how these methods are implemented.

Understanding the onPreExecute() Callback and Progress Dialog

Going back to MyLongTask implementation in Listing 15-5, in the onPreExecute() method we started a progress dialog to indicate that the task is in progress. Figure 15-1 shows an image of that dialog. (Use menu item Test Async1 to invoke this view from project download ProAndroid5_Ch15_TestAsyncTask.zip.)

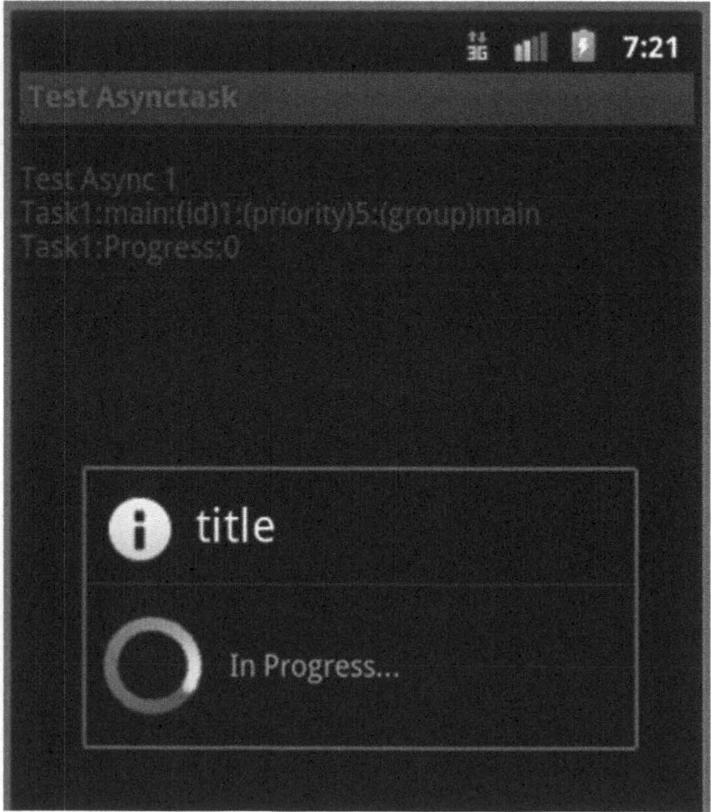

Figure 15-1. A simple progress dialog interacting with an AsyncTask

The code segment (taken from Listing 15-5) that shows the progress dialog is reproduced in Listing 15-7.

Listing 15-7. Showing an Indeterminate Progress Dialog

```
pd = ProgressDialog.show(ctx, "title", "In Progress...",true);
```

The variable pd was already declared in the constructor (see Listing 15-5). This call in Listing 15-7 will create a progress dialog and display it as shown in Figure 15-1. The last argument to the show() method in Listing 15-7 indicates if the dialog is indeterminate (whether the dialog can estimate beforehand how much work there is). We will cover the deterministic case in a later section.

> **Note** Showing progress of an AsyncTask reliably is quite involved. This is because an activity can come and go, because of either a configuration change or another UI taking precedence. We will cover this essential need and solutions later in the chapter.

Understanding the doInBackground() Method

All the background work carried out by the AsyncTask is done in the doInBackground() method. This method is orchestrated by the AsyncTask to run on a worker thread. As a result, this work is allowed to take more than five seconds, unlike the work done on a main thread.

In our example from Listing 15-5, in the doInBackground() method we simply retrieve each of the input strings to the task as if they are an array. In this method definition we haven't defined an explicit string array. However, the single argument to this function is defined as a variable-length argument, as shown in Listing 15-8.

Listing 15-8. doInBackground() Method Signature

```
protected Integer doInBackground(String...strings)
```

Java then treats the argument as if it is an array inside the function. So in our code in the doInBackground() method, we read each of the strings and log them to indicate that we know what they are. We then wait long enough to simulate a long-running operation. Because this method is running in a worker thread, we have no access to the UI functionality of Android from this worker thread. For instance, you won't be able to update any Views directly even if you have access to them from this thread. You cannot even send a Toast from here. The next two methods allow us to overcome this.

Triggering onProgressUpdate() through publishProgress()

In the doInBackground() method, you can trigger onProgressUpdate() by calling the publishProgress() method. The triggered onProgressUpdate() method then runs on the main thread. This allows the onProgressUpdate() method to update UI elements such as Views appropriately. You can also send a Toast from here. In Listing 15-5, we simply log a message. Once all the work is done, we return from the doInBackground() method with a result code.

Understanding the onPostExecute() Method

The result code from the `doInBackground()` method is then passed to the `onPostExecute()` callback method. This callback is also executed on the main thread. In this method, we tell the progress dialog to close. Being on the main thread, you can access any UI elements in this method with no restrictions.

Upgrading to a Deterministic Progress Dialog

In the previous example in Listing 15-5, we used a progress dialog (Figure 15-1) that doesn't tell us what portion of the work is complete. This progress dialog is called an indeterminate progress dialog. If you set the `indeterminate` property to `false` on this progress dialog, you will see a progress dialog that tracks progress in steps. This is shown in Figure 15-2. (Use menu item "Test Async2" to invoke this view from project download `ProAndroid5_Ch15_TestAsyncTask.zip`.)

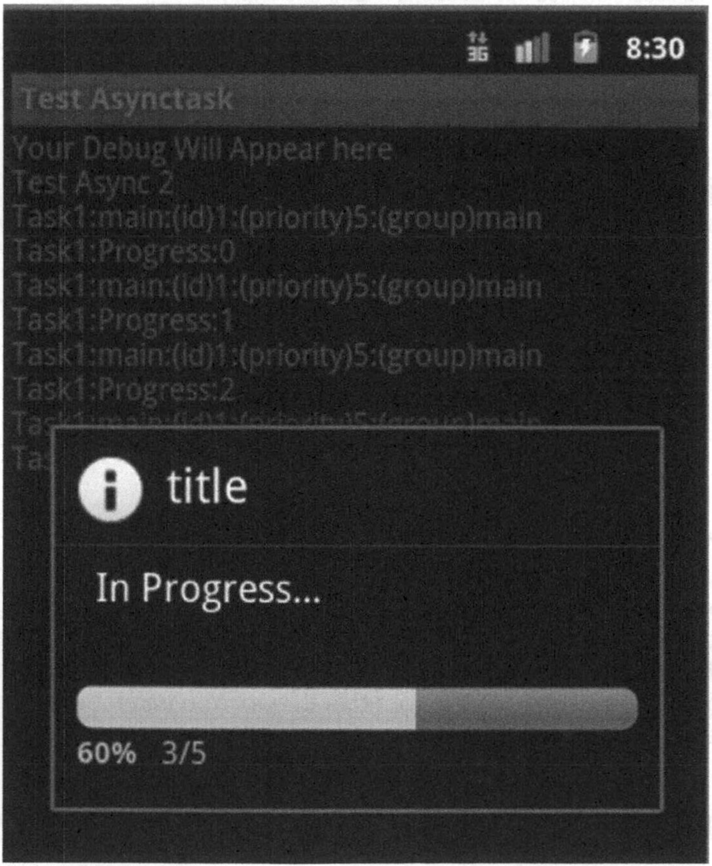

Figure 15-2. A progress dialog showing explicit progress, interacting with an AsyncTask

Listing 15-9 shows the previous task from Listing 15-5 rewritten to change the behavior of the progress dialog to a deterministic progress dialog. We have also added an onCancelListener to see if we need to cancel the task on cancelling the dialog. A user can click the back button in Figure 15-2 to cancel the dialog. Key portions of the code are given in Listing 15-9 (for the full code, see the download file ProAndroid5_Ch15_TestAsyncTask.zip).

Listing 15-9. A Long Task Utilizing a Deterministic Progress Dialog

```
//Following code is in MyLongTask1.java(ProAndroid5_Ch15_TestAsyncTask.zip)
//Use menu item: Test Async2 to invoke this code
public class MyLongTask1 extends AsyncTask<String,Integer,Integer>
implements OnCancelListener
{
    //..other code taken from Listing 15-5
    //Also refer to the java class MyLongTask1.java in the downloadable project
    //for full code listing.
    protected void onPreExecute()    {
        //....other code
        pd = new ProgressDialog(ctx);
        pd.setTitle("title");
        pd.setMessage("In Progress...");
        pd.setCancelable(true);
        pd.setOnCancelListener(this);
        pd.setIndeterminate(false);
        pd.setProgressStyle(ProgressDialog.STYLE_HORIZONTAL);
        pd.setMax(5);
        pd.show();
    }
    public void onCancel(DialogInterface d)     {
        r.reportBack(tag,"Cancel Called");
        this.cancel(true);
    }
    //..other code taken from Listing 15-5
}
```

Notice how we have prepared the progress dialog in Listing 15-9. In this case we haven't used the static method show(), in contrast to what we did in Listing 15-5, on the progress dialog. Instead, we explicitly instantiated the progress dialog. The variable ctx stands for the context (or activity) in which this UI progress dialog operates. Then we individually set the properties on the dialog, including its deterministic or indeterminate behavior. The method setMax() indicates how many steps the progress dialog has. We have also passed the self reference (the AsyncTask itself) as a listener when cancel is triggered. In the cancel callback, we explicitly issue a cancel on the AsyncTask. The cancel() method will try to stop the worker thread if we call it with the boolean argument of false. A boolean argument of true will force-stop the worker thread.

AsyncTask and Thread Pools

Consider the code in Listing 15-10, where a menu item is invoking two AsyncTasks one after the other.

Listing 15-10. Invoking Two Long-Running Tasks

```
void respondToMenuItem() {
    MyLongTask mlt = new MyLongTask(this.mReportTo,this.mContext,"Task1");
    mlt.execute("String1","String2","String3");

    MyLongTask mlt1 = new MyLongTask(this.mReportTo,this.mContext,"Task2");
    mlt1.execute("String1","String2","String3");
}
```

Here we are executing two tasks on the main thread. You may expect that both the tasks get started close to each other. The default behavior, however, is that these tasks run sequentially using a single thread drawn out of a pool of threads. If you want a parallel execution, you can use the executeOnExecutor() method on the AsyncTask. See SDK docs for details on this method. Also as per the SDK documentation, it is not valid to call the execute() method more than once on a single AsyncTask. If you want that behavior, you have to instantiate a new task and call the execute() method again.

Issues and Solutions for Correctly Showing the Progress of an AsyncTask

If your primary goal with this chapter is to learn just the essentials of AsyncTask, then what we have covered so far is sufficient. However, there are some issues when an AsyncTask is paired with a progress dialog as shown in the previous listings so far. One of those issues is that an AsyncTask will lose the correct activity reference when the device is rotated, thereby also losing its reference to the progress dialog. The other issue is that the progress dialog we used earlier in the code is not a managed dialog. Let's understand these issues now.

Dealing with Activity Pointers and Device Rotation

The activity pointer that is held by the AsyncTask becomes stale when the activity is re-created because of a configuration change. This is because Android has created a new activity and the old activity is no longer shown on the screen. So holding on to the old activity and its corresponding dialog is bad for a couple of reasons. The first is that the user is not seeing that activity or dialog that the AsyncTask is trying to update. The second reason is that the old activity needs to be garbage collected and you are stopping it from getting garbage collected because the AsyncTask is holding on to its reference. If you were to be smart and use a Java weak reference for the old activity, then you wouldn't leak memory but you would get a null pointer exception. The case of stale pointer is true not only of the activity pointer but any other pointer that indirectly points to the activity.

There are two ways to address the stale activity reference issue. The recommended way is to use headless retained fragments. (Fragments are covered in Chapter 8. Retained fragments are fragments that stay around while the activity is re-created due to a configuration change. These fragments are also called headless because they don't necessarily have to hold any UI.) Another way to solve the stale activity pointers is to use the retained objects callback from the activity. We will present both of these approaches for addressing the stale activity pointer issue.

Dealing with Managed Dialogs

Even if we are able to solve the stale activity reference issue and reestablish the connectivity to the current activity, there is a flaw in the way progress dialogs were used so far in this chapter. We have instantiated a `ProgressDialog` directly. A `ProgressDialog` created in this manner is not a "managed" dialog. If it is not a managed dialog, the activity will not re-create the dialog when the device undergoes rotation or any other configuration change. So, when the device rotates the `AsyncTask` is still running uninterrupted but the dialog will not show up. There are a couple of ways to solve this problem as well. The recommended way is not to use progress dialogs but instead use an embedded UI control in the activity itself, such as a progress bar. Because a progress bar is part of the activity view hierarchy, the hope is that it will be re-created. Although a progress bar sounds good, there are times when a modal progress dialog makes more sense. For example, that would be the case if you don't want the user to interact with any other part of the activity while the AsyncTask is running. In those cases, we see little contradiction in using fragment dialogs instead of progress bars.

It's time we step into the solutions to deal with the activity references issues and the managed dialogs issue. We will present three different solutions. The first one uses retained objects and fragment dialogs. The second one uses headless retained fragments and fragment dialogs. The third solution uses headless retained fragments and progress bars.

Testing Scenarios for a Well-Behaved Progress Dialog

Of the three solutions we have in this chapter, whichever you use to correctly display a progress dialog for an `AsyncTask`, the solution should work in all of the following test scenarios:

1. Without an orientation change the progress dialog must start, show its progress, end, and also clean up the reference to the `AsyncTask`. This must work repeatedly to show that there are no vestiges left from the previous run.
2. The solution should handle the orientation changes while the task is in the middle of its execution. The rotation should re-create the dialog and show progress where it left off. The dialog should properly finish and clean up the `AsyncTask` reference. This must work repeatedly to show that there are no vestiges left behind.
3. The back should be disabled when the task starts to run.

4. Going Home should be allowed even when the task is in the middle of execution.
5. Going Home and revisiting the activity should show the dialog and correctly reflect the current progress, and the progress should never be less than the one before.
6. Going Home and revisiting the activity also should work when the task finishes before returning. The dialog should be properly dismissed and the AsyncTask reference removed.

This set of test cases should always be performed for all activities dealing with `AsyncTasks`. Now that we have laid out how each solution should satisfy, let's start with the first solution, the one that uses retained objects and fragment dialogs.

Using Retained Objects and Fragment Dialogs

In this first solution, let's show you how to use retained objects and fragment dialogs for displaying progress correctly for an `AsyncTask`. This solution involves the following steps:

1. The activity must keep track of an external object through its `onRetainNonConfigurationInstance()` callback. This external object must stick around and its reference validated as the activity is closed and brought back. That is why this object is referred to as a retained object. This retained object can either be the `AsyncTask` object itself or an intermediate object that holds a reference to the `AsyncTask`. Let's call that a root retained activity-dependent object (or a root RADO). It is called a "root" because the `onRetainNonConfigurationInstance()` can use only one retained object reference.
2. A root RADO then will have a pointer to the `AsyncTask` and can set and reset the activity pointer on `AsyncTask` as the activity comes and goes. So, this root RADO acts as an intermediary between the activity and the `AsyncTask`.
3. The `AsyncTask` then will instantiate a fragment progress dialog instead of a plain non-managed progress dialog. The `AsyncTask` will use the activity pointer that is set by the root RADO to accomplish this, as you will need an activity to create a fragment including a fragment dialog.
4. The activity will re-create the dialog fragment as it rotates and keeps its state properly because dialog fragments are managed. The `AsyncTask` can proceed to increment progress on the fragment dialog as long as the activity is set and available. Note that this dialog fragment is not, by itself, a retained fragment. It gets re-created as part of the activity life cycle.

5. The fragment dialog can further disallow the cancel on it so that the user cannot go back to the activity from the dialog while the AsyncTask is in progress.
6. However, a user can go Home by tapping Home and use other apps. This will push our activity, and the dialog with it, into the background. This must be handled. When the user returns to the activity or app, the dialog can continue to show the progress. The AsyncTask must know how to dismiss the fragment dialog if the task finishes while the activity is hidden. Being a fragment dialog, dismissing this dialog throws an invalid state exception if the activity is not in the foreground. So, the AsyncTask has to wait until the activity is reopened and in the right state to dismiss the dialog.

Exploring Corresponding Key Code Snippets

We will present now the key pieces of code that are used to implement the outlined approach. The rest of the implementation can be found in the downloadable project ProAndroid5_Ch15_TestAsyncTaskWithConfigChanges.zip for this chapter. As all solutions for this problem require the dialog to be a fragment dialog, so that the dialog can be managed, Listing 15-11 presents the source code of this fragment dialog first.

Listing 15-11. Encapsulating a ProgressDialog in a DialogFragment

```
//The following code is in ProgressDialogFragment.java
//(ProAndroid5_Ch15_TestAsyncTaskWithConfigChanges.zip)
/**
 * A DialogFragment that encapsulates a ProgressDialog.
 * This is not expected to be a retained fragment dialog.
 * Gets re-created as activity rotates following any fragment protocol.
 */
public class ProgressDialogFragment extends DialogFragment  {
    private static String tag = "ProgressDialogFragment";
    ProgressDialog pd; //Will be set by onCreateDialog

    //This gets called from ADOs such as retained fragments
    //typically done when activity is attached back to the AsyncTask
    private IFragmentDialogCallbacks fdc;
    public void setDialogFragmentCallbacks(IFragmentDialogCallbacks infdc)  {
        Log.d(tag, "attaching dialog callbacks");
        fdc = infdc;
    }

    //This is a default constructor. Called by the framework all the time
    //for reintroduction.
    public ProgressDialogFragment()     {
        //Should be safe for me to set cancelable as false;
        //wonder if that is carried through rebirth?
        this.setCancelable(false);
    }
```

```
    //One way for the client to attach in the beginning when the fragment is reborn.
    //The reattachment is done through setFragmentDialogCallbacks
    //This is a shortcut. Your compiler if enabled for lint may throw an error.
    //You can use the newInstance pattern and setbundle (see the fragments chapter)
    public ProgressDialogFragment(IFragmentDialogCallbacks infdc)    {
        this.fdc = infdc;
        this.setCancelable(false);
    }
    /**
     * This can get called multiple times each time the fragment is
     * re-created. So storing the dialog reference in a local variable should be safe
     */
    @Override
    public Dialog onCreateDialog(Bundle savedInstanceState)    {
        Log.d(tag,"In onCreateDialog");
        pd = new ProgressDialog(getActivity());
        pd.setTitle("title");
        pd.setMessage("In Progress...");
        pd.setIndeterminate(false);
        pd.setProgressStyle(ProgressDialog.STYLE_HORIZONTAL);
        pd.setMax(15);
        return pd;
    }
    //Called when the dialog is dismissed.I should tell my corresponding task
    //to close or do the right thing! This is done through call back to fdc
    //fdc: fragment dialog callbacks could be the Task, or Activity or the rootRADO
    //See Listing 15-12 to see how FDC is implemented by the task
    @Override
    public void onDismiss(DialogInterface dialog)    {
        super.onDismiss(dialog);
        Log.d(tag,"Dialog dismissed");
        if (fdc != null)        {
            fdc.onDismiss(this, dialog);
        }
    }
    @Override
    public void onCancel(DialogInterface dialog)    {
        super.onDismiss(dialog);
        Log.d(tag,"Dialog cancelled");
        if (fdc != null)    {
            fdc.onCancel(this, dialog);
        }
    }
    //will be called by a client like the task
    public void setProgress(int value)    {
        pd.setProgress(value);
    }
}
```

Code in Listing 15-11 shows how to wrap a regular non-managed `ProgressDialog` in a managed fragment dialog. We extend a `DialogFragment` and override its `onCreateDialog()` to return the `ProgressDialog` object. In addition to that basic feature, we added the ability to monitor when the progress dialog gets dismissed or cancelled. We also provide a setProgress() method on the wrapped class to call the setProgress() on the internal ProgressDialog. You can see the source code for the IFragmentDialogCallbacks in the downloadable project (ProAndroid5_Ch15_TestAsyncTaskWithConfigChanges.zip), as it is not that critical to understanding this fragment progress dialog.

Let's see now how an AsyncTask can create and control this fragment progress dialog. Listing 15-12 presents the pseudocode for the AsyncTask in order to aid this understanding. For the complete source code, refer to downloadable project.

Listing 15-12. Pseudocode for an AsyncTask That Uses a Fragment Progress Dialog

```
//The following code is in MyLongTaskWithRADO.java
//(ProAndroid5_Ch15_TestAsyncTaskWithConfigChanges.zip)
//You can start this task through menu item: Flip Dialog with ADOs
public class MyLongTaskWithRADO extends AsyncTask<String,Integer,Integer>
implements IRetainedADO, IFragmentDialogCallbacks
{
    //....other code
    @Override public void onPreExecute()    {
        //....other code
        //get the activity as it would have been set by the root RADO
        Activity act = this.getActivity();

        //Create the progress diaolg
        ProgressDialogFragment pdf = new ProgressDialogFragment();
        //the show method will add and commit the fragment dialog
        pdf.show(act.getFragmentManager(), this.PROGRESS_DIALOG_FRAGMENT_TAG_NAME);
    }
    @Override public void onProgressUpdate()    {
        //if activity is available, get the fragment dialog from it
        //call setProgress() on it
        //otherwise ignore the progress
    }
    @Override public void onPostExecute()    {
        //if activity is in a good state
        //dismiss the dialog and tell the root RADO to drop the pointer to the AsyncTask
        //if not remember it through a flag to close it when you come back
    }
    @Override public void attach()    {
        //called when the activity is back
        //check to see if you are done
        //if so dismiss the dialog and remove yourself from the RADO
        //if not continue to update the progress
    }
}
```

Because this AsyncTask implements the idea of a retained activity-dependent object (IRetainedADO), it knows when the activity is available and when it is not. It also knows the state of the activity, such as whether the UI is ready or not. Although it takes some code to implement activity-dependent objects (ADOs), it is not a hard concept. We leave it to you due to space considerations to look into the downloadable project ProAndroid5_Ch15_TestAsyncTaskWithConfigChanges .zip and see how this is done.

This AsyncTask in Listing 15-12 also takes over the management of its fragment dialog so that it acts like a cohesive unit and thereby doesn't contaminate the main activity with the details of this AsyncTask. Another key detail in Listing 15-12 is what happens when the dialog is dismissed as the AsyncTask finishes. At this instant if the activity is hidden, or not there due to rotation, it is important to dismiss the dialog when the activity is re-created. In order to do this, the onPostExecute() remembers the last state of the AsyncTask whether it is done or in progress. This AsyncTask then waits for the attach() method, which gets called when the UI ready activity is reattached to this ADO. Once in the attach() method, the AsyncTask can then dismiss the fragment dialog.

You can download the project named ProAndroid5_Ch15_TestAsyncTaskWithConfigChanges.zip and see how the interaction presented in Listing 15-12 is fully realized.

This particular approach of using retained objects is a bit involved when compared to using retained fragments instead. But it has the elegance of solving it in a more generic form using the idea of ADOs, be they fragments or otherwise. We have links in the reference section that outline this idea and provide background. With that, let's turn our attention to the recommended idea of retained fragments in our second solution.

Using Retained Fragments and Fragment Dialogs

In the second solution, we will stick with the fragment dialogs but we will use headless retained fragments instead of simple retained objects. Android has deprecated the retained objects in favor of retained fragments. In Android a retained object is just an object and has no in-built ability to track the state of the activity. (This is why we had to invent the framework of ADOs on top.) This deficiency is not there with the introduction of fragments in later releases of Android. Although fragments are tightly woven into the fabric of UI, they can exist without UI as well. These are called headless fragments. In addition to being able to track the state of the activity, fragments can also be retained, much like retained objects.

Outlining the Retained Fragments Approach

The approach in this solution is to use a headless retained fragment as an anchor to communicate between the activity and the AsyncTask. Here are the key aspects of this approach:

1. Continue to use a fragment progress dialog, as in the solution before.
2. Have the activity create a headless retained fragment which then holds a pointer to the AsyncTask. This headless retained fragment takes the place of the retained object in the previous solution. Being a retained fragment, the fragment object sticks around while the activity is re-created with a new pointer. The AsyncTask then always relies on the retained fragment to retrieve the most current activity pointer.
3. The AsyncTask relies on the headless retained fragment to be informed of the activity state to accomplish all of the test cases indicated in the previous solution.

Exploring Corresponding Key Code Snippets

We have already shown you the code for the fragment dialog during the previous solution. As we continue to use the same object in this solution, we will focus on the retained fragment and also how the AsyncTask uses the fragment dialog through the retained fragment.

In the sample program (ProAndroid5_Ch15_TestAsyncTaskWithConfigChanges.zip) we have provided in the download, we called the retained fragment AsyncTesterFragment. Listing 15-13 shows the pseudocode for this class, which demonstrates, among other things, what makes this class a headless fragment.

Listing 15-13. Pseudocode for a Headless Fragment

```
//The following code is in AsyncTesterFragment.java
//(ProAndroid5_Ch15_TestAsyncTaskWithConfigChanges.zip)
//You can start this task through menu item: Flip Dialog with Fragment
public class AsyncTesterFragment
extends Fragment (or another object that is derived from Fragment) {

   //No need to override the key onCreateView() method
   //which otherwise would have returned a view loaded from a layout.
   //Thus having no View makes this fragment a headless fragment

   //Use this name to register with the activity
   public static String FRAGMENT_NAME="AsyncTesterRetainedFragment";

   //Local variable for the asynctask. You can use a menu to start work on this task
   //Nullify this reference when the asynctask finishes
   MyLongTaskWithFragmentDialog taskReference;

   //Have an init method to help with inheritance
   public void init(arg1, arge2, etc) {
       super.init(arg1,...); //if there is one
       setArguments(....); //or pass the bundle to the super init
   }
   public static AsyncTesterFragment newInstance(arg1, arg2, ...){
       AsyncTesterFragment f = new AsyncTesterFragment();
       f.init(arg1,arg2,...);
   }
   //have more static methods to create the fragment, locate the fragment etc.
}
```

There are three things worth mentioning about the code in Listing 15-13. By not overriding the onCreateView(), this fragment becomes a headless fragment. Because a fragment gets re-created using its default constructor, we followed the newInstance() pattern and also extended that pattern to use init() methods which can be virtual and inherited. This latter approach is useful if you are extending the Fragment class in a deeper hierarchy.

Listing 15-14 shows a static method on this AsyncTesterFragment object that can create this fragment, make it retain its state, and then register it with the activity.

Listing 15-14. Registering a Fragment as a Retained Fragment

```
//The following code is in AsyncTesterFragment.java
//(ProAndroid5_Ch15_TestAsyncTaskWithConfigChanges.zip)
//You can start this task through menu item: Flip Dialog with Fragment
public static AsyncTesterFragment createRetainedAsyncTesterFragment(Activity act) {
    AsyncTesterFragment frag = AsyncTesterFragment.newInstance();
    frag.setRetainInstance(true);
    FragmentManager fm = act.getFragmentManager();
    FragmentTransaction ft = fm.beginTransaction();
    ft.add(frag, AsyncTesterFragment.FRAGMENT_TAG);
    ft.commit();
    return frag;
}
```

Once this retained fragment is available with the activity, it can be retrieved any time and asked to start an AsyncTask. Listing 15-15 shows the pseudocode for the AsyncTask that is able to interact with this retained fragment to control the fragment dialog

Listing 15-15. An AsyncTask That Uses a Fragment Dialog Through a Retained Fragment

```
//The following code is in MyLongTaskWithFragment.java
//(ProAndroid5_Ch15_TestAsyncTaskWithConfigChanges.zip)
//You can start this task through menu item: Flip Dialog with Fragment
public class MyLongTaskWithFragment extends AsyncTask<String,Integer,Integer> {
    //...other code
    //The following reference passed in and set from the constructor
    AsyncTesterFragment retainedFragment;

    //....other code
    @Override protected void onPreExecute()    {
        ....other code
        //get the activity from the retained fragment
        Activity act = retainedFragment.getActivity();
        //Create the progress dialog
        ProgressDialogFragment pdf = new ProgressDialogFragment();
        //the show method will add and commit the fragment dialog
        pdf.show(act.getFragmentManager(), this.PROGRESS_DIALOG_FRAGMENT_TAG_NAME);
    }
    @Override protected void onProgressUpdate()    {
        //if activity is available, get the fragment dialog from it, call setProgress() on it
        //otherwise ignore the progress
    }
    @Override protected void onPostExecute()    {
        //if activity is in a good state
        //dismiss the dialog and tell the root RADO to drop the pointer to the AsyncTask
        //if not remember it through a flag to close it when you come back
    }
    @Override public void attach()    {
        //called when the activity is back. check to see if this task is done
        //if so dismiss the dialog and remove yourself from the retained fragment
        //if not continue to update the progress
    }
```

```
    @Override protected Integer doInBackground(String...strings)
    {
        //Do the actual work here which occurs on a separate thread
    }
}
```

This AsyncTask in Listing 15-15 behaves much like the AsyncTask that used the retained object. Once this task knows how to get access to the progress dialog fragment from the retained fragment, it is pretty straightforward to set the progress on it. As before, this task also needs to know when the activity is reattached in case the task is done beforehand. If this happens, the `AsyncTask` needs to remember this and close the dialog on reattach. The pseudocode in Listing 15-15 satisfies all the test conditions set forth earlier.

This concludes our second solution. Let's shift now to the third solution, where we will use a progress bar instead of a progress dialog to show the progress of an `AsyncTask`.

Using Retained Fragments and ProgressBars

Android SDK documentation on `ProgressDialog` (`http://developer.android.com/guide/topics/ui/dialogs.html`) is recommending that we use a `ProgressBar` in a number of scenarios instead as a better practice. The purported reason is that a progress bar is less intrusive, as it allows interaction with other areas of the activity. A progress bar, like a progress dialog, can be indeterminate or fixed in duration. It can also be a continuously revolving circle or a horizontal bar. You can find these modes by looking up the docs for `ProgressBar`. Listing 15-16 gives a quick rundown of a sampling of `ProgressBar` styles in a layout file.

Listing 15-16. Different Ways to Style a Progress Bar in a Layout File

```
//The following code is in spb_show_progressbars_activity_layout.xml
//(ProAndroid5_Ch15_TestAsyncTaskWithConfigChanges.zip)
//You can see these progress bars through menu item: Show Progress bars
<!--  A regular progress bar - A large spinning circle -->
<ProgressBar
    android:id="@+id/tpb_progressBar1"
    android:layout_width="match_parent"
    android:layout_height="wrap_content"
    android:background="@android:color/background_light"/>

<!--  Small spinning circle -->
<ProgressBar
    android:id="@+id/tpb_progressBar4"
    style="?android:attr/progressBarStyleSmall"
    android:layout_width="match_parent"
    android:layout_height="wrap_content"
    android:background="@android:color/background_light"/>

<!--  Horizontal indefinite Progress bar: a line -->
<ProgressBar
    android:id="@+id/tpb_progressBar3"
    style="?android:attr/progressBarStyleHorizontal"
    android:layout_width="match_parent"
```

```
    android:layout_height="wrap_content"
    android:indeterminate="true"
    />

<!-- Horizontal fixed duration Progress bar: a line -->
<ProgressBar
    android:id="@+id/tpb_progressBar3"
    style="?android:attr/progressBarStyleHorizontal"
    android:layout_width="match_parent"
    android:layout_height="wrap_content"
    android:indeterminate="false"
    android:max="50"
    android:progress="10"
    />
```

Figure 15-3 shows how the progress bar layouts shown in Listing 15-16 look when loaded into an activity. Each type of progress bar is labeled to indicate its mode or behavior. (Use menu item `Show Progress Bars` to invoke this view from project download `ProAndroid5_Ch15_TestAsyncTaskWithConfigChanges.zip`.)

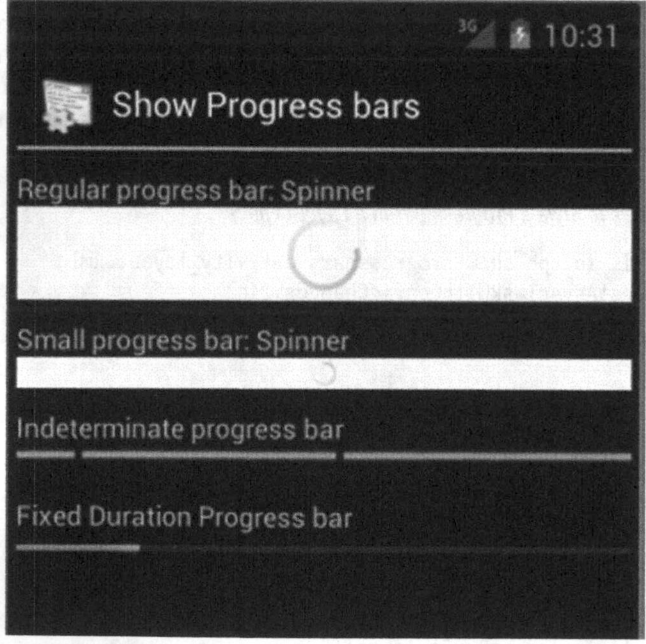

***Figure 15-3.** A sampling of progress bars in Android*

Outlining the ProgressBar Approach

The approach to report the progress of an AsyncTask through a progress bar is similar to the previous approach that used a retained headless fragment and a fragment progress dialog.

1. As in the previous solution, have the activity create a headless retained fragment that holds a pointer to the AsyncTask.
2. Embed the progress bar in the activity layout. AsyncTask will get to this progress bar through the headless retained fragment.
3. The AsyncTask relies on the headless retained fragment to be informed of the activity state to accomplish all of the test cases indicated earlier.

Walking Through Corresponding Key Code Snippets

Let's walk through the key code snippets that you would need to make this solution work. Let's begin with the local variables the AsyncTask holds to interact with the retained fragment and the activity (Listing 15-17).

Listing 15-17. Local Variables of an AsyncTask to Work with a ProgressBar

```
//The following code is in MyLongTaskWithProgressBar.java
//(ProAndroid5_Ch15_TestAsyncTaskWithConfigChanges.zip)
//You can start this task through menu item: Test ProgressBar
public class MyLongTaskWithProgressBar
extends AsyncTask<String,Integer,Integer>
implements IWorkerObject
{
    public String tag = null;    //Debug tag
    private MonitoredFragment retainedFragment; //Reference to the retained fragment
    int curProgress = 0; //To track current progress
....
```

Listing 15-18 shows how the AsyncTask initializes the progress bar when it starts.

Listing 15-18. Initializing a ProgressBar

```
//Part of MyLongTaskWithProgressBar.java
private void showProgressBar()    {
    Activity act = retainedFragment.getActivity();
    ProgressBar pb = (ProgressBar) act.findViewById(R.id.tpb_progressBar1);
    pb.setProgress(0);
    pb.setMax(15);
    pb.setVisibility(View.VISIBLE);
}
```

Listing 15-19 shows how the AsyncTask sets the progress on the progress bar after locating it.

***Listing 15-19.** Setting Progress on a ProgressBar*

```
//Part of MyLongTaskWithProgressBar.java
private void setProgressOnProgressBar(int i) {
    this.curProgress = i;
    ProgressBar pbar = getProgressBar();
    if (pbar == null)  {
        Log.d(tag, "Activity is not available to set progress");
        return;
    }
    pbar.setProgress(i);
}
```

The method getProgressBar() that locates the activity is quite simple; you just use the find() method to locate the ProgressBar view. If the activity is not available due to device rotation, the ProgressBar reference will be null and we will ignore setting the progress. Listing 15-20 shows how the AsyncTask closes the progress bar.

***Listing 15-20.** Closing the ProgressBar on AsyncTask Completion*

```
//Part of MyLongTaskWithProgressBar.java
private void closeProgressBar(){
    ProgressBar pbar = getProgressBar();
    if (pbar == null)    {
        Log.d(tag, "Sorry progress bar is null to close it!");
        return;
    }
    //Dismiss the dialog
    pbar.setVisibility(View.GONE);
    detachFromParent();
}
```

Once the ProgresBar is removed from the view, the code in Listing 15-20 informs the retained fragment that it can let go of the AsyncTask pointer should it be holding it. Depending on how the retained fragment holds this pointer, this step may or may not be needed. But it is a good practice to tell the parent it no longer needs to hold on to a reference that it doesn't need anymore. So, Listing 15-21 shows how the AsyncTask informs the parent that it no longer needs to hold a pointer to the AsyncTask.

***Listing 15-21.** Informing Clients, Like the Retained Fragment, of the Completion of AsyncTask*

```
//To tell the called object that I, the AsyncTask, have finished
//The Activity or retained fragment can act as a client to this AsyncTask
//AsyncTask is imagined to be a WorkerObject and hence understands the IWorkerObjectClient

//MyLongTaskWithProgressBar implements IWorkerObject
//AsyncTesterFragment implements the IWorkerObjectClient

//Code below is taken from MyLongTaskWithProgressBar.java
//This implements the IWorkerObject contract
```

```
IWorkerObjectClient client = null;
int workerObjectPassbackIdentifier = -1;

public void registerClient(IWorkerObjectClient woc,
     int inWorkerObjectPassbackIdentifier) {
    client = woc;
    this.workerObjectPassbackIdentifier = inWorkerObjectPassbackIdentifier;
}
private void detachFromParent()    {
    if (client == null)        {
        Log.e(tag,"You have failed to register a client.");
        return;
    }
    //client is available
    client.done(this,workerObjectPassbackIdentifier);
}
```

Addressing Key Differences with the ProgressBar Solution

There are some unexpected differences you must be aware of when we use a progress bar instead of a progress dialog.

Initially, in the layout file, visibility of the progress bar is set to GONE so that it represents the state that the AsyncTask has not even started. Once the AsyncTask starts it will set the visibility to VISIBLE and subsequently set the progress as it goes along. However, when the activity is re-created, the state management of the activity requires that the control is visible coming out of the onCreate() method. Because in the layout the visibility is set to be GONE, the activity will not restore the progress bar state and you will not see the progress bar when the device is rotated. Because of this, the AsyncTask needs to take over the control of this progress bar state management and reinitialize it properly when the activity is reattached. Listing 15-22 shows how we do this in the AsyncTask code.

***Listing 15-22.** Managing the ProgressBar State from the AsyncTask*

```
//Taken from MyLongTaskWithProgressBar.java
//On activity start
public void onStart(Activity act) {
    //dismiss dialog if needed
    if (bDoneFlag == true)        {
        Log.d(tag,"On my start I notice I was done earlier");
        closeProgressBar();
        return;
    }
    Log.d(tag,"I am reattached. I am not done");
    setProgressBarRightOnReattach();
}
private void setProgressBarRightOnReattach()    {
    ProgressBar pb = getProgressBar();
    pb.setMax(15);
    pb.setProgress(curProgress);
    pb.setVisibility(View.VISIBLE);
}
```

The onStart() method in Listing 15-22 is called by the retained fragment on the AsyncTask when the activity is reattached to the retained fragment and the fragment detects that the activity's UI is ready to be used.

Another difference when using a progress bar is the behavior of the back button. Unlike a progress dialog, for the activity, you may want to allow the back button. As the back button completely removes the activity, you may want to take this opportunity to cancel the task. The releaseResources()method in Listing 15-23 is called by the retained fragment when it detects that the activity is not going to be back by monitoring the isFinishing() flag in the onDestroy() method.

Listing 15-23. Cancelling the AsyncTask on Activity Back

```
//Taken from MyLongTaskWithProgressBar.java
public void releaseResources()    {
    cancel(true); //cancel the task
    detachFromParent(); //remove myself
}
```

All three solutions outlined in this latter part of the chapter will work to correctly show the progress of an AsyncTask. The SDK-recommended approach is to use the ProgressBar as the right UI component to display the progress. Our preference for quick tasks that take just a second or two is to use the progress bars as well. For a task that takes a little longer—and you don't want the user to disturb the state of the UI—then use the ProgressDialog in conjunction with a headless retained fragment. When your solutions require a deep hierarchy of objects, then use of the ADO framework could come handy irrespective of whether you use them through retained fragments or through the retained objects. You can see all of the solutions outlined here fully implemented in the downloadable project ProAndroid5_Ch15_TestAsyncTaskWithConfigChanges.zip.

There are further considerations if the AsyncTask were doing updates and changing state. If that is the case, you may want to use a background service so that it can be restarted if the process is to be reclaimed and restarted later. The approaches presented here are adequate for quick- to medium-level reads as you are expecting the user to wait. However, for longer-time reads or writes, you may want to adapt a service-based solution.

References

The following references will help you learn more about the topics discussed in this chapter:

- http://developer.android.com/reference/android/os/AsyncTask.html: A key resource that definitively documents the behavior of AsyncTask.
- http://www.shanekirk.com/2012/04/asynctask-missteps/: Another look at a well-behaved AsyncTask.
- http://www.androidbook.com/item/3536: Research notes on AsyncTask that we gathered in preparing this chapter.
- http://www.androidbook.com/item/3537: Android uses Java generics often in its API. This URL documents a few basics on Java generics to get you started.

- http://www.androidbook.com/fragments: As this chapter has demonstrated, to work with an AsyncTask authoritatively you need to know a lot about activity life cycle, fragments, their life cycle, headless fragments, configuration changes, fragment dialogs, AsyncTask, ADOs, and more. This URL has a number of articles focusing on all these areas.
- http://www.androidbook.com/item/4660: ADO is an abstraction that one of our authors espoused as a handy tool to deal with configuration change. This URL documents what ADOs are and how they could be used, and it also provides a preliminary implementation.
- http://www.androidbook.com/item/4674: This URL documents the background, helpful URLs, code snippets, and helpful hints to work with a ProgressBar.
- http://www.androidbook.com/item/4680: This URL has a good bit of research on activity life cycle in the event of configuration changes.
- http://www.androidbook.com/item/4665: It is quite hard to write programs that work well when devices rotate. This URL outlines some basic test cases you must successfully run for validating AsyncTask.
- http://www.androidbook.com/item/4673: This URL suggests an enhanced pattern for constructing inherited fragments.
- http://www.androidbook.com/item/4629: The best way to understand a fragment, including a retained fragment, is to study its callbacks diligently. This URL provides documented sample code for all the important callbacks of a fragment.
- http://www.androidbook.com/item/4668: The best way to understand an activity life cycle is study its callbacks diligently. This URL provides documented sample code for all the important activity callbacks.
- http://www.androidbook.com/item/3634: This URL outlines our research on fragment dialogs.
- http://www.androidbook.com/proandroid5/projects: A list of downloadable projects from this book is at this URL. For this chapter, look for a zip file named ProAndroid5_Ch15_TestAsyncTask.zip and also ProAndroid5_Ch15_TestAsyncTaskWithConfigChanges. The latter zip file is the one that implements the three proposed solutions for a well-behaved AsyncTask.

Summary

In this chapter, in addition to covering AsyncTask, we have introduced you to progress dialogs, progress bars, headless retained fragments, and ADOs. Reading this chapter, you not only understood AsyncTask but also got to apply your understanding of activity life cycle and a deep understanding of fragments. We have also documented a set of key test cases that must be satisfied for a well-behaved Android application.

Chapter 16

Broadcast Receivers and Long-Running Services

A broadcast receiver is another component in an Android process, along with activities, content providers, and services. A broadcast receiver is a component that can respond to a broadcast message sent by a client. This message is modeled as an intent. Further, a broadcast message (intent) can be responded to by more than one receiver.

A client component such as an activity or a service uses the `sendBroadcast(intent)` method, available on the `Context` class, to send a broadcast. Receiving components of the broadcast intent will need to inherit from a `BroadcastReceiver` class available in the Android SDK. These broadcast receivers need to be registered in the manifest file through a `receiver` component tag to indicate that the receiver is interested in responding to a certain type of broadcast intent.

Sending a Broadcast

Listing 16-1 shows sample code that sends a broadcast event. This code creates an intent with a unique intent action string, puts an extra field called `message` on it, and calls the `sendBroadcast()` method. Putting the `extra` on the intent is optional.

Listing 16-1. Broadcasting an Intent

```
//This code is in class: TestBCRActivity.java
//Project: TestBroadcastReceiver, Download: ProAndroid5_Ch16_TestReceivers.zip
private void testSendBroadcast(Activity activity) {
    //Create an intent with a unique action string
    String uniqueActionString = "com.androidbook.intents.testbc";
    Intent broadcastIntent = new Intent(uniqueActionString);
```

```
    //Allow stand alone cross-processes that have broadcast receivers
    //in them to be started even though they are in stopped state.
    broadcastIntent.addFlags(Intent.FLAG_INCLUDE_STOPPED_PACKAGES);

    broadcastIntent.putExtra("message", "Hello world");
    activity.sendBroadcast(broadcastIntent);
}
```

In Listing 16-1, the action is an arbitrary identifier that suits your needs. To make this action string unique, you may want to use a namespace similar to a Java package. Also, we will talk about the cross-process FLAG_INCLUDE_STOPPED_PACKAGES later in this chapter in the section called "Out-of-Process Receivers."

Coding a Simple Receiver

Listing 16-2 shows a broadcast receiver that can respond to the broadcasted intent from Listing 16-1.

Listing 16-2. Sample Broadcast Receiver Code

```
//This class is in TestBroadcastReceiver project in the download
//The download for this chapter is: ProAndroid5_Ch16_TestReceivers.zip
public class TestReceiver extends BroadcastReceiver {
    private static final String tag = "TestReceiver";
    @Override
    public void onReceive(Context context, Intent intent)     {
        Log.d("TestReceiver", "intent=" + intent);
        String message = intent.getStringExtra("message");
        Log.d(tag, message);
    }
}
```

Creating a broadcast receiver is quite simple. Extend the BroadcastReceiver class and override the onReceive() method. We are able to see the intent in the receiver and extract the message from it. Next we need to register the broadcast receiver in the manifest file as a receiver.

Registering a Receiver in the Manifest File

Listing 16-3 shows how you can declare a receiver as the recipient of the intent whose action is com.androidbook.intents.testbc.

Listing 16-3. A Receiver Definition in the Manifest File

```
<!--
In filename: AndroidManifest.xml
Project: TestBroadcastReceiver, Download: ProAndroid5_Ch16_TestReceivers.zip
-->
<manifest>
<application>
```

```
...
<activity>...</activity>
...
<receiver android:name=".TestReceiver">
    <intent-filter>
        <action android:name="com.androidbook.intents.testbc"/>
    </intent-filter>
</receiver>
...
</application>
</manifest>
```

The receiver element is a child node of the application element like the other component nodes such as an activity.

With the receiver (Listing 16-2) and its registration in the manifest file (Listing 16-3) available, you can invoke the receiver using the client code in Listing 16-1. We have included a reference to the downloadable ZIP file ProAndroid5_Ch16_TestReceivers.zip for this chapter at the end of this chapter. This ZIP file has two projects. The code referenced so far is in the project TestBroadcastReceiver.

Accommodating Multiple Receivers

The idea of a broadcast is that there could be more than one receiver. Let's replicate TestReceiver (see Listing 16-2) as TestReceiver2 and see if both can respond to the same broadcast message. The code for TestReceiver2 is presented in Listing 16-4.

Listing 16-4. Source code for TestReceiver2

```
//Filename: TestReceiver2.java
//Project: TestBroadcastReceiver, Download: ProAndroid5_Ch16_TestReceivers.zip
public class TestReceiver2 extends BroadcastReceiver {
    private static final String tag = "TestReceiver2";
    @Override
    public void onReceive(Context context, Intent intent)    {
        Log.d(tag, "intent=" + intent);
        String message = intent.getStringExtra("message");
        Log.d(tag, message);
    }
}
```

Add this receiver to your manifest file as shown in Listing 16-5.

Listing 16-5. TestReceiver2 Definition in the Manifest File

```
<!--
In filename: AndroidManifest.xml
Project: TestBroadcastReceiver, Download: ProAndroid5_Ch16_TestReceivers.zip
-->
<receiver android:name=".TestReceiver2">
    <intent-filter>
        <action android:name="com.androidbook.intents.testbc"/>
    </intent-filter>
</receiver>
```

Now, if you fire off the event as in Listing 16-1, both receivers will be called.

We have indicated in Chapter 13 that the main thread runs all the broadcast receivers that belong to a single process. You can prove this by printing out the thread signature in each of the receivers, including the main line invoking code. You will see the same thread running through this code sequentially. The `sendBroadcast()` queues the broadcast message and lets the main thread get back to its queue. Response to this queued message by a receiver is carried out by the same main thread in order. When there are multiple receivers, it is not good design to rely on the order of execution as to which receiver is invoked first.

Working with Out-of-Process Receivers

The intention of a broadcast is more likely that the process responding to it is an unknown one and separate from the client process. You can prove this by replicating one of your receivers presented so far and creating a separate `.apk` file from it. Then when you fire off the event from Listing 16-1, you will see that both the in-process receivers (those that are in the same project or `.apk` file) and out-of-process receivers (those that are in a separate `.apk` file) are invoked. You will also see through the LogCat messages that the in-process and out-of-process receivers run in their respective main threads.

However, after API 12 (Android 3.1) there are some wrinkles around broadcast receivers that are in external processes. This is due to the launch model adapted by the SDK for security concerns. You can read about this more in one of the reference links provided for this chapter. With this change an application when installed will be in a stopped state. Intents that can start components can now specify to target those applications that are only in started state. By default the old behavior persists. However, for broadcast intents the system automatically adds a flag to exclude applications that are in stopped state. To overcome the previous point, one can explicitly set an intent flag on the broadcast intent to include those stopped applications as valid targets. This is what you see in code Listing 16-1.

We have included an additional separate stand-alone project called `StandaloneBroadcastReceiver` in the chapter's downloadable ZIP file `ProAndroid5_Ch16_TestReceivers.zip` to test this concept. To try it, you have to deploy both the invoking project `TestBroadcastReceiver` and the stand-alone receiver's project `StandloneBroadcastReceiver` on the emulator. You can then use the `TestBroadcastReceiver` project to send the broadcast event and monitor the LogCat for the receivers responding from the `StandaloneBroadcastReceiver`.

Using Notifications from a Receiver

Broadcast receivers often need to communicate to the user about something that happened or as a status. This is usually done by alerting the user through a notification icon in the system-wide notification bar. We will now show you how to create a notification from a broadcast receiver, send it, and view it through the notification manager.

Monitoring Notifications Through the Notification Manager

Android shows icons of notifications as alerts in the notification area. The notification area is located at the top of device in a strip that looks like Figure 16-1. The look and placement of the notification area may change based on whether the device is a tablet or a phone and may at times also change based on Android release.

Figure 16-1. Android notification icon status bar

The notification area shown in Figure 16-1 is called the *status bar*. It contains system indicators such as battery strength, signal strength, and so on. When we deliver a notification, the notification will appear as an icon in the area shown in Figure 16-1. The notification icon is illustrated in Figure 16-2.

Figure 16-2. Status bar showing a notification icon

The notification icon is an indicator to the user that something needs to be observed. To see the full notification, you have to hold a finger on the icon and drag the title strip shown in Figure 16-2 down like a curtain. This will expand the notification area, as shown in Figure 16-3.

***Figure 16-3.** Expanded notification view*

In the expanded view of the notification in Figure 16-3, you get to see the details supplied to the notification. You can click the notification detail to fire off the intent to bring up the full application to which the notification belongs. You can use this view to clear notifications. Also depending on the device and release there may be alternate ways of opening the notifications. Let's see now how to generate a notification icon like the one shown in Figures 16-2 and 16-3.

Sending a Notification

When you create a notification object, it needs to have the following elements:

- An icon to display
- Ticker text like "hello world"
- The time when it is delivered

Once you have a notification object constructed, you get the notification manager reference by asking the context for a system service named `Context.NOTIFICATION_SERVICE`. Then you ask the notification manager to send the notification. Listing 16-6 has the source code for a broadcast receiver that sends the notification shown in Figures 16-2 and 16-2.

Listing 16-6. A Receiver That Sends a Notification

```
//Filename: NotificationReceiver.java
//Project: StandaloneBroadcastReceiver, Download: ProAndroid5_Ch16_TestReceivers.zip
public class NotificationReceiver extends BroadcastReceiver {
    private static final String tag = "Notification Receiver";
    @Override
    public void onReceive(Context context, Intent intent) {
        Log.d(tag, "intent=" + intent);
        String message = intent.getStringExtra("message");
        Log.d(tag, message);
        this.sendNotification(context, message);
    }
    private void sendNotification(Context ctx, String message)   {
        //Get the notification manager
        String ns = Context.NOTIFICATION_SERVICE;
        NotificationManager nm =
            (NotificationManager)ctx.getSystemService(ns);
        //Prepare Notification Object Details
        int icon = R.drawable.robot;
        CharSequence tickerText = "Hello";
        long when = System.currentTimeMillis();
        //Get the intent to fire when the notification is selected
        Intent intent = new Intent(Intent.ACTION_VIEW);
        intent.setData(Uri.parse("http://www.google.com"));
        PendingIntent pi = PendingIntent.getActivity(ctx, 0, intent, 0);
        //Create the notification object through the builder
        Notification notification =
            new Notification.Builder(ctx)
                .setContentTitle("title")
                .setContentText(tickerText)
                .setSmallIcon(icon)
                .setWhen(when)
                .setContentIntent(pi)
                .setContentInfo("Addtional Information:Content Info")
                .build();
        //Send notification
        //The first argument is a unique id for this notification.
        //This id allows you to cancel the notification later
        //This id also allows you to update your notification
        //by creating a new notification and resending it against that id
        //This id is unique with in this application
        nm.notify(1, notification);
    }
}
```

The content view of a notification is displayed when the notification is expanded. This is what you see in Figure 16-2. The content view needs to be a RemoteViews object. However, we don't pass a content view directly. Based on the parameters passed to the Builder object, the Builder object creates an appropriate RemoteViews object and sets it on the notification. The Builder interface also has a method to directly set the content view as a whole if needed.

The steps for directly using remote views for a content view of a notification are as follows:

1. Create a layout file.
2. Create a RemoteViews object using the package name and the layout file ID.
3. Call setContent() on the Notification.Builder object before calling the build() method to create the notification object, which is then sent to the notification manager.

Keep in mind that only a limited set of controls may participate in a remote view, such as FrameLayout, LinearLayout, RelativeLayout, AnalogClock, Button, Chronometer, ImageButton, ImageView, ProgressBar, TextView.

The code in Listing 16-6 creates a notification using the Builder object to set the implicit content view (through title and text) and the intent to fire (in our case, this intent is the browser intent). A new notification can be created to be resent through the notification manager in order to update the previous instance of it using the unique ID of the notification. The ID of the notification, which is set to 1 in Listing 16-6, is unique within this application context. This uniqueness allows us to continuously update what is happening to that notification and also cancel it if needed.

You may also want to look at the various flags available while creating a notification, such as FLAG_NO_CLEAR and FLAG_ONGOING_EVENT, to control the persistence of these notifications. You can use the following URL to check these flags:

http://developer.android.com/reference/android/app/Notification.html

Starting an Activity in a Broadcast Receiver

Although you're advised to use the notification manager when a user needs to be informed, Android does allow you to spawn an activity explicitly. You can do this by using the usual startActivity() method but with the following flags added to the intent that is used as the argument to the startActivity():

- Intent.FLAG_ACTIVITY_NEW_TASK
- Intent.FLAG_FROM_BACKGROUND
- Intent.FLAG_ACTIVITY_SINGLE_TOP

Exploring Long-Running Receivers and Services

So far, we have covered the happy path of broadcast receivers where the execution of a broadcast receiver is unlikely to take more than 10 seconds. The problem space is a bit complicated if we want to perform tasks that take longer than 10 seconds.

To understand why, let's review a few facts about broadcast receivers:

- A broadcast receiver, like other components of an Android process, runs on the main thread. Hence holding up the code in a broadcast receiver will hold up the main thread and will result in ANR. The time limit on a broadcast receiver is 10 seconds compared to 5 seconds for an activity. It is a bit of a reprieve, but not very much.
- The process hosting the broadcast receiver will start and terminate along with the broadcast receiver execution. Hence the process will not stick around after the broadcast receiver's `onReceive()` method returns. Of course, this is assuming that the process contains only the broadcast receiver. If the process contains other components, such as activities or services, that are already running, then the lifetime of the process takes these component life cycles into account as well.
- Unlike a service process, a broadcast receiver process will not get restarted.
- If a broadcast receiver were to start a separate thread and return to the main thread, Android will assume that the work is complete and will shut down the process even if there are threads running, bringing those threads to an abrupt stop.
- Android automatically acquires a partial wake lock when invoking a broadcast service and releases it when it returns from the service in the main thread. A wake lock is a mechanism and an API class available in the SDK to keep the device from going to sleep or to wake it up if it is already asleep.

Given these predicates, how can we execute longer-running code in response to a broadcast event?

Understanding Long-Running Broadcast Receiver Protocol

The answer lies in resolving the following:

- We will clearly need a separate thread so that the main thread can get back and avoid ANR messages.
- To stop Android from killing the process and hence the worker thread, we need to tell Android that this process contains a component, such as a service, with a life cycle. So we need to create or start that service. The service itself cannot directly do the work for more than 5 seconds because that happens on the main thread, so the service needs to start a worker thread and let the main thread go.

- For the duration of the worker thread's execution, we need to hold on to the partial wake lock so that the device won't go to sleep. A partial wake lock will allow the device to run code without turning on the screen and so on, which allows for longer battery life.
- The partial wake lock must be obtained in the main line code of the receiver; otherwise, it will be too late. For example, you cannot do this in the service, because it may be too late between the `startService()` being issued by the broadcast receiver and the `onStartCommand()` of a service that begins execution.
- Because we are creating a service, the service itself can be brought down and brought back up because of low-memory conditions. If this happens, we need to acquire the wake lock again.
- When the worker thread started by the `onStartCommand()` method of the service completes its work, it needs to tell the service to stop so that it can be put to bed and not brought back to life by Android.
- It is also possible that more than one broadcast event can occur. Given that, we need to be cautious about how many worker threads we need to spawn.

Given these facts, the recommended protocol for extending the life of a broadcast receiver is as follows:

1. Get a (static) partial wake lock in the `onReceive()` method of the broadcast receiver. The partial wake lock needs to be static to allow communication between the broadcast receiver and the service. There is no other way of passing a reference of the wake lock to the service, as the service is invoked through a default constructor that takes no parameters.
2. Start a local service so that the process won't be killed.
3. In the service, start a worker thread to do the work. Do not do the work in the `onStart()` method of the service. If you do, you are basically holding up the main thread again.
4. When the worker thread is done, tell the service to stop itself either directly or through a handler.
5. Have the service turn off the static wake lock.

Understanding IntentService

Recognizing the need for a service to not hold up the main thread, Android has provided a utility local service implementation called `IntentService` to offload work to a worker thread so that the main thread can be released after scheduling the work to the subthread. Under this scheme, when you call `startService()` on an `IntentService`, the `IntentService` will queue that request to a subthread using a looper and a handler so that a derived method of the `IntentService` is called to do the actual work on a single worker thread.

Here is what the API documentation for IntentService says:

> *IntentService is a base class for Services that handle asynchronous requests (expressed as Intents) on demand. Clients send requests through startService(Intent) calls; the service is started as needed, handles each Intent in turn using a worker thread, and stops itself when it runs out of work. This "work queue processor" pattern is commonly used to offload tasks from an application's main thread. The IntentService class exists to simplify this pattern and take care of the mechanics. To use it, extend IntentService and implement onHandleIntent(Intent). IntentService will receive the Intents, launch a worker thread, and stop the service as appropriate. All requests are handled on a single worker thread—they may take as long as necessary (and will not block the application's main loop), but only one request will be processed at a time.*

This idea is demonstrated using a simple example in Listing 16-7. You extend the IntentService and provide what you want to do in the onHandleIntent() method.

***Listing 16-7.** Using IntentService*

```
//You can see file Test30SecBCRService.java for example
//Project: StandaloneBroadcastReceiver, Download: ProAndroid5_Ch16_TestReceivers.zip
public class MyService extends IntentService {
    public MyService()
    { super("some-java-package-like-name-used-for-debugging"); }
    protected void onHandleIntent(Intent intent)  {
        //log thread signature if you want to see that it is running on a separate thread
        //Ex: Utils.logThreadSignature("MyService");
        //do the work in this subthread
        //and return
    }
}
```

Once you have a service like this, you can register this service in the manifest file and use client code to invoke this service as context.startService(new Intent(context, MyService.class)). This will result in a call to onHandleIntent() in Listing 16-7. You will notice that if you were to use the commented out method Utils.logThreadSignature() in Listing 16-7 in your actual code, it will print the ID of the worker thread and not the main thread. You can see the Utils class in the project and download references listed in the comments section of Listing 16-7.

Extending IntentService for a Broadcast Receiver

From the perspective of a broadcast receiver, an IntentService is a wonderful thing. It lets us execute long-running code without blocking the main thread. Not only that, being a service, an IntentService provides a process that keeps running when the broadcast code returns. So can we use the IntentService for the needs of a long-running operation? Yes and no.

Yes, because the IntentService does two things: First, it keeps the process running because it is a service. Second, it lets the main thread go and avoids related ANR messages.

To understand the "no" answer, you need to understand wake locks a bit more. When a broadcast receiver is invoked through an alarm manager, the device may not be on. So the alarm manager partially turns on the device (just enough to run the code without any UI) by making a call to the power manager and requesting a wake lock. The wake lock gets released as soon as the broadcast receiver returns.

This leaves the IntentService invocation without a wake lock, so the device may go to sleep before the actual code runs. However, IntentService, being a general-purpose extension to a service, it does not acquire a wake lock. So we need further props on top of an IntentService. We need an abstraction.

Mark Murphy has created a variant of the IntentService called WakefulIntentService that keeps the semantics of using an IntentService but also acquires the wake lock and releases it properly under a variety of conditions. You can look at his implementation at http://github.com/commonsguy/cwac-wakeful.

Exploring Long-Running Broadcast Service Abstraction

WakefulIntentService is a good abstraction. However, we want to go a step further so that our abstraction parallels the method of extending IntentService as in Listing 16-7 and does everything that an IntentService does but also provides few more benefits:

- Pass the original intent that was passed to the broadcast receiver to the overridden method onHandleIntent. This allows us to largely hide the broadcast receiver, simulating a programming experience that a service is started in response to a broadcast message. This is really the goal for this abstraction while some extras are thrown in.
- Acquire and release wake locks (similar to WakefulIntentService).
- Deal with a service being restarted.
- Allow a uniform way to deal with the wake lock for multiple receivers and multiple services in the same process.

We will call this abstract class ALongRunningNonStickyBroadcastService. As the name suggests, we want this service to allow for long-running work. It will also be specifically built for a broadcast receiver. This service will also be nonsticky (we will explain this concept later in the chapter, but briefly, this indicates that Android will not start the service if there are no messages in the queue). To allow for the behavior of an IntentService, it will extend the IntentService and override the onHandleIntent method.

Combining these ideas, the abstract ALongRunningNonStickyBroadcastService service will have a signature that looks like Listing 16-8.

Listing 16-8. Long-Running Service Abstract Idea

```
public abstract class ALongRunningNonStickyBroadcastService extends IntentService {
//...other implementation details
//the following method will be called by the onHandleIntent of IntentService
//this is where the actual work happens in this derived abstract class
protected abstract void handleBroadcastIntent(Intent broadcastIntent);
//...other implementation details

}
```

The implementation details for this ALongRunningNonStickyBroadcastService are a touch involved, and we will cover them soon after we explain why we are going after this type of service. We want to demonstrate first the utility and simplicity of having it.

Once we have this abstract class of Listing 16-8, the MyService example in Listing 16-7 can be rewritten as in Listing 16-9.

Listing 16-9. Long-Running Service Sample Usage

```
public class MyService extends ALongRunningNonStickyBroadcastService {
    //..other implementation details
    protected void handleBroadcastIntent(Intent broadcastIntent)  {
        //You can use the following method to see which thread runs this code
        //Utils.logThreadSignature("MyService");
        //do the work here
        //and return
    }
    //..other implementation details
}
```

The simplicity of Listing 16-9 is that this code is invoked as soon as a client fires off a broadcast intent. Especially the fact that you are receiving directly, unmodified, the same intent that invoked the broadcast receiver. It is as if the broadcast receiver has disappeared from the solution.

As you can see, you can extend this new long-running service class (just like IntentService and WakefulIntentService) and override a single method and do very little to nothing in the broadcast receiver. Your work will be done in a worker thread (thanks to IntentService) without blocking the main thread.

Listing 16-9 is a simple example demonstrating the concept. Let's turn to a more complete implementation that implements a long-running service that can run for 60 seconds in response to a broadcast event (proving that we can run for more than 10 seconds and avoid an ANR message). We will call this service appropriately Test60SecBCRService (BCR stands for broadcast receiver), and its implementation is shown in Listing 16-10.

Listing 16-10. Source code for Test60SecBCRService

```
//Filename: Test30SecBCRService.java
//Project: StandaloneBroadcastReceiver, Download: ProAndroid5_Ch16_TestReceivers.zip
public class Test60SecBCRService extends ALongRunningNonStickyBroadcastService {
   public static String tag = "Test60SecBCRService";
```

```
    //Required by IntentService to pass the classname for debug needs
    public Test60SecBCRService(){
       super("com.androidbook.service.Test60SecBCRService");
    }
    /* Perform long-running operations in this method.
     * This is executed in a separate thread.
     */
    @Override
    protected void handleBroadcastIntent(Intent broadcastIntent)  {
       //Utils class is in the download project mentioned
       Utils.logThreadSignature(tag);
       Log.d(tag,"Sleeping for 60 secs");
       //Use the thread to sleep for 60 seconds
       Utils.sleepForInSecs(60);
       String message =
          broadcastIntent.getStringExtra("message");
       Log.d(tag,"Job completed");
       Log.d(tag,message);
    }
}
```

As you can see, this code successfully simulates doing work for 60 seconds and still avoids the ANR message. The utility methods in Listing 16-10 are self-explanatory and available in the download projects for this chapter. The project name and download filename are in the comments section of the code in Listing 16-10.

Designing A Long-Running Receiver

Once we have the long-running service in Listing 16-10, we need to be able to invoke the service from a broadcast receiver. Again we are going after an abstraction to hide the broadcast receiver as much as possible.

The first goal of a long-running broadcast receiver is to delegate the work to the long-running service. To do this, the long-running receiver will need the class name of the long-running service to invoke it. The second goal is to acquire a wake lock. The third goal is to transfer the original intent that the broadcast receiver is invoked on to the service. We will do this by sticking the original intent as a `Parcelable` in the intent extras. We will use `original_intent` as the name for this extra. The long-running service then extracts `original_intent` and passes it to the overridden method of the long-running service (you will see this later in the implementation of the long-running service). This facility thus gives the impression that the long-running service is indeed an extension of the broadcast receiver.

Let us abstract out these three things and provide a base class. The only bit of information this long-running receiver abstraction needs is the name of the long-running service class (`LRSClass`) through an abstract method called `getLRSClass()`.

Putting these needs together, source code for the implementation of the abstract class `ALongRunningReceiver` is in Listing 16-11.

Listing 16-11. ***ALongRunningReceiver Abstraction***

```
//Filename: ALongRunningReceiver.java
//Project: StandaloneBroadcastReceiver, Download: ProAndroid5_Ch16_TestReceivers.zip
public abstract class  ALongRunningReceiver extends BroadcastReceiver  {
    private static final String tag = "ALongRunningReceiver";
    @Override
    public void onReceive(Context context, Intent intent) {
       Log.d(tag,"Receiver started");
       //LightedGreenRoom abstracts the Android WakeLock
       //to keep the device partially on.
       //In short this is equivalent to turning on
       //or acquiring the wake lock.
       LightedGreenRoom.setup(context);
       startService(context,intent);
       Log.d(tag,"Receiver finished");
    }
    private void startService(Context context, Intent intent) {
       Intent serviceIntent = new Intent(context,getLRSClass());
       serviceIntent.putExtra("original_intent", intent);
       context.startService(serviceIntent);
    }
    /*
     * Override this method to return the
     * "class" object belonging to the
     * nonsticky service class.
     */
    public abstract Class getLRSClass();
}
```

In the preceding broadcast receiver code, you see references to a class called LightedGreenRoom. This is a wrapper around a static wake lock. In addition to being a wake lock, this class tries to cater to working with multiple receivers, multiple services, etc., so that all waki-ness is properly coordinated. For the purpose of understanding, you can treat it as if it is a static wake lock. This abstraction is called a LightedGreenRoom because it is aimed at saving power for the device like the various “green” movements. Furthermore it is called “Lighted” because it starts off being “lighted” first as the broadcast receiver turns it on as soon as it is kicked off. The last service to use it will turn it off.

Once the receiver abstraction is available, you'll need a receiver that works hand in hand with the 60-second long-running service in Listing 16-11. Such a receiver is provided in Listing 16-12.

Listing 16-12. ***A Sample Long-Running Broadcast Receiver, Test60SecBCR***

```
//Filename: Test60SecBCR.java
//Project: StandaloneBroadcastReceiver, Download: ProAndroid5_Ch16_TestReceivers.zip
public class Test60SecBCR extends ALongRunningReceiver {
   @Override
   public Class getLRSClass() {
     Utils.logThreadSignature("Test60SecBCR");
     return Test60SecBCRService.class;
   }
}
```

Just like the service abstraction in Listings 16-10 and 16-11, the code in Listing 16-12 uses an abstraction for the broadcast receiver. The receiver abstraction starts the service indicated by the service class returned by the `getLRSClass()` method.

Thus far, we have demonstrated why we needed the two important abstractions to implement long-running services invoked by broadcast receivers:

- `ALongRunningNonStickyBroadcastService` (Listing 16-8)
- `ALongRunningReceiver` (Listing 16-11)

Abstracting a Wake Lock with LightedGreenRoom

As mentioned earlier, the primary purpose of the `LightedGreenRoom` abstraction is to simplify the interaction with the wake lock, and a wake lock is used to keep the device on during background processing. You really don't need the details of the implementation of the LightedGreenRoom, but merely its interface and the calls that are made against it. Just keep in mind that it is a thin wrapper around the Android SDK wake lock. In its simplest implementation, it can just be as simple as turning the wake lock on (acquire) and off (release). Listing 16-13 shows how a wake lock is used typically as stated in the SDK.

Listing 16-13. Psuedocode for working with the `WakeLock` API

```
//Get access to the power manager service
PowerManager pm =
   (PowerManager)inCtx.getSystemService(Context.POWER_SERVICE);

//Get hold of a wake lock
PowerManager.WakeLock wl =
   pm.newWakeLock(PowerManager.PARTIAL_WAKE_LOCK, tag);

//Acquire the wake lock
wl.acquire();

//do some work
//while this work is being done the device will be on partially

//release the Wakelock
wl.release();
```

Given this interaction, the broadcast receiver is supposed acquire the lock, and when the long-running service is finished, it needs to release the lock. As said earlier there is no good way to pass the wake lock variable to the service from the broadcast receiver. The only way the service knows about this wake lock is to use a static or application-level variable.

Another difficulty in acquiring and releasing a wake lock is the reference count. As a broadcast receiver is invoked multiple times, if the invocations overlap, there are going to be multiple calls to acquire the wake lock. Similarly, there are going to be multiple calls to release. If the number of acquire and release calls don't match, we will end up with a wake lock that at worst keeps the device on for far longer than needed. Also, when the service is no longer needed and the garbage collection runs, if the wake lock counts are mismatched, there will be a runtime exception in the LogCat. These issues have prompted us to do our best to abstract the wake lock as a `LightedGreenRoom` to ensure proper usage. There will be one of these objects per process that keeps a wake lock and ensures it is turned on and off properly. The included project has an implementation for this class. If you find that code too complicated due to the number of conditions it takes into account, you can just start with a simple static variable and turn it on and off as the service starts and closes and refine it to suit your particular conditions.

A reasonable approach for the broadcast receiver and the service to communicate with each other is through a static variable. Instead of making `WakeLock` static, we have made the entire `LightedGreenRoom` a static instance. However, every other variable inside `LightedGreenRoom` stays local and nonstatic.

Every public method of `LightedGreenRoom` is also exposed as a static method for convenience. We have used the convention of naming these methods starting with "s_". You can choose, instead, to get rid of the static methods and directly call the single object instance of `LightedGreenRoom`.

Implementing a Long-Running Service

To present the long-running service abstraction, we have to take one more detour to explain the lifetime of a service and how it relates to the implementation of `onStartCommand`. This is the method that is ultimately responsible for starting the worker thread and the semantics of a service.

When a service is started through `startService`, the service gets created first, and its `onStartCommand` method is called. Android has provisions to keep this process in memory so that the service can be completed even when serving multiple incoming client requests. However, under demanding memory conditions, Android may choose to reclaim the process and call the `onDestroy()` method of the service.

> **Note** Android tries to call the `onDestroy()` method for a service to reclaim its resources when the service is not executing its `onCreate()`, `onStart()`, or `onDestroy()` method, or in other words when the service is idle.

However, unlike an activity that is shut down, a service is scheduled to restart again when resources are available if there are pending `startService` intents in the queue. The service will be woken up and the next intent delivered to it via `onStartCommand()`. Of course, `onCreate()` will be called when the service is brought back.

Because services are automatically restarted if they are not explicitly stopped, it is reasonable to think that, unlike activities and other components, a service component is fundamentally a sticky component.

Understanding a Nonsticky Service

A service will not be automatically restarted if a client explicitly calls stopService. Depending on how many clients are still connected, this stopService method can move the service into a stopped state, at which time the service's onDestroy method is called and the service life cycle is complete. Once a service has been stopped like this by its last client, the service will not be brought back.

This protocol works well when everything happens as per design, where start and stop methods are called and executed in sequence and without a miss. Prior to Android 2.0, devices have seen a lot of services hanging around and claiming resources even though there was no work to be done, meaning Android brought the services back into memory even though there were no messages in the queue. This would have happened when stopService was not invoked either because of an exception or because the process was taken out between onStartCommand and stopService.

Android 2.0 introduced a solution so that we can indicate to the system, if there are no pending intents, that it shouldn't bother restarting the service. This is done by returning the nonsticky flag (Service.START_NOT_STICKY) from onStartCommand.

However, nonsticky is not really that nonsticky. Even if we mark the service as nonsticky, if there are pending intents, Android will bring the service back to life. This setting applies only when there are no pending intents.

Understanding a Sticky Service

What does it mean for a service to be really sticky then? The sticky flag (Service.START_STICKY) means that Android should restart the service even if there are no pending intents. When the service is restarted, call onCreate and onStartCommand with a null intent. This will give the service an opportunity, if need be, to call stopSelf if that is appropriate. The implication is that a service that is sticky needs to deal with null intents on restarts.

Understanding Redeliver Intents Option

Local services in particular follow a pattern where onStart and stopSelf are called in pairs. A client calls onStart. The service, when it finishes that work, calls stopSelf. If a service takes, say, 30 minutes to complete a task, it will not call stopSelf for 30 minutes. Meanwhile, the service is reclaimed due to low-memory conditions and higher-priority jobs. If we use the nonsticky flag, the service will not wake up, and we would never have called stopSelf.

Many times, this is OK. However, if you want to make sure whether these two calls happen for sure, you can tell Android not to unqueue the start event until stopSelf is called. This ensures that when the service is reclaimed, there is always a pending event unless the stopSelf is called. This is called redeliver mode, and it can be indicated in reply to the onStartCommand method by returning the Service.START_REDELIVER_INTENT flag.

Coding a Long-Running Service

Now that you have the background on IntentService, service-start flags, and the lighted green room, we're ready to take a look at the long-running service in Listing 16-14.

Listing 16-14. A Long-Running Service Abstraction

```
//Filename: ALongRunningNonStickyBroadcastService.java
//Project: StandaloneBroadcastReceiver, Download: ProAndroid5_Ch16_TestReceivers.zip
public abstract class ALongRunningNonStickyBroadcastService
extends IntentService  {
    public static String tag = "ALongRunningBroadcastService";
    //This is what you override to do your work
    protected abstract void
    handleBroadcastIntent(Intent broadcastIntent);

    public ALongRunningNonStickyBroadcastService(String name){
        super(name);
    }
    /*
     * This method can be invoked under two circumstances
     * 1. When a broadcast receiver issues a "startService"
     * 2. when android restarts this service due to pending "startService" intents.
     *
     * In case 1, the broadcast receiver has already
     * set up the "lightedgreenroom" and thereby gotten the wake lock
     *
     * In case 2, we need to do the same.
     */
    @Override
    public void onCreate()   {
        super.onCreate();

        //Set up the green room
        //The setup is capable of getting called multiple times.
        LightedGreenRoom.setup(this.getApplicationContext());

        //It is possible that more than one service of this type is running.
        //Knowing the number will allow us to clean up the wake locks in ondestroy.
        LightedGreenRoom.s_registerClient();
    }
    @Override
    public int onStartCommand(Intent intent, int flag, int startId)   {
        //Call the IntentService "onstart"
        super.onStart(intent, startId);

        //Tell the green room there is a visitor
        LightedGreenRoom.s_enter();
```

```
        //mark this as nonsticky
        //Means: Don't restart the service if there are no
        //pending intents.
        return Service.START_NOT_STICKY;
    }
    /*
     * Note that this method call runs in a secondary thread setup by the IntentService.
     *
     * Override this method from IntentService.
     * Retrieve the original broadcast intent.
     * Call the derived class to handle the broadcast intent.
     * finally tell the lighted room that you are leaving.
     * if this is the last visitor then the lock
     * will be released.
     */
    @Override
    final protected void onHandleIntent(Intent intent)    {
        try {
            Intent broadcastIntent
            = intent.getParcelableExtra("original_intent");
            handleBroadcastIntent(broadcastIntent);
        }
        finally {
            //release the wake lock if you are the last one
            LightedGreenRoom.s_leave();
        }
    }
    /* If Android reclaims this process, this method will release the lock
     * irrespective of how many visitors there are.
     */
    @Override
    public void onDestroy() {
        super.onDestroy();
        //Do any cleanup, if needed, when a service no longer needs a wake lock
        LightedGreenRoom.s_unRegisterClient();
    }
}
```

This class extends IntentService and gets all the benefits of a worker thread as set up by IntentService. In addition, it specializes the IntentService further so that it is set up as a nonsticky service. From a developer's perspective, the primary method to focus on is the abstract handleBroadcastIntent() method. Listing 16-15 shows you how to set up the receiver and the corresponding service in the manifest file.

Listing 16-15. The Long-Running Receiver and Service Definition

```
<!--
In filename: AndroidManifest.xml
Project: StandaloneBroadcastReceiver, Download: ProAndroid5_Ch16_TestReceivers.zip
-->
<manifest...>
......
```

```
<application....>
<receiver android:name=".Test60SecBCR">
    <intent-filter>
       <action android:name="com.androidbook.intents.testbc"/>
    </intent-filter>
</receiver>
<service android:name=".Test60SecBCRService"/>
</application>
.....
<uses-permission android:name="android.permission.WAKE_LOCK"/>
</manifest>
```

Notice that you will need the wake lock permission to run this long-running receiver abstraction. Complete source code for all of the receivers and long-running services is available in the downloadable projects for this chapter. Listing 16-15 brings out the essence of the long-running services invoked by a broadcast receiver. This abstraction states that you write a couple of lines to create a receiver like the `Test60SecBCR` (Listing 16-12), and then write a java method similar to the one in code `Test60SecBCRService` (Listing 16-10). Given the receiver and the java method that you want to run for a long time, you can execute that method in response to the broadcast event. This abstraction ensures that the method then can run as long as it takes without producing an ARM. The abstraction takes care of a) keeping the process alive, b) calling the service, c) taking care of the wake lock, and d) transferring the broadcast intent to the service. In the end this abstraction simulates "calling a method that can execute without time limits" from a broadcast event.

Additional Topics in Broadcast Receivers

Due to space limitations, we are not able to cover all aspects of broadcast receivers in this book. One topic we haven't covered at all is the security opportunities available to restrict both sending and receiving broadcasts. You can use the export attribute on a receiver to allow whether it can be invoked from external processes or not. You can also enable or disable a receiver either through the manifest file or programmatically. We have also not covered a method called `sendOrderBroadcast` that facilitates calling broadcast receivers in an order including chaining them. You can read up on these aspects from the main API docs for the `BroadcastReceiver` class.

Furthermore, in version 4 of the Android support library SDK there is a class called `LocalBroadcastManager` that is used to optimize calls to broadcast receivers that are strictly local. Being local, all security limitations need not be considered. As per the SDK, there is also system-level optimization for when this class is used.

Also in version 4 of the Android support library SDK, there is a class called `WakefulBroadcastReceiver` that encapsulates some of the same concepts that we have covered for long-running service needs.

References

Here are helpful references to the topics that are covered in this chapter:

- http://developer.android.com/reference/android/content/BroadcastReceiver.html: The BroadcastReceiver API. You will find at this link more about ordered broadcasts and about the BroadcastReceiver life cycle. This is an excellent resource.
- http://developer.android.com/reference/android/support/v4/content/WakefulBroadcastReceiver.html: Android API reference.
- http://developer.android.com/reference/android/support/v4/content/LocalBroadcastManager.html: Android API reference.
- http://developer.android.com/reference/android/app/Service.html: The Service API. This reference is especially good to have while working with long-running services.
- http://developer.android.com/reference/android/app/NotificationManager.html: The NotificationManager API.
- http://developer.android.com/reference/android/app/Notification.html: The Notification API. You will see here the various options available for working with a notification, such as content views and sound effects.
- http://developer.android.com/reference/android/widget/RemoteViews.html: The RemoteViews API. RemoteViews are used to construct custom detailed views of notifications.
- http://www.androidbook.com/item/3514: Authors' research on long-running services.
- http://www.androidbook.com/item/3482: Authors' research on broadcast receivers. This note also explains how to start an activity from a receiver.
- http://www.androidbook.com/proandroid5/projects: A list of downloadable projects from this book. For this chapter, look for a ZIP file named ProAndroid5_Ch16_TestReceivers.zip. This ZIP file has two projects: TestBroadcastReceiver and StandaloneBroadcastReceiver. The latter is dependent on the former, so install them in that order. The source code snippets in this chapter are annotated with their filenames and in what projects they are available.

Summary

In this chapter, we have covered broadcast receivers, notification managers, and the role of service abstraction in putting broadcast receivers to their best use. We also have given a practical abstraction to simulate long running broadcast services out of broadcast receivers.

Chapter 17

Exploring the Alarm Manager

In Android an intent object is used to start a UI activity, a background service, or a broadcast receiver. Normally these intents are triggered by user actions. In Android you can also use alarms to trigger broadcast intents, mind you, only broadcast intents. The invoked broadcast receivers then can choose to start an activity or a service.

In this chapter you will learn about the alarm manager API. Alarm manager API is used to schedule a broadcast intent to go off at a particular time. We will refer to this process of scheduling a broadcast intent at a particular time as setting an alarm.

We will also show you how to schedule alarms that repeat at regular intervals. We will show you how to cancel alarms that are already set.

When an intent object is stored to be used at a later time, it is called a pending intent. As alarm managers use pending intents all the time you will get to see the usage and intricacies of pending intents as well in this chapter.

Setting Up a Simple Alarm

We will start the chapter with setting an alarm at a particular time and having it call a broadcast receiver. Once the broadcast receiver is invoked, you can use the information from Chapter 16 to perform both simple and long-running operations in that broadcast receiver.

Getting access to the alarm manager is simple and is shown in Listing 17-1.

Listing 17-1. Getting Access to an Alarm Manager

```
//In filename: SendAlarmOnceTester.java
AlarmManager am =
    (AlarmManager)
         anyContextObject.getSystemService(Context.ALARM_SERVICE);
```

The variable anyContextObject refers to a context object. For example, if you are invoking this code from an activity menu, the context variable will be the activity. To set the alarm for a particular date and time, you will need an instance in time identified by a Java Calendar object. Listing 17-2 shows a utility function that gives you a calendar object for some specified time instant after the current time.

Listing 17-2. A Few Useful Calendar Utilities

```
//In filename: Utils.java
public class Utils {
    public static Calendar getTimeAfterInSecs(int secs) {
        Calendar cal = Calendar.getInstance();
        cal.add(Calendar.SECOND,secs);
        return cal;
    }
}
```

In the downloadable project for this chapter, you will see lot more calendar-based utilities to arrive at a time instance in a number of ways. Now, we need a receiver to set against the alarm that we are planning to set. A simple receiver is shown in Listing 17-3.

Listing 17-3. TestReceiver to Test Alarm Broadcasts

```
//In filename: TestReceiver.java
public class TestReceiver extends BroadcastReceiver  {
    private static final String tag = "TestReceiver";
    @Override
    public void onReceive(Context context, Intent intent)  {
        Log.d (tag, "intent=" + intent);
        String message = intent.getStringExtra("message");
        Log.d(tag, message);
    }
}
```

You will need to register this receiver in the manifest file using the <receiver> tag, as shown in Listing 17-4. Receivers are covered in detail in Chapter 16.

Listing 17-4. Registering a Broadcast Receiver

```
<!-- In filename: AndroidManifest.xml -->
<receiver android:name=".TestReceiver"/>
```

In Android an alarm is really a broadcast intent that is scheduled for a later time. What receiver component this intent should invoke is explicitly (through its classname) specified in the intent. Listing 17-5 shows an intent that can be used to invoke the broadcast receiver that we had in Listing 17-3.

Listing 17-5. Creating an Intent Pointing to `TestReceiver`

```
//In filename: SendAlarmOnceTester.java
Intent intent = new Intent(mContext, TestReceiver.class);
intent.putExtra("message", "Single Shot Alarm");
```

We also have an opportunity to load the intent with "extras" while creating this intent. Because an alarm manager stores an intent for a later use, we need to create a pending intent out of this intent of Listing 17-5. Listing 17-6 shows how to create a pending intent from a standard intent.

Listing 17-6. Creating a Pending Intent

```
//In filename: SendAlarmOnceTester.java
PendingIntent pendingIntent =
    PendingIntent.getBroadcast(
      mContext,    //context, or activity, or service
      1,           //request id, used for disambiguating this intent
      intent,      //intent to be delivered
      0);          //pending intent flags
```

Notice that we have asked the `PendingIntent` class to construct a pending intent that is suitable for a broadcast explicitly. The other variations of creating a pending intent are listed in Listing 17-7:

Listing 17-7. Multiple APIs for Creating a Pending Intent

```
//useful to start an activity
PendingIntent activityPendingIntent = PendingIntent.getActivity(..args..);
//useful to start a service
PendingIntent servicePendingIntent = PendingIntent.getService(..args..);
```

In Listing 17-7, arguments to the methods `getActivity()` and `getService()` are similar to the arguments to the `getBroadcast()` method in Listing 17-6. Note that alarms require a broadcast pending intent and not an activity pending intent or a service pending intent.

We will discuss the `request id` argument, which we set to 1 in Listing 17-6, in greater detail later in the chapter. Briefly, it is used to separate two intent objects that are `equal` in all other respects.

Pending intent flags have little or no influence on the alarm manager. Recommendation is to use no flags at all and use `0` for their values. These intent flags are typically useful in controlling the lifetime of the pending intent. However, in this case, the lifetime is maintained by the alarm manager. For example, to cancel a pending intent, you ask the alarm manager to cancel it.

Once we have the time instance in milliseconds as a `Calendar` object and the pending intent pointing to the receiver, we can set up an alarm by calling the `set()` method of the alarm manager. This is shown in Listing 17-8.

Listing 17-8. Using the Alarm Manager set() Method

```
//In filename: SendAlarmOnceTester.java
Calendar cal = Utils.getTimeAfterInSecs(30);
//...other code that gets the pendingintent etc
am.set(AlarmManager.RTC_WAKEUP,
        cal.getTimeInMillis(),
        pendingIntent);
```

The first argument to the set()method indicates the wakeup nature of the alarm and also the reference clock that we are going to be using for the alarm. Possible values for this argument are AlarmManager.RTC_WAKEUP, AlarmManager.RTC, AlarmManager.ELAPSED_REALTIME, AlarmManager.ELAPSED_REALTIME_WAKEUP.

The elapsed word in these constants refers to the time in milliseconds since the device is recently booted. So, it refers to the device clock. The RTC time refers to the human clock/time that you see on the device when you check your clock on the device. The WAKEUP word in these constants refers to the nature of the alarm, such as whether the alarm should wake up the device or just deliver it at the first opportunity when the device eventually wakes up. Taken together, the RTC_WAKEUP indicates the use of real-time clock and the device should wake up. The constant ELAPSED_REALTIME means use the device clock and don't wake up the device; instead, deliver the alarm at the first opportunity.

When this method of Listing 17-8 is called, the alarm manager will invoke the TestReceiver in Listing 17-3, 30 seconds after the calendar time when the method was called and also wakes up the device if it is asleep.

Setting Off an Alarm Repeatedly

Let's now consider how we can set an alarm that goes of repeatedly; see Listing 17-9.

Listing 17-9. Setting a Repeating Alarm

```
public void sendRepeatingAlarm() {
    Calendar cal = Utils.getTimeAfterInSecs(30);

    //Get an intent to invoke the receiver
    Intent intent = new Intent(this.mContext, TestReceiver.class);
    intent.putExtra("message", "Repeating Alarm");

    int requestid = 2;
    PendingIntent pi = this.getDistinctPendingIntent(intent, requestid);
    // Schedule the alarm!
    AlarmManager am =
        (AlarmManager)
            this.mContext.getSystemService(Context.ALARM_SERVICE);

    am.setRepeating(AlarmManager.RTC_WAKEUP,
            cal.getTimeInMillis(),
            5*1000, //5 secs repeat
            pi);
}
```

```
protected PendingIntent getDistinctPendingIntent(Intent intent, int requestId) {
    PendingIntent pi =
        PendingIntent.getBroadcast(
          mContext,      //context, or activity
          requestId,     //request id
          intent,        //intent to be delivered
          0);
    return pi;
}
```

Key elements of the code in Listing 17-9 are highlighted. A repeating alarm is set by invoking the setRepeating() method on the alarm manager object. The primary input to this method is a pending intent pointing to a receiver. We have used the same intent that was created in Listing 17-5, the one pointing to the TestReceiver. However, when we make a pending intent out of the intent in Listing 17-5, we alter the unique request code to a value of 2. If we don't do this, we will see a bit of odd behavior which we shall explain now. Say we intend to invoke the same receiver through two different alarms: one alarm that goes off only once and another alarm that goes off repeatedly. Because both alarms target the same receiver they need to be using an intent that points to the same receiver. Two intents that point to the same receiver, without any other difference between them, is considered the same intent. So, when we tell the alarm manager to set the alarm on intent 1 as a one-time alarm and then set the alarm on intent 2 as a repeated alarm, we might be under the impression that they are two different alarms. Internally, however, both alarms point to the same intent value, as intent 1 and intent 2 are the same in their values. This is why an alarm is practically the same as its intent on which it is set (especially by value). As a result, the later alarm overrides the first alarm if the intents are equivalent.

Again, two intents are considered the same if they have the same action, type, data, categories, or class. The extras are not included in figuring out the uniqueness of intents. Further, two pending intents are considered the same if their underlying intents are the same and the request IDs match. Because we can use the request ID to distinguish two pending intents, the code in Listing 17-8 overcomes the similarity of source intents by using the request id argument. This request id argument to the PendingIntent API will separate one pending intent from the other pending intent when all else matches.

This all should make sense if you were to see the pending intent (by value not by its Java object reference) itself as the alarm on which you are setting different times.

Cancelling an Alarm

Code in Listing 17-10 is used to cancel an alarm.

Listing 17-10. Cancelling a Repeating Alarm

```
public void cancelRepeatingAlarm() {
    //Get an intent that was originally
    //used to invoke TestReceiver class
    Intent intent = new Intent(this.mContext, TestReceiver.class);
```

```
    //To cancel, extra is not necessary to be filled in
    //intent.putExtra("message", "Repeating Alarm");

    PendingIntent pi = this.getDistinctPendingIntent(intent, 2);

    // Cancel the alarm!
    AlarmManager am =
        (AlarmManager)
            this.mContext.getSystemService(Context.ALARM_SERVICE);
    am.cancel(pi);
}
```

To cancel an alarm, we have to construct a pending intent first and then pass it to the alarm manager as an argument to the `cancel()` method. However, you must pay attention to make sure that the `PendingIntent` is constructed the exact same way when setting the alarm, including the request code and targeted receiver.

In constructing the cancel intent, you can ignore the intent extras from the original intent (Listing 17-10), because intent extras don't play a role in the uniqueness of an intent, and hence cancelling that intent.

Understanding Exactness of Alarms

Prior to API 19, Android fired the alarms as close as possible to the specified time. Since API 19, alarms that are close to each other are bundled for battery life. If you need the older behavior, there is a version of `set()` method called `setExact()`. There is also a method called `setWindow()` that allows room for efficiencies and also allows a guaranteed window. Similarly, the method `setRepeating()` is now inexact. Unlike the `setExact()` method, there is no exact version for `setRepeating()`. If you have such a need, you have to use the `setExact()` and repeat it yourself multiple times.

Understanding Persistence of Alarms

Another note on alarms is that they are not saved across device reboots. This means you will need to save the alarm settings and pending intents in a persistent store and reregister them based on device reboot broadcast actions, and possibly time-change broadcast actions (e.g., `intent.ACTION_BOOT_COMPLETED`, `intent.ACTION_TIME_CHANGED`, `intent.ACTION_TIMEZONE_CHANGED`).

References

The following references will help you learn more about the topics discussed in this chapter:

- `http://developer.android.com/reference/android/app/AlarmManager.html`: The alarm manager API. You will see here signatures for methods like `set`, `setRepeating`, and `cancel`.

- http://developer.android.com/reference/android/app/PendingIntent.html: How to construct a pending intent. Don't pay too much attention to the pending intent flags; they are not that critical to the alarm manager.
- http://androidbook.com/item/1040: Quick examples and references for working with date and time classes.
- http://androidbook.com/item/3503: Our research on alarm managers.
- http://androidbook.com/proandroid5/projects: A list of downloadable projects from this book. For this chapter, look for a ZIP file named ProAndroid5_Ch17_TestAlarmManager.zip.

Summary

This chapter explored the Alarm Manager API, which you use to set up and cancel alarms. This chapter showed you how to connect an alarm to a broadcast service. This chapter also showed you how alarms are closely related to intents.

Chapter 18

Exploring 2D Animation

Animation allows an object on a screen to change its color, position, size, or orientation over time. Animation capabilities in Android are practical, fun, and simple. They are used frequently in applications.

Android 2.3 and prior releases support three types of animation: frame-by-frame animation, which occurs when a series of frames is drawn one after the other at regular intervals; layout animation, where you animate the layout of the views inside a container such as lists and tables; and view animation, in which any view can be animated. In layout animation the focus is not any given view but the way views come together to form the composite layout. Android 3.0 enhanced animation by extending it to any Java property including the properties of UI elements. We will cover the pre-2.3 features first and then cover the 3.0 features right after. Both features are applicable based on your use case.

Exploring Frame-by-Frame Animation

Frame-by-frame animation is where a series of images are shown in succession at quick intervals so that the final effect is that of an object moving or changing. Figure 18-1 shows a set of circles each with a ball at a different position. With a few of these images (which are the frames) you can use animation to have the ball going around the circle.

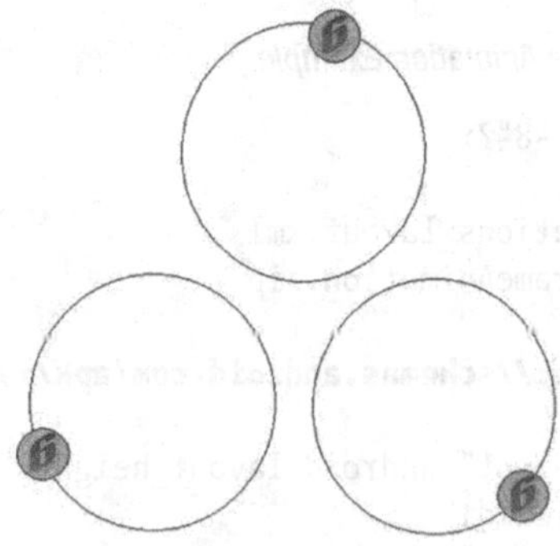

***Figure 18-1.** Example image frames for animation*

Each circle in Figure 18-1 is a separate image. Give the image a base name of `colored_ball` and store eight of these images in the `/res/drawable` subdirectory so that you can access them using their resource IDs. The name of each image will have the pattern `colored-ballN`, where `N` is the digit representing the image number. The animation activity we are planning will look like Figure 18-2.

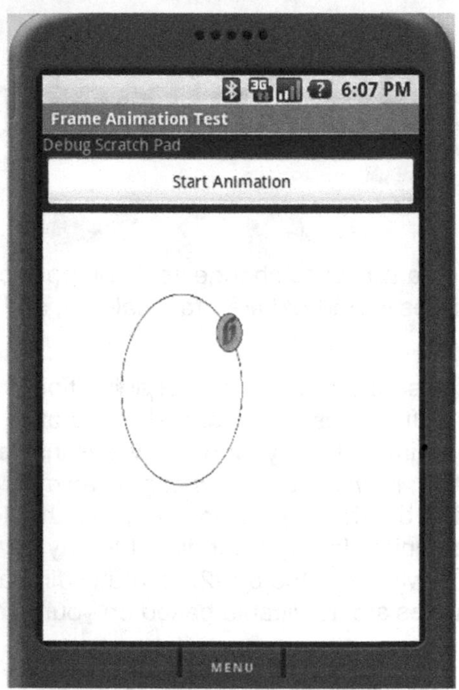

***Figure 18-2.** A frame-by-frame animation test harness*

Primary control in Figure 18-2 is the animation view showing the ball placed on an oval/circle. Button at the top is used to start and stop the animation. There is a debug scratch pad at the top to log events. Listing 18-1 shows the layout used to create the activity in Figure 18-2.

***Listing 18-1.** XML Layout File for the Frame Animation Example*

```
<?xml version="1.0" encoding="utf-8"?>
<!--
filename: /res/layout/frame_animations_layout.xml
Download: ProAndroid5_ch18_TestFrameAnimation.zip
-->
<LinearLayout xmlns:android="http://schemas.android.com/apk/res/android"
    android:orientation="vertical"
    android:layout_width="fill_parent" android:layout_height="fill_parent">
<TextView android:id="@+id/textViewId1"
    android:layout_width="fill_parent"
    android:layout_height="wrap_content" android:text="Debug Scratch Pad"/>
```

```
<Button
    android:id="@+id/startFAButtonId"
    android:layout_width="fill_parent" android:layout_height="wrap_content"
    android:text="Start Animation"/>
<ImageView
    android:id="@+id/animationImage"
    android:layout_width="fill_parent" android:layout_height="wrap_content"/>
</LinearLayout>
```

The first control is the debug-scratch text control, which is a simple TextView. You then add a button to start and stop the animation. The last view is the ImageView, which is used to play the animation.

In Android, frame-by-frame animation is implemented through the class AnimationDrawable. This class is a Drawable. These objects are commonly used as backgrounds for views. AnimationDrawable, in addition to being a Drawable, can take a list of other Drawable resources (like images) and render them at specified intervals. To use this AnimationDrawable class, start with a set of Drawable resources (for example, a set of images) placed in the /res/drawable subdirectory. You will then construct an XML file that defines the AnimationDrawable using a list of these images (see Listing 18-2). This XML file needs to be placed in the /res/drawable subdirectory as well.

Listing 18-2. XML File Defining the List of Frames to Be Animated

```
<!--
filename: /res/drawable/frame_animation.xml
Download: ProAndroid5_ch18_TestFrameAnimation.zip
-->
<animation-list xmlns:android="http://schemas.android.com/apk/res/android"
android:oneshot="false">
    <item android:drawable="@drawable/colored_ball1" android:duration="50" />
    <item android:drawable="@drawable/colored_ball2" android:duration="50" />
    <item android:drawable="@drawable/colored_ball3" android:duration="50" />
    <item android:drawable="@drawable/colored_ball4" android:duration="50" />
    <item android:drawable="@drawable/colored_ball5" android:duration="50" />
    <item android:drawable="@drawable/colored_ball6" android:duration="50" />
    <item android:drawable="@drawable/colored_ball7" android:duration="50" />
    <item android:drawable="@drawable/colored_ball8" android:duration="50" />
</animation-list>
```

Each frame points to one of the colored-ball images you have assembled through their resource IDs. The animation-list tag gets converted into an AnimationDrawable object representing the collection of images. You then need to set this AnimationDrawable as a background resource for our ImageView control in the activity layout. Assuming that the file name for this XML file is frame_animation.xml and that it resides in the /res/drawable subdirectory, you can use the following code to set the AnimationDrawable as the background of the ImageView:

```
view.setBackgroundResource(R.drawable.frame_animation); //See Listing 18-3
```

With this code, Android realizes that the resource ID `R.drawable.frame_animation` is an XML resource and accordingly constructs a suitable `AnimationDrawable` Java object for it before setting it as the background. Once this is set, you can access this `AnimationDrawable` object by doing a `get` on the `view` object like this:

```
Object  backgroundObject = view.getBackground();
AnimationDrawable ad = (AnimationDrawable)backgroundObject;
```

Once you have the `AnimationDrawable` object, you can use its `start()`and `stop()` methods to start and stop the animation. Here are two other important methods on this object:

```
setOneShot(boolean);
addFrame(drawable, duration);
```

The `setOneShot(true)` method runs the animation once and then stops. The `addFrame()` method adds a new frame using a `Drawable` object and sets its display duration. The functionality of the `addFrame()` method resembles that of the XML tag `android:drawable` in `Listing 18-2`. Put this all together to get the complete code for our frame-by-frame animation activity of Figure 18-1.

Listing 18-3. Complete Code for the Frame-by-Frame Animation Test Harness

```
// filename: FrameAnimationActivity.java
// Download: ProAndroid5_ch18_TestFrameAnimation.zip
public class FrameAnimationActivity extends Activity {
    @Override
    public void onCreate(Bundle savedInstanceState)   {
        super.onCreate(savedInstanceState);
        setContentView(R.layout.frame_animations_layout);
        this.setupButton();
    }
    private void setupButton(){
       Button b = (Button)this.findViewById(R.id.startFAButtonId);
       b.setOnClickListener(
             new Button.OnClickListener(){
                public void onClick(View v) {animate();}
             });
    }
    private void animate()  {
        ImageView imgView = (ImageView)findViewById(R.id.animationImage);
        imgView.setVisibility(ImageView.VISIBLE);
        imgView.setBackgroundResource(R.drawable.frame_animation);

        AnimationDrawable frameAnimation = (AnimationDrawable)imgView.getBackground();
        if (frameAnimation.isRunning()) {
            frameAnimation.stop();
        }
        else {
            frameAnimation.stop();
            frameAnimation.start();
        }
    }
}//eof-class
```

animate()method in Listing 18-3 locates the ImageView in the activity and sets its background to the AnimationDrawable identified by the resource R.drawable.frame_animation. This animation resource ID points to the earlier animation definition in Listing 18-3. The rest of the code in the method retrieves this AnimationDrawable object and calls animation methods on that object. In the same Listing 18-3, Start/Stop button is set up so that if animation is running, the button could stop it; if animation is not running, the button could start it. If you set the oneshot attribute in the animation definition in Listing 18-2 to true, the animation stops after once.

Exploring Layout Animation

LayoutAnimation is used to animate the views in an Android layout. You can use this type of animation for example with common layout controls like ListView and GridView. Unlike frame-by-frame animation, layout animation is not achieved through repeating frames but by changing the transformation matrix of a view. Every view in Android has a transformation matrix that maps the view to the screen. By changing this matrix you can accomplish scaling, rotation, and movement (translation) of the view. This type of animation that relies on changing properties and redrawing an image is referred to as tweening animation. Essentially LayoutAnimation is tweening animation of the transformation matrix of the views in a layout. A LayoutAnimation that is specified on a layout is applied to all the views in that layout.

These are the tweening animation types that can be applied to a layout:

- Scale animation: Used to make a view smaller or larger either along the x axis, on the y axis, or on both. You can also specify the pivot point around which you want the animation to take place.
- Rotate animation: Used to rotate a view around a pivot point by a certain number of degrees.
- Translate animation: Used to move a view along the x axis or the y axis.
- Alpha animation: Used to change the transparency of a view.

These animations are defined as XML files in the /res/anim subdirectory. Listing 18-4 shows a scale animation declared in an XML file.

Listing 18-4. A Scale Animation Defined in an XML File at /res/anim/scale.xml

```
<set xmlns:android="http://schemas.android.com/apk/res/android"
android:interpolator="@android:anim/accelerate_interpolator">
   <scale
         android:fromXScale="1"
         android:toXScale="1"
         android:fromYScale="0.1"
         android:toYScale="1.0"
         android:duration="500"
         android:pivotX="50%"
         android:pivotY="50%"
         android:startOffset="100" />
</set>
```

Parameters in the animation XMLs have a "from" and a "to" flavor to indicate start and end values of that property. Other properties of an animation also include animation duration and a time interpolator. Interpolators determine the rate of change of the animated argument such as scale in Listing 18-4 during animation. We will cover interpolators shortly. XML file in Listing 18-4 can be associated with a layout to animate that layout's constituent views.

> **Note** Animations like the `Scale` animation in Listing 18-4 are represented as Java classes in the `android.view.animation` package. Java documentation for these classes describes not only Java methods but also the allowed XML arguments for each type of animation.

We can use the `ListView` in Figure 18-3 to test a number of layout animations. This activity is what you see when you run the sample project for this chapter. `ProAndroid5_ch18_TestLayoutAnimation.zip`

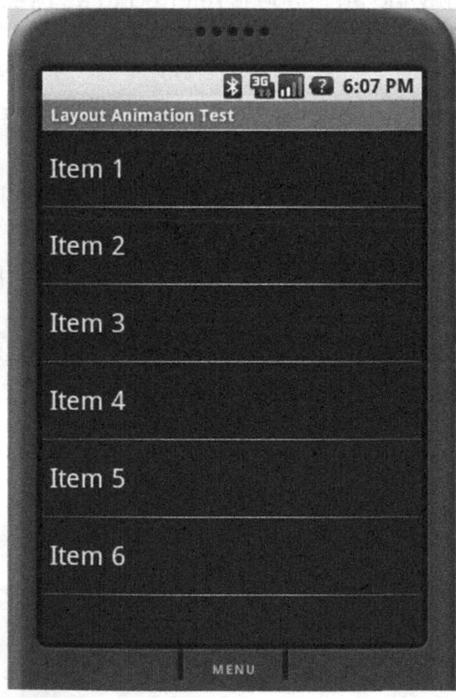

***Figure 18-3.** The `ListView` to be Animated*

The layout for this activity is in Listing 18-5.

Listing 18-5. ListView XML Layout File

```
<?xml version="1.0" encoding="utf-8"?>
<!--
filename: /res/layout/list_layout.xml
project: ProAndroid5_ch18_TestLayoutAnimation.zip
-->
<LinearLayout xmlns:android="http://schemas.android.com/apk/res/android"
    android:orientation="vertical"
    android:layout_width="fill_parent"
    android:layout_height="fill_parent">
    <ListView
        android:id="@+id/list_view_id"
        android:layout_width="fill_parent"
        android:layout_height="fill_parent"/>
</LinearLayout>
```

Listing 18-5 shows a simple `LinearLayout` with a single `ListView` in it. The activity code to show the layout from 18-5 as Figure 18-3 is in Listing 18-6.

Listing 18-6. Layout-Animation Activity Code

```
//filename: LayoutAnimationActivity.java
//project: ProAndroid5_ch18_TestLayoutAnimation.zip
public class LayoutAnimationActivity extends Activity  {
    @Override
    public void onCreate(Bundle savedInstanceState)  {
        super.onCreate(savedInstanceState);
        setContentView(R.layout.list_layout);
        setupListView();
    }
    private void setupListView()  {
      String[] listItems = new String[] {
              "Item 1", "Item 2", "Item 3", "Item 4", "Item 5", "Item 6",
      };
      ArrayAdapter<String> listItemAdapter =
       new ArrayAdapter<String>(this, android.R.layout.simple_list_item_1, listItems);
      ListView lv = (ListView)this.findViewById(R.id.list_view_id);
      lv.setAdapter(listItemAdapter);
    }
}
```

Let's see now how to apply scale animation from Listing 18-4 to this `ListView`. The `ListView` requires another XML file that acts as a mediator between itself and the scale animation in Listing 18-4. This is because the animations defined in Listing 18-4 are generic and apply to any view. On the other hand a layout is a collection of views. So the mediator layout animation XML file in Listing 18-7 reuses the generic animation XML file and specifies the additional attributes that are applicable to a collection of views. This mediator layout animation XML file is shown in Listing 18-9.

Listing 18-7. Layout-Controller XML File

```
<?xml version="1.0" encoding="utf-8"?>
<!--
filename: /res/anim/list_layout_controller.xml (ProAndroid5_ch18_TestLayoutAnimation.zip)
-->
<layoutAnimation xmlns:android="http://schemas.android.com/apk/res/android"
        android:delay="100%"
        android:animationOrder="reverse"
        android:animation="@anim/scale" />
```

This XML file needs to be in /res/anim subdirectory. This XML file specifies that the animation in the list should proceed in reverse, and the animation for each item should start with a 100% delay with respect to the total animation duration. A 100% duration ensures that the animation of one item is complete before the animation of the next item starts. You can change this percentage to suit the needs of your animation. Anything less than 100% will result in an overlapping animation of items. This mediator XML file also refers to the individual animation file, scale.xml (Listing 18-4) through the resource reference @anim/scale. Listing 18-8 shows how to attach the animation of Listing 18-4 to the activity layout of Listing 18-5 via the mediator of Listing 18-7.

Listing 18-8. The Updated Code for the list_layout.xml File

```
<?xml version="1.0" encoding="utf-8"?>
<!--
filename: /res/layout/list_layout.xml(ProAndroid5_ch18_TestLayoutAnimation.zip)
-->
<LinearLayout xmlns:android="http://schemas.android.com/apk/res/android"
    android:orientation="vertical"
    android:layout_width="fill_parent" android:layout_height="fill_parent">
    <ListView android:id="@+id/list_view_id"
        android:persistentDrawingCache="animation|scrolling"
        android:layout_width="fill_parent" android:layout_height="fill_parent"
        android:layoutAnimation="@anim/list_layout_controller" />
</LinearLayout>
```

In Listing 18-8 android:layoutAnimation is the tag that points to the mediating XML file of Listing 18-7, which in turn points to the scale.xml of Listing 18-5. In Listing 18-8 Android SDK docs recommend setting the persistentDrawingCache tag on the list view to optimize for animation and scrolling. If you were to run the application ProAndroid5_ch18_TestLayoutAnimation.zip, you would see the scale animation take effect on the individual list items as the activity gets loaded. We have set the animation duration to 500 ms so that scale change can be observed as each list item is drawn.

With this sample program you can experiment with different animation types. You can try alpha animation with the code in Listing 18-9.

Listing 18-9. The `alpha.xml` File to Test Alpha Animation

```
<?xml version="1.0" encoding="utf-8"?>
<!-- file: /res/anim/alpha.xml(ProAndroid5_ch18_TestLayoutAnimation.zip) -->
<alpha xmlns:android="http://schemas.android.com/apk/res/android"
       android:interpolator="@android:anim/accelerate_interpolator"
       android:fromAlpha="0.0" android:toAlpha="1.0" android:duration="1000" />
```

Alpha animation controls fading (of color). In Listing 18-9 alpha animation color goes from invisible to full intensity in 1 second. Don't forget to change the mediator XML file (see Listing 18-7) to point to the new animation file if you intend to use the same mediator file.

Listing 18-10 shows an animation that combines a change in position with a change in color gradient.

Listing 18-10. Combining Translate and Alpha Animations Through an Animation Set

```
<?xml version="1.0" encoding="utf-8"?>
<!-- file:/res/anim/alpha_translate.xml(ProAndroid5_ch18_TestLayoutAnimation.zip)-->
<set xmlns:android="http://schemas.android.com/apk/res/android"
  android:interpolator="@android:anim/accelerate_interpolator">
  <translate android:fromYDelta="-100%" android:toYDelta="0"android:duration="500"/>
  <alpha android:fromAlpha="0.0" android:toAlpha="1.0" android:duration="500"/>
</set>
```

Notice two animations are in the animation set of Listing 18-10. Translate animation will move the text from top to bottom in its currently allocated display space. Alpha animation will change the color gradient from invisible to visible as the text item descends into its slot. To see this animation in action, change the `layoutAnimation` mediator XML file with reference to file name `@anim/alpha_translate.xml`. Listing 18-11 shows the definition for a rotation animation.

Listing 18-11. Rotate Animation XML File

```
<!-- file: /res/anim/rotate.xml(ProAndroid5_ch18_TestLayoutAnimation.zip) -->
<rotate xmlns:android="http://schemas.android.com/apk/res/android"
      android:interpolator="@android:anim/accelerate_interpolator"
      android:fromDegrees="0.0" android:toDegrees="360"
      android:pivotX="50%"  android:pivotY="50%"
      android:duration="500" />
```

Listing 18-11 spins each text item in the list one full circle around the midpoint of the text item. Let's talk about the interpolators that you have seen used in the animation XML files.

Understanding Interpolators

Interpolators tell how a property changes over time from its start value to the end value. Will the change occur linearly or exponentially? Will the change start quickly and slow down toward the end?

Alpha animation in Listing 18-9 identifies the interpolator as `accelerate_interpolator`. There is a corresponding Java object that defines the behavior of this interpolator. As we've specified this interpolator as a resource reference in Listing 18-9, there must be a file corresponding to the `@anim/accelerate_interpolator` that describes what this Java object is and what additional parameters it might take. Listing 8-12 shows the resource XML file definition pointed to by the resource reference `@android:anim/accelerate_interpolator`:

***Listing 18-12.** An Interpolator Definition as an XML Resource*

```
<accelerateInterpolator
  xmlns:android="http://schemas.android.com/apk/res/android"
  factor="1" />
```

You can see this XML file in the subdirectory `/res/anim/accelerate_interpolator.xml` in the root Android SDK package. (Caution: This file could look differently depending on the release.) The `accelerateInterpolator` XML tag corresponds to the Java class `android.view.animation.AccelerateInterpolator`. You can look up the corresponding Java documentation to see what XML tags are available. This interpolator's goal is to provide a multiplication factor given a time interval based on a hyperbolic curve. The source code snippet in Listing 18-13 for this interpolator illustrates this. (Caution: This code could look different depending on the Android release.)

***Listing 18-13.** Sample Code from AccelerateInterpolator in the Core Android SDK*

```
public float getInterpolation(float input) {
   if (mFactor == 1.0f)   {
      return (float)(input * input);
   }
   else  {
      return (float)Math.pow(input, 2 * mFactor);
   }
}
```

Every interpolator implements the `getInterpolation` method differently. In case of the `AccelerateInterpolator`, if the interpolator is set up in the resource file with a factor of `1.0`, it will return the square of the input at each interval. Otherwise, it will return a power of the input that is further scaled by the factor amount. If the factor is `1.5`, you will see a cubic function instead of a square function.

The supported interpolators include `AccelerateDecelerateInterpolator`, `AccelerateInterpolator`, `CycleInterpolator`, `DecelerateInterpolator`, `LinearInterpolator`, `AnticipateInterpolator`, `AnticipateOvershootInterpolator`, `BounceInterpolator`, and `OvershootInterpolator`.

To see how flexible these interpolators can be, take a quick look in Listing 18-14 at the BounceInterpolator which bounces the object (that is, moves it back and forth) toward the end of the animation cycle:

Listing 18-14. ***BounceInterpolator Implementation in the Core Android SDK***

```
public class BounceInterpolator implements Interpolator {
     private static float bounce(float t) {
         return t * t * 8.0f;
     }
     public float getInterpolation(float t) {
         t *= 1.1226f;
         if (t < 0.3535f) return bounce(t);
         else if (t < 0.7408f) return bounce(t - 0.54719f) + 0.7f;
         else if (t < 0.9644f) return bounce(t - 0.8526f) + 0.9f;
         else return bounce(t - 1.0435f) + 0.95f;
     }
}
```

You can find the behavior of these various interpolators described at the following URL:

http://developer.android.com/reference/android/view/animation/package-summary.html

Java documentation for each of these classes also points out the XML tags available to control them.

Exploring View Animation

Through view animation you can animate a view by manipulating its transformation matrix. A transformation matrix is like a lens that projects a view on to the display. A transformation matrix can affect the projected views scale, size, position, and color.

Identity transformation matrix preserves the original view. You start with an identity matrix and apply a series of mathematical transformations involving size, position, and orientation. You then set the final matrix as the transformation matrix for the view you want to transform.

Android exposes the transformation matrix for a view by allowing registration of an animation object with that view. The animation object will be passed to the transformation matrix.

Consider Figure 18-4 as a demonstration of view animation. The Start Animation button animates the list view to start small in the middle of the screen and gradually fill the full space. Listing 18-15 shows the XML layout file used for this activity.

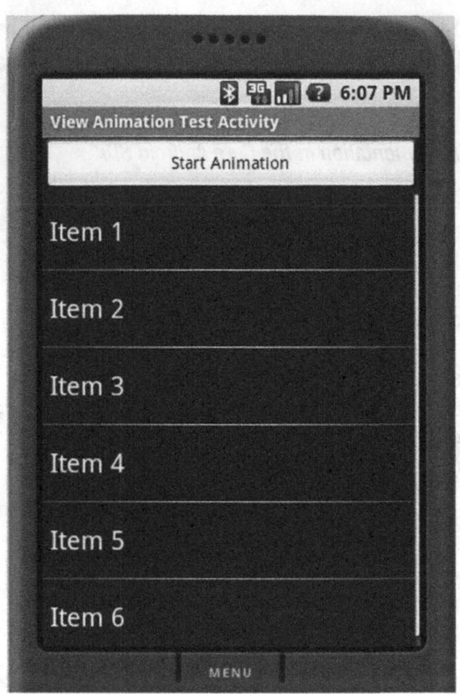

Figure 18-4. A View Animation Activity

Listing 18-15. XML Layout File for the View-Animation Activity

```
<?xml version="1.0" encoding="utf-8"?>
<!-- filen: at /res/layout/list_layout.xml(ProAndroid5_ch18_TestViewAnimation.zip) -->
<LinearLayout xmlns:android="http://schemas.android.com/apk/res/android"
    android:orientation="vertical"
    android:layout_width="fill_parent"
    android:layout_height="fill_parent">
<Button
   android:id="@+id/btn_animate"
    android:layout_width="fill_parent"
    android:layout_height="wrap_content"
    android:text="Start Animation"/>
<ListView
     android:id="@+id/list_view_id"
     android:persistentDrawingCache="animation|scrolling"
     android:layout_width="fill_parent"
     android:layout_height="fill_parent"/>
</LinearLayout>
```

Listing 18-16 shows the activity code that loads this layout.

***Listing 18-16.** Code for the View-Animation Activity, Before Animation*

```
//filename: ViewAnimationActivity.java(ProAndroid5_ch18_TestViewAnimation.zip)
public class ViewAnimationActivity extends Activity {
    @Override
    public void onCreate(Bundle savedInstanceState)      {
        super.onCreate(savedInstanceState);
        setContentView(R.layout.list_layout);
        setupListView();
        this.setupButton();
    }
    private void setupListView()      {
      String[] listItems = new String[] {
            "Item 1", "Item 2", "Item 3","Item 4", "Item 5", "Item 6",
      };
      ArrayAdapter<String> listItemAdapter =
        new ArrayAdapter<String>(this,android.R.layout.simple_list_item_1,listItems);
      ListView lv = (ListView)this.findViewById(R.id.list_view_id);
      lv.setAdapter(listItemAdapter);
    }
    private void setupButton()      {
       Button b = (Button)this.findViewById(R.id.btn_animate);
       b.setOnClickListener(
           new Button.OnClickListener(){
             public void onClick(View v)    {
                //animateListView();
             }
           });
    }
}
```

With this code you will see the UI as laid out in Figure 18-4. To add animation to the `ListView` shown in Figure 18-4 we need a class that derives from `android.view.animation.Animation`. Listing 18-17 shows this class.

***Listing 18-17.** Code for the `ViewAnimation` Class*

```
//filename: ViewAnimation.java project: ProAndroid5_ch18_TestViewAnimation.zip
public class ViewAnimation extends Animation {
 @Override
 public void initialize(int width, int height, int parentWidth, int parentHeight){
        super.initialize(width, height, parentWidth, parentHeight);
        setDuration(2500); setFillAfter(true);
        setInterpolator(new LinearInterpolator());
  }
  @Override
  protected void applyTransformation(float interpolatedTime, Transformation t) {
        final Matrix matrix = t.getMatrix();
        matrix.setScale(interpolatedTime, interpolatedTime);
  }
}
```

In Listing 18-7 `initialize` method is a callback method with the dimensions of the view. Animation parameters can be initialized here. Here the animation duration is set to 2.5 seconds. We have set the animation effect to remain intact after the animation completes by setting `FillAfter` to `true`. We've set a linear interpolator. All of these properties come from the base `android.view.animation.Animation` class.

The main part of the animation occurs in the `applyTransformation` method. Android SDK calls this method again and again to simulate animation. Every time Android calls the method, `interpolatedTime` has a different value. This value changes from `0` to `1` depending on where the animation is in the 2.5-second duration that you set during initialization. When `interpolatedTime` is `1`, the animation is at the end. Our goal in this method is to change the transformation matrix that is available through the transformation object called `t`. First get the matrix and change something about it. When the view gets painted, the new matrix will take effect. Methods available on the `Matrix` object are documented in the SDK at

`http://developer.android.com/reference/android/graphics/Matrix.html`

In Listing 18-17, the code that changes the matrix is

```
matrix.setScale(interpolatedTime, interpolatedTime);
```

`setScale` method takes two parameters: the scaling factor in the x direction and the scaling factor in the y direction. Because `interpolatedTime` goes between `0` and `1`, you can use that value directly as the scaling factor. At the start of the animation, the scaling factor is `0` in both the x and y directions. Halfway through the animation, this value will be `0.5` in both x and y directions. At the end of animation, the view will be at its full size because the scaling factor will be `1` in both the x and y directions. The end result of this animation is that the `ListView` starts out tiny and grows to full size. Listing 18-18 shows the function you need to add the activity class in Listing 18-15 and call it from the button click.

Listing 18-18. Code for the View-Animation Activity, Including Animation

```
private void animateListView()   {
   ListView lv = (ListView)this.findViewById(R.id.list_view_id);
   lv.startAnimation(new ViewAnimation());
}
```

> **Note** In this section on View Animation we are going to suggest alternate implementations for the `ViewAnimation` class of Listing 18-18. In the supplied project there are variations of this class available as `ViewAnimation`, `ViewAnimation1`, `ViewAnimation2`, and `ViewAnimation3`. Code snippets in the subsequent discussions will indicate in comments which of these classes hold that code. There is only one menu item in the sample project for animation. To test each variation you have to replace the `ViewAnimation()` class in Listing 18-18 with the respective version of it and rerun the program to see the altered animation.

When you run the code with the ViewAnimation class as in Listing 18-17, you will notice something odd. Instead of uniformly growing larger from the middle of the screen, the ListView grows larger from the top-left corner. This is because the origin for matrix operations is at the top-left corner. To get the desired effect, you first have to move the whole view so that the view's center matches the animation center (top left). Then, you apply the matrix and move the view back to the previous center. The rewritten code from Listing 18-16 for doing this is shown in Listing 18-19.

***Listing 18-19.** ViewAnimation using preTranslate and postTranslate*

```
//filename: ViewAnimation1.java project: ProAndroid5_ch18_TestViewAnimation.zip
public class ViewAnimation extends Animation {
    float centerX, centerY;
    public ViewAnimation(){}

    @Override
    public void initialize(int width, int height, int parentWidth, int parentHeight) {
        super.initialize(width, height, parentWidth, parentHeight);
        centerX = width/2.0f;  centerY = height/2.0f;
        setDuration(2500);  setFillAfter(true);
        setInterpolator(new LinearInterpolator());
    }
    @Override
    protected void applyTransformation(float interpolatedTime, Transformation t) {
        final Matrix matrix = t.getMatrix();
        matrix.setScale(interpolatedTime, interpolatedTime);
        matrix.preTranslate(-centerX, -centerY); matrix.postTranslate(centerX, centerY);
    }
}
```

The preTranslate and postTranslate methods set up a matrix before the scale operation and after the scale operation. This is equivalent to making three matrix transformations in tandem. Consider the following code in Listing 18-20

***Listing 18-20.** Standard pattern for Pre and Post Translate of Transformation Matrices*

```
matrix.setScale(interpolatedTime, interpolatedTime);
matrix.preTranslate(-centerX, -centerY);
matrix.postTranslate(centerX, centerY);
```

Code in Listing 18-20 is equivalent to

```
move to a different center
scale it
move to the original center
```

You will see this pattern of pre and post applied often. You can also accomplish this result using other methods on the Matrix class, but this technique is common as it is succinct.

The Matrix class allows you not only to scale a view but also to move it around through translate methods or change its orientation through rotate methods. You can experiment with these methods and see the resulting animations. The animations presented in the preceding "Layout Animation" section are all implemented internally using the methods on this Matrix class.

Using Camera to Provide Depth Perception in 2D

The graphics package in Android provides another transformation matrix–related feature through the Camera class. This class provides depth perception to a 2D view. You can take our ListView example and move it back from the screen by 10 pixels along the z axis and rotate it by 30 degrees around the y axis. Listing 18-21 is an example of manipulating the transformation matrix using a Camera.

Listing 18-21. Using Camera Object

```
//filename: ViewAnimation2.java project: ProAndroid5_ch18_TestViewAnimation.zip
public class ViewAnimation extends Animation {
    float centerX, centerY;
    Camera camera = new Camera();
    public ViewAnimation(float cx, float cy){
        centerX = cx;  centerY = cy;
    }
    @Override
    public void initialize(int width, int height, int parentWidth, int parentHeight) {
        super.initialize(width, height, parentWidth, parentHeight);
        setDuration(2500); setFillAfter(true);
        setInterpolator(new LinearInterpolator());
    }
    @Override
    protected void applyTransformation(float interpolatedTime, Transformation t) {
        final Matrix matrix = t.getMatrix();
        camera.save();
        camera.translate(0.0f, 0.0f, (1300 - 1300.0f * interpolatedTime));
        camera.rotateY(360 * interpolatedTime);
        camera.getMatrix(matrix);

        matrix.preTranslate(-centerX, -centerY);
        matrix.postTranslate(centerX, centerY);
        camera.restore();
    }
}
```

This code animates the ListView by first placing the view 1,300 pixels back on the z axis and then bringing it back to the plane where the z coordinate is 0. While doing this, the code also rotates the view from 0 to 360 degrees around the y axis. The camera.translate(x,y,z) method in Listing 18-21 tells the camera object to translate the view such that when interpolatedTime is 0 (at the beginning of the animation), the z value will be 1300. As the animation progresses, the z value will get smaller and smaller until the end, when the interpolatedTime becomes 1 and the z value becomes 0.

The method camera.rotateY(360 * interpolatedTime) takes advantage of 3D rotation around an axis by the camera. At the beginning of the animation, this value will be 0. At the end of the animation, it will be 360.

The method camera.getMatrix(matrix) takes the operations performed on the Camera so far and imposes those operations on the matrix that is passed in. Once the code does that, the matrix has the translations it needs to get the end effect of having a Camera. Now the Camera object is no longer necessary because the matrix has all the operations embedded in it. Then, you do the pre and post on the matrix to shift the center and bring it back. At the end, you set the Camera to its original state that was saved earlier. With this code in Listing 18-21 you will see the ListView arriving from the center of the view in a spinning manner toward the front of the screen. As this version of ViewAnimation takes additional construction arguments, Listing 18-22 shows how to invoke this version of the AnimationView:

Listing 18-22. View Animation using preTranslate and postTranslate

```
//filename: ViewAnimationActivity.java
//project: ProAndroid5_ch18_TestViewAnimation.zip
ListView lv = (ListView)this.findViewById(R.id.list_view_id);
float cx = (float)(lv.getWidth()/2.0);
float cy = (float)(lv.getHeight()/2.0);
lv.startAnimation(new ViewAnimation(cx, cy));
```

As part of our discussion about view animation, we showed you how to animate any view by extending an Animation class and then applying it to a view. In addition to letting you manipulate matrices (both directly and indirectly through a Camera class), the Animation class also lets you detect various stages in an animation. We will cover this next.

Exploring the AnimationListener Class

Android SDK has a listener interface, AnimationListener, to monitor animation events. Listing 18-23 demonstrates these animation events by implementing the AnimationListener interface.

Listing 18-23. An Implementation of the AnimationListener Interface

```
//filename: ViewAnimationListener.java
//project: ProAndroid5_ch18_TestViewAnimation.zip
public class ViewAnimationListener implements Animation.AnimationListener {
    public ViewAnimationListener(){}
    public void onAnimationStart(Animation animation) {
        Log.d("Animation Example", "onAnimationStart");
    }
    public void onAnimationEnd(Animation animation) {
        Log.d("Animation Example", "onAnimationEnd");
    }
    public void onAnimationRepeat(Animation animation) {
        Log.d("Animation Example", "onAnimationRepeat");
    }
}
```

The ViewAnimationListener class in Listing 18-23 just logs messages. Code in Listing 18-24 shows how to attach an animation listener to an Animation object.

Listing 18-24. Attaching an AnimationListener to an Animation Object

```
private void animateListView(){
   ListView lv = (ListView)this.findViewById(R.id.list_view_id);
   //Init width,height and assuming ViewAnimation from Listing 18-21
   ViewAnimation animation = new ViewAnimation(width,height);
   animation.setAnimationListener(new ViewAnimationListener());
   lv.startAnimation(animation);
}
```

Notes on Transformation Matrices

As you have seen in this chapter, matrices are key to transforming views and animations. Let's explore some key methods of the Matrix class.

- Matrix.reset(): Resets a matrix to an identity matrix, which causes no change to the view when applied
- Matrix.setScale(...args ..): Changes size
- Matrix.setTranslate(...args ..): Changes position to simulate movement
- Matrix.setRotate(... args ..): Changes orientation
- Matrix.setSkew(...args ..): Distorts a view

The last four methods have input parameters.

You can multiply matrices together to compound the effect of individual transformations. In Listing 18-25, consider three matrices, m1, m2, and m3, which are identity matrices:

Listing 18-25. View Animation using preTranslate and postTranslate

```
m1.setScale(..scale args..);
m2.setTranslate(..translate args..)
m3.setConcat(m1,m2)
```

Transforming a view by m1 and then transforming the resulting view with m2 is equivalent to transforming the same view by m3. Note that m3.setConcat(m1,m2) is different from m3.setConcat(m2,m1). setConcat(matrix1, matrix2) multiplies two matrices in that given order.

You have already seen the pattern used by the preTranslate and postTranslate methods to affect matrix transformation. In fact, pre and post methods are not unique to translate, and you have versions of pre and post for every one of the set transformation methods. Ultimately, a preTranslate such as m1.preTranslate(m2) is equivalent to

```
m1.setConcat(m2,m1)
```

In a similar manner, the method `m1.postTranslate(m2)` is equivalent to

```
m1.setConcat(m1,m2)
```

Consider the code in Listing 18-26

***Listing 18-26.** Pre and Post Translate Pattern*

```
matrix.setScale(interpolatedTime, interpolatedTime);
matrix.preTranslate(-centerX, -centerY);
matrix.postTranslate(centerX, centerY);
```

The code in this Listing 18-26 is equivalent to the code in Listing 18-27

***Listing 18-27.** Equivalence of Pre and Post Translate Pattern*

```
Matrix matrixPreTranslate = new Matrix();
matrixPreTranslate.setTranslate(-centerX, -centerY);

Matrix matrixPostTranslate = new Matrix();
matrixPostTranslate.setTranslate(centerX, centerY);

matrix.setConcat(matrixPreTranslate,matrix);
matrix.setConcat(matrix,matrixPostTranslate);
```

Exploring Property Animations: The New Animation API

The animation API is overhauled in 3.0 and 4.0 of Android. This new approach to animations is called property animation. The property animation API is extensive and different enough to refer to the previous animation API (prior to 3.x) as the legacy API even though the previous approach is still valid and not deprecated. The old animation API is in the package `android.view.animation`. The new animation API is in the package `android.animation`. Key concepts in the new property animation API are:

- Animators
- Value animators
- Object animators
- Animator sets
- Animator builders
- Animation listeners
- Property value holders
- Type evaluators
- View property animators
- Layout transitions
- Animators defined in XML files

We will cover most of these concepts in the rest of the chapter.

Understanding Property Animation

The property animation approach changes the value of a property over time. This property can be anything, such as a stand-alone integer, a float, or a specific property of an object such as a view. For example, you can change an `int` value from 10 to 200 over a time period of 5 seconds by using an animator class called `ValueAnimator` (see Listing 18-28).

Listing 18-28. A Simple Value Animator

```
//file: TestBasicValueEvaluator.java(ProAndroid5_ch18_TestPropertyAnimation.zip)
//Define an animator to change an int value from 10 to 200
ValueAnimator anim = ValueAnimator.ofInt(10, 200);

//set the duration for the animation
anim.setDuration(5000); //5 seconds, default 300 ms

//Provide a callback to monitor the changing value
anim.addUpdateListener(
    new ValueAnimator.AnimatorUpdateListener()  {
        public void onAnimationUpdate(ValueAnimator animation) {
            Integer value = (Integer) animation.getAnimatedValue();
            // this code gets called many many times for 5 seconds.
            // The value will range from 10 to 200
        }
    }
);
anim.start();
```

The idea is easy to grasp. A `ValueAnimator` is a mechanism to do something every 10 ms (this is the default framerate). Although this is the default framerate, depending on the system load you may not get called that many times. For the example given we could expect to get called 500 times over a span of 5 seconds. On an emulator our tests show that it may be as few as 10 times. However the last call will be close to the 5-second duration.

In the corresponding callback that is called for every frame (every 10 ms), you can choose to update a view or any other aspect to affect animation. In addition to the `onAnimationUpdate`, other useful callbacks are available on the general purpose `Animator.AnimatorListener` interface (Listing 18-28) from the Android SDK which can be attached to the `ValueAnimator` through its base class `Animator`. So on a `ValueAnimator`, you can do `addListener(Animator.AnimatorListener listener)`. See Listing 18-29.

Listing 18-29. `AnimatorListener` Callback Interface

```
public static interface Animator.AnimatorListener {
  abstract void onAnimationStart(Animator animation);
  abstract void onAnimationRepeat(Animator animation);
  abstract void onAnimationCancel(Animator animation);
  abstract void onAnimationEnd(Animator animation);
}
```

You can use these callbacks in Listing 18-29 to further act on objects of interest during or after an animation.

Property Animation relies on the availability of an `android.os.Looper` on the thread that is initiating the animation. This is generally the case for the UI thread. The callbacks happen on the UI thread as well when the animating thread is the main thread.

As you use `ValueAnimators` and their listeners, keep in mind the lifetime of these objects. Even if you let the reference of a `ValueAnimator` go from your local scope, the `ValueAnimator` will live on until it finishes the animation. If you were to add a listener then all the references that the listener holds are also valid for the lifetime of the `ValueAnimator`.

Planning a Test Bed for Property Animation

Starting with the basic idea of value animators, Android provides a number of derived ways to animate any arbitrary object, especially views. To demonstrate these mechanisms, we will take a simple text view in a linear layout and animate its `alpha` property (simulating transparency animation) and also the x and y positions (simulating movement). We will use Figure 18-5 as an anchor to explain property animation concepts.

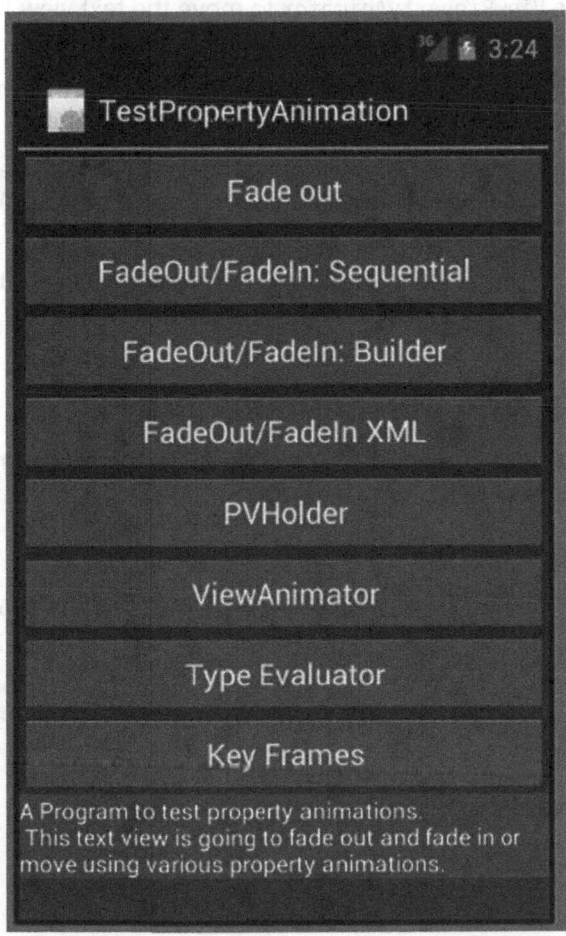

Figure 18-5. Activity to demonstrate Property animations

Each button in Figure 18-5 uses a separate mechanism to animate the text view at the bottom of the figure. The mechanisms we will demonstrate are as follows:

- Button 1: Using object animators, fade out and fade in a view alternatively at the click of a button.
- Button 2: Using an `AnimatorSet`, run a fade-out animation followed by fade-in animation in a sequential manner.
- Button 3: Use an `AnimatiorSetBuilder` object to tie multiple animations together in a "before," "after," or "with" relationship. Use this approach to run the same animation as button 2.
- Button 4: Define an XML file for button 2's sequence animation and attach it to the text view for the same animation affect.
- Button 5: Using a `PropertyValuesHolder` object, animate multiple properties of the text view in the same animation. We will change the x and y values to move the text view from bottom right to top left.
- Button 6: Use `ViewPropertyAnimator` to move the text view from bottom right to top left (same animation as button 5).
- Button 7: Use a `TypeEvaluator` on custom point objects to move the text view from bottom right to top left (same animation as button 5).
- Button 8: Use key frames to affect movement and also alpha changes on the text view (same animation as button 5, but staggered).

Constructing the activity in Figure 18-5 is straightforward. You can see the layout for this activity and the activity code in the download project file `ProAndroid5_ch18_TestPropertyAnimation.zip`. Let's start with the first button.

Animating Views with Object Animators

The first button in Figure 18-5 (Fadeout: Animator) invokes the `toggleAnimation(View)` method that is in Listing 18-30.

Listing 18-30. Basic View Animation with Object Animators

```
//file:TestPropertyAnimationActivity.java(ProAndroid5_ch18_TestPropertyAnimation.zip)
public void toggleAnimation(View btnView) {
    Button tButton = (Button)btnView; //The button we have pressed
    //m_tv: is the pointer to the text view
    //Animate the alpha from current value to 0 this will make it invisible
    if (m_tv.getAlpha() != 0)  {
        ObjectAnimator fadeOut = ObjectAnimator.ofFloat(m_tv, "alpha", 0f);
        fadeOut.setDuration(5000);
        fadeOut.start();
        tButton.setText("Fade In");
    }
```

```
    //Animate the alpha from current value to 1 this will make it visible
    else   {
        ObjectAnimator fadeIn = ObjectAnimator.ofFloat(m_tv, "alpha", 1f);
        fadeIn.setDuration(5000);
        fadeIn.start();
        tButton.setText("Fade out");
    }
}
```

The code in Listing 18-30 first examines the `alpha` value of the text view. If this value is greater than `0`, then the code assumes that the text view is visible and runs a fade-out animation. At the end of the fade-out animation, the text view will be invisible. If the `alpha` value of the text view is `0`, then the code assumes the text view is invisible and runs a fade-in animation to make the text view visible again.

The `ObjectAnimator` code in Listing 18-30 is really simple. An `ObjectAnimator` is obtained on the text view (m_tv) using the static method `ofFloat()`. The first argument to this method is an object (m_tv). The second argument is the property name of the object that you want the `ObjectAnimator` to modify or animate. In the case of the text view m_tv this property name is `alpha`. The target object needs to have a public method to match this name. For a property named `alpha`, the corresponding view object needs to have the following `set` method:

```
view.setAlpha(float f);
```

The third argument to `ofFloat()` is the value of the property at the end of the animation. If you specify a fourth argument, then the third argument is the starting value and the fourth is the target value. You can pass more arguments as long as they are all `floats`. The animation will use those values as intermediate values in the animation process.

If you specify just the "to" value, then the "from" value is taken from the current value by using

```
view.getAlpha();
```

When you play this animation, the text view will gradually disappear first. The code in Listing 18-30 then renames the button to "Fade in." Now if you click the button again, which is now called "Fade in," the second animation in Listing 18-30 is run, and the text view will appear gradually over a period of 5 seconds.

Achieving Sequential Animation with AnimatorSet

Button 2 in Figure 18-5 runs two animations one after the other: a fade-out followed by a fade-in. We could use animation listener callbacks to wait for the first animation to finish and then start the second animation. There is an automated way to run animations in tandem through the class `AnimatorSet` to get the same effect. Button 2 demonstrates this in Listing 18-31.

Listing 18-31. Sequential Animation Through an `AnimatorSet`

```
//file:TestPropertyAnimationActivity.java(ProAndroid5_ch18_TestPropertyAnimation.zip)
public void sequentialAnimation(View bView) {
    ObjectAnimator fadeOut = ObjectAnimator.ofFloat(m_tv, "alpha", 0f);
    ObjectAnimator fadeIn = ObjectAnimator.ofFloat(m_tv, "alpha", 1f);
    AnimatorSet as = new AnimatorSet();
    as.playSequentially(fadeOut,fadeIn);
    as.setDuration(5000); //5 secs
    as.start();
}
```

In Listing 18-31, we have created two animators: a fade-out animator and a fade-in animator. Then we created an animator set and tell it to play both animations sequentially.

You can also choose to play animations together using an animator set by calling the method `playTogether()`. Both of these methods, `playSequentially()` and `playTogether()`, can take a variable number of `Animator` objects.

When you play this animation, the text view will gradually disappear and then reappear, much like the animation you saw earlier.

Setting Animation Relationships with AnimatorSet.Builder

`AnimatorSet` also provides a bit more elaborate way to link animations through a utility class called `AnimatorSet.Builder`. Listing 18-32 demonstrates this.

Listing 18-32. Using an `AnimatorSetBuilder`

```
//filename: TestPropertyAnimationActivity.java (ProAndroid5_ch18_TestPropertyAnimation.zip)
public void testAnimationBuilder(View v) {
    ObjectAnimator fadeOut = ObjectAnimator.ofFloat(m_tv, "alpha", 0f);
    ObjectAnimator fadeIn = ObjectAnimator.ofFloat(m_tv, "alpha", 1f);
    AnimatorSet as = new AnimatorSet();
    //play() returns the nested class: AnimatorSet.Builder
    as.play(fadeOut).before(fadeIn);
    as.setDuration(5000); //5 secs
    as.start();
}
```

The play method on an `AnimatorSet` returns a class called `AnimatorSet.Builder`. This is purely a utility class. The methods on this class are `after(animator)`, `before(animator)`, and `with(animator)`. This class is initialized with the first animator you supply through the play method. Every other call on this object is with respect to this original animator. Consider Listing 18-33:

Listing 18-33. Using AnimationSet.Builder

```
AnimatorSet.Builder builder = someSet.play(main_animator).before(animator1);
```

With this code `animator1` will play after the `main_animator`. When we say `builder.after(animator2)`, the animation of animator2 will play before main_animator. The method `with(animator)` plays the animations together.

The key point with an AnimationBuilder is that the relationship established via before(), after(), and with() is not chained but only tied to the original animator that was obtained from play() method. Also, the animation start() method is not on the builder object but on the original animator set. When you play this animation through Button3, the text view will gradually disappear and then reappear, much as in the previous animation.

Using XML to Load Animators

It is only to be expected that the Android SDK allows animators to be described in XML resource files. Android SDK has a new resource type called R.animator to distinguish animator resource files. These XML files are stored in the /res/animator subdirectory. Listing 18-34 is an example of an animator set defined in an XML file.

Listing 18-34. An Animator XML Resource File

```
<?xml version="1.0" encoding="utf-8" ?>
<!-- file: /res/animator/fadein.xml (ProAndroid5_ch18_TestPropertyAnimation.zip) -->
<set xmlns:android="http://schemas.android.com/apk/res/android"
    android:ordering="sequentially">
<objectAnimator
    android:interpolator="@android:interpolator/accelerate_cubic"
    android:valueFrom="1"  android:valueTo="0"
    android:valueType="floatType"  android:propertyName="alpha"
    android:duration="5000" />
<objectAnimator
    android:interpolator="@android:interpolator/accelerate_cubic"
    android:valueFrom="0"  android:valueTo="1"
    android:valueType="floatType" android:propertyName="alpha"
    android:duration="5000" />
</set>
```

You will naturally wonder what XML nodes are available for you to define these animations. As of 4.0 the allowed XML tags are as follows:

- animator: Binds to ValueAnimator
- objectAnimator: Binds to ObjectAnimator
- set: Binds to AnimatorSet

You can see a basic discussion of these tags at the following Android SDK URL:

http://developer.android.com/guide/topics/graphics/prop-animation.html#declaring-xml

The complete XML reference for the animation tags can be found at the following URL:

http://developer.android.com/guide/topics/resources/animation-resource.html#Property

Once you have this XML file, you can play this animation using the method shown in Listing 18-35.

Listing 18-35. Loading an Animator XML Resource File

```
//file: TestPropertyAnimationActivity.java(ProAndroid5_ch18_TestPropertyAnimation.zip)
public void sequentialAnimationXML(View bView) {
  AnimatorSet set = (AnimatorSet)AnimatorInflater.loadAnimator(this, R.animator.fadein);
  set.setTarget(m_tv);
  set.start();
}
```

Notice how it is necessary to load the animation XML file first followed by explicitly setting the object to animate. In our case, the object to animate is the text view represented by `m_tv`. The method in Listing 18-35 is called by button 4 (FadeOut/FadeIn XML). When this animation runs, the text view will fade out first and then reappear by fading in, just as in the previous alpha animations.

Using PropertyValuesHolder

So far, we have seen how to animate a single value in a single animation. The class `PropertyValuesHolder` lets us animate multiple values during the animation cycle. Listing 18-36 demonstrates the use of the `PropertyValuesHolder` class.

Listing 18-36. Using the `PropertyValueHolder` Class

```
//file: TestPropertyAnimationActivity.java(ProAndroid5_ch18_TestPropertyAnimation.zip)
public void testPropertiesHolder(View v) {
    //Get the current coordinates of the text view.
    //This allows us to know starting and ending positions to animate
    float h = m_tv.getHeight(); float w = m_tv.getWidth();
    float x = m_tv.getX(); float y = m_tv.getY();

    //Set the view to the bottom right as a starting point
    m_tv.setX(w); m_tv.setY(h);

    //from the right bottom animate "x" to its original position: top left
    PropertyValuesHolder pvhX = PropertyValuesHolder.ofFloat("x", x);

    //from the right bottom animate "y" to its original position
    PropertyValuesHolder pvhY = PropertyValuesHolder.ofFloat("y", y);

    //when you do not specify the from position, the animation will take the current position
    //as the from position.

    //Tell the object animator to consider both
    //"x" and "y" properties to animate to their respective target values.
    ObjectAnimator oa = ObjectAnimator.ofPropertyValuesHolder(m_tv, pvhX, pvhY);

    //set the duration
    oa.setDuration(5000); //5 secs
```

```
    //here is a way to set an interpolator on any animator
    oa.setInterpolator(new  AccelerateDecelerateInterpolator());
    oa.start();
}
```

A PropertyValuesHolder class holds a property name and its target value. Then you can define many of these PropertyValuesHolders with their own property to animate. You can supply this set of PropertyValuesHolders to the object animator. The object animator will then set these properties to their respective values on the target object. With each refresh of the animation, all the values from each PropertyValuesHolder will be applied all at once. This is more efficient than applying multiple animations in parallel.

Button 5 in Figure 18-5 runs the code in Listing 18-36. When this animation runs, the text view will emerge from bottom right and migrate toward the top left in 5 seconds.

Understanding View Properties Animation

Android SDK has an optimized approach to animate various properties of views. This is done through a class called ViewPropertyAnimator. Listing 18-37 uses this class to move the text view from bottom right to top left.

Listing 18-37. Using a ViewPropertyAnimator

```
//file: TestPropertyAnimationActivity.java(ProAndroid5_ch18_TestPropertyAnimation.zip)
public void testViewAnimator(View v) {
    //Remember current boundaries
    float h = m_tv.getHeight(); float w = m_tv.getWidth();
    float x = m_tv.getX(); float y = m_tv.getY();

    //Position the view at bottom right
    m_tv.setX(w);  m_tv.setY(h);

    //Get a ViewPropertyAnimator from the text view
    ViewPropertyAnimator vpa = m_tv.animate();

    //Set as many target values you want to set
    vpa.x(x);  vpa.y(y);

    //Set duration and interpolators
    vpa.setDuration(5000); //2 secs
    vpa.setInterpolator(new  AccelerateDecelerateInterpolator());

    //The animation automatically starts when the UI thread gets to it.
    //No need to explicitly call the start method.
    //vpa.start();
}
```

The steps to use ViewPropertyAnimator are as follows:

1. Get a ViewPropertyAnimator by calling the animate() method on a view.
2. Use the ViewPropertyAnimator object to set various final properties of that view, such as x, y, scale, alpha, and so on.
3. Let the UI thread proceed by returning from the function. The animation will automatically start.

This animation is invoked by button 6. When this animation runs, the text view will migrate from bottom right to top left.

Understanding Type Evaluators

As we have seen, an object animator directly sets a particular value on a target object with each animation cycle. These values so far have been single point values such as floats, ints, and so on. What happens if your target object has a property that is an object itself? This is where type evaluators come into play.

To illustrate this consider a view on which we want to set two values such as 'x' and 'y'. Listing 18-35 shows how we encapsulate a regular view for which we know how to change x and y. The encapsulation will allow the animation to call once for both x and y through the PointF abstraction available in the Android graphics package. We will provide a setPoint(PointF) method and then, inside that method, parse out x and y and set them on the view. Take a look at Listing 18-38.

Listing 18-38. Animating a View Through a TypeEvaluator

```
//file: AnimatableView.java(ProAndroid5_ch18_TestPropertyAnimation.zip)
public class MyAnimatableView {
    PointF curPoint = null; View m_v = null;
    public MyAnimatableView(View v)    {
        curPoint = new PointF(v.getX(),v.getY());
        m_v = v;
    }
    public PointF getPoint()    {
        return curPoint;
    }
    public void setPoint(PointF p) {
        curPoint = p;
        m_v.setX(p.x);
        m_v.setY(p.y);
    }
}
```

In code Listing 18-38 TypeEvaluator is a helper object that knows how to set a composite value such as a two-dimensional or three-dimensional point during an animation cycle. In a scenario involving composite fields (represented as an object), an ObjectAnimator will take the starting composite value (like the PointF object which is a composite of x and y), an ending composite value and pass them to a TypeEvaluator helper object to get the intermediate object value. This composite value is then set on the target object. Listing 18-39 shows how a TypeEvlautor calculates this intermediate value through its evaluate method.

Listing 18-39. Coding a TypeEvaluator

```
//file: MyPointEvaluator.java(ProAndroid5_ch18_TestPropertyAnimation.zip)
public class MyPointEvaluator implements TypeEvaluator<PointF> {
  public PointF evaluate(float fraction, PointF startValue, PointF endValue) {
        PointF startPoint = (PointF) startValue;
        PointF endPoint = (PointF) endValue;
        return new PointF(
            startPoint.x + fraction * (endPoint.x - startPoint.x),
            startPoint.y + fraction * (endPoint.y - startPoint.y));
    }
}
```

From Listing 18-39 you can see that you need to inherit from the TypeEvaluator interface and implement the evaluate() method. In this method, you will be passed the fraction of the animation's total progress. You can use that fraction to adjust your intermediate composite value and return it as a typed value.

Listing 18-40 shows how an ObjectAnimator uses MyAnimatableView and the MyPointEvaluator to animate composite values for a View.

Listing 18-40. Using a TypeEvaluator

```
//file: TestPropertyAnimationActivity.java(ProAndroid5_ch18_TestPropertyAnimation.zip)
public void testTypeEvaluator(View v) {
    float h = m_tv.getHeight(); float w = m_tv.getWidth();
    float x = m_tv.getX(); float y = m_tv.getY();

    PointF startingPoint = new PointF(w,h);
    PointF endingPoint = new PointF(x,y);

    //m_atv: You will need this code in your activity earlier as a local variable:
    MyAnimatableView m_atv = new MyAnimatableView(m_tv);

    ObjectAnimator viewCompositeValueAnimator =
        ObjectAnimator.ofObject(m_atv
            ,"point", new MyPointEvaluator()
            ,startingPoint, endingPoint);

    viewCompositeValueAnimator.setDuration(5000);
    viewCompositeValueAnimator.start();
}
```

Notice in Listing 18-40 that the ObjectAnimator is using the method ofObject() as opposed to ofFloat() or ofInt(). Also notice that the starting value and ending value for the animation are composite values represented by the class PointF. The goal of the object animator is now to come up with an intermediate value for PointF and then pass it to the method setPoint(PointF) on the custom class MyAnimatableView. The class

MyAnimatableView can accordingly set the respective individual properties on the contained text view. This animation in Listing 18-40 using the TypeEvaluator is invoked by button 7. When this animation runs, the view will migrate from bottom right to top left.

Understanding Key Frames

Key frames are useful places during an animation cycle to put key time markers (significant instances in time). A key frame specifies a particular value for a property at a given moment in time. The key marker's time is between 0 (beginning of animation) and 1 (end of animation). Once you gather these key-frame values, you set them against a particular property such as alpha, x, or y. This association of key frames to their respective properties is done through the PropertyValuesHolder class. You then tell the ObjectAnimator to animate the resulting PropertyValuesHolder. Listing 18-41 demonstrates key-frame animation.

Listing 18-41. Animating a View Using Key Frames

```
//file:TestPropertyAnimationActivity.java(ProAndroid5_ch18_TestPropertyAnimation.zip)
public void testKeyFrames(View v) {
    float h = m_tv.getHeight();    float w = m_tv.getWidth();
    float x = m_tv.getX();  float y = m_tv.getY();

    //Start frame : 0.2, alpha: 0.8
    Keyframe kf0 = Keyframe.ofFloat(0.2f, 0.8f);

    //Middle frame: 0.5, alpha: 0.2
    Keyframe kf1 = Keyframe.ofFloat(.5f, 0.2f);

    //end frame: 0.8, alpha: 0.8
    Keyframe kf2 = Keyframe.ofFloat(0.8f, 0.8f);

    PropertyValuesHolder pvhAlpha =
        PropertyValuesHolder.ofKeyframe("alpha", kf0, kf1, kf2);
    PropertyValuesHolder pvhX =
        PropertyValuesHolder.ofFloat("x", w, x);

    //end frame
    ObjectAnimator anim =
        ObjectAnimator.ofPropertyValuesHolder(m_tv, pvhAlpha,pvhX);
    anim.setDuration(5000);
    anim.start();
}
```

The animation in Listing 18-41 is invoked by button 8. When this animation runs, you will see the text move from right to left. When 20% of the time has passed, alpha will change to 80%. The alpha value will reach 20% at half way and change back to 80% at the 80th percentile of the animation time.

Understanding Layout Transitions

The property animation API also provides layout-based animations through the `LayoutTransition` class. This class is well documented as part of the standard API Java doc at the following URL.

`http://developer.android.com/reference/android/animation/LayoutTransition.html`

We will summarize here only the key points of layout transitions. To enable layout transitions on a view group (most layouts are view groups), you will need to use the code shown in Listing 18-42.

***Listing 18-42.** Setting a Layout Transition*

```
viewgroup.setLayoutTransition(
  new LayoutTransition()
);
```

With the code in Listing 18-42 the layout container (ViewGroup) will exhibit default transitions as views are added and removed. A LayoutTransition object has four different default animations that cover each of the following scenarios:

- Add a view (animation for the view that is appearing due to an add or a show)
- Change appearing (animation for the rest of the items in the layout as they could change their size or appearance due to a new item being added)
- Remove a view (animation for the view that is disappearing due to a remove or a hide)
- Change disappearing (animation for the rest of the items in the layout as they could their size or appearance due to an item being removed)

If you want custom animators for each of these cases, you can set them on the `LayoutTransition` object. Here is an example in Listing 18-43.

***Listing 18-43.** Layout Transition Methods*

```
//Here is how you get a new layout transition
LayoutTransition lt = new LayoutTransition();

//You can set this layout transition on a layout
someLayout.setLayoutTransition(lt);

//obtain a default animator if you need to remember
Animator defaultAppearAnimator = lt.getAnimator(APPEARING);

//create a new animator
ObjectAnimator someNewObjectAnimator1, someOtherObjectAnimator2;
```

```
//set it as your custom animator for the allowed set of animators
lt.setAnimator(APPEARING, someNewObjectAnimator1);
lt.setAnimator(CHANGE_APPEARING, someNewObjectAnimator1);
lt.setAnimator(DISAPPEARING, someNewObjectAnimator1);
lt.setAnimator(CHANGE_DISAPPEARING, someOtherObjectAnimator2);
```

Because the animator you supply to a layout transition applies to each view, the animators are internally cloned before being applied to each view.

Resources

Here are some useful links to when you are working with the Android Animation API:

- `http://www.androidbook.com/item/3901`: Author research notes on Android property animations.
- `http://android-developers.blogspot.com/2011/02/animation-in-honeycomb.html`: A key blog on property animations.
- `http://android-developers.blogspot.com/2011/05/introducing-viewpropertyanimator.html`: A blog on view property animations.
- `http://developer.android.com/guide/topics/graphics/prop-animation.html`: Primary documentation on property animations from the Android SDK.
- `http://developer.android.com/guide/topics/graphics/animation.html`: Android documentation links to all animation types, including property animations and old-style animations.
- `http://developer.android.com/reference/android/view/animation/package-summary.html`: Java doc API for the older animation package `android.view.animation`.
- `http://developer.android.com/guide/topics/resources/animation-resource.html`: XML tags for various animation types.
- `http://www.androidbook.com/proandroid5/projects`: Downloadable test projects for this chapter. The names of the zip files are `ProAndroid5_ch18_TestFrameAnimation.zip`, `ProAndroid5_ch18_TestLayoutAnimation.zip`, `ProAndroid5_ch18_TestViewAnimation.zip`, and `ProAndroid5_ch18_TestPropertyAnimation.zip`.

Summary

In this chapter we have covered frame-by-frame animation, layout animation, view animation, interpolators, transformation matrices, Camera, and various ways of using the new property animation API. All concepts are presented with working code snippets and supported by working downloadable projects.

Chapter 19

Exploring Maps and Location-Based Services

In this chapter, we are going to talk about maps and location-based services. Location-based services form one of the more exciting pieces of the Android SDK. This portion of the SDK provides APIs to let application developers display and manipulate maps, obtain real-time device-location information, and take advantage of other exciting features. Working with maps changed significantly when Google introduced the `MapFragment` and version 2 of the Google Maps API. This chapter will go into details of the new ways of creating maps and manipulating them.

The location-based services facility in Android sits on two pillars: the mapping and location-based APIs. The mapping APIs in Android provide facilities for you to display a map and manipulate it. For example, you can zoom and pan; you can change the map mode (from satellite view to traffic view, for example); you can add markers and custom data to the map; and so on. The other end of the spectrum is Global Positioning System (GPS) data and information about locations, both of which are handled by the location package.

These APIs often reach across the Internet to invoke services from Google servers, via Google Play Services (the local uber application on the device). Therefore, you will usually need to have Internet connectivity for these to work. In addition, Google has Terms of Service that you must agree to before you can develop applications with these Google services. Read the terms carefully; Google places some restrictions on what you can do with the service data. For example, you can use location information for users' personal use, but certain commercial uses are restricted, as are applications involving automated control of vehicles. The terms will be presented to you when you sign up for a Maps API key.

In this chapter, we'll go through each of these packages. We'll start with the mapping APIs and show you how to use maps with your applications. As you'll see, mapping in Android boils down to using `MapFragment` class in addition to the mapping APIs, which integrate with Google Maps. We will also show you how to place custom data onto the maps that you display and how to show the current location of the device on a map. After talking about maps, we'll delve into location-based services, which extend the mapping concepts. We will show you how to use the Android `Geocoder` class and the `LocationServices` service. We will also touch on threading issues that surface when you use these APIs.

Understanding the Mapping Package

As we mentioned, the mapping APIs are one of the components of Android's location-based services. The mapping package contains almost everything you'll need to display a map on the screen, handle user interaction with the map (such as zooming), display custom data on top of the map, and so on. In the old version of Android Maps, your application would talk directly to the Google Maps services for everything map-related. In the new version, your application must talk to Google Play Services, which is a local app on the device, provided as part of the operating system. Your app still also makes calls over the Internet for data, but if Google Play Services is not present locally on the device, your maps will not work. If you need maps on devices that don't have Google Play Services you'll need to explore one of the other maps packages available for Android (e.g., MapQuest).

In order for your application to talk to Google Play Services, you will need to include the Google Play Services library into your application. Android Studio does this differently than Eclipse with ADT. See the References section below for a link to online instructions for the latest way to do this. Before you include the Google Play Services library in your application, you must first download it through the SDK Manager. You'll find it under Extras.

You may have noticed that your Android SDK Manager shows Google API packages in addition to the Android SDK platforms. Previously, you had to base your application on a Google APIs package in order to use maps, but that is no longer true. Instead, the Maps API integrates to Google Play Services, so your application can be based on a regular Android package. However, to test a maps-based app in the emulator, you would need to base your emulator's Android Virtual Device (AVD) on a Google APIs package. More on testing apps later.

The first step to working with the maps package is to display a map. To do that, you'll use `MapFragment` (or `SupportMapFragment` if you want backwards compatibility with versions of Android prior to API 12, a.k.a. Honeycomb 3.1). Using this class, however, requires some preparation work. Specifically, before you can use Google Maps services, you'll need to get a Maps API key from Google. The *Maps API key* enables Android to interact with Google Maps services to obtain map data. The next section explains how to obtain a Maps API key.

Obtaining a Maps API Key from Google

Google wants to be able to identify the application that is connecting to the map services. It uses a combination of the application package and the certificate used to sign the application, to generate a Maps API key that the application must then use to request service. The Maps API key can be used across a number of pairs of packages and certificates. This means you can use the same Maps API key for development and production; the package would be the same but the certificates are probably different. In theory you could use the same key across multiple applications but this practice is discouraged. You don't want to do this anyway since Google imposes certain limits on the Maps API usage and by sharing a Maps API key with multiple applications you could more easily exceed the limit.

To obtain a Maps API key, you need the certificate that you'll use to sign your application (in the case of a development version of your app, the debug certificate). You'll get the SHA-1 fingerprint of your certificate, and then you'll enter it, along with your application's package, on Google's web site to generate an associated Maps API key.

First, you must locate your debug certificate, which is generated and maintained by Eclipse. You can find the exact location using the Eclipse IDE. If you're using an IDE other than Eclipse, you just need to locate the keystore file where the certificates are held. From Eclipse's Preferences menu, go to Android ➤ Build. The debug certificate's location will be displayed in the Default Debug Keystore field, as shown in Figure 19-1.

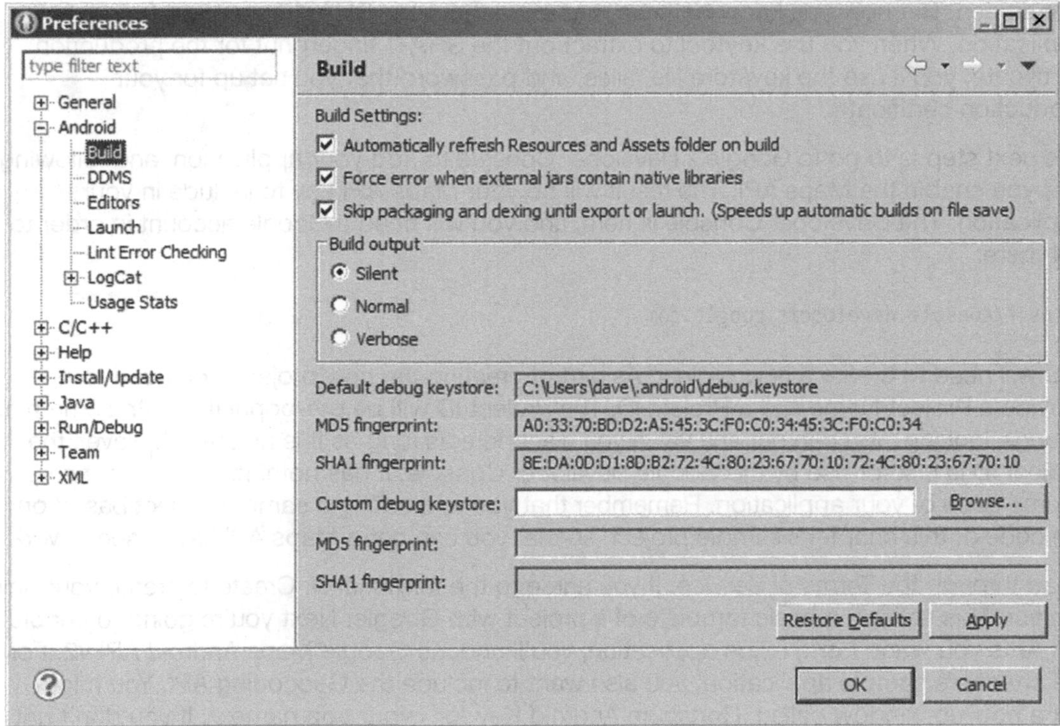

***Figure 19-1.** The debug certificate's location*

To extract the SHA-1 fingerprint, you can run the keytool with the -list option, as shown here:

```
keytool -list -alias androiddebugkey -keystore
"FULL PATH OF YOUR debug.keystore FILE" -storepass android -keypass android
```

Note that the alias you want from the debug store is androiddebugkey. Similarly, the keystore password is android, and the private key password is also android. When you run this command, the keytool provides the fingerprint (see Figure 19-2).

```
C:\Windows\system32\cmd.exe

C:\Users\dave\.android>keytool -list -alias androiddebugkey -keystore debug.keystore
Enter keystore password:
androiddebugkey, Nov 28, 2011, PrivateKeyEntry,
Certificate fingerprint (SHA1): 8E:DA:0D:D1:8D:B2:72:4C:80:23:67:70:10:72:4C:80:23:67:70:10

C:\Users\dave\.android>
```

***Figure 19-2.** The keytool output for the `list` option*

You'll notice that the fingerprint displayed by the keytool command is the same as displayed in the Preferences screen as shown in Figure 19-1 so you could have just gotten it from that screen. But now you know both ways to extract out the SHA-1 fingerprint for your application. When you use keytool to extract out the SHA-1 fingerprint for the production certificate, you'll use the keystore file, alias, and password that you set up for your production certificate.

The next step is to go to Google's Developer Console to add your application, and following that you enable the Maps API. The result will be your Maps API key to include in your application. The Developer Console is here, and you will need a Google account in order to get there:

```
https://console.developers.google.com
```

You will need to create a new project. As part of creating the new project, you need to provide a Project Name and a Project ID. The Project ID will be pre-populated with something strange-looking. You can put any value you want here as long as it is unique. However, the Project ID is just for use by the Google Developer Console; it has nothing to do with the source code of your application. Remember that you're creating a sample project based on the code of this chapter's sample project, so that you can get a Maps API key to see it work.

Read through the Terms of Service. If you agree to the terms, click Create to create your new project. This sets up a basic template of a project with Google. Next you're going to enable the APIs you want. For a maps application, you'll choose Google Maps Android API v2. For the chapter's sample application, you also want to include the Geocoding API. You might get a pop-up window called 'Configure Android Key for <your app name>'. If you don't get a pop-up, you can navigate to the APIs & auth ➤ Credentials section of your project in the Developers Console and generate an API key there. This is where you need to copy and paste in both the SHA-1 fingerprint of the application signing certificate, and the package name of the application, separated by a semicolon. The package name is the one from your source code. Note that you can copy in more than one line, so if you have the SHA-1 fingerprint from the production application signing certificate (which is typically different from the androiddebugkey used in development), you could add a second line for the production application.

Once you press the Create button on this screen you will get an API key. This is what you will include in the AndroidManifest.xml file of your application. The API key is active immediately, so you can start using it to obtain map data from Google.

Adding the Maps API Key to Your Application

To see how the Maps API key is added to the manifest file, see the bottom of Listing 19-1.

Listing 19-1. AndroidManifest.xml for a Simple Maps Application

```
<?xml version="1.0" encoding="utf-8"?>
<manifest xmlns:android="http://schemas.android.com/apk/res/android"
    package="com.androidbook.maps.whereami"
    android:versionCode="1"
    android:versionName="1.0" >

    <uses-sdk
        android:minSdkVersion="10" android:targetSdkVersion="19" />
    <uses-permission android:name="android.permission.ACCESS_FINE_LOCATION"/>
    <uses-permission android:name="android.permission.ACCESS_NETWORK_STATE" />
    <uses-permission android:name="android.permission.INTERNET"/>
    <uses-permission android:name="android.permission.WRITE_EXTERNAL_STORAGE"/>
    <uses-feature
        android:glEsVersion="0x00020000" android:required="true"/>

    <application
        android:allowBackup="true" android:icon="@drawable/ic_launcher"
        android:label="@string/app_name"
        android:theme="@style/AppTheme" >
        <activity
            android:name="com.androidbook.maps.whereami.MainActivity"
            android:label="@string/app_name" >
            <intent-filter>
                <action android:name="android.intent.action.MAIN" />
                <category android:name="android.intent.category.LAUNCHER" />
            </intent-filter>
        </activity>
        <meta-data android:name="com.google.android.gms.version"
            android:value="@integer/google_play_services_version" />
        <meta-data
            android:name="com.google.android.maps.v2.API_KEY"
            android:value="AIzaSyBDs1ZQgu9X2A4TG1a7fPl-Ge_MKlyviKM"/>
    </application>
</manifest>
```

As you no doubt noticed, there are other elements within the manifest file that must be present for a maps application to work. The `<meta-data>` tag above the Maps API key is required, as are the permissions near the top. Technically, the `ACCESS_FINE_LOCATION` permission is not needed to show maps; it is there so location functionality (e.g., GPS) will work. GPS is commonly used in maps applications. `ACCESS_NETWORK_STATE` and `INTERNET` permissions are there so the maps application can download map tile data (i.e., the map graphics) and to know what type and state of network connection the application has. The `WRITE_EXTERNAL_STORAGE` permission is there so the maps application can create a local cache of map tile files on the device's local storage space. Without caching, a maps application would likely spend a lot of time downloading map tiles over and over again, which is not only inefficient for your app, but it places an unwanted burden on the Google servers and it could consume a large portion of the user's data plan. And finally, the `glEsVersion` feature is present because rendering maps on the screen uses OpenGL, so by requiring the feature, the application avoids getting installed on devices that could not display maps.

Now, let's start playing with maps.

Understanding MapFragment

The foundational building block of a map application is the `MapFragment`. This was introduced in Honeycomb (Android 3.1) and replaced `MapView` and `MapActivity` functionality. Now you can embed a `MapFragment` inside of a regular Android activity. If you want your application to run on devices running an older version of Android, you can use `SupportMapFragment` and embed it inside a `FragmentActivity`. The `MapFragment` contains the map view to display maps, it handles user gestures to manipulate the map, and it manages the background threads that talk to the Google services to retrieve map data.

`MapFragment` is a very nice bundle of functionality, but it's not all that you need on your device to make maps work. Fortunately, the integration with Google Play Services is all handled for you; all you need to do is make a special entry into your app's AndroidManifest.xml file, which you saw in the previous section.

The first sample application for this chapter will simply show a map to the user and let the user explore the map.

> **Note** We give you a URL at the end of the chapter that you can use to download projects from this chapter. This will allow you to import these projects into your IDE directly. Also note that if you want to test these samples with an Android emulator, make sure the Android Virtual Device (AVD) is built with the Google APIs.

Please refer to the sample project called WhereAmI. The application is made up of a very basic `FragmentActivity`, a very simple layout, and a `SupportMapFragment`. The sample is using the compatibility classes, which means it will run on Gingerbread devices as well as the latest models. If your app only needs to run on devices newer than Honeycomb 3.0, you could use a regular activity and a `MapFragment` instead.

Listing 19-2 shows the activity. All that's needed is to set up the layout and, if needed, create the `MapFragment` and insert it into the layout's container (a FrameLayout).

Listing 19-2. A Basic FragmentActivity for Displaying a Map

```
public class MainActivity extends FragmentActivity {

    private static final String MAPFRAGTAG = "MAPFRAGTAG";
    private MyMapFragment myMapFrag;

    @Override
    protected void onCreate(Bundle savedInstanceState) {
        super.onCreate(savedInstanceState);
        setContentView(R.layout.activity_main);

        if ((myMapFrag = (MyMapFragment) getSupportFragmentManager()
                .findFragmentByTag(MAPFRAGTAG)) == null) {
            myMapFrag = MyMapFragment.newInstance();
            getSupportFragmentManager().beginTransaction()
                .add(R.id.container, myMapFrag, MAPFRAGTAG).commit();
        }
    }
}
```

If the activity is re-created due to an orientation change for example, the map fragment will still be available and be automatically attached to the new activity by Android. If the map fragment is not found, it means this is the first time in, or the map fragment has been destroyed, so create a new one and attach it. It doesn't get any easier than that. The layout source is shown in Listing 19-3. It is simply a FrameLayout with an id of "container" that fills the available screen space.

Listing 19-3. Layout for Simple Map Display (activity_main.xml)

```
<FrameLayout xmlns:android="http://schemas.android.com/apk/res/android"
    xmlns:tools="http://schemas.android.com/tools"
    android:id="@+id/container"
    android:layout_width="match_parent"
    android:layout_height="match_parent"
    tools:context="com.androidbook.maps.whereami.MainActivity"
    tools:ignore="MergeRootFrame" />
```

If you are including the map fragment with other items in your user interface, you can simply use the FrameLayout where you want the map fragment to appear, embedded within other layouts. The only code remaining is that of the MapFragment, which is shown in Listing 19-4. Figure 19-3 shows what the user sees.

Listing 19-4. Code for the MapFragment

```
public class MyMapFragment extends SupportMapFragment
    implements OnMapReadyCallback {
    private GoogleMap mMap = null;

    public static MyMapFragment newInstance() {
        MyMapFragment myMF = new MyMapFragment();
        return myMF;
    }
```

```
    @Override
    public void onCreate(Bundle savedInstanceState) {
        super.onCreate(savedInstanceState);
        getMapAsync(this);
    }

    @Override
    public void onActivityCreated(Bundle savedInstanceState) {
        super.onActivityCreated(savedInstanceState);
        setRetainInstance(true);
    }

    @Override
    public void onResume() {
        super.onResume();
        doWhenMapIsReady();
    }

    @Override
    public void onPause() {
        super.onPause();
        if(mMap != null)
            mMap.setMyLocationEnabled(false);
    }

    @Override
    public void onMapReady(GoogleMap arg0) {
        mMap = arg0;
        doWhenMapIsReady();
    }

    /* We have a race condition where the fragment could resume
     * before or after the map is ready. So we put all our logic
     * for initializing the map into a common method that is
     * called when the fragment is resumed or resuming and the
     * map is ready.
     */
    void doWhenMapIsReady() {
        if(mMap != null && isResumed())
            mMap.setMyLocationEnabled(true);
    }
}
```

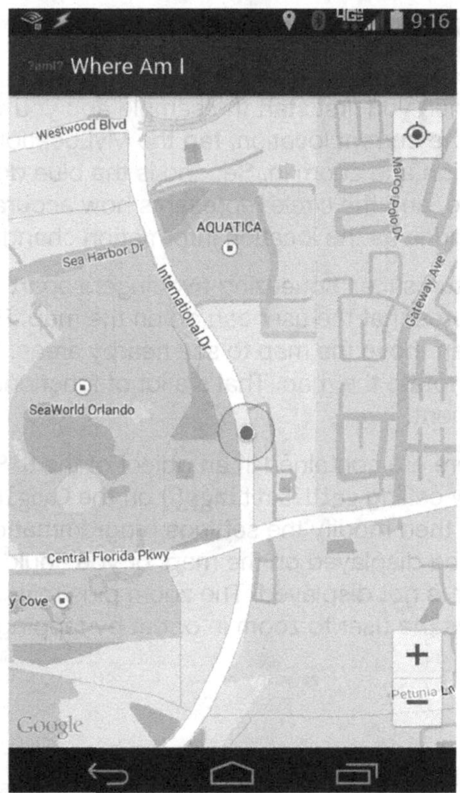

Figure 19-3. A basic MapFragment displaying your location

A recent development (Dec 2014) to the Maps API is the use of a callback to let the application know when the map is ready to be acted upon. The callback is set up using `getMapAsync()`, and the `onMapReady()` callback is called when the map can be used by the application. In between calling `getMapAsync()` and invoking the `onMapReady()` callback, Android is setting up communications, threads, etc., for the map. This means that the map may or may not be ready when `onResume()` is invoked, which tells the fragment that the UI is now being shown. Therefore, the application needs a separate method to work on the map and it needs to be called both by `onResume()` and by `onMapReady()`. For this sample application, the `doWhenMapIsReady()` method fills that role.

The application wants to show the user the device's current location, so the `setMyLocationEnabled()` method is called in `doWhenMapIsReady()`. But `doWhenMapIsReady()` needs to check that the map exists and that the fragment is resuming or has resumed. We don't know which will occur first, but both must be true before we enable location updates. The current location updates are disabled when the fragment goes out of view (see `onPause()`). The only other code line to notice is the `setRetainInstance()` method call. Since the map does not need to be destroyed and re-created for a configuration change of the activity, it makes sense to keep the fragment and reuse it, along with the threads and tiles and so on. You should remember that a configuration change will cause `onPause()` and `onResume()` to be invoked during the config change. This will correctly disable location updates and re-enable them during `onResume()`.

Map Controls: MyLocation, Zoom, Pan

There are a couple of artifacts on the user interface to notice. First is the MyLocation button in the upper-right corner. When you first start the sample app you will see a very high-level view of the world. To show the current location, tap the MyLocation button. This will relocate the map to the current position and zoom in. Second is the blue dot. The blue dot represents where the app thinks you are, and the circle represents how accurate it thinks this location is. The circle may grow or shrink as the location information changes.

The user can use pinch gestures (i.e., squeezing two fingers apart or together) to zoom in or out. There are more gestures that the user can do on the map. By swiping, the user can pan the map; that is, they can move the map to see nearby areas. Using two fingers and a rotation move, the user can rotate the map. That's a lot of functionality that's automatic from simply creating a MapFragment.

These map controls and more are contained in an object of the `UiSettings` class. You can get the map's `UiSettings` by calling `getUiSettings()` on the `GoogleMap` object (i.e., `mMap` in the sample app). You can then modify the settings programmatically. For example, you could enable a compass to be displayed on the map, or you could enable/disable the zoom plus/minus control so it is or is not displayed. The zoom plus/minus control appears in the lower-right corner and allows the user to zoom in or out by tapping the plus or minus button, respectively.

Map Types

The default map type is `MAP_TYPE _NORMAL`. This is the type that was used in Figure 19-3. It shows the roads with the basic features of the land such as where water is, where greenspace is, and some places and buildings. `MAP_TYPE_SATELLITE` shows a photographic satellite view of the ground, so the user is able to see actual buildings, cars, and even people. `MAP_TYPE_HYBRID` is a combination of these two; `MAP_TYPE_TERRAIN` is like a normal map but with topographical features added such as mountains and canyons. To really see the effect of `MAP_TYPE_TERRAIN`, zoom in on a place like Boulder, Colorado with a map set to Terrain.

You use the `setMapType()` method of a `GoogleMap` to change the type.

Adding a Traffic Layer

In the previous version of Android Maps, traffic was treated like the satellite and normal modes of maps. With API v2, traffic is enabled separately using the `setTrafficEnabled()` method of a `GoogleMap`.

Map Tiles

It's helpful to understand what's going on when your app displays a map. Google has created millions of base map tiles to represent the earth's surface. At the lowest zoom level (i.e., zero) there is one tile to show the entire world. At zoom level 1, there are four tiles in a 2x2 configuration. At zoom level 2, there are 16 tiles in a 4x4 configuration. And so on up to zoom level 21. Depending on what part of the world you want to display, and what the zoom level is, the GoogleMap object will fetch and cache the appropriate tiles. Pan to the side, and any additional tiles will be fetched and displayed. Pan back to where you were and your app can retrieve map tiles from the cache instead of making more round trips to the server.

It's interesting to note that base map tiles for the normal type of maps are not images. Google has figured out a compressed way to describe the shapes and colors within the tiles instead of just sending down images for each tile. As a result, normal map tiles are very efficient in terms of cache space as well as network bandwidth. Satellite tiles on the other hand are not as compressed, since they are images.

Now you can understand why sometimes a maps application will show a gray grid pattern and seem to function but won't show streets and other items. The GoogleMap object has been instantiated, and it knows a zoom level and where it is supposed to be displaying a map, but it is unable to retrieve and render tiles to the user. This is most often due to an invalid Maps API key, or the API key has not been set up properly. But it could also mean difficulty in reaching the Google Maps servers. However, if map tiles have been cached, those tiles can be rendered to the user even if the tile servers at Google are unreachable. There are two unfortunate things about map tile caching. The first is that there are no API calls to manage the map tile cache, either to force map tiles to be cached, or to change the size of the cache, or to evict tiles from the cache. You just have to trust that Google will do the right thing. The second is that map tiles are cached per application. So just because the Google Maps application may have cached tiles, your application does not have access to those tiles. Your application can only see the cached tiles that it has cached.

Adding Markers to Maps

Usually you'll want to identify points of interest on a map, and this is done using Markers. The points could be stationary objects like addresses, landmarks, or a parking spot. But they could also be moving objects like cars, planes, people, pets, storms, etc. You get to choose what the marker looks like and where it is positioned on a map. And you can have lots of markers all at the same time. We're going to modify the sample program from above to include a couple of markers. You'll see how to place them, and then how to manipulate the view to make sure the user sees the markers.

Now use the sample program called WhereAmIMarkers. You will need to modify the AndroidManifest.xml file as before to use your Maps API key. The source code for `MyMapFragment.java` has been modified as shown in Listing 19-5. The screen will appear similar to Figure 19-4.

Listing 19-5. Code for the MapFragment Showing Markers

```
public class MyMapFragment extends SupportMapFragment
    implements OnMapReadyCallback {

    public static MyMapFragment newInstance() {
        MyMapFragment myMF = new MyMapFragment();
        return myMF;
    }
```

```
    @Override
    public void onCreate(Bundle savedInstanceState) {
        super.onCreate(savedInstanceState);
        getMapAsync(this);
    }
    @Override
    public void onActivityCreated(Bundle savedInstanceState) {
        super.onActivityCreated(savedInstanceState);
        setRetainInstance(true);
    }

    @Override
    public void onMapReady(GoogleMap myMap) {
        LatLng disneyMagicKingdom = new LatLng(28.418971, -81.581436);
        LatLng disneySevenLagoon = new LatLng(28.410067, -81.583699);

        // Add a marker
        MarkerOptions markerOpt = new MarkerOptions()
                .draggable(false)
                .flat(false)
                .position(disneyMagicKingdom)
                .title("Magic Kingdom")
                .icon(BitmapDescriptorFactory.defaultMarker(BitmapDescriptorFactory.
                HUE_AZURE));
        myMap.addMarker(markerOpt);

        markerOpt.position(disneySevenLagoon)
                 .title("Seven Seas Lagoon");
        myMap.addMarker(markerOpt);

        // Derive a bounding box around the markers
        LatLngBounds latLngBox = LatLngBounds.builder()
                .include(disneyMagicKingdom)
                .include(disneySevenLagoon)
                .build();

        // Move the camera to zoom in on our locations
        myMap.moveCamera(CameraUpdateFactory.newLatLngBounds(latLngBox, 200, 200, 0));
    }
}
```

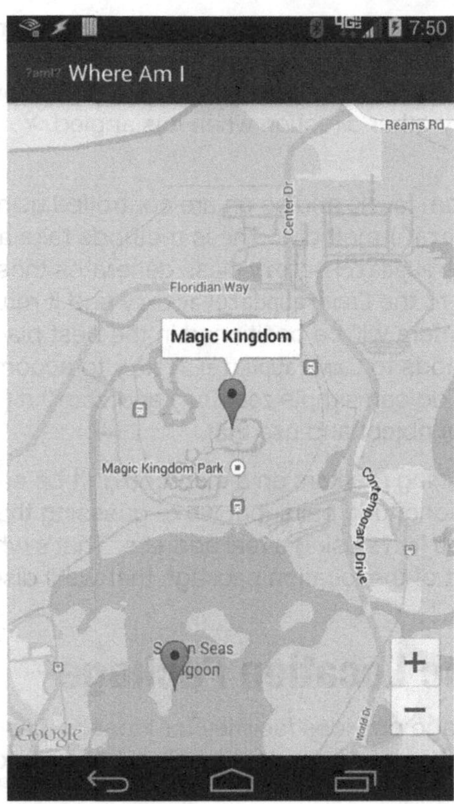

Figure 19-4. Markers on a map

Once again, everything starts from acquiring the `GoogleMap` object from the `MapFragment`. Once the map is available, you can create markers which in this case are based on a couple of fixed `LatLng` objects. You'll notice though that you don't directly instantiate a `Marker` object. Instead, you use a `MarkerOptions` object to specify how the marker should be created. It is within the `MarkerOptions` object that you decide the position, title, marker shape, color, etc. While you could instantiate a `Marker` object and then call each setter that you want, `MarkerOptions` makes things much easier, especially if you need to create multiple markers that will share common features. This sample only uses some of the `MarkerOptions` features; please see the reference documentation to learn all of the options available.

The next thing you likely want to do is show the map to the user such that all the markers are visible at the same time. This requires two things: centering the map in the middle of the markers, and setting the zoom level as high as possible without being so close that you can't fit all the markers into the view. Fortunately, a helper class is available for this purpose. The `LatLngBounds` object is created by passing it all of the `LatLng` points that should be within the view, and it calculates the smallest box that contains them all. In this sample, both points are passed in at once. You could also use a loop to pass in all the points and then invoke the `build()` method to return the bounding box.

Once you have a bounding box, you need to adjust the map's camera. In the old version of Google Maps, there was only a straight-down view of a map, as if you were above the map looking straight down. With Maps API version 2, there is the concept of a camera that can look straight down, but can also look at an angle. If you use two fingers at the same time and swipe the screen from top to bottom, you will see the viewing angle change. You have in effect pivoted the camera so you are no longer looking straight down. The camera can also look to the east, south or any other direction when it is angled. You can twist two fingers to rotate the map too.

All these camera angles, zoom levels and so on are controlled using the map's `animateCamera()` or `moveCamera()` methods. These methods take a `CameraUpdate` object as instructions, and the `CameraUpdateFactory` class generates those. In the sample, the bounding box is passed to the `CameraUpdateFactory` and it returns an appropriate `CameraUpdate` so that the camera will be positioned in the best place to see all the markers. There are several other methods to `CameraUpdateFactory` to accommodate other ways of positioning the camera. You do can simple `zoomIn()` and `zoomOut()` for example. You can also create a `CameraPosition` object and use that.

All in all, you'll agree that placing markers on a map couldn't be easier. Or could it? We don't have a database of latitude/longitude pairs, but we're guessing that we'll need to somehow create one or more `LatLng objects` using a real address. That's when you can use the `Geocoder` class, which is part of the location package that we'll discuss next.

Understanding the Location Package

The `android.location` package provides facilities for location-based services. In this section, we are going to discuss two important pieces of this package: the `Geocoder` class and the `LocationManager` service. We'll start with `Geocoder`.

Geocoding with Android

If you are going to do anything practical with maps, you'll likely have to convert an address (or location) to a latitude/longitude pair. This concept is known as *geocoding*, and the `android.location.Geocoder` class provides this facility. In fact, the `Geocoder` class provides both forward and backward conversion—it can take an address and return a latitude/longitude pair, and it can translate a latitude/longitude pair into a list of addresses. The class provides the following methods:

- `List<Address>   getFromLocation(double latitude, double longitude, int maxResults)`
- `List<Address>   getFromLocationName(String locationName, int maxResults, double lowerLeftLatitude, double lowerLeftLongitude, double upperRightLatitude, double upperRightLongitude)`
- `List<Address>   getFromLocationName(String locationName, int maxResults)`

It turns out that computing an address is not an exact science because of the various ways a location can be described. For example, the `getFromLocationName()` methods can take the name of a place, the physical address, an airport code, or simply a well-known name for the location. Thus, the methods return a list of addresses and not a single address. Because the methods return a list, which could be quite long (and take a long time to return), you are encouraged to limit the result set by providing a value for maxResults that ranges between 1 and 5. Now, let's consider an example.

Listing 19-6 shows the XML layout and corresponding code for the activity and map fragment shown in Figure 19-5. To run the example, you'll need to update the manifest with your own Maps API key.

Listing 19-6. Working with the Android Geocoder Class

```
<!-- This is activity_main.xml -->
<LinearLayout xmlns:android="http://schemas.android.com/apk/res/android"
    xmlns:tools="http://schemas.android.com/tools"
    android:layout_width="match_parent"
    android:layout_height="match_parent"
    android:orientation="vertical"
    android:paddingBottom="@dimen/activity_vertical_margin"
    android:paddingLeft="@dimen/activity_horizontal_margin"
    android:paddingRight="@dimen/activity_horizontal_margin"
    android:paddingTop="@dimen/activity_vertical_margin"
    tools:context="com.androidbook.maps.whereami.MainActivity"
    tools:ignore="MergeRootFrame" >

    <EditText android:id="@+id/locationName"
        android:layout_width="match_parent"
        android:layout_height="wrap_content"
        android:hint="Enter location name"
        android:inputType="text"
        android:imeOptions="actionGo" />

    <FrameLayout android:id="@+id/container"
        android:layout_width="match_parent"
        android:layout_height="match_parent" />

</LinearLayout>

/**
  * This is from MainActivity.java
 **/
public class MainActivity extends FragmentActivity {

    private static final String MAPFRAGTAG = "MAPFRAGTAG";
    MyMapFragment myMapFrag = null;
    private Geocoder geocoder;

    @Override
    protected void onCreate(Bundle savedInstanceState) {
        super.onCreate(savedInstanceState);
        setContentView(R.layout.activity_main);
```

```
        if ((myMapFrag = (MyMapFragment) getSupportFragmentManager()
                        .findFragmentByTag(MAPFRAGTAG)) == null) {
            myMapFrag = MyMapFragment.newInstance();
            getSupportFragmentManager().beginTransaction()
                .add(R.id.container, myMapFrag, MAPFRAGTAG).commit();
        }
        if(Build.VERSION.SDK_INT >= Build.VERSION_CODES.GINGERBREAD
                        && !Geocoder.isPresent()) {
            Toast.makeText(this, "Geocoder is not available on this device",
                        Toast.LENGTH_LONG).show();
            finish();
        }
        geocoder = new Geocoder(this);
        EditText loc = (EditText)findViewById(R.id.locationName);
        loc.setOnEditorActionListener(new OnEditorActionListener() {
            @Override
            public boolean onEditorAction(TextView v, int actionId, KeyEvent event) {
                if (actionId == EditorInfo.IME_ACTION_GO) {
                    String locationName = v.getText().toString();

                    try {
                        List<Address> addressList =
                           geocoder.getFromLocationName(locationName, 5);
                        if(addressList!=null && addressList.size()>0)
                        {
//                           Log.v(TAG, "Address: " + addressList.get(0).toString());
                            myMapFrag.gotoLocation(new LatLng(
                                addressList.get(0).getLatitude(),
                                addressList.get(0).getLongitude()),
                                locationName);
                        }
                    } catch (IOException e) {
                        e.printStackTrace();
                    }
                }
                return false;
            }
        });
    }
}

public class MyMapFragment extends SupportMapFragment
    implements OnMapReadyCallback {
    private GoogleMap mMap = null;

    public static MyMapFragment newInstance() {
        MyMapFragment myMF = new MyMapFragment();
        return myMF;
    }
```

```
    @Override
    public void onCreate(Bundle savedInstanceState) {
        super.onCreate(savedInstanceState);
        getMapAsync(this);
    }

    @Override
    public void onActivityCreated(Bundle savedInstanceState) {
        super.onActivityCreated(savedInstanceState);
        setRetainInstance(true);
    }

    public void gotoLocation(LatLng latlng, String locString) {
        if(mMap == null)
            return;
        // Add a marker for the given location
        MarkerOptions markerOpt = new MarkerOptions()
                .draggable(false)
                .flat(false)
                .position(latlng)
                .icon(BitmapDescriptorFactory.defaultMarker(BitmapDescriptorFactory.
                HUE_AZURE))
                .title("You chose:")
                .snippet(locString);
        // See the onMarkerClicked callback for why we do this
        mMap.addMarker(markerOpt);

        // Move the camera to zoom in on our location
        mMap.moveCamera(CameraUpdateFactory.newLatLngZoom(latlng, 15));
    }

    @Override
    public void onMapReady(GoogleMap arg0) {
        mMap = arg0;
    }
}
```

Figure 19-5. *Geocoding to a point given the location name*

To demonstrate the uses of geocoding in Android, type the name or address of a location in the `EditText` field and then tap the Go button on the keyboard. To find the address of a location, we call the `getFromLocationName()` method of `Geocoder`. The location can be an address or a well-known name such as "White House." Geocoding can be a prolonged operation, so we recommend that you limit the results to five, as the Android documentation suggests.

The call to `getFromLocationName()` returns a list of addresses. The sample application takes the list of addresses and processes the first one if any were found. Every address has a latitude and longitude, which you use to create a `LatLng`. You then call our `gotoLocation()` method to navigate to the point. This new method in the map fragment creates a new marker, adds it to the map, and moves the camera to the marker with a zoom level of 15. The zoom level can be set to a float between 1 and 21, inclusive. As you move from 1 toward 21 by 1's, the zoom level increases by a factor of 2. We could have presented a dialog to display multiple found locations if we wanted to, but for now, we'll just display the first location returned to us.

In our example application, we only read the latitude and longitude of our returned `Address`. In fact, there can be a ton of data about `Addresses` returned to us, including the location's common name, street, city, state, postal/ZIP code, country, and even phone number and web site URL.

You should understand a few points with respect to geocoding:

- While the Geocoder class may exist, the service may not be implemented. If the device is Gingerbread or higher, you should check with Geocoder.isPresent() before attempting to geocode in your application.
- A returned address is not always an exact address. Obviously, because the returned list of addresses depends on the accuracy of the input, you need to make every effort to provide an accurate location name to the Geocoder.
- Whenever possible, set the maxResults parameter to a value between 1 and 5.
- You should seriously consider doing the geocoding operation in a different thread from the UI thread. There are two reasons for this. The first is obvious: the operation is time-consuming, and you don't want the UI to hang while you do the geocoding, causing Android to kill your activity. The second reason is that, with a mobile device, you always need to assume that the network connection can be lost and that the connection is weak. Therefore, you need to handle input/output (I/O) exceptions and timeouts appropriately. Once you have computed the addresses, you can post the results to the UI thread. See the included sample application called WhereAmIGeocoder2 for how to do this.

Understanding Location Services

Location Services provide two main functions: a mechanism for you to obtain the device's geographical location and a facility for you to be notified (via an intent) when the device enters or exits a specified geographical location. This latter operation is known as geofencing.

In this section, you are going to learn how to find the device's current location. To use the service, you must first obtain a reference to it. Listing 19-7 shows a simple usage of the FusedLocationProviderApi service. The sample project for this is called WhereAmILocationAPI.

Listing 19-7. Using the Location Provider API

```
public class MyMapFragment extends SupportMapFragment
    implements GoogleApiClient.ConnectionCallbacks,
               GoogleApiClient.OnConnectionFailedListener,
               OnMapReadyCallback {
    private Context mContext = null;
    private GoogleMap mMap = null;
    private GoogleApiClient mClient = null;
    private LatLng mLatLng = null;
```

```
public static MyMapFragment newInstance() {
    MyMapFragment myMF = new MyMapFragment();
    return myMF;
}

@Override
public void onCreate(Bundle savedInstanceState) {
    super.onCreate(savedInstanceState);
    getMapAsync(this);
}

@Override
public void onActivityCreated(Bundle savedInstanceState) {
    super.onActivityCreated(savedInstanceState);
    if(mClient == null) { // first time in, set up this fragment
        setRetainInstance(true);

        mContext = getActivity().getApplication();
        mClient = new GoogleApiClient.Builder(mContext, this, this)
            .addApi(LocationServices.API)
            .build();
        mClient.connect();
    }
}

@Override
public void onConnectionFailed(ConnectionResult arg0) {
    Toast.makeText(mContext, "Connection failed", Toast.LENGTH_LONG).show();
}
@Override
public void onConnected(Bundle arg0) {
    // Figure out where we are (lat, long) as best as we can
    // based on the user's selections for Location Settings
    FusedLocationProviderApi locator = LocationServices.FusedLocationApi;
    Location myLocation = locator.getLastLocation(mClient);
    // if the services are not available, could get a null location
    if(myLocation == null)
        return;
    double lat = myLocation.getLatitude();
    double lng = myLocation.getLongitude();
    mLatLng = new LatLng(lat, lng);
    doWhenEverythingIsReady();
}

@Override
public void onConnectionSuspended(int arg0) {
    Toast.makeText(mContext, "Connection suspended", Toast.LENGTH_LONG).show();
}
```

```
    @Override
    public void onMapReady(GoogleMap arg0) {
        mMap = arg0;
        doWhenEverythingIsReady();
    }

    private void doWhenEverythingIsReady() {
        if(mMap == null || mLatLng == null)
            return;
        // Add a marker
        MarkerOptions markerOpt = new MarkerOptions()
                .draggable(false)
                .flat(true)
                .position(mLatLng)
                .icon(BitmapDescriptorFactory.defaultMarker(BitmapDescriptorFactory.
                HUE_AZURE));
        mMap.addMarker(markerOpt);

        // Move the camera to zoom in on our location
        mMap.moveCamera(CameraUpdateFactory.newLatLngZoom(mLatLng, 15));
    }
}
```

To acquire a location service, you first need to create a Google API client object, which makes available to you the services from Google Play Services. This is relatively easy to do, and once you have the client object, you need to call its `connect()` method. This will later invoke the `onConnected()` callback asynchronously to let your application know that the client has been connected and is now available for use. Or your application may get the `onConnectionFailed()` callback, in which case you should take appropriate action. For the sample we simply show a Toast message when the connection attempt has failed. Later on you'll see how to deal more robustly with a failed connection.

When the `onConnected()` callback is invoked, now you can work with the location provider API. Recall that at the beginning of this chapter you set permissions in the manifest file to access location information. Fine locations use GPS while coarse locations use cell towers and WiFi hotspots. Using a fused location provider API means that your application isn't worrying about what is enabled or what permissions are set. The API calls are the same. You just ask for locations and you will get the best location information that is available at the time.

For this sample, we call the `getLastLocation()` method. With luck, the location that is returned is very current; however, be aware that the last location might be from minutes or hours ago. The `Location` object can tell you, via the `getTime()` method, when this location fix was obtained. You could check to see if it is new enough for your purposes before deciding to use it. It is technically possible that `getLastLocation()` will return null so you should be prepared for that case as well. This can happen if Location Services have been disabled in Settings.

You'll see soon how to get updates to locations. For now, the sample takes whatever the last location was and creates a map marker out of it for display to the user. You should recognize the code to create a marker from the previous section of this chapter.

How to Enable Location Services

You might think there's a simple API to enable Location Services if they are not turned on when your application runs. Unfortunately, this is not the case. To get Location Services turned on, the user must do that from within the Settings screens of their device. Your application can make this a lot simpler for the user by launching that particular Settings screen. The location settings source screen is really just an activity, and this activity is set up to respond to an intent.

In the sample application just covered, you will see the code from Listing 19-8 in the activity's `onCreate()` callback.

Listing 19-8. Checking to See If Location Services Are On

```
@Override
protected void onCreate(Bundle savedInstanceState) {
    super.onCreate(savedInstanceState);
    setContentView(R.layout.activity_main);

    if ((myMapFrag = (MyMapFragment) getSupportFragmentManager()
            .findFragmentByTag(MAPFRAGTAG)) == null) {
        myMapFrag = MyMapFragment.newInstance();
        getSupportFragmentManager().beginTransaction()
            .add(R.id.container, myMapFrag, MAPFRAGTAG).commit();
    }

    if(!isLocationEnabled(this)) {
        // no location service providers are enabled
        Toast.makeText(context, "Location Services appear to be turned off." +
            " This app can't work without them. Please turn them on.",
            Toast.LENGTH_LONG).show();
        startActivityForResult(new Intent(
            android.provider.Settings.ACTION_LOCATION_SOURCE_SETTINGS), 0);
    }
}

@SuppressWarnings("deprecation")
public boolean isLocationEnabled(Context context) {
    int locationMode = Settings.Secure.LOCATION_MODE_OFF;
    String locationProviders;

    if (Build.VERSION.SDK_INT >= Build.VERSION_CODES.KITKAT){
        try {
            locationMode = Settings.Secure.getInt(
                context.getContentResolver(),
                Settings.Secure.LOCATION_MODE);
        } catch (SettingNotFoundException e) {
            e.printStackTrace();
        }
```

```
        return locationMode != Settings.Secure.LOCATION_MODE_OFF;
    }else{
        locationProviders = Settings.Secure.getString(
            context.getContentResolver(),
            Settings.Secure.LOCATION_PROVIDERS_ALLOWED);
        return !TextUtils.isEmpty(locationProviders);
    }
}
```

A change occurred in Android 19 (KitKat) where new settings values were added to the static Settings.Secure class. This made it easier to tell if Location Services were turned on or not, and which ones, but the user still needs to do the work to enable the services. There are two ways in this code to check for services: use one of the new values, or do a get on the available location providers. The first part of Listing 19-8 checks to see if the version of Android is KitKat or higher, and if so it looks for the value of the new Setting for location mode. The second part of the code (if the version of Android is older than KitKat) does a get on the allowed location providers. If location mode is not off, or if there is at least one location provider available, then Location Services are running. If not, this code launches an intent to the Location Settings screen. At that point, this activity would be paused while the Settings activity runs. When the Settings activity is done, our activity will resume.

If you want to handle a response from the Settings activity (i.e., be notified when that activity is done and presumably a setting change has been made), you must implement the onActivityResult() callback in your activity. And also keep in mind that although you hope the user turns on location services, they may not. You will need to check again to see if the user has enabled location services and take appropriate action based on the result. We'll show you how to do all of this in a later section.

Location Providers

You've seen the FusedLocationApi, but you should also be aware of the older, alternate location providers. The hardware is right there on the device for getting location information, and the location providers will give it to your application. You'll soon see how the FusedLocationApi handles your location needs at a higher level than these providers. But if you need to dig into the details, for example to check the status of the available GPS satellites, you'll be happy to know these providers exist. Google recommends that everyone switch over to the FusedLocationApi; but since it relies on Google Play Services, that means applications that use FusedLocationApi will not run on a non-Google Android device.

The LocationManager service is a system-level service. *System-level services* are services that you obtain from the context using the service name; you don't instantiate them directly. The android.app.Activity class provides a utility method called getSystemService() that you can use to obtain a system-level service. You call getSystemService() and pass in the name of the service you want, in this case, Context.LOCATION_SERVICE. You'll see this shortly in Listing 19-9.

The LocationManager service provides geographical location details by using location providers. Currently, there are three types of location providers:

- *GPS* providers use a Global Positioning System to obtain location information.
- *Network* providers use cell-phone towers or WiFi networks to obtain location information.
- The *passive* provider is like a location update sniffer, and it passes to your application location updates that are requested by other applications, without your application having to specifically request any location updates. Of course, if no one else is requesting location updates, you won't get any either.

Similar to the FusedLocationApi, the LocationManager class can provide the device's last known location, this time via the getLastKnownLocation() method. Location information is obtained from a provider, so the method takes as a parameter the name of the provider you want to use. Valid values for provider names are LocationManager.GPS_PROVIDER, LocationManager.NETWORK_PROVIDER, and LocationManager.PASSIVE_PROVIDER. Note that there is no option for a fused provider, since that is a separate location-finding capability.

In order for your application to successfully get location information, it must have the appropriate permissions in the AndroidManifest.xml file. android.permission.ACCESS_FINE_LOCATION is required for GPS and for passive providers, whereas android.permission.ACCESS_COARSE_LOCATION or android.permission.ACCESS_FINE_LOCATION can be used for network providers, depending on what you need. For instance, assume your application will use GPS or network data for location updates. Because you need ACCESS_FINE_LOCATION for GPS, you've also satisfied permissions for network access, so you do not need to also specify ACCESS_COARSE_LOCATION. If you're only going to use the network provider, you could get by with only ACCESS_COARSE_LOCATION in the manifest file.

Calling getLastKnownLocation() returns an android.location.Location instance, or null if no location is available. The Location class provides the location's latitude and longitude, the time the location was computed, and possibly the device's altitude, speed, and bearing. A Location object can also tell you which provider it came from using getProvider(), which will be either GPS_PROVIDER or NETWORK_PROVIDER. If you're getting location updates via the PASSIVE_PROVIDER, remember that you're only really sniffing location updates, so all updates are ultimately from either GPS or the network.

Because the LocationManager operates on providers, the class provides APIs to obtain providers. For example, you can get all of the known providers by calling getAllProviders(). You can obtain a specific provider by calling getProvider(), passing the name of the provider as an argument (such as LocationManager.GPS_PROVIDER). One thing to watch out for is that getAllProviders() will return providers that you may not have access to or that are currently disabled. Fortunately, you are able to determine the status of providers using other methods, such as isProviderEnabled(String providerName) or getProviders(boolean enabledOnly), which you could call with a value of true to get only providers you are able to use immediately.

There's another way to get a suitable provider, and that is to use the `getProviders(Criteria criteria, boolean enabledOnly)` method of `LocationManager`. By specifying criteria for location updates, and by setting `enabledOnly` to `true` so you get providers that are enabled and ready to go, you can get a list of provider names returned to you without having to know the specifics of which provider you got. This could be more portable, because a device may have a custom `LocationProvider` that meets your needs without you having to know about it in advance. The `Criteria` object can be set with parameters that include accuracy level and the need for information about speed, bearing, altitude, cost, and power requirements. If no providers meet your criteria, a null list will be returned, allowing you to either bail out or relax the criteria and try again.

Sending Location Updates to Your Application

When doing development testing, your application needs location information, and the emulator doesn't have access to GPS or cell towers. In order for you to test your application in the emulator, you can manually send location updates from Eclipse. Listing 19-9 shows a simple example to illustrate how to do this. We're going to stick with the LocationManager approach here, and then show the FusedLocationApi approach later.

Listing 19-9. Registering for Location Updates

```
public class LocationUpdateDemoActivity extends Activity
{
    LocationManager locMgr = null;
    LocationListener locListener = null;

    @Override
    public void onCreate(Bundle savedInstanceState)
    {
        super.onCreate(savedInstanceState);

        locMgr = (LocationManager)
            getSystemService(Context.LOCATION_SERVICE);

        locListener = new LocationListener()
        {
            public void  onLocationChanged(Location location)
            {
                if (location != null)
                {
                    Toast.makeText(getBaseContext(),
                        "New location latitude [" +
                        location.getLatitude() +
                        "] longitude [" +
                        location.getLongitude()+"]",
                        Toast.LENGTH_SHORT).show();
                }
            }
```

```
            public void  onProviderDisabled(String provider)
            {
            }

            public void  onProviderEnabled(String provider)
            {
            }

            public void  onStatusChanged(String provider,
                                int status, Bundle extras)
            {
            }        };
    }

    @Override
    public void onResume() {
        super.onResume();

        locMgr.requestLocationUpdates(
            LocationManager.GPS_PROVIDER,
            0,                  // minTime in ms
            0,                  // minDistance in meters
            locListener);
    }

    @Override
    public void onPause() {
        super.onPause();
        locMgr.removeUpdates(locListener);
    }
}
```

We're not displaying a user interface for this example, so the standard initial layout XML file will do, as well as a regular activity.

One of the primary uses of the LocationManager service is to receive notifications of the device's location. Listing 19-9 demonstrates how you can register a listener to receive location-update events. To register a listener, you call the requestLocationUpdates() method, passing the provider type as one of the parameters. When the location changes, the LocationManager calls the onLocationChanged() method of the listener with the new Location. It is very important that you remove any registrations for location updates at the appropriate time. In our example, we do registration in onResume(), and we remove that registration in onPause(). If we aren't going to be around to do anything with location updates, we should tell the provider not to send them. There's also the possibility that our activity could be destroyed (for example, if the user rotates their device and our activity is restarted), in which case our old activity could still exist, be receiving updates, displaying them with Toast, and taking up memory.

In our example, we set the minTime and minDistance to zero. This tells the LocationManager to send us updates as often as possible. These are not desired settings for your production application, or on real devices, but we use them here to make the demonstrations run better in the emulators. (In real life, you would not want the hardware trying to figure out our current position so often, as this drains the battery.) Set these values appropriately for the situation, trying to minimize how often you truly need to be notified of a change in position. Google typically recommends values no smaller than 20 seconds.

Testing Location Applications with the Emulator

Let's test this in the emulator, using the Dalvik Debug Monitor Service (DDMS) perspective that ships with the ADT plug-in for Eclipse. The DDMS UI provides a screen for you to send the emulator a new location (see Figure 19-6).

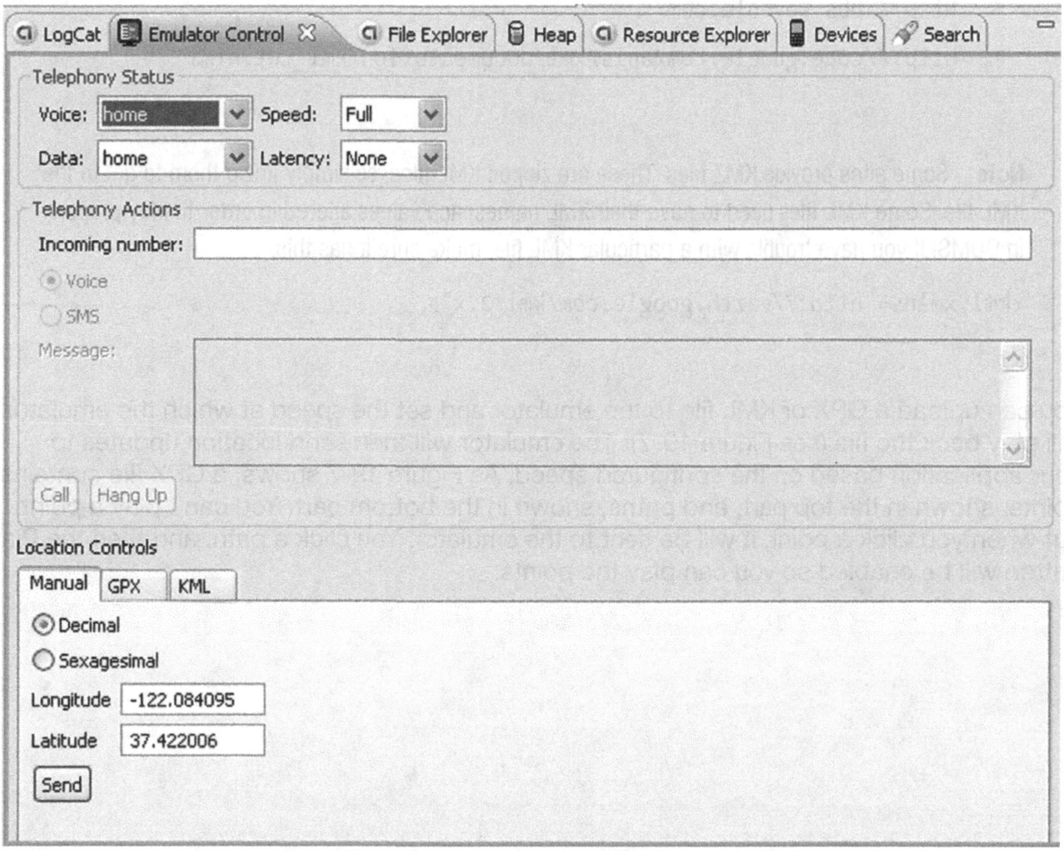

***Figure 19-6.** Using the DDMS UI in Eclipse to send location data to the emulator*

To get to the DDMS in Eclipse, use Window ➤ Open Perspective ➤ DDMS. The Emulator Control view should already be there for you, but if not, use Window ➤ Show View ➤ Other ➤ Android ➤ Emulator Control to make it visible in this perspective. You may need to scroll down in the emulator control to find the location controls. As shown in Figure 19-6, the Manual tab in the DDMS user interface allows you to send a new GPS location (latitude/longitude pair) to the emulator. Sending a new location will fire the `onLocationChanged()` method on the listener, which will result in a message to the user conveying the new location.

You can send location data to the emulator using several other techniques, as shown in the DDMS user interface (see Figure 19-6). For example, the DDMS interface allows you to submit a GPS Exchange Format (GPX) file or a Keyhole Markup Language (KML) file. You can obtain sample GPX files from these sites:

- `www.topografix.com/gpx_resources.asp`
- `http://tramper.co.nz/?view=gpxFiles`
- `www.gpsxchange.com/`

Similarly, you can use the following KML resources to obtain or create KML files:

- `http://bbs.keyhole.com/`
- `http://code.google.com/apis/kml/documentation/kml_tut.html`

> **Note** Some sites provide KMZ files. These are zipped KML files, so simply unzip them to get to the KML file. Some KML files need to have their XML namespace values altered in order to play properly in DDMS. If you have trouble with a particular KML file, make sure it has this:
>
> `<kml xmlns="http://earth.google.com/kml/2.x">.`

You can upload a GPX or KML file to the emulator and set the speed at which the emulator will play back the file (see Figure 19-7). The emulator will then send location updates to your application based on the configured speed. As Figure 19-7 shows, a GPX file contains points, shown in the top part, and paths, shown in the bottom part. You can't play a point, but when you click a point, it will be sent to the emulator. You click a path, and then the Play button will be enabled so you can play the points.

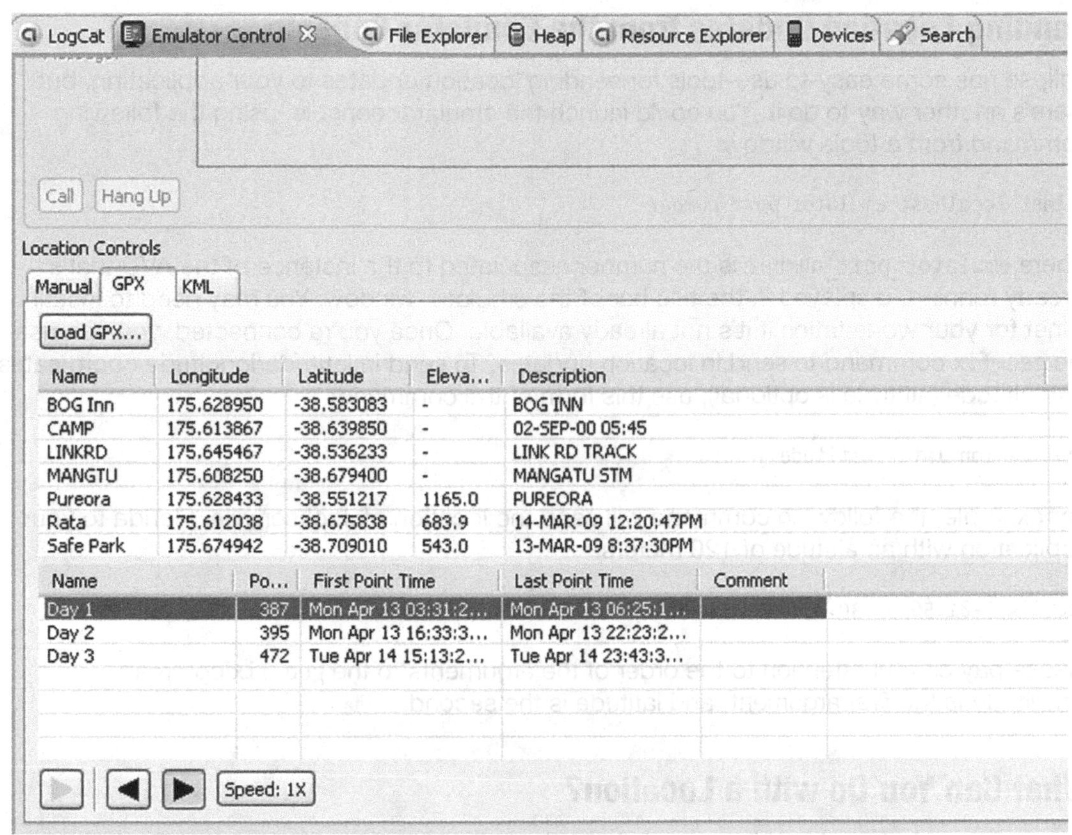

***Figure 19-7.** Uploading GPX and KML files to the emulator for playback*

> **Note** There have been reports that not all GPX files are understandable by the emulator control. If you attempt to load a GPX file and nothing happens, try a different file from a different source.

Listing 19-9 includes some additional methods for `LocationListener` we haven't mentioned yet. They are the callbacks `onProviderDisabled()`, `onProviderEnabled()`, and `onStatusChanged()`. For our sample, we did not do anything with these, but in your application, you could be notified when a location provider, such as gps, is disabled or enabled by the user, or when a status changes with one of the location providers. Statuses include `OUT_OF_SERVICE`, `TEMPORARILY_UNAVAILABLE`, and `AVAILABLE`. Even if a provider is enabled, it does not mean that it will be sending any location updates, and you can tell that using statuses. Note that `onProviderDisabled()` will be invoked immediately if a `requestLocationUpdates()` is called for a disabled provider.

Sending Location Updates from the Emulator Console

Eclipse has some easy-to use-tools for sending location updates to your application, but there's another way to do it. You could launch the emulator console, using the following command from a tools window:

```
telnet localhost emulator_port_number
```

where `emulator_port_number` is the number associated to the instance of the AVD that's already running, displayed in the title bar of the emulator window. You may need to install telnet for your workstation if it's not already available. Once you're connected, you can use the `geo fix` command to send in location updates. To send in latitude/longitude coordinates with altitude (altitude is optional), use this form of the command:

```
geo fix lon lat [ altitude ]
```

For example, the following command will send the location of Jacksonville, Florida to your application with an altitude of 120 meters.

```
geo fix  -81.5625  30.334954  120
```

Please pay careful attention to the order of the arguments to the `geo fix` command. Longitude is the *first* argument, and latitude is the second.

What Can You Do with a Location?

As mentioned before, `Locations` can tell you the latitude and longitude, when the `Location` was computed, the provider that computed this `Location`, and optionally the altitude, speed, bearing, and accuracy level. Depending on the provider where the `Location` came from, there could be extra information as well. For example, if the `Location` came from a GPS provider, there is an extras `Bundle` that will tell you how many satellites were used to compute the `Location`. The optional values may or may not be present, depending on the provider. To know if a `Location` has one of these values, the `Location` class provides a set of `has...()` methods that return a `boolean` value, for example `hasAccuracy()`. Before relying on the return value of `getAccuracy()`, it would be wise to call `hasAccuracy()` first.

The `Location` class has some other useful methods, including a static method `distanceBetween()`, which will return the shortest distance between two `Locations`. Another distance-related method is `distanceTo()`, which will return the shortest distance between the current `Location` object and the `Location` object passed to the method. Note that distances are in meters and that the distance calculations take into account the curvature of the Earth. But also be aware that the distances are not provided in terms of the distance you would have to go by car, for example.

If you want to get driving directions or driving distances, you will need to have your beginning and ending `Locations`, but to do the calculations, you will likely need to use the Google Directions API. The Directions API would allow your application to show how to get from your beginning to your ending location. This is another of the Google API client APIs that you can enable for your application.

Setting Up for Google Play Services Location Updates

You've seen how to get location updates with a LocationManager, but let's return to the FusedLocationProviderApi to see how to get location updates from it. The sample project for this section is FusedLocationApiUpdates. This one is a bit trickier because we are dealing with Google Play Services, an independent service running on the device. Therefore, you can't always be sure that you have a valid client connection, and you need to be careful when requesting location updates. For this reason, your application will need to worry about state.

In the earlier sample program (WhereAmILocationAPI), you checked to see if Location Services were turned on, but the code assumed that Google Play Services were available and ready. Now you're going to see how to check for the existence of Google Play Services and how the GooglePlayServicesUtil class can help you. The basic flow is to check each dependency for location updates to occur and, if there is a way to correct a problem, help the user fix it. If the user does not, or cannot, fix a problem, the application quits. If the user keeps fixing problems until everything is working, then location updates get requested, and the application displays location updates via Toast messages.

Listing 19-10 shows our main method for trying to connect. You will see inside this method the same Location Services check from the earlier WhereAmILocationAPI sample application. The `tryToConnect()` method will be called from the activity's `onResume()` callback, so that every time this activity is resumed, a new client connection will be established to Google Play Services. We do not want to assume that an old client is still valid and active.

Listing 19-10. Checking for the Ability to Do Location Updates

```
private void tryToConnect() {
    // Check that Google Play services is available
    int resultCode = GooglePlayServicesUtil
                    .isGooglePlayServicesAvailable(this);
    // If Google Play services is available, then we're good
    if (resultCode == ConnectionResult.SUCCESS) {
        Log.d(TAG, "Google Play services is available.");
        if(!isLocationEnabled(this)) {
            if(lastFix == FIX.LOCATION_SETTINGS) {
                // Since we're coming through again, it means
                // recovery didn't happen. Time to bail out.
                Log.e(TAG, "Location settings didn't work");
                finish();
            }
            else {
                // no location service providers are enabled
                Toast.makeText(this, "Location Services are off. " +
                    "Can't work without them. Please turn them on.",
                    Toast.LENGTH_LONG).show();
                Log.i(TAG, "Location Services need to be on. " +
                    "Launching the Settings screen");
                startActivityForResult(new Intent(
                    android.provider.Settings
                        .ACTION_LOCATION_SOURCE_SETTINGS),
```

```
                LOCATION_SETTINGS_REQUEST);
            lastFix = FIX.LOCATION_SETTINGS;
        }
    }
    else {
        client.connect();
        Log.v(TAG, "Connecting to GoogleApiClient...");
        }
    }
    // Google Play services was not available for some reason
    // See if the user can do something about it
    else if(GooglePlayServicesUtil
            .isUserRecoverableError(resultCode)) {
        if(lastFix == FIX.PLAY_SERVICES) {
            // Since we're coming through again, it means
            // recovery didn't happen. Time to bail out.
            Log.e(TAG, "Recovery doesn't seem to work");
            finish();
        }
        else {
            Log.d(TAG, "Google Play services may be available. " +
                "Asking user for help");
            // This form of the dialog call will result in either a
            // callback to onActivityResult, or a dialog onCancel.
            GooglePlayServicesUtil.showErrorDialogFragment(resultCode,
                this, PLAY_SERVICES_RECOVERY_REQUEST, this);
            lastFix = FIX.PLAY_SERVICES;
        }
    } else {
        // No hope left.
        Log.e(TAG, "Google Play Services is/are not available." +
              " No point in continuing");
        finish();
    }
}
```

The GooglePlayServicesUtil class has several static methods to help get everything set up for location updates. The first method is `isGooglePlayServicesAvailable()`, which requires a context. The result is an integer value which is either `SUCCESS` or one of several other values which could indicate for example that the services are missing, or the version is not appropriate. For most purposes, you don't really need to care about the other values that are returned, as you'll see.

If Google Play Services are available, you will check for Location Services (as before) and if they are okay, you can invoke the `connect()` method on the GoogleApiClient client. The `connect()` call is asynchronous and a separate callback will handle the results of the connect call. As before, if Location Services are not turned on, you would launch the location settings activity so the user could turn them on. In this sample, we just use a Toast message to tell the user why they are being redirected to the Settings screen. In a production application, you would probably want to show an alert dialog with an OK and Cancel button before redirecting to the Settings screen.

If Google Play Services are not available, the next check is to see if the user could resolve the issue, using the isUserRecoverableError() method. Here you pass in the result code from the earlier check, which should be something other than SUCCESS. This is why you don't need to care what other value was returned. This method decides for you if the user can do something about it or not. If the user can't correct the situation (i.e., isUserRecoverableError() returns false), then there really isn't anything else you can do and you will probably want to bail out. In this sample application a log message is written and the activity ends. You might want to be more graceful in your exit.

If the user can do something about the problem with Google Play Services, the GooglePlayServicesUtil class has yet another static method you can use: showErrorDialogFragment(). This will show a dialog to the user indicating what the problem is and what they can do about it. There are a few variations on this call, and the sample is using the one which pops a dialog fragment while listening for a dialog cancel. The dialog fragment could launch another activity, which would result in our onActivityResult() being called. For this reason, you want to pass in a request value (i.e., PLAY_SERVICES_RECOVERY_REQUEST), which will be passed to onActivityResult() later. This method is also asynchronous, and your application will see either onActivityResult() invoked later, or the onCancel() for the dialog. The second argument to showErrorDialogFragment() is the context, and the last argument is the listener for the dialog. Because we passed 'this' as the last argument, to represent this activity, the sample activity must implement DialogInterface.OnCancelListener and have an onCancel() callback.

You'll soon see the code for onActivityResult(), but you should know that when a result is passed back to your activity, you're going to have do these checks again, by calling tryToConnect(). That is why this method sets a lastFix value, to keep track of which problem is being worked on. If the same problem exists after the user has had a chance to fix it, we could assume that the user isn't interested in fixing the problem, or the system is unable to fix the problem. We do not want some sort of infinite loop that the user cannot break out of. For this sample activity, if tryToConnect() hits the same problem twice in a row, it bails out and the activity is finished. Your application might want to take alternative action, giving the user more options to continue to use the app.

To recap what has happened in tryToConnect(), you checked for the existence and readiness of Google Play Services, as well as Location Services. If everything looked good, a connect call was made on the GoogleClientApi client. If the user was able to correct anything, a suitable intent was fired to launch an activity to take care of it. And if the situation was hopeless, the activity ended. Now let's look at the various callbacks that could result from these actions.

If the connection request was successful, the onConnected() callback will fire. Listing 19-11 shows what this looks like.

Listing 19-11. Client Is Connected So Request Location Updates

```
@Override
public void onConnected(Bundle arg0) {
    // Set up location updates
    Log.v(TAG, "Connected!");
    lastFix = FIX.NO_FAIL;
    locator.requestLocationUpdates(client, locReq, this);
    Log.v(TAG, "Requesting location updates (onConnected)...");
}
```

This one is pretty straightforward. If we got a good connection to Google Play Services, start asking the FusedLocationProviderApi (locator) for location updates. You'll see more about locReq later, but for now just know that it is a LocationRequest object with parameters that define what kinds of location updates your application wants. This method also resets a state variable (lastFix) which will make more sense soon.

If the connection request was not successful, the onConnectionFailed() callback will fire. Listing 19-12 shows this callback.

Listing 19-12. Handling a Failed Connection Attempt

```
@Override
public void onConnectionFailed(ConnectionResult connectionResult) {
    /*
     * Google Play services can resolve some errors it detects.
     * If the error has a resolution, try sending an Intent to
     * start a Google Play services activity that can resolve
     * the error.
     */
    if (connectionResult.hasResolution()) {
        Log.i(TAG, "Connection failed, trying to resolve it...");
        if(lastFix == FIX.CONNECTION) {
            // Since we're coming through again, it means
            // recovery didn't happen. Time to bail out.
            Log.e(TAG, "Connection retry didn't work");
            finish();
        }
        try {
            // Start an activity that tries to resolve the error
            lastFix = FIX.CONNECTION;
            connectionResult.startResolutionForResult(
                    this,
                    CONNECTION_FAILURE_RESOLUTION_REQUEST);
        } catch (IntentSender.SendIntentException e) {
            // Log the error
            Log.e(TAG, "Could not resolve connection failure");
            e.printStackTrace();
            finish();
        }
    } else {
        /*
         * If no resolution is available, display error to the
         * user.
         */
        Log.e(TAG, "Connection failed, no resolutions available, "+
                GooglePlayServicesUtil.getErrorString(
                        connectionResult.getErrorCode() ));
        Toast.makeText(this, "Connection failed. Cannot continue",
                Toast.LENGTH_LONG).show();
        finish();
    }
}
```

If the connection request has failed, it is still possible that the situation can be corrected. Once again there is a method that can tell if there is a way to resolve the problem. The ConnectionResult object contains both an indicator if there is a resolution, as well as the intent to fire to try to resolve the situation. In this case, the application calls `startResolutionForResult()`. Similar to before, an intent will be fired, some activity will be launched, and your application will get a result back in `onActivityResult()`. Notice that here the request tag is `CONNECTION_FAILURE_RESOLUTION_REQUEST`. If nothing can be done, display an error and bail out.

There could have been several intents launched, each of which should cause your `onActivityResult()` callback to fire. Listing 19-13 shows what this callback looks like. Remember that there could have been three separate intents fired to handle problems, so this callback must expect any of the three. Also keep in mind that the intents caused an activity to run, meaning your activity got paused, and it will resume right after the `onActivityResult()` has fired. This is a major reason why the `tryToConnect()` method (shown in Listing 19-10) is only called from the activity's `onResume()` callback. Whenever this activity is being resumed, it tries to make a new connection to Google Play Services and to set up location updates. When this activity pauses, it disconnects from Google Play Services. It is easy to reconnect rather than trying to hang on to a connection while it is not needed.

Listing 19-13. Getting News Back from the Launched Intents

```
@Override
protected void onActivityResult(
        int requestCode, int resultCode, Intent data) {
    /* Decide what to do based on the original request code.
     * Note that our activity got paused to launch the other
     * activity, so after this callback runs, our activity's
     * onResume() will run.
     */
    switch (requestCode) {
    case PLAY_SERVICES_RECOVERY_REQUEST :
        Log.v(TAG, "Got a result for Play Services Recovery");
        break;
    case LOCATION_SETTINGS_REQUEST :
        Log.v(TAG, "Got a result for Location Settings");
        break;
    case CONNECTION_FAILURE_RESOLUTION_REQUEST :
        Log.v(TAG, "Got a result for connection failure");
        break;
    }
    Log.v(TAG, "resultCode was " + resultCode);
    Log.v(TAG, "End of onActivityResult");
}
```

Since onActivityResult() could be called because of a number of intents, the switch statement is used to figure out which one is being responded to. The Google Play Services corrective action might say it was successful by setting the resultCode to Activity.RESULT_OK. This doesn't necessarily mean that the user fixed the problem, but it tells you that nothing failed. If the response to the Google Play Services corrective action is Activity.RESULT_CANCELED, it could mean there was some sort of failure. Regardless if the user fixed the problem or not, you're going to return from this callback, and then onResume() will run, in which tryToConnect() will be called again. So it really doesn't matter what resultCode is. In practice, even when a setting has been properly set for location updates to occur, you could see resultCode set to RESULT_CANCELED. Similarly, if there's a response to the other fixes, log it and continue since onResume() will run next anyway.

Finally, refer back to the onConnected() callback in Listing 19-11, which calls locator.requestLocationUpdates(client, locReq, this). This is where the FusedLocationProviderApi will be asked to send location updates back to this activity. Google Play Services is up and running, and Location Services are set appropriately.

Once location updates have been requested, any new location updates will get sent to the onLocationChanged() callback. In this sample application, all that happens is that the location information is displayed in a Toast message. The next section goes into more detail on how to request location updates.

There are a few other methods in the activity that so far were not described. The onPause() callback disconnects the client after stopping the location updates. You should notice that the client is checked for connectedness before calling methods. The GoogleApiClient class has a method called isConnected(), which you will use to be sure you request or remove location updates only when there's a connected client. Otherwise, you will get an IllegalStateException. The two methods for setting up the menu are basic menu callbacks. The menu is used to allow the user to switch between the various priority values. When the user selects a menu item, the location request object is updated and passed back in to alter the location update process. The onCancel() callback can be called from the pop-up error dialog that is shown in tryToConnect (see Listing 19-10). If the user simply closes the error fragment dialog box, we infer that the user doesn't want to get updates and the application exits.

Location Updates with FusedLocationProviderApi

With the LocationManager, you had to deal with the specific location providers (i.e., GPS or cell/WiFi). With the FusedLocationProviderApi, you submit a LocationRequest and the API will make choices for you of which provider would be the best, not only initially but over time as well. In general, the trade-off when getting location updates is between power consumption and accuracy. GPS is usually more accurate but uses the most power. On the other hand, when indoors, GPS may be less accurate than cell/WiFi, and you'd want to automatically switch to be more accurate while consuming the least amount of power. The FusedLocationProviderApi could also take advantage of on-board sensors such as a gyroscope or compass. This API hides the complexities of location fixing from you.

You should write your code so you're requesting location updates only when it makes sense to do so. If you are displaying the current location on a map, and the map is not visible, you do not need to request updates. There are cases when you might want to keep getting updates even when not displaying the current position, and we'll cover that in the next section. The point is that location updates can be a big drain on the battery, so ask for them only when you really need them. You should not assume that the user is going to "be right back" and therefore keep getting updates. If they set their device down and won't be looking at it again for some time, you'd better not be draining the battery down.

Listing 19-14 shows how the sample application sets the `LocationRequest` object to make a location updates request of the `FusedLocationProviderApi`. This is done in the `onCreate()` callback of the activity.

***Listing 19-14.** Setting Up a LocationRequest Object*

```
locReq = LocationRequest.create()
        .setPriority(
            LocationRequest.PRIORITY_BALANCED_POWER_ACCURACY)
        .setInterval(10000)
        .setFastestInterval(5000);
```

Use the static `create()` method, then call the appropriate setters to fill out the request object. This object will be passed to the `requestLocationUpdates()` method of the `FusedLocationProviderApi`. A big difference from dealing with the older location providers is that this request object does not make any reference to a specific location provider. Similar to the Criteria method of finding a provider, this request object ultimately selects the frequency of updates and the consumption of power.

You can specify the desired frequency of location updates using `setInterval()` and `setFastestInterval()`; both take a long argument representing the number of milliseconds. The former is saying that you want to get a location update on a regular basis, every so many milliseconds apart. The system will try to honor this if it is able to, but there are no guarantees. You could get updates more frequently than desired, even much more frequently. That is where the second method comes in. You can specify the fastest interval for receiving location updates. More on this in a bit.

The power portion of the request is handled by the `setPriority()` setter. There are currently four options for the argument:

- `PRIORITY_NO_POWER`
- `PRIORITY_LOW_POWER`
- `PRIORITY_BALANCED_POWER_ACCURACY`
- `PRIORITY_HIGH_ACCURACY`

The `NO_POWER` option is pretty much saying that your application will be using the passive provider described earlier. The only way to not consume any power is to piggyback off of the location updates for another application. Therefore, the accuracy of the locations may not be very accurate or frequent; it all depends on what other applications are requesting. You just learned that you can request a frequency of updates using `setInterval()` and `setFastestInterval()`. If you are piggybacking off of another application, and that application is receiving location updates every 5 seconds, but you don't want updates faster than every 20 seconds, you should use `setFastestInterval(20000)` so your application is not overwhelmed with updates. At the same time you could use `setInterval(60000)` to request a desired interval of one update every minute. If there are few other location updates happening on the device, you won't have to worry about reducing the frequency from 5 seconds to 20 seconds apart, but at the same time you probably won't get updates every minute either. You need to use both of these setters to indicate what your application wants, but that doesn't mean you are guaranteed to get what you want.

The `LOW_POWER` priority in general means that location updates will be derived only via cell tower triangulation and WiFi hotspot location information. These are low-power ways of determining position, with a corresponding reduction in accuracy. You could easily find the locations to be accurate only to within 1,500 meters or worse, but then you could get a location that's accurate to 10 meters. All of the priorities will take advantage of the passive provider, so if an accurate location update happens to be requested by some other application, your application could pick it up even when your priority is set to low power.

The `BALANCED` priority will try to do a decent job of trading off accuracy for less power. It will consider using all of the available methods of determining location, except for GPS.

The `HIGH_ACCURACY` priority will potentially use all available sources of location information, including GPS. Because of the GPS radio, this priority could consume a lot of battery.

Location updates also depend on the location mode of the device. As you saw earlier, the Location Settings changed in KitKat to allow the user to specify a mode of location updates for their device. Referring now to the `Settings.Secure` class, the location mode setting values are as follows:

- `LOCATION_MODE_OFF`
- `LOCATION_MODE_BATTERY_SAVING`
- `LOCATION_MODE_HIGH_ACCURACY`
- `LOCATION_MODE_SENSORS_ONLY`

and the current value can be retrieved using the code from Listing 19-8. The mode is set by the user for the entire device, not by application. However, your application has an opportunity to request a priority to complement the mode choice made by the user. If the device has a mode of `HIGH_ACCURACY` and your application chooses a priority of `LOW_POWER`, your application will not be the one draining the battery but could still get decent location updates.

The mode can work against you however. If the user chooses a mode of `SENSORS_ONLY`, and the priority is set to `NO_POWER`, `LOW_POWER` or even `BALANCED`, location updates will be rare, regardless of what you set in the location request with `setInterval()`. The preferred mode for most useful location updates is `HIGH_ACCURACY`, because this mode will combine all possible sources of location information and provide the most accurate results. Your application will be able to get high accuracy when needed (hopefully this is a rare need) and good accuracy the rest of the time. Your application can alter the priority to `HIGH_ACCURACY` when needed, but `BALANCED` or `LOW_POWER` the other times.

Some other interesting options with a `LocationRequest` include setting a specific number of location updates to receive, or to specify a time limit when the location updates should stop. You can also set a minimum distance (in meters) within which your application does not want updates. This is a geofence of sorts, where you tell the location service that you only want a location update if the device moves a certain distance from its current location. That is in effect setting up a geofence circle around the current location. More on geofences later.

Alternate Ways of Getting Location Updates

You've seen how to get location updates sent to your activity using the `requestLocationUpdates()` method of the `LocationManager` and the `FusedLocationProviderApi`. There are actually several different signatures of this method, including ones that use a `PendingIntent`. This gives you the ability to direct location updates to services or broadcast receivers. You can also direct location updates to other `Looper` threads instead of the main thread, giving you lots of flexibility for your application, although some of these methods have been available only since Android 2.3.

Using Proximity Alerts and Geofencing

Geofencing is a popular requirement for a mobile application. It means that your application should alter its behavior depending on where it is located. A typical use case is to prevent the device from working when it is outside of a particular location. For example, a hospital application could restrict access to patient data when it is not at the hospital. Or your application might want to silence notifications when the device is at the workplace. LocationManager has a mechanism called proximity alerts, and there is a similar recent API called GeofencingApi for the newer Location Services. We'll briefly discuss the first, then address the second in detail.

We mentioned earlier that the `LocationManager` can notify you when the device enters a specified geographical location. The method to set this up is `addProximityAlert()` from the `LocationManager` class. Basically, you tell the `LocationManager` that you want an `Intent` to be fired when the location of the device goes into, or leaves, a circle of a certain radius with a center at a latitude/longitude position. The `Intent` can trigger a `BroadcastReceiver` or a `Service` to be called, or an `Activity` to be started. There is also an optional time limit placed on the alert, so it could time out before the `Intent` fires.

Internally, the code for this method registers listeners for both the GPS and network providers and sets up location updates for once per second and a `minDistance` of 1 meter. You don't have any way to override this behavior or set parameters. Therefore, if you leave this running for a long time, you could end up draining the battery very quickly. If the screen goes to sleep, proximity alerts will only be checked once every four minutes, but again, you have no control over the time duration here. For these reasons, we have included a demonstration application called ProximityAlertDemo with the sample applications, but we will not dive into the details. Instead, we will turn our attention to the Location Services approach, with another sample application called GeofencingApi. Note that the GeofencingApi sample application will look similar to the FusedLocationProviderApi sample application since both share the GoogleClientApi mechanism for activation.

The GeofencingApi API

At the time of this writing, a geofence is a circular region with a latitude/longitude center, plus some time parameters. At some point in the future, the region might not be circular but for now it is. Once a geofence has been built, it can be passed to the GeofenceApi for monitoring. Your application can even go away and your geofence can be active. Along with a geofence, or set of geofences, your application will pass a PendingIntent with an Intent to be fired when something interesting happens around a geofence. The three current events are enter, exit and dwell. Enter and exit are simple to understand; the Intent will be fired if the device goes into, or leaves, the circular region. The dwell event fires the Intent after the device remains inside of the circular region for a period of time. This loitering delay is specified in milliseconds. And that's all there is to it.

See the sample application called GeofencingApiDemo. It sets up two geofences called home and work, connects to Location Services, and registers a service intent to be fired when the device enters, exits or dwells in either of these geofences. When triggered, the service generates a notification per event to make it easier for you to see the results. Geofences are often used in the background, so a service makes a lot of sense here. That is, an application shouldn't need to be in the foreground to have geofences. In fact, the basic idea of a geofence is that you want your application to be wakened up if the device enters or leaves a specific geographic region.

The setup code used earlier to make sure that Google Play Services and Location Services are available and ready has been left out of this sample application to make it easier to follow along, but you would want to include that code in a production application. Listing 19-15 shows the `onCreate()` method of the main activity, in which the geofences and the `PendingIntent` are created.

Listing 19-15. Setting Up Geofences

```
private GoogleApiClient mClient = null;
private List<Geofence> mGeofences = new ArrayList<Geofence>();
private PendingIntent pIntent = null;

@Override
protected void onCreate(Bundle savedInstanceState) {
    super.onCreate(savedInstanceState);
    setContentView(R.layout.activity_main);

    final float radius = 0.5f * 1609.0f; // half mile times 1609 meters per mile

    Geofence.Builder gb = new Geofence.Builder();
    // Make a half mile geofence around your home
    Geofence home = gb.setCircularRegion(28.993818, -81.383816, radius)
            .setTransitionTypes(
                Geofence.GEOFENCE_TRANSITION_ENTER |
                Geofence.GEOFENCE_TRANSITION_EXIT |
                Geofence.GEOFENCE_TRANSITION_DWELL )
            .setExpirationDuration(
                12 * 60 * 60 * 1000)  // 12 hours
            .setLoiteringDelay(300000)   // 5 minutes
            .setRequestId("home")
            .setNotificationResponsiveness(5000) // 5 secs
            .build();
    mGeofences.add(home);

    // Make another geofence around your work
    Geofence work = gb.setCircularRegion(28.36631, -81.52120, radius)
            .setRequestId("work")
            .build();
```

```
    mGeofences.add(work);
    Intent intent = new Intent(this, ReceiveTransitionsIntentService.class);

    pIntent = PendingIntent.getService(getApplicationContext(), 0, intent,
            PendingIntent.FLAG_UPDATE_CURRENT);

    mClient = new GoogleApiClient.Builder(this, this, this)
            .addApi(LocationServices.API)
            .build();

    Log.v(TAG, "Activity, client are created");
}
```

See how the geofence is created as a circle around a lat/lon, with the events of interest (in this case all of them) and some time parameters. In this sample, the geofences will be active for 12 hours, or until they are removed (see `onDestroy()`). It's also possible to set geofences to never expire. The loitering delay of 5 minutes means that the dwell event will fire if the device stays inside the geofence for at least 5 minutes. The request ID will be passed back to your application with the Intent so you can identify which geofence the Intent is for. The notification responsiveness of 5 seconds means that the GeofencingApi will try to send the Intent within 5 seconds of when the event happens. However, there are no guarantees that the Intent will be that quick. The larger this value, the better it is on battery life, since the API could sleep more and check things less often. On the other hand, if this value is very long, for example several minutes, it is possible you might even miss an event if the device passes through your geofence quickly. The choice of notification responsiveness will depend on how big your geofences are and how you want your application to behave.

Similar to the previous sample application, a connection is attempted from `onResume()`, and Listing 19-16 shows what runs when the connection is successful.

Listing 19-16. Registering Geofences with the API

```
@Override
public void onConnected(Bundle arg0) {
    // Set up geofences
    Log.v(TAG, "Setting up geofences (onConnected)...");
    PendingResult<Status> pResult = mFencer.addGeofences(mClient,
            mGeofences, pIntent);
    pResult.setResultCallback(this);  // ResultCallback<Status> interface
}

@Override
public void onResult(Status status) {
    Log.v(TAG, "Got a result from addGeofences("
        + status.getStatusCode() + "): "
        + status.getStatus().getStatusMessage());
}
```

The `GeofencingApi` gets passed the API client handle, the list of geofences, and the PendingIntent. The return is a `PendingResult`. If you want to find out if the result is ultimately successful or not, you need to set a callback receiver using `setResultCallback()`. This activity has implemented the ResultCallback<Status> interface, so the onResult() callback will be invoked with the results of the addGeofences() method call. For this sample, the result is simply logged, but of course you would want to take steps if the result was not successful. That's all that the activity does. Next up is the service that receives an Intent when an interesting event occurs.

Listing 19-17 shows the interesting callbacks and methods of the ReceiveTransitionsIntentService, an IntentService for this application. It basically reports out the information received, whether that is an error or a geofence event. Events are displayed using notifications. This is for your safety since the expectation is that you will start this application at home and drive to work. We do not want you having to watch the device's screen during the trip. Instead, you will be able to review all of the notifications from each event when you are safely stopped.

Listing 19-17. Receiving Intents from the GeofencingApi

```
public void onCreate() {
    super.onCreate();
    notificationMgr = (NotificationManager)getSystemService(
            NOTIFICATION_SERVICE);
}

@Override
protected void onHandleIntent(Intent intent) {
    GeofencingEvent gfEvent = GeofencingEvent.fromIntent(intent);
    // First check for errors
    if (gfEvent.hasError()) {
        // Get the error code with a static method
        int errorCode = gfEvent.getErrorCode();
        // Log the error
        Log.e(TAG, "Location Services error: " +
                Integer.toString(errorCode));
    /*
     * If there's no error, get the transition type and the IDs
     * of the geofence or geofences that triggered the transition
     */
    } else {
        // Get the type of transition (entry or exit)
        int transitionType =
                gfEvent.getGeofenceTransition();
        String tranTypeStr = "UNKNOWN(" + transitionType + ")";
        switch(transitionType) {
        case Geofence.GEOFENCE_TRANSITION_ENTER:
            tranTypeStr = "ENTER";
            break;
        case Geofence.GEOFENCE_TRANSITION_EXIT:
            tranTypeStr = "EXIT";
            break;
        case Geofence.GEOFENCE_TRANSITION_DWELL:
            tranTypeStr = "DWELL";
            break;
        }
```

```
        Log.v(TAG, "transitionType reported: " + tranTypeStr);
        Location triggerLoc = gfEvent.getTriggeringLocation();
        Log.v(TAG, "triggering location is " + triggerLoc);

        List <Geofence> triggerList =
                gfEvent.getTriggeringGeofences();

        String[] triggerIds = new String[triggerList.size()];

        for (int i = 0; i < triggerIds.length; i++) {
            // Grab the Id of each geofence
            triggerIds[i] = triggerList.get(i).getRequestId();
            String msg = tranTypeStr + ": " + triggerLoc.getLatitude() +
                ", " + triggerLoc.getLongitude();
            String title = triggerIds[i];
            displayNotificationMessage(title, msg);
        }
    }
}

private void displayNotificationMessage(String title, String message)
{
    int notif_id = (int) (System.currentTimeMillis() & 0xFFL);

    Notification notification = new NotificationCompat.Builder(this)
    .setContentTitle(title)
    .setContentText(message)
    .setSmallIcon(android.R.drawable.ic_menu_compass)
    .setOngoing(false)
    .build();

    notificationMgr.notify(notif_id, notification);
}
```

When you replace the latitude and longitude of home and work in this application, you run it on a real device, and you then move the device, you will see notifications such as those in Figure 19-8.

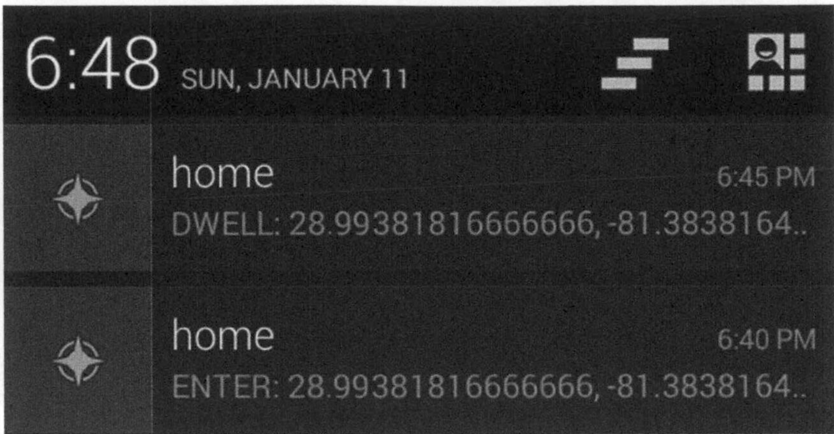

Figure 19-8. Notifications from GeofencingApi events

The first event occurred at 6:40 pm and happened because the device was already inside the home region when the app was started. The second event at 6:45 pm is a dwell event because the device is still within the home region after the loitering delay of 5 minutes. Had the device left the home region before the screenshot was captured, there would have been an exit event from home. Note that the latitude and longitude in the notification are the actual location of the device and not necessarily the center of the region.

References

Here are helpful references you may wish to explore further.

- `www.androidbook.com/proandroid5/projects`. A list of downloadable projects related to this book. For this chapter, look for a zip file called `ProAndroid5_Ch19_Maps.zip`. This zip file contains all projects from this chapter, listed in separate root directories. There is also a `README.TXT` file that describes exactly how to import projects into an IDE from one of these zip files. There are some extra sample applications in here, including WhereAmI4, which contains custom info windows for markers.
- `https://developer.android.com/guide/topics/location/index.html`. The Android developer's guide for Location and Maps.
- `https://developer.android.com/google/play-services/index.html`. The Google Play Services documentation which includes the FusedLocationProviderApi, GeofencingApi and GoogleMap.
- `https://developer.android.com/google/play-services/setup.html`. Instructions for including the Google Play Services library into your application. Note the drop-down menu to allow choosing between Android Studio and Eclipse with ADT.
- `https://developers.google.com/maps/documentation/android/`. The Maps API documentation which is separate from the rest of the online Android documentation.

Summary

Let's conclude this chapter by quickly enumerating what you have learned about maps so far:

- How to get your own Maps API key from Google.
- `MapFragment`, the main component for all maps.
- The modifications you need to make to your `AndroidManifest.xml` file to get a maps application to work.
- Defining a layout to contain a map, and how to instantiate a map.
- Zooming in and out, panning and showing the current location.
- Including different modes such as satellite and traffic.
- How map tiles are used to render maps.
- Adding markers to your maps.
- Map cameras and methods to set a zoom level that accommodates a specific set of markers.
- The Geocoder, and how it converts from address to latitude/longitude, or from latitude/longitude to addresses and places of interest.
- Putting the `Geocoder` into a background thread to avoid nasty Application Not Responding (ANR) pop-ups.
- The `LocationServices` service, which uses GPS and/or network towers to pinpoint the location of the device.
- Selecting a location provider, and what to do if the desired location service or provider is not enabled.
- Using the emulator's features to send location events to your application for testing. This includes using special files that record entire series of location events.
- Using methods of the `Location` class to, for example, calculate distances between points.
- How to do all of the checks and corrective actions to set up Google Play Services for Location Updates.
- Alerting on proximity—that is, setting up a proximity and being alerted when the device enters or leaves that proximity.
- Setting up geofences to act on enter, exit, and dwell events for one or more regions while conserving battery life.

Chapter 20

Understanding the Media Frameworks

Now we are going to explore a very interesting part of the Android SDK: the media frameworks. We will show you how to play audio and video from a variety of sources. We'll also cover in the online companion section how to take photos with the camera and record audio and video.

Using the Media APIs

Android supports playing audio and video content under the `android.media` package. In this chapter, we are going to explore the media APIs from this package.

At the heart of the `android.media` package is the `android.media.MediaPlayer` class. The `MediaPlayer` class is responsible for playing both audio and video content. The content for this class can come from the following sources:

- *Web*: You can play content from the Web via a URL.
- `.apk` *file*: You can play content that is packaged as part of your `.apk` file. You can package the media content as a resource or as an asset (within the `assets` folder).
- The *Storage Access Framework*, new to Android KitKat 4.4, which provides access to media files stored across a range of providers and internet services.
- *SD card*: You can play content that resides on the device's SD card or emulated local storage.

The MediaPlayer is capable of decoding quite a few different content formats, including 3rd Generation Partnership Project (3GPP, `.3gp`), MP3 (`.mp3`), MIDI (`.mid` and others), Ogg Vorbis (`.ogg`), PCM/WAVE (`.wav`), and MPEG-4 (`.mp4`). RTSP, HTTP/HTTPS live streaming, and M3U playlists are also supported, although playlists that include URLs are not, at least as of this writing. For a complete list of supported media formats, go to `http://developer.android.com/guide/appendix/media-formats.html`.

Whither SD Cards?

Before we dive in to the heart of the media frameworks, we should quickly address the topic of removable storage, and SD Cards in particular. Recent trends in Android devices have seen some manufacturers drop them from devices, while others continue to include them. Google itself has blurred the lines of what is and isn't removal storage by obfuscating the low-level file systems in Android.

Regardless of your personal preference as a developer, some of your users will likely still have devices that support SD Cards and want to use them. Many of the examples we'll cover here are equally applicable to sourcing media files from SD Cards. However, to save space, and spare you unneeded repetition, we've placed some extra examples that go into SD Card details and supporting material on the book's website. Be sure to check it out at `www.androidbook.com`.

Playing Media

To get started, we'll show you how to build a simple application that plays an MP3 file located on the Web (see Figure 20-1). After that, we will talk about using the `setDataSource()` method of the `MediaPlayer` class to play content from the `.apk` file. `MediaPlayer` isn't the only way to play audio, though, so we'll also cover the `SoundPool` class, as well as `JetPlayer`, `AsyncPlayer`, and, for the lowest level of working with audio, the `AudioTrack` class. After that, we will discuss some of the shortfalls of the `MediaPlayer` class. Finally, we'll see how to play video content.

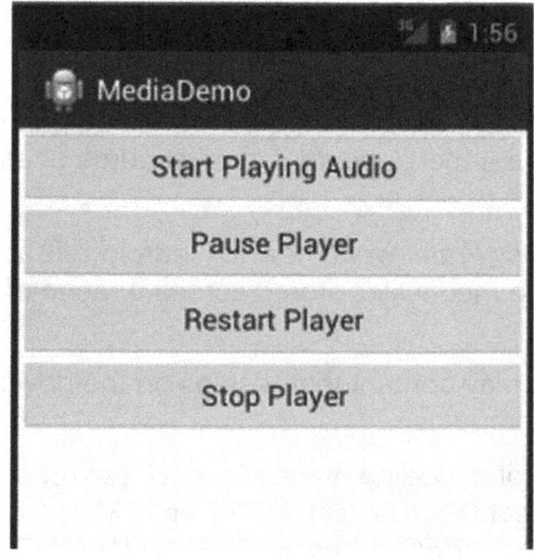

***Figure 20-1.** The user interface for the media application*

Playing Audio Content

Figure 20-1 shows the user interface for our first example. This application will demonstrate some of the fundamental uses of the `MediaPlayer` class, such as starting, pausing, restarting, and stopping the media file. Look at the layout for the application's user interface.

The user interface consists of a `RelativeLayout` with four buttons: one to start the player, one to pause the player, one to restart the player, and one to stop the player. We could have made this easy and just coupled our example with a `MediaController` widget that does the same thing, but we want to show you the inner workings of controlling things yourself. The code and layout file for the application are shown in Listing 20-1. We're going to assume you're building against Android 2.2 or later for this example, because we're using the `getExternalStoragePublicDirectory()` method of the `Environment` class. If you want to build this against an older version of Android, simply use `getExternalStorageDirectory()` instead and adjust where you put the media files so your application will find them.

> **Note** See the "References" section at the end of this chapter for the URL from which you can import these projects into Eclipse directly, instead of copying and pasting code.

Listing 20-1. The Layout and Code for the Media Application

```
<RelativeLayout xmlns:android="http://schemas.android.com/apk/res/android"
    xmlns:tools="http://schemas.android.com/tools"
    android:layout_width="match_parent"
    android:layout_height="match_parent"
    tools:context=".MainActivity"
    android:orientation="vertical" >

  <Button android:id="@+id/startPlayerBtn"
    android:layout_width="match_parent"
    android:layout_height="wrap_content"
    android:text="Start Playing Audio"
    android:onClick="doClick" />

  <Button android:id="@+id/pausePlayerBtn"
    android:layout_width="match_parent"
    android:layout_height="wrap_content"
    android:text="Pause Player"
    android:layout_below="@+id/startPlayerBtn"
    android:onClick="doClick" />

  <Button android:id="@+id/restartPlayerBtn"
    android:layout_width="match_parent"
    android:layout_height="wrap_content"
    android:text="Restart Player"
    android:layout_below="@+id/pausePlayerBtn"
    android:onClick="doClick" />
```

```
  <Button android:id="@+id/stopPlayerBtn"
    android:layout_width="match_parent"
    android:layout_height="wrap_content"
    android:text="Stop Player"
    android:layout_below="@+id/restartPlayerBtn"
    android:onClick="doClick" />

</RelativeLayout>

// This file is MainActivity.java
import android.app.Activity;
import android.content.res.AssetFileDescriptor;
import android.media.AudioManager;
import android.media.MediaPlayer;
import android.media.MediaPlayer.OnPreparedListener;
import android.os.Bundle;
import android.os.Environment;
import android.util.Log;
import android.view.View;

public class MainActivity extends Activity implements OnPreparedListener
{
    static final String AUDIO_PATH =
     "http://www.androidbook.com/akc/filestorage/android/documentfiles/3389/play.mp3";

    private MediaPlayer mediaPlayer;
    private int playbackPosition=0;

    /** Called when the activity is first created. */
    @Override
    public void onCreate(Bundle savedInstanceState) {
        super.onCreate(savedInstanceState);
        setContentView(R.layout.main);
    }

    public void doClick(View view) {
        switch(view.getId()) {
        case R.id.startPlayerBtn:
            try {
            // Only have one of these play methods uncommented
                playAudio(AUDIO_PATH);
//              playLocalAudio();
//              playLocalAudio_UsingDescriptor();
            } catch (Exception e) {
                e.printStackTrace();
            }
            break;
        case R.id.pausePlayerBtn:
            if(mediaPlayer != null && mediaPlayer.isPlaying()) {
                playbackPosition = mediaPlayer.getCurrentPosition();
                mediaPlayer.pause();
            }
            break;
```

```
        case R.id.restartPlayerBtn:
            if(mediaPlayer != null && !mediaPlayer.isPlaying()) {
                mediaPlayer.seekTo(playbackPosition);
                mediaPlayer.start();
            }
            break;
        case R.id.stopPlayerBtn:
            if(mediaPlayer != null) {
                mediaPlayer.stop();
                playbackPosition = 0;
            }
            break;
        }
    }

    private void playAudio(String url) throws Exception
    {
        killMediaPlayer();

        mediaPlayer = new MediaPlayer();
        mediaPlayer.setAudioStreamType(AudioManager.STREAM_MUSIC);
        mediaPlayer.setDataSource(url);
        mediaPlayer.setOnPreparedListener(this);
        mediaPlayer.prepareAsync();
    }

    private void playLocalAudio() throws Exception
    {
        mediaPlayer = MediaPlayer.create(this, R.raw.music_file);
        mediaPlayer.setAudioStreamType(AudioManager.STREAM_MUSIC);
        // calling prepare() is not required in this case
        mediaPlayer.start();
    }

    private void playLocalAudio_UsingDescriptor() throws Exception {

        AssetFileDescriptor fileDesc = getResources().openRawResourceFd(
                R.raw.music_file);
        if (fileDesc != null) {

            mediaPlayer = new MediaPlayer();
            mediaPlayer.setAudioStreamType(AudioManager.STREAM_MUSIC);
            mediaPlayer.setDataSource(fileDesc.getFileDescriptor(),
                    fileDesc.getStartOffset(), fileDesc.getLength());

            fileDesc.close();

            mediaPlayer.prepare();
            mediaPlayer.start();
        }
    }
```

```
    // This is called when the MediaPlayer is ready to start
    public void onPrepared(MediaPlayer mp) {
        mp.start();
    }

    @Override
    protected void onDestroy() {
        super.onDestroy();
        killMediaPlayer();
    }

    private void killMediaPlayer() {
        if(mediaPlayer!=null) {
            try {
                mediaPlayer.release();
            }
            catch(Exception e) {
                e.printStackTrace();
            }
        }
    }
}
```

In this first scenario, you are playing an MP3 file from a web address. Therefore, you will need to add android.permission.INTERNET to your manifest file. Listing 20-1 shows that the MainActivity class contains three members: a final string that points to the URL of the MP3 file, a MediaPlayer instance, and an integer member called playbackPosition. Our onCreate() method just sets up the user interface from our layout XML file. In the button-click handler, when the Start Playing Audio button is pressed, the playAudio() method is called. In the playAudio() method, a new instance of the MediaPlayer is created, and the data source of the player is set to the URL of the MP3 file.

The prepareAsync() method of the player is then called to prepare the MediaPlayer for playback. We're in the main UI thread of our activity, so we don't want to take too long to prepare the MediaPlayer. There is a prepare() method on MediaPlayer, but it blocks until the prepare is complete. If this takes a long time, or if the server takes a while to respond, the user could think the application is stuck or, worse, get an error message. Things like progress dialogs can help your user understand what is happening. The prepareAsync() method returns immediately but sets up a background thread to handle the prepare() method of the MediaPlayer. When the preparation is complete, our activity's onPrepared() callback is called. This is where we ultimately start the MediaPlayer playing. We have to tell the MediaPlayer who the listener is for the onPrepared() callback, which is why we call setOnPreparedListener() just before the call to prepareAsync(). You don't have to use the current activity as the listener; we do here because it's simpler for this demonstration.

Now look at the code for the Pause Player and Restart Player buttons. You can see that when the Pause Player button is selected, you get the current position of the player by calling getCurrentPosition(). You then pause the player by calling pause(). When the player has to be restarted, you call seekTo(), passing in the position obtained earlier from getCurrentPosition(), and then call start().

The MediaPlayer class also contains a stop() method. Note that if you stop the player by calling stop(), you need to prepare the MediaPlayer again before calling start() again. Conversely, if you call pause(), you can call start() again without having to prepare the player. Also, be sure to call the release() method of the media player once you are done using it. In this example, you do this as part of the killMediaPlayer() method.

There is a second URL in the sample application source code for an audio source, but it is not an MP3 file, it's a streaming audio feed (Radio-Mozart). This also works with the MediaPlayer and shows again why you need to call prepareAsync() instead of prepare(). Preparing an audio stream for playback can take a while, depending on the server, network traffic, and so on.

Listing 20-1 shows you how to play an audio file located on the Web. The MediaPlayer class also supports playing media local to your .apk file. Listing 20-2 shows how to reference and play back a file from the /res/raw folder of your .apk file. Go ahead and add the raw folder under /res if it's not already there in the Eclipse project. Then, copy the MP3 file of your choice into /res/raw with the file name music_file.mp3. Note also the comment in the original code to uncomment the desired call to playLocalAudio(), and commenting out playAudio().

Listing 20-2. Using the MediaPlayer to Play Back a File Local to the Application

```
private void playLocalAudio()throws Exception
{
    mediaPlayer = MediaPlayer.create(this, R.raw.music_file);
    mediaPlayer.setAudioStreamType(AudioManager.STREAM_MUSIC);
    // calling prepare() is not required in this case
    mediaPlayer.start();
}
```

If you need to include an audio or video file with your application, you should place the file in the /res/raw folder. You can then get a MediaPlayer instance for the resource by passing in the resource ID of the media file. You do this by calling the static create() method, as shown in Listing 20-2. Note that the MediaPlayer class provides a few other static create() methods that you can use to get a MediaPlayer rather than instantiating one yourself. In Listing 20-2, the create() method is equivalent to calling the constructor MediaPlayer(Context context,int resourceId) followed by a call to prepare(). You should use the create() method only when the media source is local to the device, because it always uses prepare() and not prepareAsync().

Understanding the setDataSource Method

In Listing 20-2, we called the create() method to load the audio file from a raw resource. With this approach, you don't need to call setDataSource(). Alternatively, if you instantiate the MediaPlayer yourself using the default constructor, or if your media content is not accessible through a resource ID or a URI, you'll need to call setDataSource().

The setDataSource() method has overloaded versions that you can use to customize the data source for your specific needs. For example, Listing 20-3 shows how you can load an audio file from a raw resource using a FileDescriptor.

Listing 20-3. Setting the MediaPlayer's Data Source using a `FileDescriptor`

```
private void playLocalAudio_UsingDescriptor() throws Exception {

    AssetFileDescriptor fileDesc = getResources().openRawResourceFd(
            R.raw.music_file);
    if (fileDesc != null) {

        mediaPlayer = new MediaPlayer();
        mediaPlayer.setAudioStreamType(AudioManager.STREAM_MUSIC);
        mediaPlayer.setDataSource(fileDesc.getFileDescriptor(),
                fileDesc.getStartOffset(), fileDesc.getLength());

        fileDesc.close();

        mediaPlayer.prepare();
        mediaPlayer.start();
    }
}
```

Listing 20-3 assumes that it's within the context of an activity. As shown, you call the `getResources()` method to get the application's resources and then use the `openRawResourceFd()` method to get a file descriptor for an audio file within the `/res/raw` folder. You then call the `setDataSource()` method using the `AssetFileDescriptor`, the starting position to begin playback, and the ending position. You can also use this version of `setDataSource()` if you want to play back a specific portion of an audio file. If you always want to play the entire file, you can call the simpler version of `setDataSource(FileDescriptor desc)`, which does not require the initial offset and length.

In this case, we chose to use `prepare()` followed by `start()`, only to show you what it might look like. We should be able to get away with it because the audio resource is local, but it won't hurt to use `prepareAsync()` as before.

We have one more source for audio content to talk about: the SD card. Refer to the online companion chapter for the basics on dealing with the SD card and its file system contents. In our example, we used `setDataSource()` to access content on the Internet by passing in a URL for an MP3 file. If you've got an audio file on your SD card, you can use the same `setDataSource()` method but instead pass it the path to your audio file on the SD card. For example, a file called `music_file.mp3` in the Music directory can be played with the `AUDIO_PATH` variable set like so:

```
static final String AUDIO_PATH =
Environment.getExternalStoragePublicDirectory(
    Environment.DIRECTORY_MUSIC) +
    "/music_file.mp3";
```

You may have noticed that we did not implement `onResume()` and `onPause()` in our example. This means that when our activity goes into the background, it continues to play audio—at least, until the activity is killed, or until access to the audio source is turned off. For example, if we do not hold a wake lock, the CPU could be shut down, thus ending the playing of music. Many people choose to manage media playback in a service to aid in working around these issues. In our current example, additional issues include if MediaPlayer is playing an audio stream over Wi-Fi, and if our activity does not obtain a lock on Wi-Fi, Wi-Fi could be turned off, and we'll lose our connection to the stream. MediaPlayer has a method called setWakeMode() that allows us to set a PARTIAL_WAKE_LOCK to keep the CPU alive while playing. However, in order to lock Wi-Fi, we need to do that separately through WifiManager and WifiManager.WifiLock.

The other aspect of continuing to play audio in the background is that we need to know when not to do so, perhaps because there's an incoming phone call, or because an alarm is going off. Android has an AudioManager to help with this. The methods to call include requestAudioFocus() and abandonAudioFocus(), and there's a callback method called onAudioFocusChange() in the interface AudioManager.OnAudioFocusChangeListener. For more information, see the Media page in the Android Developer's Guide.

Using SoundPool for Simultaneous Track Playing

The MediaPlayer is an essential tool in our media toolbox, but it only handles one audio or video file at a time. What if we want to play more than one audio track simultaneously? One way is to create multiple MediaPlayers and work with them at the same time. If you only have a small amount of audio to play, and you want snappy performance, Android has the SoundPool class to help you. Behind the scenes, SoundPool uses MediaPlayer, but we don't get access to the MediaPlayer API, just the SoundPool API.

One of the other differences between MediaPlayer and SoundPool is that SoundPool is designed to work with local media files only. That is, you can load audio from resource files, files elsewhere using file descriptors, or files using a pathname. There are several other nice features that SoundPool provides, such as the ability to loop an audio track, pause and resume individual audio tracks, or pause and resume all audio tracks.

There are some downsides to SoundPool, though. There is an overall audio buffer size in memory for all the tracks that SoundPool will manage of only 1MB. This might seem large when you look at MP3 files that are only a few kilobytes in size. But SoundPool expands the audio in memory to make the playback fast and easy. The size of an audio file in memory depends on the bit rate, number of channels (stereo versus mono), sample rate, and length of the audio. If you have trouble getting your sounds loaded into SoundPool, you could try playing with these parameters of your source audio file to make the audio smaller in memory.

Our example application will load and play animal sounds. One of the sounds is of crickets and it plays constantly in the background. The other sounds play at different intervals of time. Sometimes all you hear are crickets; other times you will hear several animals all at the same time. We'll also put a button in the user interface to allow for pausing and resuming. Listing 20-4 shows our layout XML file and the Java code of our activity. Your best bet is to download this from our web site, in order to get the sound files as well as the code. See the "References" section at the end of this chapter for information on how to locate the downloadable source code.

Listing 20-4. Playing Audio with SoundPool

```
<?xml version="1.0" encoding="utf-8"?>
<LinearLayout xmlns:android="http://schemas.android.com/apk/res/android"
    android:orientation="vertical"
    android:layout_width="fill_parent"  android:layout_height="fill_parent"
    >
<ToggleButton android:id="@+id/button"
    android:textOn="Pause"  android:textOff="Resume"
    android:layout_width="wrap_content"  android:layout_height="wrap_content"
    android:onClick="doClick" android:checked="true" />
</LinearLayout>

// This file is MainActivity.java
import java.io.IOException;
import android.app.Activity;
import android.content.Context;
import android.content.res.AssetFileDescriptor;
import android.media.AudioManager;
import android.media.SoundPool;
import android.os.Bundle;
import android.os.Handler;
import android.util.Log;
import android.view.View;
import android.widget.ToggleButton;

public class MainActivity extends Activity implements SoundPool.OnLoadCompleteListener {
    private static final int SRC_QUALITY = 0;
    private static final int PRIORITY = 1;
    private SoundPool soundPool = null;
    private AudioManager aMgr;

    private int sid_background;
    private int sid_roar;
    private int sid_bark;
    private int sid_chimp;
    private int sid_rooster;

    @Override
    public void onCreate(Bundle savedInstanceState) {
        super.onCreate(savedInstanceState);
        setContentView(R.layout.main);
    }

    @Override
    protected void onResume() {
        soundPool = new SoundPool(5, AudioManager.STREAM_MUSIC,
                SRC_QUALITY);
        soundPool.setOnLoadCompleteListener(this);

        aMgr =
            (AudioManager)this.getSystemService(Context.AUDIO_SERVICE);
```

```
        sid_background = soundPool.load(this, R.raw.crickets, PRIORITY);

        sid_chimp = soundPool.load(this, R.raw.chimp, PRIORITY);
        sid_rooster = soundPool.load(this, R.raw.rooster, PRIORITY);
        sid_roar = soundPool.load(this, R.raw.roar, PRIORITY);

        try {
            AssetFileDescriptor afd =
                    this.getAssets().openFd("dogbark.mp3");
            sid_bark = soundPool.load(afd.getFileDescriptor(),
                                    0, afd.getLength(), PRIORITY);
            afd.close();
        } catch (IOException e) {
            e.printStackTrace();
        }
        //sid_bark = soundPool.load("/mnt/sdcard/dogbark.mp3", PRIORITY);

        super.onResume();
    }

    public void doClick(View view) {
        switch(view.getId()) {
        case R.id.button:
            if(((ToggleButton)view).isChecked()) {
                soundPool.autoResume();
            }
            else {
                soundPool.autoPause();
            }
            break;
        }
    }

    @Override
    protected void onPause() {
        soundPool.release();
        soundPool = null;
        super.onPause();
    }

    @Override
    public void onLoadComplete(SoundPool sPool, int sid, int status) {
        Log.v("soundPool", "sid " + sid + " loaded with status " +
                status);

        final float currentVolume =
            ((float)aMgr.getStreamVolume(AudioManager.STREAM_MUSIC)) /
            ((float)aMgr.getStreamMaxVolume(AudioManager.STREAM_MUSIC));
```

```
        if(status != 0)
            return;
        if(sid == sid_background) {
            if(sPool.play(sid, currentVolume, currentVolume,
                    PRIORITY, -1, 1.0f) == 0)
                Log.v("soundPool", "Failed to start sound");
        } else if(sid == sid_chimp) {
            queueSound(sid, 5000, currentVolume);
        } else if(sid == sid_rooster) {
            queueSound(sid, 6000, currentVolume);
        } else if(sid == sid_roar) {
            queueSound(sid, 12000, currentVolume);
        } else if(sid == sid_bark) {
            queueSound(sid, 7000, currentVolume);
        }
    }

    private void queueSound(final int sid, final long delay,
        final float volume)
    {
        new Handler().postDelayed(new Runnable() {
            @Override
            public void run() {
                if(soundPool == null) return;
                if(soundPool.play(sid, volume, volume,
                        PRIORITY, 0, 1.0f) == 0)
                    Log.v("soundPool", "Failed to start sound (" + sid +
                            ")");
                queueSound(sid, delay, volume);
            }}, delay);
    }
}
```

The structure of this example is fairly straightforward. We have a user interface with a single ToggleButton on it. We'll use this to pause and resume the active audio streams. When our app starts, we create our SoundPool and load it up with audio samples. When the samples are properly loaded, we start playing them. The crickets sound plays in a neverending loop; the other samples play after a delay and then set themselves up to play again after the same delay. By choosing different delays, we get a somewhat random effect of sounds on top of sounds.

Creating a SoundPool requires three parameters:

- The first is the maximum number of samples that the SoundPool will play simultaneously. This is not how many samples the SoundPool can hold.
- The second parameter is which audio stream the samples will play on. The typical value is AudioManager.STREAM_MUSIC, but SoundPool can be used for alarms or ringtones. See the AudioManager reference page for the complete list of audio streams.
- The SRC_QUALITY value should just be set to 0 when creating the SoundPool.

The code demonstrates several different `load()` methods of `SoundPool`. The most basic is to load an audio file from `/res/raw` as a resource. We use this method for the first four audio files. Then we show how you could load an audio file from the `/assets` directory of the application. This `load()` method also takes parameters that specify the offset and the length of the audio to load. This would allow us to use a single file with multiple audio samples in it, pulling out just what we want to use. Finally, we show in comments how you might access an audio file from the SD card. Up through Android 4.0, the `PRIORITY` parameter should just be 1.

For our example, we chose to use some of the features introduced in Android 2.2, specifically the `onLoadCompleteListener` interface for our activity, and the `autoPause()` and `autoResume()` methods in our button callback.

When loading sound samples into a `SoundPool`, we must wait until they are properly loaded before we can start playing them. Within our `onLoadComplete()` callback, we check the status of the load, and, depending on which sound it is, we then set it up to play. If the sound is the crickets, we play with looping turned on (a value of `-1` for the fifth parameter). For the others, we queue the sound up to play after a short period of time. The time values are in milliseconds. Note the setting of the volume. Android provides the `AudioManager` to let us know the current volume setting. We also get the maximum volume setting from `AudioManager` so we can calculate a volume value for `play()` that is between 0 and 1 (as a float). The `play()` method actually takes a separate volume value for the left and right channels, but we just set both to the current volume. Again, `PRIORITY` should just be set to 1. The last parameter on the `play()` method is for setting the playback rate. This value should be between 0.5 and 2.0, with 1.0 being normal.

Our `queueSound()` method uses a `Handler` to basically set up an event into the future. Our `Runnable` will run after the delay period has elapsed. We check to be sure we still have a `SoundPool` to play from, then we play the sound once and schedule the same sound to play again after the same interval as before. Because we call `queueSound()` with different sound IDs and different delays, the effect is a somewhat random playing of animal sounds.

When you run this example, you'll hear crickets, a chimp, a rooster, a dog, and a roar (a bear, we think). The crickets are constantly chirping while the other animals come and go. One nice thing about `SoundPool` is that it lets us play multiple sounds at the same time with no real work on our part. Also, we're not taxing the device too badly, because the sounds were decoded at load time, and we simply need to feed the sound bits to the hardware.

If you click the button, the crickets will stop, as will any other animal sound currently being played. However, the `autoPause()` method does not prevent new sounds from being played. You'll hear the animal sounds again within seconds (except for the crickets). Because we've been queuing up sounds into the future, we will still hear those sounds. In fact, `SoundPool` does not have a way to stop all sounds now and in the future. You'll need to handle stopping on your own. The crickets will only come back if we click the button again to resume the sounds. But even then, we might have lost the crickets because `SoundPool` will throw out the oldest sound to make room for newer sounds if the maximum number of simultaneously playing samples is reached.

Playing Sounds with JetPlayer

SoundPool is not too bad a player, but the memory limitations can make it difficult to get the job done. An alternative when you need to play simultaneous sounds is JetPlayer. Tailored for games, JetPlayer is a very flexible tool for playing lots of sounds and for coordinating those sounds with user actions. The sounds are defined using Musical Instrument Digital Interface (MIDI).

JetPlayer sounds are created using a special JETCreator tool. This tool is provided under the Android SDK tools directory, although you'll also need to install Python in order to use it, and it is limited to the Mac OSX and Windows SDK packages. The resulting JET file can be read into your application, and the sounds set up for playback. The whole process is somewhat involved and beyond the scope of this book, so we'll just point you to more information in the "References" section at the end of this chapter.

Playing Background Sounds with AsyncPlayer

If all you want is some audio played, and you don't want to tie up the current thread, the AsyncPlayer may be what you're looking for. The audio source is passed as a URI to this class, so the audio file could be local or remote over the network. This class automatically creates a background thread to handle getting the audio and starting the playback. Because it is asynchronous, you won't know exactly when the audio will start. Nor will you know when it ends, or even if it's still playing. You can, however, call stop() to get the audio to stop playing. If you call play() again before the previous audio has finished playing, the previous audio will immediately stop and the new audio will begin at some time in the future when everything has been set up and fetched. This is a very simple class that provides an automatic background thread. Listing 20-5 shows how your code should look to implement this.

Listing 20-5. ***Playing Audio with AsyncPlayer***

```
private static final String TAG = "AsyncPlayerDemo";
private AsyncPlayer mAsync = null;

[ ... ]

    mAsync = new AsyncPlayer(TAG);
    mAsync.play(this, Uri.parse("file://" + "/perry_ringtone.mp3"),
            false, AudioManager.STREAM_MUSIC);

[ ... ]

@Override
protected void onPause() {
    mAsync.stop();
    super.onPause();
}
```

Low-Level Audio Playback Using AudioTrack

So far, we've been dealing with audio from files, be they local files or remote files. If you want to get down to a lower level, perhaps playing audio from a stream, you need to investigate the AudioTrack class. Besides the usual methods like play() and pause(), AudioTrack provides methods for writing bytes to the audio hardware. This class gives you the most control over audio playback, but it is much more complicated than the audio classes discussed so far in this chapter. One of our online companion sample applications uses the AudioRecord class. The AudioRecord class is very much like the AudioTrack class, so to get a better understanding of the AudioTrack class, refer to the AudioRecord sample later on.

More About MediaPlayer

In general, the MediaPlayer is very systematic, so you need to call operations in a specific order to initialize a MediaPlayer properly and prepare it for playback. The following list summarizes some of the other details you should know for using the media APIs:

- Once you set the data source of a MediaPlayer, you cannot easily change it to another one—you'll have to create a new MediaPlayer or call the reset() method to reinitialize the state of the player.
- After you call prepare(), you can call getCurrentPosition(), getDuration(), and isPlaying() to get the current state of the player. You can also call the setLooping() and setVolume() methods after the call to prepare(). If you used prepareAsync(), you should wait until onPrepared() is called before using any of these other methods.
- After you call start(), you can call pause(), stop(), and seekTo().
- Every MediaPlayer you create uses a lot of resources, so be sure to call the release() method when you are done with the media player. The VideoView takes care of this in the case of video playback, but you'll have to do it manually if you decide to use MediaPlayer instead of VideoView. More about VideoView in the next sections.
- MediaPlayer works with several listeners you can use for additional control over the user experience, including OnCompletionListener, OnErrorListener, and OnInfoListener. For example, if you're managing a playlist of audio, OnCompletionListener will be called when a piece is finished so you can queue up the next piece.

This concludes our discussion about playing audio content. Now we'll turn our attention to playing video. As you will see, referencing video content is similar to referencing audio content.

Playing Video Content

In this section, we are going to discuss video playback using the Android SDK. Specifically, we will discuss playing a video from a web server and playing one from an SD card. As you can imagine, video playback is a bit more involved than audio playback. Fortunately, the Android SDK provides some additional abstractions that do most of the heavy lifting.

> **Note** Playing back video in the emulator is not very reliable. If it works, great. But if it doesn't, try running on a device instead. Because the emulator must use only software to run video, it can have a very hard time keeping up with video, and you will likely get unexpected results.

Playing video requires more effort than playing audio, because there's a visual component to take care of in addition to the audio. To take some of the pain away, Android provides a specialized view control called `android.widget.VideoView` that encapsulates creating and initializing the `MediaPlayer`. To play video, you create a `VideoView` widget in your user interface. You then set the path or URI of the video and fire the `start()` method. Listing 20-6 demonstrates video playback in Android.

Listing 20-6. Playing Video Using the Media APIs

```
<?xml version="1.0" encoding="utf-8"?>
<!-- This file is /res/layout/main.xml -->
<LinearLayout
 android:layout_width="fill_parent" android:layout_height="fill_parent"
 xmlns:android="http://schemas.android.com/apk/res/android">

    <VideoView  android:id="@+id/videoView"
        android:layout_width="200px"  android:layout_height="200px" />

</LinearLayout>

// This file is MainActivity.java
import android.app.Activity;
import android.net.Uri;
import android.os.Bundle;
import android.widget.MediaController;
import android.widget.VideoView;

public class MainActivity extends Activity {
    /** Called when the activity is first created. */
    @Override
    protected void onCreate(Bundle savedInstanceState) {
        super.onCreate(savedInstanceState);
        this.setContentView(R.layout.main);

        VideoView videoView =
               (VideoView)this.findViewById(R.id.videoView);
        MediaController mc = new MediaController(this);
        videoView.setMediaController(mc);
        videoView.setVideoURI(Uri.parse(
              "http://www.androidbook.com/akc/filestorage/android/" +
               "documentfiles/3389/movie.mp4"));
 /* videoView.setVideoPath(
    Environment.getExternalStoragePublicDirectory(
    Environment.DIRECTORY_MOVIES) +
    "/movie.mp4");
```

```
*/
        videoView.requestFocus();
        videoView.start();
    }
}
```

Listing 20-6 demonstrates video playback of a file located on the Web at www.androidbook.com/akc/filestorage/android/documentfiles/3389/movie.mp4, which means the application running the code will need to request the android.permission.INTERNET permission. All of the playback functionality is hidden behind the VideoView class. In fact, all you have to do is feed the video content to the video player. The user interface of the application is shown in Figure 20-2.

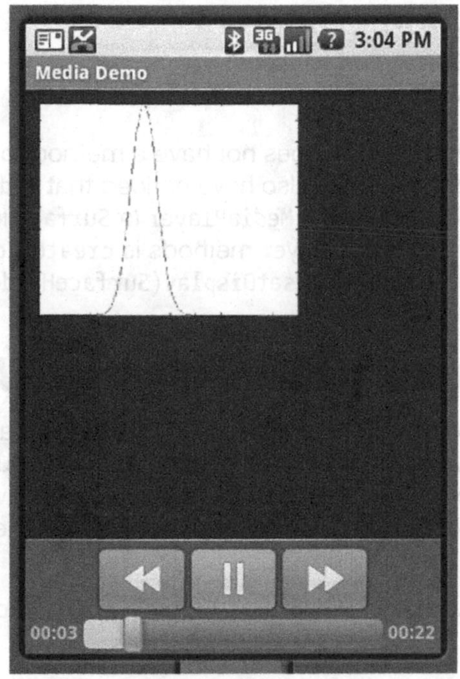

***Figure 20-2.** The video playback UI with media controls enabled*

When this application runs, you will see the button controls along the bottom of the screen for about three seconds, and then they disappear. You get them back by clicking anywhere within the video frame. When we were doing playback of audio content, we needed to display the button controls only to start, pause, and restart the audio. We did not need a view component for the audio itself. With video, of course, we need button controls as well as something to view the video in. For this example, we're using a VideoView component to display the video content. But instead of creating our own button controls (which we could still do if we chose to), we create a MediaController that provides the buttons for us. As shown in Figure 20-2 and Listing 20-6, you set the VideoView's media controller by calling setMediaController() to enable the play, pause, and seek-to controls. If you want to manipulate the video programmatically with your own buttons, you can call the start(), pause(), stopPlayback(), and seekTo() methods.

Keep in mind that we're still using a MediaPlayer in this example—we just don't see it. You can in fact "play" videos directly in MediaPlayer. If you go back to the example from Listing 20-1, put a movie file on your SD card, and plug in the movie's file path in AUDIO_PATH, you will find that it plays the audio quite nicely even though you can't see the video.

Whereas MediaPlayer has a setDataSource() method, VideoView does not. VideoView instead uses the setVideoPath() or setVideoURI() methods. Assuming you put a movie file onto your SD card, you change the code from Listing 20-6 to comment out the setVideoURI() call and uncomment the setVideoPath() call, adjusting the path to the movie file as necessary. When you run the application again, you will now hear *and see* the video in the VideoView. Technically, we could have called setVideoURI() with the following to get the same effect as setVideoPath():

```
videoView.setVideoURI(Uri.parse("file://" +
    Environment.getExternalStoragePublicDirectory(
    Environment.DIRECTORY_MOVIES) + "/movie.mp4"));
```

You might have noticed that VideoView does not have a method to read data from a file descriptor as MediaPlayer did. You may also have noticed that MediaPlayer has a couple of methods for adding a SurfaceHolder to a MediaPlayer (a SurfaceHolder is like a view port for images or video). One of the MediaPlayer methods is create(Context context, Uri uri, SurfaceHolder holder), and the other is setDisplay(SurfaceHolder holder).

Bonus Online Chapter on Recording and Advanced Media

Now that you have mastered many of the aspects of media playback, including the variety of methods to build your own audio and video capabilities into your application, there are a few more areas to explore on the topic that are almost a book's worth of content in their own right. So we have put them together into another bonus online chapter that explores the following:

- Audio recording with MediaRecorder, AudioRecord, and other techniques
- Video recording from the ground up
- Camera and camcorder profiles for video recording
- Using intents and the MediaStore class to have other applications do all your recording for you!

Take a look at the online material for the Audio and Video Recording bonus chapter.

References

Here are some helpful references to topics you may wish to explore further:

- www.androidbook.com/proandroid5/projects: A list of downloadable projects related to this book. For the projects in this chapter, look for a zip file called ProAndroid5_Ch20_Media.zip. This zip file contains all the projects from this chapter, listed in separate root directories. There is also a README.TXT file that describes exactly how to import projects into Eclipse from one of these zip files.
- http://developer.android.com/guide/topics/media/jet/jetcreator_manual.html: The user manual for the JETCreator tool. You can use this to create a JET sound file to be played using the JetPlayer. JETCreator is only available for Windows and Mac OS. To see JetPlayer in action, load the JetBoy sample project from the Android SDK into Eclipse, build it, and run it. Note that the Fire button is the center directional pad key.

Summary

Here is a summary the topics covered in this media chapter on audio and video:

- Playing audio through a MediaPlayer
- Several ways to source audio for MediaPlayer, from local application resources, to files, to streaming over the network
- Steps to take with a MediaPlayer to get the audio to come out properly
- SoundPool and its ability to play several sounds simultaneously
- SoundPool's limitations in terms of the amount of audio it can handle
- AsyncPlayer, which is useful because sounds generally need to be managed in the background
- AudioTrack, which provides low-level access to audioPlaying video using VideoView

Chapter 21

Home Screen Widgets

Home screen widgets in Android present frequently changing information on the home screen of Android. Home screen widgets are disconnected views displayed on the home screen. Data content of these views is updated at regular intervals by background processes or just kept as a static view.

For example, an e-mail home screen widget might alert you to the number of outstanding e-mails to be read. The widget may just show you the number of e-mails and not the messages themselves. Clicking the e-mail count may then take you to the activity that displays actual e-mails. These could even be external e-mail sources such as Yahoo, Gmail, and Hotmail, as long as the device has a way to access the counts through HTTP or other connectivity mechanisms.

In the Android SDK a widget is declaratively defined. A widget definition contains the following:

- A view layout to be displayed on the home screen, along with how big it should be to fit on a home page.
- A timer that specifies the frequency of updates.
- A broadcast receiver Java class called a widget provider that can respond to timer updates in order to alter the view in some fashion by populating with data.
- An activity class that is responsible for collecting the input necessary to further configure the widget to be displayed.

The timer, the receiver, and the configuration activity are optional. Once a widget is defined and the Java classes are provided, the widget will be available for the user to drag onto a home page. The view and the corresponding Java classes are architected in such a way that they are disconnected from each other. For example, any Android service or activity can retrieve the view using its layout ID, populate that view with data (just like populating a template), and send it to the home screen. Once the view is sent to the home screen, it is dislodged from the underlying Java code.

Before we show you how to implement a widget, we'll first give you an overview of how a widget is used by an end user.

User Experience with Home Screen Widgets

Home screen widget functionality in Android allows you to choose a preprogrammed widget to be placed on the home screen. When placed, the widget will allow you to configure it using an activity (defined as part of the widget package), if necessary. It is important to understand this interaction before actually going into the details of how a widget is implemented.

We are going to walk you through a widget called Birthday Widget that we have created for this chapter. We will present the source code for it later in the chapter. First, we are going to use this widget as an example for our walkthrough. As a consequence of source code coming later, we need your consideration to read along and follow the pictures and not look for this widget on your screen. If you follow the provided figures and explanation, you will know the nature and behavior of the Birthday Widget, which will make things clear when we code it subsequently.

Let's start this tour by locating the widget we want and creating an instance of it on the home screen. The way you access the available widget list is different depending on the Android release. Usually though, the list of widgets is kept alongside the list of applications available on your device. Here is an example from API 16 (or Jellybean version of Android) in Figure 21-1.

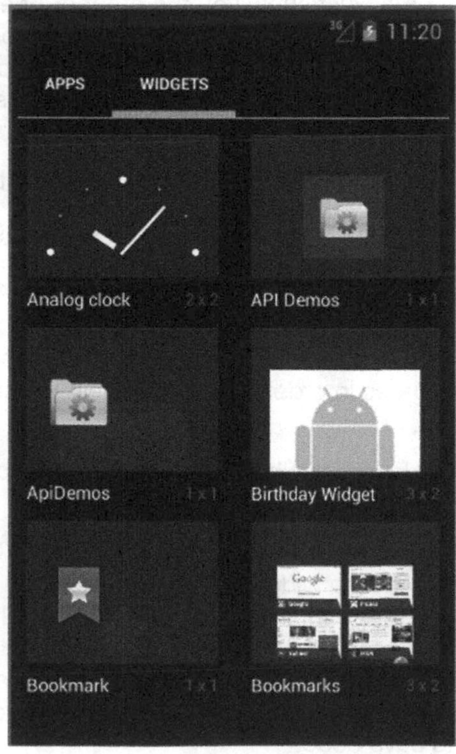

***Figure 21-1.** Home screen widget pick list*

In the list of widgets in Figure 21-1, the *Birthday Widget* is designed for this chapter. If you choose this widget, Android allows you to drag it to one of pages of your home screen. Android will create a corresponding widget instance on the home screen that looks like the example Birthday Widget shown in Figure 21-2.

***Figure 21-2.** An example Birthday Widget*

Birthday Widget in Figure 21-2 will indicate in its header the name of the person, how many days away this person's birthday is, when the date of birth falls this year, and a link to buy gifts. You may be wondering how the name of the person and date of birth were configured. What if you want two instances of this widget, each with the name and date of birth for a different person? This is where the widget configuration activity comes into play and is the topic we are covering next.

Understanding Widget Configuration Activity

A widget definition optionally includes a specification of an activity called a widget configuration activity. When you choose a widget from the home page widget pick list to create the widget instance, Android invokes the corresponding widget configuration activity if one is defined for it. This activity is something you need to code.

In case of our `BirthdayWidget`, this configuration activity will prompt you for the name of the person and the upcoming birth date, as shown in Figure 21-3. It is the responsibility of the configuration activity to save this information in a persistent place so that when an update is called on the widget provider, the widget provider will be able to locate this information and update the number of days until the birthday.

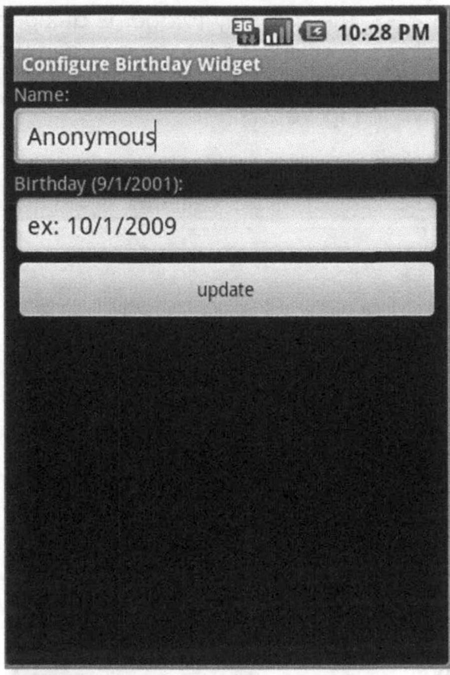

Figure 21-3. Birthday Widget configuration activity

> **Note** When a user chooses to create two Birthday Widget instances on the home screen, the configuration activity will be called twice (once for each widget instance).

Internally, Android keeps track of the widget instances by allocating them unique IDs. This unique widget instance ID is passed to the Java callbacks and to the configurator Java class so that initial configuration and updates can be directed to the right instance of the widget on the homepage. In Figure 21-2, in the later part of the string `satya:3`, the `3` is the widget instance ID.

Understanding the Life Cycle of a Widget

The life cycle of a widget has the following phases:

1. Widget definition
2. Widget instance creation
3. `onUpdate()` (when the time interval expires)
4. Responses to clicks (on the widget view on the home screen)
5. Widget deletion (from the home screen)
6. Uninstallation

We will go through these phases in detail now.

Understanding Widget Definition Phase

Widget definition starts with the definition of the widget provider class in the Android manifest file. Listing 21-1 shows the definition for the AppWidgetProvider that we have designed for this chapter called BDayWidgetProvider in the manifest file.

Listing 21-1. Widget Definition in Android Manifest File

```
<!-- filename: AndroidManifest.xml, project: ProAndroid5_ch21_TestWidgets.zip -->
<manifest..>
<application>
....
   <receiver android:name=".BDayWidgetProvider">
      <meta-data android:name="android.appwidget.provider"
            android:resource="@xml/bday_appwidget_provider" />
      <intent-filter>
            <action android:name="android.appwidget.action.APPWIDGET_UPDATE" />
      </intent-filter>
   </receiver>
   ...
   <activity>
      .....
   </activity>
</application>
</manifest>
```

This definition indicates that there is a broadcast receiver Java class called BDayWidgetProvider which receives application widget broadcast update messages. The widget class definition in Listing 21-1 also points to an XML file @xml/bday_appwidget_provider which is /res/xml/bday_appwidget_provider.xml. This XML file is in Listing 21-2. This widget definition file has a number of things about this widget such as its layout resource file, update frequency, etc.

Listing 21-2. Widget View Definition in Widget Provider Information XML File

```
<!-- /res/xml/bday_appwidget_provider.xml(ProAndroid5_ch21_TestWidgets.zip) -->
<appwidget-provider xmlns:android="http://schemas.android.com/apk/res/android"
    android:minWidth="150dp"
    android:minHeight="120dp"
    android:updatePeriodMillis="43200000"
    android:initialLayout="@layout/bday_widget"
    android:configure="com.androidbook.BDayWidget.ConfigureBDayWidgetActivity"
    android:resizeMode="horizontal|vertical"
    android:previewImage="@drawable/some_preview_image_icon"
    >
</appwidget-provider>
```

This XML file is called the App widget provider information file. Internally, this gets translated to the AppWidgetProviderInfo Java class. This file identifies the width and height of the layout to be 150dp and 120dp, respectively. This definition file also indicates the update frequency to be 12 hours translated to milliseconds. The widget definition also points to a layout file through the initialLayout attribute. This layout file (see future Listing 21-6) produces the widget look that is shown in Figure 21-2.

Understanding resize Mode Attribute

Starting with SDK 3.1, users have the ability to resize a widget that is placed on one of their images. The user sees resize handles when they long-click the widget and can then use these handles to resize. This resize can be horizontal, vertical, or none. You can combine horizontal and vertical to resize the widget in both dimensions, as shown in Listing 21-2. However, to take advantage of this, your widget controls should be laid out in such a way that they can expand and contract using their layout parameters. There is no callback to tell you what size your widget is.

Understanding previewImage Attribute

The preview image attribute in Listing 21-2 indicates what image or icon is used to show your widget in the list of available widgets. If you omit it, the default behavior is to show the main icon for your application package, which is indicated in the manifest file.

Understanding Widget Layout: initialLayout Attribute

The layout for widget views is restricted to contain only certain types of view elements. The views allowed in a widget layout are exposed through an interface called `RemoteViews`, and only certain views can be composed into this layout. Some of the allowed view elements are shown in Listing 21-3. Note that their subclasses are not supported—only those that are included in Listing 21-3.

Listing 21-3. Allowed View Controls in `RemoteViews`

```
FrameLayout
LinearLayout
RelativeLayout
GridLayout
AnalogClock
Button
Chronometer
ImageButton
ImageView
ProgressBar
TextView
ViewFlipper
ListView
GridView
StackView
AdapterViewFlipper
```

This list may grow with each release. The primary reason for restricting what is allowed in a remote view is that these views are disconnected from the processes that actually control them. These widget views are hosted by an application like the Home application. The controllers for these views are background processes that get invoked by timers. For this reason, these views are called remote views. There is a corresponding Java class called

RemoteViews that allows access to these views. In other words, programmers do not have direct access to these views to call methods on them. You have access to these views only through the RemoteViews (like a gatekeeper).

We will cover the relevant methods of a RemoteViews class when we explore the example in the next main section. For now, remember that only a limited set of views in Listing 21-3 are allowed in the widget layout file.

Understanding configure Attribute

The widget definition (Listing 21-2) uses the configure attribute to specify the configuration activity that needs to be invoked when the user creates a widget instance. This configuration activity specified in Listing 21-2 is the ConfigureBDayWidgetActivity. This activity (Figure 21-3) is like any other Android activity. Form fields on this activity are used to collect the information needed by a widget instance.

Understanding Widget Instance Creation Phase

When a user chooses a widget to create a widget instance, Android invokes the configuration activity (Figure 21-3) if it is defined in the configuration XML file for the widget. If this configuration activity is not defined then this phase skipped and the widget is presented directly on the home page. When invoked this configuration activity does the following:

1. Receive the widget instance ID from the invoking intent that started the configuration activity.
2. Prompt the user through form fields to collect the widget-instance–specific information.
3. Persist the widget instance information so that subsequent calls to AppWidgetProvider's onUpdate method have access to this information.
4. Prepare to display the widget view for the first time by retrieving the widget view layout and create a RemoteViews object with it.
5. Call methods on the RemoteViews object to set values on individual view objects, such as text and images.
6. Also use the RemoteViews object to register any onClick events on any of the subviews of the widget.
7. Tell the AppWidgetManager to paint the RemoteViews on the home screen using the instance ID of that widget.
8. Return the widget ID, and close.

Notice that the first population of the widget in this case is done by the configuration activity and not AppWidgetProvider's onUpdate() method.

> **Note** The configuration activity is optional. If the configuration activity is not specified, the call goes directly to the onUpdate() method of the AppWidgetProvider. It is up to onUpdate() to update the view.

Android will undertake this process for each widget instance that the user creates. Besides invoking the configuration activity, Android also invokes the onEnabled callback of the AppWidgetProvider. Let's briefly consider the callbacks on an AppWidgetProvider class by taking a look at the shell of our BDayWidgetProvider (see Listing 21-4). We will examine the complete listing of this file later in Listing 21-10.

Listing 21-4. A Widget Provider Shell

```
// filename: BDayWidgetProvider.java(ProAndroid5_ch21_TestWidgets.zip)
public class BDayWidgetProvider extends AppWidgetProvider {
    public void onUpdate(Context context, AppWidgetManager appWidgetManager,
                        int[] appWidgetIds){}
    public void onDeleted(Context context, int[] appWidgetIds){}
    public void onEnabled(Context context){}
    public void onDisabled(Context context) {}
}
```

The onEnabled() callback method indicates that there is at least one instance of the widget up and running on the home screen. This means a user must have dropped the widget on the home page at least once. In this call, you will need to enable receiving messages for this broadcast receiver component (you will see this in Listing 21-10). The SDK base class AppWidgetProvider has the functionality to enable or disable receiving broadcast messages.

The onDeleted() callback method is called when a user drags the widget instance view to the trash can. This is where you will need to delete any persistent values you are holding for that widget instance.

The onDisabled() callback method is called after the last widget instance is removed from the home screen. This happens when a user drags the last instance of a widget to the trash. You should use this method to unregister your interest in receiving any broadcast messages intended for this component (you will see this in Listing 21-9).

The onUpdate() callback method is called every time the timer specified in Listing 21-2 expires. This method is also called the very first time the widget instance is created if there is no configuration activity. If there is a configuration activity, this method is not called at the creation of a widget instance. This method will subsequently be called when the timer expires at the frequency indicated.

Understanding onUpdate Phase

Once the widget instance is on the home screen, the next significant event is the expiration of the timer. Android will call `onUpdate()` in response to that timer. Because `onUpdate()` is called is through a broadcast receiver, the corresponding Java process will be loaded and will remain live until the end of that call. Once the call returns, the process will be ready to be taken down.

Once you have the necessary data available to update the widget in the `onUpdate()` method, you can invoke the `AppWidgetManager` to paint the remote view. This goes to show that the `AppWidgetProvider` class is stateless and may even be incapable of maintaining static variables between invocations. This is because the Java process containing this broadcast receiver class could be taken down and reconstructed between two invocations, resulting in re-initialization of static variables.

As a result, you will need to come up with a scheme to remember state if that is required. You can save the state of the widget instance in a persistent store such as a file, shared preferences, or a SQLite database. In the examples in this chapter, we used shared preferences as the persistence API.

> **Caution** To save power, Google recommends that the duration of the updates be more than an hour, so the device won't wake up too often. Starting with the 2.0 API, there is a restriction of 30 minutes or more for the update timeout.

For durations that are shorter, such as only seconds, you need to call this `onUpdate()` method yourself by using the facilities in the `AlarmManager` class. When you use `AlarmManager`, you also have the option not to call `onUpdate()` but, instead, do the work of `onUpdate()` in alarm callbacks. Refer to Chapter 17 for working with the alarm manager.

This is what you typically need to do in an `onUpdate()` method:

1. Make sure the configurator has finished its work; otherwise, just return. This should not be problem in releases 2.0 and above, where the duration is expected to be longer. Otherwise, based on the update interval (when it is too small) it is possible that `onUpdate()` will be called before the user has finished configuring the widget in the configurator.
2. Retrieve the persisted data for that widget instance.
3. Retrieve the widget view layout, and create a `RemoteViews` object with it.
4. Call methods on the `RemoteViews` to set values on individual view objects such as text and images.

5. Register any `onClick` events on any of the views by using pending intents.
6. Tell the `AppWidgetManager` to paint the updated `RemoteViews` using the instance ID.

As you can see, there is a lot of overlap between what a configurator does initially and what the `onUpdate()` method does. You may want to reuse this functionality between the two places.

Understanding Widget View Mouse Click Event Callbacks

As stated, the `onUpdate()` method keeps the widget views up to date. The widget view and subelements in that view could have callbacks registered for a mouse click. Typically, the `onUpdate()` method uses a pending intent to register an action for an event like a mouse click. This action could then start a service or start an activity such as opening up a browser.

This invoked service or activity can then communicate back with the view, if needed, using the widget instance ID and the `AppWidgetManager`. Hence, it is important that the pending intent carries with it the widget instance ID.

Deleting a Widget Instance

Another distinct event that can happen to a widget instance is that it can get deleted. To do this, a user has to long-press the widget on the home screen. This will enable the trash can to show on the home screen. The user can then drag the widget instance to the trash can to delete the widget instance from the screen.

Doing so calls the `onDelete()` method of the widget provider. If you have saved any state information for this widget instance, you will need to delete that data in this `onDelete` method.

Android also calls `onDisable()` if the widget instance that has just been deleted is the last of the widget instances of this type. You will use this callback to clean up any persistence attributes that are stored for all widget instances and also unregister for callbacks from the widget `onUpdate()` broadcasts.

Uninstalling Widget Packages

There is a need to clean up the widgets if you are planning to uninstall and install a new release of your `.apk` file containing these widgets.

It is recommended that you remove or delete all widget instances before trying to uninstall the package. Follow the directions in the "Deleting a Widget Instance" section to delete each widget instance until none remain.

Then, you can uninstall and install the new release. This is especially important if you are using the Eclipse ADT to develop your widgets, because during the development time, ADT tries to do this every time you run the application. So, between runs, make sure you remove the widget instances.

Implementing A Sample Widget Application

So far, we have covered the theory and approach behind widgets. Let's create the sample widget whose behavior has been used as the example to explain widget architecture. We will develop, test, and deploy this Birthday Widget.

Each Birthday Widget instance will show a name, the date of the next birthday, and how many days from today until the birthday. It will also create an `onClick` area where you can click to buy gifts. This click will open a browser and take you to `www.google.com`.

The layout of the finished widget should look like Figure 21-4.

***Figure 21-4.** Birthday Widget look and feel*

The implementation of this widget consists of the following widget-related files. The entire project is also available for download at the URL mentioned in the "References" section of this chapter.

The basic files are

- `AndroidManifest.xml`: Where the `AppWidgetProvider` is defined (see Listing 21-5)
- `res/xml/bday_appwidget_provider.xml`: Widget dimensions and layout (see Listing 21-2)
- `res/layout/bday_widget.xml`: The widget layout (see Listing 21-6)
- `res/drawable/box1.xml`: Provides boxes for sections of the widget layout (see Listing 21-7)
- `src/.../BdayWidgetProvider.java`: Implementation of the AppWidgetProvider class (see Listing 21-10)

These files implement the widget configuration activity:

- `src/.../ConfigureBDayWidgetActivity.java`: Configuration activity (see Listing 21-8)
- `layout/edit_bday_widget.xml`: Layout for taking the name and birthday (see Listing 21-9)

These files store/retrieve the state of a widget instance using preferences:

- `src/.../IWidgetModelSaveContract.java`: Contract for saving and retrieving a widget's data (See in downloadable project)
- `src/.../APrefWidgetModel.java`: Abstract preference-based widget model that saves widget data in preferences (see in downloadable project)
- `src/.../BDayWidgetModel.java`: Widget model holding the data for a widget view (see in downloadable project)
- `src/.../Utils.java`: A few utility classes (see in downloadable project)

We will walk through some of the key files and explain any additional concepts that bear further consideration. You can get the rest of the files from the downloadable project for this chapter.

Defining the Widget Provider

For the Birthday Widget project the manifest file is in Listing 21-5. It has the declarations for the widget provider `BDayAppWidgetProvider` as a broadcast receiver and also the definition for the configuration activity `ConfigureBDayWidgetActivity`. Notice how the widget provider definition also points to the widget definition XML file `@xml/bday_appwidget_provider`.

Listing 21-5. Android Manifest File for `BDayWidget` Sample Application

```
<?xml version="1.0" encoding="utf-8"?>
<!-- file: AndroidManifest.xml(ProAndroid5_ch21_TestWidgets.zip) -->
<manifest xmlns:android="http://schemas.android.com/apk/res/android"
      package="com.androidbook.BDayWidget"
      android:versionCode="1"
      android:versionName="1.0.0">
<application android:icon="@drawable/icon"
             android:label="Birthday Widget">
<!--
*********************************************************************
*  Birthday Widget Provider Receiver
*********************************************************************
 -->
   <receiver android:name=".BDayWidgetProvider">
      <meta-data android:name="android.appwidget.provider"
             android:resource="@xml/bday_appwidget_provider"/>
      <intent-filter>
           <action android:name="android.appwidget.action.APPWIDGET_UPDATE"/>
      </intent-filter>
   </receiver>
```

```
<!--
*******************************************************************
*  Birthday Provider Configuration activity
*******************************************************************
 -->
   <activity android:name=".ConfigureBDayWidgetActivity"
             android:label="Configure Birthday Widget">
       <intent-filter>
           <action android:name="android.appwidget.action.APPWIDGET_CONFIGURE"/>
       </intent-filter>
   </activity>

    </application>
    <uses-sdk android:minSdkVersion="3"/>
</manifest>
```

The application label identified by "Birthday Widget" in the following line

```
<application android:icon="@drawable/icon" android:label="Birthday Widget">
```

is what shows up in the widget pick list (see Figure 21-2) of the home page. You can also indicate in the widget definition XML file (Listing 21-2) an alternate icon to be shown when the widget is listed (also called a preview). The configuration activity definition is like any other normal activity, except that it needs to declare itself as capable of responding to android.appwidget.action.APPWIDGET_CONFIGURE actions.

Refer to the widget definition file @xml/bday_appwidget_provider in Listing 21-2 to see how the widget size and a path to the layout file are specified. This layout file is just like any other layout file for a view in Android. Listing 21-6 shows the layout file we used to produce the widget layout shown in Figure 21-4.

***Listing 21-6.** Widget View Layout Definition for BDayWidget*

```
<?xml version="1.0" encoding="utf-8"?>
<!-- res/layout/bday_widget.xml -->
<LinearLayout xmlns:android="http://schemas.android.com/apk/res/android"
    android:orientation="vertical"
    android:layout_width="fill_parent"  android:layout_height="fill_parent"
    android:background="@drawable/box1">
<TextView
    android:id="@+id/bdw_w_name"
    android:layout_width="fill_parent" android:layout_height="40sp"
    android:text="Anonymous"  android:background="@drawable/box1"
    android:gravity="center"  android:layout_weight="0"/>
<LinearLayout
    android:orientation="horizontal"
    android:layout_width="fill_parent" android:layout_height="fill_parent"
    android:layout_weight="1">
       <TextView
           android:id="@+id/bdw_w_days"
           android:layout_width="wrap_content" android:layout_height="fill_parent"
           android:gravity="center" android:layout_weight="50"
                  android:text="0" android:textSize="30sp" />
```

```
        <TextView
            android:id="@+id/bdw_w_button_buy"
            android:layout_width="wrap_content"  android:layout_height="fill_parent"
            android:layout_weight="50"  android:gravity="center"
            android:textSize="20sp"  android:text="Buy"
            android:background="#FF6633"/>
</LinearLayout>
<TextView
    android:id="@+id/bdw_w_date"
    android:layout_width="fill_parent"  android:layout_height="40sp"
    android:gravity="center" android:layout_weight="0"
    android:text="1/1/2000" android:background="@drawable/box1"/>
</LinearLayout>
```

Some of the controls also use a shape definition file called box1.xml to define the borders. The code for the shape definition file is shown in Listing 21-7.

Listing 21-7. A Boundary Box Shape Definition

```
<!-- res/drawable/box1.xml -->
<shape xmlns:android="http://schemas.android.com/apk/res/android">
    <stroke android:width="4dp" android:color="#888888"/>
    <padding android:left="2dp" android:top="2dp"
            android:right="2dp" android:bottom="2dp"/>
    <corners android:radius="4dp"/>
</shape>
```

Implementing Widget Configuration Activity

For the Birthday Widget example, the configuration of the widget responsibilities are implemented in ConfigureBDayWidgetActivity. Source code for this class is in Listing 21-8.

Listing 21-8. Implementing a Configuration Activity

```
// file: ConfigureBDayWidgetActivity.java(ProAndroid5_ch21_TestWidgets.zip)
public class ConfigureBDayWidgetActivity extends Activity
{
   private static String tag = "ConfigureBDayWidgetActivity";
   private int mAppWidgetId = AppWidgetManager.INVALID_APPWIDGET_ID;

    @Override
    public void onCreate(Bundle savedInstanceState) {
        super.onCreate(savedInstanceState);
        setContentView(R.layout.edit_bday_widget);
        setupButton(); //setup the save button

        //Get the widget instanceid from the intent extra
        Intent intent = getIntent();
        Bundle extras = intent.getExtras();
```

```
        if (extras != null) {
            mAppWidgetId = extras.getInt(
                    AppWidgetManager.EXTRA_APPWIDGET_ID,
                    AppWidgetManager.INVALID_APPWIDGET_ID);
        }
    }
    private void setupButton(){
       Button b = (Button)this.findViewById(R.id.bdw_button_update_bday_widget);
       b.setOnClickListener(
             new Button.OnClickListener(){
                public void onClick(View v)  {
                   saveConfiguration(v);
                }
             });
    }
    //Read name and date.
    //Call updateAppWidgetLocal to save the values for this instance
    //in that method also send the view to the homepage.
    //Return the result of the configuration activity to the SDK
    //finish the activity.
    private void saveConfiguration(View v){
       String name = this.getName();
       String date = this.getDate();
       if (Utils.validateDate(date) == false){
          this.setDate("wrong date:" + date);
          return;
       }
       if (this.mAppWidgetId == AppWidgetManager.INVALID_APPWIDGET_ID){
          return;
       }
       updateAppWidgetLocal(name,date);
       Intent resultValue = new Intent();
       resultValue.putExtra(AppWidgetManager.EXTRA_APPWIDGET_ID, mAppWidgetId);
       setResult(RESULT_OK, resultValue);
       finish();
    }
    private String getName(){
        EditText nameEdit =
            (EditText)this.findViewById(R.id.bdw_bday_name_id);
        String name = nameEdit.getText().toString();
        return name;
    }
    private String getDate(){
        EditText dateEdit = (EditText)this.findViewById(R.id.bdw_bday_date_id);
        String dateString = dateEdit.getText().toString();
        return dateString;
    }
    private void setDate(String errorDate){
        EditText dateEdit = (EditText)this.findViewById(R.id.bdw_bday_date_id);
        dateEdit.setText("error");
        dateEdit.requestFocus();
    }
```

```
    private void updateAppWidgetLocal(String name, String dob){
       //Create an object to hold the data: widgetid, name, and dob
       BDayWidgetModel m = new BDayWidgetModel(mAppWidgetId,name,dob);
       //Create the view and send it to the home screen
       updateAppWidget(this,AppWidgetManager.getInstance(this),m);
       //Use the data model object to save the id, name, and dob in prefs
       m.savePreferences(this);
    }
    //A key method where a lot of magic happens
    public static void updateAppWidget(Context context,
            AppWidgetManager appWidgetManager,
            BDayWidgetModel widgetModel)
    {
      //Construct a RemoteViews Object from the widget layout file
      RemoteViews views = new RemoteViews(context.getPackageName(),
                    R.layout.bday_widget);

      //Use the control ids in the layout to set values on them.
      //Notice that these methods are limited and available on the
      //on the RemoteViews object. In other words we are not using the
      //TextView directly to set these values.
      views.setTextViewText(R.id.bdw_w_name
         , widgetModel.getName() + ":" + widgetModel.iid);

      views.setTextViewText(R.id.bdw_w_date
            , widgetModel.getBday());

      //update the name
      views.setTextViewText(R.id.bdw_w_days,
                          Long.toString(widgetModel.howManyDays()));

      //Set intents to invoke other activities when widget is clicked on
      Intent defineIntent = new Intent(Intent.ACTION_VIEW,
              Uri.parse("http://www.google.com"));
      PendingIntent pendingIntent =
           PendingIntent.getActivity(context,
                    0 /* no requestCode */,
                    defineIntent,
                    0 /* no flags */);
       views.setOnClickPendingIntent(R.id.bdw_w_button_buy, pendingIntent);

      // Tell the widget manager to paint the remote view
      appWidgetManager.updateAppWidget(widgetModel.iid, views);
   }
}
```

Before we cover what this code does, the layout used by this widget configuration activity is in Listing 21-9. This layout is straightforward. You can also see this visually in Figure 21-3.

Listing 21-9. Layout Definition for Configuration Activity

```
<?xml version="1.0" encoding="utf-8"?>
<!-- res/layout/edit_bday_widget.xml -->
<LinearLayout xmlns:android="http://schemas.android.com/apk/res/android"
   android:id="@+id/root_layout_id" android:orientation="vertical"
   android:layout_width="fill_parent" android:layout_height="fill_parent">
<TextView
    android:id="@+id/bdw_text1" android:layout_width="fill_parent"
    android:layout_height="wrap_content" android:text="Name:" />
<EditText
    android:id="@+id/bdw_bday_name_id" android:layout_width="fill_parent"
    android:layout_height="wrap_content" android:text="Anonymous" />
<TextView
    android:id="@+id/bdw_text2" android:layout_width="fill_parent"
    android:layout_height="wrap_content" android:text="Birthday (9/1/2001):" />
<EditText
    android:id="@+id/bdw_bday_date_id" android:layout_width="fill_parent"
    android:layout_height="wrap_content"  android:text="ex: 10/1/2009" />
<Button
    android:id="@+id/bdw_button_update_bday_widget" android:layout_width="fill_parent"
    android:layout_height="wrap_content" android:text="update"/>
</LinearLayout>
```

Going back to the configuration activity code in Listing 21-8, it accomplishes the following tasks:

- Reading the widget instance ID from invoking intent
- Collecting the name and date of birth using form fields
- Obtaining `RemoteViews` by loading widget layout file
- Setting text values on the `RemoteViews`
- Registering a pending intent through `RemoteViews`
- Invoking the `AppWidgetManager` to send the `RemoteViews` to the widget
- Saving the name and date of birth in preferences against this widget instance ID. This is done through the class `BDayWidgetModel`. We will talk about this shortly.
- Returning at the end with a result.

> **Note** The static function `udpateAppWidget` can be called from anywhere as long as you know the widget ID. This suggests that you can update a widget from anywhere on your device and from any process, both visual and nonvisual.

Notice how we are passing the widget ID back to the invoker of this configuration activity. This is how `AppWidgetManager` knows that the configuration activity is completed for that widget instance.

Let's talk about saving and retrieval of the widget instance state through BDayWidgetModel object in Listing 21-8. The role of BDayWidgetModel object is to store and retrieve three values: The widget instance ID (primary key), name, and date of birth. This class uses the preferences API to persist and read back these values. Alternatively, you can use any persistence mechanism for this need. We are not including the source code for this class as it is quite a simple need to implement. In the downloadable project for this chapter we have an implementation for this class that is a bit more extensive, where we coded a reusable framework to store values for any java object in the preferences. We have amply documented the source code so that you can use it as is for other needs or tweak it further and use reflection to simplify further. In the end you will have a model framework that is quite extensible. As this is not the primary goal of this chapter we have not gotten into those details here. What matters for this chapter is that these three values, the instance ID, name, and dob be saved and retrieved. You can follow the names on the BDayWidgetModel as a guide.

Implementing a Widget Provider

Let's see now how we will respond to the life cycle events of widgets by examining the widget provider class. Listing 21-10 implements the widget provider class.

Listing 21-10. Source code for Sample Widget Provider: BDayWidgetProvider

```
// file: BDayWidgetProvider.java(ProAndroid5_ch21_TestWidgets.zip)
public class BDayWidgetProvider extends AppWidgetProvider  {
    private static final String tag = "BDayWidgetProvider";
    public void onUpdate(Context context, AppWidgetManager appWidgetManager,
                    int[] appWidgetIds)  {
        final int N = appWidgetIds.length;
        for (int i=0; i<N; i++)  {
            int appWidgetId = appWidgetIds[i];
            updateAppWidget(context, appWidgetManager, appWidgetId);
        }
    }
    public void onDeleted(Context context, int[] appWidgetIds) {
        final int N = appWidgetIds.length;
        for (int i=0; i<N; i++) {
              BDayWidgetModel bwm = BDayWidgetModel.retrieveModel(context,
appWidgetIds[i]);
              bwm.removePrefs(context);
        }
    }
    public void onEnabled(Context context) {
        BDayWidgetModel.clearAllPreferences(context);
        PackageManager pm = context.getPackageManager();
        pm.setComponentEnabledSetting(
                new ComponentName("com.androidbook.BDayWidget",
                     ".BDayWidgetProvider"),
                PackageManager.COMPONENT_ENABLED_STATE_ENABLED,
                PackageManager.DONT_KILL_APP);
    }
```

```
    public void onDisabled(Context context) {
        BDayWidgetModel.clearAllPreferences(context);
        PackageManager pm = context.getPackageManager();
        pm.setComponentEnabledSetting(
                new ComponentName("com.androidbook.BDayWidget",
                        ".BDayWidgetProvider"),
                PackageManager.COMPONENT_ENABLED_STATE_DISABLED,
                PackageManager.DONT_KILL_APP);
    }
    private void updateAppWidget(Context context, AppWidgetManager appWidgetManager,
                        int appWidgetId) {
       BDayWidgetModel bwm = BDayWidgetModel.retrieveModel(context, appWidgetId);
       if (bwm == null) {return;}
       ConfigureBDayWidgetActivity.updateAppWidget(context, appWidgetManager, bwm);
   }
}
```

In the "Life Cycle of a Widget" section we discussed the responsibilities of these methods. For the Birthday Widget, all these methods make use of the `BDayWidgetModel` to retrieve the data associated with a widget instance for which the callbacks are called. Some of these methods on the `BDayWidgetModel` are `removePrefs()`, `retrievePrefs()`, and `clearAllPreferences()`.

The update callback method is called for all the widget instances of this widget type. This method must update all the widget instances. The widget instances are passed in as an array of IDs. For each `id`, the `onUpdate()` method will locate the corresponding widget instance model and call the same method that is used by the configuration activity (see Listing 21-8) to display the retrieved widget model.

In the `onDeleted()` method, we have instantiated a `BDayWidgetModel` and then asked it to remove itself from the preferences persistence store.

In the `onEnabled()` method, because it is called only once when the first instance comes into play, we have cleared all persistence of the widget models so that we start with a clean slate. We do the same in the `onDisabled()` method so that no memory of widget instances exists.

In the `onEnabled()` method, we enable the widget provider component so that it can receive broadcast messages. In the `onDisabled()` method, we disable the component so that it won't look for any broadcast messages.

Collection-Based Widgets

Starting with SDK 3.0, Android has expanded the widgets to include widgets based on collections. We don't have room in the print copy of this book. We will include the chapter from the previous edition on collection widgets at our online site for download.

Resources

Here are helpful references to the topics that are covered in this chapter:

- `http://developer.android.com/guide/topics/appwidgets/index.html`: Official Android SDK documentation on app widgets.
- `http://developer.android.com/reference/android/content/SharedPreferences.html`: `SharedPreferences` API for managing state.
- `http://developer.android.com/reference/android/content/SharedPreferences.Editor.html`: The `SharedPreferences.Editor` API, which is related to shared preferences.
- `http://developer.android.com/guide/practices/ui_guidelines/widget_design.html`: Design pleasing widget layouts.
- `http://developer.android.com/reference/android/widget/RemoteViews.html`: `RemoteViews` API, used to paint and manipulate widget views.
- `http://developer.android.com/reference/android/appwidget/AppWidgetManager.html`: Widgets themselves are managed by a widget manager class.
- `http://www.androidbook.com/item/3938`: Research notes used while writing this chapter, including a summary, research logs, code snippets, and useful URLs.
- `http://www.androidbook.com/free-android-chapters`: You can use this URL to download a detailed chapter on list widgets.
- `http://www.androidbook.com/proandroid5/projects`: Downloadable test projects for this chapter. The name of the ZIP file for this chapter is `ProAndroid5_ch21_TestWidgets.zip`.

Summary

Widgets are often used alongside your applications in Android. This chapter has covered the essentials you need to create and configure widgets. A supplemental chapter on list widgets is provided online.

Chapter 22

Touch Screens

Many Android devices incorporate touch screens. When a device does not have a physical keyboard, much of the user input *must* come through the touch screen. Therefore your applications will often need to be able to deal with touch input from the user. You've most likely already seen the virtual keyboard that displays on the screen when text input is required from the user. We used touch with mapping applications in Chapter 19. The implementations of the touch screen interface have been hidden from you so far, but now we'll show you how to take advantage of the touch screen.

This chapter is made up of three major parts. The first section will deal with `MotionEvent` objects, which is how Android tells an application that the user is touching a touch screen. We'll also cover the `VelocityTracker`. The second section will deal with multitouch, where a user can have more than one finger at a time on the touch screen. Finally, we will include a section on gestures, a specialized type of capability in which touch sequences can be interpreted as commands.

Understanding MotionEvents

In this section, we're going to cover how Android tells applications about touch events from the user. For now, we will only be concerned with touching the screen one finger at a time (we'll cover multitouch in a later section).

At the hardware level, a touch screen is made up of special materials that can pick up pressure and convert that to screen coordinates. The information about the touch is turned into data, and that data is passed to the software to deal with it.

The MotionEvent Object

When a user touches the touch screen of an Android device, a `MotionEvent` object is created. The `MotionEvent` contains information about where and when the touch took place, as well as other details of the touch event. The `MotionEvent` object gets passed to an appropriate method in your application. This could be the `onTouchEvent()` method of a

View object. Remember that the View class is the parent of quite a few classes in Android, including Layouts, Buttons, Lists, Clocks, and more. This means we can interact with all of these different types of View objects using touch events. When the method is called, it can inspect the MotionEvent object to decide what to do. For example, a GoogleMap could use touch events to move the map sideways to allow the user to pan the map to other points of interest. A virtual keyboard object could receive touch events to activate the virtual keys to provide text input to some other part of the user interface (UI).

Receiving MotionEvent Objects

A MotionEvent object is one of a sequence of events related to a touch by the user. The sequence starts when the user first touches the touch screen, continues through any movements of the finger across the surface of the touch screen, and ends when the finger is lifted from the touch screen. The initial touch (an ACTION_DOWN action), the movements sideways (ACTION_MOVE actions), and the up event (an ACTION_UP action) of the finger all create MotionEvent objects. You could receive quite a few ACTION_MOVE events as the finger moves across the surface before you receive the final ACTION_UP event. Each MotionEvent object contains information about what action is being performed, where the touch is taking place, how much pressure was applied, how big the touch was, when the action occurred, and when the initial ACTION_DOWN occurred. There is a fourth possible action, which is ACTION_CANCEL. This action is used to indicate that a touch sequence is ending without actually doing anything. Finally, there is ACTION_OUTSIDE, which is set in a special case where a touch occurs outside of our window but we still get to find out about it.

There is another way to receive touch events, and that is to register a callback handler for touch events on a View object. The class to receive the events must implement the View.OnTouchListener interface, and the View object's setOnTouchListener() method must be called to set up the handler for that View. The implementing class of the View.OnTouchListener must implement the onTouch() method. Whereas the onTouchEvent() method takes just a MotionEvent object as a parameter, onTouch() takes both a View and a MotionEvent object as parameters. This is because the OnTouchListener could receive MotionEvent objects for multiple views. This will become clearer with our next example application.

If a MotionEvent handler (either through the onTouchEvent() or onTouch() method) consumes the event and no one else needs to know about it, the method should return true. This tells Android that the event does not need to be passed to any other views. If the View object is not interested in this event *or any future events related to this touch sequence*, it returns false. The onTouchEvent() method of the base class View doesn't do anything and returns false. Subclasses of View may or may not do the same. For example, a Button object will consume a touch event, because a touch is equivalent to a click, and therefore returns true from the onTouchEvent() method. Upon receiving an ACTION_DOWN event, the Button will change its color to indicate that it is in the process of being clicked. The Button also wants to receive the ACTION_UP event to know when the user has let go, so it can initiate the logic of clicking the button. If a Button object returned false from onTouchEvent(), it would not receive any more MotionEvent objects to tell it when the user lifted a finger from the touch screen.

When we want touch events to do something new with a particular View object, we can extend the class, override the onTouchEvent() method, and put our logic there. We can also implement the View.OnTouchListener interface and set up a callback handler on the View object. By setting up a callback handler with onTouch(), MotionEvents will be delivered there first before they go to the View's onTouchEvent() method. Only if the onTouch() method returned false would our View's onTouchEvent() method get called. Let's get to our example application where this should be easier to see.

> **Note** We will give you a URL at the end of the chapter which you can use to download projects of this chapter. This will allow you to import these projects into your IDE directly.

Setting Up an Example Application

Listing 22-1 shows the XML of a layout file. Create a new Android project starting with this layout.

Listing 22-1. XML Layout File for TouchDemo1

```
<?xml version="1.0" encoding="utf-8"?>
<!-- This file is res/layout/main.xml -->
<LinearLayout xmlns:android="http://schemas.android.com/apk/res/android"
    android:layout_width="match_parent"
    android:layout_height="match_parent"
    android:orientation="vertical" >

  <RelativeLayout  android:id="@+id/layout1"
    android:tag="trueLayoutTop"  android:orientation="vertical"
    android:layout_width="match_parent"
    android:layout_height="wrap_content"
    android:layout_weight="1" >

    <com.androidbook.touch.demo1.TrueButton android:text="Returns True"
    android:id="@+id/trueBtn1"  android:tag="trueBtnTop"
    android:layout_width="wrap_content"
    android:layout_height="wrap_content" />

    <com.androidbook.touch.demo1.FalseButton android:text="Returns False"
    android:id="@+id/falseBtn1"  android:tag="falseBtnTop"
    android:layout_width="wrap_content"
    android:layout_height="wrap_content"
    android:layout_below="@id/trueBtn1" />

  </RelativeLayout>
  <RelativeLayout  android:id="@+id/layout2"
    android:tag="falseLayoutBottom"  android:orientation="vertical"
    android:layout_width="match_parent"
    android:layout_height="wrap_content"
    android:layout_weight="1"  android:background="#FF00FF" >
```

```
    <com.androidbook.touch.demo1.TrueButton android:text="Returns True"
    android:id="@+id/trueBtn2"  android:tag="trueBtnBottom"
    android:layout_width="wrap_content"
    android:layout_height="wrap_content" />

    <com.androidbook.touch.demo1.FalseButton android:text="Returns False"
    android:id="@+id/falseBtn2"  android:tag="falseBtnBottom"
    android:layout_width="wrap_content"
    android:layout_height="wrap_content"
    android:layout_below="@id/trueBtn2" />

  </RelativeLayout>
</LinearLayout>
```

There are a couple of things to point out about this layout. We've incorporated tags on our UI objects, and we'll be able to refer to these tags in our code as events occur on them. We've used custom objects (`TrueButton` and `FalseButton`). You'll see in the Java code that these are classes extended from the `Button` class. Because these are `Buttons`, we can use all of the same XML attributes we would use on other buttons. Figure 22-1 shows what this layout looks like, and Listing 22-2 shows our button Java code.

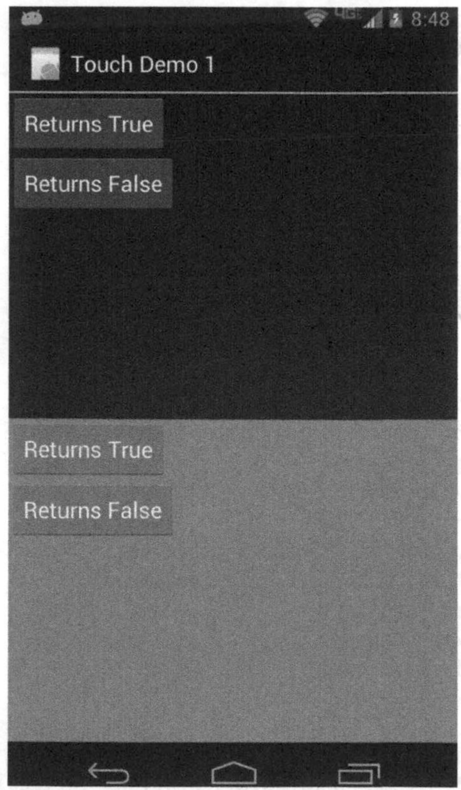

***Figure 22-1.** The UI of our TouchDemo1 application*

Listing 22-2. Java Code for the Button Classes for TouchDemo1

```
// This file is BooleanButton.java
public abstract class BooleanButton extends Button {
    protected boolean myValue() {
        return false;
    }

    public BooleanButton(Context context, AttributeSet attrs) {
        super(context, attrs);
    }

    @Override
    public boolean onTouchEvent(MotionEvent event) {
        String myTag = this.getTag().toString();
        Log.v(myTag, "-----------------------------------");
        Log.v(myTag, MainActivity.describeEvent(this, event));
        Log.v(myTag, "super onTouchEvent() returns " +
                super.onTouchEvent(event));
        Log.v(myTag, "and I'm returning " + myValue());
        return(myValue());
    }
}

// This file is TrueButton.java
public class TrueButton extends BooleanButton {
    protected boolean myValue() {
        return true;
    }

    public TrueButton(Context context, AttributeSet attrs) {
        super(context, attrs);
    }
}

// This file is FalseButton.java
public class FalseButton extends BooleanButton {

    public FalseButton(Context context, AttributeSet attrs) {
        super(context, attrs);
    }
}
```

The `BooleanButton` class was built so we can reuse the `onTouchEvent()` method, which we've customized by adding the logging. Then, we created `TrueButton` and `FalseButton`, which will respond differently to the `MotionEvents` passed to them. This will be made clearer when you look at the main activity code, which is shown in Listing 22-3.

Listing 22-3. Java Code for Our Main Activity

```
// This file is MainActivity.java
import android.view.MotionEvent;
import android.view.View.OnTouchListener;
public class MainActivity extends Activity implements OnTouchListener {
    /** Called when the activity is first created. */
    @Override
    public void onCreate(Bundle savedInstanceState) {
        super.onCreate(savedInstanceState);
        setContentView(R.layout.main);

        RelativeLayout layout1 =
                (RelativeLayout) findViewById(R.id.layout1);
        layout1.setOnTouchListener(this);
        Button trueBtn1 = (Button)findViewById(R.id.trueBtn1);
        trueBtn1.setOnTouchListener(this);
        Button falseBtn1 = (Button)findViewById(R.id.falseBtn1);
        falseBtn1.setOnTouchListener(this);

        RelativeLayout layout2 =
                (RelativeLayout) findViewById(R.id.layout2);
        layout2.setOnTouchListener(this);
        Button trueBtn2 = (Button)findViewById(R.id.trueBtn2);
        trueBtn2.setOnTouchListener(this);
        Button falseBtn2 = (Button)findViewById(R.id.falseBtn2);
        falseBtn2.setOnTouchListener(this);
    }

    @Override
    public boolean onTouch(View v, MotionEvent event) {
        String myTag = v.getTag().toString();
        Log.v(myTag, "-----------------------------");
        Log.v(myTag, "Got view " + myTag + " in onTouch");
        Log.v(myTag, describeEvent(v, event));
        if( "true".equals(myTag.substring(0, 4))) {
        /*  Log.v(myTag, "*** calling my onTouchEvent() method ***");
            v.onTouchEvent(event);
            Log.v(myTag, "*** back from onTouchEvent() method ***"); */
            Log.v(myTag, "and I'm returning true");
            return true;
        }
        else {
            Log.v(myTag, "and I'm returning false");
            return false;
        }
    }
```

```
    protected static String describeEvent(View view, MotionEvent event) {
        StringBuilder result = new StringBuilder(300);
        result.append("Action: ").append(event.getAction()).append("\n");
        result.append("Location: ").append(event.getX()).append(" x ")
                 .append(event.getY()).append("\n");
        if(    event.getX() < 0 || event.getX() > view.getWidth() ||
               event.getY() < 0 || event.getY() > view.getHeight()) {
            result.append(">>> Touch has left the view <<<\n");
        }
        result.append("Edge flags: ").append(event.getEdgeFlags());
        result.append("\n");
        result.append("Pressure: ").append(event.getPressure());
        result.append("   ").append("Size: ").append(event.getSize());
        result.append("\n").append("Down time: ");
        result.append(event.getDownTime()).append("ms\n");
        result.append("Event time: ").append(event.getEventTime());
        result.append("ms").append("  Elapsed: ");
        result.append(event.getEventTime()-event.getDownTime());
        result.append(" ms\n");
        return result.toString();
    }
}
```

Our main activity code sets up callbacks on our buttons and the layouts so we can process the touch events (the `MotionEvent` objects) for everything in our UI. We've added lots of logging, so you'll be able to tell exactly what's going on as touch events occur. One other good idea is to add the following tag to your manifest file so Google Play Store will know your application requires a touch screen to work: `<uses-configuration android:reqTouchScreen="finger" />`. For example, Google TVs don't have touch screens, so it wouldn't make sense to try to run this app there. When you compile and run this application, you should see a screen that looks like Figure 22-1.

Running the Example Application

To get the most out of this application, you need to open LogCat in your IDE (Eclipse or Android Studio) to watch the messages fly by as you touch the touch screen. This works in the emulator as well as on a real device. We also advise you to maximize the LogCat window, so you can more easily scroll up and down to see all of the generated events from this application. To maximize the window, just double-click the LogCat tab. Now, go to the application UI, and touch and release on the topmost button marked Returns True (if you're using the emulator, use your mouse to click and release the button). You should see at least two events logged in LogCat. The messages are tagged as coming from `trueBtnTop` and were logged from the `onTouch()` method in `MainActivity`. See `MainActivity.java` for the `onTouch()` method's code. As you view the LogCat output, see which method calls are producing the values. For example, the value displayed after Action comes from the `getAction()` method. Listing 22-4 shows a sample of what you might see in LogCat from the sample application.

Listing 22-4. Sample LogCat Messages from TouchDemo1

```
trueBtnTop       ----------------------------
trueBtnTop       Got view trueBtnTop in onTouch
trueBtnTop       Action: 0
trueBtnTop       Location: 42.8374 x 25.293747
trueBtnTop       Edge flags: 0
trueBtnTop       Pressure: 0.05490196   Size: 0.2
trueBtnTop       Down time: 24959412ms
trueBtnTop       Event time: 24959412ms  Elapsed: 0 ms
trueBtnTop       and I'm returning true
trueBtnTop       ----------------------------
trueBtnTop       Got view trueBtnTop in onTouch
trueBtnTop       Action: 2
trueBtnTop       Location: 42.8374 x 25.293747
trueBtnTop       Edge flags: 0
trueBtnTop       Pressure: 0.05490196   Size: 0.2
trueBtnTop       Down time: 24959412ms
trueBtnTop       Event time: 24959530ms  Elapsed: 118 ms
trueBtnTop       and I'm returning true
trueBtnTop       ----------------------------
trueBtnTop       Got view trueBtnTop in onTouch
trueBtnTop       Action: 1
trueBtnTop       Location: 42.8374 x 25.293747
trueBtnTop       Edge flags: 0
trueBtnTop       Pressure: 0.05490196   Size: 0.2
trueBtnTop       Down time: 24959412ms
trueBtnTop       Event time: 24959567ms  Elapsed: 155 ms
trueBtnTop       and I'm returning true
```

Understanding MotionEvent Contents

The first event has an action of 0, which is ACTION_DOWN. The last event has an action of 1, which is ACTION_UP. If you used a real device, you might see more than two events. Any events in between ACTION_DOWN and ACTION_UP will most likely have an action of 2, which is ACTION_MOVE. The other possibilities are an action of 3, which is ACTION_CANCEL, or 4, which is ACTION_OUTSIDE. When using real fingers on a real touch screen, you can't always touch and release without a slight movement on the surface, so expect some ACTION_MOVE events.

Notice the Location values. The location for a MotionEvent has an x and y component, where x represents the distance from the left-hand side of the View object to the point touched and y represents the distance from the top of the View object to the point touched.

In the emulator, pressure is likely 1.0 and size is likely 0.0. For a real device, the pressure represents how hard the finger pressed down, and size represents how large the touch is. If you touch lightly with the tip of your pinky finger, the values for pressure and size will be small. If you press hard with your thumb, both pressure and size will be larger. Pressing lightly with your thumb should result in a small value for pressure but a large value for size. The documentation says that the values of pressure and size will be between 0 and 1. However, due to differences in hardware, it may be very difficult to use any absolute numbers in your application for making decisions about pressure and size. It would be fine to compare pressure and size between MotionEvents as they occur in your application, but you may run into trouble if you decide that pressure must exceed a value such as 0.8 to be considered a hard press. On that particular device, you might never get a value above 0.8. You might not even get a value above 0.2.

The down time and event time values operate in the same way between the emulator and a real device, the only difference being that the real device has much larger values. The elapsed times work the same.

The edge flags are for detecting when a touch has reached the edge of the physical screen. The Android SDK documentation says that the flags are set to indicate that a touch has intersected with an edge of the display (top, bottom, left, or right). However, the getEdgeFlags() method may always return zero, depending on what device or emulator it is used on. With some hardware, it is too difficult to actually detect a touch at the edge of the display, so Android is supposed to pin the location to the edge and set the appropriate edge flag for you. This doesn't always happen, so you should not rely on the edge flags being set properly. The MotionEvent class provides a setEdgeFlags() method so you can set the flags yourself if you want to.

The last thing to notice is that our onTouch() method returns true, because our TrueButton is coded to return true. Returning true tells Android that the MotionEvent object has been consumed and there is no reason to give it to someone else. It also tells Android to keep sending touch events from this touch sequence to this method. That's why we got the ACTION_UP event, as well as the ACTION_MOVE event in the case of the real device.

Now touch the Returns False button near the top of the screen. Listing 22-5 shows a sample LogCat output for your Returns False touch.

Listing 22-5. ***Sample LogCat from Touching the Top Returns False Button***

```
falseBtnTop     -----------------------------
falseBtnTop     Got view falseBtnTop in onTouch
falseBtnTop     Action: 0
falseBtnTop     Location: 61.309372 x 44.281494
falseBtnTop     Edge flags: 0
falseBtnTop     Pressure: 0.0627451   Size: 0.26666668
falseBtnTop     Down time: 28612178ms
falseBtnTop     Event time: 28612178ms  Elapsed: 0 ms
falseBtnTop     and I'm returning false
falseBtnTop     -----------------------------------
falseBtnTop     Action: 0
falseBtnTop     Location: 61.309372 x 44.281494
falseBtnTop     Edge flags: 0
falseBtnTop     Pressure: 0.0627451   Size: 0.26666668
falseBtnTop     Down time: 28612178ms
falseBtnTop     Event time: 28612178ms  Elapsed: 0 ms
falseBtnTop     super onTouchEvent() returns true
falseBtnTop     and I'm returning false
trueLayoutTop     -----------------------------
trueLayoutTop     Got view trueLayoutTop in onTouch
trueLayoutTop     Action: 0
trueLayoutTop     Location: 61.309372 x 116.281494
```

```
trueLayoutTop        Edge flags: 0
trueLayoutTop        Pressure: 0.0627451   Size: 0.26666668
trueLayoutTop        Down time: 28612178ms
trueLayoutTop        Event time: 28612178ms  Elapsed: 0 ms
trueLayoutTop        and I'm returning true
trueLayoutTop        ----------------------------
trueLayoutTop        Got view trueLayoutTop in onTouch
trueLayoutTop        Action: 2
trueLayoutTop        Location: 61.309372 x 111.90039
trueLayoutTop        Edge flags: 0
trueLayoutTop        Pressure: 0.0627451   Size: 0.26666668
trueLayoutTop        Down time: 28612178ms
trueLayoutTop        Event time: 28612217ms  Elapsed: 39 ms
trueLayoutTop        and I'm returning true
trueLayoutTop        ----------------------------
trueLayoutTop        Got view trueLayoutTop in onTouch
trueLayoutTop        Action: 1
trueLayoutTop        Location: 55.08958 x 115.30792
trueLayoutTop        Edge flags: 0
trueLayoutTop        Pressure: 0.0627451   Size: 0.26666668
trueLayoutTop        Down time: 28612178ms
trueLayoutTop        Event time: 28612361ms  Elapsed: 183 ms
trueLayoutTop        and I'm returning true
```

Now you're seeing very different behavior, so we'll explain what happened. Android receives the ACTION_DOWN event in a MotionEvent object and passes it to our onTouch() method in the MainActivity class. Our onTouch() method records the information in LogCat and returns false. This tells Android that our onTouch() method did not consume the event, so Android looks to the next method to call, which in our case is the overridden onTouchEvent() method of our FalseButton class. Because FalseButton is an extension of the BooleanButton class, refer to the onTouchEvent() method in BooleanButton.java to see the code. In the onTouchEvent() method, we again write information to LogCat, we call the parent class's onTouchEvent() method, and then we also return false. Notice that the location information in LogCat is exactly the same as before. This should be expected because we're still in the same View object, the FalseButton. We see that our parent class wants to return true from onTouchEvent(), and we can see why. If you look at the button in the UI, it should be a different color from the Returns True button. Our Returns False button now looks like it's partway through being pressed. That is, it looks like a button looks when it has been pressed but has not been released. Our custom method returned false instead of true. Because we again told Android that we did not consume this event, by returning false, Android never sends the ACTION_UP event to our button, so our button doesn't know that the finger ever lifted from the touch screen. Therefore, our button is still in the pressed state. If we had returned true like our parent wanted to, we would eventually have received the ACTION_UP event, so we could change the color back to the normal button color. To recap, every time we return false from a UI object for a received MotionEvent object, Android stops sending MotionEvent objects to that UI object, and Android keeps looking for another UI object to consume our MotionEvent object.

You might have realized that when we touched our Returns True button, we didn't get a color change in the button. Why is that? Well, our onTouch() method was called before any actual button methods got called, and onTouch() returned true, so Android never bothered to call the Returns True button's onTouchEvent() method. If you add a v.onTouchEvent(event); line to the onTouch() method just before returning true, you will see the button change color. You will also see more log lines in LogCat, because our onTouchEvent() method is also writing information to LogCat.

Let's keep going through the LogCat output. Now that Android has tried twice to find a consumer for the ACTION_DOWN event and failed, it goes to the next View in the application that could possibly receive the event, which in our case is the layout underneath the button. We called our top layout trueLayoutTop, and we can see that it received the ACTION_DOWN event.

Notice that our onTouch() method got called again, although now with the layout view and not the button view. Everything about the MotionEvent object passed to onTouch() for trueLayoutTop is the same as before, including the times, except for the y coordinate of the location. The y coordinate changed from 44.281494 for the button to 116.281494 for the layout. This makes sense because the Returns False button is not in the upper-left corner of the layout, it's below the Returns True button. Therefore the y coordinate of the touch relative to the layout is larger than the y coordinate of the same touch relative to the button; the touch is further away from the top edge of the layout than it is from the top edge of the button. Because onTouch() for the trueLayoutTop returns true, Android sends the rest of the touch events to the layout, and we see the log records corresponding to the ACTION_MOVE and the ACTION_UP events. Go ahead and touch the top Returns False button again, and notice that the same set of log records occurs. That is, onTouch() is called for falseBtnTop, onTouchEvent() is called for falseBtnTop, and then onTouch() is called for trueLayoutTop for the rest of the events. Android only stops sending the events to the button for one touch sequence at a time. For a new sequence of touch events, Android will send to the button unless it gets another return of false from the called method, which it still does in our sample application.

Now touch your finger on the top layout but not on either button, and then drag your finger around a bit and lift it off the touch screen (if you're using the emulator, just use your mouse to make a similar motion). Notice a stream of log messages in LogCat, where the first record has an action of ACTION_DOWN, and then many ACTION_MOVE events are followed by an ACTION_UP event.

Now, touch the top Returns True button, and before lifting your finger from the button, drag your finger around the screen and then lift it off. Listing 22-6 shows some new information in LogCat.

Listing 22-6. LogCat Records Showing a Touch Outside of Our View

```
[ ... log messages of an ACTION_DOWN event followed by some ACTION_MOVE events ... ]

trueBtnTop          Got view trueBtnTop in onTouch
trueBtnTop          Action: 2
trueBtnTop          Location: 150.41768 x 22.628128
trueBtnTop          >>> Touch has left the view <<<
trueBtnTop          Edge flags: 0
trueBtnTop          Pressure: 0.047058824   Size: 0.13333334
trueBtnTop          Down time: 31690859ms
trueBtnTop          Event time: 31691344ms  Elapsed: 485 ms
trueBtnTop          and I'm returning true
```

```
[ ... more ACTION_MOVE events logged ... ]
trueBtnTop        Got view trueBtnTop in onTouch
trueBtnTop        Action: 1
trueBtnTop        Location: 291.5864 x 223.43854
trueBtnTop        >>> Touch has left the view <<<
trueBtnTop        Edge flags: 0
trueBtnTop        Pressure: 0.047058824   Size: 0.13333334
trueBtnTop        Down time: 31690859ms
trueBtnTop        Event time: 31692493ms  Elapsed: 1634 ms
trueBtnTop        and I'm returning true
```

Even after your finger drags itself off of the button, we continue to get notified of touch events related to the button. The first record in Listing 22-6 shows an event record where we're no longer on the button. In this case, the x coordinate of the touch event is to the right of the edge of our button object. However, we keep getting called with MotionEvent objects until we get an ACTION_UP event, because we continue to return true from the onTouch() method. Even when you finally lift your finger off of the touch screen, and even if your finger isn't on the button, our onTouch() method still gets called to give us the ACTION_UP event because we keep returning true. This is something to keep in mind when dealing with MotionEvents. When the finger has moved off of the view, we could decide to cancel whatever operation might have been performed and return false from the onTouch() method, so we don't get notified of further events. Or we could choose to continue to receive events (by returning true from the onTouch() method) and only perform the logic if the finger returns to our view before lifting off.

The touch sequence of events got associated to our top Returns True button when we returned true from onTouch(). This told Android that it could stop looking for an object to receive the MotionEvent objects and just send all future MotionEvent objects for this touch sequence to us. Even if we encounter another view when dragging our finger, we're still tied to the original view for this sequence.

Exercising the Bottom Half of the Example Application

Let's see what happens with the lower half of our application. Go ahead and touch the Returns True button in the bottom half. We see the same thing as happened with the top Returns True button. Because onTouch() returns true, Android sends us the rest of the events in the touch sequence until the finger is lifted from the touch screen. Now, touch the bottom Returns False button. Once again, the onTouch() method and onTouchEvent() methods return false (both associated with the falseBtnBottom view object). But this time, the next view to receive the MotionEvent object is the falseLayoutBottom object, and it also returns false. Now, we're finished.

Because the onTouchEvent() method called the super's onTouchEvent() method, the button has changed color to indicate it's halfway through being pressed. Again, the button will stay this way, because we never get the ACTION_UP event in this touch sequence, because our methods return false all the time. Unlike before, even the layout is not interested in this event. If you were to touch the bottom Returns False button and hold it down and then drag your finger around the display, you would not see any extra records in LogCat, because no more MotionEvent objects are sent to us. We returned false, so Android won't bother us with any more events for this touch sequence. Again, if we start a new touch sequence, we can see new LogCat records showing up. If you initiate a touch sequence in the bottom layout and not on a button, you will see a single event in LogCat for falseLayoutBottom that returns false and then nothing after that (until you start a new touch sequence).

So far, we've used buttons to show you the effects of MotionEvent events from touch screens. It's worth pointing out that, normally, you would implement logic on buttons using the onClick() method. We used buttons for this sample application, because they're easy to create and they are subclasses of View that can therefore receive touch events just like any other view. Remember that these techniques apply to any View object in your application, be it a standard or customized view class.

Recycling MotionEvents

You may have noticed the recycle() method of the MotionEvent class in the Android reference documentation. It is tempting to want to recycle the MotionEvents that you receive in onTouch() or onTouchEvent(), but don't do it. If your callback method is not consuming the MotionEvent object and you're returning false, the MotionEvent object is likely to be handed to some other method or view or our activity, so you don't want Android recycling it yet. Even if you consumed the event and returned true, the event object doesn't belong to you, so you should not recycle it.

If you look at MotionEvent documentation, you will see a few variations of a method called obtain(). This is either creating a copy of a MotionEvent or a brand new MotionEvent. Your copy, or your brand-new event object, is the event object that you should recycle when you are done with it. For example, if you want to hang onto an event object that is passed to you via a callback, you should use obtain() to make a copy, because once you return from the callback, that event object will be recycled by Android, and you may get strange results if you continue to use it. When you are finished using *your copy*, you invoke recycle() on it.

Using VelocityTracker

Android provides a class to help handle touch screen sequences, and that class is VelocityTracker. When a finger is in motion on a touch screen, it might be nice to know how fast it is moving across the surface. For example, if the user is dragging an object across the screen and lets go, your application probably wants to show that object flying across the screen accordingly. Android provides VelocityTracker to help with the math involved.

To use VelocityTracker, you first get an instance of a VelocityTracker by calling the static method VelocityTracker.obtain(). You can then add MotionEvent objects to it with the addMovement(MotionEvent ev) method. You would call this method in your handler that receives MotionEvent objects, from a handler method such as onTouch(), or from a view's onTouchEvent(). The VelocityTracker uses the MotionEvent objects to figure out what is going on with the user's touch sequence. Once VelocityTracker has at least two MotionEvent objects in it, we can use the other methods to find out what's happening.

The two VelocityTracker methods—getXVelocity() and getYVelocity()—return the corresponding velocity of the finger in the x and y directions, respectively. The value returned from these two methods will represent pixels per time period. This could be pixels per millisecond or per second or really anything you want. To tell the VelocityTracker what time period to use, and before you can call these two getter methods, you need to invoke the VelocityTracker's computeCurrentVelocity(int units) method. The value of units represents how many milliseconds are in the time period for measuring the velocity. If you want pixels per millisecond, use a units value of 1; if you want pixels per second, use a units value of 1000. The value returned by the getXVelocity() and getYVelocity() methods will be positive if the velocity is toward the right (for x) or down (for y). The value returned will be negative if the velocity is toward the left (for x) or up (for y).

When you are finished with the VelocityTracker object you got with the obtain() method, call the VelocityTracker object's recycle() method. Listing 22-7 shows a sample onTouchEvent() handler for an activity. It turns out that an activity has an onTouchEvent() callback, which is called whenever no views have handled the touch event. Because we're using a stock, empty layout, we have no views consuming our touch events.

Listing 22-7. Sample Activity That Uses VelocityTracker

```
import android.view.MotionEvent;
import android.view.VelocityTracker;

public class MainActivity extends Activity {
    private static final String TAG = "VelocityTracker";

    /** Called when the activity is first created. */
    @Override
    public void onCreate(Bundle savedInstanceState) {
        super.onCreate(savedInstanceState);
        setContentView(R.layout.main);
    }

    private VelocityTracker vTracker = null;

    public boolean onTouchEvent(MotionEvent event) {
        int action = event.getAction();
        switch(action) {
            case MotionEvent.ACTION_DOWN:
                if(vTracker == null) {
                    vTracker = VelocityTracker.obtain();
                }
                else {
                    vTracker.clear();
                }
                vTracker.addMovement(event);
                break;
            case MotionEvent.ACTION_MOVE:
                vTracker.addMovement(event);
                vTracker.computeCurrentVelocity(1000);
```

```
                Log.v(TAG, "X velocity is " + vTracker.getXVelocity() +
                        " pixels per second");
                Log.v(TAG, "Y velocity is " + vTracker.getYVelocity() +
                        " pixels per second");
                break;
            case MotionEvent.ACTION_UP:
            case MotionEvent.ACTION_CANCEL:
                Log.v(TAG, "Final X velocity is " + vTracker.getXVelocity() +
                        " pixels per second");
                Log.v(TAG, "Final Y velocity is " + vTracker.getYVelocity() +
                        " pixels per second");
                vTracker.recycle();
                vTracker = null;
                break;
        }
        return true;
    }
}
```

Obviously, when you've only added one MotionEvent to a VelocityTracker (the ACTION_DOWN event), the velocities cannot be computed as anything other than zero. But we need to add the starting point so that the subsequent ACTION_MOVE events can calculate velocities then.

VelocityTracker is somewhat costly in terms of performance, so use it sparingly. Also, make sure that you recycle it as soon as you are done with it. There can be more than one VelocityTracker in use in Android, but they can take up a lot of memory, so give yours back if you're not going to continue to use it. In Listing 22-7, we also use the clear() method if we're starting a new touch sequence (that is, if we get an ACTION_DOWN event and our VelocityTracker object already exists) instead of recycling this one and obtaining a new one.

Multitouch

Now that you've seen single touches in action, let's move on to multitouch. Multitouch has gained a lot of interest ever since the TED conference in 2006 at which Jeff Han demonstrated a multitouch surface for a computer user interface. Using multiple fingers on a screen opens up a lot of possibilities for manipulating what's on the screen. For example, putting two fingers on an image and moving them apart could zoom in on the image. By placing multiple fingers on an image and turning clockwise, you could rotate the image on the screen. These are standard touch operations in Google Maps, for instance.

If you think about it, though, there is no magic to this. If the screen hardware can detect multiple touches as they initiate on the screen, notify your application as those touches move in time across the surface of the screen, and notify you when those touches lift off of the screen, your application can figure out what the user is trying to do with those touches. Although it's not magic, it isn't easy either. We're going to help you understand multitouch in this section.

The Basics of Multitouch

The basics of multitouch are exactly the same as for single touches. `MotionEvent` objects get created for touches, and these `MotionEvent` objects are passed to your methods just like before. Your code can read the data about the touches and decide what to do. At a basic level, the methods of `MotionEvent` are the same; that is, we call `getAction()`, `getDownTime()`, `getX()`, and so on. However, when more than one finger is touching the screen, the `MotionEvent` object must include information from all fingers, with some caveats. The action value from `getAction()` is for one finger, not all. The down time value is for the very first finger down and measures the time as long as at least one finger is down. The location values `getX()` and `getY()`, as well as `getPressure()` and `getSize()`, can take an argument for the finger; therefore, you need to use a pointer index value to request the information for the finger you're interested in. There are method calls that we used previously that did not take any argument to specify a finger (for example, `getX()`, `getY()`), so which finger would the values be for if we used those methods? You can figure it out, but it takes some work. Therefore, if you don't take into account multiple fingers all of the time, you might end up with some strange results. Let's dig into this to figure out what to do.

The first method of `MotionEvent` you need to know about for multitouch is `getPointerCount()`. This tells you how many fingers are represented in the `MotionEvent` object but doesn't necessarily tell you how many fingers are actually touching the screen; that depends on the hardware and on the implementation of Android on that hardware. You may find that, on certain devices, `getPointerCount()` does not report all fingers that are touching, just some. But let's press on. As soon as you've got more than one finger being reported in `MotionEvent` objects, you need to start dealing with the pointer indexes and the pointer IDs.

The `MotionEvent` object contains information for pointers starting at index 0 and going up to the number of fingers being reported in that object. The pointer index always starts at 0; if three fingers are being reported, pointer indexes will be 0, 1, and 2. Calls to methods such as `getX()` must include the pointer index for the finger you want information about. Pointer IDs are integer values representing which finger is being tracked. Pointer IDs start at 0 for the first finger down but don't always start at 0 once fingers are coming and going on the screen. Think of a pointer ID as the name of that finger while it is being tracked by Android. For example, imagine a pair of touch sequences for two fingers, starting with finger 1 down, and followed by finger 2 down, finger 1 up, and finger 2 up. The first finger down will get pointer ID 0. The second finger down will get pointer ID 1. Once the first finger goes up, the second finger will still be pointer ID 1. At that point, the pointer index for the second finger becomes 0, because the pointer index always starts at 0. In this example, the second finger (pointer ID 1) starts as pointer index 1 when it first touches down and then shifts to pointer index 0 once the first finger leaves the screen. Even when the second finger is the only finger on the screen, it remains as pointer ID 1. Your applications will use pointer IDs to link together the events associated to a particular finger even as other fingers are involved. Let's look at an example.

Listing 22-8 shows our new XML layout plus our Java code for a multitouch application. This is the application called MultiTouchDemo1. Figure 22-2 shows what it should look like.

Listing 22-8. XML Layout and Java for a Multitouch Demonstration

```
<?xml version="1.0" encoding="utf-8"?>
<!-- This file is /res/layout/main.xml -->
<RelativeLayout  xmlns:android="http://schemas.android.com/apk/res/android"
    android:id="@+id/layout1"
    android:tag="trueLayout"  android:orientation="vertical"
    android:layout_width="match_parent"
    android:layout_height="wrap_content"
    android:layout_weight="1"
    >

    <TextView android:text="Touch fingers on the screen and look at LogCat"
    android:id="@+id/message"
    android:tag="trueText"
    android:layout_width="wrap_content"
    android:layout_height="wrap_content"
    android:layout_alignParentBottom="true" />

</RelativeLayout>

// This file is MainActivity.java
import android.view.MotionEvent;
import android.view.View.OnTouchListener;

public class MainActivity extends Activity implements OnTouchListener {
    /** Called when the activity is first created. */
    @Override
    public void onCreate(Bundle savedInstanceState) {
        super.onCreate(savedInstanceState);
        setContentView(R.layout.main);

        RelativeLayout layout1 =
                (RelativeLayout) findViewById(R.id.layout1);
        layout1.setOnTouchListener(this);
    }

    public boolean onTouch(View v, MotionEvent event) {
        String myTag = v.getTag().toString();
        Log.v(myTag, "-----------------------------");
        Log.v(myTag, "Got view " + myTag + " in onTouch");
        Log.v(myTag, describeEvent(event));
        logAction(event);
        if( "true".equals(myTag.substring(0, 4))) {
            return true;
        }
        else {
            return false;
        }
    }
```

```
    protected static String describeEvent(MotionEvent event) {
        StringBuilder result = new StringBuilder(500);
        result.append("Action: ").append(event.getAction()).append("\n");
        int numPointers = event.getPointerCount();
        result.append("Number of pointers: ");
        result.append(numPointers).append("\n");
        int ptrIdx = 0;
        while (ptrIdx < numPointers) {
            int ptrId = event.getPointerId(ptrIdx);
            result.append("Pointer Index: ").append(ptrIdx);
            result.append(", Pointer Id: ").append(ptrId).append("\n");
            result.append("   Location: ").append(event.getX(ptrIdx));
            result.append(" x ").append(event.getY(ptrIdx)).append("\n");
            result.append("   Pressure: ");
            result.append(event.getPressure(ptrIdx));
            result.append("   Size: ").append(event.getSize(ptrIdx));
            result.append("\n");

            ptrIdx++;
        }
        result.append("Down time: ").append(event.getDownTime());
        result.append("ms\n").append("Event time: ");
        result.append(event.getEventTime()).append("ms");
        result.append("  Elapsed: ");
        result.append(event.getEventTime()-event.getDownTime());
        result.append(" ms\n");
        return result.toString();
    }

    private void logAction(MotionEvent event) {
        int action = event.getActionMasked();
        int ptrIndex = event.getActionIndex();
        int ptrId = event.getPointerId(ptrIndex);

        if(action == 5 || action == 6)
            action = action - 5;

        Log.v("Action", "Pointer index: " + ptrIndex);
        Log.v("Action", "Pointer Id: " + ptrId);
        Log.v("Action", "True action value: " + action);
    }
}
```

***Figure 22-2.** Our multitouch demonstration application*

If you only have the emulator, this application will still work, but you won't be able to get multiple fingers simultaneously on the screen. You'll see output similar to what we saw in the previous application. Listing 22-9 shows sample LogCat messages for a touch sequence like we described earlier. That is, the first finger presses on the screen, and then the second finger presses, the first finger leaves the screen, and the second finger leaves the screen.

***Listing 22-9.** Sample LogCat Output for a Multitouch Application*

```
trueLayout        -----------------------------
trueLayout        Got view trueLayout in onTouch
trueLayout        Action: 0
trueLayout        Number of pointers: 1
trueLayout        Pointer Index: 0, Pointer Id: 0
trueLayout           Location: 114.88211 x 499.77502
trueLayout           Pressure: 0.047058824   Size: 0.13333334
trueLayout        Down time: 33733650ms
trueLayout        Event time: 33733650ms  Elapsed: 0 ms
Action            Pointer index: 0
Action            Pointer Id: 0
Action            True Action value: 0
```

```
trueLayout      -----------------------------
trueLayout      Got view trueLayout in onTouch
trueLayout      Action: 2
trueLayout      Number of pointers: 1
trueLayout      Pointer Index: 0, Pointer Id: 0
trueLayout         Location: 114.88211 x 499.77502
trueLayout         Pressure: 0.05882353   Size: 0.13333334
trueLayout      Down time: 33733650ms
trueLayout      Event time: 33733740ms  Elapsed: 90 ms
Action          Pointer index: 0
Action          Pointer Id: 0
Action          True Action value: 2
trueLayout      -----------------------------
trueLayout      Got view trueLayout in onTouch
trueLayout      Action: 261
trueLayout      Number of pointers: 2
trueLayout      Pointer Index: 0, Pointer Id: 0
trueLayout         Location: 114.88211 x 499.77502
trueLayout         Pressure: 0.05882353   Size: 0.13333334
trueLayout      Pointer Index: 1, Pointer Id: 1
trueLayout         Location: 320.30692 x 189.67395
trueLayout         Pressure: 0.050980393   Size: 0.13333334
trueLayout      Down time: 33733650ms
trueLayout      Event time: 33733962ms  Elapsed: 312 ms
Action          Pointer index: 1
Action          Pointer Id: 1
Action          True Action value: 0
trueLayout      -----------------------------
trueLayout      Got view trueLayout in onTouch
trueLayout      Action: 2
trueLayout      Number of pointers: 2
trueLayout      Pointer Index: 0, Pointer Id: 0
trueLayout         Location: 111.474594 x 499.77502
trueLayout         Pressure: 0.05882353   Size: 0.13333334
trueLayout      Pointer Index: 1, Pointer Id: 1
trueLayout         Location: 320.30692 x 189.67395
trueLayout         Pressure: 0.050980393   Size: 0.13333334
trueLayout      Down time: 33733650ms
trueLayout      Event time: 33734189ms  Elapsed: 539 ms
Action          Pointer index: 0
Action          Pointer Id: 0
Action          True Action value: 2
trueLayout      -----------------------------
trueLayout      Got view trueLayout in onTouch
trueLayout      Action: 6
trueLayout      Number of pointers: 2
trueLayout      Pointer Index: 0, Pointer Id: 0
trueLayout         Location: 111.474594 x 499.77502
trueLayout         Pressure: 0.05882353   Size: 0.13333334
trueLayout      Pointer Index: 1, Pointer Id: 1
trueLayout         Location: 320.30692 x 189.67395
trueLayout         Pressure: 0.050980393   Size: 0.13333334
```

```
trueLayout      Down time: 33733650ms
trueLayout      Event time: 33734228ms  Elapsed: 578 ms
Action          Pointer index: 0
Action          Pointer Id: 0
Action          True Action value: 1
trueLayout      ----------------------------
trueLayout      Got view trueLayout in onTouch
trueLayout      Action: 2
trueLayout      Number of pointers: 1
trueLayout      Pointer Index: 0, Pointer Id: 1
trueLayout         Location: 318.84656 x 191.45105
trueLayout         Pressure: 0.050980393   Size: 0.13333334
trueLayout      Down time: 33733650ms
trueLayout      Event time: 33734240ms  Elapsed: 590 ms
Action          Pointer index: 0
Action          Pointer Id: 1
Action          True Action value: 2
trueLayout      ----------------------------
trueLayout      Got view trueLayout in onTouch
trueLayout      Action: 1
trueLayout      Number of pointers: 1
trueLayout      Pointer Index: 0, Pointer Id: 1
trueLayout         Location: 314.95224 x 190.5625
trueLayout         Pressure: 0.050980393   Size: 0.13333334
trueLayout      Down time: 33733650ms
trueLayout      Event time: 33734549ms  Elapsed: 899 ms
Action          Pointer index: 0
Action          Pointer Id: 1
Action          True Action value: 1
```

Understanding Multitouch Contents

We'll now discuss what is going on with this application. The first event we see is the ACTION_DOWN (action value of 0) of the first finger. We learn about this using the getAction() method. Please refer to the describeEvent() method in MainActivity.java to follow along with which methods produce which output. We get one pointer with index 0 and pointer ID 0. After that, you'll probably see several ACTION_MOVE events (action value of 2) for this first finger, even though we're only showing one of these in Listing 22-9. We still only have one pointer and the index and ID are still both 0.

A little later we get the second finger touching the screen. The action is now a decimal value of 261. What does this mean? The action value is actually made up of two parts: an indicator of which pointer the action is for and what action that pointer is doing. Converting decimal 261 to hexadecimal, we get 0x00000105. The action is the smallest byte (5 in this case), and the pointer index is the next byte over (1 in this case). Note that this tells us the pointer index but not the pointer ID. If you pressed a third finger onto the screen, the action would be 0x00000205 (or decimal 517). A fourth finger would be 0x00000305 (or decimal 773) and so on. You haven't seen an action value of 5 yet, but it's known as ACTION_POINTER_DOWN. It's just like ACTION_DOWN except that it's used in multitouch situations.

Now, look at the next pair of records from LogCat in Listing 22-9. The first record is for an ACTION_MOVE event (action value of 2). Remember that it is difficult to keep fingers from moving on a real screen. We're only showing one ACTION_MOVE event, but you might see several when you try this for yourself. When the first finger is lifted off of the screen, we get an action value of 0x00000006 (or decimal 6). Like before, we have pointer index 0 and an action value that is ACTION_POINTER_UP (similar to ACTION_UP but for multitouch situations). If the second finger was lifted in a multitouch situation, we would get an action value of 0x00000106 (or decimal 262). Notice how we still have information for two fingers when we get the ACTION_UP for one of them.

The last pair of records in Listing 22-9 shows one more ACTION_MOVE event for the second finger, followed by an ACTION_UP for the second finger. This time, we see an action value of 1 (ACTION_UP). We didn't get an action value of 262, but we'll explain that next. Also, notice that once the first finger left the screen, the pointer index for the second finger has changed from 1 to 0, but the pointer ID has remained as 1.

ACTION_MOVE events do not tell you which finger moved. You will always get an action value of 2 for a move regardless of how many fingers are down or which finger is doing the moving. All down finger positions are available within the MotionEvent object, so you need to read the positions and then figure things out. If there's only one finger left on the screen, the pointer ID will tell you which finger it is that's still moving because it's the only finger left. In Listing 22-9, when the second finger was the only one left on the screen, the ACTION_MOVE event had a pointer index of 0 and a pointer ID of 1, so we knew it was the second finger that was moving.

Not only can a MotionEvent object contain move events for more than one finger, but it can also contain multiple move events per finger. It does this using historical values contained within the object. Android should report all history since the last MotionEvent object. See getHistoricalSize() and the other getHistorical...() methods.

Going back to the beginning of Listing 22-9, the first finger down is pointer index 0 and pointer ID 0, so why don't we get 0x00000005 (or decimal 5) for the action value when the first finger is pressed to the screen before any other fingers? Unfortunately, this question doesn't have a happy answer. We can get an action value of 5 in the following scenario: press the first finger to the screen and then the second finger, resulting in action values of 0 and 261 (ignoring the ACTION_MOVE events for the moment). Now, lift the first finger (action value of 6), and press it back down on the screen. The pointer ID of the second finger remained as 1. For the moment when the first finger was in the air, our application knew about pointer ID 1 only. Once the first finger touched the screen again, Android reassigned pointer ID 0 to the first finger and gave it pointer index 0 as well. Because now we know there are multiple fingers involved, we get an action value of 5 (pointer index of 0 and the action value of 5). The answer to the question, therefore, is backward compatibility, but it is not a happy answer. The action values of 0 and 1 are pre-multitouch.

When only one finger remains on the screen, Android treats it like a single-touch case. So we get the old ACTION_UP value of 1 instead of a multitouch ACTION_UP value of 6. Our code will need to consider these cases carefully. A pointer index of 0 could result in an ACTION_DOWN value of 0 or 5, depending on which pointers are in play. The last finger up will get an ACTION_UP value of 1 no matter which pointer ID it has.

There is another action we haven't mentioned so far: ACTION_SCROLL (value of 8), introduced in Android 3.1. This comes from an input device like a mouse, not a touch screen. In fact, as you can see from the methods in MotionEvent, these objects can be used for lots of things other than touch screen touches. We won't be covering these other input devices in this book.

Gestures

Gestures are a special type of a touch screen event. The term *gesture* is used for a variety of things in Android, from a simple touch sequence like a fling or a pinch to the formal Gesture class. Flings, pinches, long presses, and scrolls have expected behaviors with expected triggers. That is, it is pretty clear to most people that a fling is a gesture where a finger touches the screen, drags somewhat quickly off in a single direction, and then lifts up. For example, when someone uses a fling in the Gallery application (the one that shows images in a left-to-right chain), the images will move sideways to show new images to the user.

In the following sections, you will learn how to implement a pinch gesture, from which you can easily implement the other common gestures. The formal Gesture class refers to gestures drawn by a user on a touch screen, so that an application can react to those gestures. The typical example includes drawing letters of the alphabet which the application can understand as letters. The formal Gesture class is not covered in this book. Let's learn to pinch!

The Pinch Gesture

One of the cool applications of multitouch is the pinch gesture, which is used for zooming. The idea is that if you place two fingers on the screen and spread them apart, the application should respond by zooming in. If your fingers come together, the application should zoom out. The application is usually showing images, which could be maps.

Before we get to the pinch gesture's native support, we first need to cover a class that's been around from the beginning—GestureDetector.

GestureDetector and OnGestureListeners

The first class to help us with gestures is GestureDetector, which has been around from the very beginning of Android. Its purpose in life is to receive MotionEvent objects and tell us when a sequence of events looks like a common gesture. We pass all of our event objects to the GestureDetector from our callback, and it calls other callbacks when it recognizes a gesture, such as a fling or long press. We need to register a listener for the callbacks from the GestureDetector, and this is where we put our logic that says what to do if the user has performed one of these common gestures. Unfortunately, this class does not tell us if a pinch gesture is taking place; for that, we need to use a new class, which we'll get to shortly.

There are a few ways to build the listener side. Your first option is to write a new class that implements the appropriate gesture listener interface: for example, the GestureDetector.OnGestureListener interface. There are several abstract methods that must be implemented for each of the possible callbacks.

Your second option is to pick one of the simple implementations of a listener and override the appropriate callback methods that you care about. For example, the `GestureDetector.SimpleOnGestureListener` class has implemented all of the abstract methods to do nothing and return `false`. All you have to do is extend that class and override the few methods you need to act on those few gestures you care about. The other methods have their default implementations. It's more future-proof to choose the second option even if you decide to override all of the callback methods, because if a future version of Android adds another abstract callback method to the interface, the simple implementation will provide a default callback method, so you're covered.

We're going to explore `ScaleGestureDetector`, plus the corresponding listener class, to see how to use the pinch gesture to resize an image. In this example, we extend the simple implementation (`ScaleGestureDetector.SimpleOnScaleGestureListener`) for our listener. Listing 22-10 has the XML layout and the Java code for our `MainActivity`.

***Listing 22-10.* Layout and Java Code for the Pinch Gesture Using `ScaleGestureDetector`**

```
<?xml version="1.0" encoding="utf-8"?>
<LinearLayout xmlns:android="http://schemas.android.com/apk/res/android"
    android:id="@+id/layout"  android:orientation="vertical"
    android:layout_width="match_parent"
    android:layout_height="match_parent" >

  <TextView  android:text=
        "Use the pinch gesture to change the image size"
    android:layout_width="match_parent"
    android:layout_height="wrap_content" />

  <ImageView android:id="@+id/image"  android:src="@drawable/icon"
    android:layout_width="match_parent"
    android:layout_height="match_parent"
    android:scaleType="matrix" />

</LinearLayout>

// This file is MainActivity.java
public class MainActivity extends Activity {
    private static final String TAG = "ScaleDetector";
    private ImageView image;
    private ScaleGestureDetector mScaleDetector;
    private float mScaleFactor = 1f;
    private Matrix mMatrix = new Matrix();
    @Override
    public void onCreate(Bundle savedInstanceState) {
        super.onCreate(savedInstanceState);
        setContentView(R.layout.main);

        image = (ImageView)findViewById(R.id.image);
        mScaleDetector = new ScaleGestureDetector(this,
                new ScaleListener());
    }
```

```
    @Override
    public boolean onTouchEvent(MotionEvent ev) {
        Log.v(TAG, "in onTouchEvent");
        // Give all events to ScaleGestureDetector
        mScaleDetector.onTouchEvent(ev);

        return true;
    }

    private class ScaleListener extends
            ScaleGestureDetector.SimpleOnScaleGestureListener {
        @Override
        public boolean onScale(ScaleGestureDetector detector) {
            mScaleFactor *= detector.getScaleFactor();

            // Make sure we don't get too small or too big
            mScaleFactor = Math.max(0.1f, Math.min(mScaleFactor, 5.0f));

            Log.v(TAG, "in onScale, scale factor = " + mScaleFactor);
            mMatrix.setScale(mScaleFactor, mScaleFactor);

            image.setImageMatrix(mMatrix);
            image.invalidate();
            return true;
        }
    }
}
```

Our layout is straightforward. We have a simple `TextView` with our message to use the pinch gesture, and we have our `ImageView` with the standard Android icon. We're going to resize this icon image using a pinch gesture. Of course, feel free to substitute your own image file instead of the icon. Just copy your image file into a drawable folder, and be sure to change the `android:src` attribute in the layout file. Notice the `android:scaleType` attribute in the XML layout for our image. This tells Android that we'll be using a graphics matrix to do scaling operations on the image. Although a graphics matrix can also do movement of our image within the layout, we're only going to focus on scaling for now. Also notice that we set the `ImageView` size to as big as possible. As we scale the image, we don't want it clipped by the boundaries of the `ImageView`.

The code is also straightforward. Within `onCreate()`, we get a reference to our image and create our `ScaleGestureDetector`. Within our `onTouchEvent()` callback, all we do is pass every event object we get to the `ScaleGestureDetector`'s `onTouchEvent()` method and return `true` so we keep getting new events. This allows the `ScaleGestureDetector` to see all events and decide when to notify us of gestures.

The `ScaleListener` is where the zooming happens. There are actually three callbacks within the listener class: `onScaleBegin()`, `onScale()`, and `onScaleEnd()`. We don't need to do anything special with the begin and end methods, so we didn't implement them here.

Within onScale(), the detector passed in can be used to find out lots of information about the scaling operation. The scale factor is a value that hovers around 1. That is, as the fingers pinch closer together, this value is slightly below 1; as the fingers move apart, this value is slightly larger than 1. Our mScaleFactor member starts at 1, so it gets progressively smaller or larger than 1 as the fingers move together or apart. If mScaleFactor equals 1, our image will be normal size. Otherwise, our image will be smaller or larger than normal as mScaleFactor moves below or above 1. We set some bounds on mScaleFactor with the elegant min/max function combination. This prevents our image from getting too small or too large. We then use mScaleFactor to scale the graphics matrix, and we apply the newly scaled matrix to our image. The invalidate() call forces a redraw of the image on the screen.

To work with the OnGestureListener interface, you'd do something very similar to what we've done here with our ScaleListener, except that the callbacks will be for different common gestures such as single tap, double tap, long press, and fling.

References

Here are some helpful references to topics you may wish to explore further.

- www.androidbook.com/proandroid5/projects: Downloadable projects related to this book. For this chapter, look for a zip file called ProAndroid5_Ch22_Touchscreens.zip. This zip file contains all projects from this chapter, listed in separate root directories. There is also a README.TXT file that describes exactly how to import projects into your IDE from one of these zip files.
- www.ted.com/talks/jeff_han_demos_his_breakthrough_touchscreen.html: Jeff Han demonstrates his multitouch computer user interface at TED in 2006—very cool.
- http://android-developers.blogspot.com/2010/06/making-sense-of-multitouch.html: An Android blog post about multitouch offers yet another way to implement a GestureDetector inside an extension of a view.

Summary

Let's conclude this chapter by quickly enumerating what you have learned about touch screens so far:

- MotionEvent as the foundation on which touch handling is done
- Different callbacks that handle touch events on a View object and through an OnTouchListener
- Different types of events that occur during a touch sequence
- How touch events travel through an entire view hierarchy, unless handled along the way

- Information that a `MotionEvent` object contains about touches, including for multiple fingers
- When to recycle a `MotionEvent` object and when not to
- Determining the speed at which a finger drags across a screen
- The wonderful world of multitouch, and the internal details of how it works
- Implementing the pinch gesture, as well as other common gestures

Chapter 23

Implementing Drag and Drop

In the last chapter, we covered touchscreens, the `MotionEvent` class, and gestures. You learned how to use touch to make things happen in your application. One area that we didn't cover was drag and drop. On the surface, drag and drop seems like it should be fairly simple: touch an object on the screen, drag it across the screen (usually over some other object), and let go, and the application should take the appropriate action. In many computer operating systems, this is a common way to delete a file from the desktop; you just drag the file's icon to the trash-bin icon, and the file gets deleted. In Android, you may have seen how to rearrange icons on the home screen by dragging them to new locations or to the trash.

This chapter is going to go in depth into drag and drop. Prior to Android 3.0, developers were on their own when it came to drag and drop. But because there are still quite a few phones out there running Android 2.3, we'll show you how to do drag and drop on them. We'll show you the old way in the first section of this chapter, and then we'll show you the new way in the second part.

Exploring Drag and Drop

In this next example application, we're going to take a white dot and drag it to a new location in our user interface. We're also going to place three counters in our user interface, and if the user drags the white dot to one of the counters, that counter will increment and the dot will return back to its starting place. If the dot is dragged somewhere else on the screen, we'll just leave it there.

> **Note** See the "References" section at the end of this chapter for the URL from which you can import these projects into your IDE directly. We'll only show code in the text to explain concepts. You'll need to download the code to create a working example application.

The first sample application for this chapter is called TouchDragDemo. There are two key files we want to talk about in this section:

- /res/layout/main.xml
- /src/com/androidbook/touch/dragdemo/Dot.java

The main.xml file contains our layout for the drag-and-drop demo. It is shown in Listing 23-1. Some of the key concepts we want you to notice are the use of a FrameLayout as the top-level layout, inside of which is a LinearLayout containing TextViews and a custom View class called Dot. Because the LinearLayout and Dot coexist within the FrameLayout, their positions and sizes don't really impact each other, but they will be sharing the screen real estate, one on top of the other. The UI for this application is shown in Figure 23-1.

Listing 23-1. Example Layout XML for Our Drag Example

```
<?xml version="1.0" encoding="utf-8"?>
<!-- This file is res/layout/main.xml -->
<FrameLayout xmlns:android="http://schemas.android.com/apk/res/android"
    android:layout_width="match_parent"
    android:layout_height="match_parent"
    android:background="#0000ff" >

  <LinearLayout android:id="@+id/counters"
    android:orientation="vertical"
    android:layout_width="match_parent"
    android:layout_height="match_parent" >

    <TextView android:id="@+id/top" android:text="0"
      android:background="#111111"
      android:layout_height="wrap_content"
      android:layout_width="60dp"
      android:layout_gravity="right"
      android:layout_marginTop="30dp"
      android:layout_marginBottom="30dp"
      android:padding="10dp" />

    <TextView android:id="@+id/middle" android:text="0"
      android:background="#111111"
      android:layout_height="wrap_content"
      android:layout_width="60dp"
      android:layout_gravity="right"
      android:layout_marginBottom="30dp"
      android:padding="10dp" />

    <TextView android:id="@+id/bottom" android:text="0"
      android:background="#111111"
      android:layout_height="wrap_content"
      android:layout_width="60dp"
      android:layout_gravity="right"
      android:padding="10dp" />
  </LinearLayout>
```

```
    <com.androidbook.touch.dragdemo.Dot android:id="@+id/dot"
      android:layout_width="match_parent"
      android:layout_height="match_parent" />

</FrameLayout>
```

Figure 23-1. *User interface for TouchDragDemo*

Note that the package name in the layout XML file for the Dot element must match the package name you use for your application. As mentioned, the layout of Dot is separated from the LinearLayout. This is because we want the freedom to move the dot around the screen, which is why we chose the layout_width and layout_height of "match_parent". When we draw the dot on the screen, we want it to be visible, and if we constrict the size of our dot's view to the diameter of the dot, we won't be able to see it when we drag it away from our starting place.

> **Note** Technically, we could set android:clipChildren to true in the FrameLayout tag and set the layout width and height of the dot to wrap_content, but that doesn't feel as clean.

For each of the counters, we simply lay them out with a background, padding, margins, and gravity to get them to show up along the right-hand side of the screen. We start them off at zero, but as you'll soon see, we'll be incrementing those values as dots are dragged over to them. Although we chose to use TextViews in this example, you could use just about any View object as a drop target. Now we will look at the Java code for our Dot class in Listing 23-2.

Listing 23-2. Java Code for Our Dot Class

```
public class Dot extends View {
    private static final String TAG = "TouchDrag";
    private float left = 0;
    private float top = 0;
    private float radius = 20;
    private float offsetX;
    private float offsetY;
    private Paint myPaint;
    private Context myContext;

    public Dot(Context context, AttributeSet attrs) {
        super(context, attrs);

        // Save the context (the activity)
        myContext = context;

        myPaint = new Paint();
        myPaint.setColor(Color.WHITE);
        myPaint.setAntiAlias(true);
    }

    public boolean onTouchEvent(MotionEvent event) {
        int action = event.getAction();
        float eventX = event.getX();
        float eventY = event.getY();
        switch(action) {
        case MotionEvent.ACTION_DOWN:
            // First make sure the touch is on our dot,
            // since the size of the dot's view is
            // technically the whole layout. If the
            // touch is *not* within, then return false
            // indicating we don't want any more events.
            if( !(left-20 < eventX && eventX < left+radius*2+20 &&
                top-20 < eventY && eventY < top+radius*2+20))
                return false;

            // Remember the offset of the touch as compared
            // to our left and top edges.
            offsetX = eventX - left;
            offsetY = eventY - top;
            break;
        case MotionEvent.ACTION_MOVE:
        case MotionEvent.ACTION_UP:
        case MotionEvent.ACTION_CANCEL:
            left = eventX - offsetX;
            top = eventY - offsetY;
            if(action == MotionEvent.ACTION_UP) {
                checkDrop(eventX, eventY);
            }
            break;
```

```
        }
        invalidate();
        return true;
    }

    private void checkDrop(float x, float y) {
        // See if the x,y of our drop location is near to
        // one of our counters. If so, increment it, and
        // reset the dot back to its starting position
        Log.v(TAG, "checking drop target for " + x + ", " + y);

        int viewCount = ((MainActivity)myContext).counterLayout
                .getChildCount();
        for(int i = 0; i<viewCount; i++) {
            View view = ((MainActivity)myContext).counterLayout
                    .getChildAt(i);
            if(view.getClass() == TextView.class){
                Log.v(TAG, "Is the drop to the right of " +
                            (view.getLeft()-20));
                Log.v(TAG, "  and vertically between " +
                         (view.getTop()-20) +
                         " and " + (view.getBottom()+20) + "?");
                if(x > view.getLeft()-20 &&
                        view.getTop()-20 < y &&
                        y < view.getBottom()+20) {
                    Log.v(TAG, "     Yes. Yes it is.");

                    // Increase the count value in the TextView by one
                    int count =
                        Integer.parseInt(
                            ((TextView)view).getText().toString());
                    ((TextView)view).setText(String.valueOf( ++count ));

                    // Reset the dot back to starting position
                    left = top = 0;
                    break;
                }
            }
        }
    }

    public void draw(Canvas canvas) {
        canvas.drawCircle(left + radius, top + radius, radius, myPaint);
    }
}
```

When you run this application, you will see a white dot on a blue background. You can touch the dot and drag it around the screen. When you lift your finger, the dot stays where it is until you touch it again and drag it somewhere else. The `draw()` method puts the dot at its current location of left and top, adjusted by the dot's radius. By receiving `MotionEvent` objects in the `onTouchEvent()` method, we can modify the left and top values by the movement of our touch.

Because the user won't always touch the exact center of the object, the touch coordinates will not be the same as the location coordinates of the object. That is the purpose of the offset values: to get us back to the left and top edges of our dot from the position of the touch. But even before we start a drag operation, we want to be sure that the user's touch is considered close enough to the dot to be valid. If the user touches the screen far away from the dot, which is technically within the view layout of the dot, we don't want that to start a drag sequence. That is why we look to see if the touch is within the white dot itself; if it is not, we simply return `false`, which prevents receiving any more touch events in that touch sequence.

When your finger starts moving across the screen, we adjust the location of the object by the deltas in x and y based on the `MotionEvents` that we get. When you stop moving (`ACTION_UP`), we finalize our location using the last coordinates of your touch. We don't have to worry about scrollbars in this example, which could complicate the calculation of the object's position of our object on the screen. But the basic principle is still the same. By knowing the starting location of the object to be moved and keeping track of the delta values of a touch from `ACTION_DOWN` through to `ACTION_UP`, we can adjust the location of the object on the screen.

Dropping an object onto another object on the screen has much less to do with touch than it does with knowing where things are on the screen. As we drag an object around the screen, we are aware of its position relative to one or more reference points. We can also interrogate objects on the screen for their locations and sizes. We can then determine if our dragged object is "over" another object. The typical process of figuring out a drop target for a dragged object is to iterate through the available objects that can be dropped on and determine if our current position overlaps with that object. Each object's size and position (and sometimes shape) can be used to make this determination. If we get an `ACTION_UP` event, meaning that the user has let go of our dragged object, and the object is over something we can drop onto, we can fire the logic to process the drop action.

We used this approach in our sample application. When the ACTION_UP action is detected, we then look through the child views of the `LinearLayout`, and for each `TextView` that is found, we compare the location of the touch to the edges of the `TextView` (plus a little bit extra). If the touch is within that `TextView`, we grab the current numeric value of the `TextView`, increment it by one, and write it back. If this happens, the position of the dot is reset back to its starting place (left = 0, top = 0) for the next drag.

Our example shows you the basics of a way to do drag and drop in Android prior to 3.0. With this you could implement drag-and-drop features in your application. This might be the action of dragging something to the trash can, where the object being dragged should be deleted, or it could be dragging a file to a folder for the purposes of moving or copying it. To embellish your application, you could pre-identify which views are potential drop targets and cause them to visually change as a drag starts. If you wanted the dragged object to disappear from the screen when it is dropped, you could always programmatically remove it from the layout (see the various `removeView` methods in `ViewGroup`).

Now that you've seen the hard way to do drag and drop, we'd like to show you the drag-and-drop support that was added in Android 3.0.

Basics of Drag and Drop in 3.0+

Prior to Android 3.0, there was no direct support for drag and drop. You learned in the first section of this chapter how to drag a View around the screen; you also learned that it was possible to use the current location of the dragged object to determine if there was a drop target underneath. When the MotionEvent for the finger-up event was received, your code could figure out if that meant a drop had occurred. Although this was doable, it certainly wasn't as easy as having direct support in Android for the drag-and-drop operation. You now have that direct support.

At its most basic, the drag-and-drop operation starts with a view declaring that a drag has started; then all interested parties watch the drag take place until the drop event is fired. If a view catches the drop event and wants to receive it, then a drag and drop has just occurred. If there is no view to receive the drop, or if the view that receives it doesn't want it, then no drop takes place. Dragging is communicated through the use of a DragEvent object, which is passed to all of the drag listeners available.

Within the DragEvent object are descriptors for lots of information, depending on the initiator of the drag sequence. For example, the DragEvent can contain object references to the initiator itself, state information, textual data, URIs, or pretty much whatever you want to pass through the drag sequence.

Information could be passed that results in view-to-view dynamic communication; however, the originator data in a DragEvent object is set when the DragEvent is created, and it stays the same thereafter. In addition to this data, the DragEvent has an action value indicating what is going on with the drag sequence, and location information indicating where the drag is on the screen.

A DragEvent has six possible actions:

- ACTION_DRAG_STARTED indicates that a new drag sequence has begun.
- ACTION_DRAG_ENTERED indicates that the dragged object has been dragged into the boundaries of a specific view.
- ACTION_DRAG_LOCATION indicates that the dragged object has been dragged on the screen to a new location.
- ACTION_DRAG_EXITED indicates that the dragged object has been dragged outside the boundaries of a specific view.
- ACTION_DROP indicates that the user has let go of the dragged object. It is up to the receiver of this event to determine whether this truly means a drop has occurred.
- ACTION_DRAG_ENDED tells all drag listeners that the previous drag sequence has ended. The DragEvent.getResult() method indicates a successful drop or failure.

You might think that you need to set up a drag listener on each view in the system that could participate in a drag sequence; but, in fact, you can define a drag listener on just about anything in your application, and it will receive all of the drag events for all views in the system. This can make things a little confusing because the drag listener does not need to be associated with either the object being dragged or the drop target. The listener can manage all of the coordination of the drag and drop.

In fact, if you inspect the drag-and-drop example project that comes with the Android SDK, you will see that it sets up a listener on a `TextView` that has nothing to do with the actual dragging and dropping. The upcoming example project uses drag listeners that are tied to specific views. These drag listeners each receive a `DragEvent` object for the drag events that occur in the drag sequence. This means a view could receive a `DragEvent` object that can be ignored because it is really about a different view. This also means the drag listener must make that determination in code and that there must be enough information within the `DragEvent` object for the drag listener to figure out what to do.

If a drag listener got a `DragEvent` object that merely said there's an unknown object being dragged and it's at coordinates (15, 57), there isn't much the drag listener can do with it. It is much more helpful to get a `DragEvent` object that says a particular object is being dragged, it's at coordinates (15, 57), it's a copy operation, and the data is a specific URI. When that drops, there's enough information to be able to initiate a copy operation.

We're actually seeing two different kinds of dragging going on. In our first example application, we dragged a view across a frame layout, and we could let go and that view would stay where it was. We only got drag-and-drop behavior when we dropped our view on top of something else. The supported form of drag and drop works differently than this. Now, when you drag a view as part of a drag-and-drop sequence, the dragged view doesn't move at all. We get a shadow image of the dragged view which does travel across the screen, but if we let go of it, that shadow view goes away. What this means is that you might still have occasion to use the technique from the beginning of this chapter in an Android 3.0+ application, to move images around on the screen perhaps, without necessarily doing drag and drop.

Drag-and-Drop Example Application

For your next example application, you're going to employ a staple of 3.0, the fragment. This, among other things, will prove that drags can cross fragment boundaries. You'll create a palette of dots on the left and a square target on the right. When a dot is grabbed using a long click, you'll change the color of that dot in the palette and Android will show a shadow of the dot as you drag. When the dragged dot reaches the square target, the target will begin to glow. If you drop the dot on the square target, a message will indicate that you've just added one more drop to the drop count, the glowing will stop, and the original dot will go back to its original color.

List of Files

This application builds upon concepts we've covered throughout this book. We're only going to include the interesting files in the text. For the others, just look at them in your IDE at your leisure. Here are the ones that we've included in the text:

- `palette.xml` is the fragment layout for the dots on the left side (see Listing 23-3).
- `dropzone.xml` is the fragment layout for the square target on the right side, plus the drop-count message (see Listing 23-4).

- DropZone.java inflates the dropzone.xml fragment layout file and then implements the drag listener for the drop target (see Listing 23-5).
- Dot.java is your custom view class for the objects you're going to drag. It handles beginning the drag sequence, watching drag events, and drawing the dots (see Listing 23-6).

Laying Out the Example Drag-and-Drop Application

Before we get into the code, Figure 23-2 shows what the application will look like.

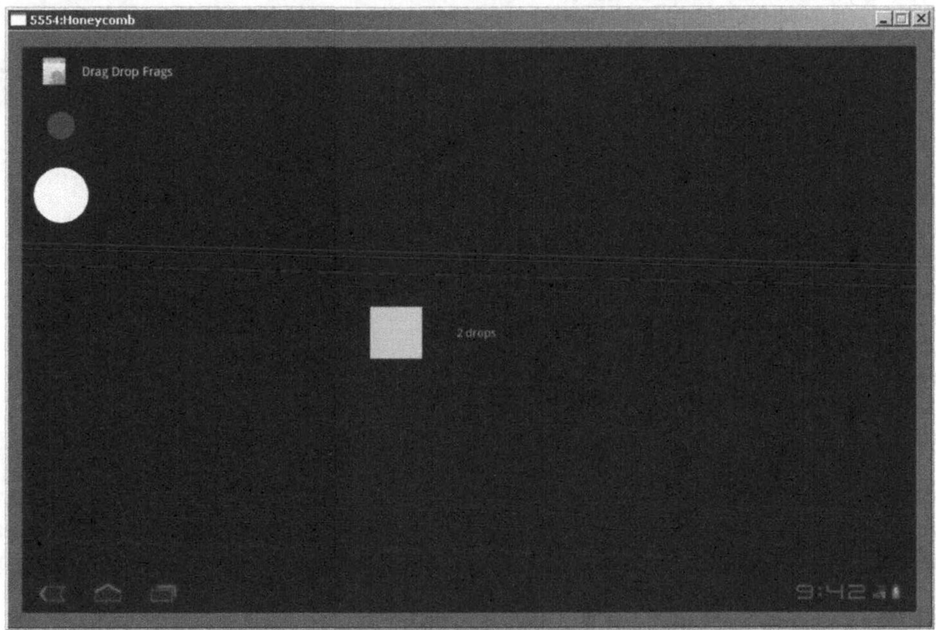

***Figure 23-2.** Drag Drop Frags example application user interface*

The main layout file has a simple horizontal linear layout and two fragment specifications. The first fragment will be for the palette of dots and the second will be for the dropzone.

The palette fragment layout file (Listing 23-3) gets a bit more interesting. Although this layout represents a fragment, you don't need to include a fragment tag within this layout. This layout will be inflated to become the view hierarchy for your palette fragment. The dots are specified as custom dots, and there are two of them arranged vertically. Notice that there are a couple of custom XML attributes in the definition of your dots (`dot:color` and `dot:radius`). As you can see, these attributes specify the color and the radius of your dots. You might also have noticed that the layout width and height are `wrap_content`, not `match_parent` as in the earlier example application in this chapter. The new drag-and-drop support makes things much easier.

Listing 23-3. The `palette.xml` Layout File for the Dots

```
<?xml version="1.0" encoding="utf-8"?>
<!-- This file is res/layout/palette.xml -->
<LinearLayout
  xmlns:android="http://schemas.android.com/apk/res/android"
  xmlns:dot=
    "http://schemas.android.com/apk/res/com.androidbook.drag.drop.demo"
  android:layout_width="match_parent"
  android:layout_height="match_parent"
  android:orientation="vertical">

  <com.androidbook.drag.drop.demo.Dot android:id="@+id/dot1"
    android:layout_width="wrap_content"
    android:layout_height="wrap_content"
    android:padding="30dp"
    android:tag="Blue dot"
    dot:color="#ff1111ff"
    dot:radius="20dp"  />

  <com.androidbook.drag.drop.demo.Dot android:id="@+id/dot2"
    android:layout_width="wrap_content"
    android:layout_height="wrap_content"
    android:padding="10dp"
    android:tag="White dot"
    dot:color="#ffffffff"
    dot:radius="40dp"  />

</LinearLayout>
```

The dropzone fragment layout file in Listing 23-4 is also easy to understand. There's a green square and a text message arranged horizontally. This will be the dropzone for the dots you'll be dragging. The text message will be used to display a running count of the drops.

Listing 23-4. The `dropzone.xml` Layout File

```
<?xml version="1.0" encoding="utf-8"?>
<!-- This file is res/layout/dropzone.xml -->
<LinearLayout
  xmlns:android="http://schemas.android.com/apk/res/android"
  android:layout_width="match_parent"
  android:layout_height="match_parent"
  android:orientation="horizontal" >

  <View android:id="@+id/droptarget"
    android:layout_width="75dp"
    android:layout_height="75dp"
    android:layout_gravity="center_vertical"
    android:background="#00ff00" />
```

```
  <TextView android:id="@+id/dropmessage"
    android:text="0 drops"
    android:layout_width="wrap_content"
    android:layout_height="wrap_content"
    android:layout_gravity="center_vertical"
    android:paddingLeft="50dp"
    android:textSize="17sp" />

</LinearLayout>
```

Responding to onDrag in the Dropzone

Now that you have the main application layout set, let's see how the drop target needs to be organized by examining Listing 23-5.

Listing 23-5. The `DropZone.java` File

```
public class DropZone extends Fragment {

    private View dropTarget;
    private TextView dropMessage;

    @Override
    public View onCreateView(LayoutInflater inflater,
            ViewGroup container, Bundle icicle)
    {
        View v = inflater.inflate(R.layout.dropzone, container, false);

        dropMessage = (TextView)v.findViewById(R.id.dropmessage);

        dropTarget = (View)v.findViewById(R.id.droptarget);
        dropTarget.setOnDragListener(new View.OnDragListener() {
            private static final String DROPTAG = "DropTarget";
            private int dropCount = 0;
            private ObjectAnimator anim;

            public boolean onDrag(View v, DragEvent event) {
                int action = event.getAction();
                boolean result = true;
                switch(action) {
                case DragEvent.ACTION_DRAG_STARTED:
                    Log.v(DROPTAG, "drag started in dropTarget");
                    break;
                case DragEvent.ACTION_DRAG_ENTERED:
                    Log.v(DROPTAG, "drag entered dropTarget");
                    anim = ObjectAnimator.ofFloat(
                                (Object)v, "alpha", 1f, 0.5f);
                    anim.setInterpolator(new CycleInterpolator(40));
                    anim.setDuration(30*1000); // 30 seconds
                    anim.start();
                    break;
```

```
                case DragEvent.ACTION_DRAG_EXITED:
                    Log.v(DROPTAG, "drag exited dropTarget");
                    if(anim != null) {
                        anim.end();
                        anim = null;
                    }
                    break;
                case DragEvent.ACTION_DRAG_LOCATION:
                    Log.v(DROPTAG, "drag proceeding in dropTarget: " +
                            event.getX() + ", " + event.getY());
                    break;
                case DragEvent.ACTION_DROP:
                    Log.v(DROPTAG, "drag drop in dropTarget");
                    if(anim != null) {
                        anim.end();
                        anim = null;
                    }

                    ClipData data = event.getClipData();
                    Log.v(DROPTAG, "Item data is " +
                           data.getItemAt(0).getText());

                    dropCount++;
                    String message = dropCount + " drop";
                    if(dropCount > 1)
                        message += "s";
                    dropMessage.setText(message);
                    break;
                case DragEvent.ACTION_DRAG_ENDED:
                    Log.v(DROPTAG, "drag ended in dropTarget");
                    if(anim != null) {
                        anim.end();
                        anim = null;
                    }
                    break;
                default:
                    Log.v(DROPTAG, "other action in dropzone: " +
                                   action);
                    result = false;
                }
                return result;
            }
        });
        return v;
    }
}
```

Now you're starting to get into interesting code. For the dropzone, you need to create the target upon which you want to drag the dots. As you saw earlier, the layout specifies a green square on the screen with a text message next to it. Because the dropzone is also a fragment, you're overriding the `onCreateView()` method of `DropZone`. The first thing to do is inflate the dropzone layout and then extract out the view reference for the square target (dropTarget) and for the text message (dropMessage). Then you need to set up a drag listener on the target so it will know when a drag is underway.

The drop-target drag listener has a single callback method in it: onDrag(). This callback will receive a view reference as well as a DragEvent object. The view reference relates to the view that the DragEvent is related to. As mentioned, the drag listener is not necessarily connected to the view that will be interacting with the drag event, so this callback must identify the view for which the drag event is taking place.

One of the first things you likely want to do in any onDrag() callback is read the action from the DragEvent object. This will tell you what's going on. For the most part, the only thing you want to do in this callback is log the fact that a drag event is taking place. You don't need to actually do anything for ACTION_DRAG_LOCATION, for example. But you do want to have some special logic for when the object is dragged within your boundaries (ACTION_DRAG_ENTERED) that will be turned off either when the object is dragged outside of your boundaries (ACTION_DRAG_EXITED) or when the object is dropped (ACTION_DROP).

You're using the ObjectAnimator class that was introduced in Chapter 18, only here you're using it in code to specify a cyclic interpolator that modifies the target's alpha. This will have the effect of pulsing the transparency of the green target square, which will be the visual indication that the target is willing to accept a drop of the object onto it. Because you turn on the animation, you must make sure to also turn it off when the object leaves or is dropped, or the drag and drop is ended. In theory, you shouldn't need to stop the animation on ACTION_DRAG_ENDED, but it's wise to do it anyway.

For this particular drag listener, you're going to get ACTION_DRAG_ENTERED and ACTION_DRAG_EXITED only if the dragged object interacts with the view with which you're associated. And as you'll see, the ACTION_DRAG_LOCATION events happen only if the dragged object is inside your target view.

The only other interesting condition is the ACTION_DROP itself (notice that DRAG_ is not part of the name of this action). If a drop has occurred on your view, it means the user has let go of the dot over the green square. Because you're expecting this object to be dropped on the green square, you can just go ahead and read the data from the first item and then log it to LogCat. In a production application, you might pay closer attention to the ClipData object that is contained in the drag event itself. By inspecting its properties, you could decide if you even want to accept the drop or not.

This is a good time to point out the result boolean in this onDrag() callback method. Depending on how things go, you want to let Android know either that you took care of the drag event (by returning true) or that you didn't (by returning false). If you don't see what you want to see inside of the drag event object, you could certainly return false from this callback, which would tell Android that this drop was not handled.

Once you log the information from the drag event in LogCat, you increment the count of the drops received; this is updated in the user interface, and that's about it for DropZone.

If you look this class over, it's really rather simple. You don't actually have any code in here that deals with MotionEvents, nor do you even need to make your own determination of whether there is a drag going on. You just get appropriate callback calls as a drag sequence unfolds.

Setting Up the Drag Source Views

Let's now consider how views corresponding to a drag source are organized, starting by looking at Listing 23-6.

Listing 23-6. The Java for the Custom View: Dot

```
public class Dot extends View
    implements View.OnDragListener
{
    private static final int DEFAULT_RADIUS = 20;
    private static final int DEFAULT_COLOR = Color.WHITE;
    private static final int SELECTED_COLOR = Color.MAGENTA;
    protected static final String DOTTAG = "DragDot";
    private Paint mNormalPaint;
    private Paint mDraggingPaint;
    private int mColor = DEFAULT_COLOR;
    private int mRadius = DEFAULT_RADIUS;
    private boolean inDrag;

    public Dot(Context context, AttributeSet attrs) {
        super(context, attrs);

        // Apply attribute settings from the layout file.
        // Note: these could change on a reconfiguration
        // such as a screen rotation.
        TypedArray myAttrs = context.obtainStyledAttributes(attrs,
                R.styleable.Dot);

        final int numAttrs = myAttrs.getIndexCount();
        for (int i = 0; i < numAttrs; i++) {
            int attr = myAttrs.getIndex(i);
            switch (attr) {
            case R.styleable.Dot_radius:
                mRadius = myAttrs.getDimensionPixelSize(attr,
                          DEFAULT_RADIUS);
                break;
            case R.styleable.Dot_color:
                mColor = myAttrs.getColor(attr, DEFAULT_COLOR);
                break;
            }
        }
        myAttrs.recycle();

        // Setup paint colors
        mNormalPaint = new Paint();
        mNormalPaint.setColor(mColor);
        mNormalPaint.setAntiAlias(true);

        mDraggingPaint = new Paint();
        mDraggingPaint.setColor(SELECTED_COLOR);
        mDraggingPaint.setAntiAlias(true);
```

```
        // Start a drag on a long click on the dot
        setOnLongClickListener(lcListener);
        setOnDragListener(this);
    }

    private static View.OnLongClickListener lcListener =
        new View.OnLongClickListener() {
        private boolean mDragInProgress;

        public boolean onLongClick(View v) {
            ClipData data =
            ClipData.newPlainText("DragData", (String)v.getTag());

            mDragInProgress =
            v.startDrag(data, new View.DragShadowBuilder(v),
                    (Object)v, 0);

            Log.v((String) v.getTag(),
              "starting drag? " + mDragInProgress);

            return true;
        }
    };

    @Override
    protected void onMeasure(int widthSpec, int heightSpec) {
        int size = 2*mRadius + getPaddingLeft() + getPaddingRight();
        setMeasuredDimension(size, size);
    }

    // The dragging functionality
    public boolean onDrag(View v, DragEvent event) {
        String dotTAG = (String) getTag();
        // Only worry about drag events if this is us being dragged
        if(event.getLocalState() != this) {
            Log.v(dotTAG, "This drag event is not for us");
            return false;
        }
        boolean result = true;

        // get event values to work with
        int action = event.getAction();
        float x = event.getX();
        float y = event.getY();

        switch(action) {
        case DragEvent.ACTION_DRAG_STARTED:
            Log.v(dotTAG, "drag started. X: " + x + ", Y: " + y);
            inDrag = true; // used in draw() below to change color
            break;
```

```
        case DragEvent.ACTION_DRAG_LOCATION:
            Log.v(dotTAG, "drag proceeding… At: " + x + ", " + y);
            break;
        case DragEvent.ACTION_DRAG_ENTERED:
            Log.v(dotTAG, "drag entered. At: " + x + ", " + y);
            break;
        case DragEvent.ACTION_DRAG_EXITED:
            Log.v(dotTAG, "drag exited. At: " + x + ", " + y);
            break;
        case DragEvent.ACTION_DROP:
            Log.v(dotTAG, "drag dropped. At: " + x + ", " + y);
            // Return false because we don't accept the drop in Dot.
            result = false;
            break;
        case DragEvent.ACTION_DRAG_ENDED:
            Log.v(dotTAG, "drag ended. Success? " + event.getResult());
            inDrag = false; // change color of original dot back
            break;
        default:
            Log.v(dotTAG, "some other drag action: " + action);
            result = false;
            break;
        }
        return result;
    }

    // Here is where you draw our dot, and where you change the color if
    // you're in the process of being dragged. Note: the color change
    // affects the original dot only, not the shadow.
    public void draw(Canvas canvas) {
        float cx = this.getWidth()/2 + getLeftPaddingOffset();
        float cy = this.getHeight()/2 + getTopPaddingOffset();
        Paint paint = mNormalPaint;
        if(inDrag)
            paint = mDraggingPaint;
        canvas.drawCircle(cx, cy, mRadius, paint);
        invalidate();
    }
}
```

The Dot code looks somewhat similar to the code for DropZone. This is in part because you're also receiving drag events in this class. The constructor for a Dot figures out the attributes in order to set the correct radius and color, and then it sets up the two listeners: one for long clicks and another for the drag events.

The two paints are going to be used to draw your circle. You use the normal paint when the dot is just sitting there. But when the dot is being dragged, you want to indicate that by changing the color of the original to magenta.

The long-click listener is where you initiate a drag sequence. The only way you let the user start dragging a dot is if the user clicks and holds on a dot. When the long-click listener is firing, you create a new `ClipData` object using a string and the dot's tag. You happen to know that the tag is the name of the dot as specified in the XML layout file. There are several other ways to specify data into a `ClipData` object, so feel free to read the reference documentation on other ways to store data in a `ClipData` object.

The next statement is the critical one: `startDrag()`. This is where Android will take over and start the process of dragging. Note that the first argument is the `ClipData` object from before; then it's the drag-shadow object, then a local-state object, and finally the number zero.

The drag-shadow object is the image that will be displayed as the dragging is taking place. In your case, this does not replace the original dot image on the screen but shows a shadow of a dot as the dragging is taking place, in addition to the original dot on the screen. The default `DragShadowBuilder` behavior is to create a shadow that looks very much like the original, so for your purposes, you merely call it and pass in your view. You can get fancy here and create whatever sort of shadow view you want, but if you do override this class, you'll need to implement a few methods to make it work.

The `onMeasure()` method is here to supply dimension information to Android for the custom view you're using here. You have to tell Android how big your view is so it knows how to lay it out with everything else. This is standard practice for a custom view.

Finally, there's the `onDrag()` callback. As mentioned, each drag listener can receive drag events. They all get `ACTION_DRAG_STARTED` and `ACTION_DRAG_ENDED`, for example. So, when events happen, you must be careful what you do with the information. Because there are two dots in play in this example application, whenever you do something with the dots, you must be careful that you're affecting the correct one.

When both dots receive the `ACTION_DRAG_STARTED` action, only one should set the color of itself to magenta. To figure out which one is correct, compare the local state object passed in with yourself. If you look back where you set the local-state object, you passed the current view in. So now, when you've received the local-state object out, you compare it to yourself to see if you're the view that initiated the drag sequence.

If you aren't the same view, you write a log message to LogCat saying this is not for you, and you return `false` to say you're not handling this message.

If you are the view that should be receiving this drag event, you collect some values from the drag event, then you mostly just log the event to LogCat. The first exception to this is `ACTION_DRAG_STARTED`. If you got this action and it's for you, you then know that your dot has begun a drag sequence. Therefore, you set the `inDrag` boolean so the `draw()` method later on will do the right thing and display a different-colored dot. This different color only lasts until `ACTION_DRAG_ENDED` is received, at which time you restore the original color of the dot.

If a dot gets the `ACTION_DROP` action, this means the user tried to drop a dot on a dot—maybe even the original dot. This shouldn't do anything, so you just return `false` from this callback in this case.

Finally, the draw() method of your custom view figures out the location of the center point of your circle (dot) and then draws it with the appropriate paint. The invalidate() method is there to tell Android that you've modified the view and that Android should redraw the user interface. By calling invalidate(), you ensure that the user interface will be updated very shortly with whatever is new.

You now have all the files and the background necessary to compile and deploy this example drag-and-drop application.

Testing the Example Drag-and-Drop Application

Following is some example output from LogCat when we ran this example application. Notice how the log message used Blue dot to indicate messages from the blue dot, White dot for messages from the white dot, and DropTarget for the view where the drops are allowed to go.

```
White dot:  starting drag? true
Blue dot:   This drag event is not for us
White dot:  drag started. X: 53.0, Y: 206.0
DropTarget: drag started in dropTarget
DropTarget: drag entered dropTarget
DropTarget: drag proceeding in dropTarget: 29.0, 36.0
DropTarget: drag proceeding in dropTarget: 48.0, 39.0
DropTarget: drag proceeding in dropTarget: 45.0, 39.0
DropTarget: drag proceeding in dropTarget: 41.0, 39.0
DropTarget: drag proceeding in dropTarget: 40.0, 39.0
DropTarget: drag drop in dropTarget
DropTarget: Item data is White dot
ViewRoot:   Reporting drop result: true
White dot:  drag ended. Success? true
Blue dot:   This drag event is not for us
DropTarget: drag ended in dropTarget
```

In this particular case, the drag was started with the white dot. Once the long click has triggered the beginning of the drag sequence, we get the starting drag message.

Notice how the next three lines all indicate that an ACTION_DRAG_STARTED action was received in three different views. Blue dot determined that the callback was not for it. It was also not for DropTarget.

Next, notice how the drag-proceeding messages show the drag happening through DropTarget, beginning with the ACTION_DRAG_ENTERED action. This means the dot was being dragged on top of the green square. The x and y coordinates reported in the drag event object are the coordinates of the drag point relative to the upper-left corner of the view. So, in the example app, the first record of the drag in the drop target is at (x, y) = (29, 36), and the drop occurred at (40, 39). See how the drop target was able to extract the tag name of the white dot from the event's ClipData to write it to LogCat.

Also see how once again, all drag listeners received the ACTION_DRAG_ENDED action. Only White dot determined that it's okay to display the results using getResult().

Feel free to experiment with this example application. Drag a dot to the other dot, or even to itself. Go ahead and add another dot to palette.xml. Notice how when the dragged dot leaves the green square, there's a message saying that the drag exited. Note also that if you drop a dot somewhere other than the green square, the drop is considered failed.

References

Here are some helpful references to topics you may wish to explore further:

- www.androidbook.com/proandroid5/projects: A list of downloadable projects related to this book. For this chapter, look for a zip file called ProAndroid5_Ch23_DragnDrop.zip. This zip file contains all the projects from this chapter, listed in separate root directories. There is also a README.TXT file that describes exactly how to import projects into your IDE from one of these zip files.
- http://developer.android.com/guide/topics/ui/drag-drop.html: The Android developer's guide to drag and drop.

Summary

Let's summarize the topics covered in this chapter:

- Drag-and-drop support in Android 3.0, and implementing it prior to 3.0 using other methods
- Iterating through possible drop targets to see if a drop (that is, finger leaving the screen after dragging) occurred
- The difficulty of doing the math to keep track of where a dragged object is and whether it's over a drop target
- Drag-and-drop support in Android 3.0+, which is much nicer because it eliminates a lot of guesswork
- Drag listeners, which can be any objects and do not need to be draggables or drop-target views
- The fact that a drag can occur across fragments
- The DragEvent object, which can contain lots of great information about what is being dragged and why
- How Android takes care of the math to determine whether a drop is occurring on top of a view

Chapter 24

Using Sensors

Android devices often come with hardware sensors built in, and Android provides a framework for working with those sensors. Sensors can be fun. Measuring the outside world and using that in software in a device is pretty cool. It is the kind of programming experience you just don't get on a regular computer that sits on a desk or in a server room. The possibilities for new applications that use sensors are huge, and we hope you are inspired to realize them.

In this chapter, we'll explore the Android sensor framework. We'll explain what sensors are and how we get sensor data, and then discuss some specifics of the kinds of data we can get from sensors and what we can do with it. While Android has defined several sensor types already, there are no doubt more sensors in Android's future, and we expect that future sensors will get incorporated into the sensor framework.

What Is a Sensor?

In Android, a *sensor* is a source of data events from the physical world. This is typically a piece of hardware that has been wired into the device, but Android also provides some logical sensors that combine data from multiple physical sensors. Applications in turn use the sensor data to inform the user about the physical world, to control game play, to do augmented reality, or to provide useful tools for working in the real world. Sensors operate in one direction only; they're read-only. That makes using them fairly straightforward. You set up a listener to receive sensor data, and then you process the data as it comes in. GPS hardware is like the sensors we cover in this chapter. In Chapter 19, we set up listeners for GPS location updates, and we processed those location updates as they came in. But although GPS is similar to a sensor, it is not part of the sensor framework that is provided by Android.

Some of the sensor types that can appear in an Android device include

- Light sensor
- Proximity sensor
- Temperature sensor
- Pressure sensor

- Gyroscope sensor
- Accelerometer
- Magnetic field sensor
- Gravity sensor
- Linear acceleration sensor
- Rotation vector sensor
- Relative humidity sensor

Detecting Sensors

Please don't assume, however, that all Android devices have all of these sensors. In fact, many devices have just some of these sensors. The Android emulator, for example, has only an accelerometer. So how do you know which sensors are available on a device? There are two ways, one direct and one indirect.

The first way is that you ask the `SensorManager` for a list of the available sensors. It will respond with a list of sensor objects that you can then set up listeners for and get data from. We'll show you how a bit later in this chapter. This method assumes that the user has already installed your application onto a device, but what if the device doesn't have a sensor that your application needs?

That's where the second method comes in. Within the `AndroidManifest.xml` file, you can specify the features a device must have in order to properly support your application. If your application needs a proximity sensor, you specify that in your manifest file with a line such as the following:

```
<uses-feature android:name="android.hardware.sensor.proximity" />
```

The Google Play Store will only install your app on a device that has a proximity sensor, so you know it's there when your application runs. The same cannot be said for all other Android app stores. That is, some Android app stores do not perform that kind of check to make sure your app can only be installed onto a device that supports the sensors you specify.

What Can We Know About a Sensor?

While using the `uses-feature` tags in the manifest file lets you know that a sensor your application requires exists on a device, it doesn't tell you everything you may want to know about the actual sensor. Let's build a simple application that queries the device for sensor information. Listing 24-1 shows the Java code of our `MainActivity`.

> **Note** You can download this chapter's projects. We will give you the URL at the end of the chapter. This will allow you to import these projects into your IDE directly.

Listing 24-1. Java for a Sensor List App

```
public class MainActivity extends Activity {
    @Override
    public void onCreate(Bundle savedInstanceState) {
        super.onCreate(savedInstanceState);
        setContentView(R.layout.main);

        TextView text = (TextView)findViewById(R.id.text);

        SensorManager mgr =
            (SensorManager) this.getSystemService(SENSOR_SERVICE);

        List<Sensor> sensors = mgr.getSensorList(Sensor.TYPE_ALL);

        StringBuilder message = new StringBuilder(2048);
        message.append("The sensors on this device are:\n");

        for(Sensor sensor : sensors) {
            message.append(sensor.getName() + "\n");
            message.append("  Type: " +
                    sensorTypes.get(sensor.getType()) + "\n");
            message.append("  Vendor: " +
                    sensor.getVendor() + "\n");
            message.append("  Version: " +
                    sensor.getVersion() + "\n");
            try {
                message.append("  Min Delay: " +
                    sensor.getMinDelay() + "\n");
            } catch(NoSuchMethodError e) {} // ignore if not found
            try {
                message.append("  FIFO Max Event Count: " +
                    sensor.getFifoMaxEventCount() + "\n");
            } catch(NoSuchMethodError e) {} // ignore if not found
            message.append("  Resolution: " +
                    sensor.getResolution() + "\n");
            message.append("  Max Range: " +
                    sensor.getMaximumRange() + "\n");
            message.append("  Power: " +
                    sensor.getPower() + " mA\n");
        }
        text.setText(message);
    }

    private HashMap<Integer, String> sensorTypes =
                    new HashMap<Integer, String>();

    {
      sensorTypes.put(Sensor.TYPE_ACCELEROMETER,"TYPE_ACCELEROMETER");
      sensorTypes.put(Sensor.TYPE_AMBIENT_TEMPERATURE,
                          "TYPE_AMBIENT_TEMPERATURE");
      /* ... the rest is omitted to save space ... */
    }
}
```

Within our onCreate() method, we start by getting a reference to the SensorManager. There can be only one of these, so we retrieve it as a system service. We then call its getSensorList() method to get a list of sensors. For each sensor, we write out information about it. The output will look something like Figure 24-1.

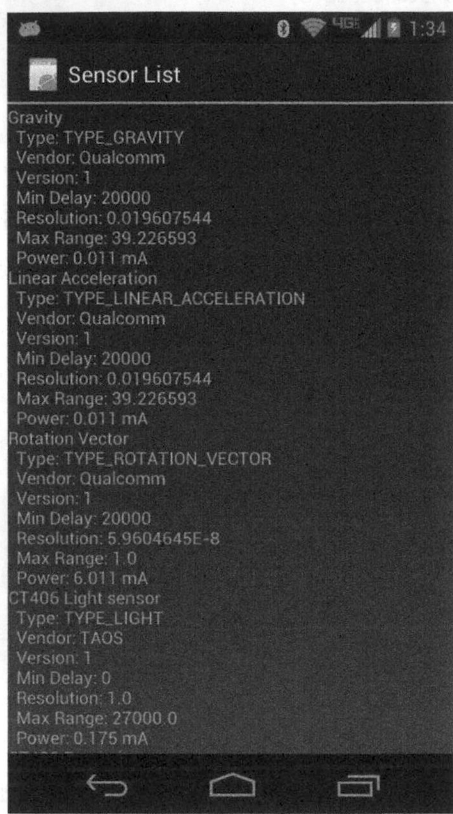

Figure 24-1. *Output from our sensor list app*

There are a few things to know about this sensor information. The type value tells you the basic type of the sensor without getting specific. A light sensor is a light sensor, but you could get variations in light sensors from one device to another. For example, the resolution of a light sensor on one device could be different from that on another device. When you specify that your app needs a light sensor in a <uses-feature> tag, you don't know in advance exactly what type of light sensor you're going to get. If it matters to your application, you'll need to query the device to find out and adjust your code accordingly.

The values you get for resolution and maximum range will be in the appropriate units for that sensor. The power measurement is in milliamperes (mA) and represents the electrical current that the sensor draws from the device's battery; smaller is better.

Now that we know what sensors we have available to us, how do we go about getting data from them? As we explained earlier, we set up a listener in order to get sensor data sent to us. Let's explore that now.

Getting Sensor Events

Sensors provide data to our application once we register a listener to receive the data. When our listener is not listening, the sensor can be turned off, conserving battery life, so make sure you only listen when you really need to. Setting up a sensor listener is easy to do. Let's say that we want to measure the light levels from the light sensor. Listing 24-2 shows the Java code for a sample app that does this.

***Listing 24-2.** Java Code for a Light Sensor Monitor App*

```
public class MainActivity extends Activity implements SensorEventListener {
    private SensorManager mgr;
    private Sensor light;
    private TextView text;
    private StringBuilder msg = new StringBuilder(2048);

    @Override
    public void onCreate(Bundle savedInstanceState) {
        super.onCreate(savedInstanceState);
        setContentView(R.layout.main);

        mgr = (SensorManager) this.getSystemService(SENSOR_SERVICE);
        light = mgr.getDefaultSensor(Sensor.TYPE_LIGHT);
        text = (TextView) findViewById(R.id.text);
    }

    @Override
    protected void onResume() {
        mgr.registerListener(this, light,
                SensorManager.SENSOR_DELAY_NORMAL);
        super.onResume();
    }

    @Override
    protected void onPause() {
        mgr.unregisterListener(this, light);
        super.onPause();
    }

    public void onAccuracyChanged(Sensor sensor, int accuracy) {
        msg.insert(0, sensor.getName() + " accuracy changed: " +
            accuracy + (accuracy==1?" (LOW)":(accuracy==2?" (MED)":
            " (HIGH)")) + "\n");
        text.setText(msg);
        text.invalidate();
    }
```

```
    public void onSensorChanged(SensorEvent event) {
        msg.insert(0, "Got a sensor event: " + event.values[0] +
        " SI lux units\n");
        text.setText(msg);
        text.invalidate();
    }
}
```

In this sample app, we again get a reference to the SensorManager, but instead of getting a list of sensors, we query specifically for the light sensor. We then set up a listener in the onResume() method of our activity, and we unregister the listener in the onPause() method. We don't want to be worrying about the light levels when our application is not in the foreground.

For the registerListener() method, we pass in a value representing how often we want to be notified of sensor value changes. This parameter could be

- SENSOR_DELAY_NORMAL (represents 200,000 microsecond delay)
- SENSOR_DELAY_UI (represents 60,000 microsecond delay)
- SENSOR_DELAY_GAME (represents 20,000 microsecond delay)
- SENSOR_DELAY_FASTEST (represents as fast as possible)

You can also specify a specific microsecond delay using one of the other registerListener methods, as long as it's larger than 3 microseconds; however anything less than 20,000 is not likely to be honored. It is important to select an appropriate value for this parameter. Some sensors are very sensitive and will generate a lot of events in a short amount of time. If you choose SENSOR_DELAY_FASTEST, you might even overrun your application's ability to keep up. Depending on what your application does with each sensor event, it is possible that you will be creating and destroying so many objects in memory that garbage collection will cause noticeable slowdowns and hiccups on the device. On the other hand, certain sensors pretty much demand to be read as often as possible; this is true of the rotation vector sensor in particular. Also, don't rely on this parameter to generate events with precise timing. The events could come a little faster or slower.

Because our activity implements the SensorEventListener interface, we have two callbacks for sensor events: onAccuracyChanged() and onSensorChanged(). The first method will let us know if the accuracy changes on our sensor (or sensors, since it could be called for more than one). The value of the accuracy parameter will be SENSOR_STATUS_UNRELIABLE, SENSOR_STATUS_ACCURACY_LOW, SENSOR_STATUS_ACCURACY_MEDIUM, or SENSOR_STATUS_ACCURACY_HIGH. Unreliable accuracy does not mean that the device is broken; it normally means that the sensor needs to be calibrated. The second callback method tells us when the light level has changed, and we get a SensorEvent object to tell us the details of the new value or values from the sensor.

A SensorEvent object has several members, one of them being an array of float values. For a light sensor event, only the first float value has meaning, which is the SI lux value of the light that was detected by the sensor. For our sample app, we build up a message string by inserting the new messages on top of the older messages, and then we display the batch of messages in a TextView. Our newest sensor values will always be displayed at the top of the screen.

When you run this application (on a real device, of course, since the emulator does not have a light sensor), you may notice that nothing is displayed at first. Just change the light that is shining on the upper-left corner of your device. This is most likely where your light sensor is. If you look very carefully, you might see the dot behind the screen that is the light sensor. If you cover this dot with your finger, the light level will probably change to a very small value (although it may not reach zero). The messages should display on the screen, telling you about the changing light levels.

> **Note** You might also notice that when the light sensor is covered, your buttons light up (if you have a device with lighted buttons). This is because Android has detected the darkness and lights up the buttons to make the device easier to use "in the dark."

Issues with Getting Sensor Data

The Android sensor framework has problems that you need to be aware of. This is the part that's not fun. In some cases, we have ways of working around the problem; in others we don't, or it's very difficult.

No Direct Access to Sensor Values

You may have noticed that there is no direct way to query the sensor's current value. The only way to get data from a sensor is through a listener. There are two kinds of sensors: those that are streaming and those that are not. Streaming sensors will send values on a regular basis, such as the accelerometer. The method call `getMinDelay()` will return a nonzero value for streaming sensors, to tell you the minimum number of microseconds that a sensor will use to sense the environment. For non-streaming sensors the return value is zero, so even once you've set up the listener, there are no guarantees that you'll get a new datum within a set period of time. At least the callback is asynchronous so you won't block the UI thread waiting for a piece of data from a sensor. However, your application has to accommodate the fact that sensor data may not be available at the exact moment that you want it. Revisiting Figure 24-1, you'll notice that the light sensor is non-streaming. Therefore, your app will get an event only if the light level changes. For the other sensors shown, the delay between events will be a minimum of 20 milliseconds, but could be more.

It is possible to directly access sensors using native code and the JNI feature of Android. You'll need to know the low-level native API calls for the sensor driver you're interested in, plus be able to set up the interface back to Android. So it can be done, but it's not easy.

Sensor Values Not Sent Fast Enough

Even at `SENSOR_DELAY_FASTEST`, you probably won't get new values more often than every 20 ms (it depends on the device and the sensor). If you need more rapid sensor data than you can get with a rate setting of `SENSOR_DELAY_FASTEST`, it is possible to use native code and JNI to get to the sensor data faster, but similar to the previous situation, it is not easy.

Sensors Turn Off with the Screen

There have been problems in Android 2.x with sensor updates that get turned off when the screen is turned off. Apparently someone thought it was a good idea to not send sensor updates if the screen is off, even if your application (most likely using a service) has a wake lock. Basically, your listener gets unregistered when the screen turns off.

There are several workarounds to this problem. For more information on this issue and possible resolutions and workarounds, please refer to Android Issue 11028:

```
http://code.google.com/p/android/issues/detail?id=11028
```

Now that you know how to get data from sensors, what can you do with the data? As we said earlier, depending on which sensor you're getting data from, the values returned in the values array mean different things. The next section will explore each of the sensor types and what their values mean.

Interpreting Sensor Data

Now that you understand how to get data from a sensor, you'll want to do something meaningful with the data. The data you get, however, will depend on which sensor you're getting the data from. Some sensors are simpler than others. In the sections that follow, we will describe the data that you'll get from the sensors we currently know about. As new devices come into being, new sensors will undoubtedly be introduced as well. The sensor framework is very likely to remain the same, so the techniques we show here should apply equally well to the new sensors.

Light Sensors

The light sensor is one of the simplest sensors on a device, and one you've used in the first sample applications of this chapter. The sensor gives a reading of the light level detected by the light sensor of the device. As the light level changes, the sensor readings change. The units of the data are in SI lux units. To learn more about what this means, please see the "References" section at the end of this chapter for links to more information.

For the values array in the `SensorEvent` object, a light sensor uses just the first element, `values[0]`. This value is a `float` and ranges technically from `0` to the maximum value for the particular sensor. We say *technically* because the sensor may only send very small values when there's no light, and never actually send a value of `0`.

Remember also that the sensor can tell us the maximum value that it can return and that different sensors can have different maximums. For this reason, it may not be useful to consider the light-related constants in the `SensorManager` class. For example, `SensorManager` has a constant called `LIGHT_SUNLIGHT_MAX`, which is a `float` value of 120,000; however, when we queried our device earlier, the maximum value returned was 10,240, clearly much less than this constant value. There's another one called `LIGHT_SHADE` at 20,000, which is also above the maximum of the device we tested. So keep this in mind when writing code that uses light sensor data.

Proximity Sensors

The proximity sensor either measures the distance that some object is from the device (in centimeters) or represents a flag to say whether an object is close or far. Some proximity sensors will give a value ranging from `0.0` to the maximum in increments, while others return either `0.0` or the maximum value only. If the maximum range of the proximity sensor is equal to the sensor's resolution, then you know it's one of those that only returns `0.0`, or the maximum. There are devices with a maximum of `1.0` and others where it's `6.0`. Unfortunately, there's no way to tell before the application is installed and run which proximity sensor you're going to get. Even if you put a `<uses-feature>` tag in your `AndroidManifest.xml` file for the proximity sensor, you could get either kind. Unless you absolutely need to have the more granular proximity sensor, your application should accommodate both types gracefully.

Here's an interesting fact about proximity sensors: the proximity sensor is sometimes the same hardware as the light sensor. Android still treats them as logically separate sensors, though, so if you need data from both you will need to set up a listener for each one. Here's another interesting fact: the proximity sensor is often used in the phone application to detect the presence of a person's head next to the device. If the head is that close to the touchscreen, the touchscreen is disabled so no keys will be accidently pressed by the ear or cheek while the person is talking on the phone.

The source code projects for this chapter include a simple proximity sensor monitor application, which is basically the light sensor monitor application modified to use the proximity sensor instead of the light sensor. We won't include the code in this chapter, but feel free to experiment with it on your own.

Temperature Sensors

The old deprecated temperature sensor (TYPE_TEMPERATURE) provided a temperature reading and also returned just a single value in `values[0]`. This sensor usually read an internal temperature, such as at the battery. There is a new temperature sensor called `TYPE_AMBIENT_TEMPERATURE`. The new value represents the temperature outside the device in degrees Celsius.

The placement of the temperature sensor is device-dependent, and it is possible that the temperature readings could be impacted by the heat generated by the device itself. The projects for this chapter include one for the temperature sensor called `TemperatureSensor`. It takes care of calling the correct temperature sensor based on which version of Android is running.

Pressure Sensors

This sensor measures barometric pressure, which could detect altitude for example or be used for weather predictions. This sensor should not be confused with the ability of a touchscreen to generate a `MotionEvent` with a pressure value (the pressure of the touch). We covered this touch type of pressure sensing in Chapter 22. Touchscreen pressure sensing doesn't use the Android sensor framework.

The unit of measurement for a pressure sensor is atmospheric pressure in hPa (millibar), and this measurement is delivered in `values[0]`.

Gyroscope Sensors

Gyroscopes are very cool components that can measure the twist of a device about a reference frame. Said another way, gyroscopes measure the rate of rotation about an axis. When the device is not rotating, the sensor values will be zeros. When there is rotation in any direction, you'll get nonzero values from the gyroscope. Gyroscopes are often used for navigation. But by itself, a gyroscope can't tell you everything you need to know to navigate. And unfortunately, errors creep in over time. But coupled with accelerometers, you can determine the path of movement of the device.

Kalman filters can be used to link data from the two sensors together. Accelerometers are not terribly accurate in the short term, and gyroscopes are not very accurate in the long term, so combined they can be reasonably accurate all the time. While Kalman filters are very complex, there is an alternative called *complementary filters* that are easier to implement in code and produce results that are pretty good. These concepts are beyond the scope of this book.

The gyroscope sensor returns three values in the values array for the x, y, and z axes. The units are radians per second, and the values represent the rate of rotation around each of those axes. One way to work with these values is to integrate them over time to calculate an angle change. This is a similar calculation to integrating linear speed over time to calculate distance.

Accelerometers

Accelerometers are probably the most utilized of the sensors on a device. Using these sensors, your application can determine the physical orientation of the device in space relative to gravity's pull straight down, plus be aware of forces acting on the device. Providing this information allows an application to do all sorts of interesting things, from game play to augmented reality. And of course, the accelerometers tell Android when to switch the orientation of the user interface from portrait to landscape and back again.

The accelerometer coordinate system works like this: the accelerometer's x axis originates in the bottom-left corner of the device and goes across the bottom to the right. The y axis also originates in the bottom-left corner and goes up along the left of the display. The z axis originates in the bottom-left corner and goes up in space away from the device. Figure 24-2 shows what this means.

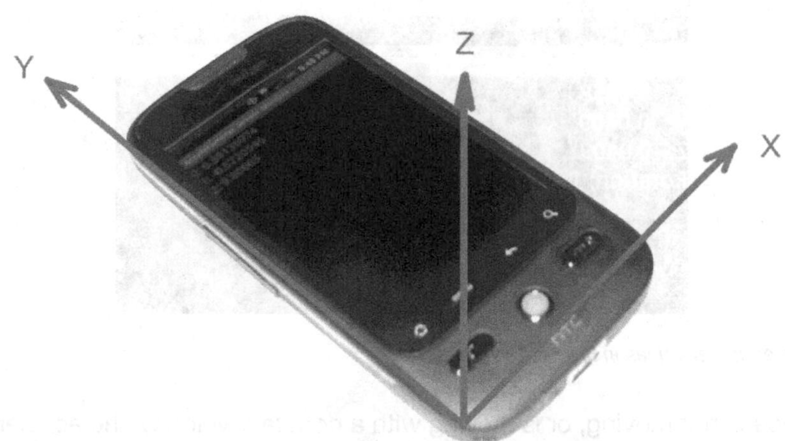

Figure 24-2. Accelerometer coordinate system

This coordinate system is different than the one used in layouts and 2D graphics. In that coordinate system, the origin (0, 0) is at the top-left corner, and y is positive in the direction down the screen from there. It is easy to get confused when dealing with coordinate systems in different frames of reference, so be careful.

We haven't yet said what the accelerometer values mean, so what *do* they mean? Acceleration is measured in meters per second squared (m/s^2). Normal Earth gravity is 9.81 m/s^2, pulling down toward the center of the Earth. From the accelerometer's point of view, the measurement of gravity is –9.81. If your device is completely at rest (not moving) and is on a perfectly flat surface, the x and y readings will be 0 and the z reading will be +9.81. Actually, the values won't be exactly these because of the sensitivity and accuracy of the accelerometer, but they will be close. Gravity is the only force acting on the device when the device is at rest, and because gravity pulls straight down, if our device is perfectly flat, its effect on the x and y axes is zero. On the z axis, the accelerometer is measuring the force on the device minus gravity. Therefore, 0 minus –9.81 is +9.81, and that's what the z value will be (a.k.a. `values[2]` in the `SensorEvent` object).

The values sent to your application by the accelerometer always represent the sum of the forces on the device minus gravity. If you were to take your perfectly flat device and lift it straight up, the z value would increase at first, because you increased the force in the up (z) direction. As soon as your lifting force stopped, the overall force would return to being just gravity. If the device were to be dropped (hypothetically—please don't do this), it would be accelerating toward the ground, which would zero out gravity so the accelerometer would read 0 force.

Let's take the device from Figure 24-2 and rotate it up so it is in portrait mode and vertical. The x axis is the same, pointing left to right. Our y axis is now straight up and down, and the z axis is pointing out of the screen straight at us. The y value will be +9.81, and both x and z will be 0.

What happens when you rotate the device to landscape mode and continue to hold it vertically, so the screen is right in front of your face? If you guessed that y and z are now 0 and x is +9.81, you'd be correct. Figure 24-3 shows what it might look like.

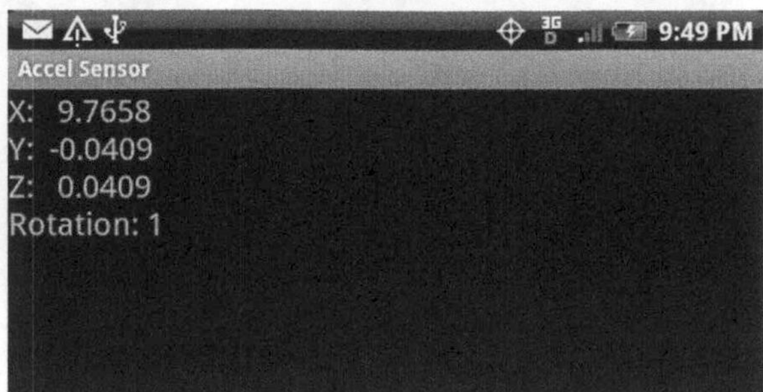

***Figure 24-3.** Accelerometer values in landscape vertical*

When the device is not moving, or is moving with a constant velocity, the accelerometers are only measuring gravity. And in each axis, the value from the accelerometer is gravity's component in that axis. Therefore, using some trigonometry, you could figure out the angles and know how the device is oriented relative to gravity's pull. That is, you could tell if the device were in portrait mode or in landscape mode or in some tilted mode. In fact, this is exactly what Android does to figure out which display mode to use (portrait or landscape). Note, however, that the accelerometers do not say how the device is oriented with respect to magnetic north. So while you could know that the device is being held in landscape mode vertically, you wouldn't know if you were facing east or west or anywhere in between. That's where the magnetic field sensor will come in, which we will cover in a later section.

Accelerometers and Display Orientation

Accelerometers in a device are hardware, and they're firmly attached, and as such have a specific orientation relative to the device that does not change as the device is turned this way or that. The values that the accelerometers send into Android will change of course as a device is moved, but the coordinate system of the accelerometers will stay the same relative to the physical device. The coordinate system of the display, however, changes as the user goes from portrait to landscape and back again. In fact depending on which way the screen is turned, portrait could be right-side up, or 180 degrees upside-down. Similarly, landscape could be in one of two different rotations 180 degrees apart.

When your application is reading accelerometer data and wanting to affect the user interface correctly, your application must know how much rotation of the display has occurred to properly compensate. As your screen is reoriented from portrait to landscape, the screen's coordinate system has rotated with respect to the coordinate system of the accelerometers. To handle this, your application must use the method `Display.getRotation()`. The return value is a simple integer but not the actual number of degrees of rotation. The value will be one of `Surface.ROTATION_0`, `Surface.ROTATION_90`, `Surface.ROTATION_180`, or `Surface.ROTATION_270`. These are constants with values of `0`, `1`, `2`, and `3`, respectively. This return value tells you how much the display has rotated from the "normal" orientation of the device. Because not all Android devices are normally in portrait mode, you cannot assume that portrait is at `ROTATION_0`.

Accelerometers and Gravity

So far, we've only briefly touched on what happens to the accelerometer values when the device is moved. Let's explore that further. All forces acting on the device will be detected by the accelerometers. If you lift the device, the initial lifting force is positive in the z direction, and you get a z value greater than +9.81. If you push the device on its left side, you'll get an initial negative reading in the x direction.

What you'd like to be able to do is separate out the force of gravity from the other forces acting on the device. There's a fairly easy way to do this, and it's called a *low-pass filter*. Forces other than gravity acting on the device will do so in a way that is typically not gradual. In other words, if the user is shaking the device, the shaking forces are reflected in the accelerometer values quickly. A low-pass filter will in effect strip out the shaking forces and leave only the steady force, which is gravity. Let's use a sample application to illustrate this concept. It's called GravityDemo. Listing 24-3 shows the Java code.

Listing 24-3. Measuring Gravity from the Accelerometers

```
// This file is MainActivity.java
public class MainActivity extends Activity implements SensorEventListener {
    private SensorManager mgr;
    private Sensor accelerometer;
    private TextView text;
    private float[] gravity = new float[3];
    private float[] motion = new float[3];
    private double ratio;
    private double mAngle;
    private int counter = 0;

    @Override
    public void onCreate(Bundle savedInstanceState) {
        super.onCreate(savedInstanceState);
        setContentView(R.layout.main);

        mgr = (SensorManager) this.getSystemService(SENSOR_SERVICE);
        accelerometer = mgr.getDefaultSensor(Sensor.TYPE_ACCELEROMETER);
        text = (TextView) findViewById(R.id.text);
    }

    @Override
    protected void onResume() {
        mgr.registerListener(this, accelerometer,
        SensorManager.SENSOR_DELAY_UI);
        super.onResume();
    }

    @Override
    protected void onPause() {
        mgr.unregisterListener(this, accelerometer);
        super.onPause();
    }
```

```
    public void onAccuracyChanged(Sensor sensor, int accuracy) {
        // ignore
    }

    public void onSensorChanged(SensorEvent event) {
        // Use a low-pass filter to get gravity.
        // Motion is what's left over
        for(int i=0; i<3; i++) {
            gravity [i] = (float) (0.1 * event.values[i] +
                                   0.9 * gravity[i]);
            motion[i] = event.values[i] - gravity[i];
        }

        // ratio is gravity on the Y axis compared to full gravity
        // should be no more than 1, no less than -1
        ratio = gravity[1]/SensorManager.GRAVITY_EARTH;
        if(ratio > 1.0) ratio = 1.0;
        if(ratio < -1.0) ratio = -1.0;

        // convert radians to degrees, make negative if facing up
        mAngle = Math.toDegrees(Math.acos(ratio));
        if(gravity[2] < 0) {
            mAngle = -mAngle;
        }

        // Display every 10th value
        if(counter++ % 10 == 0) {
            String msg = String.format(
                "Raw values\nX: %8.4f\nY: %8.4f\nZ: %8.4f\n" +
                "Gravity\nX: %8.4f\nY: %8.4f\nZ: %8.4f\n" +
                "Motion\nX: %8.4f\nY: %8.4f\nZ: %8.4f\nAngle: %8.1f",
                event.values[0], event.values[1], event.values[2],
                gravity[0], gravity[1], gravity[2],
                motion[0], motion[1], motion[2],
                mAngle);
            text.setText(msg);
            text.invalidate();
            counter=1;
        }
    }
}
```

The result of running this application is a display that looks like Figure 24-4. This screenshot was taken as the device lay flat on a table.

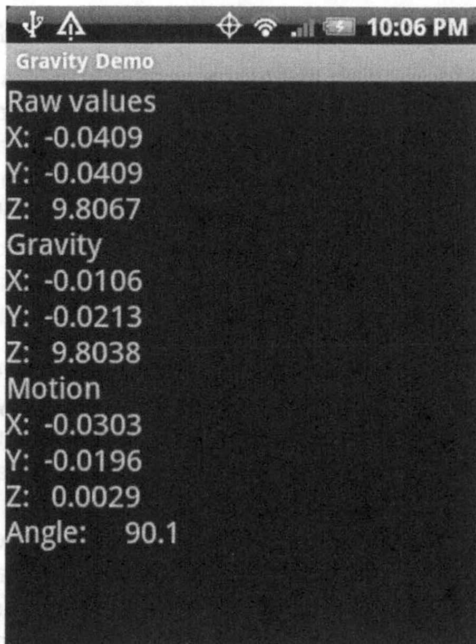

Figure 24-4. *Gravity, motion, and angle values*

Most of this sample application is the same as the Accel Sensor application from before. The differences are in the `onSensorChanged()` method. Instead of simply displaying the values from the event array, we attempt to keep track of gravity and motion. You get gravity by using only a small portion of the new value from the event array, and a large portion of the previous value of the gravity array. The two portions used must add up to 1.0. We used 0.9 and 0.1. You could try other values, too, such as 0.8 and 0.2. Our gravity array cannot possibly change as fast as the actual sensor values are changing. But this is closer to reality. And this is what a low-pass filter does. The event array values would only be changing if forces were causing the device to move, and you don't want to measure those forces as part of gravity. You only want to record into your gravity array the force of gravity itself. The math here does not mean you're magically recording only gravity, but the values you're calculating are going to be a lot closer than the raw values from the event array.

Notice also the motion array in the code. By tracking the difference between the raw event array values and the calculated gravity values, you are basically measuring the active, non-gravity, forces on the device in the motion array. If the values in the motion array are zero or very close to zero, it means the device is probably not moving. This is useful information. Technically, a device moving in a constant speed would also have values in the motion array close to zero, but the reality is that if a user is moving the device, the motion values will be somewhat larger than zero. Users can't possibly move a device at a perfect constant speed.

Lastly, please notice that this example does not produce new objects that need to be garbage collected. It is very important when dealing with sensor events to not create new objects; otherwise your application will spend too much time paused for garbage collection cycles.

Using Accelerometers to Measure the Device's Angle

We wanted to show you one more thing about the accelerometers before we move on. If we go back to our trigonometry lessons, we remember that the cosine of an angle is the ratio of the near side and the hypotenuse. If we consider the angle between the y axis and gravity itself, we could measure the force of gravity on the y axis and take the arccosine to determine the angle. We've done that in this code as well, although here we have to deal yet again with some of the messiness of sensors in Android. There are constants in `SensorManager` for different gravity constants, including Earth's. But your actual measured values could possibly exceed the defined constants. We will explain what we mean by this next.

In theory, your device at rest would measure a value for gravity equal to the constant value, but this is rarely the case. At rest, the accelerometer sensor is very likely to give us a value for gravity that is larger or smaller than the constant. Therefore, our ratio could end up greater than one, or less than negative one. This would make the `acos()` method complain, so we fix the ratio value to be no more than 1 and no less than –1. The corresponding angles in degrees range from 0 to 180. That's fine except that we don't get negative angles from 0 to –180 this way. To get the negative angles, we use another value from our gravity array, which is the z value. If the z value of gravity is negative, it means the device's face is oriented downward. For all those values where the device face is pointed down, we make our angle negative as well, with the result being that our angle goes from –180 to +180, just as we would expect.

Go ahead and experiment with this sample application. Notice that the value of the angle is 90 when the device is laid flat, and it's zero (or close to it) when the device is held straight up and down in front of us. If we keep rotating down past flat, we will see the value of the angle exceed 90. If we tilt the device up more from the 0 position, the value of angle goes negative until we're holding the device above our heads and the value of the angle is –90. Finally, you may have noticed our counter that controls how often the display is updated. Because the sensor events can come rather frequently, we decided to only display every tenth time we get values.

Magnetic Field Sensors

The magnetic field sensor measures the ambient magnetic field in the x, y, and z axes. This coordinate system is aligned just like the accelerometers, so x, y, and z are as shown in Figure 24-2. The units of the magnetic field sensor are microteslas (uT). This sensor can detect the Earth's magnetic field and therefore tell us where north is. This sensor is also referred to as the *compass*, and in fact the `<uses-feature>` tag uses `android.hardware.sensor.compass` as the name of this sensor. Because this sensor is so tiny and sensitive, it can be affected by magnetic fields generated by things near the device, and even to some extent to components within the device. Therefore the accuracy of the magnetic field sensor may at times be suspect.

We've included a simple `CompassSensor` application in the download section of the web site, so feel free to import that and play with it. If you bring metal objects close to the device while this application is running, you might notice the values changing in response. Certainly if you bring a magnet close to the device you will see the values change. In fact, the Google Cardboard "device" uses a magnet under a physical button which is then detected by the phone as a change in the magnetic field when the button is pressed.

You might be asking, can I use the compass sensor as a compass to detect where north is? And the answer is: not by itself. While the compass sensor can detect magnetic fields around the device, if the device is not being held perfectly flat in relation to the Earth's surface, you'd have no way of correctly interpreting the compass sensor values. But you have accelerometers that can tell you the orientation of the device relative to the Earth's surface! Therefore, you can create a compass from the compass sensor, but you'll need help from the accelerometers too. So let's see how to do that.

Using Accelerometers and Magnetic Field Sensors Together

The `SensorManager` provides some methods that allow us to combine the compass sensor and the accelerometers to figure out orientation. As we just discussed, you can't use just the compass sensor alone to do the job. So `SensorManager` provides a method called `getRotationMatrix()`, which takes the values from the accelerometers and from the compass and returns a matrix that can be used to determine orientation.

Another `SensorManager` method, `getOrientation()`, takes the rotation matrix from the previous step and gives an orientation matrix. The values from the orientation matrix tell you your device's rotation relative to the Earth's magnetic north, as well as the device's pitch and roll relative to the ground.

Magnetic Declination and GeomagneticField

There's another topic we want to cover with regard to orientation and devices. The compass sensor will tell you where magnetic north is, but it won't tell you where true north is (a.k.a., geographic north). Imagine you are standing at the midpoint between the magnetic north pole and the geographic north pole. They'd be 180 degrees apart. The further away you get from the two north poles, the smaller this angle difference becomes. The angle difference between magnetic north and true north is called *magnetic declination*. And the value can only be computed relative to a point on the planet's surface. That is, you have to know where you're standing to know where geographic north is in relation to magnetic north. Fortunately, Android has a way to help you out, and it's the `GeomagneticField` class.

In order to instantiate an object of the `GeomagneticField` class, you need to pass in a latitude and longitude. Therefore, in order to get a magnetic declination angle, you need to know where the point of reference is. You also need to know the time at which you want the value. Magnetic north drifts over time. Once instantiated, you simply call this method to get the declination angle (in degrees):

```
float declinationAngle = geoMagField.getDeclination();
```

The value of `declinationAngle` will be positive if magnetic north is to the east of geographic north.

Gravity Sensors

This sensor isn't a separate piece of hardware. It's a virtual sensor based on the accelerometers. In fact, this sensor uses logic similar to what we described earlier for accelerometers to produce the gravity component of the forces acting on a device. We cannot access this logic, however, so whatever factors and logic are used inside the gravity sensor class are what we must accept. It's possible, though, that the virtual sensor will take advantage of other hardware such as a gyroscope to help it calculate gravity more accurately. The values array for this sensor reports gravity just like the accelerometer sensor reports its values.

Linear Acceleration Sensors

Similar to the gravity sensor, the linear acceleration sensor is a virtual sensor that represents the accelerometer forces minus gravity. Again, we did our own calculations earlier on the accelerometer sensor values to strip out gravity to get just these linear acceleration force values. This sensor makes that more convenient for you. And it could take advantage of other hardware, such as a gyroscope, to help it calculate linear acceleration more accurately. The values array reports linear acceleration just like the accelerometer sensor reports its values.

Rotation Vector Sensors

The rotation vector sensor represents the orientation of the device in space, with angles relative to the frame of reference of the hardware accelerometer (see Figure 24-2). This sensor returns a set of values that represents the last three components of a unit quaternion. Quaternions are a subject that could fill a book, so we won't be going into them here.

Thankfully, Google has provided a few methods within `SensorManager` to help with this sensor. The `getQuaternionFromVector()` method converts a rotation vector sensor output to a normalized quaternion. The `getRotationMatrixFromVector()` method converts a rotation vector sensor output to a rotation matrix, and that can be used with `getOrientation()`. When converting rotation vector sensor output to an orientation vector, though, you need to realize that it goes from –180 degrees to +180 degrees.

The ZIP file of sample apps for this chapter includes a version of `VirtualJax` that shows the rotation vector in use.

References

Here are some helpful references to topics you may wish to explore further:

- `www.androidbook.com/proandroid5/projects`: A list of downloadable projects related to this book. For this chapter, look for a ZIP file called `ProAndroid5_Ch24_Sensors.zip`. This file contains all the projects from this chapter, listed in separate root directories. There is also a `README.TXT` file that describes exactly how to import projects into an IDE from one of these ZIP files.

- http://en.wikipedia.org/wiki/Lux: The Wikipedia entry for lux, the unit of light measurement.
- www.ngdc.noaa.gov/geomag/faqgeom.shtml: Information about geomagnetism from NOAA.
- www.youtube.com/watch?v=C7JQ7Rpwn2k: A Google Tech Talk from David Sachs on accelerometers, gyroscopes, compasses, and Android development.
- http://stackoverflow.com/questions/1586658/combine-gyroscope-and-accelerometer-data: A nice posting on stackoverflow.com that talks about combining gyroscope and accelerometer sensor data for use in applications.
- http://en.wikipedia.org/wiki/Quaternions_and_spatial_rotation: The Wikipedia page on quaternions and how they can be used in representing spatial rotation, such as an Android device.

Summary

In this chapter, we covered the following topics:

- What sensors are in Android.
- Finding out what sensors are on a device.
- Specifying the sensors that are required for an application before it will be loadable onto an Android device.
- Determining the properties of a sensor on a device.
- How to get sensor events.
- The fact that events come whenever the sensor value changes, so it is important to understand there could be a lag before you get your first value.
- The different speeds of updates from a sensor and when to use each one.
- The details of a `SensorEvent` and how these can be used for the various sensor types.
- Virtual sensors, made up of data from other sensors. The `ROTATION_VECTOR` sensor is one of these.
- Determining the angle of the device using sensors, and telling whioh direction the device is facing.

Chapter 25

Exploring Android Persistence and Content Providers

There are a number of ways of saving state in the Android SDK. Some of these are 1) shared preferences, 2) internal files, 3) external files, 4) SQLite, 5) content providers, 6) O/R mapping tools, and 7) network storage in the cloud. We will briefly introduce each of these state-saving options first and then cover in detail managing application state using SQLite and content providers.

Saving State Using Shared Preferences

We have covered shared preferences in Chapter 11. Shared preferences are key/value-based XML files owned by your application. Android has a framework on top of this general persistence mechanism to display/update/retrieve preferences without writing a lot of code. This latter aspect is the main topic of Chapter 11.

Chapter 11 also touched briefly on how an application can store any type of data using the shared preference API in XML files. In this approach data is converted to a string representation first and then stored in the preferences key/value store. This approach can be used to store any arbitrary state of your application as long as it is small to medium in size.

The shared preference XML files are internal to the application on your device. This data is not directly available to other applications. End user cannot directly manipulate this data by mounting on to a USB port. This data is removed automatically when the application is removed.

From simple to moderate application persistence needs, you can take advantage of shared preferences by storing various trees of Java objects directly in a shared preference file. In a given preference file you can have a key point to a serialized Java object tree. You can also use multiple preference files for multiple Java object trees. We have used JSON/GSON library from google to do this conversion from Java objects to their equivalent JSON string values quite effectively. In this approach a Java object tree is streamed as a JSON string using the google GSON library. This tree is then stored as a value in a key/value pair of a preference file. Keep in mind that GSON and JSON conversion of a Java object may have some limitations. Read the GSON/JSON documentation to see how complex a Java object can get to make this approach work. We are fairly confident that for most data-based Java objects this will work.

Listing 25-1 has some sample code for how to save a Java tree using GSON/JSON and shared preferences.

Listing 25-1. Saving a Java Object Tree Using JSON in Shared Preferences XML Files

```
//Implementation of storeJSON for storing any object
public void storeJSON(Context context, Object anyObject) {

    //Get a GSON instance
    Gson gson = new Gson();

    //Convert Java object to a JSON string
    String jsonString = gson.toJson(anyObject);

    //See Chapter 11 for more details on how to get a shared preferences reference
    String filename = "somefilename.xml";
    int mode = Context.MODE_PRIVATE;
    SharedPreferences sp = context.getSharedPreferences(filename,mode);

    //Save the JSON string in the shared preferences
    SharedPreferences.Editor spe = sp.edit();
    spe.putString("json", jsonString);
    spe.commit();
}
//This code can then be used by a client like this:
//Create any data object with reasonable complexity
//Ex:  MainObject mo = MainObject.createTestMainObject();
//You can then call storeJSON(some-activity, mo) below
```

Listing 25-2 shows some sample code for how to retrieve a Java tree using GSON/JSON and shared preferences.

Listing 25-2. Reading a Java Object Tree Using JSON from Shared Preferences XML Files

```
public Object retrieveJSON(Context context, String filename, Class classRef) {
    int mode = Context.MODE_PRIVATE;
    SharedPreferences sp = context.getSharedPreferences(filename,mode);
    String jsonString = sp.getString("json", null);
    if (jsonString == null)     {
        throw new RuntimeException("Not able to read the preference");
    }
    Gson gson = new Gson();
    return gson.fromJson(jsonString, classRef);
}
```

```
//You can then do this in the client code
MainObject mo = (MainObject)retrieveJSON(context,"somefilename.xml", MainObject.class);
String compareResult = MainObject.checkTestMainObject(mo);
if (compareResult != null)    {
       throw new RuntimeException("Something is wrong. Objects don't match");
}
```

This code requires that you have the GSON Java library added to your project. This GSON-based approach is covered in detail in our companion book, *Expert Android* from Apress. This is also briefly documented online at `http://androidbook.com/item/4438`.

Saving State Using Internal Files

In Android, you can also use internal files to store the state of your application. These internal files are internal to the application on your device. This data is not directly available to other applications. End user cannot directly manipulate this data by mounting on to a USB port. This data is removed automatically when the application is removed.

Listing 25-3 shows sample code for how to save a Java tree using GSON/JSON and internal files.

***Listing 25-3.** Reading/Writing JSON Strings from/to an Android Internal File*

```
private Object readFromInternalFile(Context appContext, String filename, Class classRef)
throws Exception
{
    FileInputStream fis = null;
    try {
        fis = appContext.openFileInput(filename);
        //Read the following string from the filestream fis
        String jsonString;

        Gson gson = new Gson();
        return gson.fromJson(jsonString, classRef);
}
    finally {
        // write code to closeStreamSilently(fis);
    }
}
private void saveToInternalFile(Context appContext, String filename, Object anyObject){
    Gson gson = new Gson();
    String jsonString = gson.toJson(anyObject);

    FileOutputStream fos = null;
    try {
        fos = appContext.openFileOutput(filename
                                   ,Context.MODE_PRIVATE);
        fos.write(jsonString.getBytes());
    }
    finally    {
        // closeStreamSilently(fos);
    }
}
```

This approach based on internal files and GSON is covered in detail in our companion book, *Expert Android* from Apress (`http://www.apress.com/9781430249504`). This is also briefly documented online at `http://androidbook.com/item/4439`.

Saving State Using External Files

In Android, external files are stored either on the SD card or on the device. These become public files that other apps including the user could see and read outside the context of your application. For many apps that want to manage their internal state these external files will unnecessarily pollute the public space.

Because the data you would represent as JSON is typically very specific to your application, it doesn't make sense to make this available as external storage, which is typically used for music files, video files, or files that are commonly in a format that is understandable by other applications.

Because external storage such as an SD card can be in various states (available, not mounted, full, etc.), it is harder to program this for simple apps when the data is small enough. So we could not make a good case for now that the application state be maintained on external storage.

A hybrid approach may be meaningful if the application requires music and photos and those can go on the external storage while keeping the core state data in JSON and internal.

The `android.os.Environment` class and the `android.content.Context` class have a number of methods to read and write to external files and directories. We have not included code examples because the approach is very similar to internal files once you get access to these files through the `andorid.content.Context`.

Saving State Using SQLite

Android apps can use SQLite databases to store their state. SQLite is well integrated into the fabric of Android. If you want to store the internal state of your application robustly then this is probably the best approach. However, working with any relational database including SQLite has a lot of nuances. We will cover the essentials and nuances of using SQLite on Android a little later in the chapter.

Saving State Using O/R Mapping Libraries

O/R mapping stands for Object-to-Relational Mapping. A key difficulty with storing state in a relational database from a programming language like Java is the mismatch between Java object structures and relational structures of the database. One needs to map between the names, types, and relationships of fields as they are in the Java space and their equivalents in the database space. This mapping is error prone. You will see this when we cover the SQLite in detail later.

There is a need for simplifying this mapping of data between Java and SQL. This space in the industry is called O/R mapping. A few tools are now available to solve this in Android. It is beyond the scope of this book to cover the essentials of these O/R mapping tools. But we will name a couple of these tools and give their online references now.

Two key tools in this space are GreenDAO (`http://greendao-orm.com/`) and OrmLite (`http://ormlite.com/`). There are more appearing every year. So check often to see if the new ones are faster or easier. GreenDAO uses a code generation approach based on schema definitions. It is said to be three to four times faster than OrmLite. OrmLite fuses the schema definition with Java classes through annotations. The latter approach is easier programmatically. Also OrmLite works the same on any Java platform. However, possibly due to reflection used at run time, it can be slower, but I suspect is fast enough for most applications.

We predict that using one of these O/R mapping libraries is a key need to get your apps faster to the market. We recommend that you isolate the persistence services and start with OrmLite and then move to GreenDAO if your app gains enough traction or for moving to production from your prototype.

Saving State Using Content Providers

Android provides a higher-level abstraction on top of data stores based on URIs. Using this approach any application can read or store data using REST like URIs. This abstraction also allows applications to share their data through APIs based on URI strings. In this approach submitting a URI will give back a collection of rows and columns in a database cursor. A URI can also take a set of key/value pairs and persist them in a target database if permissions are granted. This is a general-purpose mechanism for interoperability of data between Android applications. We will cover this in greater detail later in the chapter. This is a preferred mechanism if your application has data that is valuable to be shared, created, or manipulated by other applications. For example many applications that deal with notes, documents, audio, or video implement their data as content providers. This is also the case with most of Android's core data-related services.

Saving State Using Network Storage

Network storage comes into play when the data created or used by an application needs to be shared via a network by other users on either the same platform or different platforms like in a collaborative application. This back-end service facility utilized by mobile application is being called MBaaS (Mobile Back-end As A Service). Parse.com is an example of a MBAAS that provides back-end services such as user management, user logins, security, social, common network storage, server side business logic, and notifications.

Android also natively uses a concept called sync adapters to transfer data between the device and network servers. You can read more on sync adapters at `http://developer.android.com/training/sync-adapters/index.html`. This is a framework that uses asynchronous callbacks to optimize transfer of arbitrary amounts of data efficiently by scheduling and executing it at the most opportune moment. The framework sweats the detail and developers just provide the transfer code.

That concludes the overview of various ways to save state for Android mobile applications. We will cover now two of those approaches in detail: SQLite and content providers. We will start with the Android SQLite API.

Storing Data Directly Using SQLite

In this section we will explore in detail how to use SQLite effectively to manage Android application state. You will understand the extent of SQLite support in Android. We will show you the essential code snippets. We will show you best practices for using SQLite on Android. We will show you how best to load DDLs to create your database. We will show you a cleaner architectural pattern to abstract persistence services. We will show how to apply transactions through dynamic proxies. This section is a robust treatment of using SQLite on Android. We also have a sample program that you can download to see the complete working implementation. Let's start with a quick overview of SQLite packages and classes in Android.

Summarizing Key SQLite Packages and Classes

Android supports SQLite through its Java package `android.database.sqlite`. Some of the key classes you will need to understand for effectively using the Android SQLite API are listed in Listing 25-4. Note that some of the classes are outside the `android.database.sqlite` package.

Listing 25-4. Key SQLite Java Classes in the Android SDK

```
android.database.sqlite.SQLiteDatabase
android.database.sqlite.SQLiteCursor
android.database.sqlite.SQLiteQueryBuilder
android.content.ContentValues
android.database.Cursor
android.database.SQLException
android.database.sqlite.SQLiteOpenHelper
```

Let's talk about each of these packages and classes briefly.

SQLiteDatabase: `SQLiteDatabase` is a Java class that represents the database usually referring to a "`.db`" file on the file system. Using this object you can query, insert, update, or delete for a given table in that database. You can also execute a single arbitrary SQL statement. You can apply transactions. You can also use this object to define tables through DDLs (Data Definition Language). DDLs are statements that let you create database entities such as tables, views, indexes, etc. Typically there is a single instance of this object in your application representing your database.

SQLiteCursor: This Java class represents a collection of rows that are returned from an `SQLiteDatabase`. It also implements the `android.database.Cursor` interface. This object has methods to navigate the rows one at a time like a forward database cursor and retrieving the rows only as needed. This object can also jump forward or backward if needed like a random cursor by implementing windowing qualities. This is also the object you will use to read the column values for any current row.

SQLiteQueryBuilder: This is a helper Java class to construct an SQLite query string by incrementally specifying table names, column names, where clause, etc., as separate fields. This class has a number of set methods to gradually build up the query as opposed to specifying the entire SQL Query as a string. You can also use the query methods directly on the `SQLiteDatabase` class if your query is simple.

ContentValues: A Java object of this class holds a set of key/value pairs that are used by a number of SQLite classes to insert or update a row of data.

SQLException: Most Android SQLite database APIs `throw` this exception when there are errors.

SQLiteOpenHelper: This helper Java object provides access to an `SQLiteDatabase` by examining a few things: given a filename of the database, this object checks to see if that database is already installed and available. If it is available it checks to see if the version is the same. If the version is also the same it provides a reference to the `SQLiteDatabase` representing that database. If the version is different it provides a callback to migrate the database prior to providing a valid reference to the database. If the database file doesn't exist then it provides a callback to create and populate the database. You will extend this base class and provide implementations to these various callbacks. You will see this shortly in the provided code snippets.

That is a quick summary of the key classes you use to save state of your application in an SQLite database. Let us now turn to key concepts in using SQLite for managing application state. Let's start with creating a database.

Creating an SQLite Database

Creation of a database in Android is controlled through the `SQLiteOpenHelper` class. For each database in your application you will have a Java database object that is an instance of this class. This `SQLiteOpenHelper` object has a pair of get methods to get a reference to the read-optimized (configured for) or write-optimized (configured for) `SQLiteDatabase` object. Creating or getting access to your SQLite database object involves the following:

1. Extending `SQLiteOpenHelper` and supplying the database name and version to the constructor of this derived class so that those values can be passed to the base class
2. Overriding the `onCreate()`, `onUpgrade()`, and `onDowngrade()` methods from `SQLiteOpenHelper`. You get a call to `onCreate()` if this database is not there. You get a call to `onUpgrade()` if the version of the database is newer, and a call to onDowngrade() if the version of the database is older from the one that is on the device. You will use execute DDL statements in these methods to create or adjust your database. If your database is not new or has the same version, then neither of these callbacks will be invoked.
3. Have a single static reference to this derived object. Call get methods on this object to get a reference to a copy of readable or writable database. Use these database references to perform CRUD operations and transactions.

Listing 25-5 is a code snippet that demonstrates how these steps are implemented in creating a database called "booksqlite.db", a database to hold a single table of books and their detail.

Listing 25-5. Using SQLiteOpenHelper

```
// File reference in project: DirectAccessBookDBHelper.Java
/**
* A complete example of SQLiteOpenHelper demonstrating
* 1. How to create a databases
* 2. How to migrate a database
* 3. How to hold a static reference
* 4. How to give out read and write database references
*
* This class also can act as a DatabaseContext.IFactory to produce read and write
* database references. This aspect is not critical to understanding but included
* for advanced readers and for some material later in the chapter.
*/
public class DirectAccessBookDBHelper extends SQLiteOpenHelper
implements DatabaseContext.IFactory
{
    //there is one and only one of these database helpers
    //for this database for this entire application
    public static DirectAccessBookDBHelper m_self =
       new DirectAccessBookDBHelper(MyApplication.m_appContext);

    //Name of the database on the device
    private static final String DATABASE_NAME = "bookSQLite.db";

    //Name of the DDL file you want to load while creating a database
    private static final String CREATE_DATABASE_FILENAME = "create-book-db.sql";

    //Current version number of the database for the App to work
    private static final int DATABASE_VERSION = 1;

    //Just a logging tag
    private static final String TAG = "DirectAccessBookDBHelper";

    //Pass the database name and version to the base class
    //This is a non public constructor
    //Clients can just use m_self and not construct this object at all directly
    DirectAccessBookDBHelper(Context context) {
        super(context,DATABASE_NAME,null,DATABASE_VERSION);
        //Initialize anything else in your system that may need a
        //reference to this object.
        //Example: DatabaseContext.initialize(this);
    }
```

```
@Override
public void onCreate(SQLiteDatabase db) {
   try {
      //No database exists. Load DDL from a file in the assets directory
      loadSQLFrom(this.CREATE_DATABASE_FILENAME,db);
   }
   catch(Throwable t)      {
      //Problem creating database
      throw new RuntimeException(t);
   }
}
//A function to load one SQL statement at a time using execSQL method
private void loadSQLFrom(String assetFilename, SQLiteDatabase db)    {
   List<String> statements = getDDLStatementsFrom(assetFilename);
   for(String stmt: statements){
      Log.d(TAG,"Executing Statement:" + stmt);
      db.execSQL(stmt);
   }
}
//Optimize this function for robustness.
//For now it assumes there are no comments in the file
//the statements are separated by a semicolon
private List<String> getDDLStatementsFrom(String assetFilename)  {
   ArrayList<String> l = new ArrayList<String>();
   String s = getStringFromAssetFile(assetFilename);
   for (String stmt: s.split(";"))  {
      //Add the stmt if it is a valid statement
      if (isValid(stmt)) {
         l.add(stmt);
      }
   }
   return l;
}
private boolean isValid(String s)    {
    //write logic here to see if it is null, empty etc.
    return true; //for now
}
@Override
public void onUpgrade(SQLiteDatabase db, int oldVersion, int newVersion)   {
   //Use old and new version numbers to run DDL statements
   //to upgrade the database
}
//Using your specific application object to remember the application context
//Then using that application context to read assets
private String getStringFromAssetFile(String filename)    {
   Context ctx = MyApplication.m_appContext;
   if ( ctx == null)   {
      throw new RuntimeException("Sorry your app context is null");
   }
```

```
        try   {
          AssetManager am = ctx.getAssets();
          InputStream is = am.open(filename);
          String s = convertStreamToString(is);
          is.close();
          return s;
        }
        catch (IOException x)     {
           throw new RuntimeException("Sorry not able to read filename:" + filename,x);
        }
     }
     //Optimize later. This may not be an efficient read
     private String convertStreamToString(InputStream is)  throws IOException   {
        ByteArrayOutputStream baos = new ByteArrayOutputStream();
        int i = is.read();
        while (i != -1)  {
           baos.write(i);
           i = is.read();
        }
        return baos.toString();
     }
    //Here are some examples of how to get access to readable and
    //writable databases. These methods will make sense once we get through the
    //the transactions applied through dynamic proxies
    /*
    public ReadDatabaseContext createReadableDatabase() {
       return new ReadDatabaseContext(this.getReadableDatabase());
    }
    public WriteDatabaseContext createWritableDatabase() {
       return new WriteDatabaseContext(this.getWritableDatabase());
    }
    */
}//eof-class DatabaseHelper
//Here is the code for MyApplication to remember the context
public class MyApplication extends Application {
   public final static String tag="MyApplication";
   public static volatile Context m_appContext = null;

   @Override
   public void onCreate() {
       super.onCreate();
          MyApplication.m_appContext = this.getApplicationContext();
   }
}
//assets/create-book-db.sql
CREATE TABLE t_books (id INTEGER PRIMARY KEY,
                name TEXT,  isbn TEXT, author TEXT,
                created_on INTEGER, created_by TEXT,
                last_updated_on INTEGER, last_updated_by TEXT
);
```

Defining a Database Through DDLs

In Listing 25-5, the `DirectAccessBookDBHelper` is a derived class of `SQLiteOpenHelper` that allows us to examine an existing database and see if it needs to be created or just migrated based on its version.

The method `onCreate()`is called only if this database does not exist on the device. Without the `SQLiteOpenHelper` we would have had to examine the physical location of this file and see if it exists. In other words `SQLiteOpenHelper` is really a thin wrapper that is saving us a number of "if-else" clauses to examine the database and do the necessary initialization: be it creating it or migrating it.

A number of examples for creating an Android database on the Internet use embedded DDL strings in Java code to create the tables needed. As DDL statements, strings in Java code are difficult to read and error prone. A better approach is to put these database creation scripts in a text file in the assets directory. Sample code in Listing 25-5 demonstrates how to read a text file from an assets directory of your application and use the `execSQL()` function available on the `SQLiteDatabase` to initialize the database.

A limitation of `execSQL()` is it can execute only one SQL statement at a time. That is why the code in Listing 25-5 reads the script file and parses it into a series of statements using a simple syntax. You may want to scour the Internet to see better parsing utilities to allow a better script file support. Another alternative, if it works for your case, is to have a schema class whose sole purpose is contain static public strings for your DDL as it alleviates the need for parsing files. We have links to some of these Java-based libraries in the online references provided at the end of this chapter. Especially, Java-based tools using ANTLR have a lot of promise for complex database setups.

The `onCreate()` function also wraps its execution in a transaction so that the executed database is consistent.

If you have a lot of scripts it is also possible to create the database entirely and keep it in the assets folder. During deployment if the database doesn't exist you can just copy the file to its target location.

Migrating a Database

As stated the `SQLiteOpenHelper` recognizes version numbers and appropriately calls the `onUpgrade()` method to upgrade the database. Here also you may want to keep series of scripts in the assets folder that can alter the database appropriately depending on the differences in the version numbers. Keep in mind that the version number on the device may be smaller or larger than your target version. So you may need a set of scripts that are unique to each conversion sequence: Going from V1 to V3 or from V2 to V3 or V3 to V1. Going backwards may require either warnings or dynamic downloading of server-side conversions to an older version, as the source code of an older version of the app is unlikely to have the needed utilities to step down from a future version.

Inserting Rows

At its core, inserting a row with its column values into SQLiteDatabase is merely calling the insert-related methods on the SQLiteDatabase object. Pseudocode that explains this is shown in Listing 25-6.

Listing 25-6. Basics of Inserting a Row Using SQLiteDatabase

```
//Get a reference to the database object
//Depending on the framework you have there could be many ways of doing this
SQLiteDatatabase db = DirectAccessBookDBHelper.m_self.getReadableDatabase();
String tablename; //which table you want to insert the row into

//populate a structure with the needed columns and their values
ContentValues cv = new ContentValues();
cv.put(columnName1, column1Value); //etc.

//A column that could be null if 'cv' is empty if an empty row is needed
//Provide null if that behavior is not needed
String nullColumnName = null;

//Insert the row
long rowId = db.insertOrThrow(tablename, nullColumnName, cv);
```

This code is really simple. Inserting any Java object using this code is merely reading its attributes and putting those values into the ContentValues data set and just insert. As far as Android's SQLite insert capabilities are concerned, that is all you need to know.

How best to structure to get to your Java objects and how to convert those values into the content values depends on your framework. This is a tedious process to do correctly. But again, this detail is not essential for the basic understanding of insert. You will need this level of rigor for most of your applications. You can skip this if you think this is complicated, but we are including it here as we feel you will need this level of rigor for most of your applications.

So getting the right column names and values for inserting rows requires some work and you typically need the following (irrespective of the framework you use):

1. A Java object that typically represents the row in a database, for example, a Book object
2. A table name to hold a set of books
3. String names for the columns available in the Books table
4. Finally, calling the insert method to persist the Book object as a row in the Books table

We will give code snippets (some in pseudocode fashion) for each of these needs. For actual code you can download the project for this chapter. Here are a couple of classes in Listing 25-7 that represent a Book object in Java code.

Listing 25-7. Ensuring Minimal Dependency Between Domain Objects and Persistence

```
// File reference in project: BaseEntity.Java
public class BaseEntity {
   private int id; //database identifier

   private String ownedAccount = null; //Multi-tenant if needed
   private String createdBy;
   private Date createdOn;
   private String lastUpdatedBy;
   private Date lastUpdatedOn;

   public BaseEntity(String ownedAccount, String createdBy, Date createdOn,
         String lastUpdatedBy, Date lastUpdatedOn, int id) {
      super();
      this.ownedAccount = ownedAccount;
      this.createdBy = createdBy;
      this.createdOn = createdOn;
      this.lastUpdatedBy = lastUpdatedBy;
      this.lastUpdatedOn = lastUpdatedOn;
      this.id = id;
   }
   //For persistence
   public BaseEntity(){}

   //Usual generated get/set methods
   //eliminated here for space. See the downloads
}
// File reference in project: Book.Java
public class Book extends BaseEntity
{
   //Key data fields
   //*************************************
   private String name;
   private String author;
   private String isbn;
   //*************************************

   public Book(String ownedAccount, String createdBy, Date createdOn,
         String lastUpdatedBy, Date lastUpdatedOn, String name,
         String author, String isbn) {
      super(ownedAccount, createdBy, createdOn, lastUpdatedBy, lastUpdatedOn,-1);
      this.name = name;
      this.author = author;
      this.isbn = isbn;
   }
   //To help with persistence
   public Book() {}
   //Generated methods get and set methods...
   //....
   //The following method is here for testing purposes
   //and also to see how a book object is typically created
```

```
    public static Book createAMockBook() {
        String ownedAccount = "Account1";
        String createdBy = "satya";
        Date createdOn = Calendar.getInstance().getTime();
        String lastUpdatedBy = "satya";
        Date lastUpdatedOn = Calendar.getInstance().getTime();

        //See how many books I have and increment it by one
        //The following method returns a collection of books in the database
        //This is not essential for your understanding here
        //You will see this clarified when you read the section of transactions
        List<Book> books = Services.PersistenceServices.bookps.getAllBooks();
        int i = books.size();
        String name = String.format("Book %s",i);
        String author = "satya";
        String isbn   = "isbn-12344-" + i;

        return new Book(ownedAccount,createdBy,createdOn,
              lastUpdatedBy,lastUpdatedOn,
              name,author,isbn);
    }
}
```

This listing has two Java classes: a `BaseEntity` and a `Book` that extends the `BaseEntity`. Objects that look like a `Book` in Listing 25-7 are called domain objects. These are pure Java objects that can move around in the Java space of your program without being burdened by their behavior relating to persistence. However, who created these objects, when they were created, and such attributes are encapsulated in the `BaseEntity` so that all domain objects have this basic information.

Because the SQLite database methods require explicit column names for these objects that aspect is defined in a separate set of classes that describe the metadata for these objects. These supporting classes are given in Listing 25-8.

Listing 25-8. Defining Metadata for Domain Objects

```
// File reference in project: BaseEntitySQLiteSQLiteMetaData.Java
public class BaseEntitySQLiteSQLiteMetaData  {
   static public final String OWNED_ACCOUNT_COLNAME = "owned_account";
   static public final String CREATED_BY_COLNAME = "created_by";
   static public final String CREATED_ON_COLNAME = "created_on";
   static public final String LAST_UPDATED_ON = "last_updated_on";
   static public final String LAST_UPDATED_BY = "last_updated_by";
   static public final String ID_COLNAME = "id";
}
// File reference in project: BookSQLiteSQLiteMetaData.Java
public class BookSQLiteSQLiteMetaData extends BaseEntitySQLiteSQLiteMetaData {
   static public final String TABLE_NAME = "t_books";
   static public final String NAME = "name";
   static public final String AUTHOR = "author";
   static public final String ISBN = "isbn";
}
```

These two classes parallel their respective BaseEntity and Book object classes. You have to pay attention that the column names match to those in the database. So this need is fundamentally error prone. Unless you use an O/R mapping library and craft one of your own, this issue will remain and you have to test well. It is defining these classes explicitly by the programmer that is eliminated in the O/R mapping tools that we discussed earlier.

Now that we have a Java class to represent a book and its metadata definition, that tells us the table name and the fields we can proceed to write the Java code to save a book object in the database, as shown in Listing 25-9 (note that this is still pseudocode and use the download to see any missing details).

Listing 25-9. Using Android SQLite APIs to Insert a Row

```
// File reference in project: BookPSSQLite.Java
private long createBook(Book book) {
   //Get access to a read database
   SQLiteDatabase db = DirectAccessBookDBHelper.m_self.getWritableDatabase();

   //Fill fields from the book object into the content values
   ContentValues bcv = new ContentValues();
   //.... fill other fields example
   bcv.put(BookSQLiteSQLiteMetaData.NAME, book.getName());
   bcv.put(BookSQLiteSQLiteMetaData.ISBN, book.getIsbn());
   bcv.put(BookSQLiteSQLiteMetaData.AUTHOR, book.getAuthor());
   //.... fill other fields

   //if bcv is an empty set, then an empty row can possibly be inserted.
   //It is not the case for our book table. If it were though, the empty bcv
   //will result in an insert statement with no column names in it.
   //At least one column name is needed by SQL insert syntax.
   //It is one of these column names that goes below. For us this is not case so a null
   String nullColumnName = null;

    long rowId = db.insertOrThrow(BookSQLiteSQLiteMetaData.TABLE_NAME,
                     nullColumnName,
                     bcv);
    return rowId;
}
```

The logic in Listing 25-9 is quite simple. Get a reference to a Book object we want to save. Copy the field values from the book into a ContentValues key/value pair object. Use metadata classes to define the field names correctly. Use the filled-in ContentValues object and call the insert method. If we don't do anything, the insert is encapsulated in an auto commit. We will talk about how to do transactions shortly, as the theory of it is a bit involved although the code is quite simple to write. The insert method returns the newly inserted primary key ID for this table. This convention of returning the primary key of the table comes from the underlying SQLite product documentation and is not Android specific.

The nullColumnName is related to the syntax of the SQL insert statement. If the row has ten columns but only two columns and their non-null values are indicated, then a new row is inserted with those two columns, and it is expected that the remaining eight columns will allow nulls. If you want a row with every column as null it is possible to issue an insert statement with no column names at all, matching the empty content values set. However, an insert statement with no column names is not allowed. So this parameter nullColumnName can contain one of the column names that could be null so that the insert statement syntax requirement is satisfied. The rest of the columns will be made null by the database internally when this row is inserted. Usually this column name is passed in as null because it is rare that we want to insert a row where every column is empty or null.

Updating Rows

Listing 25-10 is a sample pseudocode snippet (for full code see the download project) to show how to update a row in the database. Notice how Book object and BookSQLiteMetaData classes are used to minimize errors in specifying table names and column names. The approach is similar to the insert method.

***Listing 25-10.** Android SQLite API to Update a Record*

```
// File reference in project: BookPSSQLite.Java
public void updateBook(Book book) {
   if (book.getId() < 0) {
      throw new SQLException("Book id is less than 0");
   }
   //Get access to a read database
   SQLiteDatabase db = DirectAccessBookDBHelper.m_self.getWritableDatabase();

   //Fill fields from the book object into the content values
   ContentValues bcv = new ContentValues();
   //.... fill other fields
   bcv.put(BookSQLiteSQLiteMetaData.NAME, book.getName());
   bcv.put(BookSQLiteSQLiteMetaData.ISBN, book.getIsbn());
   bcv.put(BookSQLiteSQLiteMetaData.AUTHOR, book.getAuthor());
   //.... fill other fields

   //You can do this
   String whereClause = String.format("%s = %s",BookSQLiteSQLiteMetaData.ID_COLNAME,
   book.getId());
   String whereClauseArgs = null;
   //Or the next 4 lines (this is preferred)
   String whereClause2 = BookSQLiteSQLiteMetaData.ID_COLNAME + " = ?";
   String[] whereClause2Args = new String[1];
   whereClause2Args[1] = Integer.toString(book.getId());

   int count = db.update(BookSQLiteSQLiteMetaData.TABLE_NAME, bcv, whereClause2,
   whereClause2Args);
   if (count == 0)   {
      throw new SQLException(
            String.format("Failed to update book for book id:%s",book.getId()));
   }
}
```

Deleting Rows

Listing 25-11 is an example of how to delete a row from the database.

Listing 25-11. ***Android SQLite API to Delete a Record***

```
// File reference in project: BookPSSQLite.Java
public void deleteBook(int bookid){
   //Get access to a writable database
   SQLiteDatabase db = DirectAccessBookDBHelper.m_self.getWritableDatabase();

   String tname = BookSQLiteSQLiteMetaData.TABLE_NAME;
   String whereClause =
      String.format("%s = %s;",
         BookSQLiteSQLiteMetaData.ID_COLNAME,
         bookid);
   String[] whereClauseargs = null;
   int i = db.delete(tname,whereClause, whereClauseargs);
   if (i != 1)   {
      throw new RuntimeException("The number of deleted books is not 1 but:" + i);
   }
}
```

Reading Rows

Listing 25-12 shows pseudocode snippet (for full code see the download project) to read from SQLite using the `SQLiteDatabase.query()` method. This method returns a `Cursor` object, which you can use to retrieve each row.

Listing 25-12. ***Android SQLite API to Read Records***

```
// File reference in project: BookPSSQLite.Java
public List<Book> getAllBooks()   {
   //Get access to a read database
   SQLiteDatabase db = DirectAccessBookDBHelper.m_self.getReadableDatabase();

   String tname = BookSQLiteSQLiteMetaData.TABLE_NAME;
   //Get column name array from the metadata class
   //(See the download how the column names are gathered)
   //(at the end of the day it is just a set of column names
   String[] colnames = BookSQLiteSQLiteMetaData.s_self.getColumnNames();

   //Selection
   String selection = null;      //all rows. Usually a where clause. exclude where part
   String[] selectionArgs = null; //use ?s if you need it

   String groupBy = null;        //sql group by clause: exclude group by part
   String having = null;         //similar
   String orderby = null;
   String limitClause = null; //max number of rows
```

```
   //db.query(tname, colnames)
   Cursor c = null;

   try {
      c = db.query(tname,colnames,selection,selectionArgs,groupBy,having,orderby,limitClause);
      //This may not be the optimal way to read data through a list
      //Directly pass the cursor back if your intent is to read these one row at a time
      List<Book> bookList = new ArrayList<Book>();
      for(c.moveToFirst();!c.isAfterLast();c.moveToNext()) {
         Log.d(tag,"There are books");
         Book b = new Book();

         //..fill base fields the same way
         b.setName(c.getString(c.getColumnIndex(BookSQLiteMetaData.NAME)));
         b.setAuthor(c.getString(c.getColumnIndex(BookSQLiteMetaData.AUTHOR)));
         b.setIsbn(c.getString(c.getColumnIndex(BookSQLiteMetaData.ISBN)));
         //..fill other fields

         //Or you could delegate this work to the BookSQLiteMetaData object
         //as we have done in the sample downloadable project
         //Ex: BookSQLiteSQLiteMetaData.s_self.fillFields(c,b);

         bookList.add(b);
      }
      return bookList;
   }
   finally {
      if (c!= null) c.close();
   }
}
```

Here are a few facts about an Android cursor object:

- A cursor is a collection of rows.
- You need to use `moveToFirst()` before reading any data because the cursor starts off positioned before the first row.
- You need to know the column names.
- You need to know the column types.
- All field-access methods are based on column number, so you must convert the column name to a column number first. Note that this lookup can be optimized. It's more efficient to populate the column name array in order if you wish to fetch the values and then use explicit constant indices on the cursor.
- The cursor is random (you can move forward and backward, and you can jump).
- Because the cursor is random, you can ask it for a row count.

Applying Transactions

SQLite libraries on Android support transactions. The transaction methods are available on the `SQLiteDatabase` class. These methods are shown in pseudocode snippet (for full code see the download project) in Listing 25-13.

Listing 25-13. SQLite API for Transactions

```
// File reference in project: DBServicesProxyHandler.Java
public void doSomeUpdates() {
  SQLiteDatabase db; //Get a reference to this database through helper
  db.beginTransaction();
  try {
    //...call a number of database methods
    db.setTransactionSuccessful();
  }
  finally {
    db.endTransaction();
  }
}
```

Summarizing SQLite

If you are a Java programmer with a few years of experience, what we have covered so far is sufficient to understand the SQLite API in Android. With the material covered so far, you know how to check for a database, create a database through DDL, insert rows, update rows, delete rows, or read using database cursors. We have also showed you the basic API for transactions. However, if you are not an experienced hand at Java, database transactions are tricky to implement correctly and efficiently. The next section will tell you an API-based pattern using Java dynamic proxies.

Doing Transactions Through Dynamic Proxies

You can visualize your mobile application as a collection of two bricks: An API brick and a UI brick. The API brick will have a series of stateless methods that provide logic and data to the UI brick. In this context the method in Listing 25-13 `doSomeUpdates()` is considered a reusable API by many parts of the UI or by other APIs. Because it is a reusable API the client decides whether something should be committed or not committed in that transaction. This means the API should not be dealing with transactions most of the time. It is very much like a stored procedure in a relational database. A stored procedure rarely does transactions directly. The container of the stored procedure decides to commit or not commit external to the stored procedure. The logic is this: if the stored procedure is invoked by itself then its output is committed at the stored procedure level. If the stored procedure is called by another stored procedure the commit waits until the main invoking stored procedure is complete.

It is better to use the same strategy for these APIs in your application to reduce the complexity in implementing the APIs. This is done by intercepting calls to all the APIs to make a determination if this is a direct call or being called by another API that is already being monitored for a transaction. There are a number of ways to intercept the API calls that need to be intercepted.

This is also sometimes called Aspect-Oriented Programming or AOP. AOP needs sophisticated tooling to do. Java provides a less sophisticated but straightforward way to do this through dynamic proxies. A dynamic proxy is a facility in Java, based on Java reflection, that allows you to intercept calls to an underlying object without the object being aware of it. When a client calls the object through this proxy, the client thinks it is talking to the object directly. However, the proxy can choose to apply other aspects (like security, logging, transactions, etc.) before sending the call to the real object. The included project for this chapter provides a full implementation of a dynamic proxy that automatically applies the transactional aspects.

We will show you first what your API implementations look like once a dynamic proxy is in place. This will give you an idea of the simplicity of this approach to transactions first. Then you can see if you want to take this route and use dynamic proxies. As we present the code below note that we will be including only snippets or samples and not the entire code. Use the downloadable project for full details. We have annotated the download project with a lot of comments to help your understanding. With that caveat consider the API to work with Book-based objects.

Listing 25-14. API-Based Interfaces for Working with the Book Domain Object

```
// File reference in project: IBookPS.Java
public interface IBookPS {
   public int saveBook(Book book);
   public Book getBook(int bookid);
   public void updateBook(Book book);
   public void deleteBook(int bookid);
   public List<Book> getAllBooks();
}
```

This interface defines operations using Java-based objects. The letters "PS" at the end of IBookPS service indicates that this is a persistence service API for a book. Listing 25-15 shows an SQLite implementation for the IBookPS

Listing 25-15. Implementing the Book APIs Using SQLite

```
// File reference in project: BookPSSQLite.Java
// The missing classes in this code are in the download and not essential for
// exploring the idea.
// ASQLitePS is a class that contains reusable common methods like getting access
// to the read and write databases using the singleton database helper.
public class BookPSSQLite extends ASQLitePS implements IBookPS {
   private static String tag = "BookPSSQLite";
   @Override public int saveBook(Book book)   {
      //get the database
      //case: id does not exist in the book object
      if (book.getId() == -1)  {
         //id of the book doesn't exist so create it
         return (int)createBook(book);
      }
      //case: id exists in book object
      updateBook(book);
      return book.getId();
   }
```

```
@Override public void deleteBook(int bookid){
   SQLiteDatabase db = getWriteDb();
   String tname = BookSQLiteSQLiteMetaData.TABLE_NAME;
   String whereClause =
      String.format("%s = %s;",
         BookSQLiteSQLiteMetaData.ID_COLNAME,
         bookid);
   String[] whereClauseargs = null;
   int i = db.delete(tname,whereClause, whereClauseargs);
   if (i != 1)  {
      throw new RuntimeException("The number of deleted books is not 1 but:" + i);
   }
}
private long createBook(Book book)   {
   //book doesn't exist
   //create it
   SQLiteDatabase db = getWriteDb();

   ContentValues bcv = this.getBookAsContentValuesForCreate(book);

   //I don't need to insert an empty row
   //usually any nullable column name goes here if I want to insert an empty row.
   String nullColumnNameHack = null;
   //Construct values from the Book object. SQLException is a runtime exception
   long rowId = db.insertOrThrow(BookSQLiteMetaData.TABLE_NAME, nullColumnNameHack, bcv);
   return rowId;
}
@Override  public void updateBook(Book book) {
   if (book.getId() < 0) {
      throw new SQLException("Book id is less than 0");
   }
   SQLiteDatabase db = getWriteDb();
   ContentValues bcv = this.getBookAsContentValuesForUpdate(book);
   String whereClause = String.format("%s = %s",BookSQLiteMetaData.ID_COLNAME,book.
getId());
   whereArgs[0] = BookSQLiteMetaData.ID_COLNAME;
   whereArgs[1] = Integer.toString(book.getId());

   int count = db.update(BookSQLiteMetaData.TABLE_NAME, bcv, whereClause, null);
   if (count == 0)   {
      throw new SQLException(
            String.format("Failed to update book for book id:%s",book.getId()));
   }
}
 private ContentValues getBookAsContentValuesForUpdate(Book book)  {
   ContentValues cv = new ContentValues();
   //Following code loads column values from book object to the cv
   //See the downloadable project for the mechanics of it
   BookSQLiteMetaData.s_self.fillUpdatableColumnValues(cv, book);
   return cv;
 }
```

```
private ContentValues getBookAsContentValuesForCreate(Book book)  {
    ContentValues cv = new ContentValues();
    BookSQLiteMetaData.s_self.fillAllColumnValues(cv, book);
    return cv;
}
@Override   public List<Book> getAllBooks() {
    SQLiteDatabase db = getReadDb();
    String tname = BookSQLiteMetaData.TABLE_NAME;
    String[] colnames = BookSQLiteMetaData.s_self.getColumnNames();

    //Selection
    String selection = null; //all rows. Usually a where clause. exclude where part
    String[] selectionArgs = null; //use ?s if you need it

    String groupBy = null; //sql group by clause: exclude group by part
    String having = null; //similar
    String orderby = null;
    String limitClause = null; //max number of rows
    //db.query(tname, colnames)
    Cursor c = null;

    try {
       c = db.query(tname,colnames,selection,selectionArgs,groupBy,having,orderby,
       limitClause);
       //This may not be the optimal way to read data through a list
       //Directly pass the cursor back if your intent is to read these one row at a time
       List<Book> bookList = new ArrayList<Book>();
       for(c.moveToFirst();!c.isAfterLast();c.moveToNext())
       {
          Log.d(tag,"There are books");
          Book b = new Book();
          BookSQLiteMetaData.s_self.fillFields(c,b);
          bookList.add(b);
       }
       return bookList;
    }
    finally {
       if (c!= null) c.close();
    }
}
@Override   public Book getBook(int bookid) {
    SQLiteDatabase db = getReadDb();
    String tname = BookSQLiteMetaData.TABLE_NAME;
    String[] colnames = BookSQLiteMetaData.s_self.getColumnNames();

    //Selection
    String selection =
       String.format("%s = %s",
             BookSQLiteMetaData.ID_COLNAME,
             bookid);
```

```
        //all rows. Usually a where clause. exclude where part
        String[] selectionArgs = null; //use ?s if you need it

        String groupBy = null; //sql group by clause: exclude group by part
        String having = null; //similar
        String orderby = null;
        String limitClause = null; //max number of rows
        //db.query(tname, colnames)
        Cursor c = db.query(tname,colnames,selection,
                    selectionArgs,groupBy,having,orderby,limitClause);
        try   {
           if (c.isAfterLast()) {
              Log.d(tag,"No rows for id" + bookid);
              return null;
           }
           Book b = new Book();
           BookSQLiteMetaData.s_self.fillFields(c, b);
           return b;
        }
        finally {
           c.close();
        }
    }
}//eof-class
```

Notice how the implementation of the Book persistence API does not directly deal with the transactional aspects of these methods. Instead, the transactions are handled by Java dynamic proxy, which we will show shortly. Listing 25-16 shows how a client can see these APIs and invoke these persistence APIs indirectly (again, please refer to the download projects for classes that are referenced in this code but not listed here as they are not essential for understanding).

Listing 25-16. Client Access to API-Based Services

```
// File reference in project: SQLitePersistenceTester.Java
// BaseTester is just a helper class to provider common functionality
// it implements some logging and report back methods to the UI activity
public class SQLitePersistenceTester extends BaseTester {
   private static String tag = "SQLitePersistenceTester";
   //Services is a static class that provides access to persistence services
   //Services class provides visibility to the implementer of the IBookPS
   //It demonstrates how a client gets access to the namespace of services
   //You will shortly see what this class is. Understand the intent first.
   private IBookPS bookPersistenceService = Services.PersistenceServices.bookps;
   //IReportBack is a logging interface to report loggable events back to the UI
   //UI will then choose to log those events and also show on the activity screen.
   SQLitePersistenceTester(Context ctx, IReportBack target) {
      super(ctx, target,tag);
   }
```

```
    //Add a book whose id is one larger than the books
    //in the database
    public void addBook() {
       Book book = Book.createAMockBook();
       int bookid = bookPersistenceService.saveBook(book);
       reportString(String.format("Inserted a book %s whose generated id now is %s"
             ,book.getName()
             ,bookid));
    }
    //Delete the last book
    public void removeBook() {
       List<Book> bookList = bookPersistenceService.getAllBooks();
       if( bookList.size() <= 0)
       {
          reportString("There are no books that can be deleted");
          return;
       }
       reportString(String.format("There are %s books. First one will be deleted",
       bookList.size()));

       Book b = bookList.get(0);
       bookPersistenceService.deleteBook(b.getId());
       reportString(String.format("Book with id:%s successfully deleted", b.getId()));
    }

    //write the list of books so far to the screen
    public void showBooks() {
       List<Book> bookList = bookPersistenceService.getAllBooks();
       reportString(String.format("Number of books:%s", bookList.size()));
       for(Book b: bookList) {
          reportString(String.format("id:%s name:%s author:%s isbn:%s"
                ,b.getId()
                ,b.getName()
                ,b.getAuthor()
                ,b.getIsbn()));
       }
    }

    //Count the number of books in the database
    private int getCount() {
       List<Book> bookList = bookPersistenceService.getAllBooks();
       return bookList.size();
    }
}
```

In Listing 25-16, notice how simple it is to access the APIs through the static class Services. Of course we haven't shown you the implementation of Services and also the dynamic proxy held by the static class Services. Listing 25-17 shows the source code for the static Services class in order to give you an idea of how this scheme works. The goal of many, if not all, of the listings in this chapter is to aid your understanding. For complete compilable source code we kindly request that you refer to the downloadable projects for this chapter.

Listing 25-17. Exposing APIs to Clients Through a Services Name Space

```
// File reference in project: Services.Java
/**
 * Allow a namespace for clients to discover various services
 * Usage: Services.persistenceServices.bookps.addBook(); etc.
 * Dynamic proxy will take care of transactions.
 * Dynamic proxy will take care of mock data.
 * Dynamic Proxy will allow more than one interface
 *   to apply the above aspects.
 */
public class Services {
   public static String tag = "Services";
   public static class PersistenceServices  {
      ////se this pointer during initialization
      public static IBookPS bookps = null;
      static {
         Services.init();
      }
   }
   //Although this method is empty, calling it
   //will trigger all static initialization code for this class
   public static void init() {}
   private static Object mainProxy;
   static   {
      //A utility class to compile all database-related initializations so far
      //Gets the database helper going.
      //See the download project how it uses the concepts presented so far to do this
      Database.initialize();

      //set up bookps
      ClassLoader cl = IBookPS.class.getClassLoader();
      //Add more interfaces as available
      Class[] variousServiceInterfaces = new Class[] { IBookPS.class };

      //Create a big object that can proxy all the related interfaces
      //for which similar common aspects are applied
      //In this cases it is android SQLite transactions
      mainProxy = Proxy.newProxyInstance(cl,
               variousServiceInterfaces, new DBServicesProxyHandler());

      //Preset the namespace for easy discovery
      PersistenceServices.bookps = (IBookPS)mainProxy;
   }
}
```

Notice how DBServicesProxyHandler is a proxy for the implementation of IBookPS. When called by clients, the DBServicesProxyHandler then calls the actual implementation for IBookPS. The actual implementation of IBookPS is shown in Listing 25-15. Let's turn to the implementation of the dynamic proxy in Listing 25-18. Some of the code and classes referenced in Listing 25-18 are only available in the downloadable projects. However, that should not hinder the general understanding of the architecture of the dynamic proxy.

Listing 25-18. Java Dynamic Proxy to Wrap the SQLite API Implementations

```
// File reference in project: DBServicesProxyHandler.Java
/**
 * DBServicesProxyHandler: A class to externalize SQLite Transactions.
 * It is a dynamic proxy. See Services.Java to see how a reference to this is used.
 *
 * This proxy is capable of hosting multiple persistence interfaces.
 * Each interface may represent persistence aspects of a particular entity or a domain
object
 * like a Book. Or the interface can be a composite interface dealing with multiple
entities.
 *
 * It also uses ThreadLocals to pass the DatabaseContext
 * DatabaseContext holds a reference to the database that is on this thread
 * It also knows how to apply transactions to that database
 * It also knows if the current thread also has a running transaction
 * @See DatabaseContext
 *
 * DatabaseContext provides the SQLiteDatabase reference to
 * the implementation classes.
 *
 * Related classes
 * ****************
 * Services.Java : Client access to interfaces
 * IBookPS: Client interface to deal with persisting a Book
 * BookPSSQLite: SQLite Implementation of IBookPS
 *
 * DBServicesProxyHandler: This class that is a dynamic proxy
 * DatabaseContext: Holds a db reference for BookPSSQLite implementation
 * DirectAccessBookDBHelper: Android DBHelper to construct the database
 *
 */
public class DBServicesProxyHandler implements InvocationHandler {
   private BookPSSQLite bookServiceImpl = new BookPSSQLite();
   private static String tag = "DBServicesProxyHandler";
   DBServicesProxyHandler(){}
   public Object invoke(Object proxy, Method method, Object[] args)
         throws Throwable {
      logMethodSignature(method);
      String mname = method.getName();
      if (mname.startsWith("get")){
         return this.invokeForReads(method, args);
      }
      else {
         return this.invokeForWrites(method, args);
      }
   }
   private void logMethodSignature(Method method){
      String interfaceName = method.getDeclaringClass().getName();
      String mname = method.getName();
      Log.d(tag,String.format("%s : %s", interfaceName, mname));
   }
```

```
private Object callDelegatedMethod(Method method, Object[] args)
throws Throwable{
   return method.invoke(bookServiceImpl, args);
}
private Object invokeForReads(Method method, Object[] args) throws Throwable {
   //See comments above about DatabaseContext
   if (DatabaseContext.isItAlreadyInsideATransaction() == true){
      //It is already bound
      return invokeForReadsWithoutATransactionalWrap(method, args);
   }
   else {
      //A new transaction
      return invokeForReadsWithATransactionalWrap(method, args);
   }

}
private Object invokeForReadsWithATransactionalWrap(Method method, Object[] args)
throws Throwable {
   try   {
      DatabaseContext.setReadableDatabaseContext();
      return callDelegatedMethod(method, args);
   }
   finally   {
      DatabaseContext.reset();
   }
}
private Object invokeForReadsWithoutATransactionalWrap(Method method, Object[] args)
throws Throwable {
   return callDelegatedMethod(method, args);
}
private Object invokeForWrites(Method method, Object[] args) throws Throwable   {
   if (DatabaseContext.isItAlreadyInsideATransaction() == true) {
      //It is already bound
      return invokeForWritesWithoutATransactionalWrap(method, args);
   }
   else   {
      //A new transaction
      return invokeForWritesWithATransactionalWrap(method, args);
   }
}
private Object invokeForWritesWithATransactionalWrap(Method method, Object[] args)
throws Throwable   {
   try   {
      DatabaseContext.setWritableDatabaseContext();
      DatabaseContext.beginTransaction();
      Object rtnObject = callDelegatedMethod(method, args);
      DatabaseContext.setTransactionSuccessful();
      return rtnObject;
   }
```

```
      finally   {
         try {
            DatabaseContext.endTransaction();
         }
         finally {
            DatabaseContext.reset();
         }
      }
   }
   private Object invokeForWritesWithoutATransactionalWrap(Method method, Object[] args)
   throws Throwable   {
      return callDelegatedMethod(method, args);
   }
}//eof-class
```

This code in Listing 25-18 is the dynamic proxy implementation. We have not included all the details but sufficient detail is here to understand how this dynamic proxy performs transactions in an automated aspect-oriented way. It examines the called method name through reflection to see if the method name starts with "get," and if so then it assumes the method doesn't need a transactional context. Otherwise it marks the current thread as a transactional context. At the return of the method it completes the transaction as successful. If there are other methods called in between, the dynamic proxy knows from the thread that there is a transaction in place and hence ignores that method from a transactional aspect perspective.

Now based on your need you may want to alter this protocol based on annotations or some other aspect of your interfaces, but you get the idea. This approach of separating APIs from your UI is good design and you can use any number of persistent stores without changing your client UI code. We strongly recommend that you adapt this approach irrespective of the persistence mechanism you use, including the O/R mapping tools.

Exploring Databases on the Emulator and Available Devices

As you use SQLite as your persistence mechanism either directly or through content providers (next section), you may want to examine the resulting database files on the device for debugging purposes.

The database files created by SQLite API are kept in the following directory:

/data/data/<fully-qualified-package-name>/databases

You can use Eclipse Android file explorer to locate the directory and copy the files to your local drive and use native SQLite tools provided by SQLite directly to see and manipulate that database.

You can also use tools provided both by Android and by SQLite to examine these databases. Many of these tools reside in the `\<android-sdk-install-directory>\tools` subdirectory; others are in `\<android-sdk-install-directory>\platform-tools`.

Some useful commands from these directories are

```
android list avd: To see a list of AVDs or emulators
emulator.exe @avdname: To start an emulator with a given name
adb.exe devices: To see the devices or emulators
adb shell: To open a shell on the emulator or device
```

You can use the following commands from an "adb shell." These will work on the emulator but on a real device you will need root access.

```
ls /system/bin : To see available commands
ls -l /: Root level directories
ls /data/data/com.android.providers.contacts/databases: an example
ls -R /data/data/*/databases: To see all databases on the device or emulator
```

If there were a `find` command in the included Android Unix shell, you could look at all the `*.db` files. But there is no good way to do this with `ls` alone. The nearest thing you can do is this:

```
ls -R /data/data/*/databases
```

With this command, you will notice that the Android distribution has the databases shown in Listing 25-19 (depending on your release, this list may vary):

***Listing 25-19.** A Few Sample Databases*

```
alarms.db
contacts.db
downloads.db
internal.db
settings.db
mmssms.db
telephony.db
```

You can invoke `sqlite3` on one of these databases inside the adb shell by typing this:

```
sqlite3 /data/data/com.android.providers.contacts/databases/contacts.db
```

You can exit `sqlite3` by typing this:

```
sqlite>.exit
```

Notice that the prompt for adb is # and the prompt for `sqlite3` is `sqlite>`. These prompts could be different depending on the device. You can read about the various `sqlite3` commands by visiting `www.sqlite.org/sqlite.html`. However, we will list a few important commands here so you don't have to make a trip to the Web. You can see a list of tables by typing

```
sqlite> .tables
```

This command is a shortcut for querying on the sqlite_master table as shown in Listing 25-20 (format and structure of the resulting output may vary).

Listing 25-20. Using SQLite sqlite_master Table

```
SELECT name FROM sqlite_master
WHERE type IN ('table','view') AND name NOT LIKE 'sqlite_%'
UNION ALL
SELECT name FROM sqlite_temp_master
WHERE type IN ('table','view')
ORDER BY 1
```

The table sqlite_master is a master table that keeps track of tables and views in the SQLite database. The following command line displays a create statement for a table called people in contacts.db (assuming this database exists on your device):

```
.schema people
```

This is one way to get at the column names of a table in SQLite. This will also show the column data types. While working with content providers, you should note these column types because access methods depend on them. Also note that this may not be a practical way to see these databases as you may not have access to them on real devices. In that case you have to rely on the documentation provided by the content provider.

You can issue the following command from your OS command prompt to pull down the contacts.db file to the local file system:

```
adb pull /data/data/com.android.providers.contacts/databases/contacts.db ➥
c:/somelocaldir/contacts.db
```

The sample SQL statements in Listing 25-21 could help you navigate through an SQLite database quickly (alternatively you can use any third-party SQLite browser tool):

Listing 25-21. Sample SQL Code for SQLite

```
--Set the column headers to show in the tool
sqlite>.headers on

--select all rows from a table
select * from table1;

--count the number of rows in a table
select count(*) from table1;

--select a specific set of columns
select col1, col2 from table1;

--Select distinct values in a column
select distinct col1 from table1;

--counting the distinct values
select count(col1) from (select distinct col1 from table1);
```

```
--group by
select count(*), col1 from table1 group by col1;

--regular inner join
select * from table1 t1, table2 t2
where t1.col1 = t2.col1;

--left outer join
--Give me everything in t1 even though there are no rows in t2
select * from table t1 left outer join table2 t2
on t1.col1 = t2.col1
where ....
```

Exploring Content Providers

Earlier in the chapter we touched upon content providers to share data between applications. Content providers as stated are wrappers around a data store. The data stores could be local or remote. The data stores are usually SQLite databases on the local device.

To retrieve data from a content provider or save data into a content provider, you will use a set of REST-like URIs. For example, if you were to retrieve a set of books from a content provider that is an encapsulation of a book database, you might need to use a URI like this:

```
content://com.android.book.BookProvider/books
```

To retrieve a specific book from the book database (like say book 23), you might use a URI like this:

```
content://com.android.book.BookProvider/books/23
```

You will see in this chapter how these URIs translate to underlying database-access mechanisms. Any application with the appropriate access permissions on the device can make use of these URIs to access and manipulate data.

Exploring Android's Built-in Providers

Android comes with a number of built-in content providers, which are documented in the SDK's `android.provider` Java package. You can view the list of these providers here:

```
http://developer.android.com/reference/android/provider/package-summary.html
```

The providers include, for example, Contacts and Media Store. These SQLite databases typically have an extension of `.db` and are accessible only from the implementation package. Any access outside that package must go through the content-provider interface. You can use the previous section "Exploring Databases on the Emulator and Available Devices" to explore the database files created by built-in providers on the emulator. On real devices this is not feasible unless of course you have root access on the device.

Understanding the Structure of Content Provider URIs

Each content provider on a device is registered in the Android manifest file like a web site with a string identifier called an authority (akin to a domain name). Listing 25-22 has two examples of this registration:

Listing 25-22. Example of Registering a Provider

```
<!-- File reference in project: AndroidManifest.xml -->
<provider android:name="SomeProviderJavaClass"
        android:authorities="com.your-company.SomeProvider" />

<provider android:name="BookProvider"
   android:authorities="com.androidbook.provider.BookProvider"
/>
```

The unique authority string forms the basis of a set of URIs that this content provider offers. An Android content URI has the following structure:

```
content://<authority-name>/<path-segment1>/<path-segment2>/etc...
```

Here's an example URI that identifies a book numbered 23 in a database of books:

```
content:// com.androidbook.provider.BookProvider/books/23
```

After `content:`, the URI contains the authority, which is used to locate the provider in the provider registry. In the preceding example, `com.androidbook.provider.BookProvider` is the authority portion of the URI.

`/books/23` is the path section of the URI that is specific to each provider. The `books` and `23` portions of the path section are called path segments. It is the responsibility of the provider to document and interpret the path section and path segments of the URIs. Hence content providers provide these REST-like URLs to retrieve or manipulate data. For the preceding registration, the URI to identify a directory or a collection of books in the books database is

```
content:// com.androidbook.provider.BookProvider/books
```

The URI to identify a specific note is

```
content:// com.androidbook.provider.BookProvider/books/#
```

where # is the `id` of a particular note. Listing 25-23 shows additional examples of URIs that some data providers on Android accept:

Listing 25-23. Few Sample Android Content URLs

```
content://media/internal/images
content://media/external/images
content://contacts/people/
content://contacts/people/23
```

Notice how these providers' media (`content://media`) and contacts (`content://contacts`) don't have a fully qualified authority name. This is because providers offered by Android may not carry a fully qualified authority name.

Given these content URIs, a provider is expected to retrieve rows that the URIs represent. The provider is also expected to alter content at this URI using any of the state-change methods: `insert`, `update`, or `delete`.

Implementing Content Providers

Let's fully understand content providers by implementing and using one. To write a content provider, you have to extend `android.content.ContentProvider` and implement the following key methods: `query()`, `insert()`, `update()`, `delete()`, and `getType()`.

You'll need to set up a number of things for implementing these methods. Implementing a content provider needs the following steps:

1. Plan your database, URIs, column names, and so on, and create a metadata class that defines constants for all of these metadata elements.
2. Extend the abstract class ContentProvider.
3. Implement these methods: query, insert, update, delete, and getType.
4. Register the provider in the manifest file.
5. Use the content provider.

Planning a Database

To explore this topic, we'll create a database similar to the one that we have used for the book collection that was used to illustrate the storing of data in SQLite directly. Note that to keep the databases from conflicting with each other some of the names may be different.

The book database contains only one table called `books`, and its columns are `name`, `isbn`, and `author`. These column names fall under metadata. You'll define this sort of relevant metadata in a Java class. This metadata-bearing Java class `BookProviderMetaData` is shown in Listing 25-24.

Listing 25-24. Defining Metadata for Your Database

```
// File reference in project: BookProviderMetaData.Java
public class BookProviderMetaData {
    public static final String AUTHORITY = "com.androidbook.provider.BookProvider";

    public static final String DATABASE_NAME = "book.db";
    public static final int DATABASE_VERSION = 1;
    public static final String BOOKS_TABLE_NAME = "books";

    private BookProviderMetaData() {}
```

```
    //inner class describing BookTable
    public static final class BookTableMetaData implements BaseColumns {
        private BookTableMetaData() {}
        public static final String TABLE_NAME = "books";

        //uri and MIME type definitions
        public static final Uri CONTENT_URI =
                          Uri.parse("content://" + AUTHORITY + "/books");
        public static final String CONTENT_TYPE =
                         "vnd.android.cursor.dir/vnd.androidbook.book";
        public static final String CONTENT_ITEM_TYPE =
                        "vnd.android.cursor.item/vnd.androidbook.book";

        public static final String DEFAULT_SORT_ORDER = "modified DESC";

        //Additional Columns start here.
        //string type
        public static final String BOOK_NAME = "name";
        //string type
        public static final String BOOK_ISBN = "isbn";
        //string type
        public static final String BOOK_AUTHOR = "author";
        //Integer from System.currentTimeMillis()
        public static final String CREATED_DATE = "created";
        //Integer from System.currentTimeMillis()
        public static final String MODIFIED_DATE = "modified";
    }
}
```

This BookProviderMetaData class starts by defining its authority to be com.androidbook.provider.BookProvider.

This class then proceeds to define its one table (books) as an inner BookTableMetaData class. The BookTableMetaData class then defines a URI for identifying a collection of books. Given the authority in the previous paragraph, the URI for a collection of books will look like this:

```
content://com.androidbook.provider.BookProvider/books
```

This URI is indicated by the constant

```
BookProviderMetaData.BookTableMetaData.CONTENT_URI
```

The BookTableMetaData class then proceeds to define the MIME types for a collection of books and a single book. The provider implementation will use these constants to return the MIME types for the incoming URIs. MIME types are similar to the MIME types defined by HTTP. As a guideline the primary MIME type for a collection of items returned through an Android cursor should always be vnd.android.cursor.dir, and the primary MIME type of a single item retrieved through an Android cursor should be vnd.android.cursor.item. You have more wiggle room when it comes to the subtype, as in vnd.androidbook.book in Listing 25-24.

BookTableMetaData then defines the set of columns for the book table: name, isbn, author, created (creation date), and modified (last-updated date).

The metadata class BookTableMetaData also inherits from the BaseColumns class that provides the standard _id field, which represents the row ID. With these metadata definitions in hand, we're ready to tackle the provider implementation.

Extending ContentProvider

Implementing the BookProvider involves extending the ContentProvider class and overriding onCreate() to create the database and then implement the query, insert, update, delete, and getType methods.

A query method requires the set of columns it needs to return. This is similar to a select clause that requires column names along with their as counterparts (sometimes called synonyms). As a convention Android SDK uses a map object that it calls a projection map to represent these column names and their synonyms. We will need to set up this map so we can use it later in the query-method implementation. In the code for the provider implementation (see Listing 25-26), you will see this done upfront as part of projection map setup.

Most of the methods we'll be implementing for the content provider contract take a URI as an input. Listing 25-25 shows book provider URI examples:

***Listing 25-25.** Examples of BookProvider Content URIs*

```
Uri1: content://com.androidbook.provider.BookProvider/books
Uri2: content://com.androidbook.provider.BookProvider/books/12
```

The book provider needs to distinguish each of these URIs. BookProvider is a simple case. If our book provider had been housing more objects in addition to just books, then there would be more URIs to identify those additional objects.

The provider implementation needs a mechanism to distinguish one URI from the other; Android uses a class called UriMatcher for this purpose. So we need to set up this object with all our URI variations. You will see this code in Listing 25-26 right after we define the projection map. We'll further explain the UriMatcher class in the section "Using UriMatcher to Figure Out the URIs."

The code in Listing 25-26 then overrides the onCreate() method to facilitate the database creation. The database creation is identical to the database creation we have covered as part of using SQLite directly for internal persistence needs.

The source code in Listing 25-26 then implements the insert(), query(), update(), getType(), and delete() methods. The code for all of this is presented together in Listing 25-26, but we will explain each aspect in a separate subsection.

Listing 25-26. Implementing the BookProvider Content Provider

```
// File reference in project: BookProvider.Java
public class BookProvider extends ContentProvider
{
    //Logging helper tag. No significance to providers.
    private static final String TAG = "BookProvider";

    //Setup projection Map
    //Projection maps are similar to "as" (column alias) construct
    //in an sql statement where by you can rename the
    //columns.
    private static HashMap<String, String> sBooksProjectionMap;
    static
    {
        sBooksProjectionMap = new HashMap<String, String>();
        sBooksProjectionMap.put(BookTableMetaData._ID,
                                BookTableMetaData._ID);

        //name, isbn, author
        sBooksProjectionMap.put(BookTableMetaData.BOOK_NAME,
                                BookTableMetaData.BOOK_NAME);
        sBooksProjectionMap.put(BookTableMetaData.BOOK_ISBN,
                                BookTableMetaData.BOOK_ISBN);
        sBooksProjectionMap.put(BookTableMetaData.BOOK_AUTHOR,
                                BookTableMetaData.BOOK_AUTHOR);

        //created date, modified date
        sBooksProjectionMap.put(BookTableMetaData.CREATED_DATE,
                                BookTableMetaData.CREATED_DATE);
        sBooksProjectionMap.put(BookTableMetaData.MODIFIED_DATE,
                                BookTableMetaData.MODIFIED_DATE);
    }

    //Provide a mechanism to identify all the incoming uri patterns.
    private static final UriMatcher sUriMatcher;
    private static final int INCOMING_BOOK_COLLECTION_URI_INDICATOR = 1;
    private static final int INCOMING_SINGLE_BOOK_URI_INDICATOR = 2;
    static {
        sUriMatcher = new UriMatcher(UriMatcher.NO_MATCH);
        sUriMatcher.addURI(BookProviderMetaData.AUTHORITY, "books",
                           INCOMING_BOOK_COLLECTION_URI_INDICATOR);
        sUriMatcher.addURI(BookProviderMetaData.AUTHORITY, "books/#",
                           INCOMING_SINGLE_BOOK_URI_INDICATOR);

    }
    // Setup/Create Database to use for the implementation
    private static class DatabaseHelper extends SQLiteOpenHelper {
        DatabaseHelper(Context context) {
            super(context,
                BookProviderMetaData.DATABASE_NAME,
                null,
                BookProviderMetaData.DATABASE_VERSION);
        }
```

```
    @Override
    public void onCreate(SQLiteDatabase db)     {
        Log.d(TAG,"inner oncreate called");
        db.execSQL("CREATE TABLE " + BookTableMetaData.TABLE_NAME + " ("
                + BookTableMetaData._ID + " INTEGER PRIMARY KEY,"
                + BookTableMetaData.BOOK_NAME + " TEXT,"
                + BookTableMetaData.BOOK_ISBN + " TEXT,"
                + BookTableMetaData.BOOK_AUTHOR + " TEXT,"
                + BookTableMetaData.CREATED_DATE + " INTEGER,"
                + BookTableMetaData.MODIFIED_DATE + " INTEGER"
                + ");");
    }
    @Override
    public void onUpgrade(SQLiteDatabase db, int oldVersion, int newVersion) {
        Log.d(TAG,"inner onupgrade called");
        Log.w(TAG, "Upgrading database from version "
                + oldVersion + " to "
                + newVersion + ", which will destroy all old data");
        db.execSQL("DROP TABLE IF EXISTS " +
                 BookTableMetaData.TABLE_NAME);
        onCreate(db);
    }
}//eof-inner DatabaseHelper class
//This is initialized in the onCreate() method
private DatabaseHelper mOpenHelper;

//Component creation callback
@Override
public boolean onCreate()   {
    Log.d(TAG,"main onCreate called");
    mOpenHelper = new DatabaseHelper(getContext());
    return true;
}

@Override
public Cursor query(Uri uri, String[] projection, String selection,
        String[] selectionArgs,  String sortOrder)   {
    SQLiteQueryBuilder qb = new SQLiteQueryBuilder();

    switch (sUriMatcher.match(uri)) {
    case INCOMING_BOOK_COLLECTION_URI_INDICATOR:
        qb.setTables(BookTableMetaData.TABLE_NAME);
        qb.setProjectionMap(sBooksProjectionMap);
        break;

    case INCOMING_SINGLE_BOOK_URI_INDICATOR:
        qb.setTables(BookTableMetaData.TABLE_NAME);
        qb.setProjectionMap(sBooksProjectionMap);
        qb.appendWhere(BookTableMetaData._ID + "="
                    + uri.getPathSegments().get(1));
        break;
```

```
        default:
            throw new IllegalArgumentException("Unknown URI " + uri);
        }

        // If no sort order is specified use the default
        String orderBy;
        if (TextUtils.isEmpty(sortOrder)) {
            orderBy = BookTableMetaData.DEFAULT_SORT_ORDER;
        } else {
            orderBy = sortOrder;
        }

        // Get the database and run the query
        SQLiteDatabase db = mOpenHelper.getReadableDatabase();
        Cursor c = qb.query(db, projection, selection,
                   selectionArgs, null, null, orderBy);

        //example of getting a count
        int i = c.getCount();

        // Tell the cursor what uri to watch,
        // so it knows when its source data changes
        c.setNotificationUri(getContext().getContentResolver(), uri);
        return c;
    }
    @Override
    public String getType(Uri uri)    {
        switch (sUriMatcher.match(uri)) {
        case INCOMING_BOOK_COLLECTION_URI_INDICATOR:
            return BookTableMetaData.CONTENT_TYPE;
        case INCOMING_SINGLE_BOOK_URI_INDICATOR:
            return BookTableMetaData.CONTENT_ITEM_TYPE;
        default:
            throw new IllegalArgumentException("Unknown URI " + uri);
        }
    }
    @Override
    public Uri insert(Uri uri, ContentValues initialValues)  {
        // Validate the requested uri
        if (sUriMatcher.match(uri)
                != INCOMING_BOOK_COLLECTION_URI_INDICATOR) {
            throw new IllegalArgumentException("Unknown URI " + uri);
        }
        ContentValues values;
        if (initialValues != null) {
            values = new ContentValues(initialValues);
        } else {
            values = new ContentValues();
        }
```

```
    Long now = Long.valueOf(System.currentTimeMillis());
    // Make sure that the fields are all set
    if (values.containsKey(BookTableMetaData.CREATED_DATE) == false){
        values.put(BookTableMetaData.CREATED_DATE, now);
    }
    if (values.containsKey(BookTableMetaData.MODIFIED_DATE) == false) {
        values.put(BookTableMetaData.MODIFIED_DATE, now);
    }
    if (values.containsKey(BookTableMetaData.BOOK_NAME) == false) {
        throw new SQLException(
           "Failed to insert row because Book Name is needed " + uri);
    }
    if (values.containsKey(BookTableMetaData.BOOK_ISBN) == false) {
        values.put(BookTableMetaData.BOOK_ISBN, "Unknown ISBN");
    }
    if (values.containsKey(BookTableMetaData.BOOK_AUTHOR) == false) {
        values.put(BookTableMetaData.BOOK_ISBN, "Unknown Author");
    }

    SQLiteDatabase db = mOpenHelper.getWritableDatabase();
    long rowId = db.insert(BookTableMetaData.TABLE_NAME,
            BookTableMetaData.BOOK_NAME, values);
    if (rowId > 0) {
        Uri insertedBookUri =
            ContentUris.withAppendedId(
                    BookTableMetaData.CONTENT_URI, rowId);
        getContext()
           .getContentResolver()
                .notifyChange(insertedBookUri, null);

        return insertedBookUri;
    }
    throw new SQLException("Failed to insert row into " + uri);
}
@Override
public int delete(Uri uri, String where, String[] whereArgs) {
    SQLiteDatabase db = mOpenHelper.getWritableDatabase();
    int count;
    switch (sUriMatcher.match(uri)) {
    case INCOMING_BOOK_COLLECTION_URI_INDICATOR:
        count = db.delete(BookTableMetaData.TABLE_NAME,
                where, whereArgs);
        break;
    case INCOMING_SINGLE_BOOK_URI_INDICATOR:
        String rowId = uri.getPathSegments().get(1);
        count = db.delete(BookTableMetaData.TABLE_NAME,
                BookTableMetaData._ID + "=" + rowId
                + (!TextUtils.isEmpty(where) ? " AND (" + where + ')' : ""),
                whereArgs);
        break;
```

```
        default:
            throw new IllegalArgumentException("Unknown URI " + uri);
        }

        getContext().getContentResolver().notifyChange(uri, null);
        return count;
    }
    @Override
    public int update(Uri uri, ContentValues values,
            String where, String[] whereArgs)  {
        SQLiteDatabase db = mOpenHelper.getWritableDatabase();
        int count;
        switch (sUriMatcher.match(uri)) {
        case INCOMING_BOOK_COLLECTION_URI_INDICATOR:
            count = db.update(BookTableMetaData.TABLE_NAME,
                    values, where, whereArgs);
            break;

        case INCOMING_SINGLE_BOOK_URI_INDICATOR:
            String rowId = uri.getPathSegments().get(1);
            count = db.update(BookTableMetaData.TABLE_NAME,
                    values, BookTableMetaData._ID + "=" + rowId
                    + (!TextUtils.isEmpty(where) ? " AND (" + where + ')' : ""),
                    whereArgs);
            break;

        default:
            throw new IllegalArgumentException("Unknown URI " + uri);
        }

        getContext().getContentResolver().notifyChange(uri, null);
        return count;
    }
}
```

Now, let's analyze this code section by section.

Using UriMatcher to Figure Out the URIs

We've mentioned the `UriMatcher` class several times now; let's look into it. Almost all methods in a content provider are overloaded with respect to the URI. For example, the same `query()` method is called whether you want to retrieve a single book or a list of books. It is up to the method to know which type of URI is being requested. Android's `UriMatcher` utility class helps you identify the URI types.

Here's how it works. You tell an instance of `UriMatcher` what kind of URI patterns to expect during its initialization. You will also associate a unique number with each pattern. Once these patterns are registered, you can then ask `UriMatcher` if the incoming URI matches a certain pattern.

As we've mentioned, our BookProvider content provider has two URI patterns: one for a collection of books and one for a single book. The code in Listing 25-26 registers both of these patterns using UriMatcher. It allocates 1 for a collection of books and 2 for a single book (the URI patterns themselves are defined in the metadata for the books table). You can see this in the static initialization of the variable sUriMatcher in Listing 25-26. You can then see how UriMatcher plays a part in the query() method implementation in distinguishing the URIs using the constants for each type of URI.

Using Projection Maps

A content provider acts like an intermediary between an abstract set of columns and a real set of columns in a database, yet these column sets could differ. While constructing queries, you must map between the where clause columns that a client specifies and the real database columns. You set up this projection map with the help of the SQLiteQueryBuilder class. You can see how this projection map variable sBooksProjectionMap is set for the BookProvider in Listing 25-26. You can also see in that listing how this variable sBooksProjectionMap is then used by the SQLiteQueryBuilder object.

Fulfilling MIME-Type Contracts

Let's start with the getType() method in Listing 25-26. This method returns a MIME type for a given URI. This method, like many other methods of a content provider, is sensitive to the incoming URI. As a result, the first responsibility of the getType() method is to distinguish the type of the URI. Is it a collection of books or a single book? The code used the UriMatcher to decipher this URI type. Depending on this URI, the BookTableMetaData class has defined the MIME-type constants to return for each URI.

Implementing the Query Method

Like the other methods, the query method uses UriMatcher to identify the URI type. If the URI type is a single-item type, the method retrieves the book ID from the incoming URI by looking at the first segment returned by getPathSegments().

The query method then uses the projections that we created upfront in Listing 25-26 to identify the return columns. In the end, query returns the cursor to the caller. Throughout this process, the query method uses the SQLiteQueryBuilder object to formulate and execute the query.

While reading the data one can constrain the rows returned either using the URI or through explicit where clause arguments passed to the query method as inputs. In the BookProvider implementation of Listing 25-26 we used the approach of using the URI segments to retrieve the book ID to return the values for just that book.

Instead you can use the selection parameter and the selectionArgs parameter of the query() method to explicitly pass the where clause arguments. These arguments work just like the SQLiteDatabase.query() arguments in Listing 25-12, where "?" are used as placeholders for the values passed in the selectionArgs array.

Implementing the Insert Method

The insert method in a content provider is responsible for inserting a record into the underlying database and then returning a URI that point to the newly created record.

Like the other methods, insert uses UriMatcher to identify the URI type. The code first checks whether the URI indicates the proper collection-type URI. If not, the code throws an exception.

The code then validates the optional and mandatory column parameters. The code can substitute default values for some columns if they are missing.

Next, the code uses an SQLiteDatabase object to insert the new record and returns the newly inserted ID. In the end, the code constructs the new URI using the returned ID from the database.

Implementing the Update Method

The update method in a content provider is responsible for updating a record (or records) based on the column values passed in, as well as the where clause that is passed in. The update method then returns the number of rows updated in the process.

Like the other methods, update uses UriMatcher to identify the URI type. If the URI type is a collection, the where clause is passed through so it can affect as many records as possible. If the URI type is a single-record type, then the book ID is extracted from the URI and specified as an additional where clause. In the end, the code returns the number of records updated. Also notice how this notifyChange method enables you to announce to the world that the data at that URI has changed. Potentially, you can do the same in the insert method by saying that the collection of books data at URI "…/books" has changed when a record is inserted.

Implementing the Delete Method

The delete method in a content provider is responsible for deleting a record (or records) based on the where clause that is passed in. The delete method then returns the number of rows deleted in the process.

Like the other methods, delete uses UriMatcher to identify the URI type. If the URI type is a collection type, the where clause is passed through so you can delete as many records as possible. If the where clause is null, all records will be deleted. If the URI type is a single-record type, the book ID is extracted from the URI and specified as an additional where clause. In the end, the code returns the number of records deleted.

Registering the Provider

Finally, you must register the content provider in the Android.Manifest.xml file using the tag structure in Listing 25-27. A provider is a component and hence a sibling of the other components such as an activity and a receiver. So it is a sibling node to other activities in the Android manifest file.

Listing 25-27. Registering a Provider

```
<provider android:name=".BookProvider"
   android:authorities="com.androidbook.provider.BookProvider"/>
```

Exercising the Book Provider

Now that we have a book provider, we are going to show you sample code to exercise that provider. The sample code includes adding a book, removing a book, getting a count of the books, and finally displaying all the books.

Keep in mind that these are code extracts from the sample project and will not compile, because they require additional dependency files. However, we feel this sample code is sufficient in demonstrating the concepts we have explored.

At the end of this chapter, we have included a link to the downloadable sample project, which you can use in your Eclipse environment to compile and test.

Adding a Book

The code in Listing 25-28 inserts a new book into the book database.

Listing 25-28. Exercising a Provider Insert

```
// File reference in project:ProviderTester.Java
public void addBook(Context context) {
    String tag = "Exercise BookProvider";
    Log.d(tag,"Adding a book");
    ContentValues cv = new ContentValues();
    cv.put(BookProviderMetaData.BookTableMetaData.BOOK_NAME, "book1");
    cv.put(BookProviderMetaData.BookTableMetaData.BOOK_ISBN, "isbn-1");
    cv.put(BookProviderMetaData.BookTableMetaData.BOOK_AUTHOR, "author-1");

    ContentResolver cr = context.getContentResolver();
    Uri uri = BookProviderMetaData.BookTableMetaData.CONTENT_URI;
    Log.d(tag,"book insert uri:" + uri);
    Uri insertedUri = cr.insert(uri, cv);
    Log.d(tag,"inserted uri:" + insertedUri);
}
```

Removing a Book

The code in Listing 25-29 deletes the last record from the book database.

Listing 25-29. Exercising a Provider Delete

```
// File reference in project:ProviderTester.Java
public void removeBook() {
   int firstBookId = this.getFirstBookId();
   if (firstBookId == -1) throw new SQLException("Book id is less than 0");
   ContentResolver cr = this.mContext.getContentResolver();
   Uri uri = BookProviderMetaData.BookTableMetaData.CONTENT_URI;
```

```
   Uri delUri = Uri.withAppendedPath(uri, Integer.toString(firstBookId));
   reportString("Del Uri:" + delUri);
   cr.delete(delUri, null, null);
   this.reportString("Number of Books after the delete:" + getCount());
}

private int getFirstBookId() {
   Uri uri = BookProviderMetaData.BookTableMetaData.CONTENT_URI;
   Activity a = (Activity)this.mContext;
   Cursor c = null;
   try   {
      c = a.getContentResolver().query(uri,
            null, //projection
            null, //selection string
            null, //selection args array of strings
            null); //sort order
      int numberOfRecords = c.getCount();
      if (numberOfRecords == 0) {
         return -1;
      }
      c.moveToFirst();
      int id = c.getInt(1); //id column
      return id;
   }
   finally   {
      if (c!= null) c.close();
   }
}
```

Displaying the List of Books

The code in Listing 25-30 retrieves all the records in the book database.

***Listing 25-30.** Displaying a List of Books*

```
// File reference in project:ProviderTester.Java
public void showBooks() {
   Uri uri = BookProviderMetaData.BookTableMetaData.CONTENT_URI;
   Activity a = (Activity)this.mContext;
   Cursor c = null;
   try  {
      c = a.getContentResolver().query(uri,
            null, //projection
            null, //selection string
            null, //selection args array of strings
            null); //sort order
      int iid = c.getColumnIndex(BookProviderMetaData.BookTableMetaData._ID);
      int iname = c.getColumnIndex(BookProviderMetaData.BookTableMetaData.BOOK_NAME);
      int iisbn = c.getColumnIndex(BookProviderMetaData.BookTableMetaData.BOOK_ISBN);
      int iauthor = c.getColumnIndex(BookProviderMetaData.BookTableMetaData.BOOK_AUTHOR);
```

```
        //Report your indexes
        Log.d(tag, "name,isbn,author:" + iname + iisbn + iauthor);

        //walk through the rows based on indexes
        for(c.moveToFirst();!c.isAfterLast();c.moveToNext()) {
           //Gather values
           String id = c.getString(iid);
           String name = c.getString(iname);
           String isbn = c.getString(iisbn);
           String author = c.getString(iauthor);

           //Report or log the row
           StringBuffer cbuf = new StringBuffer(id);
           cbuf.append(",").append(name);
           cbuf.append(",").append(isbn);
           cbuf.append(",").append(author);
           Log.d(tag,cbuf.toString());
        }

        //Report how many rows have been read
        int numberOfRecords = c.getCount();
        Log.d(tag,"Num of Records:" + numberOfRecords);
    }
    finally  {
        if (c!= null) c.close();
    }
}
```

Notice that the method of retrieving the books from a content provider is very similar to retrieving data from an SQLite database. In Listing 25-30 we have used the `query()` method from a `ContentResolver` object. After using the cursor object we have closed the cursor.

Instead if you were passing this cursor object to a UI component that is in the `Activity` then this cursor object needs to be managed as the activity follows its life cycle. Prior to Honeycomb, there was a method called `managedQuery()` on the `Activity` to do this automatically, which has since been deprecated in favor of CursorLoader.

When a query is thus managed through `managedQuery()`, the activity can call methods on the cursor to place it into proper state. For example, the activity will call `deactivate()` on the cursor when it is stopped and later calls `requery()` when it is started. The cursor will be closed when the activity is destroyed. You can choose to call `stopManagingCursor()` on that cursor if you want to control the behavior of the cursor yourself. Because the activity closes the cursor, don't close a managed cursor. If your intention is to read all the rows one time and close the cursor, then use the `query()` method of the `ContentResolver` as opposed to the `Activity.managedQuery()` method and explicitly close the cursor.

Since Honeycomb, the cursor reads are wrapped into a more general approach called "Loaders," which allow you to read data in an asynchronous thread through callbacks exposed to fragments or activities. This is the recommended and preferred method. We will cover this approach in the next chapter, Chapter 26, on Loaders.

You have seen how we have used update APIs on a content providers. These update operations can be inefficient if done one by one through a content provider. In Chapter 27 we will cover how these individual update operations can be sent as a batch to a content provider for efficiency reasons.

Resources

Here are some additional Android resources that can help you with the topics covered in this chapter:

- `http://developer.android.com/guide/topics/data/data-storage.html`: Various data storage options from Android documentation.
- `http://www.androidbook.com/item/4437`: A summary of options for persistence on Android.
- `http://www.androidbook.com/item/4876`: Exploring tools and techniques for direct SQL storage on Android. This includes research on O/R mapping tools as well.
- `http://www.androidbook.com/item/4877`: Storing data in the cloud through Parse for Android.
- `http://www.androidbook.com/item/4440`: Using GSON/JSON for mobile app storage.
- `http://www.androidbook.com/item/4438`: Using shared preferences for application state management.
- `http://developer.android.com/guide/topics/providers/content-providers.html`: Android documentation on content providers.
- `http://developer.android.com/reference/android/content/ContentProvider.html`: API description for a `ContentProvider`, where you can learn about `ContentProvider` contracts.
- `http://developer.android.com/reference/android/content/UriMatcher.html`: Information that is useful for understanding `UriMatcher`.
- `http://developer.android.com/reference/android/database/Cursor.html`: Information that helps you read data from a content provider or a database directly.
- `http://developer.android.com/guide/components/loaders.html`: Developer's guide for Loaders.
- `http://developer.android.com/reference/android/app/Activity.html#startManagingCursor(android.database.Cursor)`: API documentation of what a managed cursor is.

- `http://www.sqlite.org/sqlite.html`: Home page of SQLite, where you can learn more about SQLite and download tools that you can use to work with SQLite databases.
- `http://androidbook.com/proandroid5/projects`: Downloadable test project for this chapter is accessible from this URL. The name of the zip file is `ProAndroid5_Ch25_TestProvider.zip`.

Summary

This chapter has covered a lot of aspects about a vital need of your applications: persistence. We have given you a plethora of options available in Android for persistence and how to choose an appropriate option. We have covered how to use SQLite for internal persistence needs in significant detail. We have shown you an industrial-strength API pattern for persistence using SQLite which can be extended to any persistence implementation. Importantly, this pattern showed you how to externalize transactions to keep your persistence code simple. We have then covered what content providers are, the nature of content URIs, MIME types, how to use SQLite to construct providers that respond to URIs, how to write a new content provider, and how to access an existing content provider.

Chapter 26

Understanding Loaders

This chapter looks at loading data from data sources through the recommended mechanism of Loaders. The API of Loaders is designed to deal with two issues with loading data by activities and fragments.

The first is the non-deterministic nature of activities where an activity can be hidden partially or fully, restarted due to device rotation, or removed from memory when in background due to low-memory conditions. These events are called activity life cycle events. Any code that retrieves data must work in harmony with the activity life cycle events. Prior to the introduction of Loaders in 3.0 (API 11), this was handled through Managed Cursors. This mechanism is now discontinued in favor of Loaders.

The second issue with loading data in activities and fragments is that data access could take longer on the main thread resulting in application-not-responding (ANR) messages. Loaders solve this by doing the work on a worker thread and providing callbacks to the activities and fragments to respond to the asynchronous nature of data fetch.

Understanding the Architecture of Loaders

Loaders make it easy to asynchronously load data in an activity or a fragment. Multiple loaders, each with its own set of data, can be associated with an activity or a fragment. Loaders also monitor the source of their data and deliver new results when the data content changes. Loaders automatically reconnect to the previously retrieved data structure, like a cursor, when being re-created after a configuration change. As the previous cursor is not destroyed, data is not requeried.

When we talk about loaders in this chapter all aspects of loaders apply to both activities and fragments unless we indicate otherwise from now on.

Every activity uses a single LoaderManager object to manage the loaders associated with that activity. Once a loader is registered with a loader manager, the LoaderManager will facilitate the necessary callbacks to a) create and initialize the Loader, b) read the data when the Loader finishes loading the data, and c) close the resource when the loader is about to be destroyed as the activity is no longer needed. The LoaderManager is hidden from you and you work with it through callbacks and LoaderManager public APIs. The creation of the LoaderManager is controlled by the activity. LoaderManager is almost like an integral part of the activity itself.

It is the responsibility of the registered Loader to work with its data source and also with the LoaderManager to read the data and send the results back to the LoaderManager. The LoaderManager will then invoke the callbacks on the activity that data is ready. The Loader is also responsible for pausing the data access or monitoring data changes or working with the LoaderManager to understand and react to the activity life cycle events.

While you can write a loader from scratch for your specific data needs by extending the loader API, you typically use the Loaders that are already implemented in the SDK. Most loaders extend the AsyncTaskLoader which provides the basic ability to do its work on a worker thread freeing the main thread. When the worker thread returns data, the LoaderManager will invoke the main callbacks to the activity that the data is ready on the main thread.

The most used of these prebuilt loaders is the CursorLoader. With the availability of CursorLoader, using Loaders becomes really, really trivial with a few lines of code. This is because all the details are hidden behind the LoaderManager, Loader, AsyncTaskLoader, and the CursorLoader.

Listing Basic Loader API Classes

Listing 26-1 lists the key classes involved in the Loader API.

Listing 26-1. Android Loader API Key Participating Classes

```
LoaderManager
LoaderManager.LoaderCallbacks
Loader
AsyncTaskLoader
CursorLoader
```

The APIs that are most often used are the LoaderManager.LoaderCallbacks and the CursorLoader. However, let us briefly introduce each of these classes.

There is one LoaderManager object per activity. This is the object that defines the protocol of how Loaders should work. So LoaderManager is the orchestrator for the loaders associated with an activity. LoaderManager's interaction with the activity is through the LoaderManager.LoaderCallbacks. These loader callbacks are where you are given the data by the Loader via the LoaderManager and expected to interact with the activity.

The Loader class defines the protocol that must be adhered to if one wants to design their own loader. AsyncTaskLoader is one example where it implements the loader protocol in an asynchronous manner on a worker thread. It is typically the AsyncTaskLoader that is the base class to implement most of your loaders. CursorLoader is an implementation of this AsyncTaskLoader that knows how to load cursors from content providers. If one is implementing their own loader it is important to understand that all interaction with the loader from a LoaderManager happens on the main thread. Even the LoaderManager callbacks that are implemented by the activity take place on the main thread.

Demonstrating the Loaders

We will now show you how to use Loaders by implementing a simple one-page application (Figure 26-1) that loads contacts from the contact provider database on an Android device. This application is typical of how one would develop Android activities. You could even use this sample project as a starter application template.

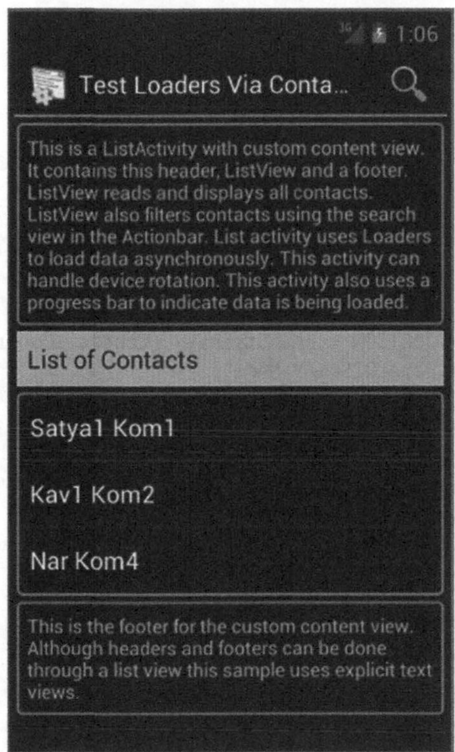

***Figure 26-1.** Filtered list of contacts loaded through loaders*

We want the activity in Figure 26-1 to exhibit the following characteristics: 1) It should display all the contacts on the device; b) It should retrieve data asynchronously; c) While data is being retrieved, the activity should show a progress bar view in place of the list view; d) On retrieving data successfully, the code should replace the progress view with the filled-in list view; e) The activity should provide a search mechanism to filter the necessary contacts; f) When the device is rotated, it should show the contacts again without making a requery to the contacts content provider; g) The code should allow us to see the order of callbacks along with the activity life cycle callbacks.

We will first present the source code for the activity and then explain each section. By the end of the chapter you will have a clear understanding of how Loaders work and how to use them in your code. With that, Listing 26-2 shows the code for the activity of Figure 26-1. Please note that the code in Listing 26-2 relies on a number of resources that are presented here. Some of these string resources you can see in Figure 26-1, but for others and the code that is not included here, please see the downloadable project. As always, the code presented here is sufficient for the topic at hand.

Listing 26-2. An Activity Loading Data with Loaders

```
public class TestLoadersActivity
extends      MonitoredListActivity //very simple class to log activity callbacks
implements   LoaderManager.LoaderCallbacks<Cursor> //Loader Manager callbacks
             ,OnQueryTextListener //Search text callback to filter contacts
{
   private static final String tag = "TestLoadersActivity";

   //Adapter for displaying the list's data
   //Initialized to null cursor in onCreate and set on the list
   //Use it in later callbacks to swap cursor
   //This is reinitialized to null cursor when rotation occurs
    SimpleCursorAdapter mAdapter;

    //Search filter working with OnQueryTextListener
    String mCurFilter;

    //Contacts columns that we will retrieve
    static final String[] PROJECTION = new String[] {ContactsContract.Data._ID,
            ContactsContract.Data.DISPLAY_NAME};

    //select criteria for the contacts URI
    static final String SELECTION = "((" +
            ContactsContract.Data.DISPLAY_NAME + " NOTNULL) AND (" +
            ContactsContract.Data.DISPLAY_NAME + " != '' ))";

    public TestLoadersActivity()  {
       super(tag);
    }
    @Override
    protected void onCreate(Bundle savedInstanceState)  {
       super.onCreate(savedInstanceState);
       this.setContentView(R.layout.test_loaders_activity_layout);

       //Initialize the adapter
       this.mAdapter = createEmptyAdapter();
       this.setListAdapter(mAdapter);

       //Hide the listview and show the progress bar
       this.showProgressbar();

       //Initialize a loader for an id of 0
       getLoaderManager().initLoader(0, null, this);
    }
    //Create a simple list adapter with a null cursor
    //The good cursor will come later in the loader callback
    private SimpleCursorAdapter createEmptyAdapter() {
       // For the cursor adapter, specify which columns go into which views
        String[] fromColumns = {ContactsContract.Data.DISPLAY_NAME};
        int[] toViews = {android.R.id.text1}; // The TextView in simple_list_item_1
        //Return the cursor
```

```
    return new SimpleCursorAdapter(this,
          android.R.layout.simple_list_item_1,
          null, //cursor
          fromColumns,
          toViews);
 }
//This is a LoaderManager callback. Return a properly constructed CursorLoader
//This gets called only if the loader does not previously exist.
//This means this method will not be called on rotation because
//a previous loader with this ID is already available and initialized.
//This also gets called when the loader is "restarted" by calling
//LoaderManager.restartLoader()
@Override
public Loader<Cursor> onCreateLoader(int id, Bundle args) {
   Log.d(tag,"onCreateLoader for loader id:" + id);
   Uri baseUri;
   if (mCurFilter != null) {
       baseUri = Uri.withAppendedPath(ContactsContract.Contacts.CONTENT_FILTER_URI,
              Uri.encode(mCurFilter));
   } else {
       baseUri = Contacts.CONTENT_URI;
   }
   String[] selectionArgs = null;
   String sortOrder = null;
   return new CursorLoader(this, baseUri,
         PROJECTION, SELECTION, selectionArgs, sortOrder);
}
//This is a LoaderManager callback. Use the data here.
//This gets called when he loader finishes. Called on the main thread.
//Can be called multiple times as the data changes underneath.
//Also gets called after rotation with out requerying the cursor.
@Override
public void onLoadFinished(Loader<Cursor> loader, Cursor cursor) {
    Log.d(tag,"onLoadFinished for loader id:" + loader.getId());
    Log.d(tag,"Number of contacts found:"+ cursor.getCount());
     this.hideProgressbar();
     this.mAdapter.swapCursor(cursor);
}
//This is a LoaderManager callback. Remove any references to this data.
//This gets called when the loader is destroyed like when activity is done.
//FYI - this does NOT get called because of loader "restart"
//This can be seen as a "destructor" for the loader.
@Override
public void onLoaderReset(Loader<Cursor> loader) {
   Log.d(tag,"onLoaderReset for loader id:" + loader.getId());
   this.showProgressbar();
   this.mAdapter.swapCursor(null);
}
```

```
    @Override
    public boolean onCreateOptionsMenu(Menu menu) {
        // Place an action bar item for searching.
        MenuItem item = menu.add("Search");
        item.setIcon(android.R.drawable.ic_menu_search);
        item.setShowAsAction(MenuItem.SHOW_AS_ACTION_IF_ROOM);
        SearchView sv = new SearchView(this);
        sv.setOnQueryTextListener(this);
        item.setActionView(sv);
        return true;
    }
    //This is a Searchview callback. Restart the loader.
    //This gets called when user enters new search text.
    //Call LoaderManager.restartLoader to trigger the onCreateLoader
    @Override
    public boolean onQueryTextChange(String newText) {
        // Called when the action bar search text has changed.  Update
        // the search filter, and restart the loader to do a new query
        // with this filter.
        mCurFilter = !TextUtils.isEmpty(newText) ? newText : null;
        Log.d(tag,"Restarting the loader");
        getLoaderManager().restartLoader(0, null, this);
        return true;
    }
    @Override
    public boolean onQueryTextSubmit(String query) {
        return true;
    }
    private void showProgressbar() {
       //show progress bar
       View pbar = this.getProgressbar();
       pbar.setVisibility(View.VISIBLE);
       //hide listview
       this.getListView().setVisibility(View.GONE);
       findViewById(android.R.id.empty).setVisibility(View.GONE);
    }
    private void hideProgressbar()  {
       //show progress bar
       View pbar = this.getProgressbar();
       pbar.setVisibility(View.GONE);
       //hide listview
       this.getListView().setVisibility(View.VISIBLE);
    }
    private View getProgressbar()  {
       return findViewById(R.id.tla_pbar);
    }
}//eof-class
```

We will explain each section from Listing 26-2 after we show you the supporting layout for the activity code in Listing 26-3. This layout in Listing 26-3 should clarify the view in Figure 26-1 (please note that a number of resources are not included here but are available in the downloadable file at apress.com/9781430246800).

Listing 26-3. A Typical ListActivity Layout for Loaders

```
<?xml version="1.0" encoding="utf-8"?>
<!--
*******************************************
* /res/layout/test_loaders_activity_layout.xml
* corresponding activity: TestLoadersActicity.java
* prefix: tla_ (Used for prefixing unique identifiers)
*
* Use:
*    Demonstrate loading a cursor using loaders
* Structure:
*    Header message: text view (tla_header)
*    ListView Heading, ListView (fixed)
*    ProgressBar (To show when data is being fetched)
*    Empty View (To show when the list is empty): ProgressBar
*    Footer: text view (tla_footer)
********************************************
-->
<LinearLayout xmlns:android="http://schemas.android.com/apk/res/android"
    android:orientation="vertical"
    android:layout_width="match_parent"  android:layout_height="match_parent"
    android:paddingLeft="2dp"  android:paddingRight="2dp">
    <!-- Header and Main documentation text -->
    <TextView android:id="@+id/tla_header"
        android:layout_width="match_parent" android:layout_height="wrap_content"
        android:background="@drawable/box2"
        android:layout_marginTop="4dp" android:padding="8dp"
        android:text="@string/tla_header"/>
    <!-- Heading for the list view -->
    <TextView android:id="@+id/tla_listview_heading"
        android:layout_width="match_parent"    android:layout_height="wrap_content"
        android:background="@color/gray"
        android:layout_marginTop="4dp"  android:padding="8dp"
        android:textColor="@color/black" style="@android:style/TextAppearance.Medium"
        android:text="List of Contacts"/>
    <!-- ListView used by the ListActivity. Uses a standard id needed by a list view -->
    <!-- Fix the height of the listview in a production setting -->
    <ListView android:id="@android:id/list"
        android:layout_width="match_parent" android:layout_height="wrap_content"
        android:background="@drawable/box2"
        android:layout_marginTop="4dp" android:layout_marginBottom="4dp"
        android:drawSelectorOnTop="false"/>
    <!-- ProgressBar: To show and hide the progress bar as loaders load data -->
    <ProgressBar android:id="@+id/tla_pbar"
        android:layout_width="match_parent" android:layout_height="wrap_content"
        android:layout_gravity="center"
        android:indeterminate="true"/>
```

```
    <!-- Empty List: Uses a standard id needed by a list view -->
    <TextView android:id="@android:id/empty"
        android:layout_width="match_parent" android:layout_height="wrap_content"
        android:visibility="gone"
        android:layout_marginTop="4dp"  android:layout_marginBottom="4dp"
        android:padding="8dp"
        android:text="No Contacts to Match the Criteria"/>
    <!-- Footer: Additional documentation text and the footer-->
    <TextView android:id="@+id/tla_footer"
        android:layout_width="match_parent"  android:layout_height="wrap_content"
        android:background="@drawable/box2"  android:padding="8dp"
        android:text="@string/tla_footer"/>
</LinearLayout>
```

Let's now turn to understanding the code in Listing 26-2. We will explain this code through a series of steps you would follow to code with loaders. Let's start with step 1, where the activity needs to be extended to support the LoaderManager callbacks.

Step 1: Preparing the Activity to Load Data

Code necessary to load data using loaders is remarkably small, because most of the work is done by the CursorLoader. The first thing you need to do is to have your activity extend the LoaderManager.LoaderCallbacks<Cursor> and implement the three needed methods: onCreateLoader(), onLoadFinished(), and onLoaderReset(). You can see how in Listing 26-2. By implementing this interface, you have enabled the activity to become a receiver for the LoaderManager events through these three callbacks.

Step 2: Initializing the Loader

Next, you have to tell the activity that you want a Loader object to load the data. This is done by registering and initializing a Loader during the onCreate() method of the activity as shown in Listing 26-4. You can also see this in the onCreate() of Listing 26-3 as well, in context of the overall code.

Listing 26-4. Initializing a Loader

```
int loaderid = 0; Bundle argBundle = null;
LoaderCallbacks<Cursor> loaderCallbacks = this; //this activity itself
getLoaderManager().initLoader(loaderid, argBundle, loaderCallbacks);
```

The loaderid argument is a developer-assigned unique number in the context of this activity to uniquely identify this Loader from other Loaders registered with this activity. Note that in the example here, we are using only one Loader.

The second argsBundle argument is used to pass additional arguments to the onCreateLoader() callback if needed. This "bundle of arguments" approach follows the usual pattern of differed factory object construction in many of the managed components in Android. Activities, fragments, and loaders are all examples of this pattern.

The third argument, loaderCallbacks, is a reference to an implementation of the callbacks required by the LoaderManager. In Listings 26-2 and 26-4, the activity itself is playing this role, so we pass this variable referring to the activity as the argument value.

Once the Loader is registered and initialized, the LoaderManager will schedule a call to the onCreateLoader() callback if necessary. If a call was previously made to the onCreateLoader() and a loader object is available corresponding to this loader ID, then the method onCreateLoader() will not be triggered. As stated earlier, the exception is if the developer overrides this behavior by calling LoaderManager.restartLoader(). You will see this call explained later when we talked about providing search-based filtering capabilities to locate a sub-selection of contacts.

Delving into the Structure of ListActivity

The ListActivity in Figure 26-1 is extending a list activity with a content view that is a custom layout through setContentView(). This gives us a lot more flexibility to place other controls in addition to the list view on the activity. For example, we have provided a header view, a footer view, and also a progress bar to show that we are in the process of fetching data. The only constraint placed by a ListActivity is to name a control with the reserved @android:id/listview to identify the list view that the list activity would be using. In addition to the listview ID, we can also provide a view that the list activity uses if the list is empty. This view is identified by the predefined ID @android:id/empty.

Working with Asynchronous Loading of Data

Loaders load data asynchronously. Because of this we have an added responsibility in the Activity.onCreate() to hide the listview and show the progress indicator until the list data is ready. To do this, we have a ProgressBar component in the layout in Listing 26-3. In the Activity.onCreate() method, we set the initial state of the layout so that the list view is hidden and the progress bar is shown. This functionality is coded in the method showProgressbar() in Listing 26-2. In the same Listing 26-2, when the data is ready we call hideProgressbar() to hide the progress bar and show the populated list view or an empty list view if there is no data.

Step 3: Implementing onCreateLoader()

The onCreateLoader() is triggered by the initialization of the loader. You can see the signature and implementation of this method in Listing 26-2. This method constructs a Loader object for the corresponding loader ID that is passed in from the initialization stemming from the call to LoaderManager.initLoader(). This method also receives the argument bundle that is provided during the loader initialization for this loader ID.

This method returns a properly typed (through Java generics) Loader object to the LoaderManager. In our case this type is Loader<Cursor>. The LoaderManager caches the Loader object and will reuse it. This is useful because when the device rotates and the loader is reinitialized due to Activity.onCreate(), LoaderManager recognizes the loader ID and the presence of an existing loader. The LoaderManager then will not trigger a duplicate call to the onCreateLoader(). However, if the activity is to realize that the input data to the loader has changed, the activity code can call the LoaderManager.restartLoader(), which will trigger a call to the onLoaderCreate() again. In that case, the LoaderManager will first destroy the old loader and use the new one returned by the onLoaderCreate(). The LoaderManager does guarantee that the older loader will hang around until the new loader is created and available.

The onCreateLoader() method has full access to the local variables of the activity. So it can use them in any conceivable manner to construct the needed loaders. In case of a CursorLoader this construction is limited to the arguments available to the constructor of the CursorLoader, which is specifically built to allow cursors from an Android content provider.

In our example, we have used the content URIs provided by the contacts content provider. Refer to Chapter 25, on content provider, for how to use content URIs to retrieve cursors from content provider data sources. It is quite simple: just indicate the URI you want to get the data from, supply the filter string as an argument or a path segment on that URI as per the documentation available for the contacts content provider, specify the columns you want, specify the where clause as a string, and construct the CursorLoader.

Step 4: Implementing onLoadFinished()

Once the CursorLoader is returned to the LoaderManager, the CursorLoader will be instructed to start its work on a worker thread and the main thread will go on to the UI chores. At a later point this method onLoadFinished() is called when the data is ready.

This method could be called multiple times. When the data from a content provider changes, as the CursorLoader has registered itself with the data source, it will be alerted. CursorLoader then will trigger the onLoadFinished() again.

In the onLoadFinished() method, all you need to do is to swap the data cursor that is held by the list adapter. The list adapter was initialized originally with a null cursor. Swapping with a populated cursor will show the new data on the list view. As we have hidden the listview in Activity.onCreate(), we need to show the listview and hide the progress bar. Subsequently we can go on swapping the new cursors for old cursors as data changes. The changes will reflect automatically on the list view.

When the device rotates, a couple of things happen. The Activity.onCreate() will be called again. This will set the list cursor to null and also hide the list view. The code in Activity.onCreate() will also initialize the loader again. The LoaderManager is programmed so that this repeat initialization is harmless. The onCreateLoader() will not be called. The Cursor will not be requeried. However, the onLoadFinished() gets called again, which is what we needed to break out of this conundrum of initializing the data to null first and wondering how and when it will be populated if we were not to requery. As the onLoadFinished() gets called again on rotation, we are able to remove the ProgressBar, show the list view, and swap the valid cursor from the null cursor. All works. Yes, it is sneaky and round-about, but it works.

Step 5: Implementing onLoaderReset()

This callback is invoked when a previously registered loader is no longer necessary and hence destroyed. This can happen when an activity is destroyed due to a back button or explicitly instructed to be finished by code. In such cases, this callback allows an opportunity to close resources or references that are no longer needed. However, it is important not to close the cursors as they are managed by the corresponding loaders and will be closed for you by the framework. This might suggest that the `LoaderManager.restartLoader()` might result in a call to the `onLoaderReset()` as the arguments to the old loader are no longer valid. But tests show that this is not the case. The method `LoaderManager.restartLoader()` will not trigger a call to the method `onLoaderReset()`. The `onLoaderReset()` method is only called when the loader is actively destroyed by the activity no longer being needed. You can also explicitly instruct the `LoaderManager` to destroy the loader by calling `LoaderManager.destroyLoader(loaderid)`.

Using Search with Loaders

We will use search in our sample application to demonstrate the dynamic nature of loaders. We have attached a search view to the menu. You can see this in the method `onCreateOptionsMenu()` in Listing 26-2. Here we have attached a `SearchView` to the menu and provided the activity as the callback to the `SearchView` when new text is provided in the `SearchView`. The `SearchView` callback is handled in the method `onQueryTextchange()` of Listing 26-2.

In the `onQueryTextChange()` method, we take the new search text and set the local variable `mCurFilter`. We then call `LoaderManager.restartLoader()` with the same arguments as the `LoaderManager.initializeLoader()`. This will trigger the `onCreateLoader()` again, which will then use the `mCurFilter` to alter the parameters to the `CursorLoader` resulting in a new cursor. This new cursor will replace the old one in the `onLoadFinished()` method.

Understanding the Order of LoaderManager Callbacks

Because Android programming is largely event-based, it is important to know the order of event callbacks. To help you understand the timing of the `LoaderManager` callbacks, we have rigged the sample program with log messages. Here are some results showing the order of callbacks.

Listing 26-5 shows the order of calls when the activity is first created.

***Listing 26-5.** Loader Callbacks on Activity Creation*

```
Application.onCreate()
Activity.onCreate()
  LoaderManager.LoaderCallbacks.onCreateLoader()
  Activity.onStart()
  Activity.onResume()
  LoaderManager.LoaderCallbacks.onLoadFinished()
```

When the search view fires a new search criteria through its callback, the order of callbacks is as shown in Listing 26-6.

Listing 26-6. Loader Callbacks on a New Search Criteria triggered by RestartLoader

```
RestartLoader //log message from onQueryTextChange
LoaderManager.LoaderCallbacks.onCreateLoader()
LoaderManager.LoaderCallbacks.onLoadFinished()
//Notice, no call to onLoaderReset()
```

Listing 26-7 shows the order of calls on configuration change.

Listing 26-7. Loader Callbacks on a Configuration Change

```
Application:config changed
Activity: onCreate
  Activity.onStart
  [No call to the onCreateLoader]
  LoaderManager.LoaderCallbacks.onLoadFinished
  [optionally if searchview has text in it]
    SearchView.onQueryChangeText
    RestartLoader //just a log message
    LoaderManager.LoaderCallbacks.onCreateLoader
    LoaderManager.LoaderCallbacks.onLoadFinished
```

Listing 26-8 shows the order of callbacks on navigating back or navigating Home as those action results in the activity are being destroyed.

Listing 26-8. Loader Callbacks when the Activity is destroyed

```
ActivityonStop()
Activity.onDestroy()
LoaderManager.LoaderCallbacks.onLoaderReset() //Notice this method is called
```

Writing Custom Loaders

As you have seen with the `CursorLoader`, `Loaders` are specific to their data sources. So you may need to write your own loaders. Very likely you will need to derive from the `AsyncTaskLoader` and specialize it using the principles and contracts laid out by the `Loader` protocol. See the SDK documentation for the `Loader` class to get more details. You can also use the `CursorLoader` source code as a guide in writing your own loaders. The source code is available online from multiple sources (you can just google it) or as part of the Android source download.

Resources

Here are additional resources for the topics covered in this chapter:

- `http://www.androidbook.com/item/4890`: Research notes on loaders. You will see here links to references, research, sample code, images, key questions, and ongoing notes.
- `http://developer.android.com/guide/components/loaders.html`: Primary guide for loaders from Android.

- http://developer.android.com/guide/components/loaders.html#callback: Key loader API callbacks to be implemented by an activity or a fragment.
- http://developer.android.com/reference/android/content/Loader.html: Loader Java class API to understand what methods are available on a loader object which is often passed to the loader API callbacks.
- http://developer.android.com/reference/android/app/LoaderManager.html: LoaderManager Java class API which is useful to control the loader, such as initialing, restarting, or removing.
- http://developer.android.com/reference/android/content/CursorLoader.html: CursorLoader Java class API which is useful to load data using cursors. CursorLoaders are also passed as arguments to the LoaderManager callbacks. You can use the public API on the CursorLoader to get its ID, cancel the load, and get the input arguments used to start the cursor.
- http://developer.android.com/guide/topics/ui/layout/listview.html: You will find here how to use loaders to populate and work with a ListView.
- http://developer.android.com/reference/android/provider/ContactsContract.Contacts.html: Content provider APIs available to work with the Android contacts database.
- http://developer.android.com/reference/android/app/Activity.html#startManagingCursor(android.database.Cursor): API documentation of what a managed cursor is. This is useful to see what is done to a cursor in a managed environment. This applies to cursors managed by loaders as well.
- http://www.androidbook.com/proandroid5/projects: Downloadable test project for this chapter is accessible from this URL. The name of the zip file is ProAndroid5_Ch26_TestLoaders.zip.

Summary

Loaders are essential to load data from data sources both from a timing perspective and also in terms of the ability to deal with the managed life cycle of activities and fragments. You have seen in this chapter how easy it is to use loaders to load data from content providers. The resulting code is responsive, able to deal with configuration changes, and simple.

Chapter 27

Exploring the Contacts API

In Chapters 25 and 26, we covered content providers and their close cousins, the loaders. We listed the benefits of exposing data through content provider abstraction. In a content provider abstraction, data is exposed as a series of URLs. These data URLs can be used to read, query, update, insert, and delete. These URLs and their corresponding cursors become the API for that content provider.

The Contacts API is one such content provider API for working with contact data. Contacts in Android are maintained in a database and exposed through a content provider whose authority is rooted at

```
content://com.android.contacts
```

The Android SDK documents the various URLs and the data they return using a set of Java interfaces and classes that are rooted at the Java package

```
android.provider.ContactsContract
```

You will see numerous classes whose parent context is `ContactsContract`; these are useful in querying, reading, updating, and inserting contacts into and from the content database. The primary documentation for using the Contacts API is available on the Android site at

```
https://developer.android.com/guide/topics/providers/contacts-provider.html
```

The primary API entry point `ContactsContract` is appropriately named because this class defines the contract between the clients of the contacts and the provider and protector of the contacts database.

This chapter explores this contract in a fair amount of detail but does not cover every nuance. The Contacts API is large and its tentacles far-reaching. However, when you approach the Contacts API, it will take a few weeks of research to realize that it is simple in its underlying structure. This is where we would like to contribute the most and explain these basics in the time it takes to read this chapter.

Android 4.0 has extended the idea of contacts to include a user profile, similar to a user profile in a social network. A user profile is a dedicated contact that represents the owner of the device. Most of the general contact-based concepts remain the same. We will cover how the Contacts API is extended to support a user profile.

Understanding Accounts

All contacts in Android work in the context of an account. What is an account? Well, for example, if you have your e-mail through Google, you are said to have an account with Google. If you set up yourself as a user of Facebook, you are said to have an account with Facebook. You will be able to set up these accounts through the “Accounts & sync” Settings option on the device. See the Android User’s Guide to get more details around accounts and how to set them up.

The contacts you manage are tied to a specific account. An account owns its set of contacts—or an account is said to be the parent of a contact. An account is identified by two strings: the account name and the account type. In case of Google, your account name is your e-mail user name at Gmail and your account type is `com.google`. The account type must be unique across the device. Your account name is unique within that account type. Together, an account type and an account name form an account, and only once the account is formed can a set of contacts be inserted for that account.

Enumerating Accounts

The Contacts API primarily deals with contacts that exist in various accounts. The mechanism of creating accounts is outside of the Contacts API, so explaining the ability to write your own account providers and how to sync the contacts within those accounts is outside the scope of this chapter. You can understand and benefit from this chapter without going into the details of how accounts get set up. However, when you want to add a contact or a list of contacts, you do need to know what accounts exist on the device. You can use the code in Listing 27-1 to enumerate the accounts and their properties (the account name and type). Code in Listing 27-1 lists the account name and type given a context variable such as an activity.

Listing 27-1. Code to Display a List of Accounts

```
public void listAccounts(Context ctx) {
    AccountManager am = AccountManager.get(ctx);
    Account[] accounts = am.getAccounts();
    for(Account ac: accounts) {
        String account_name=ac.name;
        String account_type = ac.type;
        Log.d("accountInfo", account_name + ":" + account_type);
    }
}
```

To run the code in Listing 27-1, the manifest file needs to ask for permission using the line in Listing 27-2.

Listing 27-2. Permission to Read Accounts

```
<uses-permission android:name="android.permission.GET_ACCOUNTS"/>
```

The code from Listing 27-1 will print something like the following:

```
Your-email-at-gmail:com.google
```

This assumes that you have only one account (Google) configured. If you have more than one account, all of those accounts will be listed in a similar manner.

Using the contacts application on the device you can add, edit, and delete contacts to any of your existing accounts.

Understanding Contacts

Contacts owned by an account are called raw contacts. A raw contact has a variable set of data elements (for example, e-mail address, phone number, name, and postal address). Android presents an aggregated view of raw contacts by listing only once any raw contacts that seems to match. These aggregated contacts form the set of contacts you see when you open the contacts application.

We will now examine how contacts and their related data are stored in various tables. Understanding these contact tables and their associated views is key to understanding the Contacts API.

Examining the Contacts SQLite Database

One way to understand and examine the contacts database tables is to download the contacts database from the device or the emulator and open it using one of the SQLite explorer tools.

To download the contacts database, use the File Explorer shown in Figure 30-17 and navigate to the following directory on your emulator:

```
/data/data/com.android.providers.contacts/databases
```

Depending on the release, the database file name may differ slightly, but it should be called `contacts.db`, `contacts2.db`, or something similar. In 4.0, the contacts provider uses a similarly structured but separate database file called `profile.db` to hold the contacts related to the personal profile.

Understanding Raw Contacts

The contacts you see in the contacts application are called aggregated contacts. Underneath each aggregated contact lies a set of contacts called raw contacts. An aggregated contact is a view on a set of similar raw contacts.

The set of contacts belonging to an account are called raw contacts. Each raw contact points to the details of one person in the context of that account. This is in contrast to an aggregated contact, which crosses account boundaries and belongs to the device as a whole. This relationship between an account and its set of raw contacts is maintained in the raw contacts table. Listing 27-3 shows the structure of the raw contacts table in the contacts database.

Listing 27-3. Raw Contact Table Definition

```
CREATE TABLE raw_contacts
(_id INTEGER PRIMARY KEY AUTOINCREMENT,
is_restricted          INTEGER DEFAULT 0,
account_name           STRING DEFAULT NULL,
account_type           STRING DEFAULT NULL,
sourceid               TEXT,
version                INTEGER NOT NULL DEFAULT 1,
dirty                  INTEGER NOT NULL DEFAULT 0,
deleted                INTEGER NOT NULL DEFAULT 0,
contact_id             INTEGER REFERENCES contacts(_id),
aggregation_mode       INTEGER NOT NULL DEFAULT 0,
aggregation_needed     INTEGER NOT NULL DEFAULT 1,
custom_ringtone        TEXT
send_to_voicemail      INTEGER NOT NULL DEFAULT 0,
times_contacted        INTEGER NOT NULL DEFAULT 0,
last_time_contacted    INTEGER,
starred                INTEGER NOT NULL DEFAULT 0,
display_name           TEXT,
display_name_alt       TEXT,
display_name_source    INTEGER NOT NULL DEFAULT 0,
phonetic_name          TEXT,
phonetic_name_style    TEXT,
sort_key               TEXT COLLATE PHONEBOOK,
sort_key_alt           TEXT COLLATE PHONEBOOK,
name_verified          INTEGER NOT NULL DEFAULT 0,
contact_in_visible_group  INTEGER NOT NULL DEFAULT 0,
sync1 TEXT, sync2         TEXT, sync3 TEXT, sync4 TEXT )
```

As with most Android tables, the raw contacts table has the `_ID` column that uniquely identifies a raw contact. Together, the field's `account_name` and `account_type` identify the account to which this contact (specifically, the raw contact) belongs. The `sourceid` field indicates how this raw contact is uniquely identified in the account.

The field `contact_id` refers to the aggregated contact that this raw contact is one of. An aggregated contact points to one or more similar contacts that are essentially the same person set up among multiple accounts.

The field `display_name` points to the display name of the contact. This is primarily a read-only field. It is set by triggers based on the data rows added in the data table (which is covered in the next subsection) for this raw contact.

The sync fields are used by the account to sync contacts between the device and the server-side account such as Google mail.

Although we have used SQLite tools to explore these fields, there is more than one way to discover these fields. The recommended way is to follow the class definitions as declared in the ContactsContract API. To explore the columns belonging to a raw contact, you can look at the class documentation for ContactsContract.RawContacts.

There are advantages and disadvantages to this approach. A significant advantage is that you get to know the fields published and acknowledged by the Android SDK. The database columns may get added or dropped without changing the public interface. So if you use the database columns directly, they may or may not be there. Instead, if you use the public definitions for these columns, you are safe between releases.

One disadvantage, however, is that the class documentation has many other constants interspersed with column names; we kind of got lost in figuring out what was what. These numerous class definitions give the impression that the API is complex when, in reality, 80% of the class documentation for the Contacts API is to define constants for these columns and the URIs to access these rows.

When we exercise the Contacts API in later sections, we will use the class-documentation-based constants instead of direct column names. However, we felt the direct exploration of the tables was the quickest way to help you understand the Contacts API.

Let's talk next about how the data relating to a contact (such as e-mail and phone number) is stored.

Understanding the Contacts Data Table

As seen from the raw contact table definition, the raw contact (in an anticlimactic sense) is just an ID indicating what account it belongs to. Data pertaining to the contact is not in the raw contact table but saved in the data table. Each data element, such as e-mail and phone number, is stored as separate rows in the data table tied by the raw contact ID. The data table, whose definition is shown in Listing 27-4, contains 16 generic columns that can store any type of data element such as an e-mail.

Listing 27-4. Contact Data Table Definition

```
CREATE TABLE data
(_id                INTEGER PRIMARY KEY AUTOINCREMENT,
package_id          INTEGER REFERENCES package(_id),
mimetype_id         INTEGER REFERENCES mimetype(_id) NOT NULL,
raw_contact_id      INTEGER REFERENCES raw_contacts(_id) NOT NULL,
is_primary          INTEGER NOT NULL DEFAULT 0,
is_super_primary    INTEGER NOT NULL DEFAULT 0,
data_version        INTEGER NOT NULL DEFAULT 0,
data1 TEXT,data2 TEXT,data3 TEXT,data4 TEXT,data5 TEXT,
data6 TEXT,data7 TEXT,data8 TEXT,data9 TEXT,data10 TEXT,
data11 TEXT,data12 TEXT,data13 TEXT,data14 TEXT,data15 TEXT,
data_sync1 TEXT, data_sync2 TEXT, data_sync3 TEXT, data_sync4 TEXT )
```

The raw_contact_id points to the raw contact to which this data row belongs. The mimetype_id points to the MIME type entry indicating one of the types identified in the contact data types in Listing 27-4. The columns data1 through data15 are generic string-based tables that can store anything that is necessary based on the MIME type. The sync fields support contact syncing. The table that resolves the MIME type IDs is in Listing 27-5.

Listing 27-5. Contacts MIME Type Lookup Table Definition

```
CREATE TABLE mimetypes
(_id INTEGER PRIMARY KEY AUTOINCREMENT,
mimetype TEXT NOT NULL)
```

As with the raw contacts table, you can discover the data table columns through the helper class documentation for `ContactsContract.Data`. Although you can figure out the columns from this class definition, you will not know what is stored in each of the generic columns from `data1` through `data15`. To know this, you will need to see the class definitions for a number of classes under the namespace `ContactsContract.CommonDataKinds`.

Some examples of these classes follow:

- `ContactsContract.CommonDataKinds.Email`
- `ContactsContract.CommonDataKinds.Phone`

In fact, you will see one class for each of the predefined MIME types. These classes are as follows: `Email`, `Event`, `GroupMembership`, `Identity`, `Im`, `Nickname`, `Note`, `Organization`, `Phone`, `Photo`, `Relation`, `SipAddress`, `StructuredName`, `StructuredPostal`, `Website`. Ultimately, all the `CommonDataKinds` classes do is indicate which generic data fields (`data1` through `data15`) are in use and what for.

Understanding Aggregated Contacts

Ultimately, a contact and its related data are unambiguously stored in the raw contacts table and the data table. An aggregated contact, on the other hand, is heuristic and could be ambiguous.

When there is a contact that is the same between multiple accounts, you may want to see one name instead of seeing the same or similar name repeated once for every account. Android addresses this by aggregating contacts into a read-only view. Android stores these aggregated contacts in a table called contacts. Android uses a number of triggers on the raw contact table and the data table to populate or change this aggregated contact table.

Before going into explaining the logic behind aggregation, let us show you the contact table definition (see Listing 27-6).

Listing 27-6. Aggregated Contact Table Definition

```
CREATE TABLE contacts
(_id                 INTEGER PRIMARY KEY AUTOINCREMENT,
name_raw_contact_id  INTEGER REFERENCES raw_contacts(_id),
photo_id             INTEGER REFERENCES data(_id),
custom_ringtone      TEXT,
send_to_voicemail    INTEGER NOT NULL DEFAULT 0,
times_contacted      INTEGER NOT NULL DEFAULT 0,
last_time_contacted  INTEGER,
starred              INTEGER NOT NULL DEFAULT 0,
```

```
in_visible_group        INTEGER NOT NULL DEFAULT 1,
has_phone_number        INTEGER NOT NULL DEFAULT 0,
lookup                  TEXT,
status_update_id        INTEGER REFERENCES data(_id),
single_is_restricted    INTEGER NOT NULL DEFAULT 0)
```

No client directly updates this table. When a raw contact is added with its detail, Android searches other raw contacts to see if there are similar raw contacts. If there is one, it will use the aggregated contact ID of that raw contact as the aggregated contact ID of the new raw contact as well. No entry is made into the aggregated contact table. If none is found, it will create an aggregated contact and use that aggregated contact as the contact ID for that raw contact.

Android uses the following algorithm to determine which raw contacts are similar:

1. The two raw contacts have matching names, both first and last.
2. The words in the name are the same but vary in order: "first last" or "first, last" or "last, first."
3. The shorter versions of the names match, such as "Bob" for "Robert."
4. If one of the raw contacts has just a first or last name, this will trigger a search for other attributes, such as phone number or e-mail, and if the other attributes match, the contact will be aggregated.
5. If one of the raw contacts is missing the name altogether, this will also trigger a search for other attributes as in step 4.

Because these rules are heuristic, some contacts may be aggregated unintentionally. The client applications need to provide a mechanism to separate the contacts in such a case. If you refer to the Android User's Guide, you will see that the default contacts application allows you to separate contacts that are unintentionally merged.

You can also prevent the aggregation by setting the aggregation mode when you insert the raw contact. The aggregation modes are shown in Listing 27-7.

Listing 27-7. Aggregation Mode Constants

```
AGGREGATION_MODE_DEFAULT
AGGREGATION_MODE_DISABLED
AGGREGATION_MODE_SUSPENDED
```

The first option is obvious; it is how aggregation works.

The second option (`disabled`) keeps this raw contact out of aggregation. Even if it is aggregated already, Android will pull it out of aggregation and allocate a new aggregated contact ID dedicated to this raw contact.

The third option (`suspended`) indicates that even though the properties of the contact may change, which will make it invalid for the aggregation into that batch of contacts, it should be kept tied to that aggregated contact.

The last point brings out the volatile dimension of the aggregated contact. Say you have a unique raw contact with a first name and a last name. Right now, it doesn't match any other raw contact, so this unique raw contact gets its own allocation of an aggregated contact. The aggregated contact ID will be stored in the raw contact table against that raw contact row.

However, you go and change the last name of this raw contact, which makes it a match to another set of contacts that are aggregated. In that case, Android will remove the raw contact from this aggregated contact and move it to the other one, abandoning this single aggregated contact by itself. In this case, the ID of the aggregated contact becomes entirely abandoned, as it will not match anything in the future because it is just an ID without an underlying raw contact.

So an aggregated contact is volatile. There is not a significant value to hold on to this aggregated contact ID over time.

Android offers some respite from this predicament by providing a field called `lookup` in the aggregated contacts tables. This lookup field is an aggregation (concatenation) of the account and the unique ID of this raw contact in that account for each raw contact. This information is further codified so that it can be passed as a URL parameter to retrieve the latest aggregated contact ID. Android looks at the lookup key and sees which underlying raw contact IDs are there for this lookup key. It then uses a best-fit algorithm to return a suitable (or perhaps new) aggregated contact ID.

While we are explicitly examining the contacts database, let's consider a couple of contact-related database views that are useful.

Exploring view_contacts

The first of these views is the `view_contacts`. Although there is a table that holds the aggregated contacts (contacts table), the API doesn't expose the contacts table directly. Instead, it uses `view_contacts` as the target for reading the aggregated contacts. When you query based on the URI `ContactsContract.Contacts.CONTENT_URI`, the columns returned are based on this view `view_contacts`. The definition of `view_contacts` view is shown in Listing 27-8.

Listing 27-8. A View to Read Aggregated Contacts

```
CREATE VIEW view_contacts AS

SELECT contacts._id AS _id,
contacts.custom_ringtone                   AS custom_ringtone,
name_raw_contact.display_name_source       AS display_name_source,
name_raw_contact.display_name              AS display_name,
name_raw_contact.display_name_alt          AS display_name_alt,
name_raw_contact.phonetic_name             AS phonetic_name,
name_raw_contact.phonetic_name_style       AS phonetic_name_style,
name_raw_contact.sort_key                  AS sort_key,
name_raw_contact.sort_key_alt              AS sort_key_alt,
name_raw_contact.contact_in_visible_group AS in_visible_group,
has_phone_number,
lookup,
photo_id,
```

```
contacts.last_time_contacted           AS last_time_contacted,
contacts.send_to_voicemail             AS send_to_voicemail,
contacts.starred                       AS starred,
contacts.times_contacted               AS times_contacted, status_update_id

FROM contacts JOIN raw_contacts AS name_raw_contact
ON(name_raw_contact_id=name_raw_contact._id)
```

Notice that the view_contacts view combines the contacts table with the raw contact table based on the aggregated contact ID.

Exploring contact_entities_view

Another useful view is the contact_entities_view that combines the raw contacts table with the data table. This view allows us to retrieve all the data elements of a given raw contact one time, or even the data elements of multiple raw contacts belonging to the same aggregated contact. Listing 27-9 presents the definition of this view based on contact entities.

Listing 27-9. Contact Entities View

```
CREATE VIEW contact_entities_view AS

SELECT raw_contacts.account_name      AS account_name,
raw_contacts.account_type             AS account_type,
raw_contacts.sourceid                 AS sourceid,
raw_contacts.version                  AS version,
raw_contacts.dirty                    AS dirty,
raw_contacts.deleted                  AS deleted,
raw_contacts.name_verified            AS name_verified,
package                               AS res_package,
contact_id,
raw_contacts.sync1                    AS sync1,
raw_contacts.sync2                    AS sync2,
raw_contacts.sync3                    AS sync3,
raw_contacts.sync4                    AS sync4,
mimetype, data1, data2, data3, data4, data5, data6, data7, data8,
data9, data10, data11, data12, data13, data14, data15,
data_sync1, data_sync2, data_sync3, data_sync4,

raw_contacts._id                      AS _id,

is_primary, is_super_primary,
data_version,
data._id                              AS data_id,
raw_contacts.starred                  AS starred,
raw_contacts.is_restricted            AS is_restricted,
groups.sourceid                       AS group_sourceid

FROM raw_contacts LEFT OUTER JOIN data
   ON (data.raw_contact_id=raw_contacts._id)
LEFT OUTER JOIN packages
  ON (data.package_id=packages._id)
```

```
LEFT OUTER JOIN mimetypes
  ON (data.mimetype_id=mimetypes._id)
LEFT OUTER JOIN groups
  ON (mimetypes.mimetype='vnd.android.cursor.item/group_membership'
    AND groups._id=data.data1)
```

The URIs needed to access this view are available in the class `ContactsContract.RawContactsEntity`.

Working with the Contacts API

So far, we have explored the basic idea behind the Contacts API by exploring its tables and views. We will now present a number of code snippets that can be used to explore contacts. These snippets are taken from the sample application that is developed to support this chapter. Although the snippets are taken from the sample application, they are sufficient to aid the understanding of how the Contacts API work. You can download the full sample program using the project download URL at the end of this chapter.

Exploring Accounts

We will start our exercise by writing a program that can print out the list of accounts. We have already given the code snippets necessary to get a list of accounts. Consider the class `AccountsFunctionTester` in Listing 27-10.

Listing 27-10. `AccountsFunctionTester` That Prints Available Accounts

```
//Java class: AccountsFunctionTester.java
//Menu to invoke this: Accounts
//BaseTester is a supporting base class holding the parent activity
// and some reused common variables. See the source code if you are more curious.
public class AccountsFunctionTester extends BaseTester {
    private static String tag = "tc>";

    //IReportBack is a simple logging interface that writes log messages
    //to the main activity and also to the log.
    public AccountsFunctionTester(Context ctx, IReportBack target) {
        super(ctx, target);
    }
    public void testAccounts() {
        AccountManager am = AccountManager.get(this.mContext);
        Account[] accounts = am.getAccounts();
        for(Account ac: accounts) {
            String acname=ac.name;
            String actype = ac.type;
            this.mReportTo.reportBack(tag,acname + ":" + actype);
        }
    }
}
```

> **Note** As we present and explore the Java code necessary to work with contacts, you will see three variables repeatedly used in the presented source code:
>
> mContext: A variable pointing to an activity
>
> mReportTo: A variable implementing a logging interface (IReportBack—you can see this Java file in the downloadable project) that can be used to log messages to the test activity that is used for this chapter
>
> Utils: A static class that encapsulates very simple utility methods
>
> We have chosen not to list these classes here because they will distract you from understanding the core functionality of the Contacts API. You can examine these classes in the downloadable project.
>
> All the code in this chapter uses an unmanaged query against the content provider. This is done by calling Activity.getContentResolver().query(). This is because we merely read the data and print out the results right away. If your goal instead is to use UI (through activities or fragments) as a target to display your contacts then read Chapter 27 on loaders. Loaders show the right way to display cursors from any content provider.

When you run the sample program that you can download for this chapter, you will see a main activity that appears with a number of menu options. The menu option "Accounts" will print the list of accounts available on the device.

Exploring Aggregated Contacts

Let's see how we can explore aggregated contacts through code snippets. To read contacts, you need to request the following permission in the manifest file:

```
android.permission.READ_CONTACTS
```

As the functionality we are testing deals with content providers, URIs, and cursors, let's look at some useful code snippets presented in Listing 27-11. (These code snippets are available either in utils.java or in some of the base classes derived from BaseTester in the chapter's downloadable project.)

***Listing 27-11.** Getting a Cursor Given a URI and a where Clause*

```
//Utils.java
//Retrieve a column from a cursor
public static String getColumnValue(Cursor cc, String cname) {
   int i = cc.getColumnIndex(cname);
   return cc.getString(i);
}
```

```
//See what columns are there  in a cursor
protected static String getCursorColumnNames(Cursor c) {
   int count = c.getColumnCount();
   StringBuffer cnamesBuffer = new StringBuffer();
    for (int i=0;i<count;i++) {
       String cname = c.getColumnName(i);
       cnamesBuffer.append(cname).append(';');
    }
    return cnamesBuffer.toString();
}

//From URIFunctionTester.java, baseclass of some of the other testers
//Given a URI and a where clause return a cursor
protected Cursor getACursor(Uri uri,String clause) {
   Activity a = (Activity)this.mContext; //mContext coming from BaseTester
   return a.getContentResolver().query(uri, null, clause, null, null);
}
```

In this section, we are primarily exploring the cursor returned by aggregated contact URIs. Each row returned by the resulting contact cursor will have a number of fields. For our example, we are not interested in all the fields but only a few. You can abstract this out into another class called an AggregatedContact. Listing 27-12 shows this class.

Listing 27-12. An Object Definition for a Few Fields of an Aggregated Contact

```
//AggregatedContact.java
public class AggregatedContact {
    public String id;
    public String lookupUri;
    public String lookupKey;
    public String displayName;
    public void fillinFrom(Cursor c) {
        id = Utils.getColumnValue(c,"_ID");
        lookupKey = Utils.getColumnValue(c,ContactsContract.Contacts.LOOKUP_KEY);
        lookupUri = ContactsContract.Contacts.CONTENT_LOOKUP_URI + "/" + lookupKey;
        displayName = Utils.getColumnValue(c,ContactsContract.Contacts.DISPLAY_NAME);
    }
}
```

In Listing 27-12 we use the cursor to load up the fields that we are interested in.

Getting the Aggregated Contacts Cursor

Listing 27-13 shows how to retrieve a cursor that is a collection of aggregated contacts.

Listing 27-13. Getting a Cursor for All Aggregated Contacts

```
//Get a cursor of all contacts. Specify the where clause as null to indicate all rows.
//Java class: AggregatedContactFunctionTester.java
//Menu item to invoke: Contacts Cursor
private Cursor getContacts() {
    Uri uri = ContactsContract.Contacts.CONTENT_URI;
    //Specify ascending or descending way to sort names
    String sortOrder = ContactsContract.Contacts.DISPLAY_NAME
                        + " COLLATE LOCALIZED ASC";
    Activity a = (Activity)this.mContext; //Local variable pointing to an activity
    return a.getContentResolver().query(uri, null, null, null, sortOrder);
}
```

The URI used to read all the contacts is `ContactsContract.Contacts.CONTENT_URI`. You can pass this URI to the `query()`function to retrieve a cursor. You can pass null as the column projection to receive all columns. Although this is not recommended in practice, in our case, it makes sense because we want to know about all the columns it returns. We have also used the display name of the contact as the sort order. Notice how, again, we have used `ContactContract.Contacts` to get the column name for the contact display name. If you were to print the field names from this cursor you will see the returned fields as those shown in Listing 27-14. Depending on the release the order may be different and more columns may be added. It is a good practice to explicitly specify a projection to the query clause; that way your code will work across releases.

Listing 27-14. Aggregated Contacts Content URI Cursor Columns

```
times_contacted; contact_status; custom_ringtone; has_phone_number; phonetic_name;
phonetic_name_style; contact_status_label; lookup; contact_status_icon; last_time_contacted;
display_name; sort_key_alt; in_visible_group; _id; starred; sort_key; display_name_alt;
contact_presence; display_name_source; contact_status_res_package; contact_status_ts;
photo_id; send_to_voicemail;
```

Reading Aggregated Contact Details

Now that we've explored the columns available with the contacts content URI, let's pick a few columns and see what contact rows are available. We are interested in the following columns from a contact cursor: display name, lookup key, and lookup URI. We are considering these fields because we want to see what the lookup key and lookup key URI look like based on what is covered in the theory part of this chapter. Specifically, we are interested in firing off the lookup URI to see what type of a cursor it returns.

The function `listContacts()` in Listing 27-15 gets a contacts cursor and prints these three columns for each row of the cursor. Note that this listing is taken from a class that holds a local variable called `mContext` to indicate the activity and a local variable called `mReportTo` to be able to log any messages to the activity.

Listing 27-15. Printing the Lookup Keys for an Aggregated Contact

```
//Java class: AggregatedContactFunctionTester.java
//Menu item to invoke: Contacts
public void listContacts() {
    Cursor c = null;
    try {
        c = getContacts();
        int i = c.getColumnCount();
        this.mReportTo.reportBack(tag, "Number of columns:" + i);
        this.printLookupKeys(c);
    }
   finally { if (c!= null) c.close(); }
}
private void printLookupKeys(Cursor c) {
    for(c.moveToFirst();!c.isAfterLast();c.moveToNext()) {
        String name=this.getContactName(c);
        String lookupKey = this.getLookupKey(c);
        String luri = this.getLookupUri(lookupKey);
        this.mReportTo.reportBack(tag, name + ":" + lookupKey); //log
        this.mReportTo.reportBack(tag, name + ":" + luri); //log
    }
}
private String getLookupKey(Cursor cc) {
    int lookupkeyIndex = cc.getColumnIndex(ContactsContract.Contacts.LOOKUP_KEY);
    return cc.getString(lookupkeyIndex);
}
private String getContactName(Cursor cc){
    return Utils.getColumnValue(cc,ContactsContract.Contacts.DISPLAY_NAME);
}
private String getLookupUri(String lookupkey) {
    String luri = ContactsContract.Contacts.CONTENT_LOOKUP_URI + "/" + lookupkey;
    return luri;
}
```

Exploring the Lookup URI-Based Cursor

Now that we know how to extract lookup URIs for a given aggregated contact, let's see what we can do with a lookup URI.

The function `listLookupUriColumns()` in Listing 27-16 will take the first contact from the list of all contacts and then formulate a lookup URI for that contact and fire off the URI to see what kind of a cursor it returns by printing the column names from that cursor.

Listing 27-16. Exploring the Lookup URI Cursor

```
//Class: AggregatedContactFunctionTester.java, Menu item to invoke: Single Contact Cursor
public void listLookupUriColumns() {
    Cursor c = null;
    try {
        c = getContacts();
        String firstContactLookupUri = getFirstLookupUri(c);
        printLookupUriColumns(firstContactLookupUri);
    }
    finally { if (c!= null) c.close(); }
}
private String getFirstLookupUri(Cursor c) {
    c.moveToFirst();
    if (c.isAfterLast()) {
        Log.d(tag,"No rows to get the first contact");
        return null;
    }
    String lookupKey = this.getLookupKey(c);
    return  this.getLookupUri(lookupKey);
}
public void printLookupUriColumns(String lookupuri) {
    Cursor c = null;
    try {
        c = getASingleContact(lookupuri);
        int i = c.getColumnCount();
        this.mReportTo.reportBack(tag, "Number of columns:" + i);
        int j = c.getCount();
        this.mReportTo.reportBack(tag, "Number of rows:" + j);
        this.printCursorColumnNames(c);
    }
    finally { if (c!=null)c.close(); }
}
// Use the lookup uri, retrieve a single aggregated contact
private Cursor getASingleContact(String lookupUri) {
    Activity a = (Activity)this.mContext;
    return a.getContentResolver().query(Uri.parse(lookupUri), null, null, null, null);
}
```

As it turns out, it just returns a cursor (as in Listing 27-14) that is identical in columns for that of the aggregated contact cursor as in Listing 27-13, except that it has only one row pointing to the contact for which this is the lookup key. Also notice that we have used the following lookup URI definition:

```
ContactsContract.Contacts.CONTENT_LOOKUP_URI
```

You know from the discussion of the contact lookup URIs that each lookup URI represents a collection of raw contact identities that have been concatenated. That being the case, you might have expected the lookup URI to return a series of matching raw contacts. However, the test in Listing 27-16 is showing that it is not returning a cursor of raw contacts but instead a cursor of contacts.

> **Note** A lookup based on the contact lookup URI returns an aggregated contact and not a raw contact.

Another tidbit is that the lookup process for the aggregated contact based on the lookup URI is not linear or exact. This means Android will not look for an exact match of the lookup key. Instead, Android parses the lookup key into its constituent raw contacts and then finds the aggregated contact ID that matches the most of the raw contact records and returns that aggregated contact record.

One consequence of this is that no public mechanism is available to go from the lookup key to its constituent raw contacts. Instead, you have to find the contact ID for that lookup key and then fire off a raw contact URI for that contact ID to retrieve the corresponding raw contacts.

Here is another code snippet that shows what is returned from a cursor as an object instead of as a set of columns. The code in Listing 27-17 returns the first aggregated contact as an object.

Listing 27-17. Code Testing Aggregated Contacts

```
//Java class: AggregatedContactFunctionTester.java
protected AggregatedContact getFirstContact() {
    Cursor c=null;
    try {
        c = getContacts(); c.moveToFirst();
        if (c.isAfterLast()) {
            Log.d(tag,"No contacts");
            return null;
        }
        AggregatedContact firstcontact = new AggregatedContact();
        firstcontact.fillinFrom(c);
        return firstcontact;
    }
    finally { if (c!=null) c.close(); }
}
```

Exploring Raw Contacts

In Listing 27-18, the file RawContact.java, captures a few important fields from the raw contacts table cursor. (This file, like all other code snippets in this chapter, is available in the downloadable project for this chapter.)

Listing 27-18. Source code for RawContact.java

```
//Class: RawContact.java
public class RawContact  {
    public String rawContactId;
    public String aggregatedContactId;
    public String accountName;
    public String accountType;
    public String displayName;
```

```
    public void fillinFrom(Cursor c) {
        rawContactId = Utils.getColumnValue(c,"_ID");
        accountName = Utils.getColumnValue(c,ContactsContract.RawContacts.ACCOUNT_NAME);
        accountType = Utils.getColumnValue(c,ContactsContract.RawContacts.ACCOUNT_TYPE);
        aggregatedContactId = Utils.getColumnValue(c,
                                    ContactsContract.RawContacts.CONTACT_ID);
        displayName = Utils.getColumnValue(c,"display_name");
    }
    public String toString() { //..prints the public fields. See the download project for
details }
}//eof-class
```

Showing the Raw Contacts Cursor

As with the aggregated contact URIs, let's first examine the nature of the raw contact URI and what it returns. The signature for the raw contact URI is defined as follows:

```
ContactsContract.RawContacts.CONTENT_URI
```

The function showRawContactsCursor() in Listing 27-19 prints the cursor columns for a raw contacts URI.

Listing 27-19. Exploring the Raw Contacts Cursor

```
//Java class: RawContactFunctionTester.java; Menu item: Raw Contacts Cursor
public void showRawContactsCursor() {
    Cursor c = null;
    try {
        c = this.getACursor(ContactsContract.RawContacts.CONTENT_URI,null);
        this.printCursorColumnNames(c);
    }
    finally { if (c!=null) c.close(); }
}
```

Code in Listing 27-19 will show that the raw contact cursor has the fields shown in Listing 27-20 (this list seem to vary somewhat with each device).

Listing 27-20. Raw Contacts Cursor Fields

```
times_contacted; phonetic_name; phonetic_name_style; contact_id;version; last_time_contacted;
aggregation_mode; _id; name_verified; display_name_source; dirty; send_to_voicemail;
account_type; custom_ringtone; sync4;sync3;sync2;sync1; deleted; account_name; display_name;
sort_key_alt; starred; sort_key; display_name_alt; sourceid;
```

Seeing the Data Returned by a Raw Contacts Cursor

Listing 27-21 shows the method showAllRawContacts(), which prints all the rows in the raw contacts cursor.

Listing 27-21. Displaying Raw Contacts

```
//Java class: RawContactFunctionTester.java; Menu item: All Raw Contacts
public void showAllRawContacts(){
    Cursor c = null;
    try {
        c = this.getACursor(getRawContactsUri(), null);
        this.printRawContacts(c);
    }
    finally { if (c!=null) c.close(); }
}
private void printRawContacts(Cursor c) {
    for(c.moveToFirst();!c.isAfterLast();c.moveToNext()) {
        RawContact rc = new RawContact();
        rc.fillinFrom(c);
        this.mReportTo.reportBack(tag, rc.toString()); //log
    }
}
```

Constraining Raw Contacts with a Corresponding Set of Aggregated Contacts

Using the columns of the cursor in Listing 27-20, let's see if we can refine our query to retrieve the contacts for a given aggregated contact ID. The code in Listing 27-22 will look up the first aggregated contact and then issue a raw contact URI with a where clause specifying a value for the contact_id column.

Listing 27-22. Getting Raw Contacts for an Aggregated Contact

```
//Java class: RawContactFunctionTester.java; Menu item: Raw Contacts
public void showRawContactsForFirstAggregatedContact(){
    AggregatedContact ac = getFirstContact();
    Cursor c = null;
    try {
        c = this.getACursor(getRawContactsUri(), getClause(ac.id));
        this.printRawContacts(c);
    }
    finally { if (c!=null) c.close(); }
}
private String getClause(String contactId) {
    return "contact_id = " + contactId;
}
```

Exploring Raw Contact Data

Because a data row belonging to a raw contact contains a number of fields, we have created a Java class called ContactData.java, shown in Listing 27-23, to capture a representative set of the contact data, and not all fields.

Listing 27-23. Source code for `ContactData.java`

```
//ContactData.java
public class ContactData {
    public String rawContactId;
    public String aggregatedContactId;
    public String dataId;
    public String accountName;
    public String accountType;
    public String mimetype;
    public String data1;

    public void fillinFrom(Cursor c) {
        rawContactId = Utils.getColumnValue(c,"_ID");
        accountName = Utils.getColumnValue(c,ContactsContract.RawContacts.ACCOUNT_NAME);
        accountType = Utils.getColumnValue(c,ContactsContract.RawContacts.ACCOUNT_TYPE);
        aggregatedContactId =
              Utils.getColumnValue(c,ContactsContract.RawContacts.CONTACT_ID);
        mimetype = Utils.getColumnValue(c,ContactsContract.RawContactsEntity.MIMETYPE);
        data1 = Utils.getColumnValue(c,ContactsContract.RawContactsEntity.DATA1);
        dataId = Utils.getColumnValue(c,ContactsContract.RawContactsEntity.DATA_ID);
    }
    public String toString()   {//just a concatenation of fields for logging }
}
```

Android uses a view called a `RawContactEntity` view to retrieve data from a raw contact table and the corresponding data tables as indicated in the section "contact_entities_view" in this chapter. The URI to access this view is in Listing 27-24.

Listing 27-24. Raw Entities Content URI

```
ContactsContract.RawContactsEntity.CONTENT_URI
```

Let's see how this URI can be used to discover field names returned by this URI:

```
//Java class: ContactDataFunctionTester.java; Menu item: Contact Entity Cursor
public void showRawContactsEntityCursor(){
    Cursor c = null;
    try {
        Uri uri = ContactsContract.RawContactsEntity.CONTENT_URI;
        c = this.getACursor(uri,null);
        this.printCursorColumnNames(c);
    }
    finally { if (c!=null) c.close(); }
}
```

The code in Listing 27-24 prints out the list of columns shown in Listing 27-25. So the columns in Listing 27-25 are the columns that are returned by the raw contacts entity cursor. There may be additional columns depending on vendor-specific implementations.

Listing 27-25. Contact Entities Cursor Columns

```
data_version; contact_id; version; data12;data11;data10; mimetype; res_package;
_id; data15;data14;data13; name_verified; is_restricted; is_super_primary;
data_sync1;dirty;data_sync3;data_sync2; data_sync4;account_type;data1;sync4;sync3;
data4;sync2;data5;sync1; data2;data3;data8;data9; deleted; group_sourceid; data6;data7;
account_name; data_id; starred; sourceid; is_primary;
```

Once you know this set of columns, you can filter the result set of this cursor by formulating a proper where clause. However, you want to use the ContactsContract Java class to use the definitions for these column names. For example, in Listing 27-26 we retrieve the data elements pertaining to contact IDs 3, 4, and 5.

Listing 27-26. Displaying Data Elements from RawContactsEntity

```
//Java class: ContactDataFunctionTester.java; Menu item: Contact Data
public void showRawContactsData(){
    Cursor c = null;
    try {
        Uri uri = ContactsContract.RawContactsEntity.CONTENT_URI;
        c = this.getACursor(uri,"contact_id in (3,4,5)");
        this.printRawContactsData(c);
    }
    finally { if (c!=null) c.close(); }
}
protected void printRawContactsData(Cursor c) {
    for(c.moveToFirst();!c.isAfterLast();c.moveToNext()) {
        ContactData dataRecord = new ContactData();
        dataRecord.fillinFrom(c);
        this.mReportTo.reportBack(tag, dataRecord.toString());
    }
}
```

Code in Listing 27-26 will print such things as name, e-mail address, and MIME type as defined in the ContactData object in Listing 27-23.

Adding a Contact with Its Details

Let's look at a code snippet to add a contact with name, e-mail, and phone number. To write to contacts, you need the following permission in the manifest file:

```
android.permission.WRITE_CONTACTS
```

Code in Listing 27-27 adds a raw contact followed by adding two data rows (name and phone number) for that contact.

Listing 27-27. Adding a Contact

```
//Java class: AddContactFunctionTester.java; Menu item: Add Contact
public void addContact(){
    long rawContactId = insertRawContact();
    this.mReportTo.reportBack(tag, "RawcontactId:" + rawContactId);
    insertName(rawContactId);
    insertPhoneNumber(rawContactId);
    showRawContactsDataForRawContact(rawContactId);
}
private long insertRawContact(){
    ContentValues cv = new ContentValues();
    cv.put(RawContacts.ACCOUNT_TYPE, "com.google");
    cv.put(RawContacts.ACCOUNT_NAME, "--use your gmail id -- ");
    Uri rawContactUri =
        this.mContext.getContentResolver()
            .insert(RawContacts.CONTENT_URI, cv);
    long rawContactId = ContentUris.parseId(rawContactUri);
    return rawContactId;
}
private void insertName(long rawContactId) {
    ContentValues cv = new ContentValues();
    cv.put(Data.RAW_CONTACT_ID, rawContactId);
    cv.put(Data.MIMETYPE, StructuredName.CONTENT_ITEM_TYPE);
    cv.put(StructuredName.DISPLAY_NAME,"John Doe_" + rawContactId);
    this.mContext.getContentResolver().insert(Data.CONTENT_URI, cv);
}
private void insertPhoneNumber(long rawContactId) {
    ContentValues cv = new ContentValues();
    cv.put(Data.RAW_CONTACT_ID, rawContactId);
    cv.put(Data.MIMETYPE, Phone.CONTENT_ITEM_TYPE);
    cv.put(Phone.NUMBER,"123 123 " + rawContactId);
    cv.put(Phone.TYPE,Phone.TYPE_HOME);
    this.mContext.getContentResolver().insert(Data.CONTENT_URI, cv);
}
private void showRawContactsDataForRawContact(long rawContactId) {
    Cursor c = null;
    try {
        Uri uri = ContactsContract.RawContactsEntity.CONTENT_URI;
        c = this.getACursor(uri,"_id = " + rawContactId);
        this.printRawContactsData(c);
    }
    finally { if (c!=null) c.close(); }
}
```

Code in Listing 27-27 does the following:

1. Adds a new raw contact for a predefined account using the account's name and type, represented by the method insertRawContact(). Notice how it uses the URI RawContact.CONTENT_URI.
2. Takes the raw contact ID from step 1 and inserts a name record using the insertName() method in the data table. Notice how it uses the URI Data.CONTENT_URI.
3. Takes the raw contact ID from step 1 and inserts a phone number record using the insertPhoneNumber() method in the data table. Being a data row, it uses Data.CONTENT_URI as the URI.

Listing 27-27 also demonstrates the column aliases used in inserting records. Notice how constants like Phone.TYPE and Phone.NUMBER point to the generic data table column names data1 and data2.

Controlling Aggregation of Contacts

Clients that update or insert contacts do not explicitly change the contacts table. The contacts table is updated by triggers that look into the raw contact table and raw contact data table.

Raw contacts that get added or changed, in turn, affect the aggregated contacts in the contacts table. However, you may not want to allow two contacts to be aggregated.

You can control the aggregation behavior of a raw contact by setting the aggregation mode when that contract is created. As you can see from the raw contact table columns in Listing 27-20, the raw contact table contains a field called aggregation_mode. Values for the aggregation mode are shown in Listing 27-7 and explained in the section "Aggregated Contacts."

You can also keep two contacts always apart by inserting rows into a table called agg_exceptions. The URIs needed to insert into this table are defined in the Java class ContactsContract.AggregationExceptions. The table structure of agg_exceptions is shown in Listing 27-28.

Listing 27-28. Aggregate Exceptions Table Definition

```
CREATE TABLE agg_exceptions
(_id INTEGER PRIMARY KEY AUTOINCREMENT,
type INTEGER NOT NULL,
raw_contact_id1 INTEGER REFERENCES raw_contacts(_id),
raw_contact_id2 INTEGER REFERENCES raw_contacts(_id))
```

The type column in Listing 27-28 holds one of the integer constants in Listing 27-29.

Listing 27-29. Aggregation Types in the Aggregation Exception Table

```
ContactsContract.AggregationExceptions.TYPE_KEEP_TOGETHER
ContactsContract.AggregationExceptions.TYPE_KEEP_SEPARATE
ContactsContract.AggregationExceptions.TYPE_AUTOMATIC
```

TYPE_KEEP_TOGETHER says the two raw contacts should never be broken apart. TYPE_KEEP_SEPARATE says that these raw contacts should never be joined. TYPE_AUTOMATIC says to use the default algorithm to aggregate contacts.

The URI you will use to insert, read, and update this table is defined as

```
ContactsContract.AggregationExceptions.CONTENT_URI
```

Constants for field definitions to work with this table are also available in the Java class ContactsContract.AggregationExceptions.

Understanding Personal Profile

A personal profile, introduced in API 14, is like a contact, except there is only one personal profile contact. That is the singular you, on your device.

However, as an implementation detail, all data pertaining to the singular personal profile contact is maintained in a separate database called profile.db. Our research shows that this database has a structure identical to contacts2.db. This means you already know what relevant tables are available and what the columns of each table are.

Being a single contact, the aggregation is straightforward. Every raw contact that is added to the personal profile is expected to belong to the singular aggregated contact. If one doesn't exist, then a new aggregated contact is created and placed in the new raw contact. If one exists, that contact ID is used as the aggregated contact ID for the raw contact.

The Android SDK uses the same base class ContactsContract to define the necessary URIs to read/update/delete/add raw contacts to the personal profile. These URIs parallel their counterparts but with the string "PROFILE" somewhere in them. Listing 27-30 shows a few of these URIs.

Listing 27-30. Profile-Based URIs Introduced in 4.0

```
//Relates to profile aggregated contact
ContactsContract.Profile.CONTENT_URI

//Relates to profile based raw contact
ContactsContract.Profile.CONTENT_RAW_CONTACTS_URI

//Relates to profile based raw contact + profile based data table
ContactsContract.RawContactsEntity.PROFILE_CONTENT_URI
```

Listing 27-30 shows we have separate URIs when dealing with aggregated contact and a raw contact. However, there isn't a corresponding personal profile URI for the Data table. The same Data URI, Data.CONTENT_URI, is applicable to both regular contact data and also the profile contact data.

Also note that the same content provider serves the needs of both the personal profile and regular contacts. Internally, this content provider knows based on the raw contact ID if the data URI belongs to the profile data or the regular contact data.

Let's look next at code snippets to read and add contact data to the personal profile. You will need the permissions from Listing 27-31 to read from and write to the profile data.

Listing 27-31. Permissions Reading/Writing Profile Data

```
<uses-permission android:name="android.permission.READ_PROFILE"/>
<uses-permission android:name="android.permission.WRITE_PROFILE"/>
```

Reading Profile Raw Contacts

Let's use the following URI to read the raw contacts that belong to the personal profile:

```
ContactsContract.Profile.CONTENT_RAW_CONTACTS_URI
```

Listing 27-32 shows how to read profile raw contact entries.

Listing 27-32. Showing All Profile Raw Contacts

```
//Java class: ProfileRawContactFunctionTester.java; Menu item: PRaw Contacts
//In the download this method is named showAllRawContacts
//It is expanded here for clarity.
public void showAllRawProfileContacts() {
    Cursor c = null;
    try {
        String whereClause = null;
        c = this.getACursor(ContactsContract.Profile.CONTENT_RAW_CONTACTS_URI,
            whereClause);
        this.printRawContacts(c);
    }
    finally { if (c!=null) c.close(); }
}
//In the download this method is named printRawContacts
//It is expanded here for clarity.
private void printRawProfileContacts(Cursor c) {
    for(c.moveToFirst();!c.isAfterLast();c.moveToNext()) {
        RawContact rc = new RawContact();
        rc.fillinFrom(c);
        this.mReportTo.reportBack(tag, rc.toString());
    }
}
```

Notice that once we retrieve the cursor, the data it contains matches the `RawContact` that we defined earlier for a regular raw contact.

Reading Profile Contact Data

Let's use the following URI to read the various data elements (such as e-mail, MIME type, and so on) of raw contacts that belong to the personal profile:

```
ContactsContract.RawContactsEntity.PROFILE_CONTENT_URI
```

Notice how we are using a similar view as in the case of regular contacts. The RawContactEntity is a join between raw contacts and the data rows belonging to that raw contact. We will see one row for each data element such as name, e-mail, MIME type, and so on.

Listing 27-33 shows the code snippet to read profile raw contact entries.

Listing 27-33. Showing Data Elements for Profile Contacts

```
//Java class: ProfileContactDataFunctionTester.java; Menu item: all p raw contacts
public void showProfileRawContactsData() {
    Cursor c = null;
    try {
        Uri uri = ContactsContract.RawContactsEntity.PROFILE_CONTENT_URI;
        String whereClause = null;
        c = this.getACursor(uri,whereClause);
        this.printProfileRawContactsData(c);
    }
    finally { if (c!=null) c.close(); }
}
protected void printProfileRawContactsData(Cursor c) {
    for(c.moveToFirst();!c.isAfterLast();c.moveToNext()) {
        ContactData dataRecord = new ContactData();
        dataRecord.fillinFrom(c);
        this.mReportTo.reportBack(tag, dataRecord.toString());
    }
}
```

Notice that once we retrieve the cursor, the data it contains matches the ContactData object (Listing 27-23) that we defined earlier for a regular raw contact data element.

Adding Data to the Personal Profile

Let's use the following URI to add a raw contact to a personal profile:

```
ContactsContract.RawContactsEntity.PROFILE_CONTENT_URI
```

We will also add a few data elements such as a phone number and a nickname to that raw contact so they appear in the details of your personal profile on the device. Listing 27-34 shows the code snippet.

Listing 27-34. Adding a Profile Raw Contact

```
//Java class: AddProfileContactFunctionTester.java; Menu item: all p raw contacts
//In the source code you won't see the word "profile" in the following method names
//It is added here to add clarity as the whole class is not included
public void addProfileContact() {
    long rawContactId = insertProfileRawContact();
    this.mReportTo.reportBack(tag, "RawcontactId:" + rawContactId);
    insertProfileNickName(rawContactId);
    insertProfilePhoneNumber(rawContactId);
    showProfileRawContactsDataForRawContact(rawContactId);
}
private void insertProfileNickName(long rawContactId) {
    ContentValues cv = new ContentValues();
    cv.put(Data.RAW_CONTACT_ID, rawContactId);
    //cv.put(Data.IS_USER_PROFILE, "1");
    cv.put(Data.MIMETYPE, CommonDataKinds.Nickname.CONTENT_ITEM_TYPE);
    cv.put(CommonDataKinds.Nickname.NAME,"PJohn Nickname_" + rawContactId);
    this.mContext.getContentResolver().insert(Data.CONTENT_URI, cv);
}
private void insertProfilePhoneNumber(long rawContactId) {
    ContentValues cv = new ContentValues();
    cv.put(Data.RAW_CONTACT_ID, rawContactId);
    cv.put(Data.MIMETYPE, Phone.CONTENT_ITEM_TYPE);
    cv.put(Phone.NUMBER,"P123 123 " + rawContactId);
    cv.put(Phone.TYPE,Phone.TYPE_HOME);
    this.mContext.getContentResolver().insert(Data.CONTENT_URI, cv);
}
private long insertProfileRawContact() {
    ContentValues cv = new ContentValues();
    cv.put(RawContacts.ACCOUNT_TYPE, "com.google");
    cv.put(RawContacts.ACCOUNT_NAME, "--use your gmail id --");
    Uri rawContactUri =
        this.mContext.getContentResolver()
             .insert(ContactsContract.Profile.CONTENT_RAW_CONTACTS_URI, cv);
    long rawContactId = ContentUris.parseId(rawContactUri);
    return rawContactId;
}
private void showProfileRawContactsDataForRawContact(long rawContactId) {
    Cursor c = null;
    try {
        Uri uri = ContactsContract.RawContactsEntity.PROFILE_CONTENT_URI;
        c = this.getACursor(uri,"_id = " + rawContactId);
        this.printRawContactsData(c);
    }
    finally { if (c!=null) c.close(); }
}
```

The code in Listing 27-34 parallels the code we used to add a regular contact and its details (Listing 27-27). Although we have used a profile-specific URI to add a raw contact, we have used the same `Data.CONTENT_URI` to add the individual data elements.

Note the following commented-out code in Listing 27-34:

```
//cv.put(Data.IS_USER_PROFILE, "1");
```

Because `Data.CONTENT_URI` is not specific to the profile, how does the underlying content provider know whether to insert this data into a regular raw contact or a personal profile raw contact? We thought that specifying a column called `IS_USER_PROFILE` would help the content provider. Apparently not. This new column is available primarily for read purposes. Your inserts will fail if you specify this during inserts. The only conclusion then is that the content provider is relying on the raw contact ID to see whether that raw contact came from `profile.db` or `contacts2.db`.

Role of Sync Adapters

So far, we have mainly talked about manipulating the contacts on the device. However, accounts and their contacts on Android work hand in hand with server-based contacts. For example, if you have created a Google account on your Android phone, the Google account will pull your Gmail contacts and make them available on the device. To do this syncing Android provides a synchronization framework which does most of the groundwork as long as you write a conforming Sync adapter. Android's synchronization framework takes care of network availability, optional authentication, and scheduling.

Implementing a sync adapter involves implementing a service by extending the SDK class `AbstractThreadedSyncAdapter` and doing the work in the method `onPerformSync()`. Work involved in this method is to load data from servers and update the contacts using the Contacts API that is discussed in this chapter. Then, a sync-adapter resource file (XML) needs to be created on the device that will describe how this service is tied to the account that needs to be synched.

Outside of this basic understanding, due to space limitations we have not covered the syncing API in this edition of the book. Android SDK documentation has some documentation and samples.

Synchronization of contacts has impacts on deleting contacts on the device. When you delete a contact using the aggregated contact URI, it will delete all its corresponding raw contacts and the data elements of each of those raw contacts. However, Android will only mark them as deleted on the device and expects the background sync to actually sync with the server and then delete the contacts permanently from the device. This cascading of deletes also happens at the raw contact level where the corresponding data elements of that raw contact are deleted.

Using Batch Operations to Optimize ContentProvider Updates

While covering content providers in Chapter 26 we indicated that we would cover the batch operations in this chapter.

Reconsider how a raw contact and its associated data elements are created earlier in the chapter. Notice the multiple commands we need to send to the contacts provider to insert a raw contact. First we have to insert raw contact. Then use that ID to insert multiple data elements belonging to that raw contact. Each of these inserts is a separate command sent to the content provider independently.

There are two issues when we send these multiple commands sequentially. The first issue is that the content provider is not aware that they belong to a single commit unit. The second issue is that it will take longer to update the content provider database as each transaction is committed by itself.

These two issues are addressed by the batch update API available for any content provider including the contact provider.

Idea of Batching Content Provider Updates

In the batching approach, each content provider update operation is encapsulated in an object called "ContentProviderOperation" along with the URI and all the necessary key/value pairs to perform that operation. Then you gather these operations into a list object. You then tell the content resolver to send the entire batch or list of commands to the content provider at the same time. Because the content provider knows these commands are in a batch, it applies the transactions appropriately either at the end or so often based on hints.

If an operation indicates that a transaction can be applied at the end of that operation, then the operations completed thus far will be committed. This allows you to sub-batch long updates of many rows in to smaller set of sub-rows. You can also indicate in an operation that one of the columns to be updated needs to use the key returned by an indexed previous operation. We will present now some sample code showing how these ideas work.

Listing 27-35 shows an example of creating a list object to hold a list of operations.

Listing 27-35. A Container for Content Provider Operations

```
ArrayList<ContentProviderOperation> ops =  new ArrayList<ContentProviderOperation>();
```

Let us see now how to construct the individual operations to be added to that list in Listing 27-36.

Listing 27-36. Batching ContentProviderOperations

```
ContentProviderOperation.Builder op = ContentProviderOperation.newInsert(a content URI);
op.withValue(key, value);
//...more of these
ContentProviderOperation op1 = op.build();
ops.add(op1);
```

The key class is `ContentProviderOperation` and its corresponding Builder object. In the example here we are using the insert operation. For the rest of the methods see the class reference. Once we have a builder along with its associated content URI, we tell the builder to add set of key/value pairs that go along with that content URI. Once finished adding all the key/value pairs we produce the ContentProviderOperation from the builder and add it to the list. We then ask the content resolver to apply the batch of operations using the code in Listing 27-37.

Listing 27-37. Using a Content Resolved to Apply the Batch of Operations

```
activity.getContentResolver().applyBatch(contentProviderAuthority, ops);
```

In Listing 27-37 the argument contentProviderAuthority is the authority string pointing the content provider and the argument ops is the list of operations that should be applied as a batch to that content provider. This is an example of adding a series of update operations as a single transaction. Let us see now how to provide commit hints to so that commit operations can be done on smaller subsets from the given batch.

Batching Commits by Yielding

One problem with committing a large batch of commands as a single transaction is that this work can block other operations on the database. To help with this and also to help with too much work to be committed in a single transaction you can instruct an operation to yield. When the content provider recognizes the yield parameter on an operation it commits the work done and pauses to yield for other processes to run.

Notice how in the code in Listing 27-38 one of the operations is set to allow yield.

Listing 27-38. Using Yield in a ContentProviderOperation

```
ContentProviderOperation.Builder operationBuilder =
      ContentProviderOperation.newInsert(a content URI);
operationBuilder.withValue(key, value);
//...more of these key/value pairs when you have them
ContentProviderOperation op1 = operationBuilder.build();

//... Add More operations

//Mark the next operation as yield allowed
operationBuilder = ContentProviderOperation.newInsert(a content URI);
operationBuilder.withValue(key, value);
operationBuilder.withYieldAllowed(true); //it is ok to commit
ContentProviderOperation operationWithYield = operationBuilder.build();
ops.add(operationWithYield);

//... Add More operations and yield points as needed

//Finally apply the list of operations
activity.getContentResolver().apply(contentProviderAuthority, ops);
```

Using Back References

For one of the operations above you can use a back reference as shown in Listing 27-39.

Listing 27-39. Using a Back Reference in a ContentProviderOperation

```
//Take the key coming out of op1 and add it as the value
int indexOfTheOperationWhoseKeyYouNeed = 0;
op.withValueBackReference(mykey, indexOfTheOperationWhoseKeyYouNeed);
```

Code in Listing 27-39 is asking the content provider to run the operation indicated by list index indexOfTheOperationWhoseKeyYouNeed and take its generated primary key and use it as a value for the column that is set on the target operation. This is how you take the insert from raw contact and use its primary key as the key value for the data items belonging to that raw contact.

Optimistic Locking

In optimistic locking, you first apply the transactions without locking the underlying repository and see if any updates have been made since you know its value before. If so, cancel the transaction and retry it.

To make this in the batch mode, the API offers a type of operation called an assert query. In this type of operation the content provider makes the query and compares the values of the retrieved cursor for either the count or the values of certain keys. If they don't match, it rolls back the transaction and raises an exception breaking the code flow. See this demonstrated in the code shown in Listing 27-40.

Listing 27-40. Using Optimistic Locking through newAssertQuery

```
try {
  //Read a raw contact for a particular raw contact id
  ContentProviderOperation.Builder assertOpBuilder =
            ContentProviderOperation.newAssertQuery(rawContactUri);
  //Make sure there is only one raw contact with that details
  assertOpBuilder.withExpectedCount(1);
  //Make sure the version column matches with you started with
  //If not throw an exception. We chose to compare the version number
  //column (field) in the raw contacts table to assert.
  assertOpBuilder.withValue(SyncColumns.VERSION, mVersion);
  //get this operation and add it to the operations list at the end
  //Apply the batch ...
  activityInstance.getContentResolver().applyBatch(...);
}
//for this or other exceptions
catch (OperationApplicationException e) {
  //The batch is already cancelled
  //Tell the user the update failed
  //Show the user the new details and repeat the process
}
```

Reusing the Contact Provider UI

Contact provider capability in Android also defines a set of intents that can be used to reuse the UI available in the contacts application.

There are three kinds of intents. There is a set of intents that the contact provider fires based on the events taking place in the content provider UI application. For example, the intent INVITE_CONTACT is fired when the user clicks the "invite to the network" button on a contact in the contact application. An application can register for this event and read the contact details.

There is another set of intents that are used when the contact provider acts as a search provider for your custom activities. Using this facility you can search for a contact in your custom application through search suggestions.

There is another set of intents that external applications can fire to reuse the UI that is provided by the contact application. You can use these intents to pick from a list of contacts, or from a list of phone numbers, or from a list of addresses, or from a list of e-mails. You can also use these intents to update a contact or create a contact using the UI provided the Android application.

These intents are documented in the class reference for `ContactsContract.Intents`.

Using Group Features

Contacts API provides the contracts shown in Listing 27-41 to work with the Group Features of contacts

***Listing 27-41.** Group Contact Contracts*

```
ContactsContract.Groups
ContactsContract.CommonDataKinds.GroupMembership
```

The groups table holds things like name of the group, notes about that group, and some group level counts of the membership. The groups a raw contact belongs to are kept in the data tables.

Using Photo Features

You can explore the photo-related information for a contact using the class contract shown in Listing 27-42.

***Listing 27-42.** Contact Photo Contracts*

```
ContactsContract.Contacts.Photo
ContactsContract.RawContacts.DisplayPhoto
```

The class documentation for these contracts has sample code that describes how to use these features.

References

Here are additional resources for the topics covered in this chapter:

- `https://developer.android.com/guide/topics/providers/contacts-provider.html`: The primary documentation for all aspects of the Contacts API from Google. This URL also includes a section on performing batch operations on the contacts database, optimistic locking, and reusing the contacts application UI.
- `http://developer.android.com/reference/android/provider/ContactsContract.html`: Java doc for the key Java class `ContactsContract`. You will need this URL often as you code to the Contacts API.
- `https://play.google.com/store/books/details/Google_Android_Quick_Start_Guide_Android_5_0_Lolli?id=dnzVBAAAQBAJ`: Android 5.0 Quick Start guide. These Android user guides that are prepared for each release are useful in understanding how the stock contacts application work from a UI perspective.
- `https://developer.android.com/guide/topics/providers/contacts-provider.html#SyncAdapters`: Sync Adapters are documented here.
- `http://developer.android.com/sdk/android-4.0.html#Contacts`: Documentation for the changes to the Contacts API in 4.0.
- `http://developer.android.com/reference/android/provider/ContactsContract.Profile.html`: A reference on how to use the new Profile URIs introduced in 4.0.
- `http://www.androidbook.com/item/3917`: Entry point for our research on the Contacts API. You will find here our research, a summary of the Contacts API, tables used in the contacts database, how to explore the contacts databases, contacts application screenshots, how to explore sources for contact providers, and other useful links.
- `http://developer.android.com/guide/topics/search/index.html`: SDK docs on Search API. Useful to review this to know how to search for contacts.
- `http://www.androidbook.com/proandroid5/projects`: You can use this URL to download the test project dedicated for this chapter. The name of the ZIP file is `ProAndroid5_ch27_TestContacts.zip`.

Summary

In this chapter, we have covered the following: the nature of the Contacts API, exploring the contacts database, exploring the Contacts API URIs and their cursors, reading and adding contacts, aggregating raw contacts, the relationship between the personal profile and contacts, and reading and adding contacts to a personal profile. We have also briefly covered batching provider operations, using the contact provider as a search provider for contacts.

Chapter 28

Exploring Security and Permissions

No exploration of modern development platforms or operating systems is complete without discussing security. In Android, security spans all phases of the application life cycle—from design-time policy considerations to runtime boundary checks. In this chapter you'll learn Android's security architecture and understand how to design secure applications.

Let's get started with the Android security model.

Understanding the Android Security Model

Let's dive right in, to cover security during the deployment and execution of any Android application. To deploy an Android application, it must be signed with a digital certificate in order for you to install it onto a device. With respect to execution, Android runs each application within a separate process, where each process has a unique and permanent user ID (assigned at install time). This places a boundary around the process and prevents one application from having direct access to another's data. Moreover, Android defines a declarative permission model that protects sensitive features (such as the contact list).

In the next several sections, we are going to discuss these topics. But before we get started, let's provide an overview of some of the security concepts that we'll refer to later.

Overview of Security Concepts

Android requires that applications be signed with a digital certificate. One of the benefits of this requirement is that an application cannot be updated with a version that was not published by the original author or holder of the signing certificate. If we publish an application, for example, then you cannot update our application with your version (unless, of course, you somehow obtain our certificate). That said, what does it mean for an application to be signed? And what is the process of signing an application?

You sign an application with a digital certificate. A *digital certificate* is an artifact that contains information about you, such as your company name, address, and so on. A few important attributes of a digital certificate include its signature and public/private key. A public/private key is also called a *key pair*. Note that although you use digital certificates here to sign `.apk` files, you can also use them for other purposes (such as encrypted communication, signing documents, and so forth). You can obtain a digital certificate from a trusted certificate authority (CA) and you can also generate one yourself using tools such as the `keytool`, which we'll discuss shortly. Digital certificates are stored in keystores. A *keystore* contains a list of digital certificates, each of which has an alias that you can use to refer to it in the keystore.

Signing an Android application requires three things: a digital certificate, the `.apk` file for the application you wish to sign, and a utility that knows how to apply a digital signature to the `.apk` file. We use a free utility that is part of the Java Development Kit (JDK) distribution called the `jarsigner`. This utility is a command-line tool that knows how to sign a `.jar` file using a digital certificate, and an .apk file is really just a zip-formatted file that collects together .jar files and a few other resources for your project. Other signing tools are available, so you are free to choose the tool that works best for you.

Now, let's move on and talk about how you can sign an `.apk` file with a digital certificate.

Signing Applications for Deployment

To install an Android application onto a device, you first need to sign the Android package (`.apk` file) using a digital certificate. The certificate, however, can be self-signed—you do not need to purchase a certificate from a certificate authority such as VeriSign. Be aware that self-signed certificates are generally considered less trustworthy, and in some environments are considered insecure.

Signing your application for deployment involves three steps. The first step is to generate a certificate using `keytool` (or a similar tool). The second step involves using the `jarsigner` tool to sign the `.apk` file with the generated certificate. The third step aligns portions of your application on memory boundaries for more efficient memory usage when running on a device. Note that during development, both the ADT plug-in for Eclipse and Android Developer Studio take care of everything for you: signing your `.apk` file and doing the memory alignment, before deploying onto the emulator or a device.

Generating a Self-Signed Certificate Using the Keytool

The `keytool` utility manages a database of private keys and their corresponding X.509 certificates (a standard for digital certificates). This utility ships with the JDK and resides under the JDK `bin` directory. If you followed the instructions in Chapter 2 regarding changing your `PATH`, the JDK `bin` directory should already be in your `PATH`. In this section, we'll show you how to generate a keystore with a single entry, which you'll later use to sign an Android `.apk` file. To generate a keystore entry, do the following:

1. Create a folder to hold the keystore, such as `c:\android\release\.` or `/opt/android/release` (depending on your operating system).

2. Open a shell or command window, and execute the `keytool` utility with the parameters shown in Listing 28-1.

Listing 28-1. Generating a Keystore Entry Using the keytool Utility

```
keytool -genkey -v -keystore "c:\android\release\release.keystore"
-alias androidbook -keyalg RSA
-validity 14000
```

All of the arguments passed to the keytool are summarized in Table 28-1.

Table 28-1. Arguments Passed to the keytool Utility

Argument	Description
genkey	Tells keytool to generate a public/private key pair.
v	Tells keytool to emit verbose output during key generation.
keystore	Path to the keystore database (in this case, a file). The file will be created if necessary.
alias	Unique name for the keystore entry. This alias is used later to refer to the keystore entry.
keyalg	Algorithm.
validity	Validity period.

keytool will prompt you for two passwords during the creation of the keystore and the entry you are creating. The first password prompted is for the keystore itself and controls access to all the key material you will store. This can also be specified using the storepass parameter. The second password is the password for the private key and related certificate you are creating, also available via the keypass parameter. You should get used to *not* including these as parameters on the command line, and instead prefer to allow keytool to prompt you as good general security practice.

Be aware, that if you do use the parameters for password to keytool, anyone who gets access to your shell or command-line history can see the passwords, as can anyone who can list the running processes on your machine while keytool runs. The command in Listing 28-1 will generate a keystore database file in your keystore folder. The database will be a file named release.keystore. The validity of the entry will be 14,000 days (or approximately 38 years)—which is a long time from now. You should understand the reason for this. The Android documentation recommends that you specify a validity period long enough to surpass the entire lifespan of the application, which will include many updates to the application. It recommends that the validity be at least 25 years. If you plan to publish the application on Google Play, your certificate will need to be valid through at least October 22, 2033. Google Play checks each application when uploaded to make sure it will be valid at least until then.

> **Caution** Because your certificate in any application update must match the certificate you used the first time, make sure you safeguard your key material. Keep either your keystore file, or the key pair if you choose to export them, safe! If you lose access to the keystore or underlying keys, and you can't re-create it, you won't be able to update your application, and you'll have to issue a whole new application instead.

Going back to the keytool, the argument alias is a unique name given to the entry in the keystore database; you will use this name later to refer to the entry. When you run the keytool command in Listing 28-1, keytool will ask you a few questions (see Figure 28-1) and then generate the keystore database and entry.

```
sh-4.3$ keytool -genkey -v -keystore "/opt/android/release/release.keystore" -alias androidbook
-keyalg RSA -validity 14000
Enter keystore password:
Re-enter new password:
What is your first and last name?
  [Unknown]:  Grant Allen
What is the name of your organizational unit?
  [Unknown]:  Authors
What is the name of your organization?
  [Unknown]:  Apress
What is the name of your City or Locality?
  [Unknown]:  New York
What is the name of your State or Province?
  [Unknown]:  NY
What is the two-letter country code for this unit?
  [Unknown]:  US
Is CN=Grant Allen, OU=Authors, O=Apress, L=New York, ST=NY, C=US correct?
  [no]:  yes

Generating 2,048 bit RSA key pair and self-signed certificate (SHA256withRSA) with a validity of
 14,000 days
        for: CN=Grant Allen, OU=Authors, O=Apress, L=New York, ST=NY, C=US
Enter key password for <androidbook>
        (RETURN if same as keystore password):
Re-enter new password:
[Storing /opt/android/release/release.keystore]
sh-4.3$
```

Figure 28-1. Additional questions asked by keytool

Once you have a keystore file for your production certificates, you can reuse this file to add more certificates. Just use keytool again, and specify your existing keystore file.

The Debug Keystore and the Development Certificate

We mentioned that the ADT plug-in for Eclipse, and Android Developer Studio, both take care of setting up a development keystore for you. However, the default certificate used for signing during development cannot be used for production deployment onto a real device. This is partly because the automatically generated development certificate is only valid for 365 days, which clearly does not get you past October 22, 2033. So what happens on the three hundred sixty-sixth day of development? You'll get a build error. Your existing applications should still run, but to build a new version of an application, you need to generate a new certificate. The easiest way to do this is to delete the existing debug.keystore file, and as soon as it is needed again, the ADT (for instance) will generate a new file and certificate valid for another 365 days.

To find your debug.keystore file, assuming you are using Eclipse with ADT, open the Preferences screen of Eclipse and go to Android ➤ Build. The debug certificate's location will be displayed in the Default Debug Keystore field, as shown in Figure 28-2 (see Chapter 2 if you have trouble finding the Preferences menu).

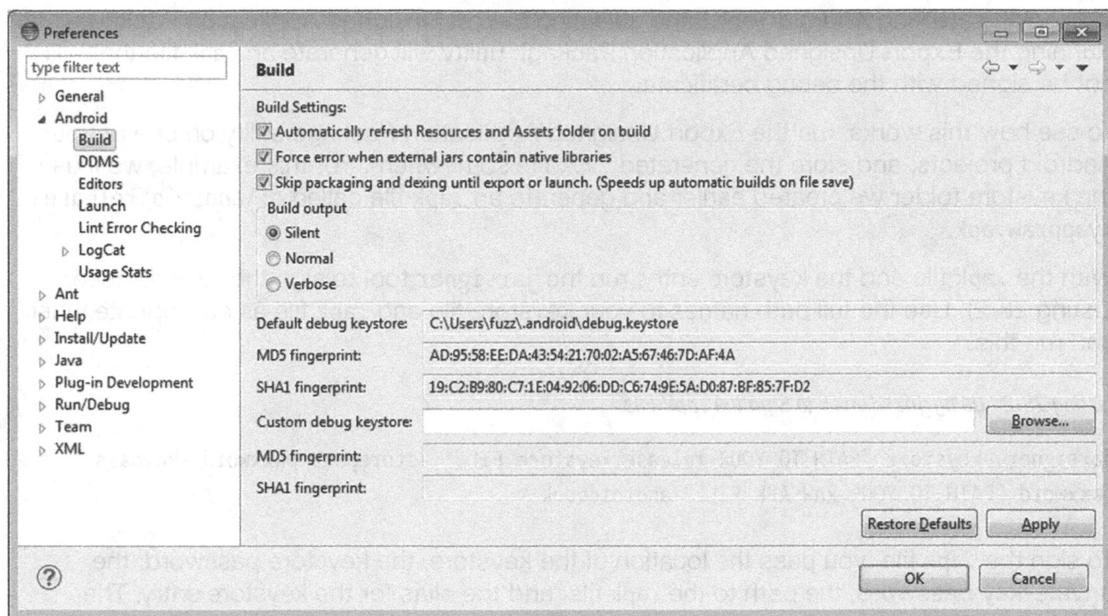

***Figure 28-2.** The debug certificate's location*

Of course, now that you've got a new development certificate, you cannot update your existing applications in Android Virtual Devices (AVDs) or on devices using a new development certificate. Eclipse will provide messages in the Console telling you to uninstall the existing application first using adb, which you can certainly do. If you have a lot of your applications installed onto an AVD, you may feel it is easier to simply re-create the AVD, so it does not contain any of your applications and you can start fresh. To avoid this problem a year from now, you could generate your own debug.keystore file with whatever validity period you desire. Obviously, it needs to have the same file name and be in the same directory as the file that ADT would create. The certificate alias is androiddebugkey, and the storepass and keypass are both "android". ADT sets the first and last name on the certificate as "Android Debug", the organizational unit as "Android", and the two-letter country code as "US". You can leave the organization, city, and state values as "Unknown".

If you acquired a map-api key from Google using the old debug certificate, you will need to get a new map-api key to match the new debug certificate. We covered map-api keys in Chapter 19.

Now that you have a digital certificate that you can use to sign your production .apk file, you need to use the jarsigner tool to do the signing. Here's how to do that.

Using the Jarsigner Tool to Sign the .apk File

The keytool utility described in the previous section created a digital certificate, which is one of the parameters for the jarsigner tool. The other parameter for jarsigner is the actual Android package to be signed. To generate an Android package, you need to use the Export Unsigned Application Package utility in the ADT plug-in for Eclipse (or equivalent function in Android Developer Studio). You access the utility by right-clicking an Android project in Eclipse, selecting Android Tools, and selecting Export Unsigned Application Package. Running the Export Unsigned Application Package utility will generate an .apk file that will not be signed with the debug certificate.

To see how this works, run the Export Unsigned Application Package utility on one of your Android projects, and store the generated .apk file somewhere. For this example, we'll use the keystore folder we created earlier and generate an .apk file called c:\android\release\myappraw.apk.

With the .apk file and the keystore entry, run the jarsigner tool to sign the .apk file (see Listing 28-2). Use the full path names to your keystore file and .apk file as appropriate when you run this.

Listing 28-2. *Using* `jarsigner` *to Sign the* `.apk` *File*

```
jarsigner -keystore "PATH TO YOUR release.keystore FILE" -storepass paxxword -keypass
paxxword "PATH TO YOUR RAW APK FILE" androidbook
```

To sign the .apk file, you pass the location of the keystore, the keystore password, the private-key password, the path to the .apk file, and the alias for the keystore entry. The jarsigner will then sign the .apk file with the digital certificate from the keystore entry. To run the jarsigner tool, you will need to either open a tools window (as explained in Chapter 2) or open a command or Terminal window and either navigate to the JDK bin directory or ensure that your JDK bin directory is on the system path. For security reasons, it is safer to leave off the password arguments to the command and simply let jarsigner prompt you as necessary for passwords. Figure 28-3 shows what the jarsigner tool invocation looks like. You may have noticed that jarsigner prompted for only one password in Figure 28-3. Jarsigner figures out not to ask for the keypass password when the storepass and keypass are the same. Strictly speaking, the jarsigner command in Listing 28-2 only needs -keypass if it has a different password than -storepass.

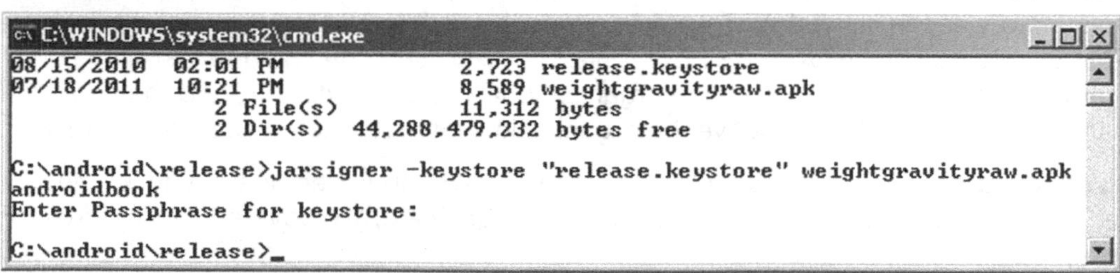

Figure 28-3. *Using* `jarsigner`

As we pointed out earlier, Android requires that an application be signed with a digital signature to prevent a malicious programmer from updating your application with their version. For this to work, Android requires that updates to an application be signed with the same signature as the original. If you sign the application with a different signature, Android treats them as two different applications. So we remind you again, be careful with your keystore file so it's available to you later when you need to provide an update to your application.

Aligning Your Application with zipalign

You want your application to be as memory efficient as possible when running on a device. If your application contains uncompressed data (perhaps certain image types or data files) at runtime, Android can map this data straight into memory using the `mmap()` call. For this to work, though, the data must be aligned on a 4-byte memory boundary. The CPUs in Android devices are 32-bit processors, and 32 bits equals 4 bytes. The `mmap()` call makes the data in your `.apk` file look like memory, but if the data is not aligned on a 4-byte boundary, it can't do that and extra copying of data must occur at runtime. The `zipalign` tool, found in the Android SDK `build` or `build-tools/<version>` directory, looks through your application and moves slightly any uncompressed data not already on a 4-byte memory boundary to a 4-byte memory boundary. You may see the file size of your application increase slightly but not significantly. To perform an alignment on your `.apk` file, use this command in a tools window (see also Figure 28-4):

```
zipalign -v 4 infile.apk outfile.apk
```

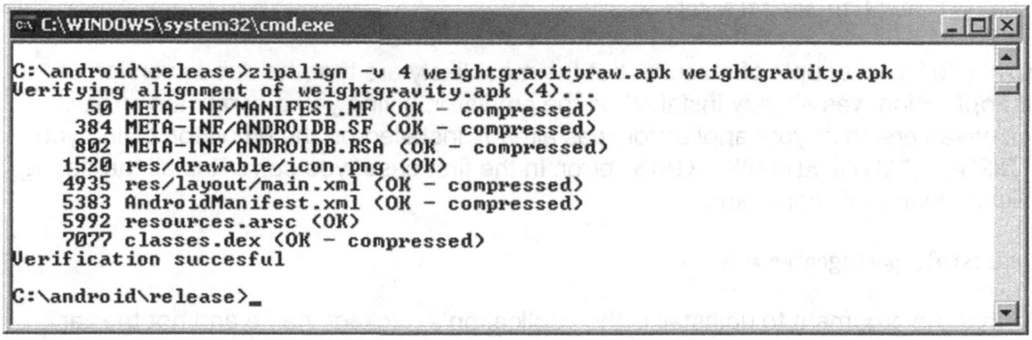

```
C:\WINDOWS\system32\cmd.exe
C:\android\release>zipalign -v 4 weightgravityraw.apk weightgravity.apk
Verifying alignment of weightgravity.apk (4)...
      50 META-INF/MANIFEST.MF (OK - compressed)
     384 META-INF/ANDROIDB.SF (OK - compressed)
     802 META-INF/ANDROIDB.RSA (OK - compressed)
    1520 res/drawable/icon.png (OK)
    4935 res/layout/main.xml (OK - compressed)
    5383 AndroidManifest.xml (OK - compressed)
    5992 resources.arsc (OK)
    7077 classes.dex (OK - compressed)
Verification succesful

C:\android\release>_
```

***Figure 28-4.** Using `zipalign`*

Note that `zipalign` does not modify the input file, so this is why we chose to use "raw" as part of our file name when exporting from Eclipse. Now, our output file has an appropriate name for deployment. If you need to overwrite an existing `outfile.apk` file, you can use the `-f` option. Also note that `zipalign` performs a verification of the alignment when you create your aligned file. To verify that an existing file is properly aligned, use `zipalign` in the following way:

```
zipalign -c -v 4 filename.apk
```

It is very important that you align *after* signing; otherwise, signing could cause things to go back out of alignment. This does not mean your application would crash, but it could use more memory than it needs to.

Using the Export Wizard

In Eclipse, you may have noticed a menu choice under Android Tools called Export Signed Application Package. This launches what is called the *export wizard*, and it does all of the previous steps for you, prompting only for the path to your keystore file, key alias, the passwords, and the name of your output .apk file. It will even create a new keystore or new key if you need one. You may find it easier to use the wizard, or you may prefer to script the steps yourself to operate on an exported unsigned application package. Now that you know how each works, you can decide which is better for you.

Manually Installing Apps

Once you have signed and aligned an `.apk` file, you can install it onto the virtual device manually using the `adb` tool. As an exercise, start the virtual device from the AVD Manager, which will start without copying over any of your development projects from Eclipse. Now, open a tools window and run the `adb` tool with the `install` command:

```
adb install "PATH TO APK FILE GOES HERE"
```

This may fail for a couple of reasons, but the most likely are that the debug version of your application was already installed on the emulator, giving you a certificate error, or the release version of your application was already installed on the emulator, giving you an `"INSTALL_FAILED_ALREADY_EXISTS"` error. In the first case, you can uninstall the debug application with this command:

```
adb uninstall packagename
```

Note that the argument to uninstall is the application's package name and not the `.apk` file name. The package name is defined in the `AndroidManifest.xml` file of the installed application.

For the second case, you can use this command, where `-r` says to reinstall the application while keeping its data on the device (or emulator):

```
adb install -r "PATH TO APK FILE GOES HERE"
```

Now, let's see how signing affects the process of updating an application.

Installing Updates to an Application and Signing

Earlier, we mentioned that a certificate has an expiration date and that Google recommends you set expiration dates far into the future, to account for a lot of application updates. That said, what happens if the certificate does expire? Would Android still run the application? Fortunately, yes—Android tests the certificate's expiration only at install time. Once your application is installed, it will continue to run even if the certificate expires.

But what about updates? Unfortunately, you will not be able to update the application once the certificate expires. In other words, as Google suggests, you need to make sure the life of the certificate is long enough to support the entire life of the application. If a certificate does expire, Android will not install an update to the application. The only choice left will be for you to create another application—an application with a different package name—and sign it with a new certificate. So as you can see, it is critical for you to consider the expiration date of the certificate when you generate it.

Now that you understand security with respect to deployment and installation, let's move on to runtime security in Android.

Performing Runtime Security Checks

Runtime security in Android happens at the process and operation levels. At the process level, Android prevents one application from directly accessing another application's data. It does this by running each application within a different process and under a unique and permanent user ID. At the operational level, Android defines a list of protected features and resources. For your application to access this information, you have to add one or more permission requests to your `AndroidManifest.xml` file. You can also define custom permissions with your application.

In the sections that follow, we will talk about process-boundary security and how to declare and use predefined permissions. We will also discuss creating custom permissions and enforcing them within your application. Let's start by dissecting Android security at the process boundary.

Understanding Security at the Process Boundary

Unlike your desktop environment, where most of the applications run under the same user ID, each Android application generally runs under its own unique ID. By running each application under a different ID, Android creates an isolation boundary around each process. This prevents one application from directly accessing another application's data.

Although each process has a boundary around it, data sharing between applications is obviously possible but has to be explicit. In other words, to get data from another application, you have to go through the components of that application. For example, you can query a content provider of another application, you can invoke an activity in another application, or—as you'll see in Chapter 15—you can communicate with a service of another application. All of these facilities provide methods for you to share information between applications, but they do so in an explicit manner because you don't directly access the underlying database, files, and so on.

Android's security at the process boundary is clear and simple. Things get interesting when we start talking about protecting resources (such as contact data), features (such as the device's camera), and our own components. To provide this protection, Android defines a permission scheme. Let's dissect that now.

Declaring and Using Permissions

Android defines a permission scheme meant to protect resources and features on the device. For example, applications, by default, cannot access the contacts list, make phone calls, and so on. To protect the user from malicious applications, Android requires applications to request permissions if they need to use a protected feature or resource. From the introduction of Android Kit Kat, and continuing in Android Lollipop, permissions when presented to the end user are now clustered into groups to address their constantly growing number and complexity. This grouping brings with it some compromises as you will observe.

As we will cover shortly, permission requests go in the manifest file. At install time, the APK installer either grants or denies the requested permissions based on the signature of the `.apk` file and/or feedback from the user. If permission is not granted, any attempt to execute or access the associated feature will result in a permission failure.

Table 28-2 shows some commonly used features and the permissions they require. Although you are not yet familiar with all the features listed, you will learn about them later (either in this chapter or in subsequent chapters).

Table 28-2. *Features and Resources and the Permissions They Require*

Feature/Resource	Required Permission	Description
Camera	`android.permission.CAMERA`	Enables you to access the device's camera.
Internet	`android.permission.INTERNET`	Enables you to make a network connection.
User's contact data	`android.permission.READ_CONTACTS` `android.permission.WRITE_CONTACTS`	Enables you to read from or write to the user's contact data.
User's calendar data	`android.permission.READ_CALENDAR` `android.permission.WRITE_CALENDAR`	Enables you to read from or write to the user's calendar data.
Recording audio	`android.permission.RECORD_AUDIO`	Enables you to record audio.
Wi-Fi location information	`android.permission.ACCESS_COARSE_LOCATION`	Enables you to access coarse-grained location information from Wi-Fi and cell towers.
GPS location information	`android.permission.ACCESS_FINE_LOCATION`	Enables you to access fine-grained location information. This includes GPS location information. It is also sufficient for Wi-Fi and cell towers.
Battery information	`android.permission.BATTERY_STATS`	Enables you to obtain battery-state information.
Bluetooth	`android.permission.BLUETOOTH`	Enables you to connect to paired Bluetooth devices.

For a complete list of permissions, see the following URL:

http://developer.android.com/reference/android/Manifest.permission.html

Application developers can request permissions by adding entries to the AndroidManifest.xml file. For example, Listing 28-3 asks to access the camera on the device, to read the list of contacts, and to read the calendar.

Listing 28-3. Permissions in `AndroidManifest.xml`

```
<manifest ... >
    <application>
        ...
    </application>
    <uses-permission android:name="android.permission.CAMERA" />
    <uses-permission android:name="android.permission.READ_CONTACTS"/>
    <uses-permission android:name="android.permission.READ_CALENDAR" />
</manifest>
```

Note that you can either hard-code permissions in the AndroidManifest.xml file or use the manifest editor. The manifest editor is wired up to launch when you open (double-click) the manifest file. The manifest editor contains a drop-down list that has all of the permissions preloaded to prevent you from making a mistake. As shown in Figure 28-5, you can access the permissions list by selecting the Permissions tab in the manifest editor.

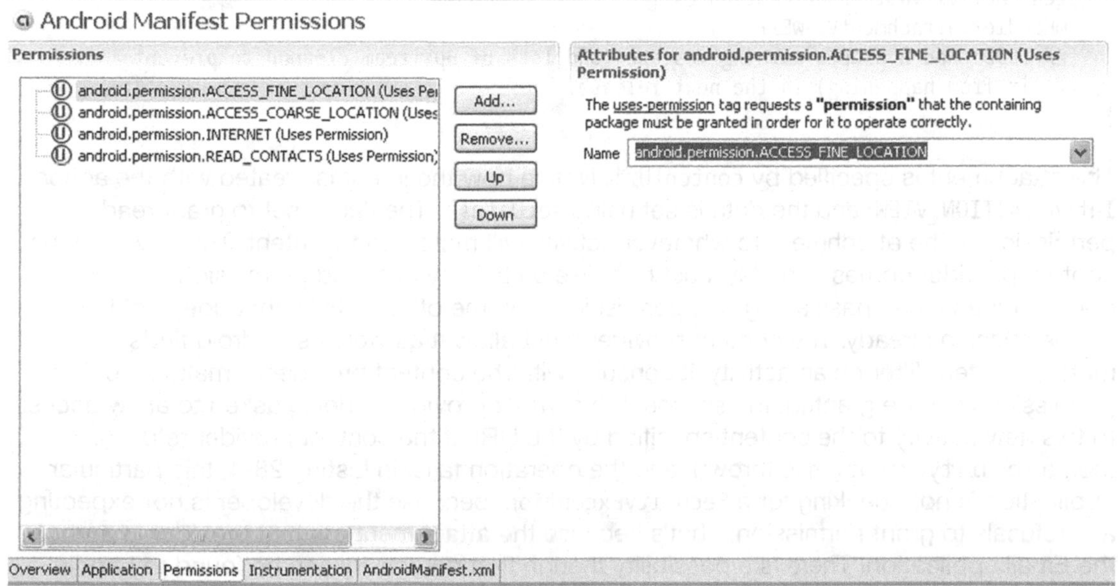

Figure 28-5. ***The Android manifest editor tool in Eclipse***

You now know that Android defines a set of permissions that protects a set of features and resources. Similarly, you can define and enforce custom permissions with your application. Let's see how that works.

Understanding and Using URI Permissions

Content providers (discussed in Chapter 4) often need to control access at a finer level than all or nothing. Fortunately, Android provides a mechanism for this. Think about e-mail attachments. The attachment may need to be read by another activity to display it. But the other activity should not get access to all of the e-mail data and does not need access even to all attachments. This is where URI permissions come in.

Passing URI Permissions in Intents

When invoking another activity and passing a URI, your application can specify that it is granting permissions to the URI being passed. But before your application can do this, it needs permission itself to the URI, and the URI content provider must cooperate and allow the granting of permissions to another activity. The code to invoke an activity with granting of permissions looks like Listing 28-4, which is actually from the Android Email program, where it is launching an activity to view an e-mail attachment.

Listing 28-4. Code to Launch an Activity with Granting of Permission

```
try {
    Intent intent = new Intent(Intent.ACTION_VIEW);
    intent.setData(contentUri);
    intent.addFlags(Intent.FLAG_GRANT_READ_URI_PERMISSION);
    startActivity(intent);
} catch (ActivityNotFoundException e) {
    mHandler.attachmentViewError();
    // TODO: Add a proper warning message (and lots of upstream cleanup to prevent
    // it from happening) in the next release.
}
```

The attachment is specified by `contentUri`. Notice how the intent is created with the action `Intent.ACTION_VIEW`, and the data is set using `setData()`. The flag is set to grant read permission of the attachment to whatever activity will match on the intent. This is where the content provider comes into play. Just because an activity has read permission to content doesn't mean it can pass along that permission to some other activity that does not have the permission already. The content provider must allow it as well. As Android finds a matching intent filter on an activity, it consults with the content provider to make sure that permissions can be granted. In essence, the content provider is being asked to allow access to this new activity to the content specified by the URI. If the content provider refuses, then a `SecurityException` is thrown, and the operation fails. In Listing 28-4, this particular application is not checking for a `SecurityException`, because the developer is not expecting any refusals to grant permission. That's because the attachment content provider is part of the Email application! There is a possibility though that no activity can be found to handle the attachment, so that is the only exception being watched for.

In the case where the activity being called to process the URI already has permission to access that URI, the content provider does not get to deny access. That is, the calling activity can grant permission, and if the activity on the receiving end of the intent already has the necessary permissions for `contentURI`, the called activity will be allowed to proceed with no problems.

In addition to Intent.FLAG_GRANT_READ_URI_PERMISSION, there is a flag for write permissions: Intent.FLAG_GRANT_WRITE_URI_PERMISSION. It is possible to specify both in an Intent. Also, these flags can apply to services and BroadcastReceivers as well as activities because they can receive intents too.

Specifying URI Permissions in Content Providers

So how does a content provider specify URI permissions? It does so in the AndroidManifest.xml file in one of two ways:

- In the <provider> tag, the android:grantUriPermissions attribute can be set to either true or false. If true, any content from this content provider can be granted. If false, the second way of specifying URI permissions can happen, or the content provider can decide not to let anyone else grant permissions.
- Specify permissions with child tags of <provider>. The child tag is <grant-uri-permission>, and you can have more than one within <provider>. <grant-uri-permission> has three possible attributes:
    - Using the android:path attribute, you can specify a complete path which will then have permissions that are grantable.
    - Similarly, android:pathPrefix specifies the beginning of a URI path.
    - android:pathPattern allows wildcards (the asterisk, *, character) to specify a path.

As we stated before, the granting entity must also have appropriate permissions to the content before being allowed to grant them to some other entity. Content providers have additional ways of controlling access to their content, through the android:readPermission attribute of the <provider> tag, the android:writePermission attribute, and the android:permission attribute (a convenient way to specify both read and write permissions with one permission String value). The value for any of these three attributes is a String that represents the permission a caller must have in order to read or write with this content provider. Before an activity could grant read permission to a content URI, that activity must have read permission first, as specified by either the android:readPermission attribute or the android:permission attribute. The entity wanting these permissions would declare them in their manifest file with the <uses-permissions> tag.

References

Here are some helpful references to topics you may wish to explore further:

- http://developer.android.com/guide/topics/security/security.html: The *Android Developer's Guide* section "Security Tips." It provides an overview with links to lots of reference pages.
- http://developer.android.com/guide/publishing/app-signing.html: The *Android Developer's Guide* section "Signing Your Applications."

Summary

This security chapter covered the following topics:

- Unique application user IDs that help separate apps from each other to protect processing and data
- Digital certificates and their use in signing Android applications
- That an application can only be updated if the update is signed with the same digital certificate as the original
- Managing certificates in a keystore using `keytool`
- Running `jarsigner` to apply a certificate to an application `.apk` file
- `zipalign` and memory boundaries
- The Eclipse plug-in wizard takes care of generating the apk, applying the certificate and `zipalign`-ing for you
- Manually installing apps onto devices and emulators
- Permissions that applications can declare and use
- URI permissions and how content providers use them

Chapter 29

Using Google Cloud Messaging with Android

As we approach the end of the book, you will have already developed a good understanding of, and appreciation for, the many communication protocols and architectural options you have available within Android when it comes to dealing with off-device services. In this chapter, we will explore Google's Cloud Messaging (or GCM) platform and how you can use it as the plumbing for your application's remote communication and service interaction needs.

What Is Google Cloud Messaging?

GCM is a service offered by Google to enable you to write multiple applications across different platforms that exchange messages in order to further their functionality. The primary examples of the multiple applications are an Android client application exchanging messages with a remote server application.

The actual messages sent, and their purpose, are up to you as a developer. It could be a message from the remote server letting your client application know (a "downstream" message) that a new update to a news feed, music service, or similar subscription is available. Messages from the client to the server (an "upstream" message) could be sending a chat message, picture thumbnail, or other new piece of data your user has captured or generated on the client. These are just examples—you are free to imagine any use, and any payload, for the messages exchanged in GCM.

Understanding the Key Building Blocks of GCM

Having read the introduction to GCM, you are already aware of two of the key components in any complete GCM configuration. The final part to complete the picture is the GCM server (in fact, servers) hosted by Google that perform the message queuing, forwarding, and so forth.

To recap, the three key building blocks for GCM are as follows:

- Client Application—An application you write, such as an Android application, that sends and/or receives messages from a remote server to help with functionality.
- GCM Connection Servers—Google's messaging infrastructure, which manages all messaging traffic, message queuing in the event of delivery delays, ultimate delivery guarantees, etc.
- Remote Application Server—An application your write as a server, hosted in an Internet-accessible fashion, responsible for sending and/or receiving messages from client applications.

We can also represent this architecture in visual form. Figure 29-1 shows the components and message flow in a complete GCM setup.

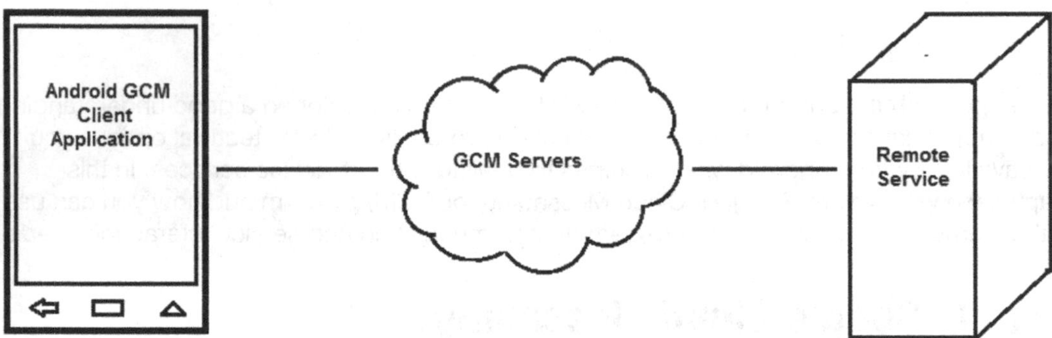

Figure 29-1. GCM architectural overview

Preparing to Use GCM in Your Application

Where previously we have jumped straight into Java code, layout XML, and so forth when constructing example applications, for GCM-based development we need to undertake a few preparatory steps in order to have Google's servers accept traffic from our client and server.

Creating or Confirming Your GCM Project in Google Developer Console

To use any of Google's online services and APIs, including GCM, you will need to create an API Project within the Google Developer Console, at cloud.google.com/console. You might already have a project you can reuse, but let's assume you are creating one for the first time. Navigate to the console URL and click the Create Project button. Follow the prompts for account and billing details, etc., and you should end up with a new project (or confirm an existing one) as shown in Figure 29-2.

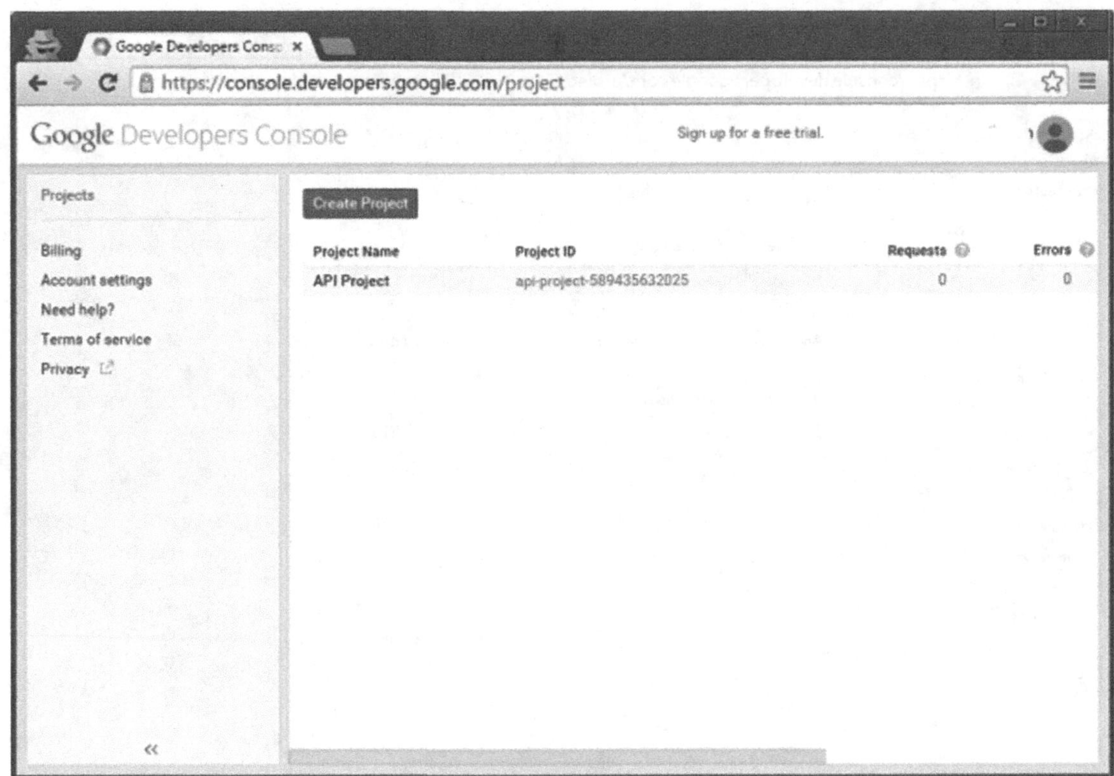

Figure 29-2. Your Google Developer Console with API Project in Place

Activating the GCM APIs for Your Project

With the API Project in place, you now need to activate the specific GCM APIs. Google supports dozens of separate APIs, all of which are disabled by default to ensure you do not accidentally trigger behavior or incur costs you were not expecting. Click on your API Project (in our case, api-project-589435632025) and under the APIs & Auth section on the left side, select APIs and scroll until you see Google Cloud Messaging for Android. Turn this on using the Enable API button. You will know you have successfully enabled the GCM API when the button changes from Enable API to Disable API, as shown in Figure 29-3.

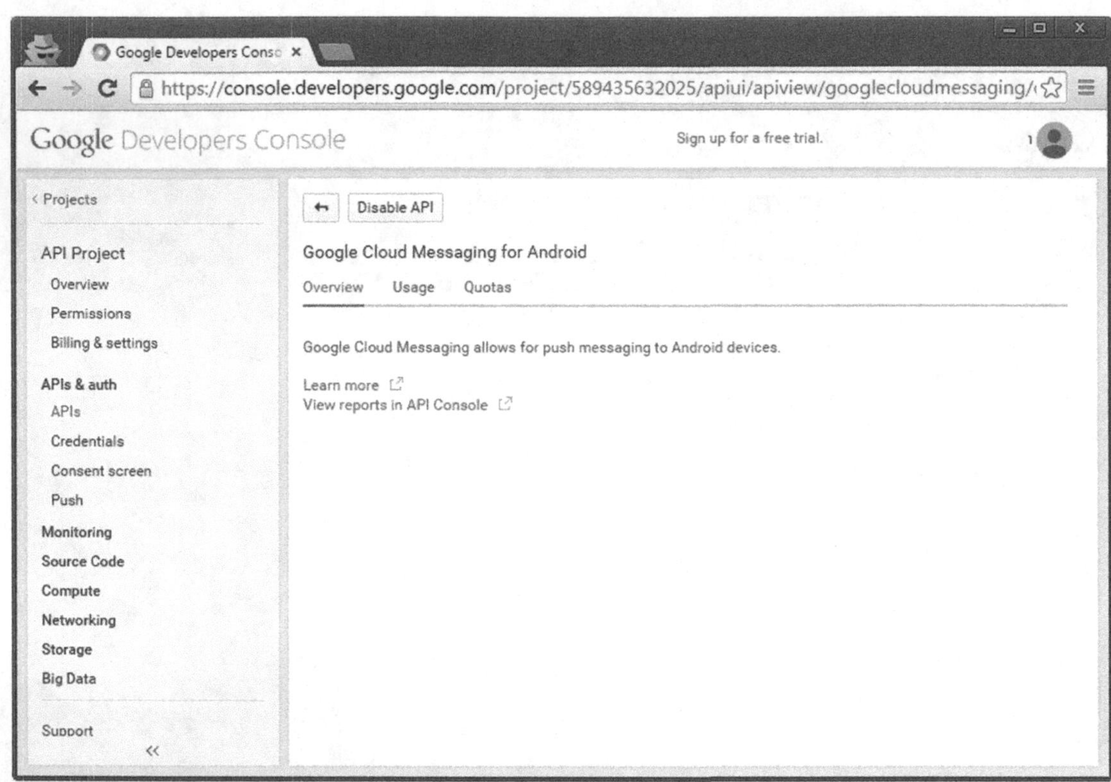

Figure 29-3. Your Google Developer Console API Project with GCM Enabled

Generating Your API Key

As with other Google APIs, access to the GCM API for your project requires your key. This helps ensure everything from traffic separation, so your GCM messages are not inadvertently mixed with those of other applications, through to billing, analytics, and so forth.

To generate your key, choose the Credentials option under APIs & Auth. Choose the Create New Key option, and when prompted for key properties, select Server for the key type. If you know the public IP address of your intended server, you can use that in the configuration section, otherwise you can use 0.0.0.0/0 for testing purposes. Then choose Create to have the key generated. When you are returned to the console, you should see your API key available under the Credentials submenu. Note down the key value as you will need it shortly.

Authenticating GCM Communication

The API key is not the only piece of identifying information used to authenticate and authorize message transfer within a GCM environment. You can find more detail on the uses of GCM tokens and keys on the `developer.google.com` website. In brief, the following four token types are used in your GCM applications:

- **Sender ID** The project ID code available from the Google developer console. Your server application will use this as part of the registration process with Google's GCM servers to enable it to send messages to the Android client application and your users.
- **Sender Auth Token** Your API key, used in every message sent to the GCM servers to demonstrate the authenticity of the message and its provenance from your server application.
- **Application ID** For your Android application, this is the fully qualified Java package name, for instance `com.androidbook.gcm`. Because this is unique across all Android applications, it allows the GCM ecosystem to know which applications receive which types of messages.
- **Registration ID** Allocated to your client Android application when it registers with the GCM servers for message delivery. The registration ID is sensitive information and should be stored securely and not disclosed.

All of these items in combination allow client and server applications to register with GCM and be identified by it, and also to uniquely identify the applications and their messages.

Building an Android GCM-Enabled Application

Building a meaningful GCM-based Android application and the supporting server-side third-party service is a large undertaking—so large that we could almost write a small book just on that topic. Below we will cover the main configuration and coding points you need to consider when building the application, and you can check the book website for a more in-depth discussion on GCM with full examples.

Coding the Client Component for GCM

The client Android application needs to consider three broad areas. First, have your development environment set up correctly. Second, configure the Android project to include the right dependencies and privileges. Lastly, write the GCM registration methods and message handling methods into your Java code for your activity (or activities).

Configure Project Dependencies for Your Project

Before we can write the actual Java code and any related XML layout for our desired GCM-based application, we need to configure our project to have the necessary APIs available and invoke your IDE's build tool (e.g., gradle) with the necessary dependencies to ensure a successful build.

Your development environment (Android Studio, Eclipse, etc.) will need to have the Google Play Services SDK installed. Double-check this with the SDK Manager from the IDE or command prompt.

Next, your project will need to be configured to work with the `GoogleCloudMessaging` API provided by the Google Play Services SDK. As an example, to add this to an Android Studio project, open your project's `build.gradle` file and ensure the API is included as a dependency, as shown in Listing 29-1.

***Listing 29-1.** build.gradle file Fragment Showing Play Services Dependency*

```
dependencies {
    // your other dependencies here
    compile "com.google.android.gms:play-services:3.1.+"
}
```

For Eclipse users, the equivalent task is to add `google-play-services.jar` as an external library dependency to your project, from your Google Play Services library collection. Lastly, any GCM application must run on Android 2.2 (with Play Store installed) or later. Update your manifest's `uses-sdk` element to set `android:minSdkVersion` to at least 8.

Setting Manifest Properties for GCM

Over and above the minimum SDK version required for GCM, your application will require specific permissions in order to do the following:

- Register with GCM servers to receive messages, using `com.google.android.c2dm.permission.RECEIVE` permission.
- Use the device's internet connection to send messages, using `android.permission.INTERNET` permission.
- Exclusively reserve messages intended for the application and prevent other applications registering for them. This uses the custom C2D_MESSAGE permission block with the application name prepended.
- GCM-specific permissions for the receiver you will also define, so that the GCM servers are allowed to send messages to your application. This uses the com.google.android.c2dm.permission.RECEIVE setting.

> **Note** The earlier incarnation of GCM was known as C2DM, or Cloud to Device Messaging. Thus the references to the earlier name of C2DM and C2D.

The receiver you define should declare its intent-filter to act on `com.google.android.c2dm.intent.RECEIVE` and use the `applicationPackage` name as its category.

It can often be better to peruse a snippet of an example AndroidManifest.xml file to see all of these settings in place. Listing 29-2 shows example settings from the four key permissions your GCM application will require.

Listing 29-2. Sample AndroidManifest.xml Entries for a GCM Android Application

```
<manifest xmlns:android="http://schemas.android.com/apk/res/android"
    package="com.androidbook.gcm">

    ...

    <uses-sdk android:minSdkVersion="8" android:targetSdkVersion="21"/>
    <uses-permission android:name="android.permission.INTERNET" />
    <uses-permission android:name="android.permission.GET_ACCOUNTS" />
    <uses-permission android:name="com.google.android.c2dm.permission.RECEIVE" />

    ...

    <permission android:name="com.androidbook.gcm.permission.C2D_MESSAGE"
        android:protectionLevel="signature" />
    <uses-permission android:name="com.androidbook.gcm.permission.C2D_MESSAGE" />

    ...

   <application ...>
        <receiver
            android:name=".GcmBroadcastReceiver"
            android:permission="com.google.android.c2dm.permission.SEND" >
            <intent-filter>
                <action android:name="com.google.android.c2dm.intent.RECEIVE" />
                <category android:name="com.androidbook.gcm" />
            </intent-filter>
        </receiver>
        <service android:name=".GcmIntentService" />
    </application>
...
</manifest>
```

Coding Your Main Activity to Register for GCM

Before your application can receive messages from GCM servers (and your server-side application that sends them), and before it can send messages of its own back through GCM, your application must register with the GCM servers. This is so the GCM infrastructure knows how to route your messages, prevent traffic mix-ups, and so on. Listing 29-3 shows an example activity fragment that initiates registration in the `onCreate()` override. This example code is modeled on the github example GCM project Google makes available at `developer.android.com`.

Listing 29-3. Registering with GCM from Java

```
package com.google.android.gcm.demo.app;

// imports from a default activity, and the GCM specific libraries

public class GCMExampleActivity extends Activity {
```

```
public static final String EXTRA_MESSAGE = "message";
public static final String PROPERTY_REG_ID = "registration_id";
private static final int PLAY_SERVICES_RESOLUTION_REQUEST = 9000;

String SENDER_ID = "a123b456c789d012"; // Remember to use your ID

TextView myMessageDisplay;
GoogleCloudMessaging gcm;
AtomicInteger messageID = new AtomicInteger();
Context context;
String registrationID;

@Override
public void onCreate(Bundle savedInstanceState) {
    super.onCreate(savedInstanceState);

    setContentView(R.layout.main);
    myMessageDisplay = (TextView) findViewById(R.id.display);
    context = getApplicationContext();

    // Register with GCM servers
    gcm = GoogleCloudMessaging.getInstance(this);
    final SharedPreferences myAppPrefs = getGcmPreferences(context);
    registrationID = myAppPrefs.getString(PROPERTY_REG_ID, "");
    // you could also perform version and other checks if desired

    if (registrationID.isEmpty()) {
        // Not registered, do so async so as not to block main thread
        try {
            registerAppInBackground();
        } catch (NameNotFoundException e)  {
            // log details here, as something failed during registration
        }
    }
}

private void registerAppInBackground() {
    new AsyncTask<Void, Void, String>() {
        @Override
        protected String doInBackground(Void... params) {
            String regStatus = "Unregistered";
            try {
                if (gcm == null) {
                    gcm = GoogleCloudMessaging.getInstance(context);
                }
                registrationID = gcm.register(SENDER_ID);
                regStatus = "Registered with ID: " + registrationID;
                // add your call to securely store the registrationID for later reuse
                // ...
            } catch (IOException ex) {
                // perform your error handling here, e.g. retry
            }
```

```
                return regStatus;
            }

        }.execute(null, null, null);
    }
...
```

This is a greatly simplified example so you can focus on the absolutely mandatory components and build from there. Our `onCreate()` method first instantiates a `gcm` object and a `SharedPreferences` object. It then retrieves the `registration_id` from the preferences. At this point your application may not be registered, which would mean the returned value from the preferences would be empty. We test for this empty value, and where an empty `registration_id` is detected we initiate our registration process by invoking the private method `registerAppInBackground()`.

The implementation of `registerAppInBackground()` follows Google's recommendation of performing the first-time registration asynchronously. We do this because we don't want to block the main thread while we wait for the handshake and registration process to complete. The process could potentially take several seconds or more. You could enhance the application here by adding a range of intermediate status updates, error checking, and more.

Once we have an application that's registered, we can carry out message exchange, and then all the other logic you might want your application to have, based on or driven by the messaging aspect. Listing 29-4 shows an example method to send a message based on a Bundle object constructed to hold your message details.

***Listing 29-4.** Example Message Sending from Your Android Client*

```
private void sendMessage(Bundle messagePayload) {
    new AsyncTask<Void, Void, String>() {
        @Override
        protected String doInBackground(Void... params) {
            String status = "";
            try {
                String id = Integer.toString(messageID.incrementAndGet());
                gcm.send(SENDER_ID + "@gcm.googleapis.com", id, messagePayload);
                status = "message sent";
            } catch (IOException ex) {
                // your error handling here
                // set status string
            }
            return status;
        }
    }
}
```

The logic of the `sendMessage()` method is entirely concerned with sending whatever it is you have constructed in the `messagePayload` parameter. This `Bundle` object is left to your imagination, but it could be the instant message, photo, voice message, or other content that your application is actually helping the user with.

We once again use `AsyncTask` to ensure we don't block on message delivery. This is a universal design pattern when working with any kind of message bus or message delivery service. Within the asynchronous logic, we generate a unique message identifier with the `messageID.incrementAndGet()` method and then invoke the `gcm.send()` method, passing it the unique ID and our message payload.

Error trapping and retry logic are easy to add at this point. If you are going to assume any higher value to the message ID (which is normally not recommended), it is best to place the retry logic within the `sendMessage()` method so as to be able to reuse the message ID generated before it falls out of scope on method return.

Coding the Server Component for GCM

Your third-party service can be written in basically any language, so long as it can make calls to the GCM cloud endpoints and support the authorization message protocols we have described in the earlier sections of this chapter.

Because such services are not strictly Android products or code, we will save some precious pages from the book and point you to excellent examples that Google provides to give you inspiration into writing the back-end services.

You can review the options and approaches for this non-Android third-party service at `developer.android.com/google/gcm/server.html`.

Moving Beyond the GCM Introduction

Such a short chapter cannot cover the enormous breadth of possibilities and nuances for GCM-based applications. For more details on what is possible, check out the Android Stack Exhange site, `android.stackechange.com`, and the `developer.android.com` site.

Chapter 30

Deploying Your Application: Google Play Store and Beyond

Creating a great application that people will love is one thing, but you also need an easy way for people to find and download it. Google created the Play Store for this purpose. From an icon right on the device, users can click straight into the Play Store to browse, search, review, and download applications. Users can also access Play Store over the Internet to do those same things, although the downloading is not to the computer but rather apps are sent directly to the user's device. Many applications are free; for those that are not, the Play Store provides payment mechanisms for easy purchasing.

The Play Store is even accessible from intents inside of applications, making it easy for applications to reach out to the Play Store to guide users into getting what they need for your application to be successful. For example, when a new version of your application becomes available, you can make it easy for the user to go straight to that Play Store page to get or buy the new version. Google Play Store is not the only way to get applications to devices, however; other channels are all over the Internet.

The Google Play Store application is not available from within the emulator (although hacks exist to make it available). This makes things a little more difficult for a developer. Ideally you will have a device of your own that you can use with Google Play Store. In this chapter, we'll explore how to get you set up for publishing applications to the Play Store; how to prepare your application for sale through the Play Store; how you can protect yourself from piracy; how users will find, download, and use your applications; and finally, alternative ways to make your applications available.

Becoming a Publisher

Before you can upload an application to Google Play Store, you need to become a publisher. To do so, you must create a Google Play Publisher Account. Once that's done, you will be able to upload your applications to the Play Store so they can be found and downloaded by users. If you will be charging money for your app, or accepting in-app purchases, you will also need to set up a Google Wallet Merchant Account. Google has made the process to get these accounts relatively painless and reasonably priced.

A good place to start is this page: `http://developer.android.com/distribute/googleplay/start.html`. From here you can click the big Start button to begin the process. If you don't already have a Google Account you will be prompted to create one. To be a publisher, you will also need to provide a developer name, an e-mail address, a web site address, and a phone number where you can be contacted. You will be able to change these values later, once your account is set up. You will also need to pay the registration fee. This is done via Google Wallet. In order to complete the payment transaction, you will need to use your Google account.

One of the options presented to you during the payment process is "Keep my email address confidential." This refers to the current transaction between you and Google Play Store to purchase publisher access. If you choose yes, you'll keep your e-mail address secret from Google Play Store. This has nothing to do with keeping your e-mail address secret from buyers of your application. Buyers' ability to see your e-mail address has nothing to do with this option. More on that later.

Next up is the Google Play Developer Distribution Agreement (GPDDA). This is the legal contract between Google and you. It spells out the rules for distributing apps, collecting payments, granting refunds, feedback, ratings, user rights, developer rights, and so on. There's more on these in the "Following the Rules" section of this chapter.

Upon accepting the Agreement, you will be taken to a page commonly called the Developer Console at `https://play.google.com/apps/publish/`.

Following the Rules

The GPDDA spells out a lot of rules. You might want legal counsel to review the contract before agreeing to it, depending on how seriously you plan to operate within the Google Play Store. This section describes some highlights you might be interested in:

- You have to be a developer in good standing to use the Google Play Store. This means you must go through the process as described to get registered, you must accept the Agreement, and you must abide by the rules in the Agreement. Breaking the rules could get you barred and your products removed from the Play Store.
- You can distribute products for free or for a price. The Agreement applies either way. Payments must be collected via an authorized Google Play Store Payment Processor. This includes Google Checkout (credit, debit, Google Play gift cards), carrier billing (e.g., Verizon, AT&T), and PayPal.
- Paid apps will incur a transaction fee, and possibly a fee from the device carrier, to be deducted from the sale price. As of March 2015, the transaction fee is 30 percent, so if the sale price is $10, Google collects $3 and you get $7 (assuming no carrier fees).

- For EU countries, Google is required to remit the taxes for you. Outside of the EU, it is your responsibility to remit appropriate taxes to your taxing authorities. For some of those non-EU countries, you can choose to let Google remit the taxes for you. When you set up your merchant account, you specify the appropriate tax rates to apply to purchases. Google Checkout will collect the appropriate taxes based on how you set up Google Checkout. This money will be provided to you if Google is not remitting for you, and you must remit it appropriately. For additional information on sales taxes in the United States, try `http://biztaxlaw.about.com/od/businesstaxes/f/onlinesalestax.htm` and `www.thestc.com`.
- You are allowed to distribute a free demo version of your application, with an option to pay to unlock the application's full set of features; however, you must collect the payment via an authorized Google Play Store Payment Processor. You are not allowed to redirect users of your free application to some other payment processor to collect upgrade fees. You could think of it this way: if you're making money via Google Play Store, Google wants its share.
- In-app billing allows an application to charge for digital goods or assets used within the application. A digital asset could be something like a virtual weapon or new levels for a game, or a music or graphics file. The checkout process is the same as for purchasing applications.
- If your application requires a user to have a login on a web server somewhere, and that web server charges the user a subscription fee, that web server could collect the subscription fee any way it wants to. In this way, you have disconnected the subscription fee from the application, and it's OK by Google to make the application available in Google Play Store—as long as your free application is not directing users to the web site. Some people just decide to distribute their free Android app from the same web server as the service, but this does require the user to enable installation of apps from unknown sources, which can discourage some users from installing.
- It seems that you can use alternate payment processors to accept donations from users of your free app, but you cannot create incentives within your app to encourage those donations.
- While the GPDDA says refunds can be requested up to 48 hours after purchase, as of March 2015 refunds can be requested by the user up to 2 hours after purchasing for an automatic refund. Refunds are not given to users who can preview the product prior to download. This includes ringtones and wallpapers.
- Google Checkout, however, does allow the developer to issue a refund even if the refund window has passed. The user can go to their Google Play activity history, and from there can request a refund even well after the initial 2 hours. If it is less than 48 hours from the purchase, the refund will probably be automatic. Otherwise, it is up to the developer whether or not to return any money.

- You are required to provide adequate support for your product. If adequate support is not provided, users can request refunds through Google, and these will be charged back to you, possibly including handling fees.
- Users get unlimited reinstalls of applications downloaded from the Google Play Store. If a user does a factory reset of their device, this feature allows them to get all their apps back without having to repurchase.
- Developers agree to protect the privacy and legal rights of users. This includes protecting (securing) any data that might be collected in the process of using the application. It is possible to change the rules regarding users' data protection, but only by displaying and having the user accept a separate agreement between you and that user.
- Your application must not compete with the Google Play Store. Google does not want an application from within Google Play Store to sell Android products from outside Google Play Store, thus bypassing its payment processor. This does not mean that you can't also sell your application through other channels, but your application on Google Play Store cannot itself be doing the selling of Android products outside of Google Play Store.
- Google will assign product ratings to your products. The ratings could be based on user feedback, install rates, uninstall rates, refund rates, and/or a Developer Composite Score. The Developer Composite Score may be calculated by Google using past history across applications, and this could influence the rating of new applications. For this reason, it is important to release good-quality applications associated with you, even the free ones. It's not clear that the Developer Composite Score even exists, but if it does there's no way to see yours.
- By selling your application through Google Play Store, you are granting the user a "non-exclusive, worldwide, perpetual license to perform, display and use the Product on the device." However, it is quite alright for you to write a separate End User License Agreement (EULA) that supersedes this statement. Make this EULA available on your web site, or provide another way for shoppers and users to be able to read it.
- Google requires that you abide by the branding rules for Android. These include restrictions on the use of the word *Android*, as well as use of the robot graphic, logo, and custom typeface. For more details, go to `http://developer.android.com/distribute/tools/promote/brand.html`.

Developer Console

The Developer Console is your landing page for controlling your applications in Google Play Store. From the Developer Console, you can set up a merchant account in Google Checkout (so you can charge for your applications), upload applications, and get information about your uploaded applications. You can also edit your account details including developer name, e-mail address, web address, and phone number. Figure 30-1 shows the Developer Console.

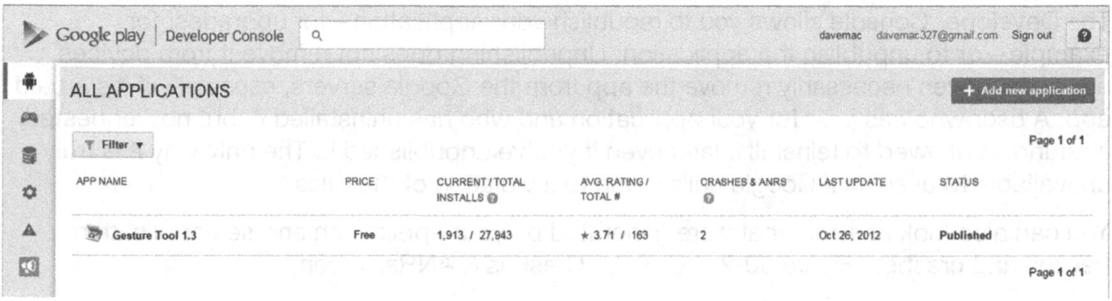

***Figure 30-1.** The Google Play Store Developer Console*

If you do not set up a merchant account, you will be unable to charge for your products in Google Play Store. Setting up a merchant account is not difficult. Click the link from the Developer Console, fill out the application, agree to the Terms of Service, and you're all set. You will need to provide a US Federal tax ID (EIN), a credit card number plus a US Social Security Number (SSN), or just a credit card number. The tax information is used to verify your credit status to ensure timely deposits. The credit card information is used to handle chargebacks due to buyer disputes when there are insufficient funds in your Google Checkout account. You can also supply bank account information to enable electronic funds transfers from the proceeds of your sales.

Note that Google Checkout is a service for more than just Google Play Store. Therefore, do not get confused by the transaction fee information for Google Checkout for non–Google Play Store sales. The 30 percent mentioned previously is the transaction fee rate for Google Play Store. There is also additional Google Checkout transaction fee information for non–Google Play Store sales, and those do not apply to Google Play Store.

Uploading and monitoring your applications are probably the main functions of the Developer Console that you will use, although the Console is also where you can sign up for access to Google APIs and game services and link to your AdWords account(s).

For monitoring, the Play Store provides tools to see how your application is doing in terms of total downloads and how many users still have it installed. You can see the overall rating of your apps in terms of 0 to 5 stars, and how many people have submitted a rating. There are various reports, charts, and graphs in the Developer Console so you can see how your application is doing in different versions of Android, on different devices, in different countries, and in different languages.

Users can submit comments in addition to rating your application. It is in your best interest to read the comments in order to address any problems quickly. Included with a comment is the user's rating of your app, a name of the user as typed by them, and the date the comment was submitted. You are able to reply to specific comments and that user will receive an e-mail to let them know. You can only leave one reply per review, but you can always edit your reply later. In an extreme case, where a comment is particularly harmful or inappropriate, you can contact Google support by starting here at the Help Center web site: `https://support.google.com/googleplay/android-developer/`.

The Developer Console allows you to republish your application—for upgrades, for example—or to unpublish the application. Unpublishing does not remove it from devices, nor does it even necessarily remove the app from the Google servers, especially if it's a paid app. A user who has paid for your application and who has uninstalled it, but not requested a refund, is allowed to reinstall it later even if you've unpublished it. The only way it is truly unavailable to users is if Google pulls it due to a violation of the rules.

You can also look at errors that were generated by your application and see application freezes and crashes. Figure 30-2 shows the Crashes & ANRs screen.

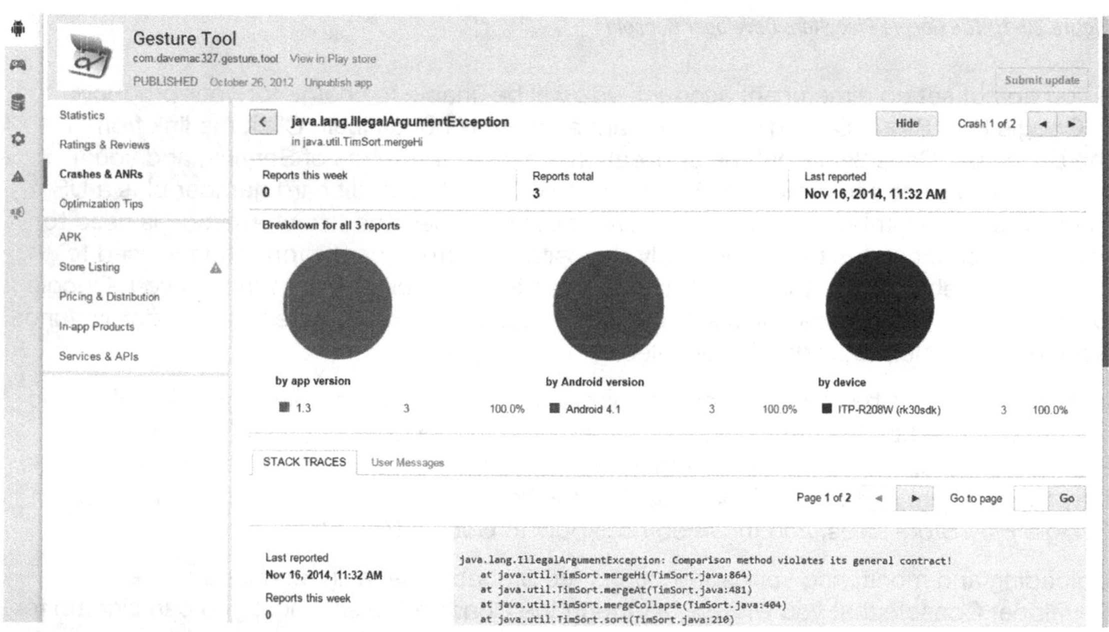

***Figure 30-2.** The Crashes & ANRs screen*

Drilling into the details of a crash report, you can see the stack trace of the crash, as well as which type of device was running the application and the time of the crash. Unfortunately, you cannot communicate back to the user who experienced the problem to get additional details or to help them get the issue resolved. You have to hope that the affected users will get in touch with you through comments, e-mail, or your web site. Otherwise, you'll just have to figure out from the crash report what went wrong and try to fix it.

If you really want to know how a user got to a crash, you'll want to implement one of the mobile analytics packages into your app. These will generate event records as a user steps through your application, and will also report crashes. The breadcrumbs (event records) will let you know the steps a user took up to the point of the crash. This capability is separate from the Google Play Store, however.

There's one more feature of the Developer Console you may need to use: the Help portion of the web site. The Help button is in the upper-right corner. Clicking it shows you some inline help, but also has a link to the Help Center web site. There are also links for submitting e-mail or for an online chat (during business hours).

We've now introduced you to some of the nice features of the Developer Console, but you probably want to get into the most useful part, which is getting your applications into the Google Play Store so users can find them and download them. But before we do that, let's go over how to prepare your application for upload and sale.

Preparing Your Application for Sale

There are quite a few things to think about and do to take an application from code complete to Google Play Store. This section will help you through those items.

Testing for Different Devices

With more and more Android devices becoming available, and each one potentially having some new hardware configuration, it is very important that you test for a variety of devices you want to support. You could purchase some of the devices that you want to support, but you probably can't purchase them all. There are some online services that make real devices available over the Internet. Your other option is to configure Android Virtual Devices (AVDs) for each type of device, specify the appropriate hardware configuration, and then test with the emulator and each AVD. Some device manufacturers make Android emulator packages available that are specific to their devices, so check out their web sites for download options.

The Android SDK provides various classes to assist with testing, as well as the UI/Application Exerciser Monkey. These tools will help you do automated testing so you don't spend forever testing your application manually. See these web pages for more details:

```
https://developer.android.com/tools/testing/index.html
https://developer.android.com/tools/testing-support-library/index.html
```

Before you begin testing, you probably want to remove from your code any development artifacts that you no longer need, and also any development artifacts from `/res`. You want your application to be as small as possible and to run as quickly as possible with the least amount of memory. Finally, be sure to disable or remove any debugging features from your application that you don't want distributed to production.

Supporting Different Screen Sizes

Android supports many screen sizes. In order to run on the smallest size, you must set a specific `<supports-screens>` element as a child element of `<manifest>` within the `AndroidManifest.xml` file. Without this tag specifying that your application supports the small screen size, your application will not be visible in the Play Store to devices that have a small screen.

To support different screen sizes, you may need to create alternate resource files under `/res`. For example, for files in `/res/layout`, you may need to create corresponding files in `/res/layout-small` to support small screens. This does not mean you must also create corresponding files in `/res/layout-large` and `/res/layout-normal`, since Android will look in `/res/layout` if it can't find what it needs in a more specific resource directory such as `/res/layout-large`. Remember, too, that you can have combinations of qualifiers for these resource files; for example, `/res/layout-small-land` would contain layouts for small screens in landscape mode. Supporting small screens probably means creating alternate versions of drawables such as icons, too. For drawables, you may need to create alternate resource directories, taking into account screen resolution as well as screen size.

Tablets of course go in the opposite direction in terms of screen size, using the label `xlarge`. The same `<supports-screens>` tag as before is used to specify if your application will run on extra-large screens, and the attribute to use inside of this tag is `android:xlargeScreens`. In some cases, you may have a tablet-only application, in which case you would specifically indicate that for the other sizes, the attribute value is `false`.

Preparing AndroidManifest.xml for Uploading

Your `AndroidManifest.xml` file may need to be tweaked a little bit before you can upload it to Google Play Store. ADT normally puts the `android:icon` attribute in the `<application>` tag, and not in `<activity>` tags. If you have more than one activity that can be launched, you'll want to specify separate icons for each activity so the user can more easily tell them apart. But you'll still need an icon specified in `<application>`, which also serves as the default activity icon for any activities that don't specify their own icon. Your application will work fine on devices and in the emulator with the `android:icon` only specified in the `<activity>` tags, but when Google Play Store inspects your application's `.apk` file when uploading, it looks for icon information in the `<application>` tag.

Google Play Store prevents uploading your application if the package name you've used starts with `com.google`, `com.android`, `android`, or `com.example`, but we hope you didn't use one of those in your application.

There are many other compatibilities to consider for your application. Some devices have cameras, some don't have physical keyboards, and some have trackballs instead of directional pads. Use `<uses-configuration>` and `<uses-feature>` tags in your `AndroidManifest.xml` file as needed to define what hardware/platform requirements your application has. Google Play Store will enforce this and not let your application be shown to a user on a device that won't support your application. Note that these tags are different and separate from the `<uses-permission>` tags of the `AndroidManifest.xml` file. In most cases, you would end up with both tags in your AndroidManifest.xml file, for specifying that a camera is required, and for specifying that permission to use the camera is required. But not all features require permission, so it is in your best interest to specify the features you need.

There is another big difference between <uses-permission> and <uses-feature>: the <uses-feature> tag can say that your application requires that feature or that your application can function without it. That is, there is an attribute called android:required that can be set to either true or false; by default it's true. If there is a permission for a feature, but you don't supply the corresponding <uses-feature> tag, then by default it's as if you specified <uses-feature> and the feature is required. For example, your application may take advantage of Bluetooth if it's available, but will work just fine if it is not. Therefore, in the manifest file, in addition to the Bluetooth permission element, you'd have something like this:

```
<uses-feature android:name="android.hardware.bluetooth" android:required="false" />
```

Within your application's code, you should make a call to the PackageManager to find out if Bluetooth is available or not, which you could do with the following:

```
boolean hasBluetooth = getPackageManager().hasSystemFeature(
                PackageManager.FEATURE_BLUETOOTH);
```

Then take appropriate action in your application if Bluetooth is not there. The Android documentation can be confusing in this area. If you look at the Developer Guide page for <uses-feature>, you will not see as many features as are described on the PackageManager reference page, which defines a FEATURE_* constant for each available feature.

The <uses-configuration> tag is a little different. It specifies what sort of keyboard, touchscreen, and/or navigational controls the device must have. But instead of being independent choices such as <uses-feature>, you would put the combinations of configuration choices together into what your application requires. For example, if your application requires a five-way navigation control (that is, a D-pad or a trackball) and a touchscreen (using either a stylus or a finger), you would specify two tags as follows:

```
<uses-configuration android:reqFiveWayNav="true" android:reqTouchScreen="stylus" />
<uses-configuration android:reqFiveWayNav="true" android:reqTouchScreen="finger" />
```

Localizing Your Application

If your application will be used in other countries, you might want to consider localizing it. This is relatively easy to do technically. Finding someone to do the localizing is another matter. From the technical point of view, you simply create another folder under /res—for example, /res/values-fr to hold a French version of strings.xml. Take your existing strings.xml file, translate the string values to the new language, and save the new translated file under the new resource folder using the same file name as the original file. At runtime, if the device's language is set to French, Android will look for strings that were placed under /res/values-fr. If it can't find strings from there, it will then look for strings from /res/values.

The same technique works for the other types of resource files—for example, drawables and menus. Images and colors may work better for your users if they are different for different countries or cultures. For this reason, it is a good idea to not use true color names for your resource names for colors. In the online documentation for colors, it is common to see something like this:

```
<color name="solid_red">#f00</color>
```

This means that in your code or other resource files, you're referring to the color by the actual name of the color, in this case, `solid_red`. In order to localize the color to something more appropriate for the other country or culture, it would be better to use a color name such as `accent_color1` or `alert_color`. In English, red might be the appropriate color value to use, while in Spanish it might be better to use a shade of yellow. Because a color name like `alert_color` does not reveal the actual color that you're using, it is less confusing when you want to change the actual color value to something else. At the same time, you can design a pleasing color scheme, with base colors and accent colors, and be more confident that you're using the correct colors in the correct places.

Menu choices might need to be changed in different countries, using fewer or more menu items, or be organized differently, depending on where the application is being used. Menus are typically stored under `/res/menu`. If you are faced with this situation, you are probably better off putting all your string text into `strings.xml`, or other files located under the `/res/values` directory, and using string IDs in the appropriate resource files everywhere else. This makes it far less likely that you will miss translating a string value in some obscure resource file. Your language translation work is then limited to the files under `/res/values`.

Preparing Your Application Icon

Shoppers and your users will see your application's icon and label prominently in both Google Play Store and on their device once they've downloaded it. Please take special care to create good icons and good labels for your application and its activities. Localize them as necessary or desired. And remember that for different screen sizes, your icons may need to be tweaked to look good. Check out what other developers have done with their icons, especially those applications in the same category as your application. You want your application to get noticed, so it's better not to blend in with all the others. At the same time, you want your icon and label to work well on a device when surrounded by lots of other application icons that do other things. You don't want a user to be confused about what your application does, so make the icon representative of the functionality of your application.

When creating any image for your application, but especially your icon, you need to consider the screen density of the target device. *Density* means the number of pixels per inch. Don't think that a small screen is low density and a large screen is high density—you could see any combination of size and density. For a high-density screen, you will probably choose an icon with 72 × 72 pixels. The medium-density icon will usually be of size 48 × 48 pixels. And for extra-high density, it's 96 × 96 pixels. For a low-density screen, making an icon appear to be the right size means making the icon with fewer pixels, typically 36 × 36. Android helps you in the low-density case because it will automatically downscale your HDPI icon by half, so you don't need to provide a low-density icon yourself. In general, you'll find it easiest to only worry about density for images such as icons. You'll worry about screen size when defining layouts.

Directing Users Back to the Play Store

Android has a URI scheme to help facilitate finding applications in Google Play Store: `market://`. [Google Play Store was formerly called Android Market.] For example, if you want to direct your users to the Play Store to locate a needed component, or to upsell to an additional app that unlocks features in your application, you would do something as shown here, where `MY_PACKAGE_NAME` would be replaced by your real package name:

```
Intent intent = new Intent(Intent.ACTION_VIEW,
        Uri.parse("market://search?q=pname:MY_PACKAGE_NAME"));
startActivity(intent);
```

This will launch the Play Store app on the device and take the user to that package name. The user can then choose to download or buy the application. Note that this scheme does not work in a normal web browser. In addition to searching using package name (`pname`), you can search by developer name using `market://search?q=pub:\"Fname Lname\"` or against any of the public fields (application title, developer name, and application description) in Google Play Store using `market://search?q=<querystring>`.

The Android Licensing Service

The way that Android apps are constructed unfortunately makes them targets for piracy. It is possible to make copies of Android apps that can then be distributed to other devices. So how can you ensure that users who have not purchased your application cannot run it? The Android team has created something called the License Verification Library (LVL) to meet this need. Here's how it works.

If your application was downloaded via Google Play Store, then there must be a copy of the Google Play Store app on the device. In addition, the Google Play Store app has elevated permissions to be able to read values from the device such as the user's Google account name, the IMSI, and other information. The Google Play Store app will respond to a license verification request from an application. You make calls into the LVL from your application, LVL communicates with the Google Play Store app, the Google Play Store app communicates with Google servers, and your application gets an answer back indicating whether or not this user on this device is licensed to use your application. This means the app must have been purchased through Google Play Store; otherwise the Google servers won't know about it. There are settings under your control to decide what to do if the network is unavailable. A full description of the process of implementing LVL can be found at `https://developer.android.com/google/play/licensing/index.html`.

One thing to be aware of, though, is that the LVL mechanism is subject to hacking. If someone can get to your application's `.apk` file, they can disassemble the app and then patch it if they know where to look for the return value from the LVL call. If you use the obvious pattern of a `switch` statement after getting the response from LVL, to branch to the appropriate logic based on the return code, a hacker can simply force a successful return code value, and they own your app. For this reason, the Android team highly recommends that you implement obfuscation of your app to hide the part of your application where you check the return code from LVL. This gets fairly complicated, as you can imagine.

Using ProGuard for Optimization, Fighting Piracy

Google provides some support for obfuscation in the form of the ProGuard feature. ProGuard is not a Google product, but has been integrated into ADT and Android Studio so it's easy to use. ProGuard does more than just provide obfuscation for fighting piracy; it also makes your application smaller and faster. It does all this by stripping out debugging information, cutting out code that will never run, and changing names (of classes, methods, and so on) to meaningless strings. Examples of code that will never run include library classes and methods that are never called, and logging that depends on a constant that you set to `false` (for production). It can also recognize optimizations such as binary-shifting a value left by one bit position instead of multiplying it by 2. By stripping out debugging information and changing the names, the resulting compiled `.apk` file won't reveal variable names, class names, methods, and so on, so it becomes extremely difficult to figure out what the code does and therefore how to steal it, modify it, and release it as something else.

When you create your application, it should automatically get a `proguard-project.txt` file. The default file will look something like Listing 30-1.

Listing 30-1. Sample `proguard-project.txt` File

```
# To enable ProGuard in your project, edit project.properties
# to define the proguard.config property as described in that file.
#
# Add project specific ProGuard rules here.
# By default, the flags in this file are appended to flags specified
# in ${sdk.dir}/tools/proguard/proguard-android.txt
# You can edit the include path and order by changing the ProGuard
# include property in project.properties.
#
# For more details, see
#   http://developer.android.com/guide/developing/tools/proguard.html

# Add any project specific keep options here:

# If your project uses WebView with JS, uncomment the following
# and specify the fully qualified class name to the JavaScript interface
# class:
#-keepclassmembers class fqcn.of.javascript.interface.for.webview {
#   public *;
#}
```

You also need to uncomment the `proguard.config` property in the application's `project.properties` file to the location of the `proguard-project.txt` file. The line looks like this:

```
proguard.config=${sdk.dir}/tools/proguard/proguard-android.txt:proguard-project.txt
```

As you can see, there is a stock set of ProGuard configurations provided to you by a file under the `tools/proguard` directory of the Android SDK. You can then augment the ProGuard configuration in the `proguard-project.txt` file as part of your application project. Note that the provided configuration does not in fact enable optimizations, as these require more testing to be sure that your application still works correctly. If you want to try optimizations, change the reference in the `project.properties` file to `${sdk.dir}/tools/proguard/proguard-android-optimize.txt`.

As mentioned, ProGuard does its work by stripping stuff out. Sometimes it strips out too much, and that is why you see the `-keep` options specified in the `proguard-android.txt` file. When you produce an `.apk` file, you need to test it to make sure ProGuard didn't take out too much. If you find errors due to missing classes or methods, you can edit the `proguard-project.txt` file to include another `-keep` option for the item you're missing. Rebuild your `.apk` file, and test again. We recommend using the Export Signed Application Package option under the Android Tools menu option in Eclipse, because it will take care of calling ProGuard for you as it builds the `.apk` file. Exporting is covered in the next section.

You can also configure Ant to obfuscate using ProGuard if you use Ant to do your builds.

When ProGuard does its thing, you'll get a file called `mapping.txt` along with your `.apk` file. Hang on to this file because you will need it to de-obfuscate a stack trace from your application. If you use Eclipse to export your `.apk` file, you will see a new `proguard` directory created within your Eclipse project. The `mapping.txt` file will be in there. The command to use is `retrace`, and it's located in the Android SDK directory under `tools/proguard/bin`. The arguments to retrace include the `mapping.txt` file and the stacktrace file, but be aware that you need to specify the full pathname to each. Also, you should keep track of which version of your application goes with which `mapping.txt` file.

One more caution about testing your application. Android KitKat introduced an experimental runtime engine called the Android RunTime (ART), and in Lollipop it became the one and only runtime engine. You should test your application with both, especially if you use ProGuard and do optimizations.

Preparing Your .apk File for Uploading

To get your tested application ready for uploading—that is, to create the `.apk` file to upload—you need to create a signed export of your application. This can be done a number of ways, but the simplest are to use the built-in IDE features. For Eclipse you would right-click on the project name and choose Android Tools ➤ Export Signed Application Package.... For Android Studio, you would select the project name and choose the Build menu ➤ Generate Signed APK... Follow the dialogs to choose a proper signing certificate key and create your production APK.

Uploading Your Application

Uploading is easy to do but takes some preparation. Before you begin an upload, there are some things you will need to have ready and decisions you have to make. This section covers that preparation and those decisions. Then, when you've got everything you need, go to the Developer Console and choose + Add new application. You'll be prompted to supply lots of information about your application, the Play Store will run some processing on your application and the information, and then your application will be ready to publish to the Play Store.

The previous section covered preparing your application `.apk` file for uploading. Making your application attractive to shoppers requires some marketing on your part. You need good descriptions of what it is and does, and you need good images so shoppers understand what they might download.

The Google Play Store understands that you could market your application in different countries. Therefore, you have the ability to provide text and graphics localized for the different countries with just one application.

Graphics

You'll be asked to upload screenshots for your application. The easiest way to capture screenshots of your application is to use DDMS. Fire up Eclipse, launch your application in the emulator or on a real device, and then switch Eclipse perspectives to DDMS and the Device view. From within the Device view, select the device where your application is running and then click the Screen Capture button (it looks like a little camera in the upper-right corner) or choose it from the View menu. If you have a choice when saving, choose 24-bit color. The Android Device Monitor is very similar to DDMS and is available as a stand-alone tool (called monitor) from under the SDK tools directory, or from the Tools menu of Android Studio.

Google Play Store will convert your screenshots to compressed JPEG; starting with 24-bit will produce better results than starting with 8-bit color. Choose screenshots that will make your application stand out from the rest but that also show the important functionality. You must supply at least two screenshots, and you can provide up to eight. Be aware that you have the ability to upload screenshots for your application for other languages. If your application has been localized for another country and/or language, you'll want the screenshots to correspond.

Next up is a high-res application icon. This could be the exact same design as your application icon, but Google Play Store wants a 512 × 512 pixel icon image. This is required.

The feature graphic is required and is a large 1024 × 500 pixels in size. This graphic is used in the Featured section of Google Play Store so you want this to look really good.

You can provide a promotional graphic as well, but its size is smaller than a screenshot. Although this graphic is optional, it is a good idea to include it. You never know when the graphic could be displayed; without one, you don't know what will be displayed in its place, if anything. One place the Promo Graphic appears is at the top of your application's Details page in Google Play Store.

By the time you read this, there could be other graphics you could upload. For example, Google now accepts a TV Banner graphic for apps that would be viewed on a TV.

The last bit of graphics related to your application is an optional video that you can put out on YouTube and link to from your Google Play Store page.

Listing Details

The Google Play Store asks for textual information about your application to display to shoppers, including the title, short description (formerly called promotional text), and full description.

There's a Short Description field that has only 80 characters, and it's mandatory. When your app is shown at the top of a list in Google Play Store, it's the Promo Graphic and the Short Description that get displayed.

The full description is also mandatory, and it allows up to 4,000 characters. If you have written a separate EULA for your users, provide a link to it in your full description text so shoppers can view it prior to downloading your application. Consider that shoppers will likely use search to locate applications, so be sure to put appropriate words into your text to maximize your hit rate on searches related to your application's functionality. It's worthwhile to put a short comment in the text that says to e-mail you if the user runs into problems. Without this simple prompt, people are more likely to leave a negative comment, and a negative comment really limits your ability to troubleshoot and solve the problem, as compared to an e-mail exchange with the affected user.

One drawback to the user comments mechanism described earlier is that it does not distinguish to users the specific version of your application. If negative reviews are received against version 1, and you release version 2 with everything fixed, the reviews from version 1 are still there, and shoppers may not realize that those comments don't apply to the new version. When releasing a new version of an application, the application rating (number of stars) does not get reset, either. Partly for this reason, Google started providing a Recent Changes text field where you can describe what's new in this release. This is where you could indicate that a certain problem has been fixed or tell what the new features are. The Play Store also provides the ability to see just the reviews/comments for the latest version, but by default the reviews and comments are shown for all versions.

One of your responsibilities when writing the text for your application is to disclose the permissions that are required. These are the same permissions as set in the `<uses-permission>` tags of your `AndroidManifest.xml` file within your application. When the user downloads your application to their device, Android will check the `AndroidManifest.xml` file and ask the user about all of the `uses-permission` requirements before completing the install. So you might as well disclose this up front. Otherwise, you risk negative reviews from users surprised that an application requires some permission that they are not prepared to grant, not to mention the refunds, which also count against your Developer Composite Score. Similar to permissions, if your application requires a certain type of screen, a camera, or other device feature, this should be disclosed in your text descriptions of your application. As a best practice, you should disclose not only what permissions and features your application needs, but also what your application will do with them. You should answer the user's question in advance: why does this app require *X*?

When uploading your application, you will need to choose an application type and a category. As these values change with time, we won't list them here, but it's easy to go to the Add new application screen to see what they are.

Publishing Options

You must choose two content ratings. The idea is to give consumers an idea of the appropriateness of an application for certain age groups. The scale for the first (older) content rating includes High, Medium, and Low Maturity, and Everyone. Choosing the right level depends on the content in your application and how much of that content there is. Google has rules about location-awareness and posting or publishing locations. It's best to read the rules for yourself here: `https://support.google.com/googleplay/android-developer/answer/188189`. The second content rating is derived after you complete a questionnaire. You will actually get several content ratings, by country, depending on how you answer the questionnaire. The questionnaire takes some of the subjectivity out of the content rating.

Next you set the price of your application. By default the price is Free, and you must have previously set up a Merchant Account in Google Checkout if you want to charge for your application. Setting the right price for an application is tricky, unless you've got some sophisticated market research capabilities, and even then it's still tricky. Prices set too high could turn people off, and you risk the effects of refunds if people don't feel the price was worth it. Prices set too low could also turn people off because they might think it's a cheap application.

One of the last decisions to make before uploading your application is to choose the locations and carriers for your application to be visible to. By choosing All, your application will be available everywhere. However, you may want to restrict distribution geographically or by carrier. Depending on what functionality is in your application, you may need to restrict by location in order to comply with US export law. You may choose to restrict your application by carrier if your application has compatibility issues with certain carriers' devices or policies. To see carriers, click the Show options link next to the country, and the available carriers for that country will be displayed, allowing you to choose the ones you want. Choosing all also means that any new locations or carriers that Google adds will automatically see your application with no intervention from you.

In addition to country and carrier choices, Google Play Store also allows you to restrict your application to certain devices. By default, the devices list is filtered based on your manifest file, in which you've specified the features and so on that your application requires. This section of the Upload screen allows you to further restrict other devices. You would probably only want to do this if there was a known issue with a particular device such that you were unable to get your application to work on that device even though it ought to.

Android also offers the option to upload multiple APKs for the same application. It enables you to have a single entry on Google Play Store but to have separate build for phones and tablets. See `http://android-developers.blogspot.com/2011/07/multiple-apk-support-in-android-market.html` and `http://developer.android.com/google/play/publishing/multiple-apks.html`.

Contact Information

Even though your developer profile contains your contact information, you can set different information when uploading each application. The Play Store asks for a web site, e-mail address, and phone number as contact information related to this application. You must supply at least one of these so buyers can get support, but you don't need to supply all three. It is a good idea to *not* use your personal e-mail address here, just as you probably wouldn't really want to give out your personal phone number. When you've made millions of dollars from selling your application, you'll want to let someone else receive and deal with the e-mails from users. By setting up an application-support type of e-mail address in advance, you can easily separate the support e-mails from your personal e-mails. Of course, you can always change these values later if you need/want to.

Consent

With all these decisions made, you must then attest that your application abides by Android's Content Guidelines (basically no nasty stuff) and make a second attestation that the software is OK for export from the United States. US export laws apply because Google's servers are located inside the United States, even if you are outside of the United States, and even if both you and your customer are outside of the United States. Remember that you can always choose to distribute your application through other channels. When all your information is in and your graphics are uploaded, go ahead and click the Save button. This will prepare everything for your application to be ready to go live.

You can then publish your application by clicking the Publish button. Google Play Store will perform some checks on your application—for instance, checking your application's certificate for the expiration date. If all goes well, your application will soon be available for download. Congratulations!

User Experience on Google Play Store

The Play Store app has been available on devices for some time now, and it is available over the Internet. Developers don't have any control over how Google Play Store works, other than to provide good text and graphics for their application's listing in the Play Store. Therefore, the user experience is pretty much up to Google. From a device, a user can search by keyword; look at top downloaded applications (both free and paid), featured applications, or new applications; or browse by categories. Once they find an application they want, they simply select it, which pops up an item details screen allowing them to install it or buy it. Buying will take the user to Google Checkout to conduct the financial part of the transaction. Once downloaded, the new application shows up with all the other applications.

From the Internet web site for Google Play Store (`https://play.google.com`), the user interface looks about the same, albeit much larger than most device screens. One difference is that the web-based Google Play Store expects the user to log in to their Google account to use the Play Store. This allows Google to connect your web experience on Google Play Store to your actual device. This means two things: when using the web site, Google Play Store knows what applications are already installed on your device; and when you make a purchase on the Google Play Store web site, the download can be sent to your device (or devices) and not to whatever computer you happen to be browsing on.

Google Play Store has an option to view downloaded applications in My Apps. This area contains all installed apps and any apps that you've purchased, even if you've removed them (perhaps you removed them just to make room for other applications). This means you could delete a paid app from your phone and then reinstall it later without having to repurchase it. Of course, if you opted for a refund, the app will not show up in My Apps.

The list of apps in My Apps is tied to your Google Account used across all your devices. This means you could switch to a new physical device and still have access to all the apps you've paid for. But beware. Since you might have multiple identities with Google, you must use the exact same identity as before to get your apps on a new device. When viewing apps in My Apps, any that have upgrades available will indicate this and allow you to get the upgrade.

Google Play Store filters applications available to users. It does this in a number of ways. Users in some countries can only see free applications because of the commerce legalities involved for Google in that country. Google is trying hard to overcome commerce hurdles so all paid apps will be available everywhere. Until that time comes, users in some countries will be unable to access paid apps. Users with devices running older versions of Android will not be able to see applications that require a newer version of the Android SDK. Users with device configurations that are not compatible with the requirements of the application (expressed via `<uses-feature>` tags in the `AndroidManifest.xml` file) will not be able to see those applications. For example, applications not specifically supporting small screens cannot be seen in Google Play Store by users on devices with small screens. This filtering is mostly intended to protect users from downloading applications that will not work on their device.

If you are purchasing apps in Google Play Store from other countries, your transaction may be subject to currency conversion, which can also carry an additional fee, unless the seller has specified pricing in your local currency. You're really purchasing using the Google Checkout from the seller's country. Google Play Store will display an approximate amount, but the actual charges could vary depending on when the transaction is placed and with which payment processor. Buyers may notice a pending transaction against their account for a small amount (for example, US $1). This is done by Google to ensure that the payment information provided is correct, and this pending charge will not actually go through.

A few web sites are available that mirror the Google Play Store app listings. Shoppers can search, browse categories, and find out about Google Play Store applications over the Internet without having a device. This gets around the filtering that Google Play Store does based on your device configuration and location. However, this does not get apps onto your device. Examples of these mirror sites are `www.androlib.com`, and `www.appszoom.com`.

Beyond Google Play Store

Google's Play Store is not the only game in town. You are not forced into using Google Play Store at all. You should consider utilizing other channels of distribution, not only to make your app available to more people in more countries, but also to take advantage of other payment processors and opportunities to make money.

There are Android app stores completely separate from Google Play Store, the biggest of which is probably Amazon. Other examples of Android app stores are `http://mall.soc.io/apps`, `http://slideme.org`, `www.getjar.com`, and `https://f-droid.org/`. From these sites, you can search, browse, find out about apps, and also download apps, either from a device or via a web browser. These sites don't have to abide by Google's rules, including the transaction fees for paid apps and methods of payment. PayPal and other payment processors can be used to purchase apps on these separate sites. These sites also don't necessarily restrict by location or device configuration. Some of them provide an Android client that can be installed, or in some cases may come preinstalled on a device. Users can simply launch a browser on their device and find the app they want to download via the web site; when the file is saved to the device, Android knows what to do with it. That is to say, a downloaded `.apk` file is treated as an Android application. If you click it in the Download history of the browser (not to be confused with My Apps, covered earlier), you will be prompted to see if you want to install it or not. This freedom means you can set up your own methods of downloading Android applications to users, even from your own web site and with your own payment methods. You must still deal though with collecting any necessary sales tax and remitting it to the appropriate authorities.

While not restricted by Google's rules, these alternate methods of app distribution may not offer the same sort of buyer protections that are found in Google Play Store. It may be possible to purchase an application through an alternate market that will not work on the buyer's device. Buyers may be at greater risk of malware on the alternate markets. The buyer may also be responsible for creating backups, in case they lose the application from their device, or for transferring applications if they switch to a new device.

These other markets allow you to make money on the sale of each app. You've also got the ability within these other markets to implement alternate payment mechanisms, or to implement ads and make money that way.

Remember that Google does not restrict developers from selling their applications in multiple markets at the same time they sell through Google Play Store. So consider all your options to make the most of your efforts.

References

Here are some helpful references to topics you may wish to explore further:

- `http://developer.android.com/guide/topics/manifest/manifest-intro.html`: The Developer Guide page to the `AndroidManifest.xml` file, with descriptions of how to use the `supports-screens`, `uses-configuration`, and `uses-feature` tags.
- `http://developer.android.com/guide/practices/screens_support.html`: The Developer Guide page "Supporting Multiple Screens," which contains lots of good information on dealing with different screen sizes and densities.
- `http://developer.android.com/design/style/iconography.html`: The Design Guide page "Iconography," which contains lots of good information on designing effective icons for your application.
- `http://android-developers.blogspot.com/2010/09/securing-android-lvl-applications.html` and `http://android-developers.blogspot.com/2010/09/proguard-android-and-licensing-server.html`: Blog posts on how to use the License Verification Library (LVL) in ways that prevent piracy.
- `http://proguard.sourceforge.net/`: The main site for ProGuard, which includes documentation.

Summary

You are now equipped to take on the world with your Android applications! Here is a rundown of the topics we covered in this chapter:

- How to get established as a Google Play Store Publisher (that is, Developer) so you can publish to Google Play Store.
- The rules as laid out in the Google Play Developer Distribution Agreement.
- Giving Google its share of your revenue if you are selling through Google Play Store. We also discussed how Google does not want to see competition from within the Play Store.
- Your responsibility for paying taxes on revenues from your applications.
- The Google Play Store refund policy, both the published and the real one.
- How users can get copies of your application anytime in the future as long as they paid for it once.
- The Android branding rules. Make sure you don't violate any copyright associated with Android, images, or fonts.
- The Developer Console and its features. The Developer Console collects user feedback and error reports from users.
- Preparing your application for production, including testing, LVL and ProGuard to fight piracy, and using resource variations and tags in `AndroidManifest.xml` to filter which devices your application will be available to.
- Advice regarding localizing your application by language and/or culture.
- The Google Play Store user interface, both on device and on the Internet/Web.
- The fact that Google Play Store is not the only game in town, and that you can sell your application in other places on the Internet, all at the same time.

Index

C

F

G

H

I

J, K

L

M

N

O

P

Q

R

S

T

U

V

W

X, Y

Z

Printed in the United States
By Bookmasters

Printed in the United States
By Bookmasters